ENCYCLOPEDIA OF
BIRTH CONTROL

ENCYCLOPEDIA OF BIRTH CONTROL

Vern L. Bullough, Editor

Brenda Appleby, Gwen Brewer,
Cathy Moran Hajo, and Esther Katz, Associate Editors

with James A. Brundage, Martha Cornog,
Stacy Elliott, Peter Engelman, Fang Fu Ruan,
Tom Flynn, Peter Frost,
Indumati Parikh, and Lois Robin

A B C 〜 C L I O

8-14-02

Library of Congress Cataloging-in-Publication Data
Encyclopedia of birth control/Vern L. Bullough, editor ; Brenda
Appleby . . . [et al.], associate editors ; with James A. Brundage . . . [et
al.].
    p. cm.
Includes bibliographical references and index.
  ISBN 1-57607-181-2 (alk. paper)—1-57607-533-8 (e-book)
  1. Birth control—Encylopedias. 2. Contraception—Encyclopedias.
  [DNLM: 1. Contraception—Encyclopedias—English. 2. Contraception
Behavior—Encyclopedias—English. 3. Abortion,
Induced—Encyclopedias—English. 4. Contraceptive
Agents—Encyclopedias—English. 5. Contraceptive
Devices—Encyclopedias—English. HQ 766 E56 2001] I. Bullough, Vern L.
HQ766.E52 2001
363.9'6'03—dc21   2001001345

This book is also available on the World Wide Web as an e-book. Visit www.abc-clio.com for details.

06 05 04 03 02 01 00 10 09 8 7 6 5 4 3 2 1
ABC-CLIO, Inc.
130 Cremona Drive, P.O. Box 1911
Santa Barbara, California 93116-1911
This book is printed on acid-free paper.
Manufactured in the United States of America

To Planned Parenthood organizations worldwide

CONTENTS

ENCYCLOPEDIA OF BIRTH CONTROL

PREFACE

The *Encyclopedia of Birth Control* is part of an ABC-CLIO series of encyclopedias on science-related topics. It is, at least as far as I know, the first encyclopedia on birth control and it was this that led me to undertake the project. This book differs from a standard history or sociological text in that it is topical. To help readers find what they want, there are referrals to other entries, and the index breaks down the subject matter further. In general, the topics are historical and sociological, but many of them are also broken into periods, for example, ancient or classical. The encyclopedia also includes biographies of key figures in the birth control movement in the United States and Great Britain. Most of the entries were written by the editor, but significant contributions were made by the associate editors and by contributors who went beyond the limitations of the editor.

No work like this could have been accomplished without relying on the pioneering work of others such as John Riddle or Norman Himes. The feminist movement has also spawned a number of writers who brought about a rethinking of the birth control movement, and their ideas are incorporated in the entries in this volume. Cathy Moran Hajo, Esther Katz, and Peter Engelman of the Margaret Sanger Papers project proved particularly helpful. Gwen Brewer compiled the information for Appendix 1. Martha Cornog compiled the information for Appendix 2. Brenda Appleby added a Canadian perspective to the encyclopedia that otherwise would not be there. My contributors, listed separately, wrote their articles with dispatch, which brought this book in on time. One reason this encyclopedia was possible was because of the valuable collection of books and articles on contraception available in the Bullough collection in the Center for Sex Research library at California State University, Northridge. Encyclopedias have to rely on a dedicated editorial staff and special thanks are due to the individuals at ABC-CLIO: Kevin Downing, acquisitions editor; Melanie Stafford, production editor; and Liz Kincaid, art director.

Vern L. Bullough

INTRODUCTION

All living things from microbes to humans have to reproduce themselves to maintain survival of the species. In the higher animals, although it takes two individuals of different sex to engage in reproduction, most of the burden falls on the female, from the egg-laying birds to the pregnant mammals. Pregnancy then is a natural, although not necessarily inevitable, biological process for most females. Any human female who engages in intercourse with any regularity could spend most of the years of her life between the ages of fifteen and forty-five either pregnant or nursing a newborn infant. It is estimated that under optimal circumstances the average woman would become pregnant every other year during her reproductive life and, if she did not give birth to twins or have other forms of multiple births and if she nursed her infants, she would give birth to fifteen children during her lifetime. Obviously some women would become pregnant more often than others, with a theoretical maximum of about twenty pregnancies for one woman. But what is theoretical is not always actual. The largest number of live births recorded for any one woman is sixty-nine by the first wife of Feodor Vassilyev (her first name does not appear in the records), a peasant from the village of Shula, 150 miles east of Moscow. She had thirty-seven pregnancies: ten individual births, sixteen pairs of twins, seven sets of triplets, and four sets of quadruplets, all born between 1725 and 1765, and almost all of them survived beyond the first year. Although we can wonder about the historical accuracy of such reports, we know that the leading mother of the twentieth century, Leontina Espinossa

Albina (b. 1925) of San Antonio, Chile, in 1981 gave birth to the last of her fifty-five children, forty of whom were still alive in the 1990s. Most natural pregnancies, that is, before fertility drugs, result in only one baby. At least three women in the twentieth century have been reported as having given birth in one pregnancy to ten infants, all of whom were stillborn. An equal number of women gave birth to nine, none of whom survived beyond a few days.

Although few women beyond their mid-forties, without fertility drugs, give birth, many have become pregnant at later ages. There are several claims of women having given birth at age seventy or older but historians have been reluctant to accept such cases because when investigation has been possible it turned out to be an instance of a mother or grandmother claiming as her own the illegitimate child of a daughter or granddaughter. The best documented incident of an older woman giving birth was the case of Ruth Alice Taylor Shephard Kistler (1899–1982), whose daughter Suzan was born in Glendale, California, on October 18, 1956, when Kistler was 57 years and 129 days old. It is also possible for pregnancies to occur at very young ages, and births have been reported to girls under ten, and one to a girl perhaps as young as five, all the result of incest. The record books are reluctant to publish such pregnancies in the fear that some will attempt to try to establish a new record.

If the female reproductive potential is limited to offspring numbering in the double digits, that of the male can number into four digits. The man who is recorded as having fathered the most children is the polygamous Moulay Ismail (1672–1727), the last Sharfan emperor of Morocco. He was reported as having had 525 sons and 341 daughters by 1703, and in 1721 he recorded the birth of his seven hundredth son. Apparently by then he no longer recorded the number of his daughters. The European holder of the title is probably Augustus the Strong (1670–1733), king of Poland and elector of Saxony, who recognized 365 individuals as his children, only one of whom was legitimate. The record holders are the exception, but it is clear that few peoples and societies ever reached the theoretical maximum.

Statisticians talk of a total maternity ratio, defined as the average number of previous live births per women age forty-five or over, regardless of whether a particular woman has children. Obviously, not all women can or do have children, and maternity ratio excludes abortions, whether induced or spontaneous. Though several societies have at different times registered as high as seven or eight, the highest rate recorded is among the Hutterites, 10.6 per woman in the first part of the twentieth century. The Hutterites are a communal religious group dating from the sixteenth century that settled in South Dakota between 1874 and 1877. They now live in more than a hundred different religious colonies in the Dakotas, Montana, and Washington in the United States and in Alberta, Saskatchewan, and Manitoba in Canada. Interestingly, their maternity ratio declined somewhat in the last part of the twentieth century. Having children, however, did not necessarily mean having a large family of adult children, and, as Thomas Malthus pointed out at the end of the eighteenth century, one result of unchecked birthrates was misery, wars, and suffering.

Although infant mortality figures of the past are notoriously difficult to determine accurately, our best estimates are that somewhere between 25 and 40 percent of the infants born before the nineteenth century did not live beyond their first birthday. One of the best sources of evidence we have about infant and child mortality is in the progeny of European royalty, where a high rate of infant mortality can be documented. Infant mortality rates began to decline in the nineteenth century, but at the beginning of the twentieth they were still between 15 and 17 percent of live births in countries such as the United States and Great Britain.

Though infant mortality is not a form of birth control, there is considerable evidence that the high mortality rate of newborns and infants in many societies has not necessarily been a result of natural causes, but rather has resulted from actions that either intentionally or unintentionally would lead to a higher death rate. In few societies would infants be deliberately murdered, although the father in many societies had the right to accept or reject an infant's membership in the family, and rejection meant abandonment of the infant. This practice allowed the individuals involved to rationalize that the possible death of a child was up to the gods because whether the child lived (by being found and raised by someone else) or died was out of their hands. Such practices have often been continued today.

I had a personal experience in Egypt with an abandoned newborn that was found by a policeman. When he tried to turn it over to the hospital, he was told that he had found it so it was his responsibility and I remember the man mumbling that it was not his and what should he do. As I talked to him later, he implied that he would just ignore the next case he saw. In short, few of the societal institutions were willing to take responsibility for an infant's survival and the chance of one surviving were highly problematic. Even if the infant ended up in a foundling home, as they often did in medieval Europe and later, mortality statistics were extremely high in such places because contagious diseases, neglect, and infection killed most of the infants early on. The problem of nursing infants in such institutions was a serious one. Again, in Egypt when I lived there, infants in such institutions were nursed by wet nurses who were paid monthly to be wet nurses. Some of the wet nurses had very little milk but the need was so desperate that almost any woman was accepted, even older women beyond childbearing age. When the wet nurses came in for the monthly checkup, they brought the infants or corpses of the infants with them. Many of the infants had died weeks before but the wet nurses waited until the end of the month in order to get maximum pay. Again, it was claimed it was God's will whether the infant lived or died.

Many upper income residents of eighteenth- and nineteenth-century Paris turned to wet nurses until the infant reached the age when it could take solid foods. Undoubtedly infant mortality in the city (and in fact most major cities) was high because of poor sanitation, likelihood of contagious diseases, and other difficulties of city living, but dependence on country wet nurses probably increased rather than decreased infant mortality. This is because wet nurses by definition usually had infants of their own to feed, and milk production was not always enough to support more than one, although it might have been the child of the wet nurse who died because she might have neglected her own for the money available for the other. Some estimate that the total mortality rate of wet-nursed babies sent out from Paris was more than 40 percent.

Fertility was also curtailed by many societies, whether consciously or unconsciously, by providing for periods of abstinence during some seasons of the year such as Lent or by prohibiting intercourse with women during certain periods of their lives, as when they were lactating or menstruating. Because fertility among men is highest when they are between sixteen and twenty, another way of controlling population growth is to delay the age of marriage for both sexes and make the age higher for men. Ireland, for example, discouraged early marriages for much of the twentieth century. Such a delay is based on the assumption that women will remain abstinent until marriage. Such assump-

tions are not usually made about men, who remain free to visit prostitutes or engage in temporary liaisons. Such practices work most effectively in cutting down the total maternity ratio in countries with a high tolerance for a double standard of sexual conduct or where government or religious control and interference in the private lives of its citizens is very great.

Another factor in keeping the maternity ratio down was sexually transmitted diseases. Gonorrhea in women—transmitted, it was usually claimed, by an errant husband—could cause infertility, as could other sexually transmitted diseases that were finally diagnosed only in the twentieth century. Fertility is controlled also by the health of the mother. Women on protein- and iron-poor diets are more likely to be anemic than are women on diets with adequate protein and iron, and those with anemia are less likely to become pregnant and, if pregnant, less able to carry the baby to term. They also tend to die younger. Maternal mortality has usually been very high in the past, and inadequate diet has been a major factor along with too many pregnancies too close together or difficulties in child birth. Most women are not believed to have lived long enough to reach the menopause, particularly if they had very many children.

Another societal custom that could limit the total maternity ratio is polygamy. It has the effect of cutting the young men who are the most fertile out of the marriage market because the polygamists are the older and more politically powerful men. If the number of wives or concubines is very large, in spite of the example of Moulay Ismail, it is difficult for an aging man to keep them pregnant. Because on a random basis of active sexual activity, without any understanding of the fertility period, a woman is likely to become pregnant about one out of every thirty-three times she has intercourse, the women in a harem would not always be pregnant. Even if there were only three or four wives, the pregnancy rate would decline, especially if there was discrepancy in age between the husband and his wives.

Whether any of these customs were deliberately adopted as a means of birth control is unclear, but it seems clear that throughout history various methods have been tried to space births, prevent pregnancy, or induce an abortion if pregnancy occurred. Contemporary peoples who live in tribal of nomadic groups, for example, are known to use douches and drugs believed to prevent or cure pregnancy, to practice withdrawal (coitus interruptus), and to insert vaginal suppositories of one kind or another as well use magic and herbs. Some of the methods were probably effective. For example, the suppositories might have had resins that blocked the entrance to the cervix or oils that reduced the motility of the sperm. Subincision was also practiced in some groups. It involves an operation that creates a hole in the male urethra at the base of the penis near the scrotum so that during ejaculation semen dribbles over the scrotum instead of entering the vagina. Urine also dribbles out but if a finger is placed over the hole it acts as a plug, allowing both the urine and semen to come out in the normal way. Whether subincision was done originally for ritualistic reasons or contraceptive purposes is not clear. Although some semen when the hole is unplugged might spill out onto the labia of the woman and some semen and sperm might spill into the vagina, it certainly lessened the likelihood of pregnancy. We also know that many peoples engaged in what can be called nonfertile intercourse: anal, oral, or with a partner of the same sex. Certainly such behavior was not rare and was even common in classical antiquity, as indicated in vase paintings and in literary works.

The oldest birth control prescription we have dates from the second millennium (between 2000 and 1000 B.C.E.). One of the difficulties with the written record, however, is that it was mostly written by men, and it is believed by most historians, including me, that women in the past were far more involved than men in trying to establish some kind of family planning, if only for their own welfare. This so-called folk medicine passed orally by women has occasionally been preserved.

Usually it involves the use of various plants or minerals, many of which have been found to have some effect on lowering the total maternity ratio. Unfortunately much of this oral tradition has not survived. Still, many of these traditional recipes made their way into the medical works. And we can now test to see how effective they were. Some have been found to be rather effective as abortifacients and some might well have acted to lessen the potentiality of becoming pregnant. These recipes are examined in detail in this book under herbal remedies.

We know that effective birth control is based on a mindset that allows a person to believe that it is possible to control or limit birth, and probably for long stretches of history that mindset was held by only a few. Others simply acted in desperation. Part of the difficulty was that people knew little about the process of reproduction, although they knew it was dependent on sexual intercourse. Semen was visible but sperm and ova were not. Sperm was first seen at the end of the seventeenth century, and although there was speculation by the beginning of the nineteenth century that women had something like an egg, the process of fertilization was first observed in the starfish in 1877. Not until the discovery of hormones in the 1920s and 1930s was the process of menstruation and fertilization fully understood. This understanding ultimately led to the various hormonal methods of birth control and to a more accurate definition of a safe period.

There was, however, a recognition even in ancient Egypt of the need to slow the motility of the sperm and block off the cervix, the entrance to the uterus. In the nineteenth century a concentrated effort was made to make such methods more effective, although many of them were very similar to devices used centuries earlier. It was not enough, however, to find more effective means of contraception or to bring about an abortion; it was also necessary to convince the public, especially women, that they could control the use of their bodies. It was Sigmund Freud who said biology was destiny, implying that there was little that women could do to avoid their mission in life to be wives and mothers. Convincing women that they could control their own bodies, knowing that many wanted to do so, has been the mission of birth control advocates, both women and men, throughout the twentieth century and into the beginning of the twenty-first.

All of this is by way of introduction to this encyclopedia, which is a historical-sociological study of birth control throughout history. Although the general history of birth control worldwide is covered, the concentration here is on the political efforts in the United Kingdom and the United States that made modern birth control possible. Although Appendix 1 provides a country-by-country survey of present-day birth control practices, this encyclopedia does not discuss many of the world's leaders in the birth control movement; for example, individuals in the Scandinavian countries such as Elise Ottesen-Jensen are not discussed in any detail. Each country had its own leaders and advocates, although the general leadership of the movement worldwide was basically American and British. Space limitations and the difficulties of covering all of the people who could be potentially included have led to a decision to somewhat narrow the focus. The *Encyclopedia of Birth Control* still, however, is the most comprehensive historical survey of birth control, contraception, and abortion available. It is designed for the average reader, but the specialist, I believe, will also find it helpful, and everyone will find it interesting.

Vern L. Bullough

A

Abortion

Historically, abortion has been widely used as a method of limiting births, although the methods prescribed were not always effective. Perhaps the earliest recorded incident of an abortive technique is found in the royal archives of China about five thousand years ago. Abortifacients were included in an Egyptian medical papyrus of 1550 B.C.E. Technically both the laws of Hammurabi dating from 1728 B.C.E. and Jews during the period of Exodus established penalties against abortion but these were strictly limited to payment of compensation to a husband when an assault on his pregnant wife resulted in miscarriage. Overall, however, it can be said that abortion was not a subject to which persons in antiquity attached any deep feeling of condemnation or immorality.

Abortion was part of official policy in many of the Greek states, and Plato (427–347 B.C.E.), for example, insisted on abortion for every woman over forty who became pregnant. Aristotle (384–322 B.C.E.) held that when couples had children in excess and they were averse to having more offspring, abortion should be "procured before life and sense have begun."

As indicated in the entry on classical medicine, the Greek and Roman medical literature mentions a number of abortifacients and menstrual regulators. The major exception is the provision in the so-called Hippocratic Oath. Attributing the text to Hippocrates (c. 460–370 B.C.E.) is questionable, and most scholars read the prohibition as a later addition, perhaps one inserted under the influence of a Pythagorean sect that believed that the body and soul were fused into one at concep-

tion, an idea with which the various writers of the Hippocratic corpus did not agree.

Roman law did not oppose abortion since the basic legal principle was that the fetus was not a human being and it was only at birth that it became one. A husband, as the *pater familias,* father of the family, even had the authority to order his wife to abort, but if she purposely terminated a pregnancy without his consent, he could punish her or divorce her. In general, it can be said that the laws and tradition of abortion were well entrenched in the Roman Empire, and in spite of Christian opposition the tradition remained until 374 M.E., more than a half century after the legal establishment of Christianity, that the killing of an infant was declared by law to be homicide.

The early theologians of the Christian Church, however, had long agitated for just such legislation. The *Didache,* or *The Teaching of the Twelve Apostles,* dating from the first century, condemns abortion and this condemnation was continued through the writings of Tertullian (155–222), Cyprian (200–258), Saint Basil (320–379), and others. Early church councils followed suit beginning with the Council of Ancyra in 314, which stipulated a ten-year penance for women who fornicated and then destroyed the product of their intercourse, although this might have been a later interpolation. Most Christian theologians, however, followed Aristotle in the belief that the soul developed in three stages: vegetable at conception, followed by a higher stage of animal soul, and finally by a rational soul. The rational soul took place some time after conception, forty days for a male soul and eighty or ninety days for a female. This belief in the delayed beginning of life, what John T. Noonan called "vivified," was reaffirmed by Pope Innocent III (1198–1216) and entered into canon law through the writings of Pope Gregory IX (1227–1241).

Canon law influenced civil law on the continent and common law in England. Although the Anglo Saxons had probably regarded abortion solely as an ecclesiastical offense, Henry de Bracton (d. 1268) in his *Laws and Customs of England* carried over the provision of canon law on this topic into civil law, but condemned abortion only if the fetus had been formed and animated. When this occurred, however, was never defined by him. This continued to be the standard for English law until the nineteenth century. William Blackstone (1723–1780), whose commentaries had a great influence on American law, upheld the common law tradition of abortion only after quickening. Lawrence Lader held that after England's break with Rome under Henry VIII English ecclesiastical courts seem to have lost all interest in the question, leaving the subject to be a matter of common law.

This was not true of the papal view, however, and in 1588 under Sixtus V (1585–1590) the old rule of quickening was eliminated and all abortions were classed as murder at any period of fetal development. This proved to be an aberration. John T. Noonan called Sixtus V "an extremist in pursuit of virtue," and his successors must have felt the same because Gregory XIV, who succeeded Sixtus, abandoned his policy on the grounds that the edict had not produced the hope for changes. He revoked all the penalties applied by Sixtus and the old policy went back into effect.

In 1869, Pope Pius IX returned to the sanctions of Sixtus V and eliminated the distinction between a nonanimated and animated fetus. All abortions, according to Pius IX, should be regarded as murder. One of the reasons for the change was quite clearly an effort for consistency because the doctrine of Mary's Immaculate Conception promulgated by Pius IX in 1854 had stated that "from the very first moment of her conception" in her mother's womb she had been preserved from all stain of an original sin. This seemed to imply that Aristotle's old distinction of the changing nature of the soul was no longer valid. In fact, in a sense, the pope was reflecting new developments in biology. William Harvey had argued that all life came from the egg but this had been challenged by the discovery of spermatozoa in 1677. Although there had been a debate between the ovists and spermists over the importance of each, there had been a growing belief that fertilization took place when the sperm and egg met. Some by the middle of the nineteenth century were even arguing that the sperm penetrated the egg, although this was not documented until Oscar Hertwig observed it in sea urchins in 1875. Still, it seemed that life itself might begin with the earliest successful mixture of the male element with the female. Probably ultimately, however, it was not biology that decided which direction the pope would go but the necessity for consistency. If life for the Virgin Mary began at the moment of her conception, then all life must begin at the same time.

Moreover, the pope's rulings in a sense were reflecting a growing hostility to abortion. In 1803, the English parliament had replaced the common law about abortion with legislation that classed abortion (after quickening) as murder. Much of the impetus for the secular legislation against abortion was to preserve lives. American physicians, in their attempt to gain status over their rivals, such as midwives, also condemned the procedure, and their professional societies not only prohibited their members from engaging in abortion but had such prohibitions enacted into law. All of the states enacted laws prohibiting physicians from performing abortions.

See also Abortion in the Nineteenth Century; Classical Medical and Scientific Writers on Birth Control; Quickening

References
Devereux, George. *A Study of Abortion in Primitive Societies.* New York: Julian Press, 1955.

Dombrowski, Daniel A., and Robert Deltete. *A Brief, Liberal, Catholic Defense of Abortion.* Champaign, IL: University of Illinois Press, 2000.

Farley, John. *Gametes and Spores: Ideas about Sexual Reproduction.* Baltimore: Johns Hopkins University Press, 1982.

Himes, Norman. *Medical History of Contraception.* New York: Schocken Books, 1970.

Jakobovits, Immanuel. *Jewish Medical Ethics.* New York: Philosophical Library, 1959.

Lader, Lawrence. *Abortion.* Boston: Beacon Press, 1966.

Noonan, John T. *Contraception: A History of Its Treatment by the Catholic Theologians and Canonists.* Cambridge, MA: Harvard University Press, 1966.

————, ed. *The Morality of Abortion.* Cambridge, MA: Harvard University Press, 1970.

Abortion and Birth Control Clinics

When the first birth control clinics in the United States were opened in the 1920s, there was concern over what was called "overdues," that is, women who came to the clinic after having missed a menstrual period and were usually pregnant. Hannah Stone, as medical director of the Clinical Research Bureau in New York City, had established the policy that staff members should refuse to examine overdue applicants. She feared that, if an overdue woman was examined at the clinic and found pregnant and later decided to have an abortion, the clinic might be portrayed by its enemies as sanctioning abortion. She and her staff were worried that decoys seeking abortions were occasionally sent by the Roman Catholic Church or the police in an effort to close the clinic. Margaret Sanger in the 1930s became concerned over this policy because the overdue patients were being turned away without any counseling. In 1933, Sanger wanted to conduct a study of all overdue patients applying to the clinic in person or over the telephone who were interviewed and given special counseling. She believed that documenting 1,000 cases showing economic, psychological, and medical justification for abortion would make a more humane policy toward these women possible. She was unable to conduct the study, and as a general rule most clinics remained reluctant to deal with overdue women. The policy did not change until after abortion was declared legal in 1973.

Reference

Reed, James. *From Private Vice to Public Virtue: The Birth Control Movement and American Society Since 1830.* New York: Basic Books, 1978.

Abortion in the Nineteenth Century

Until the nineteenth century, folk remedies for abortion and superstitions about abortion essentially remained unchanged over the centuries. In the nineteenth century the selling of abortive products became a commercial business, although older more interventionist methods continued to be available. Technically, most of the remedies available did not mention the word abortion but went under such suggestive names as the "Female Regulator," "Uterine Regulator," "Woman's Friend," "The Samaritan's Gift for Females," and many others. Most of the remedies were described as having the imprimatur of science behind them. The label on Graves Pills for Amenorrhea stated, for example,

> These pills have been approved by the École de Médecin, fully sanctioned by the M.R.C.S. of London, Edinburgh, Dublin, as a never-failing remedy for producing the catamenial or monthly flow. Though perfectly harmless to the most delicate, yet ladies are earnestly requested not to mistake their condition [if pregnant] as MISCARRIAGE WOULD CERTAINLY ENSUE. (Quoted by Brodie, 1994, p. 225)

Many of the pills simply commercialized traditional remedies such as tansy, pennyroyal, aloes, hellebore, rue, ergot, and cotton root. The medicines were often effective. In fact, as late as 1939, the Federal Trade Commission forbade the sale and advertisement of a number of compounds designed to regulate menstruation on the grounds that the compounds posed serious health hazards. If advertised drugs and

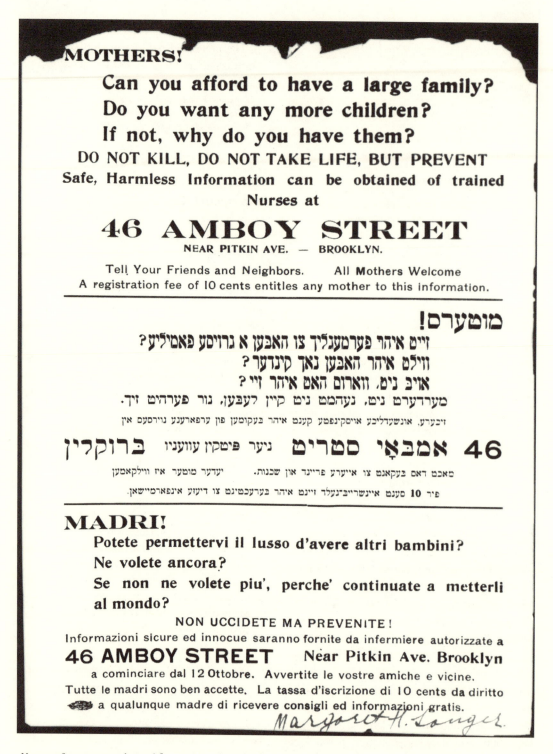

MOTHERS!

Can you afford to have a large family?

Do you want any more children?

If not, why do you have them?

DO NOT KILL, DO NOT TAKE LIFE, BUT PREVENT

Safe, Harmless Information can be obtained of trained

Nurses at

46 AMBOY STREET

NEAR PITKIN AVE. — BROOKLYN.

Tell Your Friends and Neighbors.   All Mothers Welcome

A registration fee of 10 cents entitles any mother to this information.

מוטערם!

זייט איהר פערמעגליך צו האבען א גרויסע פאמיליע?

ווילט איהר האבען נאך קינדער?

אויב ניט, ווארום האט איהר זיי?

מערדערט ניט, נעהמט ניט קיין לעבען, נור פערהיט זיך.

זיכערע, אונשעדליכע אויסקינפטע קענט איהר בעקומען פון ערפארענע נירסעם אין

46 אמבאי סטרים ניער פיטקין עוועניו **ברוקלין**

מאכט דאם בעקאנט צו אייערע פריינד און שכנות.   יעדער מוטער איז ווילקאמען

פיר 10 סענט איינשרייב־געלד זיינט איהר בערעכטיגט צו דיעזע אינפארמיישאן.

MADRI!

Potete permettervi il lusso d'avere altri bambini?

Ne volete ancora?

Se non ne volete piu', perche' continuate a metterli
al mondo?

NON UCCIDETE MA PREVENITE!

Informazioni sicure ed innocue saranno fornite da infermiere autorizzate a

46 AMBOY STREET   Near Pitkin Ave. Brooklyn

a cominciare dal 12 Ottobre. Avvertite le vostre amiche e vicine.

Tutte le madri sono ben accette. La tassa d'iscrizione di 10 cents da diritto
a qualunque madre di ricevere consigli ed informazioni gratis.

Margaret H. Sanger.

Margaret Sanger, seeing the need for women to obtain birth control instead of seeking back-alley or self-induced abortions, opened the Brownsville Clinic in Brooklyn, New York, in 1916. (Courtesy of the Sophia Smith Collection, Smith College) potions were not effective, there were instruments available to assist. *The American Medical Times* in 1863, under the title of "Instruments of a Notorious Abortionist," described forty simple instruments ranging from spoon handles bent in various shapes to pen holders with attached wires to actual forceps (Brodie, 1994, 226). There were also professional abortionists who were not yet forced underground.

A physician in the small farming town of Atkinson, Illinois (population 300) wrote in 1874 that he knew three respectable married women who were notorious for giving instructions to their younger sisters on ways of getting rid of an unwanted pregnancy. If tansy, savin, ergot, cotton root, lifting, or riding trotting horses failed, a knitting needle was a good standby. Other enterprising individuals developed their own methods. Frank Harris in his erotic biography described how he and his lover made a pencil of ingredients that swelled slowly with body heat so that once inserted into the cervix it caused an abortion.

Increasingly, however, there were legal restrictions put on abortion. For much of American history, abortion had been treated according to the common-law tradition in which abortions before quickening were not punishable. Those procured later in pregnancy might be high misdemeanors if the woman died, but not felonies. As criminal code revisions began in the various states, replacing the common law, abortion was often singled out for attention. The laws varied. In Connecticut, Missouri, and Illinois, abortion restrictions came in the form of tighter laws against the use of poisons. The first state to make an abortion a crime was New York, which in 1829 prohibited anyone, including a physician, from attempting abortion at any period of pregnancy except to save a woman's life. The state then proceeded to legalize abortions done by physicians when the mother's life was at stake, delegating to the medical profession the control of abortion. Most states followed this same delegation of authority.

Inevitably abortion began to go underground. Many of those providing such abortions were women. Perhaps the best illustration of the prevalence of women abortionists is the case of Elizabeth Blackwell, who is generally recognized as the first woman in the United States to graduate from a medical school. When she tried to establish her practice in New York City in the 1850s, she was denied rental at the first few boarding houses she approached because the landlords mistook her for an abortionist.

Probably the best-documented abortionist was Madame Restell, actually Ann Trow Lohaman (1812–1877), who ran a mail order business and abortion service in New York City from the 1840s through the 1870s. Because technically, as indicated above, abortion by non-physicians was illegal in New York state, Restell was often arrested, although only once was she sentenced to a term in prison. Mostly she was tolerated by the law enforcement officials, and she grew famous and wealthy, leaving an estate of more than a half-million dollars when she died. She was not alone, and abortionists who were arrested were often not found guilty, particularly if abortion took place before quickening.

See also Herbal Contraceptives and Abortifacients; Opponents of Birth Control and Abortion; Quickening; Social Purity Movement

References
Brodie, Janet Farrell. *Contraception and Abortion in 19th Century America.* Ithaca, NY: Cornell University Press, 1994.
Haller, John S., and Robin M. Haller. *The Physician and Sexuality in Victorian America.* Urbana: University of Illinois Press, 1974.
Lader, Lawrence. *Abortion.* Boston: Beacon Press, 1966.

Abortion in the Twentieth Century

The first country to legalize abortion in the twentieth century was the Soviet Union. In November 1920, after Vladimir Lenin, the first head of the USSR, insisted that no woman should be forced to bear a child against her will

In the 1980s and 1990s, when state legislatures and supreme courts began to impose limits on the right to choose abortion guaranteed in Roe v. Wade *(1973), many marches such as this one were held to demonstrate public support for upholding reproductive rights. (Courtesy of Planned Parenthood)*

and that women should be guaranteed the right of deciding pregnancy for themselves, abortion was made legal. A second motivating factor, however, was the government's effort to eliminate the medical havoc of widespread criminal abortion. The Soviets estimated that up to 50 percent of women became infected during the course of undergoing an illegal abortion and perhaps as many as 4 percent of them died. Interestingly, the Malthusian belief in the dangers of overpopulation that was so prevalent in the west was not an issue in the new Soviet state because Karl Marx, and for that matter Lenin, regarded such concerns as a unique problem of capitalism. Once legalized, the number of legal abortions rose rapidly, whereas illegal abortions dropped drastically. American observers of the Soviet experience reported almost an assembly line procedure, with abortions in a Moscow hospital being done every eight minutes by a two-person team. What was most upsetting to the observers, however, was the lack of any counseling or the availability of any contraceptive materials.

Without warning and for no apparent reason, in 1936 the Soviet government reversed itself and banned legalized abortion. This coincided with a general effort to abandon many of the human rights victories originally established by the early Bolsheviks such as easy divorce, progressive education, and avant-garde schools of music and literature. The ban also indicated the increasing power of Soviet premier Joseph Stalin and it was not until after his death that the Soviet state in 1955 again legalized abortion. Again the official explanation was to eliminate the harm caused by illegal abortions and to allow women to decide for themselves the question of motherhood. Although contraceptives were more available in the Soviet Union than they were earlier, there was no concentrated contraceptive information until after the collapse of the Soviet Union. Abortion, however, since its legalization, has remained widespread.

Following the Soviet example, other Eastern bloc nations followed suit. Bulgaria, Hungary, and Poland legalized abortion in 1956, Rumania legalized it in 1957, and Czechoslovakia started with unrestricted abortions but tightened its controls in 1962. Yugoslavia, not in the bloc but influenced by Soviet examples, established modified controls over abortion in 1960. East Germany was the last to legalize it but one reason for the delay is that it had the most effective contraceptive educational and dissemination system among the Communist countries. When the Soviet Union collapsed, there were efforts to criminalize abortions, particularly in Poland, but generally such efforts proved unsuccessful in the long run.

It was the threat of population growth, combined with the devastation resulting from Japan's defeat in World War II, that led the Japanese Diet (parliament) to enact in May 1948 the Eugenic Protection Law. The original law legalized abortion only for women whose health might be impaired from the "physical or economic viewpoint," but these laws were soon extended to allow abortion at the woman's request. Abortion became the standard method of birth control in Japan, with the result that the Japanese birthrate, 34.3 per 1,000 in 1947, had dropped to 16.9 by 1961. Like the Soviet Union, the Japanese paid little attention to contraception alternatives even though Margaret Sanger had been invited to Japan as early as 1922. The government, which opposed the invitation but eventually allowed her to enter, was then dominated by a militarist bloc and proponents of territorial and population expansion, who opposed the efforts of various women's groups to encourage the use of contraceptives. With the government still in opposition, Sanger's initial effort in Japan to popularize

birth control was a failure. Sanger was again invited in 1950 by a revived Birth Control Association but her initial invitation was blocked by General Douglas MacArthur under pressure from the Catholic Women's Club of Tokyo. After MacArthur's removal from command, Sanger made a triumphal return to the country. The favored method of family planning, however, remained abortion.

In Europe, the first country to legalize abortion was Iceland in 1934. Sweden followed in 1938, Denmark in 1939, Finland in 1950, and Norway in 1960, although the actual Norwegian practice of abortion generally followed that of the other Scandinavian countries even before the law was changed. Various modifications were made in the laws of all the countries, but all of them have a rather formalized procedure for approving abortions, and it is known that those women denied approval often get illegal ones anyway.

In Great Britain, the early advocates of birth control were antiabortion, although a number of spokespersons for legalized abortion began to appear in the 1920s. Their numbers grew large enough by 1936 to found the Abortion Law Reform Association. A turning point in British public opinion about abortion was a 1938 legal case involving a London surgeon, Aleck Bourne. Bourne was convinced that it was good medical practice for a physician to perform an abortion on a woman under certain circumstances but he wanted to make certain the courts agreed. He tested his beliefs by giving an abortion to a fourteen-year-old girl who had been raped by soldiers and who had been referred to him by the Abortion Law Reform Association. When the operation was completed, he notified the police, was arrested, and went to trial. The case attracted much attention and Bourne received support from not only a significant portion of the medical community but from important individuals and groups from all segments of society. The jury agreed and acquitted him on the grounds that the operation had been necessary to preserve the life of the woman who otherwise, based on psychiatric testimony, might have suffered a physical or mental trauma. Other court cases strengthened the Bourne decision and Canada and other Commonwealth nations subsequently passed laws justifying abortion if it was necessary to preserve the mental health of a patient, as well as for physical or health reasons.

In the United States, even when abortion was outlawed, therapeutic abortions were permitted when in the physician's opinion continued pregnancy was dangerous to the mother's life. Decisions in such cases depended on both the individual physicians and the medical communities in which the operation took place. The number of such abortions began to grow in the 1950s and 1960s as many physicians took into consideration the emotional health of the woman as well as her physical problems. Still, the overwhelming number of abortions were illegal ones, and in the early 1960s minimal estimates were that at least between 400,000 and 640,000 illegal abortions took place every year. The growing ability to lessen by the use of antibiotics the danger of infections was a major factor in changing attitudes about abortion in the medical community and probably made the profession more willing to extend the definition of what constituted therapeutic abortions. The difficulty was that such procedures were more likely to be limited to the well-to-do, who often had a relationship with their private physician, and this left most of the poor and most needy excluded.

The first move for change came from the legal rather than the medical community, with the publication of the Model Penal Code adopted by the American Law Institute in the 1950s. The proposals were modest, providing for termination of pregnancy when the physical or mental health of the mother was greatly impaired; when the child might be born with a grave physical or mental defect; or when pregnancy resulted from rape, incest, or other felonious intercourse, including illicit intercourse with a girl under the age of sixteen.

Public interest focused on abortion laws in 1962 with the case of Sherri Finkbine, a Phoenix, Arizona, mother of four, who had tak-en the tranquilizer thalidomide during the first few months of her fifth pregnancy. Because the drug had not been approved by the Food and Drug Administration (FDA), it had not been marketed in the United States. Finkbine's husband, however, had returned from Europe with a bottle of thalidomide, which still contained some pills he had taken, which she used. Two months later the news of the deformities that the pill was causing in European children—notably stunted or missing arms and legs—was made public. Finkbine panicked, fearful that her child would be deformed, something with which she believed she could not cope. She consulted her physician, who estimated that the chances of her infant being born deformed were at least 50 percent. He then arranged to admit her to the hospital for a therapeutic abortion. The story reached the newspapers through a friend of Finkbine's, and the news of a potential thalidomide baby in the United States received national publicity. Fearful of publicity about an abortion being performed by its staff, the hospital canceled the abortion. The distraught Finkbines flew to Los Angeles, planning to travel to Japan for the abortion, but the Japanese consulate, also afraid of negative publicity, refused them a visa. The couple then flew to Sweden, where Sherri had the abortion. The fetus was found to be deformed.

The publicity led to a greater focus on the abortion issue and gave publicity to groups encouraging a change. The American Civil Liberties Union went on record as regarding abortion as part of a woman's right to have control of her own body. In California, the Committee for Therapeutic Abortion, a coalition of civil libertarians, women's organizations, physicians, and liberal religious groups, was established in 1965. The next year the National Organization for Women was established, with reproductive rights as one of its major concerns. The National Association for the Repeal of Abortion Laws was established in 1968.

Beginning in 1967, several states modified their antiabortion laws, using all or part of the proposals of the American Law Institute. By 1970 thirteen states had passed such legislation and others were considering it. The advocates for legal reform also worked through the courts, so that by 1972 federal court decisions had liberalized abortion privileges in three jurisdictions. In 1973, the case of *Roe v. Wade* (one of several abortion cases being appealed) was decided by the U.S. Supreme Court, which ruled that abortions were a constitutional right and laws prohibiting them were null and void, although the rights of states to regulate abortions under certain conditions were recognized. The anonymous Jane Roe, who brought the suit in Texas, was later identified as Norma McCorvey. The decision did not help her because the court procedure took so long that she had already delivered her baby and put it up for adoption by the time the Supreme Court rendered its decision. In its ruling, the Court held that for the first three months of pregnancy the matter of abortion was to be decided by the woman and her physician. During the remaining six months the states were permitted to regulate the procedures used in order to ensure reasonable standards of care. Only in the last ten weeks of pregnancy, however, could the state ban abortion unless it was necessary to preserve the life of the mother. In spite of various legal challenges that have emphasized the power of the states to regulate abortions, this is essentially the law that remains today.

Most of the opposition coalesced under the collective title of "right to life." The radical fringe of these groups bombed abortion clinics or chained themselves to clinic doors to block entrances, and even murdered physicians who performed abortions. More mainstream members worked through the political process to weaken the right to abortion by passing restrictive state laws requiring the husband's consent, requiring parental consent for minors, cutting off public funding, and/or adding procedural requirements such as waiting periods.

The ideological and political make up of the Supreme Court as well as other federal courts changed during the administration of Ronald Reagan (1981–1989), who insisted on an antiabortion litmus test for his court appointees. President George H. W. Bush (1989–1993) followed the same path but not quite as zealously. Bill Clinton's ascendancy to the presidency in 1993 marked the abandonment of such a policy, although the battle continues as it did for any method of birth control. George W. Bush, elected in the year 2000, is openly antiabortion, and has talked about appointing one of the antiabortion justices as Chief Justice.

Increasingly, countries in Latin America, Africa, and Asia have allowed abortion. China uses it extensively; India, less so. Abortion still remains a controversial issue in many parts of the world.

When performed under aseptic conditions by a competent professional, abortion is a relatively safe procedure. When performed by inexperienced people or under unhygienic conditions, as so often happens in the case of illegal abortions, it is much more dangerous, not only in terms of maternal deaths, but in terms of long-term complications. Techniques vary with the stage of fetal development at which an abortion is sought. It is easiest during the early stages of pregnancy and both more complicated and dangerous in later stages.

Early abortion, sometimes called by its advocates postcoital contraception or menstrual regulation, can be brought about by several methods that rely on hormones or mechanical techniques. Various combinations of the hormones estrogen and progesterone (components of the oral contraceptive) are capable of terminating a pregnancy or bringing on the menses, although this has not been widely publicized. The FDA has been reluctant to formally approve any hormones for this purpose, more from political considerations than safety concerns, but in recent years has become more public about it, and in the year 2000 approved RU-486. There are many people who consider any contraceptive administered after an unprotected act of intercourse to be an abortifacient, and given this assumption, there are many clinics that do not prescribe any postcoital contraceptives, whereas others may limit their use to rape victims.

For contraceptive pills such as Orval, with 50 micrograms of estrogen and 0.5 milligrams of progestin, a total of four tablets should be taken in divided doses, an initial two, and then two twelve hours later. The series must start within seventy-two hours of the incident of unprotected intercourse, but preferably within twenty-four hours. Other pills vary in the doses. A postcoital insertion of a copper intrauterine device (IUD) has also proved effective in regulating menses by preventing implantation of the fertilized ovum in the uterus. IUDs that release hormones would have the same effect. All these procedures can be called menstrual regulators rather than abortifacients because no egg has been implanted.

Another method of bringing about an early abortion is menstrual extraction. This involves the insertion of a Karman cannula (tube) into the uterus and the removal of menstrual blood and tissue. A syringe or a suction machine is used to extract the uterine lining. This method is also regarded as a menstrual regulator and is often prescribed for a woman whose period is late; in fact, some women have used it to shorten the length of a menstrual period. No pregnancy test is required but casual use of the technique is not recommended because of the risk of hemorrhage and infection. The method was originally developed by Sir James Simpson in the nineteenth century to regulate menstruation and has been improved upon by later generations of physicians, most of whom refused to regard it as an abortion technique even though it was used for that purpose. It was not until the late 1950s, when a Chinese medical journal referred to it as a way of performing abortions, that Western medical journals were willing to discuss this use.

A traditional abortion technique, known by the ancient Greeks, is dilation and curettage (D&C). It is also used for a variety of purposes other than abortion, including taking biopsies to detect malignancies, dealing with prolonged bleeding from the uterus, and removing unex-

pelled placenta after childbirth. It involves dilation of the cervix and cleaning out the uterus with a curette. In unskilled hands it can lead to infection. Usually laminaria (cervical tampons that swell to three or five times their original diameter when placed in a moist environment) are used to dilate the cervix.

Midtrimester abortions (between the fourth and sixth months) are more difficult. Although D&C and vacuum aspirations are used early in this three-month period, both become increasingly risky and difficult as pregnancy advances. For most such late abortions a hypertonic saline solution is used. This method was first described in 1939 by a Rumanian physician but it was not used in the United States or in Western Europe until the 1960s. It involves the instillation of hypertonic saline (a 20 percent sodium chloride solution) in the amniotic sac or into the extraovular space (between the amniotic sac and uterus). A second method is the administration of prostaglandins, which encourage uterine contractions and are administered similarly to the hypertonic saline solution. Prostaglandins can also be given intravenously, intramuscularly, intravaginally, orally, or rectally. Third-quarter abortions require major surgical intervention and should generally be avoided unless the life of the mother is threatened.

See also Emergency Contraceptives; Oral Contraceptives; RU-486; Violence against Abortion Providers

References

Bullough, Vern L., and Bonnie Bullough. *Contraception: A Guide to Birth Control Methods.* Amherst, NY: Prometheus Books, 1997.

———. *Sexual Attitudes: Myths and Realities.* Amherst, NY: Prometheus Books, 1995.

Garrow, David J. *Liberty and Sexuality: The Right to Privacy and the Making of* Roe v. Wade. New York: Macmillan, 1994.

Gordon, Linda. *Woman's Body, Woman's Right.* New York: Penguin Books, 1977.

Lader, Lawrence. *Abortion.* Boston: Beacon Press, 1966.

———. *Abortion* II. Boston: Beacon Press, 1974.

McCorvey, Norma. *I Am Roe.* New York: HarperCollins, 1994.

Messer, Ellen, and Kathryn May. *Back Rooms: Voice from the Illegal Abortion Era.* Buffalo, NY: Prometheus Books, 1994.

Poppema, Suzanne T., with Mike Henderson. *Why I Am an Abortion Doctor.* Buffalo, NY: Prometheus Books, 1994.

"Pregnancy Termination in Mid-trimester: Review of Major Methods." *Population Reports,* Series F, No. 5 (September 1976).

Abstinence

The most obvious way to avoid either becoming pregnant or getting someone pregnant is to abstain from sex. This in essence has been the Christian remedy, and lifelong abstinence is still encouraged among such groups as Catholic priests and nuns. In the past, however, only a few societies have been either willing or able to impose long periods of abstinence upon more than a small minority of their members. Some religious groups such as the Manichaeans, a rival of Christianity, are said to have practiced abstinence, and their ideas had a great influence upon Saint Augustine and early Christians. In American history, the Shakers, a religious sect, took a vow of celibacy and abstinence. A small number of Shakers still exist as of this writing, but they were a much larger group in the nineteenth century. They kept their membership by proselytizing and by adopting unwanted children, many of whom elected to take a vow of abstinence when they reached adulthood. Many societies, on the other hand, have adopted periods of abstinence by imposing prohibitions on sexual intercourse during certain times of the year, such as Lent and various feast days, or during certain periods of a woman's life, such as when a woman is lactating or menstruating. It is highly unlikely that such prohibitions originally were established as birth control measures, although they undoubtedly helped to cut down the pregnancy rate. The belief that women had certain phases of their menstrual cycles when they were unlikely to get pregnant was widespread, although the necessary physiological data to calculate such periods was unknown until the twentieth century. Still, the belief entailed regular periods of abstinence.

Some religious groups have imposed vows of abstinence and celibacy upon a certain segment of their membership. In the case of the Catholic Church this was priests, monks, and nuns, those who enter religious orders or are ordained as priests. Again, this was not done as a means of birth control, but the result nonetheless was that of birth control because a significant number of individuals remained childless, in some periods as many as 10 percent of the population.

Many societies have encouraged adolescents, particularly females, to be abstinent until they were married, but few societies attempted to enforce such rules on the males. Instead, as this book emphasizes, most societies have hunted for various formulas to curtail the incidence of pregnancy, more or less admitting that abstinence, although perhaps a worthy goal, is one few can achieve.

See also Augustine, Saint; Sterile Period (Rhythm Method)

Reference
Abbott, Elizabeth. *A History of Celibacy.* New York: Scribner, 2000.

African Slaves in the United States and Birth Control

Little appears in the source material about contraceptives used by African slaves in America, but it was certainly believed by their European owners that their slaves used something. Herbert Guttman (1976, pp. 80–81) quotes a Georgia physician in the 1840s saying that abortion and miscarriage were more common among slaves than they were among free white woman. The physician believed that this was either due to the harsh conditions of slavery or that the "blacks are possessed of a secret by which they destroy the fetus at an early stage of gestation." The known remedies used by the slaves were tansy, rue, roots and seeds of the cotton plant, pennyroyal, cedar gum, and camphor. A brew made from cotton root is certainly an excellent emmenagogue. The slaves were also reported as using violent exercise, external and internal manipulation, and occasional tampons of various sorts. Vaginal douches made of a tea brewed from cocklebur roots mixed with bluestone was used both as a menstrual regulator and to wash out the fetus.

How effective such efforts were is perhaps debatable, but the white owners were convinced that their slaves were doing something. Guttman records a story of a slave owner who kept between four and six slave women of the "proper age to breed" for some twenty-five years and only "two children" had been born over that period as a result of full-term pregnancies. The other pregnancies had all been terminated by miscarriages. Whatever the reason, it seems that among the slaves some form of birth control was widely used, particularly among slave women who were more or less forced consorts of their owners. Birth control was in a sense a matter of quiet rebellion.

See also Herbal Contraceptives and Abortifacients

Reference

Guttman, Herbert G. *The Black Family in Slavery and Freedom, 1750–1925.* New York: Pantheon Books, 1976.

ingly older ages. This was the case with Arceli Keh, who delivered a baby in late 1996 at age sixty-three. Hers, however, was an assisted pregnancy. She did not conceive naturally but was implanted with another woman's fertilized egg. Such pregnancies could not have taken place in the past and even with fertility drugs are rare.

It is also possible for girls at very young ages to become pregnant. Several births have been reported and verified to girls under ten, and perhaps as young as five. The record books, however, have been reluctant to publicize such pregnancies for fear that someone will attempt to establish a new record. Most of these early pregnancies have been the result of incest.

Reference

McFarlan, Donald, ed. *Guinness Book of Records, 1989.* New York: Sterling Publishing, 1988. (Later editions do not always include such data, in part because of the difficulty of determining whether or not hormone treatments were involved.)

Age at Pregnancy

In the past, few women beyond their middle forties have given birth to children, although a small minority have become pregnant at still later dates. There are several undocumented claims of women in their seventies having children, but historians have been reluctant to accept such cases, if only because those that have been investigated in any detail have not turned out to be true. Usually it was a case of a mother or grandmother claiming as her own the child born out of wedlock to a daughter or granddaughter. Still, some cases of older women becoming pregnant have turned out to be true. The best documented is Ruth Alice Taylor Shephard Kistler (1899–1982), whose daughter Suzan was born in Glendale, California, on October 18, 1956, when Kistler was 57 years and 129 days old.

Kistler gave birth before fertility drugs were available but since that time other women given fertility drugs have had children at increas-

American Birth Control League

The American Birth Control League was established by Margaret Sanger in 1921, and she served as its president until 1928. Its first conference was held in New York City in 1921, timed to coincide with the convention of the American Public Health Association. Before the main event of the conference could be held, the entrance to the Town Hall Auditorium was closed by police through the instigation of the Catholic archbishop of New York. The closing of the meeting gave Sanger and her group national publicity and led to a rapid growth in the organization. By 1923 it had more than 18,000 dues-paying members and it needed a staff of from three to seven just to answer Sanger's voluminous correspondence.

The main strategy of the organization was to open birth control clinics and provide, under medical guidance, contraceptive materials to all women who sought them. The control of the

The American Birth Control League, founded by Margaret Sanger in 1921, later became the Planned Parenthood Federation of America. The slogan "every child a wanted child" has not changed much in nearly a century. (Library of Congress)

clinics by medical personnel was contrary to what Sanger had originally intended but she had come to believe that the only way to be successful in her task was to make concessions to the self-conscious professionalism of the physician. Her strategy was opposed by Mary Ware Dennett and the Voluntary Parenthood League. To emphasize physician importance, the American Birth Control League insisted on prescribing the diaphragm as the most effective means of birth control, a policy that also necessitated physician dominance under the laws of the time.

As a result of Sanger's ultimately successful strategy, both physicians and academics, many of them believers in eugenics, joined the organization. Increasingly the message of the American Birth Control League changed from simple emphasis on birth control to offering greater choice for all, and to emphasize this, in the 1930s the clinics began offering infertility therapy as well as contraception information.

In 1939 the American Birth Control League merged with the educational department of the Clinical Research Bureau and changed its name to the Birth Control Federation of America. In 1942 the name was again changed to the Planned Parenthood Federation of America, a name change opposed by Sanger. She later accepted the term as the movement became international and she was the first president of the International Planned Parenthood Federation organized in 1953.

See also Birth Control Clinical Research Bureau; Eugenics

References

Clarke, Adelle E. *Disciplining Reproduction.* Berkeley: University of California Press, 1998.

Reed, James. *From Private Vice to Public Virtue: The Birth Control Movement and American Society since 1830.* New York: Basic Books, 1978.

American Medical Association

Though much of the contraceptive information of the past is known through medical writings, in the United States organized medicine, for the last part of the nineteenth century and first part of the twentieth, was among the major opponents of the dissemination of contraceptive information. In part, this was because American medicine in the nineteenth century was a battleground of various medical theorists, each of whom had a system to preserve health and overcome disease. These systems ranged from water cures to animal magnetism, from naturopaths to homeopaths, from the followers of Sylvester Graham to those of Samuel Thomson, to outright charlatans. Medical schools of various types sprang up all over the United States. State licensing laws were nonexistent and the patient was advised to beware. Some areas of medicine such as surgery required specialized skills, but surgery itself was limited to amputations and minor excisions; penetration of body cavities did not come until almost the twentieth century. Apothecaries, free of any medical interference, developed a wide variety of tonics, salves, and pills. Because the names and contents of these preparations could be patented, many makers of nostrums made a fortune, with their success often being more dependent on their advertising ability than on the efficacy of their cures. One of the more influential regular physicians of the nineteenth century, Oliver Wendell Holmes, tried to distinguish between the quacks and the real physicians. The quack, he said, pretended to be a trained physician when he was not; he fabricated testimonials, he created diseases, and he gave his nostrums foreign names and claimed they were imported from abroad or made of rare and expensive ingredients. Statistical evidence was usually faked. Still, people often turned to them.

Complicating the problem was that traditional medicine had relied upon heroic cures such as blood letting, harsh purgatives, and other treatments that often turned out to be ineffective and even harmful. The germ theory had not yet been established, and the knowledge of physiology among even the best of practitioners was still rudimentary. On the other hand the new medical sects were generally not invasive in their techniques but emphasized diet, regularity of the bowels, and especially hygiene. The result was that their recommendations of frequent bathing, eating whole grain cereals and more vegetables and less animal foods, wearing loose and warm clothing, getting fresh air and exercise, and avoiding tobacco and alcohol were often more sound than the advice of the "more learned" physicians. New health-oriented practitioners such as chiropractors, naturopaths, osteopaths, and Christian Science healers added to the distrust of traditional medicine. Individual practitioners of any school or group could set up in practice after attending only a few lectures or reading a few medical texts, although there were more traditional schools in Philadelphia, Boston, New York, and other areas that tried to keep abreast of the changing developments of medicine on the continent. Much of the information, both good and bad, about birth control formulas and abortions had been produced by those who have since been called irregular practitioners, and any move against them tended to deprive the public of any information about such topics.

The panacea of quick cures gradually lost support in much of the United States, and there were increasing demands for some kind of standards. Struggling to fulfill this need was the American Medical Association (AMA), which had been organized in 1847 by delegates representing what then passed for regular medicine. Their mission was to raise the standards of American medicine as well as the moral quality of Americans. The battle to achieve the first objective was not complete until well into the twentieth century, and the second, in spite of their efforts, was never quite successful. In their role as moral guardians, the physicians condemned many medical practices, including abortion and birth control, as immoral. As a group, they were strong supporters of Anthony Comstock, the moral reformer, in his opposition to abortion.

The pioneer in the United States in this medical campaign was Hugh Lenox Hodge, chair of obstetrics at the University of Pennsylvania Medical School and a representative of the more orthodox medical practitioners. In 1839 he published a pamphlet, *An Introductory Lecture to a Course on Obstetrics,* in which he held that the embryo could think and perceive right and wrong. This is not accepted today, but from his conclusions it was clear that abortion was wrong. When Hodge republished the pamphlet thirty years later, he retitled it *Foeticide, or Criminal Abortion,* symbolic of the growing hostility to abortion by the AMA-affiliated physicians.

This hostility became institutionalized in the AMA through the leadership of Horatio Robinson Storer. Storer had begun his campaign to set a new moral tone on questions of abortion and birth control by gathering, from colleagues nationwide, material and statistics on still births, abortions, and maternal deaths. His report to the AMA in 1857 led the members to accept his recommendation that state legislatures and state medical societies make abortion more difficult, because he believed abortion was (and in this he was correct) a major cause of maternal deaths. He also believed that contraception was not only medically dangerous but criminal. He held that in the United States numerous instances of nervous disease and uterine problems had been caused either by abortion or the "systemic prevention of conception." Contraception was not only dangerous for women but for men because the use of condoms or the practice of coitus interruptus was not only dangerous to male health but could cause impotency. By the 1870s the AMA had launched a major campaign against abortion and contraception, effectively equating

such practices with quacks, medical irregulars, and others. For Storer, the true physician should become the moral arbiter of society, a role envisioned for physicians earlier by Benjamin Rush, the physician signer of the Declaration of Independence and a goal in which Storer and most other members of the AMA believed. Even though some of Storer's colleagues disagreed with him, they did not organize any group to oppose the AMA stands. Some spoke individually against his notions and that of the AMA and so did advocates of free love, social reformers, and even for a time some of the emerging feminist leaders such as Elizabeth Cady Stanton. Stanton, in her speeches to small groups of women, emphasized the need for women to have "self sovereignty" over their bodies and their sexual lives, but she did not officially oppose the stands of the AMA, the social purity movement, or Comstock.

Giving strength to the AMA were changes in medical theory and practice brought about by discoveries made by Louis Pasteur, Robert Koch, and others. The discovery not only of germs but of particular bacteria causing specific diseases gave medicine a stronger scientific bent than it ever had before. New aseptic techniques and the development of anesthesia allowed physicians to do more direct interventions, aided by an emerging pharmaceutical industry that provided new drugs such as aspirin, which had been laboratory tested and had clear benefits. Almost all of these breakthroughs occurred in Europe, particularly in Germany, and the better U.S. medical schools were either reorganized or newly established on the German model. The best example of this new trend was the founding in Baltimore of the Johns Hopkins University Hospital, which was the first effort in a long campaign to raise the level and sophistication of medical education. Medical schools that had earlier identified with universities, but that operated more or less independently of them, were given stronger direction by the universities and their curricula radically reformed. The hospital, the traditional bastion of medical education, itself became more important in medical treatment, and literally thousands of new hospitals were established in the United States in the last two decades of the nineteenth century and first decade of the twentieth century. The emergence of modern nursing gave the hospitals free labor in the form of students, and increasingly more procedures once done in the home moved into the hospital. For the most part, control of who would be on the staff of the hospital fell to physicians who belonged to the AMA. Medical reform became a major agenda of many of the newly emerging charitable foundations in the United States such as those established by Andrew Carnegie, John D. Rockefeller, and others.

Part of the reforms required greater state intervention in licensing and registration of physicians, setting standards for hospitals, and requiring physician prescription for drugs, and the effect of all of these was to allow the physicians who were affiliated with the AMA to squeeze out most of their rivals. In the middle of the nineteenth century, for example, almost all babies were delivered by midwives, and only a few physicians regarded themselves as experts in this. The development of anesthesia, the establishment of maternity hospitals with only AMA accredited physicians, and the gradual disappearance of home deliveries rapidly increased medical control in the gynecological and obstetrical fields. But the AMA also mounted a campaign against what they called ignorant and untrained midwives with whom they associated abortion and dangerous use of contraceptives. The midwives were not organized well enough to counter the AMA assault, and for a time they almost disappeared in the United States. Those competitors who survived, such as the osteopaths, had to establish their own medical schools and hospitals to do so. Others, such as chiropractors, tried to find a niche they could fill and rarely challenged the AMA openly. It was not until after World War I with the massive closing of what were regarded as

dubious medical schools and the setting of minimum standards for medical schools that the AMA had won the battle.

One effect was an appreciable decline in the quality of contraceptive advice literature. What existed, except underground, gave few specific descriptions of what to do. In fact, by the last decade of the nineteenth century it became almost impossible to publish and distribute even the most proper books touching on reproduction or reproduction control. Edward Bond Foote, the physician son of Edward Bliss Foote, whose writing on contraception was among the most sophisticated in the last part of the nineteenth century, reported that regular physicians like himself could no longer legally prescribe or advise contraceptives to save a mother's life, but that they could legally perform an abortion to do so. In effect the medical community had emerged to a position of legal control of reproduction, even if therapeutic abortion was the ultimate end.

One effect of the battle was official medical opposition to both abortion and contraception. In the process the practical midwife and many of the medical sectarians were accused of being abortionists or of secretly giving out to women recipes for birth control. From the first, the AMA was staunchly antiabortionist as much on moral grounds as was the medical belief that abortion was bad medicine because so many women were killed or maimed in the process. But the AMA also opposed contraception so strongly that they did not even pay attention to medical developments in the field. Morris Fishbein, the editor of the *Journal of the American Medical Association* and the major voice for organized medicine, as late as 1925 wrote that there were no safe and effective birth control methods and classified such efforts among what he considered as medical follies.

Although there was always a handful of physicians who were open advocates of contraception, it was not until well into the twentieth century that the AMA finally accepted its important role in the lives of women. To gain medical backing, contraception too had to be put in moral terms, and William Robinson and Robert Latou Dickinson were important in doing so. The struggle for rights to contraception in the United States was waged by lay people, and the medical community was only reluctantly pushed and shoved to finally accepting contraception, but by the time it did, the birth control movement itself had to change to more or less rid itself of its radical background and its association with anarchy and socialism.

See also Comstock, Anthony, and Comstockery; Dickinson, Robert Latou; Foote, Edward Bliss; Robinson, William Josephus; Social Purity Movement

References

Brodie, Janet Farrell. *Contraception and Abortion in Nineteenth Century America.* Ithaca, NY: Cornell University Press, 1994.

Fishbein, Morris. *Medical Follies.* New York: Boni and Liveright, 1925.

Gordon, Linda. *Woman's Body, Woman's Right: Birth Control in America.* New York: Penguin Books, 1990.

Kett, Joseph. *The Formation of the American Medical Profession.* New Haven, CT: Yale University Press, 1968.

Reed, James. *From Private Vice to Public Virtue: The Birth Control Movement and American Society since 1830.* New York: Basic Books, 1978.

Young, James Harvey. *The Toadstool Millionaires.* Princeton, NJ: Princeton University Press, 1961.

Anal Intercourse

Historically, one of the ways in which individuals have avoided becoming pregnant is through anal instead of vaginal penetration by the penis. Because the anus is rich in nerve endings and is involved in the sexual response whether or not it is directly stimulated, some people enjoy this form of intercourse. One of the best-documented uses of anal intercourse is among the Manichaeans, a religious rival to early Christianity and about whom we know a lot from the writings of Saint Augustine. The Manichaeans held that its members should not engage in reproductive activity, and for those who could not be continent, anal intercourse seemed a way of having sex without the consequence of pregnancy. Augus-

tine, who mentions the practice several times, seems to imply that this practice was followed only by heretical Manichaeans and reported that it was engaged in by both male and female partners, that is, homosexual and heterosexual couples.

Because the anus does not lubricate very well, some form of lubrication, such as K-Y Jelly or other forms of sterile, water-soluble solutions, has to be provided. Petroleum-based lubricants should not be used in the rectum, or for that matter in the vagina, because they tend to accumulate and are not as easily discharged as those that are water soluble. Oil-based lubricants also weaken barrier contraceptive devices, including the condom.

The anal sphincter responds to penetration with an initial contraction that may be uncomfortable. In a tense, inexperienced person, the contraction may last for a minute or longer, whereas those experienced in this form of intercourse appear to relax much more quickly, and the spasm lasts less than thirty seconds. Usually, when the spasm has run its course, the discomfort disappears. William Masters and Virginia Johnson in their studies of the human sexual response found that in eleven of fourteen episodes involving penetration of a female anus by a male, the female had an orgasm. Some researchers have found that 25 percent of American women have engaged in anal intercourse at least once, and ten percent do so regularly for pleasure. Most respondents, however, do not find it appealing.

Rectal intercourse carries risks and discomfort that can be overcome by proper care. Feces that could become smeared externally or block entry should be emptied from the rectum beforehand by an enema. The anal canal and rectum are easily damaged, so vigorous thrusting may tear the anal or rectal wall, causing hemorrhage or a serious local infection.

Heterosexual couples who engage in anal intercourse should be cautioned that vaginal intercourse ought not to be started immediately after anal sex. The penis should be thoroughly washed first. The anus contains bacteria that can cause infection if introduced to the vagina.

See also Augustine, Saint

References

Bullough, Vern L. *Sexual Variance in Society and History.* Chicago: University of Chicago Press, 1976.

Masters, William H., and Virginia E. Johnson. *Human Sexual Response.* Boston: Little, Brown, 1966.

————. *Homosexuality in Perspective.* Boston: Little, Brown, 1979.

Voeller, B. "AIDS and Heterosexual Anal Intercourse." *Archives of Sexual Behavior* 20 (1991): 233–276.

Ancient Civilizations and Birth Control

The earliest medical writing from Egypt, the Kahun Medical Papyrus, dates from 1850 B.C.E. It includes three fragments of prescriptions designed to prevent pregnancy. All of them deal with suppositories. One provides for the feces of crocodile to be smashed up and mixed with fermented dough; another provides for honey mixed with soda or saltpeter; a third one with unreadable ingredients instructs to mash them up and mix them with fermented dough.

The crocodile feces recipe is difficult to explain, although its use might have kept the squeamish away, and dung from various animals is used in other ancient cultures. Certainly any sticky barrier might hinder the penetration of some sperm. But some substances might have encouraged contraception. For example, the pH of crocodile dung is 7.9, which makes it somewhat alkaline, and by lessening the vaginal acidity it increases the chance of pregnancy because the optimum conditions for pregnancy are pH 8.5 to 9.5 and the normative pH for the vagina is 3.86 to 4.45. It might be, however, that crocodile dung was used for religious reasons because the crocodile is associated with the Egyptian god Seth, who in turn is associated with hemorrhaging, miscarriage, and abortion. The other two prescriptions include soda or saltpeter, which besides serving as barrier methods might well change the pH level, but not as much as crocodile dung.

Other medical papyruses including the Ramesseum Papyrus (1784–1662 B.C.E.) also advise crocodile dung as a suppository. Quite different is the Ebers Medical Papyrus (1875 B.C.E.), which describes a mixture of acacia berries and colocynth mixed with honey to form a suppository that is placed in the vagina. When acacia is compounded, lactic anhydride is produced and lactic acid is often a component in modern contraceptive jellies. Colocynth is usually interpreted as being *Citrullus colocynthis Schrad,* which is known to have abortifacient properties and is still taken by modern Arabic women. Other prescriptions for abortifacients include the use of fumigants, salves, and drinks, as well as the suppositories. The earliest description of an oral contraceptive dates from 1300 B.C.E. in the Berlin Medical Papyrus and includes among other things celery seeds, oil, and sweet bear (Riddle, 1992).

The realization of the Egyptian medical writers that certain agents can prevent conception and cause an abortion emphasizes the antiquity of human efforts to prevent or destroy unwanted pregnancies. Although there is less surviving evidence from the Tigris-Euphrates valley, there are tantalizing references. A Sumerian tablet written earlier than the Kahun Medical Papyrus has a fragment of a recipe for a woman who wants to abort a fetus, but the instructions are lost. A cuneiform recipe from Assur advises inserting wool soaked in pomegranate juice in the uterus probably as a abortifacient or contraceptive.

Indirect evidence indicates that the Sumerians and their successors knew that certain diets, such as ergot-infected wheat, caused abortions. Ergot is a toxin derived from a fungus that grows on many plants including rye. Its growth is heavily influenced by climatic factors such as cold winters, and there are references in cuneiform texts of predictions of miscarriages based on climatic factors and predictions with a different set of weather conditions that women would carry their fetuses to full term.

A chief source of information about the attitudes of people in Mesopotamian civilization and their successors are the surviving law codes, some dating from 2110 B.C.E. These law codes give credence to John Riddle, a historian of contraception who argued that there is little indication that the people of either Egypt or the Tigris-Euphrates valley regarded the fetus as a human persona. Damaging a fetus was damaging a woman, and the rights to compensation belonged to the father, not the mother. Miscarriages caused by others required reimbursement to the husband of the woman. A late Assyrian law prescribed a penalty of impalement of a woman for procuring her own abortion and it is clear that what was being protected was the asserted right of the husband to receive a child he sired. In general, greater penalties existed for what might be called late-term abortions than for early ones.

In China, coitus interruptus was believed to strengthen the store of the male yang and ultimately lead to more male children. Although not done for contraceptive purposes, it probably had contraceptive value. Ancient Chinese believed that the key to a long life for males was preserving the yang that was lost through sexual intercourse. By using coitus interruptus, or withdrawal, the man could gain some of the woman's yin (if she had orgasm) without losing his yang. Besides advocating coitus interruptus, the Taoists also advocated blocking the male urethra by pressing the point between the scrotum and anus and diverting the semen from the vas into the bladder instead of the urethra.

Intellectually and culturally the ancient Chinese were much more centralized than the other early civilizations. There was one polity and one elite culture and historical records were accumulated in a single language. The record of the past was conceived as that of a single people and the early availability of paper and the development of printing made literature much more subject to ideological control and more central to political and social concerns. The plethora of varied source materials available in either Egypt or Mesopotamia is therefore less evident in China. Because birth control and abortion were

subjects not usually discussed in the official literature, we have less information on those subjects. One of the earliest references is in the historical annals *Shi Chi,* compiled by Ssu Ma Ch'ien (second century B.C.E.). He noted that a mythical founder of China, Shen Nung, adopted a policy of population control (Watson, 1961, Ssu-Mac Chien, ii, 188), but what that entailed is unclear.

The earliest references to actual methods date from the seventh century C.E. work of Sun Ssu-ma entitled *Ch'ien chin fang* (literally Thousand of Gold Prescriptions), which might describe the prescriptions and methods used as birth control or abortifacients or "menstrual regulators" earlier in China as well. One involves mixing oil and quicksilver (mercury) and taking it as a potion on an empty stomach. It was said to prevent pregnancy without harming the individual, a rather dubious claim. Another involves taking a mixture of barley gruel, and still another involves rape seeds. Obviously the Chinese from an early date were attempting to prevent pregnancy or have abortions.

Sex texts are plentiful in India but they do not always contain information on contraception or abortion. There is, however, considerable discussion of nonprocreative sexual activities such as oral-genital contacts, much more so than in the other cultural areas discussed. Some Tantric sects of Hinduism also practiced the coitus interruptus methods discussed in China as a means of avoiding conception, although this might not have been the motivating purpose of such procedures.

The *Ananga Rama* dates from the fifteenth century of the modern era but it includes recipes and concepts from earlier periods including several to make a woman sterile. The twelfth century *Koka Shastra,* compiled by Kakkoka, has a whole section devoted to abortifacients and contraceptives. There are many other similar collections. Norman Himes, in his summary of the various recipes, held that most were not particularly effective. However, as indicated in the article on herbal remedies, many might have been more effective than he realized. In addition to various concoctions taken orally, the Indians used vaginal fumigations and various kinds of obstructive devices including insertion into the vagina of honey and ghee (oil), rock salt dipped in oil, and tampons of ground ajowan seeds and rock salt with oil. The use of rock salt was a particularly effective spermicide (and could be used even today) because an eight percent solution kills sperm rapidly.

The difficulty with all the prescriptions is that some were effective and others were not and there was really no way for the ancients to determine which except by trial and error. Moreover, even if some were more effective than others, dosages also were important and these often remain unclear. We know that the ancient peoples wanted to control pregnancies or eliminate unwanted fetuses but they were not always successful.

See also Herbal Contraceptives and Abortifacients

References

Biggs, R. D. "Ergotism and other mycotoxicoses in ancient Mesopotamia." *Aula Orientalis* 11 (1991): 15–21.

Bullough, Vern L. *Sexual Variance in Society and History.* Chicago: University of Chicago Press, 1976, pp. 52–53.

Driver, G. R., and J. C. Miles. *The Assyrian Laws.* Oxford, UK: Clarendon Press, 1955.

Ebers, G., trans. *Papyrus Ebers das hermetische Buch ber die Arzneimittel der alten gypter in hieratischer Schriften.* Leipzig: n.p., 1875.

Himes, Norman E. *Medical History of Contraception.* New York: Schocken Books, 1970.

Kahun, No. 21, 22 (3,7), in *Grundriss der Medizin der alten gypter,* edited by Hildegard von Deines, Herman Graprow, and Wolfhart Westendorf, 7 vols. Berlin, 1954–1962, vol. 4, pt. 5.1, p. 277; note pt. 2, p. 211; vol. 5, p. 477.

Kakkoka. *Koka Shastra,* edited by T. N. Roy. Calcutta: Medical Book Co., 1960. (This includes the section missing in the more available translation listed below with a slightly different spelling of the name of the compiler.)

Kokkoka. *Koka Shastra,* translated by Alex Comfort. New York: Stein & Day, 1964. (Unfortunately this particular translation only summarizes the section.)

Kalanmalia. *Ananga Rama,* translated by Tribidnath Ray. New York: Citadel Press, 1964.

Ricks, S. D. "Abortion." In *Anchor Bible Dictionary,* 1st ed., edited by David Noel Freedman et al. New York: Doubleday, 1992, pp. 31–32.

Riddle, John M. *Contraception and Abortion from the Ancient World to the Renaissance.* Cambridge, MA: Harvard University Press, 1992.

———. *Eve's Herbs.* Cambridge, MA: Harvard University Press, 1997.

Ssu-Ma Chien, ed., and B. Watson, trans. *Records of the Grand Historian of China, Ssu-Ma-Chien.* New York: Columbia University Press, 1961.

Thompson, R. Campbell. *A Dictionary of Assyrian Botany.* London: British Academy, 1949, p. 315.

Anemia, Diet, and Pregnancy

In the Middle Ages, although there seems to have been a slight numerical predominance of males over females at birth, the sex ratios increased in adulthood and, as David Herlihy said, there "was a spirited competition for scarce women." Several factors have been suggested to explain this shortage of females, including widespread female infanticide, abandonment, and simply underreporting or lack of reporting of females. Although all of these factors might have been at work for much of the Middle Ages, and probably for other periods as well, much of the discrepancy was a result of female anemia. This resulted in a high female mortality, and this in itself worked to cut down family size.

Even though the nutrition of Paleolithic times has sometimes been used as a reference standard for modern nutrition and a model for defense against certain "diseases of civilization," it seems clear that no such use can be made of the diet of either the classical or early medieval period. In fact, from what we can reconstruct of the Roman and early medieval diet, proteins and iron, the essential components for building hemoglobin, were in short supply. Though the protein content of the diet increased gradually in the medieval period as meat became more plentiful and beans (a good source of protein) became a standard fare, the lack of iron was slow to be remedied until the use of iron pots became common.

Although iron is present in many foods, the amount that can be absorbed from grains and vegetables in general is less than that absorbed from iron salts, liver, and muscle. It is not possible to determine precisely what the amount of iron absorption from the early medieval diet was but it has been estimated to have been between 0.25 and 0.75 mg per day. This amount would have been marginal for men and less than adequate for women between the beginning of the menarche and until the menopause began. For women, before menarche and after menopause, the needs are the same as men, but the loss of iron in the menstrual flow adds substantially to this loss, resulting in a total replacement need of 1–2 mg per day. In sum, a woman during her years of menstruation requires at least twice as much iron as a man. During pregnancy, a woman's need for replacement iron is even greater than when she is not pregnant because the demands of the pregnancy increase the need until, during the last two-thirds of the pregnancy, somewhere between 3 and 7.5 mg per day are required. This demand continues until breast-feeding is terminated.

Anemia is seldom the primary cause of death, rather it is a predisposing factor, and anemic women are more likely to get pneumonia, bronchitis, and emphysema, and in fact more women died during the medieval bubonic plague than did men. Because the average age of menarche in the medieval period was fourteen years, the net loss of iron per year for a woman over fourteen on the average diet would have been 274 mg per year, which would have reduced body stores of iron to near zero within eight years. Pregnancy would have complicated matters still further because a single pregnancy would result in losses of 1,467 mg of iron in two years (680 mg for 9 months of pregnancy, 765 mg for 14 months of lactation, and 22 mg for each month of normal menstruation). At this rate a woman's iron stores would be reduced to zero by the time she was twenty-two. The result was a high rate of female mortality and a tendency to have spontaneous abortions when pregnant. Overall this would lead to both a shortage of women and to smaller family size. Conditions conducive to anemia began to ameliorate with diet change in the later Middle Ages and women began to live

longer than men and the number of children surviving infancy also increased. Still in many parts of the world, female anemia has to be regarded as a major factor in controlling family size and in curtailing the life span of women.

References

Bullough, Vern L. "Nutrition, Women, and Sex Ratios." *Perspectives in Biology and Medicine* 30(3) (1987): 450–458.

Bullough, Vern L., and Colin Campbell. "Female Longevity and Diet in the Middle Ages." *Speculum* 55 (1980): 317–325.

Eaton, S. B., and M. Koner. "Paleolithic Nutrition." *New England Journal of Medicine* 312 (1981): 283–289.

Herlihy, David. "Life Expectancies for Women in Medieval Society." In *The Role of Women in the Middle Ages,* edited by R. T. Morewedge. Albany: SUNY Press, 1975.

Apothecaries, Abortifacients, Contraceptives, and Patent Medicines

As indicated in the entry on herbal contraceptives and abortifacients, many plants and other items were believed to have contraceptive and abortifacient value. Much of this information was oral tradition, although some crept into the medical writings. People in the Middle Ages studied plants for medicinal purposes and "wise" women or midwives often kept alive the ancient tradition. When the medical universities developed in Europe in the twelfth and thirteenth centuries, ancient classics were studied and new data were added. In the sixteenth century, modern botany was born in northern universities where German was spoken and the result, because of the difference in the language used, was a division between botany and pharmaceuticals, although much overlap remained. The main source about abortifacients and contraceptives became the recipe books intended for use by apothecaries, and much oral tradition came to be more widely disseminated.

The transition from the classical to the medieval to the modern tradition to a new type of recipe book is the *Dispensatorium* of Valerius Cordus. Issued in 1546, the *Dispensatorium* became a standard for apothecaries throughout much of Europe, with others adding to it or basing their own book upon it. Although no contraceptives or abortifacients are specifically listed as such by Cordus, there were many substances that had that effect, mainly in his listing of menstrual stimulants. Many of his recipes included multiple herbs such as myrtle, lupine, rue, wild mint, pennyroyal, cumin, blackberries, asafetida, sagapenia, opopanax, geraniums, and artemisia. All told he gave nearly a dozen recipes for menstrual regulation, all of them containing familiar abortifacient drugs.

Mostly the recipe books used very discrete language, avoiding the words for abortion or birth control, but there are major exceptions. Hans Jakob Wecker (1528–1586) openly listed some forty-five plants and three animal products that had abortifacient or contraceptive value. He also began to produce new distillates and prepared medicines, a sign of the changing nature of the apothecary art. Johann Schroeder in 1641 updated the recipes and added many new distillates and extractions. He also continued to list abortifacient drugs, many of them the classical herbs such as artemisia, calamint, juniper, squirting cucumber, and others familiar to the classical and medieval world.

Increasingly physicians began to write about obstetrical subjects. Eucharius Rosslin (c. 1500–1526), who started as a pharmacist before becoming a physician, wrote a book in German that would translate into English as *The Pregnant Woman's and Midwife's Rose Garden*. He also dealt openly with abortion, arguing that if a woman's life was in peril, even if she just thought it was, such a belief would justify medical intervention to bring about an abortion. Some signs of danger for the physician to look for were trances, general weakness and feebleness, an inability to eat meat, and a rapid pulse. Rosslin advised first using recipes beginning with fumigants (drugs administered by inhalation) and then graduating, if needed, to oral drugs, followed by pessaries, and if all failed, surgical intervention was the final alternative.

Most sixteenth and seventeenth century books by physicians dealing with diseases of women

started with menstruation and a list of drugs to relieve menstrual retention, many of which were traditional abortifacients. Some books, such as that by the English physician James Primrose (1598–1659), mentioned drugs that induce sterility, which is another way of describing contraception especially if it was for short-term sterility. One of the early books by a woman was that by Jane Sharp, who in 1671 published a guide for midwives. She did not mention contraceptives directly but rather described things harmful to conception such as ivy berries or wearing sapphire or emerald stones, a mixture of reality and magic. She was, however, more serious in her list of menstrual stimulants (and abortifacients), including artemisia, tansy, pennyroyal, and catnip. She also made mention of alpine snakeroot, which also has abortifacient activity.

Was there a distinction between a contraceptive and abortifacient in the minds of the women involved? One indication that at least some lay persons tried to distinguish the difference appears in the play *Matrimonial Whoredom* by Daniel Defoe (1727). One scene portrays a bride discussing with her cousin what might be called family planning. The cousins equated abortion and contraception, claiming that it was the "same thing to prevent a conception as to destroye [sic] the child after it is conceived." The cousin recommended the bride take a physick, which would kill an unwanted conceptus. The bride replied that she would not do that but she would take a contraceptive. The cousin responded that she could not understand the niceties involved: "I would not be with Child, that's all; there's no harm in that, I hope."

John Riddle has argued that, in spite of the lack of listing about contraceptives, there had almost always been a widespread folk knowledge about them that women passed down from generation to generation, but now adding to this unwritten tradition among women were herbals aimed at a general public. Although most printed herbals were intended for apothecaries and physicians and were usually written in Latin, not all were. One that was aimed at the general public was written by Nicholas Culpeper (1650), and being ever cautious he usually listed contraceptives and abortifacients in negative terms. For example, he warned that the fern called fililx as well as laurel were dangerous for pregnant women because they might cause a miscarriage. Dittany and iris might have the same consequences. Other plants or plant products derived from artemisia, carrot seeds, lilies, myrrh, and tamarisk were to be taken to stimulate menstruation. Two contraceptives are listed in even more negative ways: rue and wild mint, both of which were said to be an enemy to generation for those who consumed their seeds. Culpeper later translated a medicinal guide that intended to give guidance to the poor and originally was written by the continental physician Jean Prevost (1662). It included a list of drugs to extinguish a man's semen and to impede generation such as chaste tree, rue, juniper, ginger, and willow, as well as drugs to stimulate menstruation. Again the subject of abortion is not specifically mentioned.

Obviously information was available, some of it quite accurate, and the midwives and apothecaries knew about it, and so increasingly did the literary public. But there were gaps, and the professional physician often seemed to be ignorant, or at least had to appear to be ignorant. Riddle mentioned the case of a French Dr. Olivier who wrote in 1760 about an interesting case in his medical practice. A woman six months pregnant came to him and explained that she no longer felt any movement. After an examination, he concluded that her fetus was dead but he did not know what to do. He then turned to some of the classical texts to read about expulsives or abortifacients and on the basis of these texts prepared a decoction, which she drank. The same day she aborted. The implications of this are that the medical training for physicians avoided such topics and his solution was considered important enough to be published in a medical journal.

Even though the nineteenth century saw increasing legal objections to abortion, it seems clear that most of the drugs used for abortion

and contraception continued to be sold in pharmacies and drug stores. Usually the various guides said that certain drugs, most of those mentioned above, were not to be given to pregnant women and used only to treat amenorrhea or absence of menstruation. The popular medical and sexual advice manual entitled *Aristotle's Masterpiece,* which was widespread in colonial America and continued to be printed up to the twentieth century, included a long list of menstrual stimulators. With the development of patent medicines in the nineteenth century, nearly every newspaper carried advertisements for women's medicines designed to deal with menstrual problems. So widespread was the recognition of the potential use for abortion of some of these pills that one German proprietor of an apothecary shop required his customers to sign a statement that they were not taking the menstrual regulators to terminate pregnancy but only to restore the monthly cycle.

Though physicians were increasingly dubious about many of the remedies, interviews of some 2,000 women conducted by James Whitehead at the Manchester Lying-in Hospital in the 1840s found that 747 reported that they had aborted at least once; and some, many times, mostly by taking strong purgatives, emmenagogues (menstrual regulators), or mercurial medicines. Whitehead doubted that some of the medicines actually caused the abortion without other predisposing causes, but what these might have been are unclear.

What seems clear is that, in spite of a growing medical reticence to become involved in abortion and birth control, especially in nineteenth century United States, there was a widespread availability of pills and remedies, which women were led to believe could restore their menstrual flow, even though the preparations were not labeled as abortifacients or contraceptives.

See also Herbal Contraceptives and Abortifacients

References

Culpeper, Nicholas. *A Physical Director: or, A Translation of the Dispensatory Made by the College of Physicians of London.* London: n.p., 1650.

Defoe, Daniel. *Conjugal Lewdness: or, Matrimonial Whoredom.* Reprinted London: Menston, 1970, pp. 138–140.

Prevost, Jean. *Medicaments for the Poor: or, Physick for the Common People, Containing Excellent Recipes for Most Common Diseases,* 2d ed., translated by Nicholas Culpeper. London: n.p., 1662.

Riddle, John. *Eve's Herbs: A History of Contraception and Abortion in the West.* Cambridge, MA: Harvard University Press, 1997.

Whitehead, James. *On the Causes and Treatment of Abortion and Sterility.* London: n.p., 1847.

Augustine, Saint (d. 430)

Saint Augustine was the most influential early Christian writer on contraception, abortion, and sex in general. His writings have proved to be a dominant influence on Western attitudes. Born in North Africa of a pagan father and Christian mother (Saint Monica), Augustine received a Christian education and went on to advanced studies in Carthage, where he devoted himself at first to rhetoric and then to philosophy. While in Carthage, he converted to Manichaeanism, a dualistic religion that was a main rival of Christianity at the time. In Manichaean cosmology, the universe was divided into two pantheistic portions, the kingdoms of Light and Darkness, which were in juxtaposition, each reaching out into infinity. Light and Darkness were both eternal and uncreated power in everlasting opposition and conflict, although the God of Light was alone able to know the future. Eventually Light would overcome Darkness and this was represented in earthly forms as the struggle between the material and spiritual, or ideal. Humans represented the material, or darkness, but they retained an element of light and were in a sense prisoners because the earthly life was a testing one in which they were to struggle to overcome the elements of darkness and to gain the full light. This struggle could be aided or impeded by, among other things, sexual actions, and one of the worst things humans could do was to procreate because procreation kept imprisoning the light in new physical bodies, children of loins. The Manichaeans taught that concupiscence (lust) as well as covetousness were signs of darkness, and the true believers refused to eat flesh, drink wine, eat any products of sexual union such as milk (they did not know about the birds and bees in fertilization), or have sexual intercourse.

According to the Manichaeans, the human race was divided into three classes. The first were the Adepts, the Elect who renounced private property, practiced abstinence, observed strict vegetarianism, and never engaged in trade. The second were the Auditors, men and women of good will who as yet could not control their material desires and who earned money, owned property, ate flesh, and had procreative intercourse, but also served and supported the Elect and strove to reach the Adept status themselves. The rest of society was totally lost in wickedness because they rejected the gospel of Manes.

Interestingly, because the Manichaeans believed that procreation continued the imprisonment of the Light contained in the seed, they were often charged by their opponents of engaging in sexual intercourse without procreative purpose, including coitus interruptus and anal intercourse. The Elect themselves were also charged with engaging in a ritual in which they ate human semen to free part of the God of Light still imprisoned in their seed. Augustine mentioned this charge against them several times and it is one of the early references to oral-genital contact as a means of preventing conception. Sometimes, at least according to their opponents, males engaged in fellatio with other males, and females engaged in oral-genital contact with other females. Auditors, who were allowed to marry, were encouraged to avoid pregnancy in order to avoid imprisoning more souls of light. They did so by abstaining from sex for a period after menstruation when they believed conception was most likely to take place, but they also used coitus interruptus in addition to fellatio, according to Augustine, and probably various barrier methods and herbal contraceptives and abortifacients as well.

Augustine was a Manichaean for some eleven years but never reached the Elect stage, in part because of his difficulties with abstaining from sex. He remained an Auditor, living with a female lover and growing increasingly uncomfortable about his inability to control his lustful desires. His failure was emphasized by the fact that he had a son, something even Auditors were supposed to avoid.

We know of his anguish and concern over his inability to control his sexual activity because he wrote about it in detail in a unique autobiographical account entitled *Confessions*. He emphasized that he regularly prayed to God to help him control his lustful desires, but at the end of each prayer he concluded "Give me chastity, and continence, but do not give it yet."

Reluctantly, Augustine arrived at the conclusion that the only way he could control his venereal desires was by marriage, and after kicking out both his lover and his son, he became engaged to a girl who was not yet of age (twelve was the legal minimum age; fourteen was the custom). While waiting for the girl to reach the eligible age, Augustine found he could not control his sexuality and turned to prostitutes for his pleasure. At this juncture he went through a personal crisis, in part brought to a head by his growing lack of faith in Manichaeanism, as well as personal contact with Saint Ambrose, one of the Christian intellectuals of the time. Augustine's problems were solved by his conversion to Christianity. Somewhat miraculously, he felt himself purified, purged of his sexual desire, and the celibacy and continence that he had so much difficulty in achieving earlier, he now found easy.

He soon was made a priest; and within a few years, Bishop of Hippo, and he threw himself into the controversies of the church. His ideas and extensive writings essentially became the major foundation of western Christianity. As far as sex was concerned, what he did was to carry over into Christianity the Manichaean ideas about lust and coitus and establish them as main points of Christian doctrine. He held that the true Christian life, and the most desirable mod-

After converting to Christianity, Saint Augustine concluded that sex for any purpose other than reproduction, and sex using any form of birth control, was a sin, a philosophy that carried down through the centuries in Western Christianity. (North Wind Picture Archives)

el for all, was a life of continence. There was nothing that brought the "manly mind"—he always wrote from a male viewpoint—"down from the heights than a woman's caresses and that joining of bodies without which one cannot have a wife." He held that before Adam and Eve had fallen from Paradise, the two had been able to control their genitals, although if they had chosen to do so, they could have managed to have sex without lascivious heat or unseemly passion. It was after they had entered the real world that the genitals lost the docility of innocence and were no longer amenable to the will. Augustine termed this impulse "concupiscence" or *"lust."* Though he was forced to conclude, in part because of the biblical commandment to be fruitful and multiply, that coitus must be regarded as a "good," every concrete act of intercourse was evil, with the result that every child could literally be said to have been conceived in the sin of its parents.

Augustine concluded that sexual intercourse of a married couple was permissible only when it was employed for human generation. All intercourse between the unmarried was condemned by Augustine, although he held that true wedlock could exist without a ceremony. All forms of sex not leading to procreation were condemned and the only position acceptable was with the woman on her back and the man on top and using the orifice, the vagina, and the instrument, the penis, God had designed for such purposes. Sexual intercourse undertaken simply for pleasure, even with one's spouse, was a sin. To use any method of fertility control that permitted pleasure but prevented children was condemned.

Moreover, there was no particular reason for Christians to have children. The biblical injunction to increase and multiply was interpreted as not a requirement to have large families but rather to grow in reason. Perfection was to be sought in abstinence and virginity rather than in the married state. In fact, it was under Christian influence that Constantine revoked the laws put in place by the Emperor Augustus in the first century to penalize childlessness. Contraception and abortion were both condemned because they represented attempts to have sexual pleasure without bearing children.

References

Augustine. *Confessions,* edited and translated by William Watts. London: Heinemann, 1919.

———. "The Way of Life of the Manichaeans (De moribus Manichaeorum)." In *The Fathers of the Church,* vol. 56, edited and translated by D. A. Gallagher and I. J. Gallagher. Washington, DC: Catholic University of America, 1948.

Bullough, Vern L. *Sexual Variance in Society and History.* Chicago: University of Chicago Press, 1976.

McLaren, Angus. *A History of Contraception.* Oxford, England: Blackwell, 1990.

B

Barrier Contraceptives

Barrier contraceptives for women involve placing some kind of obstacle in the vagina to prevent the passage of sperm into the uterus. Perhaps because long before recorded history there was recognition that the seed the man planted needed to reach the uterus, barrier methods of pregnancy prevention are not only a modern but also a traditional method of contraception. Some of the historical attempts of women to establish a barrier employed materials similar in shape to those currently used.

In Sumatra, for example, women molded opium into a cuplike shape and inserted it into the uterus to cover the cervix. Chinese and Japanese women covered the cervix with oiled silky paper (*misugami*). Hungarian women used beeswax melted into 5- to 10-cm-wide disks (roughly 1.5 to 3 inches wide). Some historical barrier devices were quite ingenious. Giovanni Casanova, whose *Memoirs* record his numerous sexual encounters, recommended that women squeeze half a lemon and then insert the lemon rind into their vaginas, fitting it over the cervix. In terms of what we now know about how contraceptives work, the lemon rind would act as a contraceptive cup while the citric acid remaining in the pulp would serve as a spermicide. The problem was to make sure the cup stayed in place.

Rubber, even before the techniques had been developed to vulcanize it, was widely used in the form of pessaries, devices inserted into the vagina to support a prolapsed (fallen) uterus or for alleviating symptoms of abnormal retroversion (a backward displacement of the uterus), ante-version (tipping forward of the uterus), anteflexion (bending forward of the neck of the uterus), or other similar problems. Because a tipped uterus does not ordinarily cause problems, the variety of devices designed to deal with such conditions is understandable only when such devices are also seen as having contraceptive implications. For example, those designed to correct a displacement included a splint to press the uterus forward or backward, which could serve the same function as a modern intrauterine device, or rings designed to cover the cervix, enabling them to serve in the same ways as a modern diaphragm or cervical cap. In retrospect, it seems that many of the so-called female complaints of the past, which led physicians to describe a variety of devices, might well have been efforts to find some socially acceptable way of avoiding pregnancy. Such devices are much easier to document because they could be patented and advertised, whereas devices claiming to have contraceptive value were not patent protected until well into the twentieth century and could not be advertised as contraceptives either.

One of the earliest medical references to the contraceptive value of pessaries was by Friedrich Adolph Wilde, a German physician in the first part of the nineteenth century. Two developments in the last part of the nineteenth century—the invention of a method to make latex rubber and the discovery of effective spermicides—made the barrier contraceptives the most effective of all contraceptives until the last half of the twentieth century.

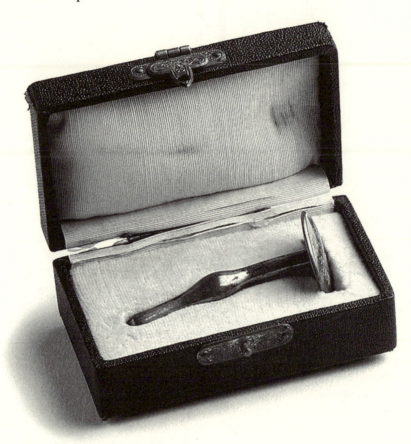

This cervical plug from the Museum of Contraception in Toronto, Ontario, is a crude form of barrier contraceptive. (Janssen-Ortho, Inc.)

As anxiety over sexually transmitted diseases mounted in the 1980s, various barrier contraceptives specifically designed for women entered the market, which when combined with nonoxynol 9 or other spermicides also lessened the chances of acquiring a sexually transmitted disease. The Food and Drug Administration in 1992 approved the female condom, technically a sheath. It is 7.8 cm (approximately 3 inches) in diameter and 17 cm (slightly more than 6.5 inches) long and made of polyurethane (some are made of latex). The soft, loose-fitting sheath contains two flexible rings. One ring lies inside at the closed end of the sheath and is fitted over the cervix in much the same way a diaphragm is.

The external ring covers the perineum and provides protection to the labia and the base of the penis during intercourse. The sheath is prelubricated with a silicone-based lubricant. The lubricant does not contain spermicide and the sheath is approved only for one-time use. The polyurethane sheath is more desirable than the latex one because it is soft, has good heat transfer characteristics, and is less likely to tear or break. It is no less likely to deteriorate during storage than latex. The female condom should not be used in conjunction with the male condom. Its big advantage is that it is for sale without a prescription and when used with a spermicide offers great protection against sexually transmitted disease as well as acting as an effective barrier contraceptive. Some say that some women have stronger orgasms using it, perhaps because the traction of the device stimulates the clitoris.

The bikini female condom has also been marketed. It is designed to be slipped on like standard panties but inside is a rolled pouch that is then unrolled inside the vagina. Because the panties part of the condom covers the external labia, both partners are also protected against herpes, genital warts, and other sexually transmitted diseases, a protection that the standard male condom does not provide. The bikini female condom too can be and should be used with a spermicide.

There is also a sponge that acts as a barrier. One called Today was on the market in the early 1990s but then withdrawn, although a similar one has again appeared. One called Protectaid combines three spermicides along with a viricide (which kills viruses) and is designed to counter sexually transmitted diseases as well as act as a contraceptive. Various shields and new varieties of caps that block the cervix are also being marketed. The standard male barrier contraceptive is the condom.

See also Cervical Cap; Condom; Diaphragm; Food and Drug Administration (United States); Pessary; Sponges, Tampons, and Vaginal Inserts

References

Bullough, Vern L., and Bonnie Bullough. *Contraception: A Guide to Birth Control Methods,* 2nd ed. Amherst, MA: Prometheus Books, 1997.

Finch, B. E. "Balls, Feathers and Caps." In *Contraception through the Ages,* edited by B. E. Finch and H. Green. Springfield, IL: Charles C. Thomas, 1963.

Hatcher, Robert A. *Contraceptive Technology.* New York: Irvington Publishers. (This is an ongoing series that appears every other year in a new edition.)

Wortman, Judith. "The Diaphragm and Other Intravaginal Barriers: A Review." *Population Reports,* ser. H, no. 4 (January 1976).

Besant, Annie (1847–1933)

Annie Besant, born Annie Wood, was one of the first women, if not the first, to be publicly involved in the public dissemination of information about birth control. Born in London, she was very well educated by her teacher, Ellen Marryat, the sister of a well-known novelist, who wanted her pupils to think for themselves. After flirting briefly with free thought, and totally ignorant of what marriage might mean, Wood drifted into marriage with the Reverend Frank Besant. She was at first frightened and then outraged when her husband pocketed a check for thirty shillings she had earned for a short story. She became further upset when she found out that any money a wife earned belonged, according to the law, to her husband.

In January 1869, Besant gave birth to a son, Arthur Digby. A daughter, Mabel Emily, nineteenth months later was born prematurely as a result of a blow from Frank Besant while Annie was pleading with him to limit the size of their family. Annie Besant still remained faithful to her husband but began to again question his religion, and she wrote an unsigned essay, *On the Deity of Jesus of Nazareth* (1873). The two quarreled over her changing beliefs, and after once threatening to throw her over a stile, Frank issued an ultimatum that she must resume attendance at Communion or leave home. She left, but found herself penniless.

While briefly serving as a tutor, Besant began writing free thought pamphlets. Charles Bradlaugh, the editor of the *National Reformer,* offered her a paid position on his newspaper, which she accepted. She also began to give public lectures on various topics. This activity enraged her estranged husband, who challenged the custodianship she had of their daughter. Under the deed of separation, he had retained custody of their son, while she had custody of their daughter until she came of age. In 1878, when Besant was in the midst of a trial involving herself and Bradlaugh over contraception—the famous Bradlaugh-Besant trial—her husband went to court to get the custody of their daughter transferred to him on the grounds that Besant was propagating atheism. She argued her case in person and lost. The judge told her that

Annie Besant was one of the first women to be involved in the public dissemination of information about birth control; her booklet The Law of Population *sold more than 175,000 copies in England. (Library of Congress)*

her character was tainted and that modest women could not be expected to associate with her. The child was torn from her arms and carried away. Eventually the court of appeal granted Besant the right of access, but the child, indoctrinated by the father, was upset by her visits. Besant therefore resolved not to see or write to either of her children until they were old enough to understand and judge for themselves. Eleven years later, both children chose to return to her. She also gave birth to a daughter fathered by Bradlaugh.

From free thought Besant moved to socialism, became a member of the Fabian Society, edited a literary magazine, and campaigned for women's rights as well as contraception. Her writings included a booklet on birth control, *The Law of Population,* most of which was first published in the *National Reformer* and then issued as a separate pamphlet in November 1877. It went through many reprintings and by the time Besant withdrew it, it had sold more than 175,000 copies in England. Separate editions were published in the United States. Continually seeking answers, in 1889 she believed she had received a vision telling her that the end to her quest was near. Shortly after this she was asked to review *The Secret Doctrine* by Madame Helen Petrovna Blavatsky (1831–1891) and was converted to Theosophy and joined the Theosophical Society. Besant resigned from most of her secular groups, withdrew *The Law of Population,* and refused to sell the copyright to others who wanted it. This was unfortunate because Besant had kept up with changes in the technology of contraception. In the 1887 edition of her book she included the soluble pessary (suppository) and the Indian rubber pessary (cervical cap) as well as the sponge. She also recommended soaking the sponge in a solution of quinine (20 grains of quinine to a pint of water) and douching with this solution as well. Unfortunately quinine is not the most effective spermicide, but it was then believed to be.

Besant became deeply involved in the Theosophical Society and went to India, where she became an advocate for Indian independence. She had removed herself from the Malthusian League with her new conversion, but she returned to the league later, although she now believed in self-restraint within marriage and the gradual restriction of the sexual relation to the perpetuation of the race. Besant died in India on September 20, 1933, and her body was burnt in a funeral pyre.

See also Bradlaugh-Besant Trial

References

Fryer, Peter. *The Birth Controllers.* London: Secker and Warburg, 1965.

Nethercott, A. H. *First Five Lives of Annie Besant.* Chicago: University of Chicago Press, 1960.

———. *The Last Four Lives of Annie Besant.* Chicago: University of Chicago Press, 1963.

Birth Control

The term birth control was popularized by Margaret Sanger. There are two different versions of how the term came to be used. In one version, Sanger tells how a few friends and supporters of the *Woman Rebel,* her radical monthly publication, gathered together in her apartment one evening to select a distinctive name. In this early version of the origin of the term, Sanger herself in her book *My Fight for Birth Control* claimed she coined it:

> We debated in turn: "Malthusianism," "conscious generation," "voluntary parenthood," "voluntary motherhood," "preventception," "the new motherhood," "constructive generation," etc, etc.
>
> All of these names were cast aside as not meeting the demands. Then we got a little nearer when "family control" and "race control" and "birth rate control" were suggested.
>
> Finally it came to me out of the blue— "Birth Control!"
>
> We all knew at once that we had found the perfect name for the cause.

In her autobiography, Sanger was less possessive of the term, although the same evening meeting was recounted: "We tried population control, race control, and birth rate control. Then someone suggested, 'Drop the rate.' Birth control was the answer; we knew we had it."

The term first appeared in the fourth issue of the *Woman Rebel* in June 1914 and was used by Sanger and her followers thereafter.

References

Sanger, Margaret. *My Fight for Birth Control.* New York: Farrar & Rinehart, 1931, p. 83.

————. *Margaret Sanger: An Autobiography.* New York: W. W. Norton, 1938, 1939, p. 105.

Birth Control Clinical Research Bureau

The Birth Control Clinical Research Bureau, founded in 1923, was the first legal U.S. birth control clinic and an influential model for the spread of clinics in the United States. It was founded by Margaret Sanger and was called the Clinical Research Bureau (CRB) to meet the requirements of a New York State law that held that doctors could prescribe contraceptives to married women only "for the cure and prevention of disease." The bureau operated under the license of its medical director, Dorothy Bocker, but Sanger, as the director, determined the policies and oversaw operations for the clinic. Sanger's goals in creating the clinic were several: to provide birth control to New York City women who could not afford or obtain it, to prove through detailed record keeping that contraceptives could be both safe and effective, and to create a model for other cities to follow. Because the American Birth Control League (ABCL) as a membership organization could not operate a medical dispensary, the solution was to have Bocker open a private practice in the same building as the ABCL. The CRB retained this link to Sanger's ABCL until 1928. The CRB rapidly succeeded in its first two objectives.

Patients at the bureau were interviewed by lay workers, who questioned them about their reproductive history, family size and income, and education level. Doctors then examined the patients to determine whether by law they could be treated. Women who were already pregnant or who could not present a medical indication for contraception (and the clinic stretched the definition as broadly as possible) were turned away or referred to a private physician who might help. Those who were accepted were fitted for diaphragms and instructed in their use by a nurse and the doctor.

Careful records were kept on the success rates of the treatment. Bocker, however, was not seen by Sanger to be the right person to carry out the necessary research. Bocker had tried a number of different contraceptive regimens with 1,208 women seen, but it was not clear what the success rate was. Her contract was not renewed and in 1925, with the appointment of Hannah Mayer Stone as medical director, the CRB began producing convincing evidence of the effectiveness of the diaphragm when combined with contraceptive jelly. Sanger fostered statistical studies, including two independent analyses, *Birth Control in Practice* (Marie Kopp, 1931) and *Controlled Fertility* (Regine Stix and Frank Notestein, 1940) that confirmed her own findings.

After Sanger's 1929 resignation from the ABCL, the CRB was reconstituted as an independent entity. Sanger expanded her work by opening a Harlem branch to cater to African American patients. Run essentially along the same lines as the downtown clinic, the Harlem clinic was never as successful. It was born during the depression in 1930 and securing funding was a continual problem. Finally, in 1936 the clinic was taken over by the ABCL and closed shortly afterward.

Though Sanger hoped to use her clinic as a model for other cities, it was unique. Because of the press that Sanger and the CRB received, it served to convince the public that birth control was a medical and social issue rather than a moral one. The public images of birth control clinics drew on the example of the CRB: professional and caring female doctors, a clinic that served any woman regardless of her ability to pay, and a guarantee that the methods prescribed were the best and most effective. In fact, however, the CRB was in many ways an anomaly. Everything about the CRB was bigger and costlier than other clinics—from the size of its paid staff to its research department, which analyzed various contraceptives sent by manufacturers; or its correspondence and literature departments, responsible for answering the thousands of requests for aid sent annually to Sanger.

Because most of Sanger's staff, doctors, social workers, and nurses were on payroll, she was able to retain far more personal control over the clinic's policies and practices than the majority of clinic reformers, who relied on volunteer work at almost all positions. Sanger's clinic was opened daily, with multiple doctors on duty, whereas most clinics were open between once and twice a week, for short two- to four-hour sessions. Many

of the clinics in other cities restricted patients based upon income, desiring to serve only those who could not afford a private physician. In contrast, the CRB had a sliding scale of charges based upon the income of the patient and used the larger fees paid by wealthier patients to subsidize the treatment of the poor. In one important way, however, the CRB was more restrictive than clinics in other cities. Because of its location in New York State, the CRB could see patients only when they had a medical reason for avoiding pregnancy, such as tuberculosis, heart disease, or previous gynecological damage. In other cities, patients could be seen without any difficulty for economic reasons, child spacing, or eugenic reasons, in addition to health concerns.

In April 1929, the CRB was the center of a controversy when it was raided by police. Four physicians were arrested and several patient records and 150 patient names were seized and never returned. The charges against the clinic were quickly dropped when it was found that the undercover policewoman whose treatment had been the basis of the case was found to have the proper medical indications for contraception. Investigations into the raid also showed that it had been instigated by Catholic officials and that one of the aims was to gain access to names of Catholic patients of the CRB. When physicians from the prestigious New York Academy of Medicine rallied to the defense of the CRB, birth control clinics had turned an important corner in their improving relations with the medical profession.

In the 1930s, the CRB began taking a more formal lead in helping other birth control organizations found clinics. It provided guidelines, samples of case histories, and organizers and in 1935 began a formal affiliation program whereby clinics that met certain standards could join a data exchange and receive startup grants and other benefits. In this and other aspects of the work, the CRB began to compete with the ABCL, and after almost ten years of independence, the two organizations merged in 1939. As part of the new organization, the

The Birth Control Review, *founded by Margaret Sanger in 1917, was the first publication in the United States advocating ways for women to control their fertility; it was taken to court by Postmaster General Anthony Comstock for promoting "obscenity." (Courtesy of Planned Parenthood)*

Birth Control Federation of America (BCFA), the CRB focused on research and the development of new contraceptive methods. In 1940 the CRB was renamed the Margaret Sanger Research Bureau (MSRB) in honor of its founder, but by then Sanger was less involved in the day-to-day operations. Despite its merger, the CRB was only loosely affiliated with the BCFA (which changed its name in 1942 to the Planned Parenthood Federation of America) and continued as the largest provider of contraceptive and fertility services in the world. It fostered research and testing of new forms of contraceptives, including the anovulant pill and intrauterine devices. Under the direction of Abraham Stone after 1940, the MSRB expanded its services into fertility treatment; marriage counseling; and increased educational services for physicians, medical students, and

nurses. At the forefront of clinic development, the MSRB was offering patients the birth control pill as early as 1961. By the 1950s, the MSRB was brought more closely under the supervision and budgetary control of Planned Parenthood, and as contraceptives became more widely available, attendance began to fall. In 1973 the MSRB merged with Planned Parenthood of New York City and was renamed Margaret Sanger Center.

The Margaret Sanger Papers contain the records of the Clinical Research Bureau and are located at the Sophia Smith Collection, Smith College; and the Library of Congress. They are also available on microfilm: Esther Katz et. al, eds., *The Margaret Sanger Papers Microfilm Edition* (Bethesda, MD: University Publications of America, 1996–1997). Clinic records can also be found in the records of the

Margaret Sanger Research Bureau and the Planned Parenthood Federation of America, both located at the Sophia Smith Collection, Smith College.

References

McCann, Carole. *Birth Control Politics in the United States, 1916–1945*. Ithaca, NY: Cornell University Press, 1996.

Reed, James. *Birth Control in American Society*. New York, Basic Books, 1977.

Birth Control Review

Margaret Sanger founded *Birth Control Review,* a monthly journal, in 1917, and it was regarded by her as the first step in establishing a national organization. A group of women led by Juliet Rublee and Frances Ackermann organized the New York Women's Publishing Company to support the *Review.* Its financial deficits were covered by special contributions from women's groups. The staff of the magazine was involved in setting up the American Birth Control League in 1921 and the journal became the voice of the league. By 1923 the *Review* had a budget of $24,565. It continued to be published until 1940.

Bradlaugh, Charles (1833–1891)

A son of a solicitor's clerk, Charles Bradlaugh attended schools in London until he was eleven, when he went to work in his father's office. After that he had a mixture of jobs but spent most of his spare time attending open air meetings in London parks listening to the open discussion of social, political, and theological questions. On Sundays he taught Sunday school but as he was being prepared for confirmation, he began to express some of his doubts about the 39 Articles of the Church of England, and when he expressed these, the minister denounced him to his parents as atheistic and suspended him from Sunday school. The minister did not stop there, but also convinced his employer to fire Bradlaugh unless he changed his opinions. Bradlaugh

found shelter with the widow of Richard Carlile and tried to support himself by selling coal, all the time spending his time trying to learn Greek and Hebrew. Unable to support himself and in debt, he joined the army, where he served for three years before a legacy from a great aunt enabled him to buy his way out of the army.

Bradlaugh gained fame and popularity as a powerful and pugnacious lecturer, debater, and pamphleteer, always seeming to hunt for causes that he believed would help the worker. He began publishing a newspaper, the *National Reformer* (1869–1893), but refused to deposit the required 800 pounds in sureties against blasphemous or seditious libel. When ordered to stop publishing, he took the matter to court, won his case, and saw the statute repealed. Often his efforts in court were stymied because judges refused to hear freethinkers (read "atheists"), but Bradlaugh continued to fight until they did so. He stood for Parliament in 1868, even though, as an avowed atheist, he knew he would not be allowed to sit there. Defeated in the original election, he continued to run at every opportunity until in 1880 he was elected. When the House of Commons refused to seat him because he would not take an oath of loyalty on the Bible, Bradlaugh went to court. The result was a six-year legal action during which he continued to win reelection until in 1886, when a new Speaker allowed him to enter without swearing on the Bible. Bradlaugh continued to serve until his death in 1891.

Among his causes was birth control, and early on he had published articles in the *National Reformer* by the birth control reformer George Drysdale. Though his coeditor, Joseph Barker, had broken with him on this issue, Bradlaugh declared that he would persist in his advocacy of Malthusian views. He got his chance to do more than publish Drysdale when in 1876 a Bristol bookseller named Henry Cook was sentenced to two years in prison for publishing an edition of Charles Knowlton's *Fruits of Philosophy*. Even though the book had been published in London without interference for more than forty years,

Charles Bradlaugh, a freethinker and member of the British Parliament, was taken to court for selling books containing information about birth control. (Hulton Getty Collection / Archive Photos)

the London authorities, emboldened by the Bristol case, decided to prosecute the current publisher Charles Watts (1836–1906).

As part of a deal with the prosecution to let him off with a suspended sentence and court costs, Watts pleaded guilty to publishing an obscene book. Bradlaugh then severed his connections with Watts, a free thought publisher, and went on the offensive. Bradlaugh and Annie Besant formed the Free Thought Publishing Company, republished *Fruits of Philosophy* with medical notes by George Drysdale, and notified the police when he and Besant would appear in public to sell the book in person. Some five hundred copies were sold in the first twenty minutes, after which the two were arrested and a trial was held. Found guilty in 1877, they were sentenced to six months' imprisonment and fined 200 pounds. On appeal the decision was overturned and Bradlaugh, determined to continue publishing, sued the police to get the copies they had confiscated returned. He was successful and sold them with the words "Recovered from the police" stamped in red across the cover.

Though freethinkers had been in the forefront of the activity for birth control, not all agreed with what Bradlaugh was doing. A group of disgruntled freethinkers issued a scurrilous *Life of Bradlaugh,* in which Bradlaugh was accused, among other things, of advocating prostitution (by publishing Drysdale's articles), trying to establish a universal female harem, and encouraging homosexuality. The book was suppressed by the court as a result of a libel action Bradlaugh brought against the authors and publisher of the book.

After he won his battle to sit in Parliament, the militant firebrand came to be acknowledged as a respected reformer because most of the things he advocated and did in his life came to be accepted.

See also Besant, Annie; Bradlaugh-Besant Trial; Knowlton, Charles

References

Fryer, Peter. *The Birth Controllers.* London: Secker and Warburg, 1965.

Bradlaugh-Besant Trial

A turning point in the movement for the dissemination of information about contraceptives was the Bradlaugh-Besant trial in 1877 involving Charles Bradlaugh and Annie Besant. The publicity surrounding the trial radically increased the demand for information about contraception and spurred people to be interested. Norman Himes, in his standard history of contraception, labeled his chapter on the topic as "Democratization by Publicity."

Charles Knowlton's *Fruits of Philosophy* had been published and distributed in London for more than 40 years without interference, but when a Bristol publisher, Henry Cook, published it, the authorities there, encouraged by the local Society for the Suppression of Vice, charged him with publishing a book with obscene illustrations (probably illustrations of the male and female genital organs). Cook was convicted and sentenced to two years at hard labor. Encouraged by the Bristol case, and probably again encouraged by the Society for the Suppression of Vice, authorities decided to prosecute the current London publisher, Charles Watts (1836–1906). Watts, in order to avoid prison, pleaded guilty to publishing an obscene book and was let off with a suspended sentence and court costs. Bradlaugh, highly upset, responded with a strong editorial in his newspaper, the *National Reformer:*

> The Knowlton pamphlet is either decent or indecent. If decent, it ought to be defended; if indecent, it should never have been published . . .I hold the work to be defensible, and I deny the right of anyone to interfere with the full and free discussion of social questions affecting the happiness of the nation. The struggle for a free press has been one of the marks of the Free thought party throughout its history, and as long as the Party permit me to hold its flag, I will never voluntarily lower it. I have no right and no power to dictate to Mr. Watts the course he should pursue, but I have the right and duty to refuse to associate my name with a submission which is utterly repugnant to my nature and

inconsistent with my whole career. (Quoted from the *National Reformer,* January 18, 1877, by Fryer, 1965, p. 161)

To provoke a test case, Bradlaugh, with Annie Besant, his associate at the *National Reformer,* formed the Free Thought Publishing Company and republished *Fruits of Philosophy* with medical notes by George Drysdale. The book was distributed at the Guildhall and the two notified the police that they would be there themselves to sell copies. They sold some five hundred in the first twenty minutes, after which they were arrested. In the three-month interval between their arrest and trial they had sold no fewer than 125,000 copies.

The trial began in June 1877. After some maneuvering Bradlaugh convinced the Lord Chief Justice, Sir Alexander Cockburn, whose name traditionally had been associated with a definition of what constituted obscenity, to agree that whether *Fruits of Philosophy* was an obscene work or had scientific merit should be decided by a judge and jury over which Cockburn himself would preside. Bradlaugh and Besant conducted their own defense very effectively. Cockburn allowed them a great deal of freedom with only occasional interruptions. Besant seemed to be particularly effective in her lengthy address in which she included references to poor women's need to purchase inexpensive contraceptives. C. R. Drysdale, a physician and brother of George Drysdale, argued that the attempt of women to better space their children by engaging in long lactation periods (eighteen months or two years) was harmful to the children because it deprived infants of proper food. Moreover, if, in spite of her effort to avoid becoming pregnant, the woman conceived anyway, the unborn child would suffer from want of nourishment. He said he knew of women with as many as twenty, twenty-one, twenty-two, and even one woman with twenty-five children, and he held that this was one of the greatest social crimes a man could permit. Another witness, H. G. Bohn, who published English translations

of the Greek and Roman classics, reported that the Society for the Suppression of Vice was constantly trying to prevent him from publishing the classics because they held they were obscene.

The solicitor general was not convinced by the witnesses and held that the real issue was publication of "a dirty, filthy book" that no one would willingly allow to lie on his table and no English husband would allow even his wife to have it. He said the only object of the book was to enable a person to have sexual intercourse and not have that which "in the order of Providence is the natural result . . . ." Cockburn in his summary called the prosecution "ill advised" and that a more injudicious proceeding in the way of a prosecution had probably never been brought into a court of justice. He wanted to know who had initiated the prosecution, but the solicitor general refused to say.

The jury after discussing the case for ninety-five minutes reported that they were unanimous in the opinion that the book was calculated to deprave public morals, but at the same time said that they "entirely exonerate the defendants from any corrupt motives in publishing it." Cockburn replied that this must mean that the jury found them guilty, a statement that the foreman immediately agreed to without consulting his colleagues. Later, one of the jurors reported to Besant that six of them had not intended to agree to a verdict of guilty and it had been arranged for them to return to further deliberations if the judge had not accepted their tortured decision, which they believed would be the case. Besant held that the decision amounted to saying "Not guilty, but don't do it again."

At their sentencing a week later, they refused to surrender the book and insisted they would go on selling it. They were each sentenced to six months' imprisonment, fined 200 pounds, and had to each post 500 pounds as bond that they would not again publish the book for a period of at least two years. Execution of the sentence was delayed pending an appeal on condition that publication be suspended. The appeal in February 1878 was decided in their favor on strictly technical grounds that the words alleged by the prosecution to be obscene had never been expressly set out in the indictment. One of the justices warned the couple that, if the book was republished and the appellants were convicted on a properly framed indictment, such a repetition of the offense would have to be met by greater punishment. Bradlaugh and Besant ignored the warning and continued to publish. The overall effect of the trial was to make large numbers of people aware of the potential available for better planning of the size of their families.

See also Besant, Annie; Bradlaugh, Charles; Drysdale, George; Knowlton, Charles

References

Fryer, Peter. *The Birth Controllers.* London: Secker and Warburg, 1965.

Himes, Norman. *Medical History of Contraception.* New York: Schocken Books, 1970.

same cultures believed that children should be nursed at least for three years, long periods of abstinence would have been associated with breast-feeding. Other factors are involved as well. The onset of menstruation, even with lactating women, is closely associated with levels of nutrition and physical well-being. A comparative study of Bostonian and Taiwanese women who breast-feed indicated that a higher percentage of Boston women had begun to menstruate within six months of weaning than had Taiwanese women. The best advice today for women who are breast-feeding and who are also engaging in sexual intercourse is to use one of the methods of contraception available as well.

References

Knodel, J. J., and H. Kitchner. "The Impact of Breast Feeding on the Biometric Analysis of Infant Mortality." *Demography* 14 (1977): 391–401.

Masnick, G. S. "The Demographic Impact of Breast Feeding: A Critical Review." *Human Biology* 51 (1979): 109–125.

Breast-feeding as a Method of Birth Control

Because breast-feeding delays the onset of menstruation after pregnancy, a phenomenon that is easily observed, it has often been regarded as a form of birth control. It is, however, only a relatively short-term one. Modern studies in developing countries show that mothers who breast-feed for an extended period do not begin menstruating until an average of ten months after delivery as compared with three months for mothers who do not breast-feed for a long period. It also takes breast-feeding mothers longer to conceive a child after their most recent birth event, perhaps because fertility is not at its height. This sterility is based on the assumption that the infant has little solid food and is entirely dependent on breast-feeding. If solid foods are offered, the window of nonfertility is lessened. Some practices associated with breast-feeding, however, might have lengthened this window. Many peoples including the Greeks and the Romans held that sexual intercourse spoiled the milk and, because some of these

Brownsville Birth Control Clinic

Margaret Sanger was intensely competitive and she much resented that while she had been abroad (to avoid prosecution) Mary Ware Dennett had established the first national birth control group, the National Birth Control League. After the charges for which she had fled the country had been dropped on February 18, 1916, Sanger moved to resume control of what she regarded as her movement. Whereas Dennett labored to change the law, Sanger preferred to confront it head on. On October 16, 1916, along with her sister and nurse Ethel Byrne and Fania Mindell, Sanger opened the first public birth control clinic in the United States at 46 Amboy Street in the Brownsville section of Brooklyn, New York.

Unable to recruit a licensed physician to operate the clinic, Sanger decided to go ahead without one and widely publicized the opening of the new clinic. On the day the clinic opened there was a long line of women waiting to get in, as well as several vice officers. After ten days

Margaret Sanger opened this clinic, the first birth control clinic in the United States, in 1916 in New York's Brownsville neighborhood and was promptly arrested. (Courtesy of the Margaret Sanger Papers)

of disseminating information and devices, the clinic was raided, its supplies confiscated, and Sanger, Mindell, and Byrne were arrested and taken to jail. Released on bail after a night in jail, Sanger reopened the clinic and was arrested again.

Byrne was tried first and sentenced to thirty days in jail, whereupon she promptly went on a hunger strike. She was pardoned by the governor of New York after ten days because of rapidly failing health. Fania Mindell was convicted but only fined $50. Both trials received considerable publicity. By the time Sanger's trial came up, the prosecution was willing to drop the charges against Sanger providing she agree to not open another clinic. She refused and was convicted and sentenced to thirty days in jail or a fine of $5,000. She chose jail and appealed. Her conviction was affirmed by the highest court in New York but the court also stated in January 1918 that New York's anticontraception statute could not prevent a physician from prescribing birth control to a married woman for the "cure and prevention of disease," a word that the court then defined in a most broad and inclusive manner. Though her case was appealed to the U.S. Supreme Court, the appeal was dismissed. Sanger, however, quickly seized upon the court's ruling holding that a fear of unwanted pregnancy could cause disease and that pregnancy itself under such conditions was a disease.

The New York court's emphasis on physician's right and obligations was a factor in the changing nature of Sanger's campaign. Mary Ware Dennett was committed to advocating the complete repeal of all state and federal anticontraceptive statutes and in 1919 had created the Voluntary Parenthood League—largely a successor to her earlier National Birth Control League—to help recruit sponsors for a federal repeal bill. Sanger, however, increasingly turned to relying on physicians for prescribing contraceptives and leaving lay people to carry out the educational and information campaigns.

See also Comstock, Anthony, and Comstockery

Reference
Gordon, Linda. *Woman's Body, Woman's Right: Birth Control in America*. New York: Penguin, 1990.

C

Cadbury, George (1907–1995) and Barbara (1910–)

George and Barbara Cadbury were prominent Canadian birth control advocates. Barbara Cadbury was a founder of the Planned Parenthood Association of Toronto in 1961. In her capacity as secretary, she wrote a letter to the minister of justice in December 1963 outlining the association's support for decriminalizing birth control services. George Cadbury was the executive director of the International Planned Parenthood Federation. Both were instrumental in forming in 1963 the Canadian Federation of Societies for Population Planning. This federation allowed Canada to participate in the International Planned Federation for the first time in 1964. By 1966, this federation had become the Family Planning Parenthood Federation of Canada; George Cadbury was an executive member and one of the Federation's representatives to Canada's Standing Committee on Health and Welfare. In the 1970s, the federation became known as the Planned Parenthood Federation of Canada. Also during these years, George Cadbury was the president of the New Democratic Party of Ontario (1961–1966).

See also Canada and Birth Control

Canada and Birth Control

Canada's first Criminal Code was enacted by Parliament in 1892. It was a federal statute that established as criminal acts offenses against the person, offenses against property, and offenses involving currency and conspiracies. From its earliest formulation within the 1892 Criminal Code, as Section 179, conception prevention came under the heading of "Offences Against Morality." Other offenses that came under this heading included sodomy, incest, and indecency; immoral or obscene books, pictures, publications, and theatrical performances; and seduction, corruption of children, and prostitution. Although there were frequent minor amendments to the Criminal Code, and more substantial consolidations in 1906, 1927, and 1953, no fundamental revisions to this Section were made until 1969.

In the 1953 formulation of the Criminal Code, Section 150, Offences Tending to Corrupt Morals, was situated in Part IV, Sexual Offences, Public Morals and Disorderly Conduct. Section 150, subsection 2(c) said that

> Every one commits an offence who knowingly, without lawful justification or excuse, . . .(c) offers to sell, advertises, publishes an advertisement of, or has for sale or disposal any means, instructions, medicine, drug or article intended or represented as a method of preventing conception or causing abortion or miscarriage.

This was modified, however, by a subsection that stated that no one shall be convicted of any offense mentioned in this section if that person proves that the public good was served by the acts alleged to have been done and that there was no excess in the acts alleged beyond what the public good required. This subsection was commonly referred to as the *pro bono publico* clause.

The inclusion of conception prevention in Canada's earliest Criminal Code indicates two things: first, that preventing conception was regarded by the lawmakers as an immoral act, and second, that committing this immoral act would lead to public offense and corruption. What must be set against this inference, however, are statistics that indicate that some people were in fact managing to exercise some measure of control over their fertility. By 1936, the fertility of American women had fallen below replacement level in a trend that could be seen throughout western Europe and the New World. According to Angus McLaren and Arlene Tigar McLaren, a decline in the birthrate had begun by the mid-1800s, with a more rapid decline during the 1920s and 1930s. Some social analysts attribute the Great Depression beginning in 1929 to economic stagnation induced primarily by this declining population growth. Yet for individual families, lower fertility was linked with greater economic stability and a desire for higher standards of living. Factors that more directly contributed to a particularly low birthrate during the depression were fewer marriages, later marriages, and delays in starting families.

Before the depression, public defenders of birth control in Canada were numbered among left-wing movements. As Angus McLaren's research has shown, in Canada there were three separate left-wing movements with distinct views on the relation between birth control and class oppression. First, the anarchists or individual libertarians saw birth control as a means of providing individual control over one's life, freeing oneself and one's family from poverty and from the imposed morality of the churches. (According to official Roman Catholic teaching and the Lambeth Conferences of the Church of England, preventing conception was immoral and contravened the will of God.) Speaking in Toronto in 1927, anarchist Emma Goldman

affirmed the right of the individual woman to control her own body. Birth control would also help to prevent abortions, strengthen marriages, encourage a greater equality between spouses, and benefit the working class by allowing for smaller families.

Second, the socialists focused more on the connection between the ability to limit family size and the struggle of labor within the capitalist system. They rejected the imposition of birth control on the working class by the middle and upper classes as undue interference, yet at the same time they regarded withholding birth control services from the working class as a means of defending the privilege of the wealthy. Within the women's movement in Canadian socialism, the main public issue was suffrage. However, it was clear that working women wanted to prevent unwanted pregnancies, did not want more children than their families could provide for, desired strong marriages, and wanted to preserve the health of women. Agrarian socialists were the most responsive to these feminist concerns—in 1929, the women's section of the United Farmers of Canada made the first public call on the government to provide contraceptive information, set up birth control clinics, and decriminalize birth control. Maternal feminists, in contrast, argued that contraception could decrease the power that was women's by their maternal role and could even increase the demands on women by men who would have no reason to exercise conjugal continence.

Third, the Communist Party in Canada feared that feminist concerns would detract from the class struggle. Communists charged that capitalists wanted to deprive working women of maternity, to control the labor supply, and to place the responsibility for poverty on the shoulders of the worker. By the mid-1930s, however, Communists saw birth control as an issue that could be used to win wider support for Communism among working, farming, and middle-class women. None of the three left-wing movements placed birth control at the top of their programs, but they shared the basic assumption that limiting the size of families had political and social consequences while helping defend individual voluntarism over force.

It is most unlikely that the positions on birth control taken by libertarians, anarchists, socialist feminists, or Communists would have been influential among more than a handful of members of the Protestant churches in Canada. Even where a growing number of people were willing to consider the benefits of access to information about effective means of preventing conception, the reasons used to justify birth limitation were radically divergent and often in opposition to one another. And yet support for birth control, even among the churches, did grow during the 1920s and 1930s.

Within the Anglican Communion, a decisive break in tradition was introduced by the Lambeth Conference of 1930. Although it inspired controversy, a resolution was passed indicating that, in situations in which spouses had a moral obligation to limit or avoid parenthood, methods of conception prevention could be used. Within months of the conference, Pope Pius XI issued *Casti connubii,* reiterating the Roman Catholic Church's opposition to any act or device used to deliberately frustrate the procreative potential of sexual intercourse.

The first group to concur with the Anglicans was the U.S. Federal Council of Churches. At its 1931 gathering, the council approved the practice of birth regulation to promote the stability of the family, to protect the health of mothers and children, and to facilitate spacing and limiting of children. When Margaret Sanger gathered evidence in favor of birth control to present to a U.S. congressional committee in 1934, the Federal Council of Churches was one of nearly one thousand American organizations to publicly endorse her statement.

A number of subsequent statements by church groups made use of the concept of "voluntariness" in parenthood. These documents included two reports prepared by the United Church of Canada—"The Meaning and Responsibilities of Christian Marriage" (1932) and "Vol-

untary Parenthood and Sterilization" (1936). The notion of voluntary and conscientious choice as an appropriate mode of participating in the creativity of God through parenthood became the hallmark of the United Church's documents of the time. Although some people in Canada believed that birth control clinics would remain ineffective as long as Section 207 of the 1927 Criminal Code banned the sale of contraceptive devices, the 1936 report countered that there had as yet been no challenge to existing clinics. Specific reference was made to the provision under Section 207(c) regarding exceptions to the ban in cases in which the public good had been served.

There was no Canadian feminist birth controller of the stature of Marie Stopes of England or Margaret Sanger of the United States, though there were some influential figures. When Sanger first visited Vancouver in 1923, she found allies among trade unionists, labor parties, and socialist feminists, who worked together to form the Canadian Birth Control League, establishing the first clinics in the early 1930s. Mary Hawkins began her work in Hamilton, Ontario, in 1929. By March 1932, she had established the Hamilton Birth Control Society, won the support of many respectable elite local women as members, and opened the Hamilton birth control clinic. Although there was considerable opposition among some doctors, Hawkins claimed the support of the medical profession and recruited Dr. Elizabeth Bagshaw, who directed the clinic for thirty-one years.

The reasons for birth control were twofold. First, women needed it to prevent unwanted pregnancies, miscarriages, abortions, and infant and maternal deaths. Dr. Margaret Batt, medical director of the Toronto Birth Control Clinic, argued that infant and maternal mortality rates improved when there was a two-year interval between births. She supported a woman's right to choose whether or not and when to have children and testified that, in spite of their church's rejection of birth control, many Catholic women came to her clinic.

The second reason for birth control was the "eugenic argument." Dr. William Hutton, a president of the Eugenics Society of Canada, promulgated the view that people of lesser intelligence had greater fertility. He claimed that, if birth control was not introduced to less intelligent people, the country would experience a lowering of its average intelligence, as well as greater social unrest. Economists and social workers alike claimed that large families caused poverty, and the solution would lie in birth control and sterilization, which would reduce venereal disease, tuberculosis, mental illness, and the resulting tax burden on the middle class. The philanthropy of the movement's supporters was partially based on the view that the poor were responsible for their own poverty. The eugenicists blamed social problems, including disease, mental deficiency, alcoholism, delinquency, and criminal activity on individual failings rather than societal structures.

Preeminent among the birth control advocates in Ontario was Alvin Ratz Kaufman, owner of the Kaufman Rubber Company of Kitchener, Ontario. In December of 1929, he laid off workers, who subsequently complained that those laid off were the most needy. Kaufman sent the company nurse, Anna Weber, to visit their homes. She reported that she found one or both spouses to be mentally deficient, that less intelligence led to larger families, and that help offered would only result in more unfortunate, feeble-minded children. She recommended that Kaufman offer the laid-off workers free sterilization, birth control information, and diaphragm fittings.

Kaufman's involvement in the birth control movement was preceded in central Canada by efforts of an Anglican cleric named A. H. Tyrer, who saw birth control as a response to the social misery that became widespread during the depression. On Tyrer's initiative, a pamphlet on birth control was mailed to every Protestant minister in Canada. When Kaufman provided financial support to Tyrer in 1931 and 1932, Tyrer began to advocate eugenic sterilization as part of the birth control agenda. Kaufman formed the Parents' Information Bureau in 1931, with Anna Weber as its director. By the mid-1930s, Kaufman's home visiting system was operating across Canada, serving those whom Kaufman believed should be encouraged to limit their fertility: poor laborers, the unemployed, and those on relief, particularly if they already had large families.

As a prominent member of the entrepreneurial middle class in English-speaking southern Ontario, Kaufman is representative of many social conservatives of his time. Conservative middle-class people had largely opposed the public availability of contraceptives, while using them themselves. This phenomenon was what lay behind fears about "race suicide." Sociologist Edward A. Ross had introduced the notion that when a "higher race" diminished its numbers while a "lesser breed" continued to propagate, society would degenerate. In the United States, Theodore Roosevelt had exhorted the American middle class not to commit "race suicide" by choosing to have smaller families than the lower classes. Many Canadians shared his sentiments.

The shift toward public acceptance of birth control was largely based on its utility in mitigating social, class, and racial tensions in a way that would preserve the privilege of English-speaking, white, Anglo-Saxon Canadians of the middle and upper classes. Among English-speaking Canadians, this concern appeared to be widespread. An editorial in the 1 September 1937 edition of *Maclean's* magazine introduced the reader to an article on the "Decline of the Anglo-Saxon Canadian" by W. Burton Hurd, a professor at McMaster University. Hurd warned readers that Canadians of "Anglo-Saxon stock" would number less than half of the population by the end of the year, would remain "virtually stationary" over the next thirty-five years, and by the end of the century, would be "outnumbered two to one by those of non-Anglo-Saxon descent" (Hurd, 1937). Of particular concern was the projected increase in French Canadians and continental European and other non-British immigrants and loss of Anglo-Saxon Canadians to the United States.

On 14 September 1936, Dorothea Palmer, an employee of Kaufman's Parents' Information Bureau, was arrested and charged under the Criminal Code. She had been visiting families in a French-Canadian section of Eastview, Ontario, providing information about birth control and offering to send them a sample packet of contraceptives. Kaufman arranged for an Ottawa attorney, A. W. Beament, to post bail and join Kaufman's company lawyer, F. W. Wegenast, in preparing Palmer's defense. When it became clear that Palmer did not herself sell or distribute any contraceptives, the police offered to drop all charges. Kaufman, however, was eager to test Subsection 2 of Section 207 (of the 1927 Criminal Code) in the courts, for he had long assumed that the *pro bono publico* clause would protect the activities of birth control advocates.

The defense strategy was to provide numerous expert witnesses representing Protestant clergy, social workers, eugenicists, and the medical profession, alongside the twenty-one visited Eastview women who were sympathetic to Palmer's cause. The officiating judge at the Ontario district court trial was Senior Magistrate Clayton. The trial, which ran from 21 October 1936 to 17 February 1937, served as a public forum on birth control in central Canada.

Judge Clayton held that Dorothea Palmer had indeed, without lawful justification and with full knowledge, advertised methods of contraception. However, the question remained whether the public good was served by her acts. According to Senior Magistrate Clayton, the public good was indeed served by "the acts alleged to have been done"—namely, providing conception prevention to women who were poor, received relief, had large families, were of lesser intelligence, and, in this particular case, were Francophone and Catholic. On 17 March 1937, Clayton handed down his decision, acquitting Palmer of the charges against her. On 2 June 1937, the

Ontario Court of Appeal upheld the magistrate's decision and dismissed the Crown's appeal. Palmer and Kaufman had won their case.

Respectability for the birth control movement would never be secured until it was sanctioned by the medical profession. Some private physicians did give contraceptive advice to married women who were already mothers, but not to the poor. Public clinics offered the poor better access, but were unpopular with the medical establishment, as were rate-reduced or subsidized services and lay involvement in the provision of care. Further, birth control was linked with the disrepute of prostitution, venereal disease, and illegal abortions performed by quacks. Doctors were quicker to respond to eugenic arguments regarding sterilization of the unfit than to the use of contraceptives.

The first public discussion about birth control among Canadian medical practitioners took place in June 1937 when the Canadian Medical Association met for its General Council in Ottawa. The publicity surrounding Palmer's trial was probably instrumental in placing the topic on the agenda. In 1930, just months before the Lambeth Conference, the British government had passed a bill permitting doctors to provide birth control information. In January 1937 in the United States, the American Medical Association had approved contraception as a subject of medical research and a legitimate medical service. Although support for birth control among doctors was preferable to opposition, support came with all of the accompanying trappings of the medical profession: paternalism, medicalization, and exclusive professional monopoly on services offered.

Originally supported by some feminists and leftist groups, birth control was associated in the minds of the middle class with abortion, the emancipation of women, declining birthrates among the upper and middle classes, and sexual promiscuity. With the coalescence of eugenicist, Neo-Malthusian, and socially conservative concerns relating to poverty, mental illness, class unrest, and fertility differentials, birth control came to be seen as a respectable means of response.

No sooner had the eugenic agenda embraced birth control as a means to improving the human race, than the abuses of eugenics, carried out in Adolph Hitler's Germany, came to light at the end of the Second World War. This necessitated a transition in the reasons for mainstream support for birth control. Immediately after the Second World War, birthrates began to rise: postponed marriages took place, deferred families were begun, and young women chose to bear more children. Throughout the 1950s, birthrates remained high, reflecting a "baby boom" throughout Canada and elsewhere. These "baby boom" families were raised during a period of comparative economic stability and prosperity: employment levels were high; housing and household costs were low; and unemployment insurance, family allowances, and pension plans were begun under a strong, centralized Liberal government.

Throughout Africa, Asia, and Latin America, fertility rates rose even more quickly, but within a context of inadequate economic, social, and resource development. By the mid-1950s, the United Nations (UN) began to attend to the global population explosion. It convened the first international Conference on Population in Rome from 31 August to 10 September 1954. Four hundred fifty delegates representing a broad range of social and scientific disciplines met to discuss population growth and development issues. Study sessions met to hear and discuss papers on mortality and fertility trends, international and internal migration, population projections, and demographic statistics. Although there was no study group on family planning or birth control, two of the six observers were members of the International Planned Parenthood Federation, first formed in 1948.

At the second UN population conference in 1965, a section on family planning met to consider the benefits of conception control. Among Canada's seventeen participants was George Cadbury, representing the International Planned Parenthood Federation. By 1968, at the UN Conference on Human Rights in Tehran, family planning was recognized as a basic human right for all people.

According to Canada's Criminal Code, both population planning and family planning programs were dependent on activities that were deemed to be criminal offenses. Neither contraceptives nor abortifacients could lawfully be advertised, distributed, or sold; even providing instructions for preventing conception or causing an abortion or miscarriage was a criminal offense.

In the technological realm, before 1960, efforts to prevent conception relied on barrier methods such as the diaphragm, cervical cap, and condom, sometimes in combination with spermicides and douches, withdrawal before ejaculation, or periodic continence. Condoms, withdrawal, and continence all relied on mutual compliance to prevent conception, and withdrawal was particularly unreliable. Barrier methods needed to be medically fitted, and the diaphragm, spermicides, and douches required attention at the time of intercourse.

The oral contraceptives and the modern generation of intrauterine devices (IUDs) differed significantly. Oral contraceptive use was controlled by the woman, did not depend on male compliance, and did not require any attention at the time of intercourse. IUDs required medical advice and insertion, but again avoided the necessities of male compliance and required no additional measures at the time of intercourse. These new contraceptives were perceived as medical advances in fertility control and were accorded the respectability of medical therapies. Both the anovulant pill and IUDs were highly effective, providing conception control that depended on little or no knowledge about fertility by their users and minimized the need for detailed sexual knowledge or discussion between physician and patient. As a result of these characteristics, contraception became incorporated into the categories of medical research and primary health care.

A minor and local development also served as a catalyst for change. In 1960, Canadian pharmacist Harold Fine was convicted and fined for selling contraceptives. Commentary on his conviction emphasized the archaic nature of the law against obscenity, noting that preventing conception was no longer offensive to many Canadians. Moreover, even if because of privately held moral or religious beliefs some Canadians refrained from practicing conception prevention, it was inappropriate to preserve a criminal statute to prevent all Canadians from using contraceptives. Although these discussions were being held in greater depth among legal communities in England and throughout the Western world, the concrete consequences of the present Canadian law were highlighted by Fine's conviction.

Prominent among birth control advocates mobilized by the case were George and Barbara Cadbury. Various Canadian organizations began to mobilize to bring about a change in the law, initially through correspondence with the federal minister of justice and the prime minister and later in submissions to the House of Commons Standing Committee on Health and Welfare. Global population problems continued to be of concern for most groups. The Canadian ambassador to the UN abstained during a vote on population programs in 1962. Yet during a session of the UN Economic and Social Council on 30 July 1965, he voted in favor of UN assistance for resolving population problems. This meant that the Criminal Code prohibitions no longer completely blocked Canada from supporting foreign population programs, though Canadian foreign policy on population was not formulated until after the law had been changed and the Canadian International Development Agency had been formed.

With regard to conception prevention as a component of family planning, most Canadians came to agree that legally married couples had a fundamental right to practice family planning.

Even the most conservative church groups recognized the right of couples to make their own decisions about parenthood. To the extent that Section 150(2)(c) of the 1953 Criminal Code interfered with this fundamental right, it was a bad law. Public consensus was that the ability to prevent conception in the context of family planning always served the public good; the *pro bono publico* clause was thus irrelevant, and the law itself was unjust. To the extent that family planning advocates and service providers acted under the belief that their actions served the public good, it was unjustifiable that the threat of criminal prosecution should remain.

If married couples were to be free to exercise their sexual activities and procreative capacities in a responsible manner, they required legal access to education and advice to guide their decisions, as well as instruction and means to carry them out. Unless these conditions were all present, spouses could not reasonably be held accountable for the children they bore and their resultant needs. These affirmations were at the core of the family planning movement. From there, it was only a small step to asserting that married couples had a moral and legal right to make their own decisions about conceiving and raising children. Family planning advocates believed that, if conception prevention were decriminalized, family planning clinics could be established throughout the country. All classes of Canadian couples would have access to the means for making their parenthood a responsible decision. No matter what their geographical location or their financial means, birth control services could be made universally available.

The welfare of poor families could be significantly improved by legal access to family planning. If family size could be limited, it was thought that poverty could be reduced. Spouses who were able to practice family planning could limit the number of children according to their ability to provide for their basic needs. Poor couples had a right to family planning services equal to that of more advantaged couples and stood to make greater gains in their living conditions. The costs of making such services widely available would surely be matched by reduced health and welfare costs for all levels of government. In addition, if contraceptives were more readily available, then it was expected that the numbers of abortions (self-induced, illegal, or physician-induced) would fall.

By the mid-1960s, doctors, nurses, public clinics, and family planning agencies provided family planning services despite the threat of criminal prosecution. If they were charged, it would be up to them to prove that their actions served the public good; that is, they were guilty until proven innocent. This constituted a legal injustice that was furthermore hypocritical when it became apparent that declining birthrates and a generally inverse proportion between wealth and family size indicated that economic resources often determined access to such services.

The strongest argument against conception control was that it would be difficult to ensure that only legally married couples practiced it. The churches remained the strongest defenders of the social institution of marriage as divinely ordained for the purposes of faithful love, covenant relationship, and procreation of children. Because the churches did not stand in the way of an amendment to decriminalize conception prevention (which in practice could not be confined to marital use), then their positive support for family planning as an essential component of responsible parenthood was very persuasive. In effect, this support served to silence the few voices that continued to predict moral degeneration as a consequence of any legal amendment.

On 24 January 1966, four private members' bills were introduced and received first reading in the House of Commons. Bill C-22 (Robert Stanbury, Liberal) and Bill C-64 (Ronald Basford, Liberal) were both designed to create a legal exemption from prosecution for authorized agents of family planning associations, public agencies and social workers, and medical professionals. Bill C-71 (Robert Prittie, New Democratic Party) and Bill C-40 (Ian Wahn, Liberal) proposed to delete the words "preventing conception or" from Section 150(2)(c) of the 1953 Criminal Code. Upon second reading on 21 February 1966, all four bills were referred to the newly established Standing Committee on Health and Welfare. The committee heard evidence from numerous national and regional witnesses including the Canadian Medical Association, the Canadian Bar Association, the Family Planning Federation of Canada, the Canadian Welfare Council, the Voice of Women of Canada, the National Council of Women, the Young Women's Christian Association, the Consumers' Association of Canada, church representatives (Anglican, United, Unitarian, Lutheran, Nazarene, Pentecostal), and the Canadian Catholic Conference of Bishops. The Canadian Catholic Conference stated that it was not appropriate for criminal law to be used to impose religious belief or morality from one group on all the citizens of Canada. When Pope Paul VI's *Humanae vitae* was issued on 25 July 1968, maintaining official Catholic opposition to birth control, the public debate in Canada was already over. Of all the witnesses heard by the committee, only the Pentecostal Church opposed decriminalizing conception prevention.

In its final report to the House of Commons on 5 December 1966, the Standing Committee made three recommendations: first, that birth control be removed from the Criminal Code altogether by deleting the words "preventing conception or"; second, that the wording of the Food and Drugs Act be amended to clearly include contraceptive devices; and third, that controls over the marketing and advertising of contraceptives should be included in the Food and Drugs Act regulations. A new bill (Bill S-15, Fred McGrand, Liberal) that would implement all three recommendations was formulated, this time originating in the Senate. After being debated and passed in the Senate, it was introduced in the House of Commons on 21 November 1968. With minor amendments it was passed by the House on 20 May 1969 and received Royal Assent on 27 June 1969.

Family planning advocates expected that the new legislation would be swiftly implemented. Minister of National Health and Welfare John Munro drafted a detailed memorandum to the cabinet in August 1969, seeking its direction on the development of a federal family planning policy and the role of his department. Munro proposed to create a family planning unit within his department. On 18 September 1970, the new minister, Marc Lalonde, announced the establishment of the Family Planning Division to provide information, training, and resources about family planning to the provinces and nongovernmental organizations.

The federal government had no intentions of providing family planning services itself. Constitutionally, the federal government could not insist that the provincial governments develop universally accessible birth control clinics or family planning services. Politically, the federal government was unwilling to establish its own programs and services because of the growing prominence of the abortion controversy. Health and welfare publications continued to maintain that implementing family planning services was a provincial responsibility. Even within federal jurisdictions, such as services for Native peoples, the government was concerned that promotion of family planning would be interpreted as a form of racial genocide.

Lalonde instructed the Canadian International Development Agency to develop an international assistance program for population and family planning initiatives in developing countries. Within Canada, the Family Planning Division would give federal grants to selected nongovernmental family planning groups: to SERENA (Service de Regulation des Naissances), in an attempt to placate antiabortion activists (who they wrongly suspected were all Catholics), and to the Family Planning Federation (later named the Planned Parenthood Federation), which the government hoped would establish the services and become the target of antiabortion protests.

At the First National Conference on Family Planning, held from 28 February to 2 March 1972, family planning was described as a broad range of services including fertility, genetic, marriage, and family counseling; and the provision of contraceptives, sterilization, and abortion. In response to the conference, Lalonde's office was deluged with letters from antiabortion protesters. On 11 September 1973, Lalonde attempted to smooth over the conflict with a statement in the House of Commons. He stated that abortion was not an acceptable form of birth control, but where birth control failed or was not used, recourse to abortion was appropriate if Criminal Code conditions for a legal abortion had been met.

Because subsidized provision of contraceptives to welfare recipients might be interpreted as an effort to oppress minority groups, no effective public assistance programs were implemented. Contraceptive access was often restricted to legally married couples, so abortion rates increased. Lack of education of the young on sexuality and fertility resulted in an increase in teenage pregnancies. Refusal to establish a national population policy to undertake a national program on fertility and contraceptive research caused birth regulation to remain a privilege of class, residential location, and marital status.

The expected consequences of the removal of contraception from the Criminal Code failed to materialize. Ideally, advocates of family planning wanted Ottawa (the capital) to develop a population policy for the country, including basic research into fertility and conception prevention, birthrates, contraceptive effectiveness, and ability to actualize personal choices in choosing or deferring pregnancy. Social welfare reformers wanted the government to initiate studies on the relationship between poverty and family size, as well as to ensure that people who relied on public health and welfare had access to the instruction and means that would allow them to limit their family to a size that was appropriate to their financial and personal means. From its earliest deliberations, the Liberal government refused to establish a national fertility study or a population policy. No fundamental research into conception prevention or conception-enhancing technologies or treatments was undertaken.

On 4 March 1977, Lalonde announced that the Family Planning Division would take a more active role in promoting family planning. He recommended that the provinces establish women's clinics for counseling in family planning and fertility, abortions, cancer screening, and maternal and family health. Antiabortion activists again rallied in protest, and the proposal was immediately canceled. During the summer of 1977, Lalonde was replaced by Monique Bégin, and the government began to dismantle the Family Planning Division; by September 1978 the division had been completely eliminated.

Brenda Margaret Appleby

See also Cadbury, George and Barbara; Eugenics; Sanger, Margaret Louise (Higgins); Stopes, Marie Charlotte Carmichael

References

Appleby, Brenda Margaret. *Responsible Parenthood: Decriminalizing Contraception in Canada.* Toronto: University of Toronto Press, 1999.

McLaren, Angus. "What Has This to Do with Working-Class Women?: Birth Control and the Canadian Left, 1900–1939." *Histoire sociale/Social History* 14:28 (November 1981), 437–447.

McLaren, Angus, and Arlene Tigar McLaren. *The Bedroom and the State.* Toronto: McClelland & Stewart Ltd., 1986.

Canon Law and Abortion

The Christian church from the outset condemned abortion. Christianity's earliest disciplinary rule book, the *Didache* (probably written for a Syrian Christian community, perhaps as early as 60 C.E., in which case it would antedate the surviving Gospel texts) specifically forbade Christians to procure the abortion of a fetus. Other early collections of rules for Christians from the second century prohibited the production, supply, or use of abortifacient potions because, as John Noonan translated it, one of them declared, "The fetus in the womb is not an animal and it is God's providence that he exist."

Christian opposition to abortion was scarcely unique. Causing a pregnant woman to miscarry was punishable as a serious offense according to the Mosaic Law (Exodus 23:22–25), as well as later rabbinical authorities. Many pagan writers, likewise, strongly disapproved of abortion. The Hippocratic oath, as it has come down to us, forbade physicians to administer certain kinds of abortifacient drugs. Aristotle (384–322 B.C.E.) deemed that abortion "before sense and life have begun" was morally acceptable, but after that point was wrong. Of course, some disagreed. Socrates (469–399 B.C.E.), for one, according to Plato (c. 429–397 B.C.E.), thought of abortion as a routine method to prevent births that seemed unwanted or unwise for any number of reasons. Still, Socrates, as he himself admitted, was a gadfly, and was put to death for impiety.

Roman jurists and lawmakers, perhaps influenced by Stoic views on the subject, adopted much the same approach as the writer of Exodus. The Aquilian Law (early third century B.C.E.) provided a civil remedy against the person who induced an involuntary abortion. Jurists also treated abortion as a crime. Cicero (106–43 B.C.E.) maintained that death was an appropriate penalty for a woman who procured an abortion against the will of the father of the fetus. Classical jurists, pagans every one, agreed that abortion was a heinous crime, but were inclined to substitute exile for execution, at least if the offender were a member of the social elite and the mother survived the experience.

Prohibitions of abortion by Christian theology and canon law seem unexceptional against this background. Canon 21 of the Council of Ancyra (314 M.E.) forbade abortion, and early medieval compilers often included this decree in their collections of canon law. The *Decretum* of Gratian (originally composed c. 1140), which became the leading canon law textbook of the high and later Middle Ages, included statements from numerous other authorities on the subject. One of them bluntly declared that abortion at any stage of pregnancy was a form of homicide, although others distinguished between early term and late term abortions. Abortion in the early stages of pregnancy, before the soul was infused into the fetus, according to these authorities, was not homicide, although abortion after ensoulment had occurred and the fetus had assumed human form was murder.

The teaching that abortion constituted a form of homicide was reaffirmed by the *Decretals of Gregory IX,* a compilation of additional canons not found in Gratian's book and promulgated by the pope in 1234. One chapter in this collection reiterated the proposition that abortion was tantamount to murder, whereas another added the qualification that this was true only if the aborted fetus had been viable at the time of the miscarriage.

The teachings found in Gratian's *Decretum* and the *Decretals of Gregory IX* remained the basic law of the Roman Catholic Church until 1917, when Pope Benedict XV (1854–1922) promulgated the *Codex juris canonici,* a restatement of the church's canon law. Although the new code did not explicitly label abortion as homicide, it treated the topic in a title that dealt with that subject and subjected all those who procured or participated in the act of abortion to excommunication, the most severe penalty available to the twentieth-century church. The code applied this penalty flatly to all involved and made no distinctions about the stage of pregnancy at which the abortion took place. The new code of canon law, promulgated in 1983 by Pope John Paul II (1920–), repeated the earlier prohibition and penalty in substantially similar terms. John Paul II subsequently reiterated the teaching in greater detail in 1995 in his encyclical letter, *Evangelium vitae.*

James A. Brundage

References

Aristotle. *The Politics,* translated by Ernest Barker. Oxford, UK: Clarendon Press, 1946, 7:16.15, 1335b 19–26.

Brundage, James A. *Medieval Canon Law.* London: Longman, 1995.

Cicero. *Pro Cluentio,* edited and translated by H. G. Hodge. Cambridge, MA: Harvard University Press, Loeb Classical Library, 1979, 11.32.

Codex iuris canonici. Rome: Typis Polyglottis Vaticanis, 1917, can. 2350, par. 1, can. 1049, par. 2.

Codex iuris canonici, 1983. Vatican City: Libreria Editrice Vaticana, 1983.

Cohen, J. *"Be Fertile and Increase, Fill the Earth and Master It":* *The Ancient and Medieval Career of a Biblical Text.* Ithaca, NY: Cornell University Press, 1989.

Corpus juris canonici, edited by Emil Friedberg, 2 vols. Graz, Austria: Akademische Druck-u. Verlagsanstalt, 1959.

Decretales Gregorii IX. In *Corpus juris canonici,* vol. 2, edited by Emil Friedberg. Graz, Austria: Akademische Druck-u. Verlagsanstalt, 1959, 5.17.5; 5.12.20.

Didache. In *The Apostolic Fathers, vol. 2,* edited and translated by K. Lake. Cambridge, MA: Harvard University Press, Loeb Classical Library, 1985.

Digest, edited by T. Mommsen and translated by P. Kruger, A. Watson, et al., 4 vols., Philadelphia: University of Pennsylvania Press, 1985, 0/2/18/22 (Ulpian), 48.19.39 (Tryphonius), 47:11.4 (Marcian), 48.8.8 (Ulpian), and 48.19.38.5 (Paul).

Gratian. *Dedcretum Gratiani.* In *Corpus juris canonici,* vol. 1, edited by Emil Friedberg. Graz, Austria: Akademische Druck-u. Verlagsanstalt, 1959, C. 2 q.5 c20; C.32 q.2c. 8–10.

John Paul II. <http://www.vatican.va/holy_father/john_paul_ii/encyclicals/> 1995.

Miller, W. P. *Die Anfänge des modernen abtreibungsverbots in spätern Mittelalter.* Princeton, NJ: Princeton University Press, 1997.

Noonan, John T., Jr. *The Morality of Abortion: Legal and Historical Perspectives.* Cambridge, MA: Harvard University Press, 1970.

Plato. *Apologia,* edited and translated by H. N. Fowler. London: Heinemann, Loeb Classical Library, 30.

———. *Laws,* edited and translated by R. G. Bury, 2 vols. London: Heinemann, Loeb Classical Library, 1926, 5:740.

———. *The Republic,* edited and translated by P. Shorey, 2 vols. Cambridge, MA: Harvard University Press, Loeb Classical Library, 1978, 5.461c.

———. *Theaetetus,* edited and translated by H. N. Fowler. London: Heinemann, Loeb Classical Library, 1921, 149d.

Riddle, John M. *Contraception and Abortion from the Ancient World to the Renaissance.* Cambridge, MA: Harvard University Press, 1992.

Canon Law and Contraception

Although Jesus of Nazareth referred only rarely to moral problems posed by sexual behavior of any kind and is not known to have said anything at all about the control of reproduction, his followers have not been nearly so reticent on these matters. Saint Augustine (354–430), whose views on sexual behavior have profoundly influenced, and often dominated, most subsequent Western discussions of the subject, saw the procreation of children as one of the three justifications for Christian marriage. The morality of sexual intercourse, he taught, was largely determined by the intentions of the spouses. If a married couple had sex with the specific intention of engendering offspring, they did so without sin. If they engaged in intercourse in some way calculated to avoid procreation, however, they committed a grave sin. Because Augustine was well aware that raising children was difficult, time-consuming, and expensive, he counseled married couples to cease having sexual relations as soon as they had produced one or two children. Abstinence, as Augustine saw things, was the only morally acceptable method of birth control.

Augustine's views were shared by Saint Jerome (c. 347–419 or 420) and other contemporary church authorities and formed the basis for most subsequent treatments of contraception in the medieval church. The penitential handbooks, which supplied guidance for priests who heard the confessions of the faithful, instructed confessors to impose heavy penance upon women who engaged in contraceptive practices, such as drinking herbal potions or wearing magical charms that they thought would prevent impregnation. The penitentials likewise condemned men who engaged in coitus interruptus, oral sex, or anal intercourse.

Contraception first appeared as an issue in canon law (as distinct from theology) in the tenth-century treatise, *Libri duo de synodalibus causis* by Abbot Regino of Prüm (d. 915). Regino's work included a list of questions that bishops were to ask when visiting the local churches in their dioceses. Among those items, one that became known from its opening words as *Si aliquis* stated:

> If someone to satisfy his lust or in deliberate hatred does something to a man or woman so that no children can be born of him or her, or gives them to drink, so that he cannot impregnate

or she cannot conceive, let this be treated as homicide (Regino of Prüm 1840, 2.89).

Authors of later anthologies of canon law, notably the *Decretum* of Burchard, bishop of Worms (1000–1025), included *Si aliquis* in their collections, although they usually identified it as the decree of a church council.

Another text on contraceptive practices, which opened with the word *Aliquando,* was also destined to have a long life in canon law. *Aliquando* was a passage taken from Saint Augustine's treatise *On Marriage and Concupiscence,* in which Augustine declared:

> Sometimes this lustful cruelty or cruel lust even causes [couples] to procure poisons of sterility and if they are unable to extinguish or destroy the fetus in the womb, preferring that their child die rather than live, if it is already alive in the womb, they choose to kill it before it is born (Augustine of Hippo, 1902, 1.15.17).

Ivo, Bishop of Chartres (1091–1116), included *Aliquando* in one of his canonical collections entitled the *Decretum.* Ivo's work, however, was not widely circulated. *Aliquando* became more broadly known only when it reappeared in a much more widely available work composed around 1140 by a canonist known as Master Gratian.

Gratian named his book *A Harmony of Clashing Canons (Concordia discordantium canonum).* That colorful but cumbersome title soon gave way in common usage to the shorter and more conventional name *Decretum.* Although it was not officially commissioned or approved by any pope, Gratian's *Decretum* quickly emerged in practice as the basic textbook for the study of canon law in the western church. Every canon lawyer needed to be familiar with the book and from it every canon lawyer learned as a student that contraceptive intercourse was incompatible with Christian marriage and was, in fact, a species of fornication. It followed that everyone who practiced contraception, married or not,

Dutch women protest outside the residence of the Papal Nuncio on the fifth anniversary of the pope's encyclical forbidding mechanical means of birth control. (Hulton Getty Collection / Archive Photos)

should be subject to punishment. Canonists discovered this not only from *Aliquando,* but also from other texts that Gratian brought together with it under the heading "Those who procure poisons of sterility are not spouses but fornicators" (Gratian 1959, C. 32 q. 7 c. 11; for the canonistic citation system employed here see Brundage, 1995, 190–205). Law students also learned from this section of Gratian's book that contraception was contrary to natural law and thus constituted a serious offense against God, against the church, against marriage, and against the rightful order of Christian society. In short, contraceptive intercourse or even the intention to engage in contraceptive intercourse, whether within marriage or outside of it, was a crime, and a major crime at that.

Gratian, for whatever reason, had not chosen to include the other major condemnation of contraceptive practices, *Si aliquis,* in his collection of canon law. As the papal chancery continued to issue new laws, mainly in the form of decretals, after Gratian's *Decretum* was completed, it became increasingly urgent to compile a supplement to Gratian's work. In 1230, accordingly, Pope Gregory IX (1227–1241) commissioned Raymond of Penyafort (c.1180–1275) to put together an official collection of the new law. The terms of Raymond's commission, among other things, authorized him to incorporate in the new work any earlier canons that seemed to merit inclusion. One of the older canons that Raymond selected for inclusion was *Si aliquis.* Thus in 1234, when Gregory IX promulgated the new collection, under the formal title of the *Decretals of Gregory IX,* this canon reappeared, this time with papal authority behind it. Because *Si aliquis* described as homicide sexual techniques that were designed to avoid conception, Raymond of Penyafort placed in book five of the *Decretals,* which dealt with criminal law, a section that contained other canons that dealt with homicide. Contraception thus remained legally a type of homicide in the canon law of the Roman Catholic Church until 1917.

In addition to these two older canons, Raymond added a new canon, *Si conditiones,* dealing with contraception. Whereas both of the older canons on the subject treated contraception as a crime, *Si conditiones* placed the practice in the context of matrimonial law. The new canon ruled that, if a person married with the intention of avoiding having children, the marriage was invalid.

The addition of *Si conditiones* to the two older canons that prohibited contraception completed the legislative basis for medieval canonistic treatments of the matter. Academic lawyers could explore the limits and implications of the policy that these canons expressed, and often did so at length, but their analysis added little of substance to it.

As a practical matter the two canons that criminalized contraception, *Aliquando* and *Si aliquis,* were virtually impossible to enforce by formal judicial process. In the present state of knowledge of the records of the medieval ecclesiastical courts (Donahue, 1989, 1994) it is impossible to say with certainty whether any defendants were ever prosecuted in ecclesiastical courts for fornication or homicide because they had practiced contraception. It is highly unlikely, however, that such actions, even if brought, could often have succeeded, given the stringent standards of the canonical law of proof.

Criminal prosecutions based on either of these canons were thus extremely rare. The force of *Si aliquis* and *Aliquando* was felt instead, not in the courts that punished crimes publicly, but rather in confession, the private court of conscience. From 1215 onward, canon 21 of the Fourth Lateran Council required western Christians to confess their sins to a priest at least once a year. Evidence concerning the effectiveness of this decree is fairly sparse, but what there is of it seems to show that its provisions were in fact often observed, and prosecutions were certainly brought in church courts to punish those who failed to comply with them. Confessors were directed to question penitents closely, among other things, about the use of methods to avoid procreation and, so far as one can tell, apparently did so routinely.

The consequences of *Si conditiones,* at least in theory, were entirely different. This canon formed part of the church's matrimonial law and potentially furnished grounds for the annulment of marriages from which one or both of the parties wished to escape. Medieval and early modern ecclesiastical courts, however, seem to have heard few, if any, annulment cases based on this canon. Indeed, they heard remarkably few annulment cases based on any grounds. It was not until 1904, in fact, that we learn of a case in which the practice of contraception under the terms of *Si conditiones* was successfully invoked as grounds for an ecclesiastical annulment in the courts of the Roman curia.

The emergence at the beginning of the twentieth century of the use of contraception as grounds for invalidating a marital union reflected changes in society and technology in the modern world. Beginning in France during the late eighteenth century the practice of voluntary birth control spread rapidly to other parts of Europe, to the United States, and more slowly through the remainder of the industrialized world. This spread reflected in part the social consequences of the Industrial Revolution, which for many couples made it less necessary, and less attractive, to produce numerous progeny. The increased frequency of the use of contraceptive techniques also stemmed in part from the appearance of new, more effective, and cheaper methods of birth control.

Religious authorities, especially among Roman Catholics, at first reacted to these developments cautiously, advising confessors not to pry too deeply into the sexual practices of married penitents, many of whom no doubt genuinely felt that no sin was involved in adopting prudent measures to control the size of their families. Leading bishops and theologians, however, increasingly harked back to the Augustinian notion that procreation was a primary goal of marriage. From this premise, they concluded that efforts to limit family size contradicted fundamental Christian values. This led church authorities during the nineteenth and early twentieth centuries to attack contraception with increasing zeal and vigor.

At the same time, the Catholic Church was in the process of reorganizing its legal system. Codification was all the rage among European jurists in the late nineteenth and early twentieth centuries. One nation after another sought to restructure its existing legal system in a more systematic and "scientific" form. France had led the way when it enacted the Napoleonic *Code civil* in 1804. Two generations later Italy adopted the *Codice civile* in 1865, and then Spain created its *Código civil* in 1889. After tumultuous debates the German Reichstag approved the *Bürgerliches Gesetzbuch* in 1895, and Switzerland replaced its cantonal laws with a common civil code in 1907. Most other European countries revised their laws as well, as did all the nations of Latin America and others even further removed from European traditions, such as Japan in 1898 and Turkey in 1926. It was thus no great surprise when Pope Pius X (1835–1914) in 1903 authorized Pietro Gasparri (1852–1934) to undertake a codification of the laws of the Catholic Church.

In the process of constructing the new code, Gasparri and the commission that he headed necessarily had to confront the confusing, and largely inoperable, treatment of contraception in the existing law. What Gasparri did, first of all, was to scrap the unworkable criminal approach enunciated in *Aliquando* and *Si aliquis.* Neither of those canons had ever been seriously enforced. Gasparri, sensibly enough, saw no future in continuing those failed approaches. Instead he chose to conflate the policy enunciated in *Si conditiones,* which made the practice of contraception grounds for matrimonial annulment, with the provisions of another thirteenth-century canon, *Tua nos,* which dealt with simulated consent to marriage. By combining the policies that undergirded these two decretals, Gasparri was able to formulate a new canon that in effect enabled canonical courts to invalidate any marriage where either partner from the outset intended to use contraceptive practices to limit family size.

This formulation became part of the *Code of Canon Law* that Pope Benedict XV (1854–1922) promulgated on 27 May 1917 and that took effect on 19 May 1918. The revised *Code of Canon Law,* promulgated by Pope John Paul II (1920–) on 25 January 1983, repeated this canon with one slight, but significant, alteration. The 1917 version provided that

> If, however, either or both of the parties by a positive willful act exclude marriage itself, or all right to the conjugal act, or some essential element, or any essential property of marriage, that party contracts invalidly (*Codex iuris canonici,* 1917, can. 1086 § 2).

The 1983 version omitted the phrase "or all right to the conjugal act," which potentially left the door ever so slightly ajar for a possible revision of the church's ban on contraception.

Canonical opposition to contraception rested ultimately upon theological doctrines, which approached the subject as a moral, rather than a legal, issue. Catholic theologians until the end of the nineteenth century unreservedly condemned all attempts at birth control as inherently sinful. Some theologians, to be sure, were hesitantly prepared to tolerate what they called *amplexus reservatus,* by which they meant unconsummated marital intercourse, in which the couple terminated coitus before they achieved orgasm. *Amplexus reservatus* was first discussed by the canonist Huguccio (d. 1210) late in the twelfth century, but the idea was not widely accepted, or even widely discussed, by theologians until the twentieth century. Few couples felt much inclined to adopt it, for understandable reasons, and its importance was more theoretical than practical.

Modern Catholic theologians have been considerably more intrigued by the moral implications of the so-called rhythm method of birth control. This stemmed from the discovery by nineteenth-century biologists that female mammals, including humans, can conceive only during certain periods. Theologians vigorously debated the question of whether it was sinful for married couples to deliberately limit their sexual activity only to those periods when conception was impossible. Such a practice, according to some, was "natural" and hence morally acceptable, as opposed to all other methods of reproductive control, which they described as "artificial" and therefore morally wrong. In 1930 Pope Pius XI (1857–1935) in the encyclical *Casti connubii* ruled that deliberate avoidance of reproduction through use of the sterile period was sinful. His successor, Pius XII (1876–1958), substantially modified this position, however, when he declared in 1951 that use of the sterile period to avoid procreation might be appropriate, at least for certain couples under certain conditions.

Catholic doctrine on contraception has become the subject of repeated controversy, both among Catholic and non-Catholic theologians, throughout the second half of the twentieth century. In March 1963 Pope John XXIII (1881–1963) appointed an international commission to study the whole matter. By the time the commission finished its work, however, John XXIII had been succeeded by Pope Paul VI (1897–1978). The final report of the commission on contraception placed Paul VI in a dilemma, because the commission, as well as a number of bishops, suggested that the ban on "artificial" birth control seemed itself suspiciously artificial and that the issue of contraception should be left to the consciences of individual married couples. To adopt that advice would have meant reversing what was by this time an embarrassing chain of earlier papal pronouncements, which Paul VI declined to do. Instead, on 25 July 1968, he issued a new encyclical, *Humanae vitae,* in which he once again condemned

> [E]very action which, either in anticipation of the conjugal act, or in its accomplishment, or in the development of its natural consequences, proposes,

whether as an end or as a means, to render procreation impossible (Paul VI 1968, § 14).

He did, however, reaffirm that in some vaguely defined situations that might arise "from the physical or psychological conditions of husband and wife, or from external conditions" it might be permissible for couples

[T]o take into account the natural rhythms immanent in the generative functions, for the use of marriage in the infecund periods only, and in this way to regulate birth without offending the moral principles which have been recalled earlier (Paul VI 1968 § 16).

John Paul II has repeatedly reaffirmed this doctrine. It thus remains the unyielding position of the Roman Catholic magisterium to this day.

Most other Christian churches, however, have rejected Rome's teachings on contraception. In the Anglican Communion, for example, the 1930 Lambeth Conference held that married couples had a moral right to employ contraceptive measures when they deemed that there was "a morally sound reason" for them to do so, and the 1968 Lambeth Conference explicitly repudiated the teachings of *Humanae vitae*. Among the Orthodox churches there appears to be no firm agreement on the issue.

The belief that the procreation of children is a divinely mandated duty of married couples has a long, rich history that stretches back into the furthest depths of Judeo-Christian culture. That strand of belief, however, does not intrinsically require couples to have as many children as possible, much less that conjugal intercourse be directed exclusively toward reproduction. Catholic law and theology adopted those views neither from Mosaic law nor from the teachings of Jesus. These doctrines originated instead in pagan beliefs, more specifically in Stoic philosophy. Their persistence in the Catholic law and theology is one of the stranger ironies in the history of western morality.

James A. Brundage

References

Augustine of Hippo, St. *De bono conjugali*. In *Corpus Scriptorum Ecclesiasticorum Latinorum, vol. 41,* edited by Joseph Zycha. Vienna: F. Tempsky, 1900, 3.3.

———. *De nuptiis et consupiscentia*. In*Corpus Scriptorum Ecclesiasticorum Latinorum, vol. 42,* edited by K. F. Urba and Joseph Zycha. Vienna: F. Tempsky, 1902.

Biller, Peter, and A. J. Minnis. *Handling Sin: Confession in the Middle Ages.* Rochester, NY: York Medieval Press, 1998.

Brown, Peter Robert Lamont. *The Body and Society: Men, Women, and Sexual Renunciation in Early Christianity.* New York: Columbia University Press, 1988.

Brundage, James A. *Law, Sex, and Christian Society in Medieval Europe.* Chicago: University of Chicago Press, 1987.

———. *Medieval Canon Law.* London: Longman, 1995.

———. "Proof in Canonical Criminal Law." *Continuity and Change* 11 (1996): 329–339.

———. "The Married Man's Dilemma: Sexual Morals, Canon Law, and Marital Restraint." *Studia Gratiana* 28 (1998):149–169.

Bullough, Vern L., and James A. Brundage. *Handbook of Medieval Sexuality.* New York: Garland, 1996.

Burchard of Worms. *Decretum.* In *Patrologia Latina,* 1880, vol. 140. *Codex iuris canonici.* Rome: Typis Polyglottis Vaticanis, 1917.

Codex iuris canonici, 1983. Vatican City: Libreria Editrice Vaticana, 1983.

Cohen, Jeremy. *"Be Fertile and Increase, Fill the Earth and Master It:"The Ancient and Medieval Career of a Biblical Text.* Ithaca, NY: Cornell University Press, 1989.

Corpus iuris canonici, edited by Emil Friedberg, 2 vols. Graz, Austria: Akademische Druck-u. Verlagsanstalt, 1959.

Cross, F. L., and Elizabeth A. Livingstone. *The Oxford Dictionary of the Christian Church,* 3rd ed. New York: Oxford University Press, 1998.

Donahue, Charles. *The Records of the Medieval Ecclesiastical Courts.* Part I: *The Continent.* Berlin: Duncker & Humblot, 1989.

———. *The Records of the Medieval Ecclesiastical Courts.* Part II: *England.* Berlin: Duncker & Humblot, 1994.

García y García, A. *Constitutiones Concilii quarti Lateranensis una cum commentariis glossatorum.* In *Monumenta iuris canonici, Corpus glossatorum, vol. 2.* Vatican City: Biblioteca Apostolica Vaticana, 1981.

Gratian *Decretum,* In *Corpus iuris canonici, vol. 1,* edited by Emil Friedberg. Graz, Austria: Akademische Druck-u. Verlagsanstalt. 1959, C 32 q.7 c.11.

Gregory IX. *Decretales Gregorii IX,* In *Corpus iuris canonici, vol. 2,* edited by Emil Friedberg. Graz, Austria: Akademische Druck-u. Verlagsanstalt, 1959, 4.5.7. 5.12.5.

Helmholz, R. H. *Marriage Litigation in Medieval England.* Cambridge, UK: Cambridge University Press, 1974.

Ivo of Chartres. *Decretum.* In *Patrologia Latina, vol. 161,* 1889, 10:55. John Paul II. *Fruitful and Responsible Love.* New York: Seabury Press, 1979.

John Paul II. *The Apostolic Exhortation on the Family: Familiaris consortio.* Hales Corners, WI: Priests of the Sacred Heart, 1981.

John Paul II. *Crossing the Threshold of Hope.* New York: Alfred A. Knopf, 1994.

Noonan, John Thomas. *Power to Dissolve: Lawyers and Marriages in the Courts of the Roman Curia.* Cambridge, MA: Belknap Press of Harvard University Press, 1972.

———. *Contraception: A History of Its Treatment by the Catholic Theologians and Canonists,* 2nd ed. Cambridge, MA: Belknap Press of Harvard University Press, 1986.

Patrologia Latina, edited by J.-P. Migne. 221 vols. Paris: J.-P. Migne. Reprinted numerous times, 1841–1860.

Paul VI. *On the Regulation of Birth: Humanae vitae.* Washington, DC: United States Catholic Conference, 1968.

Regino of Prüm. *Libri duo de synodalibus causis et disciplinis ecclesiasticis,* edited by F. G. A. Wasserschleben. Leipzig: Tauchnitz, 1840.

Wieacker, Franz. 1995. *A History of Private Law in Europe,* translated by Tony Weir. Oxford, UK: Clarendon Press, 1995.

Zweigert, Konrad, and Hein Kötz. *An Introduction to Comparative Law,* 2nd ed., translated by Tony Weir. Oxford, UK: Clarendon Press, 1992.

Carlile, Richard (1790–1843)

An English radical and freethinker, Richard Carlile was born in Ashburton, a town in Devon, England, and attended the village school there until he was apprenticed as a tin maker. When he completed his apprenticeship in 1813 he moved to London to find work and as a journeyman spent a large part of the next two years wandering around the country working when and where he could. He read widely and, influenced by the writings of Thomas Paine's *Rights of Man,* he became a freethinker and radical reformer. He very much wanted to become a writer and continually sent letters to the radical newspapers but was not particularly successful in getting them published. He turned briefly to book selling and in 1817 became the publisher of *Sherwin's Weekly Public Register,* a two-penny paper aimed at the working man.

Shortly after taking over the paper, Carlile was arrested for publishing a parody of the Book of Common Prayer. He was held for some eighteen weeks before being released without having a trial. Undaunted, he continued to publish his free thought publications, for which he was again arrested but this time convicted of blasphemy and sent to jail for two years. While in jail, his wife, whom he had married in 1813, took over the publication of his weekly, now renamed the *Republican,* but Carlile continued to edit from jail. His wife too was jailed (with her baby), as was her successor as publisher, Carlile's sister. In 1825 Carlile was suddenly and unconditionally released from prison, and one of his early publications after his release was *Every Woman's Book: or, What Is Love.* He had become convinced by Francis Place of the importance of publicizing birth control methods. Carlile's book, however, really a long pamphlet, was conceived not only as a way of disseminating information about contraception but as a way of helping women achieve emancipation.

Carlile emphasized that (1) a married couple need not have more children than they wanted and could maintain, (2) no unhealthy woman need endanger her life, (3) all children should be wanted children and there should be no illegitimate children, and (4) sexual intercourse could be made independent of the dread of conception. He considered several methods of birth control: the sponge, what was called the *baudruche* in France and the glove in England (the condom), withdrawal (either complete or partial), and emitting the semen in the cavity below the womb by "lying in a parallel line on the female, leg on leg, at the time of emission" (coitus interfemora).

Two of Carlile's shop workers, William Campion and Richard Haasell, also wrote about the need for using birth control but did not get involved in the discussion of how to do so. They too were jailed for selling prohibited books.

Carlile himself was again sent to prison for publishing a nonstamped journal (stamping was a government way of taxing publications). Jail, however, did not stop his activities and he continued to write and publicize his causes while in jail. He is remembered today as a pioneer advocate of almost every radical cause that appeared on the English scene in the first half of the nineteenth century. His causes included the abolition of the monarchy, elimination of the church tax as well as the role of the Church of England as a state church, establishment of secular education, and emancipation of women.

Carlile considered freedom of speech and propagation of knowledge far more important than specific social and political reform. When he died in London, he had spent a total of nine years and four months in prison, nearly a third of his adult life, because of his outspoken advocacy of causes.

References

Fryer, Peter. *The Birth Controllers.* London: Secker and Warburg, 1965.
McLaren, Angus. *Birth Control in Nineteenth Century England.* London: Croom, Helm, 1978.

Catholic Church (American) and Birth Control

Margaret Sanger and the birth control movement ran into repeated opposition with the Catholic Church, particularly in New York City. In 1921 when Sanger organized the first National Birth Control Conference in New York City, the city police closed the entrance of the auditorium and tried to evict the audience that had gathered to hear Harold Cox, a former member of the British Parliament, from speaking on the question of "Birth Control: Is It Moral?" Sanger herself was bodily removed from the stage and arrested. This particular action had been instigated by Monsignor Joseph P. Dineen, secretary to Archbishop Patrick J. Hayes, without the knowledge or authorization of any municipal official higher than a police precinct captain. This marked the entrance of the Catholic Church in full force opposition to Sanger and as the successor to Anthony Comstock, becoming the major source of opposition to the use of contraceptives.

The Catholic Church regarded Sanger as antinatalist and even antiwoman because she refused to recognize that the proper place of a married woman was in the home and that her duty was to bear many children. The rather crude attempts of the Catholic hierarchy to prevent her activities made Sanger appear a champion of civil liberties and served to give her work wider publicity than she might otherwise have received.

Catholic pressure and opposition to birth control, however, did not cease. On April 15, 1929, New York City police raided the Clinical Research Bureau, the birth control clinic founded by Margaret Sanger, and arrested its director Hannah Stone, another physician, and three nurses on charges of violating Section 11142, the statute prohibiting the dispensing of contraceptive information. The raid had been carried out with considerable brutality and open hostility by the police, who had forced their way into rooms where patients were on the examining table. The contents of drawers and file cabinets were dumped into the trash baskets and hauled away, and items such as physician's gloves and medicine droppers were seized. Index cards and patient histories were also taken.

Investigation demonstrated that the raid had originated at the precinct level when Catholic social workers on the Lower East Side sought clerical advice on the handling of Catholic mothers who wished to go to the birth control clinic. The precinct magistrate again had acted on his own to initiate the raid, and apparently the records had been seized to find out if any Catholics had been clients at the clinic. The raid was denounced by, among others, the New York Academy of Medicine, and in the aftermath the Catholic Church began to be more discrete in its opposition.

The Catholic Church has remained the bulwark of religious opposition to contraception, although much of its publicity and action in the last part of the twentieth century was directed against abortion.

See also Stone, Hannah

Reference

Gordon, Linda. *Woman's Body, Woman's Right: Birth Control in America.* New York: Penguin Books, 1990.

Cervical Cap

Barrier methods of contraception rely on placing some kind of obstacle in the vagina to prevent the passage of sperm into the uterus. Some, such as the diaphragm, covered the cervix, whereas the cervical cap was designed to fit only over the cervix and not block the vaginal canal as the diaphragm did. The problem was how to keep the cervical cap covering the cervix. The half of a lemon that Casanova used was a cervical cap but was difficult if not impossible to hold in place.

Rubber seemed a natural material for making a cap because it could be molded into place. From its first transmission into Europe from the Americas in the sixteenth century, rubber began to be used for a variety of medical products and the number of these gradually increased. Even before vulcanization it was widely used for various kinds of pessaries. One of the earliest medical references to what is clearly a cervical cap designed for contraceptive purposes was by Friedrich Wilde in 1838. He urged women who wished to avoid becoming pregnant to be fitted with a pessary made of unvulcanized rubber (or *kauthuck* in German). Wilde first took a wax impression of the cervix and then, using it as a pattern, designed a hard rubber pessary that would snugly cover the os, or entrance into the uterus (Wilde, 1838). Annie Besant prescribed its use as a contraceptive in the 1887 edition of her *Law of Population,* and other writers followed her example. Marie Stopes made the cervical cap her contraceptive of choice, and she helped design the modern ones, although a number of others were also involved.

The vaginal cup (cervical cap), popularized by Stopes, was a small thimble-shaped cup that effectively blocked the cervix when it was inserted properly. During the early years of the twentieth century, it was in competition with the diaphragm but it fell into disfavor in the United States (although not in Great Britain) in part because it took longer to fit properly and seemed more complicated to insert correctly than the diaphragm. It was also a source of discomfort for a few users. Perhaps the key reason for its failure to become the barrier contraceptive of choice in the United States is that Margaret Sanger and the American Birth Control League advocated the use of the diaphragm. Still, the cervical cap had its strong advocates and its popularity increased in the 1970s through the advocacy of many feminist health organizations. This success was short lived because it ran into serious legal problems as a result of the Medical Device Amendment Act of 1976. The intention of the U.S. government in enacting the law was not to ban the cervical cap but only to have its manufacturers submit data on its safety and efficacy to the Food and Drug Administration (FDA) and give proof that it had been marketed in the United States before the law had been passed. This requirement applied to all manufacturers of all medical devices on the market before 1976 and had not especially singled out contraceptive devices. When the British manufacturer of the cap, for some unknown reason but probably the cost involved since it was not widely used in the United States, failed to provide the needed information, the FDA had no alternative and in 1979 placed the cap on its Class III list of devices—those that represented a significant risk to the user—and ordered the seizure of all cap shipments entering the country. It was not until 1988 after tests finally had been run and the data gathered together that the FDA announced its approval of one type of cap, the Prentif cavity-rim cervical cap. Once again the device was available in the United States to those women who preferred it.

The Prentif cavity-rim cervical cap currently in use is made of a soft, pliable latex and is about half the size of the diaphragm. It is available in four sizes with inside diameters of 22, 25, 28, and 31 mm. Two other caps, the vault (or Dumas) cap and the Vimule cap, have also been approved. Although they are not much used in the United States, they are in other countries. The vault, or Dumas, cap is made of rubber or plastic and shaped like a circular bowl with a thick rim and thin center. It clings by suction to the vault or roof of the vagina, following the contour of the cervix. It is useful for the woman who cannot accommodate a diaphragm because of poor muscle tone and for the woman who cannot use the Prentif cervical cap because her cervix is either too long or too short. The Dumas cap is available in five sizes ranging from 50 to 75 mm, and although the diameters are larger than those of the Prentif cavity-rim cup, this is because it, like the Vimule cap, covers the cervix and part of the upper vaginal vault, whereas the Prentif covers only the cervix. The Vimule cap is a longer bell-shaped cap made of thick rubber or plastic (more like the early ones) with a deep dome. It fits around the cervix but has a flanged rim that permits it to be pressed more firmly onto the roof of the vagina. It is most useful for a woman who has poor vaginal muscle tone, a cystocele, or a longer than average cervix. It is available in three sizes: 42, 48, and 54 mm. Like the diaphragm, the cup must be fitted by a professional.

Since the development of spermicides, users of the cup are also advised to put spermicidal jelly in the cup (until it is about one-third full) before inserting. Although barrier methods are no longer as widely used as they were for much of the twentieth century, the cap has some characteristics that its users believed, once they had mastered the insertion techniques, made it their contraceptive of choice. It can be left in longer (two to three days at a time) than the diaphragm, it does not create pressure on the bladder, and it does not block the stimulation of the anterior vaginal wall, which some researchers have identified as the site of the Grafenburg, or "G," spot, a particularly sensitive area of sexual pleasure for some women. Failure rates are similar to those found by users of the diaphragm, that is, about ten per one hundred woman-years of use. This means that for every one hundred women using the cup with spermicide for one year, fewer than ten will become pregnant. However, improper fitting or insertion, which might cause the cap to be dislodged, is more likely than that among diaphragm users.

As with the diaphragm, more experienced users have lower failure rates and some would claim no more than two or three per one hundred woman-years.

See also Barrier Contraceptives; Besant, Annie; Food and Drug Administration (United States); German Medical Contributors; Pessary; Stopes, Marie Charlotte Carmichael

References

Bullough, Vern L., and Bonnie Bullough. *Contraception: A Guide to Birth Control Methods.* Buffalo, NY: Prometheus Books, 1997.

Himes, Norman E. *Medical History of Contraception.* New York: Schocken Books, 1970.

Klitsch, Michael. "FDA Approval Ends a New Look at the Old Standby." *Family Planning Perspectives* 20 (May–June, 1988): 137–138.

Wilde, F. A. *Da weibliche Gebr-unvermgen.* Berlin: In der Nicholaischen Buchhandlung, 1838.

Wortman, Judith. "The Diaphragm and Other Intravaginal Barriers: A Review," *Population Reports,* ser. H, no. 4 (January 1976).

Cervical Rings

Cervical rings, developed in the last decade of the twentieth century, are another method of distributing hormones into the female reproductive system by using the same principle as that used by the pills, the injections, and the implants. Ring diameters ranges from 50 to 75 mm; the cross-sectional diameters, from 5 to 9 mm. There are three types of rings. First are those that release the natural hormone progesterone and are intended primarily for women who are breastfeeding. These cervical rings offer long-acting contraception for women who are no longer protected by lactational amenorrhea. They are placed surrounding the cervix and can be effective for one to two years. Research and development of this type of ring was funded by the Population Council, the Contraceptive Research and Development Program, and an industrial partner, Silesia.

The second type of ring is a synthetic progestin-only ring. It uses synthetic progestins such as Nesterone or levonorgestrel and is formulated to last a year. The third type is a combined ring that contains both a progestin and an estrogen. It also was developed by the Population Council and one popular formulation is that of norethindrone acetate and ethinyl estradiol. The advantage of the combined rings is that they produce fewer bleeding problems and offer more cycle-to-cycle control but they are not appropriate for women who are breastfeeding. The combined ring is used very much like a package of pills. The woman inserts the ring into her vagina, keeps it in for three weeks, and then takes it out for one week. During the three weeks it is in, its effectiveness is nearly 100 percent. During the week it is removed there is a menstrual bleed.

All the rings can be removed temporarily before intercourse, if the couple desires to do so, and then reinserted. The partner might object to the ring or the woman might take it out for normal hygiene. The rings should, however, be removed for only short periods.

References

Severy, Lawrence J., and Jeffrey Spiler. "New Methods of Family Planning." *Journal of Sex Research* 37 (2000) 3:258–265.

China and Birth Control

The conception of children, particularly of male children, was believed to constitute not only a necessary part of the order of the universe but also a sacred duty to one's ancestors in ancient China. Chinese theories of sex were closely associated with the belief in yin and yang, concepts imbedded in Taoism, the religion founded by the sixth-century B.C.E. prophet Lao Tzu, although probably many of the theories predated him. Although the ultimate purpose of sexual intercourse was to have children, it was also a method of strengthening the male's vitality if he somehow preserved his seminal essence (*ching*) and yet in the process absorbed the yin essence of his female partner, something of which women had large amounts. The secret was to avoid ejaculation as much as possible, while making certain that the woman achieved orgasm. This could be done by coitus reservatus, slowing the

thrusting when orgasm seemed imminent, but continuing to keep the penis in the vagina until the penis became quiescent. To do this took both training and experience and the way to begin, according to the Taoists, was through *huan ching pu nao,* literally making the semen return to the brain. At the moment of ejaculation, pressure was exerted on the urethra between the scrotum and anus, and this diverted the seminal secretion into the bladder, where it would later be voided with the excreted urine. The Taoists did not have the benefit of modern physiology, and, because by observation the semen was no longer there, they held that by this method and positive thinking the seminal essence could be made to ascend and rejuvenate or revivify the upper parts of the body.

To explain the secrets of intercourse, there were a number of manuals, collectively called the *fang chung,* the "art of the bedchamber." Those that have survived are mainly from copies made in Japan. Though the intent of coitus reservatus was not to prevent conception but to build up a reservoir of yin that might then guarantee a male child, the widespread adoption of such a practice would cut down on the number of children.

The Chinese also had some concept of the fertility cycle in women and advised that intercourse three to five days after the cessation of the menses was more likely to generate boys, but even if a girl child resulted she would be pure and virtuous. There were also all sorts of prohibited days for intercourse, which probably also acted to keep the pregnancy rate low. A child was not to be conceived at midnight; at the winter or summer solstice; during an eclipse, rainbow, thunder, lightning, or a crescent or full moon; when the sun was at its height; or when one or another partner was drunk.

Though both Confucianism and Buddhism became more influential as philosophical or religious movements than did Taoism, there was a strong holdover of Taoist concepts throughout Chinese history. Increasingly also Taoism became more ascetic, with its devotees practicing the

A large Chinese birth control poster at a busy walkway shows a young father and mother with their single child. China's policy of one child per family has been controversial among reproductive freedom advocates who believe the right to have children is as important as the right not to have them. (Patrick Field/Eye Ubiquitous/Corbis)

sexual alchemy through meditation and religious study instead of engaging in actual intercourse. In mainstream Chinese society, sexual segregation increased.

Many of the herbal remedies that were attempts to prevent contraception or to expel a fetus and that were mentioned in classical and other sources were also known to the Chinese. Hawthorn, for example, mentioned by Dioscorides as causing abortions, was still in use in China in the twentieth century. Regulated dosages of the root were given for menstrual pain and postpartum lower abdominal distension. Queen Anne's lace, or wild carrot (*Daucus carota*), was also mentioned. Joseph Needham reported that as early as the eleventh century Chinese medical authorities were using placental tissue, a source of estrogen, to treat amenorrhea and it could well have served as an abortifa-

cient as well. As in other areas of the world, however, it is difficult to distinguish between abortifacients and contraceptives. Some of the contraceptives are said to have greater potential danger to the mother than any injury she might have suffered in childbirth. Most of the contraceptive remedies seem to have been the property of women and only occasionally do they appear in Chinese medical texts. Several prescriptions are given by Himes. It is mentioned that prostitutes were also a source of information about birth control and abortion.

Chinese philosophers and other writers occasionally worried about population growth. Han Fei (c. 280 B.C.E.) reported that one cause of war was the growth of population and a decline in resources. Xu Guangqi (sixteenth century) reported population as doubling over a period of thirty years and worried as to what might happen, but like Malthus later did, he tended to believe that the only solution was wars and disease. At the time he was writing, the population has been estimated as 50 million and it had increased to 100 million by the beginning of the eighteenth century.

It was only in the twentieth century, when the Chinese population passed the half billion mark that population growth and birth control became a major issue. Margaret Sanger carried the contraceptive message to China in 1924 but the issue was soon overshadowed by the struggle for political control of China. Yinchu Ma, an economist and president of China from 1951 to 1958 in the Communist takeover, proposed in 1957 that it was essential that China's population be controlled. His proposals were turned down by Mao Zedong (1893–1976), who summoned some two hundred scholars together in a conference to dispute Ma's analysis. Ma persisted but was forced to resign from his post and was prohibited from publishing any of his ideas. Although Mao eventually changed his mind, before he had done so he had launched his "Great Leap Forward" campaign, downplaying birth control and emphasizing population growth. When the People's Republic of China was established in 1949, the mainland population was estimated as 540,000,000. By 1981 it had exceeded a billion.

It was Deng Xiaoping (1904–1997), who succeeded to power in 1979, who finally launched a successful campaign to cut down the size of the Chinese family. The birthrate, which had been 33.43 per thousand in 1970, dropped to 16.57 per thousand in 1997. The fertility rate for women went from 5.81 to 2. Article 25 of the revised constitution of China stipulated that the state has a right to promote family planning in order to make population growth compatible with the plan for socioeconomic development. Article 49 stipulated that each married couple had an obligation to practice family planning, whereas Article 47 indicated that women not only have the right to bear children but also the right to have no children.

China's present population policy consists of two components: decreasing and limiting the quantity of population and at the same time improving the quality of life. To reduce the numerical growth, a three-pronged program was adopted: late marriage, late childbearing, and fewer births, with the idea being a one couple–one child policy. Such a policy might be easier to enforce in China than in other areas of the world.

Under Mao Zedong, control over the people on the local level was by the *danwei*—the unit to which an individual was assigned and from whose authorities the individual had to get permission to marry or do almost anything else, even for a woman to get pregnant. This made it possible in urban areas, where party control was greatest, to insist that people not be married before the ideal age of twenty-four for women and twenty-seven for men and for women not to get pregnant before they were thirty in order to bring about healthier births. Rural areas have been more difficult to control and in order to deal with this there has been some relaxation in rules of family size both for rural areas and among ethnic minorities. A couple in a rural area with one daughter can, after a suitable interval, have a second child. The emphasis on having male children has also led to early abortions or in many cases to infanticide of female infants in order to make sure the family has a son.

Female infanticide is, however, not a new problem in China, and in 1948 there were nearly 110 males for every 100 females, whereas some rural areas such as Dalian had a ratio of 194 males to 100 females. In an effort to curb this female infanticide, the Chinese government now prevents ultrasound screening to ascertain the sex of a fetus and permits abortion only when a real medical emergency exists. Still, it is now estimated that in 2010, there will be more than 40 million men in their thirties who will be unable to find wives, which in itself is an effective means of population control.

Birth control devices and techniques are now widely available in China and the overwhelming majority of couples of childbearing age use them. Most widely used is sterilization, some of which methods are said to be reversible. Tubal ligations in 1997 were used by about 40 percent of the couples; vasectomies, by another 9 percent. The Chinese in fact developed almost a factory system of doing tubal ligation, which involves the use of acid to scar the fallopian tube. More than 43 percent of Chinese use some form of intrauterine device (the inexpensive Lippes loop is very popular); 4 percent use condoms; 2 percent use oral contraceptives; and slightly more than 1 percent, as of this writing, used implants, spermicide, or other means (figures are rounded off).

Abortion in China is not only a legal right but a legal responsibility. If a woman already has a child, she will be asked by the authorities to terminate her unplanned pregnancy by abortion in the first trimester, and if she manages to avoid detection, even as late as the second trimester. About one-third of the women who have been pregnant in China have undergone at least one abortion. Most abortions have been described as the result of failed contraception.

Even with the drastic measures that China has taken, it is estimated that the population will not be stabilized until the year 2050, when it will reach about 1.6 billion and then begin to decline.

Fang Fu Ruan

See also Malthus, Thomas Robert; Sterilization

References

Baoxia, Zhu. "Family Planning Goal Set." *China Daily,* March 17, 1998.

Bullough, Vern L. *Sexual Variance in Society and History.* Chicago: University of Chicago Press, 1976.

China Population and Research Center, <http://www.cpirc.org.cn>.

China Population Today. (An English language publication issued by the China Population and Research Center.)

Gao, Anming. "China's Population Policy Is Proving to Be Effective." *China Daily,* October 5, 1989.

Himes, Norman E. *Medical History of Contraception.* New York: Schocken Books, 1970.

Needham, Joseph, and Lu Gwei-Djen. "Sex Hormones in the Middle Ages." *Endeavor* 27 (1968): 130–132.

Ruan, Fang-Fu. *Sex in China: Studies in Sexology in Chinese Culture.* New York: Plenum Press, 1991

Christian Hostility to Birth Control

Early Christianity, at least as represented by the evangelical and patristic writers whose works have survived, sought to attain perfection through renunciation of the world and the subjugation of the body. To attain this, every means was to be employed from fasting to solitude, including prayer, mortification of the flesh, and, above all, sexual continence. All Christians were expected to meet a minimal level of spiritual achievement, but those desiring to achieve a higher life standard were expected to abstain from coitus and even from all association with members of the opposite sex.

This emphasis on sexual asceticism did not originate with the early Christians but represented a strong countercurrent present within the classical world to the dominant views expressed in society. In a sense the negative sexuality in Christianity is derived more from paganism than from Judaism, and the emphasis on celibacy and continence in the early Christian church is derived more from Greek philosophy than from the Gospel writers. Scholars have traced this asexual asceticism through the Orphic mysteries, Pythagorean and Platonic dualism, that is, a distinction between ideas and matter, to Stoicism and Neo-Platonism. There is also a religious tradition of this same kind of dualism found in Zoroastrianism and it is particularly strong in Manichaeanism and Gnosticism, both rival religions to Christianity.

Seneca, the first-century A.D. Stoic rhetorician and statesman, was cited by Saint Jerome as claiming that a wise man ought to love his wife with judgment, not affection.

Let him control his impulses and not be borne headlong into copulation. Nothing is fouler than to love a wife like an adulteress. Certainly those who say that they united themselves to wives to produce children for the sake of the state and the human race ought, at any rate, to imitate the beasts and when their wife's belly swells not destroy the offspring. Let them show themselves

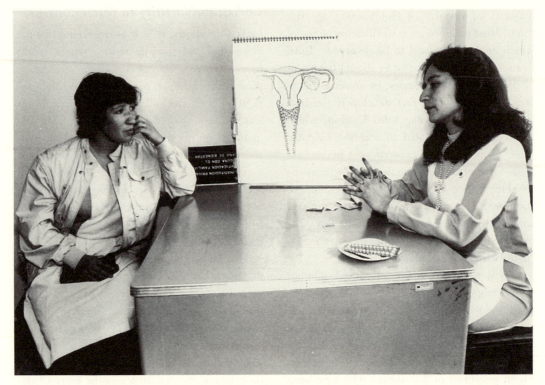

A Colombian woman receives counseling on her birth control options at a clinic in Bogota, Colombia, on the same day Pope John Paul II was scheduled to give a mass there. It is particularly difficult for women in South American countries, where the Catholic majority opposes birth control and abortion, to control their reproductive lives. (Reuters/Apichart Weerawong/Archive Photos, 1986)

to their wives not as lovers, but as husbands (Bullough, 1976, 167).

This is an argument not only for restraint in sexuality but against any form of birth control or abortion.

It is not so much Christian scriptures, that is, those teachings associated with the Bible, that reflect a hostility to sex, but the Christian theologians. Part of the difficulty is that the scriptures themselves seem ambiguous on sexual matters, even the words attributed to Jesus. When, for example, Jesus indicated that a woman remarrying another man after her husband had died is committing adultery, his disciples then questioned him whether it might be better simply for all to remain unmarried. Jesus replied:

All men cannot receive this saying, save they to whom it is given. For there are some eunuchs, which were born so from their mother's womb; and there are some eunuchs which were made eunuchs of men; and there be eunuchs which have themselves eunuchs for the kingdom of heaven's sake. He that is able to receive it, let him receive it (Matthew, 19:11).

Although the statement is unclear, it might well be interpreted to mean that service to God demanded a self-imposed continence. Occasionally it was interpreted literally by early Christians; Origen (d. about 251–254) castrated himself to more easily meet what he believed was the scriptural requirement.

Similar ambiguity is expressed in the Epistles of Saint Paul:

> It is good for a man not to touch a woman. Nevertheless, to avoid fornication, let every man have his own wife, and let every woman have her own husband. Let the husband render unto the wife due benevolence; and likewise also the wife unto the husband. For I would that all men were even as I myself. But every man hath his proper gift of God, one after this manner, and another after that. I say therefore to the unmarried and widows. It is good for them if they abide even as I. But if they cannot contain, let them marry: for it is better to marry than to burn (I Corinthians 7:1–12).

Most of the Fathers of the Church, that is, those men who established the doctrine of the Christian church between the second and fifth centuries, were bachelors, but even those, such as the second-century Tertullian, who were married tended to denigrate marriage. Tertullian later felt deep remorse over his lapse into matrimony, emphasizing that celibacy was the preferred lifestyle for Christians. Some sections of the early Christian church were so hostile to sex, as was the Christian community in Syria, that only unmarried Christians were allowed to be baptized.

Sexual pleasure in and of itself was frowned upon. Saint Ambrose (d. 397), who called marriage a "galling burden," urged all those contemplating matrimony to think about the bondage and servitude to which wedded love degenerated. He opposed the unfruitful intercourse of the old and pregnant as unnatural. Although in 325 the Council of Nicaea, the first attempt by the Roman state to draw up a uniform Christian doctrine, specifically rejected an absolute rule of clerical celibacy, later councils kept returning to it, and by the fifth century the Christian church in the west tended to hold that bishops, presbyters, deacons, and others employed before the altar were to refrain from coitus. The Christian church in the eastern portion of the Roman Empire never adopted such a position, and the growing geographical split between the eastern and western churches on celibacy, sex, and birth control seemed to be mainly a result of the influence of Saint Augustine (d. 430) in the west. It was Saint Augustine who basically set western attitudes on birth control and abortion.

Although the early Fathers of the Church condemned any kind of fertility control, particularly those practiced by women, they searched the herbals and ancient medical writings for potions that might help them preserve their continence, a task that involved serious struggles for many of them. Foods such as meat, wine, and flatulent vegetables, thought to increase potency or even lead to nocturnal emissions, were to be avoided, whereas potions from the willow and other trees believed able to extinguish every inclination for begetting children were widely prescribed.

How effective were such prohibitions? The practice of abstinence seems to have grown among the clergy and of course the growth in monasticism, which required celibacy, added to this. Infanticide was condemned and excess children, instead of being abandoned or castrated, were turned over to monasteries or convents. Marriage was not a sacrament until later in the medieval period, and although most Christians continued to marry, there was no Christian marriage as such. In the Eastern Roman Empire, marital relations changed very little. Separations of marriage partners were allowed and concubines remained common. Women continued to be segregated and secluded and married off early to protect their virtue.

See also Augustine, Saint; Classical World

References

Augustine. *Concerning the Nature of Good,* translated and edited by A. H. Newman. In *Basic Writings of St. Augustine,* edited by J. Whitney Oates. New York: Random House, 1948.

———. *De Nuptiis et concupiscentia,* translated and edited by Marcus Dodd. In *Basic Writings of St. Augustine, vol. 4, edited by* J. Whitney Oates. New York: Random House, 1948.

———. *De peccatorium meritis et remissione,* translated and edited by Marcus Dodd. In *Basic Writings of St. Augustine, vol. 4,* edited by J. Whitney Oates. New York: Random House, 1948.

Bullough, Vern L. *Sexual Variance in Society and History.* Chicago: University of Chicago Press., 1976.

McLaren, Angus. *A History of Contraception.* Oxford, England: Blackwell, 1990.

Classical Medical and Scientific Writers on Birth Control

One of the major sources for information about birth control and abortion is the classical medical and pseudomedical writers. The traditional founder of Greek medicine was a person called Hippocrates, who lived in the fifth century B.C.E. There are at least seven physicians named Hippocrates who lived at the time the collection attributed to him was being written, although one person with that name born about 460 seems to be the most likely. The biographical information about Hippocrates is mostly apocryphal. The collection of some sixty books that bear his name, entitled in Latin *Corpus Hippocraticum,* were edited by a group of scholars in Alexandria in the third century B.C.E. at the request of the ruler Ptolemy. The collection includes a number of contributions by various authors but all compiled under the name of Hippocrates. The results are miscellaneous and often contradictory texts, some of which have information about birth control and abortion, whereas others seem to condemn such practices. The most famous of the negative writings is the so-called Hippocratic oath, which states that the taker of the oath will not give a woman a pessary for an abortion, but then such remedies were usually given by midwives, and there are actually some abortifacients in other parts of the Hippocratic corpus. Among those discussed is the use of a copper solution in water, which appears in the book *On the Nature of Women.* Copper intrauterine devices are now used but whether copper taken orally was effective is unclear. It has been hypothesized that ingested copper might contaminate the vagina and continue to do so until the menses cleaned it. Interestingly, copper does not again appear until the sixth-century writings of Aetius who advised that copper would be effective only for a month, not the year the Hippocratic treatise says. This gives strength to the possibility of it becoming embedded in linings of the uterus.

The use of cantharides (Spanish fly), obtained by grinding up the cantharides beetle as an abortifacient, is mentioned in *Diseases of Women* and it is often combined with various herbal remedies such as celery seed, squirting, saltpeter, and others discussed elsewhere, primarily in the books dealing with women. Many of the herbal remedies are similar to those appearing in Egyptian recipes, indicating a continuing medical tradition. Most of the other Greek medical writings were compiled during Roman times, although they continued to be written in Greek, which was regarded by the Romans as the language of science.

Rome had a separate medical tradition early in its history but Greek medicine seemed so superior that it quickly dominated. Still, elements of the earlier tradition survived in the writing of individuals such as Pliny the Elder (23–79 M.E.). Pliny was not a physician but his encyclopedic *Natural History* came to be the source of medical and scientific ideas throughout the medieval period. It is a miscellaneous collection of information and misinformation, of myths, superstition, and practical information for menses. Pliny, like other Stoics, was personally opposed to contraceptives and abortions but this did not prevent him from giving out information under various other headings. Sometimes, for example, he listed substances that pregnant women should avoid taking because they might cause abortion. Other recipes were given for menstrual regulation, another term for abortion. He also gave several herbal prescriptions for inducing sterility, many of which have been included in the section on herbal remedies. In his list were cabbage, rue, mint, pennyroyal, hulwort, thyme, silphium, sage, galbanums, dittany, birthwort, mandrake, artemisia, wormwood, Queen Anne's lace, myrrh, pepper, scammony, and opopanax.

A more or less contemporary of Pliny was Scribonius Largus, who like Pliny was opposed to abortion, but gave several recipes for menstrual regulation and also gave a recipe for dealing with the aftereffects of an abortion. That recipe contains a number of antifertility agents. In short, what he prescribed as a treatment after abortion probably would have been an effective abortifacient.

Still another contemporary of Pliny was the first-century writer Dioscorides, who compiled a vast collection of what he called *De Materia Medica* (Material of Medicine). Dioscorides was apparently a military physician attached to the Roman army and traveled widely, collecting his medical prescriptions from a variety of sources. So great was his influence that he is regarded as largely responsible for determining modern plant nomenclature, both popular and scientific. Numerous of his medical recipes appear in modern pharmacopoeias. Determining exactly what he wrote, however, is sometimes difficult because he was so popular that others simply added their own recipes to his when they copied the work. Still, it is clear that he wrote extensively on *atokion,* which can be translated simply as contraceptives. Latin lacked a similar term, although the vague term *veneum,* meaning poison, was sometimes used. Dioscorides gave information on oral contraceptives, vaginal suppositories, and abortifacients and also offered prescriptions to smear on the penis, which would prevent conception. Many of his herbal remedies are listed in the articles on herbs.

Soranus of Ephesus, a Greek physician who practiced in Rome in the second century of the modern era, is the major writer of antiquity on gynecology. He, like other physicians of the time, traveled widely, and he was highly regarded by his contemporaries and successors. Part of his book, *Gynaecology,* is devoted to describing the necessary qualities of a midwife. He denied that women had seeds (female semen) but also held that women were not radically different from men, as Aristotle had argued. Soranus believed that conception was not possible without the woman having an orgasm since he held that during intercourse the cervix dilated to receive the seed. He also believed that the clitoris was important in arousing the woman. He

clearly distinguished between contraceptives and abortifacients and included a number of actual prescriptions, including oral herbal remedies and vaginal suppositories. Many of his suppository recipes contain pomegranate skins, which modern science has demonstrated to be effective.

The dominant medical writer in the Roman world was Galen (129–199), who provided a synthesis of Aristotelian and Hippocratic theories about conception, emphasizing the two-seed theory of conception, which Soranus had rejected. Galen set the dominant view of the importance of orgasm to women, holding that unless the female seeds and the menses were expelled they could become harmfully noxious, causing hysteria. He recommended masturbation by the women themselves or by digital manipulation of the attending physician for women not regularly having orgasms in order to expel the seeds, which might otherwise result in hysteria. Galen referenced a number of abortifacients and oral contraceptives in his work, including many of the herbal remedies. Most of his work still remains untranslated.

Medical writing did not end with Galen, in spite of his overwhelming authority. Oribasius, a fourth-century medical writer, gave recipes for both contraceptives and abortifacients, similar to those offered by his predecessors. He, however, does more than repeat the recipes of his predecessors and gives advice from his own experience. Similarly Marcellus Empiricus, a late fourth-century writer, records the familiar litany of herbs to induce menstruation but does not mention contraceptives as such. He has an immense lore of drugs but not much knowledge about medicine. Still, his work emphasizes the continuous concern with regulating childbirth in one way or another. Theodore Priscianus, another fourth-century writer, indicates that it is not right for anyone to perform an abortion but he then adds that there are times when the opening of the womb is too small or the woman is too young, and in such cases he gives prescriptions for oral compounds, plasters, and pessaries designed to produce an abortion. His work continued to circulate in Europe throughout the medieval period and it might well have been used to give a moral justification to have an abortion.

The major writer on contraceptives and abortifacients after Soranus and Dioscorides was Aetius of Amida, who wrote his magnum opus, the *Tetrabiblion,* in the sixth century. Aetius was court physician to the emperor Justinian. A Christian, born in the upper Tigris valley area, Aetius was trained in medicine at Alexandria. Many of his herbal recipes for contraceptives are derived from Soranus but he modified some and added his own. One of his prescriptions for a contraceptive, a combination of pomegranate, tannin (made from oak galls), and wormwood, would probably have been highly effective. He also includes vaginal suppositories, which he labels by a Greek word that could be translated as "unconceivers" or "sterilizers." He also prescribes ways of inducing an abortion and includes directions, when it is necessary to save the woman's life, for dismembering and extracting the fetus. He also gives recipes for various menstrual regulators. John Riddle, an expert on the topic of ancient and medieval contraceptives, believes that the prescriptions in the medical works for contraceptives and abortions seem to have improved from the time of Hippocrates and concludes that there was a continuous folk usage, experience, and change.

Aetius attributed much of his information to Aspasia, who wrote a book on gynecology in the second century. The name is apparently a pseudonym and, although the name is feminine, the book might well have been written by a man. If it was written by a woman, however, it would indicate that some of the folk medicine was working its way into the standard medical literature. Another woman who is mentioned in some of the treatises is Cleopatra. The gynecological treatise under her name was written in the late Roman period or early Middle Ages. The work is not believed to be the work of the famous Cleopatra but simply of someone attempting to use the name. The treatise recommends a number of abortifacients but not any contraceptives. Prescriptions are both for oral medications and for suppositories. The prescriptions seem to be original, although they have some of the standard ingredients.

The last of the classical medical writers was the Byzantine Paul Aegina, who lived in the seventh century. He arranged his antifertility medications for the weaker ones to be tried first and then, if these fail, increasingly stronger ones were to be tried. He gave both oral medications and suppositories. Although he repeats some of the traditional sources, he adds some of his own, again indicating a continual willingness to try new remedies if old ones do not work and to adopt old ones to the changed flora and fauna.

Obviously there was a learned tradition of contraceptives and abortifacients and also quite obviously some were quite effective. How much this learned tradition reflected real-life practices is unclear, but the changes taking place in some of the prescriptions tend to indicate a continuing refinement of methods and a willingness to discard some that apparently did not work.

From the discussion on herbal remedies we know that numerous ones probably did not work, but this might have been a result of the difficulty of maintaining a consistency in administration and preparation. This consistency was not always achieved by ancient and medieval physicians even though the state of the knowledge required more tolerance in prescriptions than modern medicine does.

See also Herbal Contraceptives and Abortifacients;
    Intrauterine Devices (IUDs)

References

Aetius of Amida. *Aetios of Amida: The Gynaecology and Obstetrics of the VIth Century.* Philadelphia: Blakiston, 1950, chaps. XVI, XVII, XVIII, XIX, XX, XXI, XXIII.

Bullough, Vern L. *Sexual Variance in Society and History.* Chicago: University of Chicago Press, 1976.

Dioscorides. *The Greek Herbal of Dioscorides,* edited by Robert T. Gunther and based on a seventeenth century translation by John Goodyer. Reprint, Oxford, England: Oxford University Press, 1959.

————. *De materia medica,* edited by Max Wellman, in Greek. Berlin: Weidman, 1958.

Galen. *Claudii Galeni: Opera omnia,* edited by Karel G. Kühn, 22 vols. Reprint, Hildesheim, Germany: Olms, 1964–1965.

————. *Hippocrates,* edited and translated by W. H. S. Jones, 6 vols. London: Heinemann, Loeb Classical Library, 1934–1988.

————. *Oeuvres completes d'Hippocrate: traduction nouvelle avec le texte grec en regard,* edited and translated by Emile Littré, 10 vols. Amsterdam: Hakkert, 1973. (This is a reprint of the original Paris edition published between 1839 and 1861.

————. *On the Usefulness of the Parts of the Body,* 2 vols. Ithaca, NY: Cornell University Press, 1968.

Paulus Aegina. *Seven Books of Paulus Aegina,* translated and edited by Francis Adams. London: C. & J. Adlard, 1844–1847.

Pliny. *Natural History,* edited and translated by W. H. S. Jones, 10 vols. Reprint, London: Heinemann, Loeb Classical Library, 1963. (See XX, xxx, 74, xxxiv, 86, 89, xli, 248, lv, 154; XXI, lxxxii, 146, lxxxix, 156; XXII, xxvi, 54; xlviii, 100, lxxi, 147; XXIV, xiii, 32; XXVI, xx, 30, xc, 151–159; XXVI, xl, 153.)

Prakash, Anand O., et al. "Anti-implantation Activity of Some Indigenous Plants in Rats." *Acta Europaea Fertilitatis* 16 (1985): 441–448.

Riddle, John M. *Contraception and Abortion from the Ancient World to the Renaissance.* Cambridge, MA: Harvard University Press, 1992.

Soranus. *Gynaecology,* edited and translated by Owsei Temkin. Baltimore: Johns Hopkins University Press, 1956.

Classical World

The world of women in ancient Greece (and for that matter in most ancient civilizations) was separate and distinct from that of the men. The Greeks of the fourth century B.C.E. demonstrated on a "scientific basis" that women were inferior. Plato, who wrote during this time, said that the womb is an animal that longs to generate children. When it remains barren too long after puberty, it is distressed and sorely disturbed, and straying about in the body and cutting off the passages of the breath, it impedes respiration and brings the sufferer into extreme anguish and provokes all manners of diseases besides (Plato *Timaeus,* 1952, 91C). The obvious solution to any such problems was to appease the womb by passion and love and to sow seeds that would grow and develop into a child.

Plato in some of his other works is somewhat more ambivalent about women and in some ways more favorable, but his pupil Aristotle was a consistent believer in the inferiority of the female. Key to Aristotle's concept about the superiority of the male was the overwhelming importance of the male in reproduction. He held that there was only male semen; female semen did not exist. It was the semen that supplied the form whereas the female supplied only the matter fit for shaping. The male was active; the female, passive. Women were a result of weak seed; men, of strong. Not all Greek scientists agreed with him and the writer of the Hippocratic text *On Generation,* for example, held that both partners produced seed, although the female's seed was thinner than the male's, and this explained why children could resemble either parent. The writer also assumed that it was important for the woman to have orgasm to produce her seed.

Far more literature has survived on attempts to ensure conception than prevent it, and usually barrenness was regarded as the fault of the woman. Still, there are references to contraceptive practices. Coitus interruptus was known and practiced, although there are remarkably few literary references to it because it apparently was assumed that all men knew about it. It might well be that husbands engaged in anal intercourse as a pregnancy preventive with their wives. Anal intercourse between men is often portrayed in the vase paintings and was probably practiced by some of the Greek courtesans.

The Greeks had a word for contraceptive—*atokion*—and many recipes for drinks containing ingredients thought to be pregnancy preventatives appear in Greek writing. Ingredients ranged from bark of hawthorn, ivy, willow, and poplar to juniper berries but also including copper sulfate. In addition barrier methods are mentioned. Dioscorides suggested anointing the genitals with cedar gum and applying alum to the uterus. These substances today would be regarded as ineffective, but in ancient Greece they were thought to make the womb a "smooth" and therefore inhospitable environment to seed. Similarly a peppermint and honey suppository employed before coitus and a peppery pessary used after were believed to be effective because they dried out the uterus.

Inevitably, most medical writings dealt with males not females. This was because women usually came under the control of the midwife, who also supervised childbirth. Only a few physicians concerned themselves with women. Plato in his *Theaetetus* has Socrates stating that midwives by means of drugs and incantations are able to arouse the pangs of labor and adds that midwives can also bring about miscarriages. In his *Laws* Plato states that there are many devices available to cause a woman to expel the fetus as well as more superstitious spells and incantations. Sometimes, however, there was more drastic intervention and several surgical instruments have survived, some designed to dismember a fetus in a breech birth, some for earlier term abortions.

The problem was that many methods of abortion did not work and so there were a variety of alternatives. The woman wanting to expel the male seed was advised to, among other things, jump up and down, touching her buttocks with her heels at each leap for seven times. When every thing seemed to fail, and apparently they often did, the Greeks practiced exposure or abandonment of infants. The Greek man had the power to declare the legitimacy of a child on his own, and if he accepted the child, then it became a member of the family and community in a ceremony known as *amphidromia*. If not accepted, the infant was abandoned and the reasons could vary from illegitimacy to frailty to deformity or simply the inability or unwillingness of a family to care for it. How widespread the practice was remains unclear and how many infants survived exposure by being raised by others as a slave or even as their own child is also uncertain.

It is possible that the Greeks used penis sheaths as a contraceptive device. Many early peoples used various forms of penis protectors for ornamentation or protection, but Greek mythology also records the possible use of them as a contraceptive device. The source of such speculation is the legend of Minos and Pasiphae as recounted in Antoninus Liberalis. Although Antoninus lived in the second century of the modern era, he compiled the Greek myths, versions of which were current in Hellenic times, that is, fourth and fifth century B.C.E. According to the myth, the semen of Minos, the legendary king of Crete, contained serpents and scorpions and all the women except Pasiphae were injured by him during sexual intercourse. Pasiphae proved immune because she was the daughter of the sun king but she still could not get pregnant. To remedy this problem, Prokris, a woman who had taken refuge in the king's court, proposed a remedy. She sought a woman of the court and had her slip the bladder of a goat into her vagina. Minos then had intercourse with her, and after getting rid of all his serpent-bearing semen, yet not injuring her, he sought out Pasiphae and had sexual intercourse with her. This time she became pregnant and gave birth to Ariadne and Phaedra, and apparently following the procedure at a later period bore him two other daughters and four sons.

This is the earliest reference to a female condom yet found, although some argue that Antoninus confused the sources, and the king himself had worn the goats bladder. Whichever is the case, it seems logical to argue that what appeared in mythology reflected, in part, reality, and barriers of one kind or another made from bladders might well have been used by the Greeks and probably their Roman successors. This use of the condom was first reported by C. E. Helbig, "Ein Condom im Altertume," *Reichs-Medizinal-Anziger,* xxv (1900), 3. The controversy over whether it was a male or female condom is reported by C. E. Helbig.

The Greeks also practiced homosexuality and it might well have been correlated with attempts to avoid having additional children. William Percy, for example, has argued that institutionalized pederasty began in the seventh century B.C.E. as a means of stemming overpopulation in the upper class. Cretan sages established a system under which a young warrior took a teenager of his own aristocratic background as a beloved until the age of thirty, when service to the state required the older partner to marry. The practice spread with significant variants to other Greek-speaking areas. The process was then repeated by the next generation, thereby limiting contact with females and curtailing the heterosexual activity of those at the height of their sexual drives.

The primary purpose of marriage in Rome was to have children, but there was also concern, particularly in imperial Rome, about having too many. In part this was because custom required the equal division of the estate among one's children. Many also came to believe that too many children posed a threat to the household. Pliny the Younger, who lived in the first century of the modern era, reported that he lived in an age when even one child was thought to be a burden. He was not alone in his thinking. Brent D. Shaw has argued that fertility control in the early Roman Empire limited itself to the practical solutions of killing, sale, or exposure of excess surviving children, but this seems to be overstated. Many of those exposed survived to be adopted by others, but many more did not. Apparently it was likely that more girl babies were exposed than boys, but what the percentage of exposed infants was is a subject of debate. Gradually also the Romans began to oppose exposure and by the third century abandonments were being described as murder and by the end of the fourth century abandonment was regarded officially as a crime.

The Romans attempted to space births and the simplest way to do so was by abstaining from sexual relations with a marital partner. Certainly there was a strong ascetic streak among the Stoics and some of the religious groups of the Roman Empire. Some such as the Manichaeans, a rival of Christianity, recommended total abstention from sex. Many of the medical writers advocated dry diets or cooling vegetables such as rue, lettuce, and linseed as a way of blunting sexual appetites. The first century writer Celsus said that sexual intercourse is "neither to be desired overmuch, nor overmuch to be feared; seldom used it braces the body, used frequently it relaxes."

Breast-feeding was rightly believed to have some contraceptive value in the ancient world but from modern studies we know that such preventatives are most effective before the infant is given solid foods. It does take breast-feeding mothers longer to conceive a child after their most recent birth. This period of nonconception might have been prolonged in the Roman period because of the Roman belief that sexual intercourse spoiled the mother's milk. Because at least some of the physicians recommended that children, at least in elite families, be breast-fed for up to three years, this implied a long period of abstinence, at least for some women. Many upper class women, however, relied on wet nurses.

Various medical writers also advised women to avoid conception in periods when they are most likely to conceive, but the problem with such advice was that there was no accurate data on when the fertile period was. Some writers said fertility was highest immediately after menstruation; others simply said women knew when they might conceive. It was not until the twentieth century that the actual time that ovulation took place was identified, and it is not right after the menses end (which is hard to determine) but usually nine or slightly more days after they begin, at least for women with any regularity, a period easier to measure. It seems likely then that no schedule of periodic abstinence, unless it extended for much of the cycle, held any greater likelihood for controlling births than pure chance.

Suppositories of various types were used. Tampons, plugs, and pessaries were made of sticky mixtures of peppermint, cedar gum, alum, and axe weed in honey. Plugs consisted of wool soaked in a viscous substance such as honey, olive oil, white lead, or alum.

See also Breast-feeding; Classical Medical and Scientific
Writers on Birth Control; Herbal Contraceptives and
Abortifacients; Sterile Period (Rhythm Method)

References

Aristotle. *Generation of Animals,* edited and translated by
A. L. Peck. London: Heinemann, Loeb Classical
Library, 1953, 729A, 25–34.

Celsus. *De medicina,* edited and translated by W. G.
Spencer. London: Heinemann, Loeb Classical Library,
1935, 1.1.

Ellinger, T. U. H. *Hippocrates on Intercourse and Pregnancy.*
New York: Abelard-Schuman, 1952.

Helbig C. E. "Zu dem Schrifttume über den Condom,"
Reichs-Medizinal Anzeiger, xxxii (1907) 405–407,
424–426.

Himes, Norman E. *A Medical History of Contraception.* New
York: Schocken Books, 1970.

Knodel, J. J., and H. Kitchner. "The Impact of Breast
Feeding on the Biometric Analysis of Infant Mortality."
Demography 14 (1977): 392–409.

McLaren, Angus. *A History of Contraception.* Oxford,
England: Blackwell, 1990.

Paulus Aegina. *Seven Books of Paulus Aeginetta,* edited and
translated by Francis Adams. London: C. & J. Adlard,
1844–1847, I.5.

Percy, William A. *Pederasty and Pedagogy in Archaic Greece.*
Urbana: University of Illinois Press, 1996.

Plato. *Laws,* edited and translated by R. G. Bury, 2 vols.
London: Heinemann, Loeb Classical Library, 1952,
5.740.

———. *Theaetetus,* edited and translated by R. G. Bury.
London: Heinemann, Loeb Classical Library, 1952, 139
c–d.

———. *Timaeus,* edited and translated by R. G. Bury.
London: Heinemann, Loeb Classical Library, 1952, 91
C.

Pliny the Younger. *Letters,* edited and translated by William
Melmoth. London: Heinemann, Loeb Classical Library,
1951, 4:15.

Riddle, John M. *Dioscorides on Pharmacy and Medicine.*
Austin: University of Texas Press, 1985.

———. *Eve's Herbs: A History of Contraception and Abortion
in the West.* Cambridge, MA: Harvard University Press,
1997.

Shaw, B. D. "The Family in Late Antiquity: The Experience
of Augustus." *Past and Present* 115 (1987): 46.

Coitus Interruptus (Withdrawal)

Coitus interruptus, or withdrawal of the penis
before the male ejaculates, is an old form of contraception. Although some semen escapes from
the Cowper's glands before the male ejaculates,
and thus pregnancy is always a theoretical possibility even with the most careful and devoted
advocates of the method, coitus interruptus
apparently was widely used in the ancient world
and in the modern world. Failure of the method
can also result from a delayed withdrawal, which
might result from psychological as well as physiological factors. In fact, the failure rate is high,
perhaps as much as 23 percent, but this still
means that it is better than not using any means
of birth control at all.

There are at least two biblical references to
coitus interruptus. One is rather ambiguous
because it could refer to a spontaneous emission
(sometimes called a "wet dream"), premature
ejaculation, or masturbation, as well as to coitus
interruptus.

> And if any man's seed of copulation go out from
> him, then he shall wash all his flesh in water, and
> be unclean until the evening. And every garment,
> and every skin, whereon is the seed of copulation
> shall be washed with water, and be unclean until
> the evening (Leviticus 15:16–18).

To become ritually pure after such emissions, a
short period of continence was normally
required.

The most well-known passage on the subject
comes from the Book of Genesis and deals with
the levirate tradition of having a surviving son
marry the widow of a deceased brother and if
she was childless to get her with child.

> And Er, Judah's first born, was wicked in the
> sight of the Lord;
> And the Lord slew him.
> And Judah said unto Onan, Go in unto thy
> brother's wife, and marry her, and raise up the
> seed to thy brother. And Onan knew that the
> seed should not be his, and it came to pass when
> he went unto his brother's wife, that he spilled it
> on the ground, lest that he should give seed to
> his brother. And the thing which he did
> displeased the Lord: wherefore He slew him also
> (Genesis 38:8–10).

Though this story has often been regarded as a prohibition against masturbation, the act described is coitus interruptus; the punishment, however, seems not so much for spilling the seed as for the refusal of Onan to obey the levirate requirement that he take his brother's wife as his own.

Coitus interruptus was practiced by the Greeks, although references to it are scarce, and apparently by the Romans. In general these ancients looked more to the female to avoid impregnation than depending upon the male. Many contemporary peoples who still live in tribal or nomadic groups are known to use it. In spite of its condemnation as onanism, or masturbation, in the Jewish, Christian, and Islamic sources, it has been widely practiced. In fact it might well be that the Bible served as a source of contraceptive information for those who might not have thought of the method by themselves.

Other historical sources occasionally refer to coitus interruptus, and in certain countries in Europe beginning with France in the eighteenth century it was widely practiced, and in fact seems to have been a common method of birth control in Europe, America, and elsewhere until the development of modern contraceptives.

A form of coitus interruptus that some Catholic writers have advocated is amplexus reservatus, which does not involve penetration and therefore not consummation even though it might involve rubbing the genitals together. The easiest way to do this is in a crouching position with the woman's back to the man. He can put his arms around her. It can also be done in the female superior position. It could be called interfemora intercourse, although the movement is supposed to cease before there is any seminal emission. Some Catholic writers have denounced it as simply withdrawal under another name, but others have accepted it as different and as acceptable to the church.

References

All biblical references are from the Authorized Version (King James Edition) because it was so influential in forming both English and American attitudes.

Bullough, Vern L., and Bonnie Bullough. *Contraception: A Guide to Birth Control Methods.* Amherst, NY: Prometheus Books, 1997.

McLaren, Angus. *A History of Contraception.* Oxford, England: Blackwell, 1990.

Noonan, John T. *Contraception: Its Treatment by Catholic Theologians.* Cambridge, MA: Harvard University Press, 1966.

Coitus Reservatus

Coitus reservatus, a method of intercourse that entails holding back ejaculation, is often associated with secret rituals and rites of ancient China and India. In these societies there was a belief that too great a loss of yang, the male's seminal essence excreted at ejaculation, would lessen a man's vigor and make him less able to have male descendants. The ways to avoid this was to have intercourse until the woman had her orgasm, and thus gain some of her yin essence. The man for his part was not to ejaculate. Instead he kept his penis in the vagina, leaving it there until the erection had passed. This took some training, and the Taoist teachers taught the man to exert pressure with his finger on the urethra between the scrotum and the anus. This would prevent the ejaculation of semen, and eventually those who became true "adepts" learned to hold up their ejaculation without the use of the finger. The Taoists believed that the unexpended semen ascended upward to the brain, where it served as a rejuvenating force for the body. Similar ideas appeared in Indian tantrism. Unfortunately, modern physiology tells a different story, namely, that the semen is diverted to the bladder, from which it is excreted as urine. Coitus reservatus does not prevent all loss of semen because there is some seepage of semen without orgasm.

Still, coitus reservatus, has some contraceptive value. It generally was a permitted form of intercourse within Catholic teaching, although there was debate about it because it involved penetration and thus was subject to the same discussion as coitus interruptus. Coitus reservatus was widely used among members of the Oneida community established by John Humphrey Noyes in upstate New York in the middle of the nineteenth century. Noyes called it "male continence," which he explained as the art of prolonging the act of intercourse without ejaculation.

Though coitus reservatus is both more physiologically and psychologically difficult to practice than withdrawal, its results would probably be the same, although, as indicated, the prolonged intercourse with this method, because of the seepage of semen, is not an entirely foolproof method and the failure rate is high for beginners.

See also Coitus Interruptus (Withdrawal)

References

Bullough, Vern L. *Sexual Variance in Society and History.* Chicago: University of Chicago Press, 1976.

Bullough, Vern L., and Bonnie Bullough. *Contraception.* Buffalo, NY: Prometheus Books, 1997.

Van Gulik, Robert Hans. *Sexual Life in Ancient China.* Leiden: E. J. Brill, 1961.

Anthony Comstock, a fanatical activist against birth control dissemination (Bettmann / Corbis)

Comstock, Anthony (1844–1915), and Comstockery

Anthony Comstock was the most eminent crusader against dissemination of literature on contraception from 1870 to his death. He was so prominent and active in the campaign against "obscene literature" that his name has come to be a synonym for moralistic censorship. Born in 1844 in New Canaan, Connecticut, Comstock was one of seven surviving children of a farmer and sawmill-owner father and devout religious mother, who died when he was ten. Educated in local schools, he was a devoted attendee and believer in the Congregational Church and Sunday schools. He enlisted in the Union army in December 1863, and became part of the Christian Commission, which meant that in his spare time he volunteered to visit soldiers and to distribute temperance and religious tracts, write letters home for the dying, and perform other acts of "Christian" compassion. He organized and conducted regular prayer meetings for his regiment, many of whom scorned and ridiculed him for his intolerance of drink, gambling, and profanity.

After the war Comstock became a dry goods clerk in New Haven, Connecticut, for a short time before moving to New York City. There, he lived in inexpensive boarding houses with other young clerks whose habits of spending evenings in saloons and brothels or reading what he regarded as pornographic literature shocked and dismayed him. Even when he had saved enough money to marry and move to Brooklyn, he maintained his interest in trying to eliminate prostitution, vice, and other moral problems from the city. Horrified by the trade in sexual goods and literature he tried to get the police to intervene, but when they refused, he began to file formal legal complaints as a citizen against individuals engaged in what he believed were nefarious activities. In 1872, his actions had brought him to the attention of Morris Ketchum Jessup, a millionaire philanthropist who, among other things, was a founder of the New York Young Men's Christian Association, the founder and a major benefactor of the Museum of Natural History, and a dedicated conservationist who worked to preserve the Adirondacks. Jessup, equally concerned with the "moral bankruptcy" of the city, put Comstock in contact with other like-minded reformers. The result, with Jessup's financial backing, was the establishment of the New York Committee for the Suppression of Vice, with Comstock as its salaried special agent. The society attracted the attention of many wealthy and powerful Americans including J. P. Morgan, who for various reasons wanted to exercise greater control over American morals. One of Comstock's first efforts was to lobby

Congress for a stronger federal antiobscenity and antireproductive control law.

Congress had more or less halfheartedly turned to the issue before. In 1842 it had enacted legislation to prohibit the importation of "indecent and obscene prints, paintings, lithographs, engravings and transparencies." Books, pamphlets, and other printed material were not mentioned. In fact the main objective was to stop the so-called French pornographic postcards. In 1857 the law was amended to include "articles." There had been other legislative efforts and actually several bills had been pending in Congress. Comstock hit Congress at an appropriate time and, though it is not clear how much of the original bill he wrote or modified, there was an almost immediate response and Comstock got the more comprehensive law he wanted within months of the initial approach.

This editorial cartoon lampoons the persistence of Anthony Comstock in attempting to squelch the birth control movement started by Margaret Sanger and Mary Ware Dennett. (Library of Congress)

So effective was the lobbying that Congress devoted less than an hour to debate, and the law was hurried through in the closing hours of an active congressional session, the final vote being taken at 2 A.M. on a Sunday morning with the clock being stopped to preserve the legislative fiction that it was still Saturday. The act provided that no obscene, lewd, or lascivious book, pamphlet, picture, or publication could be carried in the mails. For the first time, it became a felony to use the mails to carry such material and the law provided for a fine of $5,000 and imprisonment up to five years for the first offense, with $10,000 and ten years as a limit for subsequent offenses. Not only did Comstock get the law passed but he got himself appointed as a special agent of the Post Office to enforce the law. He also managed to obtain for himself or the society a portion of the fines collected on successful prosecutions.

The U.S. Supreme Court, even before the Comstock Act but in the same year (1873), had affirmed in *United States v. Botts* the right of Congress to eliminate material from the mails. In 1878 in the Orlando Jackson case, the first test of the Comstock Act itself, the court affirmed the right of Congress to enact such legislation but it left an interesting loophole in the law because it denied the authority of the postal officials to invade the privacy of first class mail.

In the first year under the law, Comstock boasted he had seized 200,000 pictures and photographs, 100,000 books, and more than 60,000 rubber articles (i.e., contraceptives). He also seized more than 50,000 packs of playing cards and 30,000 boxes of pills and powders having aphrodisiac qualities. He also managed to extend his power by becoming a consultant to the customs office for the port of New York, which allowed him to censor materials coming from overseas.

One of his first prosecutions of disseminators of birth control information was against Edward Bliss Foote in 1873. With Foote's successful prosecution, contraceptive information went

underground in the United States. Inevitably, few Americans kept up with contemporary developments taking place in England and on the continent, and though books aimed solely at the medical profession were allowed to discuss methods of contraception, the medical profession itself for the most part was reluctant to do so. The change in this situation is generally credited to a nurse, Margaret Sanger (1833–1966), whom Comstock also brought to trial but his death aborted the trial. His death also symbolized the beginning of the decline of Comstockery, which had increasingly lost the support of the wealthy and powerful communities that had originally supported it.

Underlying Comstockery, both in the United States and in large parts of Europe, though there the same ideas may have been called something else, were deep-seated fears about the drift to urban life as society in much of the Western world changed rapidly from a rural to an urban one. The growing cities offered considerable opportunities for economic advancement to ambitious and restless young men, and many went to the cities to seek their fortunes or to find more freedom to express themselves. With such moves, they left behind them the traditional source of guidance and support (and control): the family, the church, and a close knit community that tended to watch their every move. The result was not only a new freedom but also alienation and rootlessness, most noticeable among many of the immigrants to the United States and elsewhere, who had to adjust to radically changed living conditions and to different customs and language. The growing cities offered the possibility of anonymity for individuals to engage in activities, including sexual activities, that would have been severely reprimanded in their villages or rural communities. The cities also offered opportunities for individuals of like mind to come together and for homosexuals to belong to a "gay" community.

Moral reformers of the time, conscious of changing attitudes, tried to preserve the old values by putting restraints on what could be openly expressed. An 1866 Young Men's Christian Association (YMCA) survey of New York's young working men described the rootless anonymity of those who once would have lived "directly under the eye" of their employers but who now resided in rented rooms and boarding houses, devoid of restraint or guidance. Because to change conditions would have required a massive reorganization of society, the establishment in New York City and other rapidly expanding cities sought to combat symptoms, in the process ignoring root causes. It was the YMCA, for example, that launched a campaign for stricter state obscenity laws, and it was a YMCA committee in which Comstock was deeply involved. The new societies to deal with obscenity represented the establishment of the time, and to read their names today is like reading a *Who's Who* of the past. Most of the leaders had been bred in the pious atmosphere of a small town or a rural farm, and when, after making their fortunes, they faced the apparent lack of cohesiveness in the rootless urban society, what today sociologists call alienation or anomie, they thought to control things by imposing the moral influence of their past on the growing urban areas. In their campaign they invariably had the support of prominent politicians and newspapers and other official and semiofficial weapons of the establishment, since these reflected the same background as the crusaders against vice. Though the vice societies often became notorious for their lawsuits and actions—this was particularly true of Comstock—most of their influence was exercised informally. The vice societies became laughable and much less effective only as they lost their influential supporters, and as the ideas they were working for seemed no longer so desirable to more sophisticated Americans, who had adjusted to urban life and whose ideas about sex were changing.

Comstock was only the most notorious but many of the larger American cities imitated what he was doing in New York. Vice societies were organized in Boston, St. Louis, Chicago, Louisville, Cincinnati, San Francisco, and in other communities. Many followed the same title as that taken by New York City but in Boston it was known as the Watch and Ward Society. Many of the women's groups also supported Comstockery, not necessarily because they were antagonistic to birth control, but because of its vague association with indecent literature and improper devices. The Women's Christian Temperance Union in 1883 established a department for the suppression of impure literature, and the National Mothers Congress was an occasional ally of Comstock. Comstock, however, was extremely influential. It was he who was most hostile to abortion and the prevention of conception, and it was largely his focused energy that secured the criminalization of reproductive control in the federal and state antiobscenity laws. It was Comstock's doing, for example, that caused the key words "for the prevention of conception and procuring of abortion" to be inserted into the federal legislation of 1873 (Brodie, 1994, p. 263).

See also Foote, Edward Bliss; Sanger, Margaret Louise (Higgins)

References
Boyer, Paul S. *Purity in Print*. New York: Charles Scribner's Sons, 1968.
Brodie, Janet Farrell. *Contraception and Abortion in 19th Century America*. Ithaca, NY: Cornell University Press, 1994.
Broun, Heywood, and Margaret Leech. *Anthony Comstock: Foundsman of the Lord*. New York: Albert and Charles Boni, 1927. (This is a less sympathetic view of Comstock.)
Bullough, Vern L. *Sexual Variance in Society and History*. Chicago: University of Chicago Press, 1976.
Gerber, Albert B. *Sex, Pornography, and Justice*. New York: Lyle Stuart, 1965.
Trumbell, Charles G. *Anthony Comstock, Fighter*. New York: Fleming H. Revell, 1913. (This is a sympathetic account of Comstock.)

Condom

Technically the condom is a sheath designed to cover the penis and catch the ejaculate. They are different from penis protectors used to protect the penis from insect bites or as badges of rank or status, decoration, modesty, or a variety of other purposes. It is, however, possible that the sheath or condom might have evolved from these. The first use of the term in print is by John Wilmot, Earl of Rochester, who in 1665 wrote *A Panegyric upon Cundom.*

The earliest recorded use for a penis cover to catch the ejaculate is much older. It occurs in a tale told by Antoninus Liberalis (second century M.E.) of the legendary Minos and Pasiphae. Antoninus was a compiler of Greek mythology that had appeared in Hellenistic sources and he included in his text an account of the legendary king Minos, whose semen contained serpents and scorpions, which injured all the women who had cohabited with him. To solve the problem, he was advised to slip the bladder of a goat into the vagina of a woman and this would catch all the stored up serpent-bearing demons when he had sex with her, after which his semen, at least for a brief period, would be normal. It was by this method that he impregnated Pasiphae, not once but eight times, and she gave birth to four daughters and four sons.

Norman E. Himes, a historian of contraception, was not certain whether this use of what we would now call a female condom was a reflection of Roman birth control practices or not because there is no other mention of such practices in classical literature. Its mere mention, however, would indicate that animal bladders or perhaps animal cecum (intestines) were at least occasionally used by either men or women, probably as a disease preventative rather than a contraceptive. The difficulty with the use of either is holding it on to the penis or, in the case of a vaginal insert, keeping it in place. Animal cecum also deadened the sensitivity so that, if the man used it for contraceptive rather than prophylactic reasons, it was more likely to be a tight-fitting cap rather than a full sheath.

The earliest known medical description of a device similar to that used by Minos is by the Italian anatomist Fallopius (1564), which might give strength to a continuing tradition of such devices:

As often as man has intercourse, he should (if possible) wash the genitals, or wipe them with a cloth; afterward he should use a small linen cloth made to fit the glans, and draw forward the prepuce over the glans; if he can do so, it is well to moisten it with salve or with a lotion. However, it does not matter; if you fear lest caries [syphilis] be produced [in the midst of] the canal [vagina], take the sheath of linen cloth and place it in the canal. I tried the experiment on eleven hundred men, and I call immortal God to witness that not one of them was infected (Fallopius, 1564; trans. Himes, 1970).

At the end of the sixteenth century, the medical writer Hercules Saxonia described a prophylactic sheath made of linen soaked in a solution several times and then put out to dry. From then on there are a growing number of references to a penis sheath. Casimir Freschot described one made of a bladder that covered the whole length of the penis and was tied on by a ribbon. One physician reported that many a libertine would rather risk getting the "clap" than using such devices. In the eighteenth century White Kennet wrote a burlesqued poem about the condom:

> Happy the Man, who in his Pocket keeps,
>   Whether with Green or Scarlet Ribband
> bound,
>   A well made C_____ He, nor dreads the
> Ills
>   Of *Shankers* or *Cordee,* or *Buboes* Dire
>   With C_____ arm'd he wages am'rous
> Fight
>   Fearless, secure; nor Thought of future
> Pains
>   Resembling Pricks of Pin and Needle's
> Point,
>   E'er checks his Raptures, or disturbs his
> Joys(Fryer, 1965, pp. 27–28).

The very crudest of the animal condoms were made from unprocessed skins sewn or pasted together to form a sheath. They were notoriously unreliable and unaesthetic. The best condoms from animal caeca were produced by a lengthy

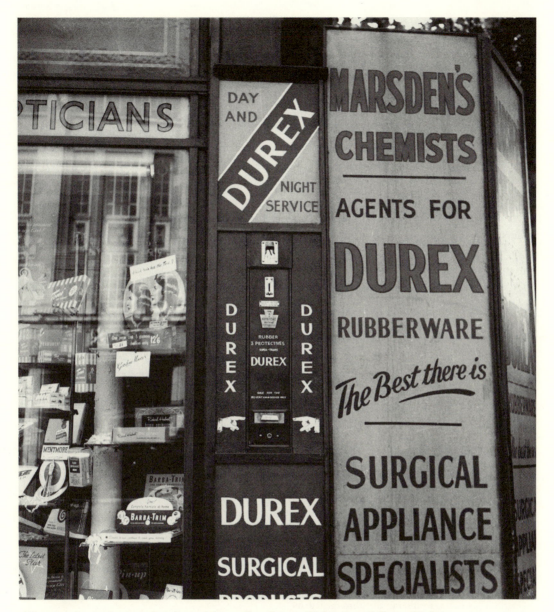

A Durex condom machine outside a chemists' shop in Great Britain. (Hulton Getty Collection/Corbis)

and somewhat expensive process that was described in Gray's *Supplement to the Pharmacopoeia* published in 1828, but the method must have been the same earlier. Sheep intestines were soaked in water for several hours; turned inside out; macerated again in a weak alkaline solution that was changed every twelve hours; scraped carefully, leaving only the peritoneal and muscu-

lar coats; and then exposed to the vapor of burning brimstone and washed in soap and water. They were then blown up to see if they could hold air. If they passed inspection, they were dried, cut to seven or eight inches, tied or sealed at one end, and bordered at the open end with a ribbon.

Baudruches were made the same way but were distinguished from ordinary condoms by undergoing further processing. In this additional finishing they were drawn smoothly and carefully onto oiled molds of appropriate size and rubbed with brimstone to make them thinner. Superfine *baudruches* were scented with essences, stretched on a glass mold, and rubbed with a glass to further polish them. There are actually some surviving condoms manufactured between 1790 and 1810 and which were found preserved in a book in an English country manor in 1953.

Perhaps because prostitutes were often regarded as carriers of disease, many of the surviving references to condoms come from the literature of prostitution. Houses of prostitution displayed a variety of condoms in the eighteenth century but they also recommended the use of sponges. Sponges did not protect from disease but did have some contraceptive value and this might indicate that condoms were sometimes also used as contraceptives as well as prophylactics.

A good description of condoms appears in the writing of the eighteenth-century Frenchman Jean Astruc, who was determined to prove that syphilis originated in America and not in France. He wrote:

> I heard from the lowest debauchees who chase without restraint after the love of prostitutes, that there are recently employed in England skins made from soft and seamless hides in the shape of a sheath, and called condoms in English, with which those about to have intercourse wrap their penis as in a coat of mail in order to render themselves safe in the dangers of an ever doubtful battle. They claim, I suppose, that thus mailed and with spears sheathed in this way, they can undergo with impunity the chances of promiscuous intercourse. But (in truth) they are greatly mistaken.

Giovanni Giacomo Casanova de Seingalt (1725–1799), whose erotic memoir lists his 116 lovers by name but leaves nameless hundreds more women and girls he had sex with ranging in age from nine to seventy and in occupation and social status from chambermaids to noblewomen. He reported having intercourse standing, sitting, and lying down in coaches, on boats, in beds, and even in alleys. He also said he knew of and used condoms and had a variety of names for them from the "English riding coat" to preservative sheaths to assurance cap. Casanova in his memoirs described one he called an "English overcoat" as being made "of very fine and transparent skin, eight inches long and closed at one end, with a narrow pink ribbon slotted through the open end." He apparently used his sheath not only for prophylactic purposes but to prevent his partners from becoming pregnant. He blew them up like balloons to test them. Some were of better quality than others. Casanova reported some broke. Some were made of animal ceca because he referred to shutting himself up in a piece of dead skin.

Apparently it was a common practice to use condoms repeatedly, washing them out after each use. The most expensive of condoms were those known as goldbeaters' skins. They got their name from the practice of beating gold into foil or leaf. Such sheaths were carefully processed by beating them until they were elasticized. Madame de Svigny, writing about contraception in a 1671 letter to her daughter, described such condoms as an "armor against enjoyment and a spider web against danger." Some condoms were made of silk that was cut, sewn, and then oiled. Condoms made of bladders were advertised in eighteenth-century England. The bladders might well be those of the blow fish common in the Rhine River and which were being described as early as 1788.

Knowledge of condoms was undoubtedly known in the American colonies in the eighteenth century but so far no historical record of them has been uncovered. It is believed that colonists probably fashioned their own condoms for personal use but it is not until 1844 that one advice book, *The United States Practical Receipt Book: or, Complete Book of Reference,* gave a detailed description on how to make condoms from the cecum of a sheep. The description was probably based on a standard recipe for homemade condoms used earlier.

In the first part of the nineteenth century, condoms began to be advertised in some newspapers as a preventive against syphilis and the seller said he would ship them anywhere in the country. Packages of fish bladder "membraneous envelope" were sold at five dollars a dozen in New York City in 1860. This would have prevented all but the extremely well-to-do from using such condoms, but the animal ones were probably cheaper because they were washed and used repeatedly.

The cost, availability, and material of condoms slowly changed with the vulcanization of rubber in 1843–1844 by Charles Goodyear and Thomas Hancock. The key development was the 1853 discovery of liquid latex, which potentially allowed for thinner and finer condoms. The first development was the use of a latex cap designed to cover the glans, not the entire penis. It was described as being made of a "delicate texture" rubber no thicker than the cuticle and shaped and bound at the open end with an India rubber ring. The tips were said to be an entirely new thing and were on the market by 1858. The cap was soon extended to a sheath, and there is a description of a full-length one in 1869 as being effective in preventing conception even though it dulled sensation and irritated the vagina. These early rubber condoms were molded from sheet crepe and carried a seam along their entire length. Making the rubber condoms more effective and useful depended on developments in rubber technology, and the key innovation was the seamless cement process, so named because the process was similar to that used in producing rubber cement. In this process natural rubber was ground up, dissolved, and then heated with solvent into which cylindrical glass molds were dipped. As the solvent evaporated, the condoms dried. They were then vulcanized by being exposed to sulfur dioxide. These new-type condoms were on the market before 1889. The major difficulty was that the finished product deteriorated rather rapidly. The advantage was that they were fairly inexpensive and disposable. By the 1870s wholesale druggists were selling rubber, skin, and imported condoms at six to sixteen cents each, and in retail outlets or from peddlers they were one to four dollars a dozen.

Condoms were increasingly being used as a means of family planning and eight of the forty-five women who filled out a sex questionnaire by Clelia Mosher, who as a student at the end of the nineteenth century began interviewing women about their sex lives. The women she interviewed between 1890 and 1920 reported that their husbands had used condoms as part of a means of preventing pregnancy. The ambiguity that some women felt about using condoms was expressed in 1878 in a letter that an Idaho woman, Mary Hallock Foote, wrote to a friend in New York to tell her how she and her husband planned to avoid another pregnancy so soon after her current one. She reported that she had learned about condoms from a friend, Mrs. Hague, who told her to have her husband go to a physician and get shields of some kind.

> They are to be had also at some druggists. It sounds perfectly revolting, but one must face anything rather than the inevitable result of Nature's methods. At all events there is nothing injurious about this. Mrs. Hague is a very fastidious woman and I hardly think she would submit to anything very bad . . .(Quoted by Brodie, 1994, p. 206).

Availability, however, did not mean widespread usage, and because condoms could not be sold for contraceptive use in the United States, they were pushed as prophylactics. In other countries, however, they were sold as contraceptives as well, and distributed widely, even through dispensing machines. Distribution in the United States was primarily through drug stores and barber shops but there were also traveling salesmen who visited industrial plants and businesses that employed large numbers of men. By 1890 packages of condoms were available at fifty cents a dozen. The main problem, however, with all contraceptive material in the United States was quality control. There was neither patent nor copyright protection for the manufacturer. None of the major rubber manufacturers, at least as indicated by the archives at the University of Akron, manufactured them, and this meant that the market was left to a number of smaller companies, some of them with a very tenuous financial base. Eventually several companies emerged with adequate quality control, including Young's Rubber, Julius Schmid, and Akwell. The entrance of Young's Rubber, founded by Merle Young (a drugstore products' salesman) in the mid-1920s, was particularly important because by promising effective quality control over his product Young was able to convince druggists to sell his condom. Young's Rubber also began a series of court suits that eventually overturned many of the state laws against condom sales.

In the 1930s, new techniques were developed that enabled rubber plantations to ship concentrated liquid natural rubber latex directly to the manufacturer, and this eliminated the need to grind and dissolve rubber back to a liquid state. Though this proved to be a less costly method of manufacture, the problem of quality control remained. In one of the first American surveys of the efficacy of condoms, that of the national Committee on Maternal Health in 1938, it was found that only about 40 percent of the rubber condoms sold in the United States were fit for use. One result of such a finding was a government decision to assign the U.S. Food and Drug Administration control over the quality of condoms sold or shipped in interstate commerce. Federal policy in effect had turned full circle; after first trying to outlaw contraceptive information and, when this was no longer possible, ignoring the existence of such things as condoms, the government finally recognized that condoms were an important consumer product. The first government effort to look at quality control found that as much as 75 percent of the condoms then on the market had small pinholes caused either by the existence of dust particles in the liquid latex or by improperly vulcanized latex. This situation changed rapidly. By the

1960s, condoms were among the most effective contraceptives on the market. They were simple to use, easy to buy, inexpensive, and did not require a physical examination or a physician's advice. Because they simply served as a container for the semen and did not interfere with any of the bodily process, they were also harmless.

The use of condoms declined after the 1960s but increased again in the 1980s with the appearance of acquired immunodeficiency syndrome (AIDS) and the recognition that condoms, used in either vaginal or anal sex, were effective in decreasing the chance of infection. The variety of condoms also increased. Originally all condoms came in one size, and the assumption of one-size-fits-all was challenged only when the United States began exporting condoms to Asian countries and found that they were too large for many Asian men. In Thailand, for example, the oversized condoms became such a publicized joke that comedians reported that men had used a "string to tie the condoms to their waist for the sake of safety." Finally, after considerable scientific investigation it was found that the median erect penis length of Thai men was between 126 mm and 150 mm (approximately 5 to 6 inches), whereas that of U.S. men was between 151 mm and 175 mm (approximately 6 to 7 inches). The median erect penis circumference of Thai men was between 101 mm and 112 mm (4 to 4.5 inches); that of U.S. men measured between 113 mm and 137 mm (4.5 to 5 inches). But researchers also found wide variations in the United States. Most large international manufacturers now produce two basic sizes, Class I, 180 mm in length and 52 mm in flat width, and Class II, 160 mm in length and 49 mm in flat width. In the United States some manufacturers, fearful of saying that some of their condoms were smaller than others, advertised them as fitting "snugger" for extra sensitivity. Rubber membranes can now be produced as thin as .03 mm but most range from .04 to .06 mm. Consumers Union has in the past issued several reports on condoms and helped change the testing procedure. Originally they used a water test, but found that the air test was more reliable. Obviously, condoms vary from one batch to another, but government regulations now provide for a random testing of each batch, and if more than 1.5 percent fail the test, the batch must be scrapped. The most effective use of the condom is with a spermicide.

As the use of condoms has grown, numerous varieties have been developed. Some are contoured, others are textured, some are ribbed, and others have an unusual pouch. They also come in a variety of color and with descriptors such as extra thin, extra strong, or lubricated with spermicides. Some manufacturers have been experimenting with new designs as well. One of the more recent ones is the Rumdum Sicher, which covers both the penis and the testicles. It is designed for male-to-male sex and features a latex band that acts as a "cock ring" to help maintain erection. It probably has more erotic than practical use.

Like any other barrier contraceptive, condoms require some skill in use. First-time users should read the instructions in the condom package in the daylight and well before planning to use one. In fact, it is a good idea to practice putting one on before trying to use one the first time (the practice condom should be discarded). Most condoms are prerolled. Those without the reservoir tip should be unrolled for about half an inch before being placed on the penis. This procedure allows for space at the end to collect the sperm. For a man who is not circumcised, the foreskin must be pulled back from the penis before putting the condom on. The condom should be placed over the erect penis and unrolled down the shaft. It should slide on easily and not get bound up. If it does, it is being put on the wrong way and another condom should be tried. Some couples find it erotically stimulating for the partner to help put on the condom before intercourse takes place. This procedure allows the condom to become part of the sexual foreplay instead of an interruption. After ejaculation, the man must withdraw his penis from the vagina before the penis becomes flaccid or soft. While withdrawing, he should hold the condom firmly in place with his fingers at the base of the penis so that it will not slip off or leak sperm. After the condom is removed the penis should not touch any part of the woman's vagina because the penis may have live sperm on it. Even though some condoms come with a spermicide in their lubricant, it is wise for women to also use an over-the-counter spermicide such as nonoxynol 9 in addition to their partner's use of the condom.

For those who use condoms with spermicides consistently and apply spermicides intervaginally as well, the pregnancy rates approximate those of the pill, less than 0.1 percent. Without the spermicide the pregnancy rate is considerably higher, even for the so-called perfect user, approaching 3 percent, whereas for the typical sporadic user it approaches 12 percent. Most failures come from inexperienced users.

Why a condom is called a condom has been a subject of much debate, with the origin of the word being attributed to several mythical physicians as well as an actual French village named Condom. The latter seems more a coincidence than actual and it was only in 1999 that this particular village held a condom festival, seeking to attract tourists to a product they had always previously denied as having anything to do with their village. If the term was not entirely made up by Lord Rochester, it might have been modified from the Latin *cunnus,* that is, the female genitals, and *dum,* implying an ability to function. Not everyone would agree, however.

See also Sponges, Tampons, and Vaginal Inserts

References

Antoninus Liberalis. "The Fox." Chap. XLI in *Metamorphoses,* edited by Edgar Martin. Leipzig: Teubner, 1896.

Astruc, Jean. *A Treatise of Venereal Disease in Nine Books.* No translator listed. London: W. Innys et al., 1754, book iii, chap. i, 2.

Brodie, Janet Farrell. *Contraception and Abortion in Nineteenth Century America.* Ithaca, NY: Cornell University Press, 1994.

Bullough, Vern L. "A Brief Note on Rubber Technology and Contraception: The Diaphragm and the

Condom." *Technology and Culture* 22 (January 1981): 104–111.

Bullough, Vern L., and Bonnie Bullough. *Contraception: A Guide to Birth Control Methods.* Amherst, NY: Prometheus Books, 1997.

Casanova, Jacques. *The Memoirs of Jacques Casanova de Seingalt,* translated by Arthur Machen. New York: A. C. Boni, 1932.

Cautley, R., G. W. Beebe, and R. L. Dickinson. "Rubber Sheaths as Venereal Disease Prophylactics: The Relation of Quality and Technique to Their Effectiveness." *American Journal of Medical Sciences* 195 (February 1948): 1550–1583.

Consumer Reports 54 (March 1989): 135–142.

———. 60 (May 1995): 322–325.

———. 61 (January 1996): 6–8.

Fallopius, Gabriele. *De morbo Gallico liber absolutismus.* Pavia, 1564, Chap. 89, p. 52.

Finch, Bernard Ephraim, and Hugh Green. *Contraception through the Ages.* Springfield, IL: Charles C Thomas, 1963.

Foote, Edward Bliss. *Medical Common Sense.* New York: n.p., 1862.

Fryer, Peter. *The Birth Controllers.* London: Secker and Warburg, 1965.

Grady, W. R., et al. *Contraceptive Failure and Continuation among Married Women in the United States, 1970–1976,* Working Paper No. 6. Hyattsville, MD: National Center of Health Statistics, 1981.

Gray, S. F. *A Supplement to the Pharmacopoeia: Being a Treatise on Pharmacology in General,* 4th ed. London: n.p., 1828.

Himes, Norman. *Medical History of Contraception.* New York: Schocken Books, 1970.

Kestleman, P., and J. Trussel. "Efficacy of the Simultaneous Use of Condoms and Spermicides." *Family Planning Perspectives* 23(5) (1991): 226–227, 232.

Redford, Myron H., Gordon W. Duncan, and Dennis J. Prager. *The Condom: Increasing Utilization in the United States.* San Francisco: San Francisco Press, 1974.

"Update on Condoms—Products, Protection, Promotion." *Population Reports,* ser. H., no. 6 (September–October 1982), vol. 10, no. 5.

W. A. Week and Company. *Illustrated Year Book.* Chicago: n.p., 1872.

Cooper, James F. *(1880–1931)*

James F. Cooper was recruited by Margaret Sanger to lecture on contraceptive practices to physicians unable to come to New York City for instruction. A physician, Cooper had been a medical missionary to China from 1913 to the end of World War I, when he returned to Boston to set up practice as an obstetrician in Boston's slums. He was convinced that this was as important a field as the Far East for a medical missionary. Hired at a salary of $10,000 a year and expenses as medical director of the Birth Control League in 1925, Cooper spoke to hundreds of county medical societies and compiled a list of several thousand physicians to whom patients could be referred by the Birth Control League for contraceptive advice. His *Techniques of Contraception,* published in 1928, was the first American medical book to deal with up-to-date methods of contraception available in the United States in the post–World War I period.

References

Cooper, James F. *Techniques of Contraception: The Principles and Practice of Anti-Conceptional Methods.* New York: Day-Nichols, 1928.

Council of Trent and Catholic Tradition

The rise of Protestantism in the sixteenth century divided western Christianity into two opposing camps. Although Protestants went their separate ways, Catholic Europe developed what might be called a two-prong attack to counter the Protestant threat. The first was to make several internal reforms, many of which had been urged for centuries. For this purpose an ecumenical council was convened by Pope Paul III in 1545 in the northern Italian city of Trento. Known as the Council of Trent, it met, with several breaks, over the next 18 years. The second prong was what might be called the Catholic Reformation, an effort to oppose Protestants both intellectually and institutionally, but also politically and militarily. The military result was a series of wars in which the Catholics for more than one hundred years tried to destroy Protestantism and vice versa until politically the two sides arrived at an uneasy truce, dividing up Europe. Intellectually and institutionally in Catholic Europe the Catholic Reformation resulted in the reorganization and reinvigoration of the Inquisition; the promulgation of an Index

The Council of Trent, shown at work in this engraving, codified Roman Catholic positions on sex and marriage, including the prohibition of birth control. (North Wind Picture Archives)

of Prohibited Books; the formation of new religious orders, the most important of which was the Society of Jesus, or the Jesuits; and efforts to convert areas of Protestantism back to Catholicism and to proselytize the recently discovered areas of the world.

The Council of Trent also debated issues of marriage and sex and finally codified them in the decree *Tametsi,* issued in 1563. The *Tametsi* and other Tridentine decrees were incorporated into the Roman Catechism issued in 1566 and this was followed by commentaries and elaborations. The most influential of these in terms of contraception was *The Holy Sacrament of Marriage* by the Spanish Jesuit Thomas Sanchez (1550–1610). In his extensive discussions of sexual enjoyment, he deals with fondling, fantasies, fellatio, and foreplay and ultimately regards them to be minor sins, or perhaps not even that, as long as they

were a prelude to "natural intercourse," with the man on top and no barriers to contraception. Not all commentators agreed with him, and there were fierce debates. Finally in 1679, Pope Innocent XI settled the matter by holding that Catholics should not engaged in any marital act simply for pleasure alone. Though such a condemnation sounds definitive, matters were not so simple, and John T. Noonan, a canon law expert, has claimed that the meaning of the pope was to use caution and prudence in teaching such beliefs.

The Catholic Church, however, continued to hold that refusal to engage in intercourse with one's spouse was a mortal sin and mutual continence was permitted and even encouraged, especially if there already had been an abundance of offspring. Some authorities went so far as to argue that one spouse alone might refuse intercourse if he or she believed it was not possible to feed more offspring or that another child might be deemed a danger or detriment to offspring already born. This concept allowed some church authorities to emphasize that it was not only the production of children that was the goal of marriage, but that it was also important if not essential to take into account the good of the offspring.

Theologians were occasionally specific in discussing various means of contraception but usually preferred generalities instead of details. Obviously for a couple to begin an act of coitus but to withdraw without ejaculation in the vagina is a conscious effort to avoid procreation. But there were distinctions made. If ejaculation follows the withdrawal, the act is coitus interruptus and was described by Catholic moralists as a sin against nature. If ejaculation after withdrawal is inhibited, the act is sometimes described as coitus reservatus or amplexus reservatus and this was treated differently by Catholic theological and legal authorities and even approved by some. It should be added, however, that modern sexologists distinguish between the two terms and coitus reservatus does not usually imply that the penis is withdrawn from the vagina. Rather it means only that motion ceases before orgasm, and after the orgasmic "crisis" diminishes, the couple can begin movement again. Amplexus coitus was generally regarded as tolerable, providing neither partner had an orgasm, but some held that amplex coitus was acceptable only if it could not involve penetration.

The use of anaphrodisiacs, substances believed to decrease libido or sexual function, were permitted and even praised, although not discussed as a means of contraception and never in any specific detail. In fact, Catholic theologians in general were careful to avoid discussion of herbal contraceptives and abortifacients, although they knew about them and some called them "poisons of sterility." As far as any further description was concerned, the theologians observed the rule that silence was the best policy. Still, the discussion of anaphrodisiacs and amplexus reservatus implies a lessening of the Augustinian view that intercourse may be initiated only for procreation and shows a glimmer of recognition that there might well be other purposes.

One male contraceptive practice casually mentioned by one authority is a method originally described by Aristotle that involved "oiling" of the genitals with a "certain unguent which would induce sterility," but what this unguent was and whether the sterility caused was permanent or temporary is not known. It has been hypothesized that the unguent might be cedar gum, and, if so, the effect would be temporary.

In general, however, the Catholic position looked askance at contraceptive information and in the new age of printing made efforts to prevent the dissemination of information about it. Among the books put on the newly established index were books of "necromancy or continuing sorceries or poisons," a common euphemism for books dealing with both birth control and abortion. There was, however, an exception made for books of "assistance to the medical arts," books written by and for physicians. There was also potentially some loopholes for those couples using some form of birth control. Noonan claimed that in the post-Tridentine church good faith was to be protected in the confessional, and the confessor should not disturb the penitent ignorantly violating natural law and unlikely to amend his or her ways. Also there were some additional loopholes for women in the confessional because it was generally agreed that a woman, who in obedience to her husband engaged in coitus interruptus with him, was not guilty of a sin. Interpretation of this was usually left up to the confessor and some were more lenient than others.

See also Canon Law and Abortion; Canon Law and Contraception; Coitus Interruptus (Withdrawal); Coitus Reservatus

References

Noonan, John T., Jr. *Contraception: A History of Its Treatment by the Catholic Theologians and Canonists.* Cambridge, MA: Belknap Press of the Harvard University Press, 1965.

Criminalizing of Abortion

The nineteenth century saw a change in laws about abortion in many parts of the Western world as various states attempted to restructure their existing legal systems into a more systematic and "scientific form." Legal traditions were either incorporated into statute law or in many cases discarded. France led the way when it enacted the Napoleonic *Code civil* in 1804 and, because French armies occupied much of Europe, it had tremendous influence. Later, after the defeat of France, many areas continued to observe the provisions of the code until they revised their own law codes as Italy, Spain, Germany, and even the Catholic Church did in the nineteenth century. Other countries of the world, including in Latin America, most of the countries of Europe, and countries outside of the European tradition such as Japan and Turkey, followed the trend.

In the process many of the states sought to regulate reproduction more effectively. In France in 1791, even before the reorganization of the law by the Napoleonic code, a new statute allowed for the prosecution of criminal abortionists. Such people were not defined and it might simply have been those without any medical degree. More drastic changes came in the aftermath of the Napoleonic code, and by 1810 prosecution was possible of anyone who by food, beverage, medicines, violence, or any other means procured an abortion on a pregnant woman, whether or not the woman had consented. Those found guilty were to be imprisoned even though the abortion attempt might not have been successful. The law, however, initially omitted the pregnant woman from punishment, providing the drugs had been self-administered, but anyone, whether physician or midwife, who assisted or advised her on what to take could be held criminally guilty. In 1817 the French law was amended to apply to women who secured their own abortions. Similar provisions were incorporated into other national law codes.

In England, in 1803, an omnibus crime bill was passed in an effort to eliminate some of the contradictions in common law about criminal activity. Among other things, abortion became a statutory offense, although there were distinctions. Abortion after quickening was classified as murder whereas before quickening it was only a felony. Over the century the laws were gradually tightened.

In the United States, Connecticut in 1821 was the first state to enact a specific law against abortion, but abortion before quickening was not made an offense until 1860. Illinois in 1827 punished only the use of poisons and did not include surgical or other means as punishable until 1867. Gradually as statutory law replaced common law, specific provisions dealing with regulation of abortion were enacted. New York, in its 1828 statute, allowed for legal abortions necessary to preserve the life of a mother but required that two physicians agree. The criminalizing of abortion but allowing therapeutic abortion was a general trend of the law, the effect of which was to give the decision to the medical professional rather than the individual involved. It also made abortion a class issue because the well-to-do with their private physicians could get a therapeutic abortion, but the poor had to turn to others. Abortion prohibitions were also more likely to be enforced against the unmarried mothers than the married ones with children.

Some saw the attempt to control abortion as a necessary corollary to protecting women from butchery by incompetent, nonmedically trained abortionists. In the nineteenth-century United States, where almost anyone could claim to be some sort of medical practitioner, simply requiring the intervention of a medical professional was not enough. The emerging American Medical Association, which came to dominate medicine by the end of the nineteenth century, however, emphasized the dangers of abortion as a way of moving against what its members believed were the untrained practitioners, ranging from midwives to naturopaths, who were active in the field. As gynecology progressed with the use of anesthetics and better aseptic techniques and moved into the emerging maternity hospitals and out of the home, the control over legal abortion lay entirely in the hands of the physician. Individual physicians who might once have performed an abortion in the privacy of the patient's home now found it difficult to even do therapeutic abortions without getting the agreement of their colleagues in the hospitals to which they were attached.

As medical sectarians and midwives were driven out of the professional field, the difficulty of finding a physician even for a therapeutic abortion increased. By 1966, fourth-fifths of all abortions were for married women and the rate of legal to illegal abortions was 1 to 110. Unfortunately, many of the illegal abortions were performed by people who operated on the fringe of society and were often carried out in unsanitary conditions in temporary offices. Because the activity was illegal, and police raids not uncommon, the equipment was kept to the bare minimum and information was passed by word of mouth. Complications were not unusual, even though an abortion is a rather simple procedure in the first trimester if carried out with good aseptic techniques by individuals who know what they are doing.

See also American Medical Association; Canon Law and Contraception

References

Brodie, Janet Farrell. *Contraception and Abortion in Nineteenth Century America.* Ithaca, NY: Cornell University Press, 1994.

Lader, Lawrence. *Abortion.* New York: Bobbs-Merrill, 1966.

Luger, Christen. *Abortion and the Politics of Motherhood.* Berkeley: University of California Press, 1984.

D

Demography and Population Control in Early Modern Europe

Many modern demographers, that is, those who gather statistical data on populations using such vital and social statistics as births, deaths, and marriages, believe that, before the eighteenth century, reproduction was independent of birth control. Rather the rate of increase or decrease of population was largely dependent upon external factors such as wars, celibacy, famine, plagues, land use, and nutrition, although these demographers also recognize that infanticide was a factor. Others have argued with what they consider demonstrable proof that at least from the seventeenth century, if not earlier, Europeans were attempting to limit their fertility. Still others believe, as does the editor of this book, that there were always attempts to limit or space child birth. Obviously not all attempts were successful because there was no easy way to distinguish the effectiveness of various folk remedies. We do know that midwives and others certainly made attempts to acquire such knowledge. Regardless of the position one holds on this issue, there is general agreement that in recent centuries there seems to have been an increasing effort toward family limitation. The question is why this might be the case.

We know that there are a lot of natural factors involved in population growth or lack of it, such as famine, wars, plagues, economic prosperity or depression, disease, diet, age at marriage, age differentials in marriage between men and women, ability or eligibility to marry, longevity, laws of heredity, long periods of marital absti-

nence dictated by religious holidays such as Lent or while a mother was nursing a baby. The list could go on. But how is it possible to determine whether there was any kind of family planning after marriage? Some evidence for this is gained from studying the birth intervals between children, the age at which women had their last child, size of families, and similar factors. From all of this data it seems clear that there was increasing use of family planning at least among some groups.

Some have argued that the explanation in the West for greater family planning was a result of the movement from the traditional authoritarian family structure, marked by arranged marriages, subordination of women, and brutal treatment of children, to the sentimental, egalitarian family of the late eighteenth century emphasizing close relationships between husbands and wives and a new concern for the well-being of children. There is a litany of factors that are said to have brought this about: growing literacy, new wage labor, social mobility, Protestantism, a nurturing of a new respect for one's spouse, a shifting of loyalties from clan and village to larger communities, and so on. Lawrence Stone argued that birth control became thinkable in the eighteenth century only with the emergence of "possessive individualism." For him, contraception marked a moral change that freed the sexuality from the restraints of theology and allowed the recognition of pleasure in sex. Individuals, or at least some of them, believed they had the right to make choices about their childbearing and no longer trust it to the will of God.

Although this ignores the existence of some sort of family planning in the ancient and medieval world, it does emphasize that at least some elements of seventeenth- and eighteenth-century society thought differently about such matters than those in an earlier period. Certainly Protestantism, as indicated, encouraged somewhat different attitudes about families than had existed before, and the Catholic attitudes after Protestantism were somewhat modified, and confessors were urged to be discrete in their probing about marital sexual activities. It might well be that such discretion was urged for fear that in their probing they might give out ideas about birth control that the penitent had not known.

In any case, family planning was an individual decision and governments certainly did not intervene and were not in a position to do so. Religious opposition to contraception or abortion was probably somewhat more effective but abortion was tolerated by the church and confessors until after quickening, and they usually did not probe too deeply into the sexual life of the penitents. It seems often that family planning was just taken for granted.

The first evidence of national concern about the possible use of birth control methods comes from France, where the French birthrate began dropping in the eighteenth century. The decline is measurable from the beginning of the nineteenth century, when the French began taking national censuses, but it began much earlier, some say the seventeenth century. We have some data for France in 1771 that have led demographers to estimate the birthrate at 38.6 per thousand, a rate that dropped to 31.3 per thousand in 1816 and continued to decline over the next hundred years. The decline is often explained as a result of the discovery of coitus interruptus by the French peasantry, but it is difficult to accept such a statement with the long tradition of such practices, including the biblical references to it. Whatever the method, the increased success at family planning by the eighteenth century was widespread and significant enough to affect population size.

But why the greater concern of the French about it? One social explanation has been offered, mainly the desire of the French peasants to avoid dividing land among heirs. Whatever the reason, inevitably there was concern about this in some quarters. Toward the end of the eighteenth century, a treatise on population, allegedly by Baron de Montyon, denounced "the pernicious secrets, unknown to all animals save man" that women used to avoid children and that were the cause of the major depopulation in the country. That women allegedly possessed the secret emphasizes the continuity of traditional herbal remedies and other things such as the sponge and douches. Not all French writers decried this drop in population, and the Marquis de Condorcet (d. 1794) argued favorably that only humans alone among the animals had the ability to set aside the law of nature. In the nineteenth century, the needs to stimulate births became a public obsession in France. Whether the French had better access to methods of birth control than did other Europeans is unclear, but it is clear that they used the methods at their disposal so effectively that population grew only sluggishly from the 1840s on, in spite of governmental efforts to increase it. In 1800, 15.7 percent of all Europe's population lived in France, whereas by 1900 the percentage had dropped to 9.7 percent, a fact that struck fear into the French military and political leaders. In contrast, England went from a population in 1550 of 4.9 percent (approximately three million) of Europe's total population to 25.1 percent in 1900.

But if France was concerned with its declining population, a new movement was beginning that was concerned with the dangers of overpopulation. The clarion call for this new movement was issued by Thomas Malthus in 1798 in an anonymous essay on population. Malthus developed what came to be called a law based on the assumption that humankind is doomed because increased prosperity is accompanied by an ever greater rise in population and the earth's capacity to produce subsistence for humans is limited. Population, when unchecked, he said, increases in a geometrical ratio (1, 2, 4, 8, 16, etc.), whereas subsistence increases only in an arithmetical ratio (1, 2, 3, 4, 5, etc.). Though he recognized that some of this could be altered (for example, agriculture might increase faster), inevitably the only options he foresaw were self-restraint from sexual intercourse, misery, and vice. Contraception was included under the category of vice. Malthus and his theories have continued to dominate any discussion of population or population control. Many of the English popularizers of population control called themselves Neo-Malthusians because they believed that birth control was possible.

See also Abortion; Canon Law and Abortion; Canon Law and Contraception; Council of Trent and Catholic Tradition; Malthus, Thomas Robert; Quickening

References
Bardet, J.-P., and H. LeBras, eds. *Histoire de la population française,* vol. 3. Paris: Presses Universitaire de France, 1988.
Coale, A. J., and S. C. Watkins, eds. *The Decline of Fertility in Europe.* Princeton, NJ: Princeton University Press, 1986. (This is a collection of articles.)
Fryer, Peter. *The Birth Controllers.* London: Secker and Warburg, 1965.
McEvedy, Colin, and Richard Jones. *Atlas of World Population.* New York: Harmondsworth, 1978.
McLaren, A. *A History of Contraception.* Oxford, England: Blackwell, 1990.
Malthus, Thomas. *An Essay on the Principle of Population as It Affects the Future Improvements of Society with Remarks on the Speculations of Mr. Godwin, M. Condorcet, and Other Writers.* London: Johnson, 1798. Reprinted 1986.
Pouthas, C. H. *La population française pendant le premier moiti du XIXe sicle,* Travaux et Documents, Cahier 25, Paris, 1956.
Riddle, J. *Eve's Herbs.* Cambridge, MA: Harvard University Press, 1997.
Stone, L. *The Family, Sex, and Marriage in England, 1500–1800.* New York: Harper & Row, 1977.

Dennett, Mary Coffin Ware (1872–1947)

Mary Coffin Ware, the second of four children of George Whitefield Ware and Livonia Coffin, was raised in Boston, Massachusetts. Her first interest was in the Arts and Crafts movement, and she studied at the Boston Museum of Fine Arts (1891–1894). She taught decoration and design at the newly established Drexel Institute in Philadelphia from 1894 to 1897. After an 1897 trip to Europe, she returned to Boston to open a handicrafts shop with her sister Clara and became an active member of the artistic community. In 1900, she married architect William Hartley Dennett (1870–1936) and worked with him, providing interior decoration for the homes he designed. The Dennetts were "utterly ignorant of the control of conception" and Mary quickly bore three sons, Carleton (1900), Appleton (1903) and Devon (1905). She described the births as "hideously difficult" and her middle son died three weeks after birth. With her third pregnancy Dennett suffered a lacerated uterus that was a major health problem until a 1907 operation corrected it. Her physician advised the Dennetts not to have any more children, but gave no practical advice. The marriage faltered as they abstained from sex. Hartley Dennett began a relationship with a client that blossomed into a life-long love affair, and by 1909 divorce and custody wrangling began. Mary Dennett won sole custody of the children.

Shaken by the breakup of her marriage, Dennett sought meaningful work in reform. In 1908 she took a job as field secretary for the Massachusetts Woman Suffrage Association and in 1910 was elected corresponding secretary of the New York City–based National American Woman Suffrage Association (NAWSA). Her work in the suffrage movement gave Dennett organizational skills and experience making political arguments. NAWSA put her in charge of the bustling literature department, where she was responsible for coordinating branch offices across the country. To take the position, Dennett moved to New York in 1910. She left her sons with family and friends in New England and visited them regularly. The Dennetts did not settle their bitter and increasingly public divorce until 1913.

While on her own in New York, Dennett took up socialist reform and Greenwich Village bohemian thought. Increasingly critical of the leadership at NAWSA, she was forced out of her position in 1914. She followed other interests, including the Twilight Sleep and single-tax

Mary Ware Dennett celebrated at home after the U.S. Circuit Court reversed the jury decision that found her guilty of sending obscene matter (sex education pamphlets) through the mail. (Corbis)

movements and regularly attended the meetings of the feminist group Heterodoxy. With the outbreak of war in Europe, Dennett and many of her colleagues devoted themselves to campaigning for peace. Dennett worked with the newly formed Women's Peace Party, the American Union Against Militarism, the People's Council of America, and other groups that fought against U.S. involvement in the war.

During this time, Dennett also became interested in birth control. She met Margaret Sanger, at the time the radical editor of *The Woman Rebel,* at a Heterodoxy meeting in the late spring or summer of 1914. Sanger's calls for broader access to contraceptive information struck a

chord with Dennett, but she deplored the use of law-defying and confrontational tactics. Sanger fled the United States in October 1914 to avoid prosecution. In her absence, Dennett helped organize the National Birth Control League (NBCL) (March 1915), using subscriber lists obtained from *The Woman Rebel* to gather members. Dennett's group argued for removing the term "prevention of conception" from the acts defined as obscene in the Comstock Law. Although her goals were similar to Sanger's at the time, Dennett used the traditional tactics she learned with the suffrage movement to accomplish them. She launched a lobbying campaign aimed at New York state politicians and circularized supporters and policy makers with propaganda and news updates.

With Sanger's return to the United States in October 1915, a rivalry was born that divided the birth control movement for the next fifteen years. Sanger resented Dennett's lack of support for her and Dennett's failure to cede leadership of the birth control movement to her upon her return. Dennett failed to understand why Sanger would not join the NBCL and work under a broader leadership. Adding to their personal differences, Sanger began to alter her views on birth control while in Europe. She began arguing for birth control in a medical setting to ensure the most effective and safe contraception using scientific methods. This brought her into conflict with Dennett, who sought to make it legal for anyone to distribute contraceptive information, not just doctors.

Dennett's economic position and her personality hampered her effectiveness in getting public support. On the surface, she and Sanger had similar histories—both had divorced and were raising sons on their own financial ability. Yet Sanger thrived on publicity and renown, undertaking combative lecture tours, writing a series of books, and dealing capably with the media. Dennett shunned public attention. She found the attention of the press uncomfortable, no doubt after the experience of her well-documented divorce. She also feared that the notoriety that came with radical ideas could jeopardize her continued custody of her sons. Rather than compete publicly with Sanger for leadership of the movement, Dennett worked quietly, focusing on attracting the support of "influential" leaders to win passage of a birth control bill. Unlike her coworkers, most of whom were upper- or middle-class society women, Dennett had to make her livelihood from reform work. The need to raise sufficient money to cover both her salary and the work of the NBCL took its toll; upon taking the full-time position of executive secretary in 1918, Dennett's salary was often in arrears and she found herself in the position of urging the NBCL toward more concentrated action.

The NBCL began its work in New York State, urging a bill that would remove contraception from a list of obscenities. Dennett orchestrated a campaign of education through literature, much as she had run with NAWSA. The NBCL worked to get a birth control bill introduced in 1917, but without the support of Republican leaders in the assembly, it failed. For a few years, Dennett's organization was the only organized birth control league in the United States. Despite that, Margaret Sanger's campaign overshadowed it. Sanger garnered headlines and fame with birth control clinics, legal challenges, and arrests. Financial woes continued to plague the NBCL, and in March 1919 the executive committee voted to cut back their work and eliminate Dennett's paid position. Dennett resigned and began a new organization, the Voluntary Parenthood League (VPL) that would focus its lobbying on a federal bill.

Dennett shifted from a state to federal focus out of practicality. Twenty-seven states had no specific laws prohibiting the distribution of contraceptives, and removing the federal obscenity ban would legalize birth control in over half the country. Dennett believed that many of the remaining states would follow the federal example and the movement could then continue where restrictions remained. She based her legislative campaign on the right to free speech, claiming that all people should have the right to decide whether they would be parents. Increasingly, Margaret Sanger challenged Dennett's theory, emphasizing clinical services and doctor-controlled contraception as the best means to get reliable information to the public. Neither woman would admit any merit in the ideas of the other and their battle polarized birth control supporters into two camps for much of the 1920s. Dennett argued that Sanger's policies were undemocratic and would create a medical monopoly on information; Dennett also claimed that Sanger herself had written birth control books that would remain obscene under her new plan. Sanger argued that Dennett's bill was unattainable—legislators would not support it. She also claimed that it would allow quacks to distribute dangerous and ineffective methods to the public.

Once Sanger formed the American Birth Control League in 1921, competition between the two women intensified. Sanger initially agreed to leave the field of federal legislation to Dennett, but by 1926 her league had representatives in Washington, lobbying her competing idea for birth control legislation. When faced with direct competition, Dennett could not muster the finances that Sanger could, and by 1925 the VPL's finances were in serious trouble. Dennett's salary was once again in arrears. She resigned her paid position as executive director and the VPL scaled back to an all-volunteer organization that never mounted another legislative campaign.

Dennett worked as an administrator for a homeopathic organization and an organic food school in the mid- and late 1920s. In the 1930s she returned to her arts and crafts work. She continued to volunteer her time as chair of VPL board of directors, but the VPL accomplished little. In 1926, Dennett published *Birth Control Laws,* which offered a detailed discussion of her birth control arguments and attacked both opponents of birth control and Margaret Sanger's doctors-only bill. Dennett refused to close the VPL for she was unwilling to leave the field to Sanger. Throughout the 1920s and early 1930s, Dennett served as a thorn in Sanger's side. Unable to mount a federal campaign of their own, Dennett and the VPL used publicity generated by Sanger's repeated legislative campaigns to publicize their alternative plan. Ultimately, neither woman succeeded in Congress. It was not until a 1936 judicial decision that Sanger won her exception for physician-controlled birth control.

In 1929, Dennett herself faced charges of obscenity, based upon a 1915 sex education essay she had written for her sons. She had reprinted the *Sex Side of Life* in pamphlet form, and in 1922, the postal authorities informed her that the book was unmailable. Dennett ignored the ruling and continued to send copies of the book through the mail. In 1929 she was indicted and was convicted. Dennett appealed and her case attracted widespread press coverage and the support of the American Civil Liberties Union. In March 1930, she won an appellate ruling. Judge Augustus Hand held that the context within which a work was written determined whether it violated the Comstock Act. Because Dennett did not aim "to arouse lust" when she wrote the pamphlet, it was not obscene. This decision was influential in setting a new standard for censorship and it vindicated Dennett. Her name splashed on newspaper headlines across the country, but Dennett eschewed publicity, refusing interviews with reporters. She published her own account of her trial, *Who's Obscene?* (1930), to get her story out in her own words. A year later, she wrote a more detailed guide, *The Sex Education of Children* (1931).

Shortly after her brief moment in the limelight, Dennett withdrew from active reform work, retiring to live with her son, and only occasionally involving herself in birth control activities. With the threat of war again on the horizon, she helped to found the pacifist World Federalists, which sought international peace through law. Dennett served as chair from 1941 until her retirement in 1944. She died in 1947.

Dennett's papers are at the Schlesinger Library, Harvard University, and available on the microfilm: *Sexuality, Sex Education, and Reproductive Rights, Papers of Mary Ware Dennett and the Voluntary Parenthood League* (Bethesda, MD: University Publications of America, 1994). Dennett's quotes about her family come from Dennett to Marie Stopes, October 31, 1921 (Reel 14: 495–497.)

See also Voluntary Parenthood League

References

Chen, Constance. *The Sex Side of Life: Mary Ware Dennett's Pioneering Battle for Birth Control and Sex Education.* New York: The New Press, 1996. (Chen's book is an uncritical biography.)

Diaphragm

The diaphragm, which became the most widely used form of barrier contraception in the United States and in much of Western Europe in the middle of the twentieth century was invented in the 1870s by the German physician, W. P. J. Mensinga. It is a soft rubber shield in circular dome-shaped form that has a covered spring rim (originally a flat spring like an old windup clock spring). It is inserted by the woman compressing together the rim, placing the bowl shape over the cervix. Once inserted, the flexible rim allows the diaphragm to resume its original molded shape. Insertion originally was with fingers, although later inserters were developed. After it is inserted, the diaphragm should be checked to see that it is properly placed, fitting securely and comfortably between the rear wall of the vagina and the upper edge of the pubic bone. The cervix should be palpated (it feels like the end of a nose) to see that it is well covered by the rubber. In the proper position, the diaphragm completely covers the cervix.

Mensinga's specific intent was to protect unhealthy women from undesired pregnancies. In his writings he dealt in some detail with the medical indications and included many contraceptive case histories. He was the first physician to do a systematic, complete study of the techniques of contraception. As information of his invention began circulating, knowledge of it reached the Netherlands. In 1881, Dr. Aletta Jacobs opened a contraceptive clinic, the first such clinic in the world, to dispense the diaphragm and information about contraceptives.

One reason the diaphragm became so popular is that those in the medical profession willing to deal with contraceptives pushed it. It had to be fitted (a variety of sizes were developed) and the physicians regarded themselves as best able to do so. The diaphragm was also promoted by Margaret Sanger.

In the 1940s and 1950s, when the use of the diaphragm was at its peak, there were several types of diaphragms on the market but in the United States three became dominant: coil spring, flat spring, and the arcing spring or Findlay spring. The most common in the United States was the coil spring, in which a spiral met-

al wire in the rim was encircled with rubber. It was and still is suitable for the average women who has strong vaginal muscles, a deep arch behind the symphysis pubis (pubic bone), no displacement of the uterus, and a normal size and contour of the vagina. The flat spring is more delicate than the coiled spring and, although it can be used by the same women who used the coiled spring type, it is particularly suitable for a woman who has a shallow arch behind the public bone. It is also most useful for a woman who has never had a child. The arcing spring diaphragm has a double spring in the rim that produces strong pressures against the vaginal walls. It gets its name because it forms an arc when the rim is compressed. It is most suitable for a woman with poor vaginal muscle tone, a moderate cystocele (a bulging of the urinary bladder into the vagina), a rectocele (a bulging of the rectum into the vagina), or a mild uterine prolapse. Because the rim exerts such strong pressure against the vaginal walls, it has to be fitted with great care in order to avoid excessive pressure either on the vaginal wall or on the urethra. Once fitted, it is next to impossible to insert it improperly.

As spermicides developed, it became standard practice to recommend that the diaphragm be used with a spermicide gel spread on the inside of the dome, fitting against the os, or mouth, of the cervix. For those who use it, the diaphragm should be left in after intercourse overnight, and when it is removed, it is recommended that the woman douche with clear water. Other types of inserts are discussed under the pessary entry. The diaphragm as of this writing is used by only a small percentage of the population.

See also Barrier Contraceptives; Pessary

References

Hatcher, Robert A., Felicia Guest, Gary K. Stewart, James Trussel, S. C. Bowen, and Willard Cates. *Contraceptive Technology 1988–89,* 14th rev. ed. New York: Irvington Publishers, 1988. (There are later editions of this because it appears every other year. This particular issue was very good on the diaphragm.)

Mensinga, Wilhelm Peter Joh. *Ueber facultative Sterilität beleuchtet vom prophylactischen und hygienischen*

Standpunkte für practische Aerzte. Neuwied und Leipzig: n.p., 1882.

———. *Ein Beitrag zum Mechanismus der Conception.* Leipzig: Ernst Fielder, 1891.

Dickinson, Robert Latou (1861–1950)

Robert Latou Dickinson presents an interesting example of a person whose major accomplishments came after his retirement from the private practice of medicine. He was a pioneer obstetrician, gynecologist, researcher into sexual behavior, and collector of all kinds of information about contraception. Norman Himes in his *Medical History of Contraception* cites him as a key reference for many of the fine points on historical and contemporary methods of birth control.

In his practice Dickinson gave instruction on contraception as part of his normal premarital counseling. More importantly he tried to get other physicians to give such advice. He was, however, initially reluctant to be too publicly identified with the birth control movement. In 1916, when Margaret Sanger asked him for the names of physicians who might be interested in her cause, he provided a list of some but deliberately left his own name off the list, supposedly because he was somewhat uneasy about becoming publicly involved with her. He believed at that time that contraception should be a matter between the physician and the patient and not left in the hands of radicals such as Margaret Sanger. Dickinson began to change his attitudes after he retired, and for a time he was active in an effort with Sanger to establish a birth control clinic with medical supervision, but the effort failed and it was not until 1930 that he formally associated himself with Sanger.

After his retirement in 1920 at age sixty, Dickinson devoted himself to causes, particularly birth control and sex education. In the process he moved from being a closeted researcher of human sexuality to being its dominant medical figure. In 1923 he founded the Committee on Maternal Health (after 1930 known as the National Committee on Maternal Health) to do research on contraception, sterility, abortion, and related issues. Some of the studies of the committee linked marriage problems to lack of effective contraceptive knowledge.

Dickinson broke ground in his presidential address to the American Gynecological Society in 1920 when he urged physicians to do more research not only in contraception, but in infertility, artificial sterilization, and similar issues. He was a persistent gadfly to the professional medical community about the need for contraception, and in 1937 he finally persuaded the American Medical Association to pass a resolution acknowledging the importance of contraception and calling for its teaching in medical schools. With Louise Stevens in 1931 he wrote *Control of Contraception,* which became the basic medical text in the field in the 1930s. It contained original studies; firsthand analysis; and discussion of contraceptive techniques, sterilization, abortion, laws, and clinical programs. Equally important was his topographical atlas, *Human Sexual Anatomy.* His case studies of single and married women were based on the women he had treated in his practice before he retired and are a gold mine of information including data on frequency of intercourse, use of contraceptives, orgasmic ability, and similar information.

References

Bullough, Vern L. *Science in the Bedroom.* New York: Basic Books, 1994.

Dickinson, Robert Latou. *Birth Atlas.* New York: Maternity Center Associations, 1940.

———. *Human Sexual Anatomy.* Baltimore: Williams & Wilkins, 1949.

Dickinson, Robert Latou, and Laura Beam. *A Thousand Marriages.* Baltimore: Williams & Wilkins, 1931.

———. *The Single Woman.* Baltimore: Williams & Wilkins, 1934.

Dickinson, Robert Latou, and Louis Stevens Bryant. *Control of Conception.* Baltimore: Williams & Wilkins, 1931.

Himes, Norman E. *Medical History of Contraception.* New York: Schocken Books, 1970. (Dickinson wrote the introduction to the original publication of this book.)

Reed, James. *From Private Vice to Public Virtue: The Birth Control Movement and American Society since 1830.* New York: Basic Books, 1978.

Distribution of Contraceptive Products in Nineteenth-Century America

Pessaries of various sorts were often sold in drug stores in the last part of the nineteenth century but they were also advertised in some of the popular media. Janet Farrel Brodie held that there are many records of women wearing stem pessaries for long periods, probably for the most part inserted by physicians because they were inserted through the cervix. Still, many of the advertisements emphasized a do-it-yourself treatment, saying that they could be "readily asserted with a minimum degree or skill [and] can be worn continually." Probably the most popular means of acquiring contraceptive devices during the first three-quarters of the century, however, was through the mail. This became increasingly true as the century progressed and the mail catalogues boosted the development of a consumer culture. Most of the popular medical books aimed at women or the family included—as did Edward Bliss Foote in his books—addresses of the author or publisher where those desiring more information about specific products or wanting to order them could do so. The mail order business served those who were unwilling to make face-to-face contact with sellers and it was a major business. This market basically ended with the Comstock laws.

When mail order became more difficult, the business was picked up by peddlers because most of the states did not have laws barring contraceptives. Some sellers even set up their own distribution centers. For example, Morris Glattstine was arrested in New York in 1877 on charges of dealing in rubber articles intended to prevent conception. Glattstine bought condoms and diaphragms from the Stuart Rubber Company in Milwaukee, Wisconsin, and sold the goods at a small store at 77 East Broadway and distributed them to outlying stores, peddlers, and other dealers. Rubber companies sometimes hired their own agents to sell their goods for them and they placed their goods almost everywhere. They were sold in tobacco, stationers', apothecary, and barber shops; at cheap book-

and newsstands; and by dealers in rubber goods and dealers in "fancy goods." Salesmen regularly visited industrial sites where large numbers of males were employed. Sometimes the products they advertised on the surface would have little to do with contraception. The Essex Syringe Manufacturing Company in Newport, Rhode Island, for example, produced several models of vaginal and uterine syringes and pessaries, clearly useful for contraceptive douching. They sold their syringes in 1860 to two "general depots" in New York City and Chicago, as well as to individual agents in Philadelphia, Boston, and New York. Druggists themselves became skilled at mail order advertising, not only for condoms, female syringes, and feminine rubber goods, but also even for abortifacient pills.

See also Comstock, Anthony, and Comstockery; Foote, Edward Bliss; Pessary

Reference
Brodie, Janet Farrell. *Contraception and Abortion in Nineteenth Century America.* Ithaca, NY: Cornell University Press, 1994.

Douching

Just when women began to use douches of various astringent solutions as a contraceptive is lost to history. Many of the herbal compounds mentioned elsewhere were probably administered as douches, although the sources do not specifically say so. Any strongly alkaline or acid condition will tend to provide a hostile environment for sperm. Alum, for example, is often mentioned in the literature of birth control and was readily available because it was used in dyeing and tanning. Both brine and vinegar are highly spermicidal. Acetic acid immobilizes human sperm in 10 to 15 seconds at a ratio of one part to two thousand. For example, ordinary vinegar is between 4 and 5 percent acetic acid, with wine vinegar running to 6 percent. Two tablespoons of vinegar to a quart of water is stronger than 1 to 1,000 and is probably the most effective home remedy for douching readily available.

Douches were well known to many eighteenth-century French women and were perhaps more widely used in France than elsewhere because of the use of the bidet among the well-to-do French. Vinegar water was used as the solution. Douching was the method most recommended by Charles Knowlton, an early advocate of birth control in the United States. He gave recommendations for a variety of douche solutions made of alum, zinc sulfate (a solution used for preserving skins and bleaching paper and as a general all-purpose astringent), bicarbonate of soda, common vinegar, and ordinary salt. His recipes for preparation usually involved small amounts (a thimble or teaspoon, or occasionally a great spoon) of the ingredients mixed with water. He did advise some testing before use and wrote that the woman should make it as strong as she could bear without producing disagreeable sensations. Douching also temporarily changes the pH of the vagina.

Rubber douching syringes were available from retail and wholesale outlets in the United States by the 1840s. When dissemination about birth control methods was either illegal or regarded as of doubtful morality in the United States, douche solutions were advertised in magazines aimed at women as a means of keeping themselves clean and fresh and as a necessity for personal feminine hygiene. One of the advertisers was the manufacturer of Lysol, which was also used to clean toilets of germs. The company advised women to

> douche regularly since without douching some minor physical irregularity plants in a woman's mind the fear of a major crisis [read: delayed menstrual period and fear of pregnancy]. Lest so devastating a fear recur again and again, and the most charming and gracious wife turns into a nerve-ridden, irritable travesty of herself. Bewildering, to say the least, to even the kindest husband. Fatal inevitably to the beauty of the marriage relation (Himes, 1970, p. 329).

All such worries and anxiety would disappear by using the Lysol method, which destroys germs in the presence of organic matter. The advertisement concluded that there was no free caustic alkali in the product, such as found in chlorine compounds. They did not add that using it or other such solutions frequently and in overstrong solutions scarred the cervix and, although it probably helped prevent pregnancy, if it was taken long enough and strong enough it might well have caused sterility.

Douching remained a major part of woman's hygiene well into the last part of the twentieth century. It was a major part of the diaphragm method of contraception for many women, and when the woman removed her diaphragm in the morning after having inserted it the evening before, she often douched to remove the spermicide that was used in conjunction with the diaphragm. Women who did so were advised to use a mild vinegar solution or plain water and to avoid strong astringent solutions.

See also Herbal Contraceptives and Abortifacients; Knowlton, Charles

References

Himes, N. *A Medical History of Contraception.* New York: Schocken Books, 1970.

Knowlton, Charles. *Fruits of Philosophy, or the Private Companion of Young Unmarried People.* Boston: A. Kneeland, 1831. (Often reprinted.)

Drysdale, George (1825–1904)

The most influential of the books dealing with contraceptives in the mid-nineteenth century, after the spate of the booklets and pamphlets that appeared after the efforts of Francis Place, was that of George Drysdale. Born in Edinburgh, the son of Sir William Drysdale, George Drysdale was a brilliant pupil, known by his fellow students as Rex, or king. He signed many of his contributions to the *National Reformer,* published by Charles Bradlaugh, as G. R. for George Rex. While studying medicine at the University of Edinburgh and having been intrigued by economic ideas of Adam Smith, David Ricardo, and Thomas Malthus, he wrote a book entitled *Physical, Sexual, Natural Religion.* Unwilling to antagonize his mother over his unorthodox religious opinions and his challenges to traditional morality, he signed it simply as "By a Student of Medicine." After some difficulty in finding a publisher, the book was finally published in 1855 by Edward Truelove, who was a prominent freethinker. Later editions of the book were entitled *The Elements of Social Science.*

Drysdale took as his mission the need to emphasize that sexual intercourse could and should be a delightful thing. Preventing it from being so, he believed, was the ever-present possibility of children, and because he believed that overpopulation itself was a major cause of poverty, he believed that birth control was a solution. He also believed that the fear of having more children not only encouraged men to turn to prostitutes but was a strong inhibitor of a woman's willingness to express her sexuality. On the other hand, Drysdale also believed that immoderate amounts of sexual activity were dangerous, and he had a horror of variant sexuality, including masturbation. Still, Havelock Ellis, the great English sexologist of the first part of the twentieth century, was greatly influenced to enter the sex field by his reading of Drysdale.

Only six pages of Drysdale's more than four hundred pages of *Physical, Sexual, and Natural Religion* were devoted to contraception. He discussed five techniques, two of which, the sponge and the douche, he advised were to be used together. His douche solution, however, was simply tepid water, which he held would flush out the sperm from the vagina, after which the sponge could be removed. He also advocated that women use a safe period, which he said was from two to three days before menstruation to eight days after but this would be useful only to women who had very regular menses because otherwise predicting the onset of menstruation two days before it begins is difficult. Moreover, the recommendation for the safe period often depended upon how the woman measured the ceasing of menstruation. If she could tell and if she tried to follow the method to the letter, she

might still get pregnant because the fertility cycle was not fully explained until well into the twentieth century. Drysdale himself was somewhat skeptical about the effectiveness of using a safe period for having intercourse but held that, although the method was not infallible, it would reduce the likelihood of conception. On the other possible procedures he discussed he was far more negative. Coitus interruptus, he wrote, was "physically injurious" because it might cause mental disorders and illness in the man and it also interfered with pleasure. The condom, in his mind, was unaesthetic, dulled enjoyment, and might even produce impotence. The section on birth control was often extracted from his major work, which by the time the thirty-fifth and last edition appeared in 1905 had sold some 88,000 copies. These extracts, or penny pamphlets, went under a wide variety of titles, and some of them were by other authors who simply adopted his methods as their own.

See also Bradlaugh, Charles; Place, Francis

References
Drysdale, G. *Physical, Sexual, and Natural Religion, by a Student of Medicine.* London: Edward Truelove, 1854. (Later editions were published under the title of *The Elements of Social Science.* The discussion here is based on the twenty-sixth edition, enlarged, London: E. Truelove, 1887.)
Fryer, Peter. *The Birth Controllers.* London: Secker and Warburg, 1965.

Dung

Dung of various animals has been used as vaginal inserts or suppositories in various cultures to prevent conception. Probably the earliest reference is from c. 1850 B.C.E. in the Kahun Medical Papyrus, which states that crocodile dung is to be mashed up and mixed with fermented dough and inserted into the vagina. Certainly any sticky barrier would handicap the penetration of sperm into the cervix but there are other factors involved as well. The optimum condition for conception in the vagina is a highly alkaline one with a pH of 8.5 to 9.5. The normative pH for the vagina is an acidic 3.86 to

4.45 and it rises in alkalinity during the fertile period. Crocodile dung has a pH of 7.9, which makes it somewhat alkaline and therefore not particularly effective chemically in preventing conception. This could of course be changed by the substances with which it is mixed and which might well decrease its alkalinity and make it more effective.

Dung of other animals, however, would probably be more effective. Indian elephant dung, for example, has a pH of 5.6 and the dung of the African elephant is 5.9. The motility of the sperm is arrested at a pH of 6.0 or below. Elephant dung is mentioned by the ninth-century Islamic physician Rhazes as an ingredient in a contraceptive suppository as well as by Avicenna in the eleventh century and others. These writing entered Europe in the eleventh century through the translations of Constantine the African.

Generally the dung suppository had disappeared from Western medical literature by the thirteenth century but various folk medical remedies advised the use of dung in other ways. Some of these must have been very ancient.

Pliny, the Roman writer of the first century of the modern era, included in his *Natural History*, a miscellaneous collection of folk medicine, gossip, superstition, mythology, and science, a reference to mouse dung applied in the form of a liniment as an anaphrodisiac. Certainly the smell would keep suitors away. Some of the use of dung are purely magical or superstitious such as the suspension of rabbit dung over a woman's bed as a method of inducing sterility, a practice recorded as late as the eighteenth century. Pigeon dung was said to have the same effect.

References

Dickinson, Robert Latou, and Louis Stevens Bryant. *The Control of Contraception.* Baltimore: Williams & Wilkins, 1931.

Himes, Norman E. *Medical History of Contraception.* New York: Schocken Books, 1970.

Kahun. No. 12, 11 [3, 7], in *Grundiss der Medizin der alten Ägypter,* edited by Hildegard von Deines, Herman Graprow, and Wolfhart Westendorf, 7 vols., Berlin: Akademie Verlag, 1954–1962, vol. 4, pt. 5, p. 277; note pt. 2, p. 211; vol. 5, p. 477.

Pliny. *Natural History,* edited and translated by W. H. S. Jones. London: Heinemann, Loeb Classical Library, 1963, 28:80.

E

Ejaculation and Pregnancy

Recent studies on infertility have thrown new light on the process of conception and, by implication, of contraception. Simply, conception relies on semen containing viable sperm to come in contact with the cervical os of an ovulating woman. Although some birth control methods rely on barrier methods of preventing exactly this, their failure rate is illustrative of the persistence of sperm and their fertilizing capacity. Penile erection was designed to penetrate the natural mechanical resistance of the vagina and to be able to achieve a vaginal depth where the ejaculated sperm would be deposited advantageously at the cervical opening. The sperm must then penetrate the cervical mucus and enter the uterine cavity on their journey to either of the fallopian tubes, at the end of which, fertilization of an ovum would normally take place. Although many factors along this latter route are important, erection is not absolutely necessary. As long as semen is deposited near or at the vaginal opening and can make it to the cervical os (through liquefaction of semen, favorable extruded vaginal fluids with alkaline pH, highly motile sperm, gravity, and intrauterine and intravaginal pressure gradients), the conception is possible. Although ejaculatory and erectile problems can lead to fertility issues, the most common coital problem associated with infertility is coital infrequency: studies have shown that fertile couples with a coital frequency of less than once per week had a pregnancy rate of 16.7 percent over six months, whereas 83.3 percent of couples with coital frequency of four times per week conceived in the same period.

Development of sperm (spermatogenesis) takes place in the body of the testes and approximately sixty days are required for the young or immature sperm to mature to spermatozoa. The spermatozoa are then held and further matured in the epididymis for another ten to fourteen days, and they line up in compartments waiting for their turn to be propelled up and out along the vas deferens. The vas deferens is a long tube that rises from the epididymis of each testicle and enters into bilateral seminal vesicles that are located at the base of the bladder on the prostate gland. Here the sperm meet with nourishing fluids and the bolus is propelled to the urethra. Prostatic fluid is also added to the seminal bolus. The nerve signals cause internal accessory organ contractions and propulsion of the bolus down the long membranous urethra to the external opening of the glans penis, the urethral meatus. Cowper's glands, small glands that exist bilaterally on either side of the urethra near the penile base, can produce varying volumes of clear fluid that lubricate the urethra; with high arousal preorgasm, varying volumes may appear at the urethral meatus and facilitate lubrication in sexual intercourse. Because sperm are continually expressed from the seminal vesicle reservoirs, occasional sperm can be found in this preejaculate; however, their low numbers make pregnancy highly unlikely, but not impossible. Semen, then, is composed of spermatozoa, seminal and prostatic fluid, and also some fluid from the Cowper's gland and the Littré's gland in the body of the penis. The first spurt or fraction of the ejaculate is usually the one that contains the highest number of sperm.

Ejaculation is a complex, highly coordinated event dependent on the autonomic, somatic, and sensory components of the nervous system, but its description can be somewhat simplified into two phases. The emission phase includes the transport of sperm from loaded epididymides along the vas deferens, into the seminal vesicles, and through the ejaculatory ducts into the prostatic urethra. This phase is under some voluntary control by the man, depending on his sexual practices and body awareness. The prostate, being vasocongested with arousal, already has a high intraprostatic pressure. With the arrival of the seminal bolus into the prostatic urethra, the intraprostatic pressure acutely arises further: this is usually interpreted by the man as "ejaculatory inevitability" or the "point of no return," as he cannot (easily) voluntarily control the neurological triggering of the second phase, propulsive ejaculations. This phase is characterized by contractions of the smooth muscles of the prostate, membranous urethra, and Cowper's glands and strong pelvic floor contractions of the striated muscles that expel the seminal bolus out of the urethral meatus. The force of this expulsion is dependent on the physics involving the urethral diameter, the volume of ejaculate, and the strength of the muscular contractions. Orgasm, the brain's interpretations of these events, usually accompanies ejaculation, but not always. Furthermore, ejaculation is not dependent on erection.

Ejaculatory disturbances lead to difficulties with conception. There may be emission but not ejaculation proper, as seen in disturbances of the autonomic nervous system. In this case the ejaculate may not appear or will dribble out with gravity some time after orgasm. Other times the nerve damage may cause the entire process to not occur (anejaculation) or to not allow complete closure of the bladder neck, thereby causing partial or complete retrograde ejaculation (low-volume ejaculate or no ejaculate but cloudy postorgasmic urine seen on voiding). There can be ejaculatory timing issues, such as very premature or rapid ejaculation that results in ejaculation occurring before vaginal penetration. The more common concern with rapid ejaculation is unwanted expulsion or ejaculate in the vagina before birth control methods are applied. Another ejaculatory disturbance is inhibited ejaculation, the inability to ejaculate despite high arousal. Situational inhibited ejaculation refers to the inability to ejaculate, despite the desire and effort to, in certain situations (such as providing a sample for assisted reproductive techniques or trying to ejaculate with intercourse on the day of ovulation). Generalized inhibited ejaculation refers to this difficulty all the time, even to the point of not ejaculating in the waking state; this is an uncommon but difficult-to-treat cause of infertility. Both fast and inhibited ejaculations are usually unwanted by the man and/or his partner.

Those men who are unable to produce an antegrade ejaculate need to undergo sperm retrieval techniques, whether they be physiological, operative, or behavioral. Sex therapy can be very beneficial in those men with ejaculatory timing difficulties but who are neurologically intact; cryopreservation of masturbatory samples may be required if timing difficulties around sexual conception become overwhelming. If there are neurological difficulties, medications (i.e., to improve the bladder neck closure) and other physiological methods (vibrostimulation and electroejaculation) can be employed to either trigger ejaculation or emission, and semen can be collected and placed in the partner. If there are anatomical problems such that the internal pathways outlined above are not patent or functional, then aspirated sperm retrieval from the epididymis or testis is possible.

The semen must also be of a minimum quality for conception to occur. Those sperm that are usually effective at fertilizing an oocyte are normally formed (normal morphology or shape), have good motility (or forward progression), and have normal fertilizing capacity. Semen quality varies considerably from one individual to the next and there is substantial variation within the individual. Typically a normal ejaculate would contain 200–300 million sperm. Semen is usually thick and requires 20–30 minutes to be liquefied by enzymes and to allow better mobility of the sperm out of the seminal bolus and into the cervical mucus, where they stay for the next few days, steadily feeding into the uterine cavity. Those sperm that are deposited near the cervical os at ejaculation have the advantage of being able to penetrate the cervical mucus within two minutes and reach their target site, the fallopian tube, in less than five minutes (Tan and Jacobs, 1991). Because of these factors, maintaining a certain sexual position or removing the ejaculate by douching will not be an effective form of birth control, nor will maintaining certain sexual positions and trying to reduce the "flow back" of liquefied semen out of the vagina ensure pregnancy. Sperm normally survive for two to four hours in the vagina but have been found up to sixteen hours after intercourse. Survival times are longer once the sperm enter the cervical canal or uterus, but in general it is believed that sperm live for forty-eight hours at least and many live for three to four days; rarely, sperm can retain their fertilizing capacity for up to seven days. It is estimated that only two hundred sperm reach the egg; several will have the ability to penetrate the outer covering of the oocyte but usually one succeeds in fusing with the oocyte.

The World Health Organization has developed standards to try to differentiate by the use of semen analysis (see chart) those men who are fertile from those who are subfertile or infertile. The basic semen analysis provides an indirect estimate of a man's fertility, but many men with subnormal values have gone on to fathering children. As the values fall away from the norm, it is more likely that difficulties with conception will be seen. In general it is accepted that there should be at least 20 million sperm per milliliter (ml) of ejaculate, with 50 percent or more moving forward in their motility and at least 30 percent having normal shape or morphology. Because the average ejaculate volume is about 3 ml, the total motile count (the total number of sperm noted with motility) estimated for intravaginal deposition of ejaculated sperm could be considered to be about 60 million. From studies of women undergoing hysterectomy it has been demonstrated that only one of every 5,000 sperm placed in the vagina during sexual intercourse reach the cervical mucus and that only one of every 14 million sperm deposited in the vagina

Semen Analysis for Fertility

Liquefaction	Complete within 60 minutes at room temperature
Appearance	Homogeneous, gray opalescent
Odor	Fresh and characteristic
Volume	2 ml or more
pH	7.2–8.0
Sperm concentration	20 million or more spermatozoa/ml
Total sperm count	40 million or more spermatozoa per ejaculate
Motility	50 percent or more with forward progression (categories "a" and "b") or 25 percent or more with rapid progression (category "c") within 60 minutes of ejaculation
Morphology	30 percent or more with normal forms
Vitality	75 percent or more live sperm
White blood cells	fewer than 1 million/ml

reach the fallopian tube. As this can be only an estimate, the information from intrauterine insemination studies as well as pregnancy rates and respective semen characteristics can be helpful in determining what numbers of sperm need to reach the uterine cavity before conception is likely. A large series of 1,100 consecutive intrauterine insemination cycles showed that men with subnormal parameters had impregnation rates similar to the rates of men with normal parameters, provided the prepared specimen contained more than 300,000 motile sperm with at least 20 percent showing category "A" progression. Several authors noted that a higher count was more efficacious for pregnancy, but although one showed that there was not significant differences in pregnancy rates above a sperm count of 800,000, another showed the threshold value to be 1,100,000. Significant problems can occur with the other parameters of volume, motility, and morphology. Hypospermia is said to exist if the volume is less than 2 ml. In severe cases of hypospermia, the ejaculate is deposited away from the cervix and the sperm do not come in contact with the cervical os. The normal acidity of the vagina (which is detrimental to sperm function) needs to be counteracted by the alkaline seminal deposition: the small volume of seminal plasma with hypospermia may be inadequate to raise the pH of the upper vagina adequately. Motility is obviously important but there must be an adequate percentage with high forward progression: sperm may move to the appropriate place in the fallopian tube but must also have the required motility characteristics to break through the oocyte barriers and deposit the DNA contained within the oocyte itself. Although nature has provided a large buffer by having many abnormal forms in a normal ejaculate, there must still be a minimum number of normally formed sperm to expect conception. This is based on the assumption that those normally formed, motile sperm have the best chance of reaching and fertilizing the oocyte.

Stacy Elliott, M.D.

References

Berg, U., C. Brucker, and F. Dieter Berg. "Effect of Mobile Sperm Count after Swim-up on Outcome of Intrauterine Insemination." *Fertility/Sterility* 67 (1997): 747–750.

Campana, A., D. Sakkas, A. Stalberg, P. G. Bianchi, I. Comte, T. Pache, et al. "Intrauterine Insemination: Evaluation of the Results According to the Woman's Age, Sperm Quality, Total Sperm Count per Insemination and Life Table Analysis." *Human Reproduction* 11 (1996): 732–736.

Macleod, J., and R. A. Gold. "The Male Factor in Fertility and Infertility: VI, Semen Quality and Certain Other Factors in the Relation to Ease of Conception." *Fertility/Sterility* 4 (1953): 10–14.

Ombelet, W., A. Cox, M. Jansen, H. Vandeput, and E. Bosmans. "Artificial Insemination (AIH). Artificial Insemination 2: Using the Husband's Sperm." In *Diagnosis and Therapy of Male Factor in Assisted Reproduction,* edited by A. A. Acosta and T. F. Kruger. Pearl River, NY: Parthenon Publishing Groups, 1995, pp. 397–410.

Settlage, D. S., M. Motoshima, and D. R. Treadway. "Sperm Transport from the External Cervical Os to the Fallopian Tubes in Women: A Time and Quantitation Study." *Gamete Research* 12 (1995): 291.

Tan, S. L., and Howard S. Jacobs. *Infertility: Your Questions Answered.* New York: McGraw-Hill, 1991.

World Health Organization. *WHO Laboratory Manual for the Examination of Human Semen and Sperm-Cervical Mucous Interaction,* 3rd ed. Cambridge, UK: Press Syndicate of the University of Cambridge, 1992.

Emergency Contraception

The term emergency contraception acquired a different meaning in the last quarter of the twentieth century than it had earlier. In a sense, the condom since its invention could be regarded as an emergency contraceptive since it was available over the counter for emergencies. So could the sponge, the various foams, and the spermicides that appeared from the late nineteenth to the twentieth century. The current use of the term essentially refers to the use of hormones to prevent conception after a woman had intercourse without using a contraceptive or for some reason did not follow her oral contraceptive regime. Since at least the 1960s, clinicians had legally prescribed oral contraceptives "off-label" to prevent pregnancy after unprotected intercourse, but the first study to demonstrate the safety and effectiveness of postcoital contraception in women was published in 1974 by the Canadian gynecologist Albert Yuzpe. He tested postcoital contraception in women by giving them two tablets containing 0.05 mg ethynyl estradiol and 0.5 mg norgestrel after an unprotected act of intercourse. The first dose was administered within seventy-two hours of unprotected intercourse, followed by a second dose twelve hours later. The Yuzpe regimen was shown to prevent 75 percent of potential pregnancies. Other researchers demonstrated the effectiveness of this method but found the procedure to be even more effective when the first dose was given prior to seventy-two hours after unprotected intercourse.

Historically, however, drug manufacturers have been reluctant to market or label their products as emergency contraception, at least in the United States, fearing this might subject them to lawsuits, protests, or even boycotts. Despite this reluctance, in February, 1997, the Food and Drug Administration (FDA) declared the use of oral emergency contraception "safe and effective" in preventing pregnancy after unprotected sexual intercourse. The FDA then requested that manufacturers submit applications to market their products as emergency contraceptives.

In September 1998, the FDA approved Prevent (manufactured by Gynetics, Inc.), the first dedicated emergency contraception product. Sold in an emergency contraceptive kit, it consists of four birth control pills (each contain 0.05 mg ethynyl estradiol and 0.25 mg levonorgestrel), a home pregnancy test, and a detailed patient information booklet. The user is advised to take the pregnancy test first to make certain she is not already pregnant. If the results are negative, the woman is instructed to take two pills within seventy-two hours and the remaining two pills a few hours after the first two. If the pregnancy test is positive, the woman is instructed to contact her health care provider as soon as possible instead of taking the pills because they are not an abortifacient. A similar procedure can be used for a woman already on

the pill: the woman is advised to get instructions about emergency contraception when her original pills are prescribed because the dosages are similar, but vary slightly according to the type of oral contraceptive.

Hormonal emergency contraceptives act by inhibiting or delaying ovulation, disturbing the normal development or function of the endometrium and thereby rendering it inhospitable for implantation; or by altering the tubal transport of sperm or ova, thereby preventing fertilization. It is also possible that the thickening of cervical mucus may result in trapping the sperm, also preventing conception.

In July 1999, the FDA approved Plan B, the first dedicated progestin-only pill developed in the United States to prevent pregnancy after unprotected intercourse. Plan B (manufactured by the Women's Capital Corporation), is intended for women who do not want to take estrogen, consists of two 0.75-mg tablets of levonorgestrel to be taken twelve hours apart, the first within seventy-two hours of unprotected intercourse. Plan B seems to be slightly more effective than the combined oral contraceptive regimen, and its users experience significantly less nausea and vomiting than those using the combined oral contraceptives.

The only nonhormonal method of emergency contraception is the insertion of a copper T380A IUD within five days of unprotected intercourse. The IUD is believed to interfere with fertilization and implantation and may be removed after the next menstrual period or may remain in place for up to ten years for prevention of conception.

At the time of publication, these pills can be obtained without a prescription in Finland, France, and Great Britain, but not in the United States. Such a possibility, however, is under consideration by the FDA, which has already approved use of the pills with a prescription. The American Medical Association endorsed the concept of a nonprescriptive plan in November, 2000. The state of Washington has already enacted legislation to allow women without a prescription access to such pills twenty-four hours a day, seven days a week at pharmacies. Other states are considering such legislation. The National Right to Life Committee, which opposes the legal use of RU-486, has not opposed these so-called emergency contraceptives because they block ovulation, which occurs before fertilization. However, the Vatican has already gone on record in opposition to such pills, calling them abortifacients although the pills cannot interrupt an established pregnancy and are best taken within twelve hours of unprotected intercourse and not effective if taken more than seventy-two hours afterward.

In a pilot program that was run in Washington State from 1998 to 1999, women who had had unprotected sex within the previous seventy-two hours were able to go to a pharmacy, have a 15-minute consultation with a pharmacist, and walk away with emergency contraceptive pills. During the sixteen months of the trial, some twelve thousand kits were given out, and this is estimated to have prevented 720 pregnancies. Since roughly half of the unwanted pregnancies in the United States result in abortion, by inference, 360 abortions were prevented. There are some precautions that need to be observed: women who have a history of migraines or of blood clots probably should not take pills that contain estrogen. Whether a 15-minute consultation with a pharmacist should be required by law is debatable, although some medical discussion will probably be necessary. Another issue under discussion is the price. Women's groups have advocated that emergency contraceptive kits be priced at $20 or less, as insurance companies may not cover their cost.

The pills are safe and effective, but information about them has not been widely disseminated. Women in those areas where a prescription is required for emergency contraceptives should ask their physician to keep the pills in stock, fill prescriptions for them, or supply the information for emergency contraception established for their existing birth control pills.

References

Emergency Contraceptive Pills: Common Legal Questions about Prescribing, Dispensing, Repackaging, and Advertising. New York: Center for Reproductive Law and Policy, 1997.

Morris, Bobby J., and Cathy Young. "Emergency Contraception." *American Journal of Nursing* 100 (9 September 2000): 46–48.

Yuzpe, Albert A. "Ethinylestradiol and dl-norgestrel as a Postcoital Contraceptive." *Fertility/Sterility* 28(9) (1977): 932–936. *http://www.ec.princeton.edu*

Eugenics

Giving a new impetus to population problems in the last part of the nineteenth century was the growth of the eugenics movement. Though this movement grew out of the Malthusian concern over excessive population growth, the eugenicists voiced concern primarily about the high birthrates among the poor and the illiterate and the low birthrates among the more intellectual classes. The word "eugenic" was coined by Francis Galton in 1885. He defined it as an applied biological science concerned with increasing from one generation to another the proportion of persons of better-than-average eugenic, that is intellectual and health endowment.

Galton (1822–1911), a cousin of Charles Darwin and a major figure in nineteenth century science, had observed that the leaders of British society were far more likely to be related to each other than chance alone might allow. From a range of possible explanations for this occurrence, Galton came to believe that heredity was the answer. Galton did not take into account the importance of contraceptives, a subject about which he apparently knew little, but he was concerned that the wealthy and gifted, terms he used more or less synonymously, were not reproducing themselves. He concentrated on urging them to engage in judicious marriages and have large families, selective breeding so to speak, which would enable the superior heredity of the British ruling classes to retain leadership positions.

To support research in the new field, Galton first endowed a fellowship and later a chair at University College, University of London. The first holder of the chair was Karl Pearson (1857–1936), a brilliant mathematician and statistician. Pearson was convinced that environment had little to do with the development of mental or emotional qualities and that both were the result of heredity. From this assumption he came to believe that the high birthrate of the poor was a threat to civilization and that the "higher races" must supplant the "lower." His use of the term "race" in this context was synonymous with a family or group of people with similar aims and ambitions. By his definition, Jews could be considered a race, and so, for that matter, could the English or a subgroup of English. Though the English Eugenic Society, founded by Galton, eventually opposed Pearson's "racist" views, large sections of the eugenic movement had racist overtones, and the American eugenic movement, founded in 1905, adopted Pearson's view wholeheartedly.

At first the eugenicists were opposed to birth control because in their view too much family planning was being used by the well-to-do, but the Neo-Malthusians and eugenicists in England ultimately closed ranks to advocate birth control for all, although the eugenicists did so to prevent the ruling classes from being grossly outnumbered. When put in this way, eugenics gave "scientific" support to those who believed in racial and class superiority. It was just such ideas that Adolph Hitler attempted to implement by genocide, his solution to the "racial" problem and which ultimately made the term "eugenics" socially unacceptable.

Eugenics could appear to give family planning a scientific base—genetics as described by the Moravian monk, Gregor Mendel. For a time many biologists wrote as if for each trait there existed a determiner in the germ plasma; environment was of negligible importance because acquired characteristics could not be inherited; the determiners were "unit characters" and were inherited and varied according to the Mendelian ratios (Cravens, 1978, p. 41).

As a group, the American eugenicists believed that the "white race" was superior to other races and that within the "white race" the Nordic "white was superior to other whites." It was also assumed that upper-class people had superior hereditary qualities, justifying their being the ruling class. To document this assumption, eugenicists turned to "science" to support their interpretation. Intelligence tests, introduced in the early 1900s by Alfred Binet (1857–1911), for example, in spite of opposition by Binet himself, were held to be measures of innate, genetic intelligence. On the basis of such tests, the eugenicists classified all people whose IQs gave them a mental age of twelve as feebleminded, or "morons," without regard to the educational background or deprived environment that might have led to such test results. Criminality was considered a concomitant of feeblemindedness. Insane, feebleminded, and epileptic persons were often sterilized, either voluntarily or involuntarily, as were, in some areas, habitual criminals, "moral perverts," and others deemed socially undesirable.

Earlier studies, such as Richard Dugdale's study, originally published in 1877, of the ancestry of large groups of criminals, prostitutes, and social misfits over seven generations of the Jukes family, were reinterpreted by eugenicists to emphasize the hereditary component of their background rather than the environmental ones originally emphasized. H. H. Goddard, who speculated that feebleminded people were a form of undeveloped humanity, traced two branches of the Kallikak family in his 1912 study. One branch descended from a feebleminded tavern prostitute who had an illicit union with the founder of the Kallikak family and whose descendants continued to be the dregs of society and the other branch was descended from a woman who was a Quaker and whose progeny included only upstanding citizens. Later much of the data was found to be misinterpreted if not fabricated. Yet such studies served as the "Bible" of the eugenics movement.

Armed with the "new" findings, eugenicists mounted campaigns to have the "better people" reproduce more, whereas the "lower elements," that is, the poor, blacks, immigrants, and so forth, were to be encouraged not to produce so much. Much of the early contraceptive movement inevitably became involved with the eugenics movement. The ideal of the eugenicists was to improve the quality of the whole population and they attracted support from a number of private foundations and had considerable influence on the development of research in genetics, demography, economics, psychology, and sociology. As a group the eugenicists initially were ambivalent about birth control, although many advocates of birth control tried to use eugenic arguments to advance their own agenda, often at the expense of women's rights. Birth control was, however, never a major agenda of the eugenicists, although they gave support to clinics and defended the right of Margaret Sanger and others to disseminate information about contraceptives.

Increasingly as the excesses of the eugenics movement, particularly in Nazi Germany,

forced a rethinking of some of the concepts of eugenics, increasing numbers of its former supporters ended up in the birth control movement, particularly in the establishment of clinics. The flirtation of the birth control movement with the eugenics movements had a long-term effect and as late as the 1970s one group of black militants condemned all contraception as racial genocide.

References

Cravens, Hamilton. *The Triumph of Evolution: American Scientists and the Heredity-Environment Controversy.* Philadelphia: University of Pennsylvania Press, 1978.

Estabrook, Arthur H. *The Jukes in 1915.* Washington, DC: Carnegie Institution, 1916.

Galton, Francis. *Inquiries into Human Faculty and Its Development.* London: J. M. Dent and Sons, 1883.

Goddard, Henry H. *The Kallikak Family: A Study in Feeblemindedness.* New York: Macmillan, 1912.

Gordon, Linda. *Woman's Body, Woman's Right: Birth Control in America.* New York: Penguin Books, 1990.

Gould, Steven J. *The Mismeasure of Man.* New York: W. W. Norton, 1981.

Kevles, Daniel J. *In the Name of Eugenics: Genetics and the Uses of Human Heredity.* Berkeley: University of California Press, 1985.

F

Family Planning as a Right (United Nations)

The rapid rise in fertility rates, particularly in those areas of the world that suffered from inadequate economic, social, and resource development, led to growing agitation within the United Nations (UN) to do something about it. The result was the convening of the first international Conference on Population, held in Rome from August 31 to September 10, 1954. Four hundred fifty delegates representing a broad range of social and scientific disciplines met to discuss population growth and development issues. Study sessions met to hear and discuss papers on mortality and fertility trends, international and internal migration, population projections, and demographic statistics. Although there was no study group on family planning or birth control, two of the six observers were members of the International Planned Parenthood Federation, first formed in 1948.

At the second UN population conference in 1965, a section on family planning met to consider the benefits of conception control and representatives of the International Planned Parenthood Federation were again active. In 1968, at the UN Conference on Human Rights in Tehran, family planning was recognized as a basic human right for all people.

Fellatio as Contraceptive Technique

Oral-genital sex has an ancient history, and it was widespread in the Greco-Roman world. The question is whether it was deliberately used

EVERY CHILD a WANTED CHILD

MOTHER'S DAY
1938

This Mother's Day poster from 1938 contains a favorite slogan of the birth control movement, but family planning was not recognized as a right until thirty years later at the third United Nations conference on population in 1968. (Courtesy of Planned Parenthood)

as a means of birth control instead of simply foreplay or erotic arousal. Clearly it was and one of the early references to the use of fellatio as a deliberate contraceptive technique is in the writings of Saint Augustine (d. 430), who described the practice among the Manichaeans. The Elect, those Manichaeans who among other things had subscribed to a life of continence, pacifism, and refusal to eat any product of sexual union, often engaged in fellatio as a means of preventing conception, something they were also supposed to avoid. In fact oral-genital sex (both fellatio and cunnilingus) was regarded as ritual in which they ate human semen to free part of the God of Light still imprisoned in their seed. Some are said to have engaged in same-sex fellatio as well as heterosexual fellatio.

Other historical references to it are not always so clear that it was deliberately used as a means of birth control, but knowledge of it was widespread and the assumption is that it was. One of the best pieces of evidence is that many men in the past who turned to prostitutes as sex partners, often had them engage in fellatio with them.

See also Augustine, Saint

References

Brooten, Bernadette J. *Love between Women: Early Christian Responses to Female Homoeroticism.* Chicago: University of Chicago Press, 1996.

Bullough, Vern L. *Sexual Variance in Society and History.* Chicago: University of Chicago Press, 1976.

Fertile Period

One of the most discussed concepts in birth control literature is that of a safe period in the female cycle when a woman will not conceive. The problem with humans is that women do not have a notable estrus like the female of almost all other mammalian creatures. Although menses take place every twenty-eight or twenty-nine days in most women (a period that was early on associated with the moon), periods can be erratic and many women have longer or shorter periods and many have irregular ones. Thus the advice of most of the writers dealt with the ending of menstruation and usually advised a period of abstinence. The problem then is determining the end of menstruation, which is not always easy to do, but even if this is determined, it is not clear when ovulation takes place in most women. Occasionally there is something called mittelschmerz (literally middle pain), when the

egg has been expelled from the ovary and is still in the abdominal cavity, and this might be an indicator of the onset of the fertile period but, if so, it does not occur in every menstrual period nor in most women. It is therefore not a reliable marker and most women are not conscious of it.

In fact it was not until the twentieth century that it became possible to identify the time of ovulation. Usually this takes place about fourteen days before the onset of the next menstrual period but this is not particularly helpful to the women who are trying to determine their fertile period. Technically it was not until the 1920s when Kyusaku Ogino in Japan and Hermann Knaus in Austria independently identified the time of ovulation in the menstrual cycle that any kind of periodic abstinence held a better chance for controlling births than pure chance (Ogino, 1934; Knaus, 1934). It is necessary to calculate from the beginning of the latest menstrual period (which is easier to determine than its end). For women with any regularity, their fertile period begins usually about nine days after the menses began, but for women with irregular periods the issue is more complicated because they have to calculate from both the longest and shortest time periods to achieve any accuracy. Some calculations require more than two weeks of abstinence.

See also Sterile Period (Rhythm Method)

References

Knaus, Hermann. *Periodic Fertility and Sterility in Women,* translated by D. H. Kitchen. Hobart, IN: Concip Co., 1930. (It appeared earlier in German.)

Ogino, Kyusaku. *Conception Period in Women.* Harrisburg, PA: Medical Arts Co., 1934. (This is the English translation. It originally appeared in Japanese in 1924.)

Fertility in Males

Researchers at the British universities of Bristol and Brunel by using data from the Avon Longitudinal Study of Pregnancy and Childhood have found that male fertility begins to decrease after the age of twenty-four. The Avon study was set up to investigate the factors affecting the health and development of thousands of babies born in the period between April 1991 and December 1992.

Based on the data, the author found that the chances of a couple conceiving within six months of unprotected intercourse began decreasing by 2 percent for ever year that the man was over twenty-four. Even though fertility decreased in both sexes with age, there, nonetheless, was still an 85 percent chance on average of a couple in their mid-thirties conceiving within a year of attempting to do so.

See also Ejaculation and Pregnancy

References

"Biological Clock Starts Ticking for Men in 30s." *The Guardian*, August 1, 2000.

Food and Drug Administration (United States)

The United States entered into the contraceptive field only reluctantly. None of the early birth control devices except for the pessary could be patented, and though many devices and means were available, the Comstock laws made dissemination of them difficult. Often they were publicly sold as having other uses such as menstrual regulators or for disease prevention. This meant that there was little quality control, and this was especially true of condoms and other rubber articles but also even of intrauterine devices (IUDs). The Food and Drug Administration (FDA) early in the twentieth century did not classify contraceptive devices as drugs and those that were claimed they served other purposes.

Even after the repeal of the Comstock laws, FDA approval was not always easy to obtain. When Upjohn applied for FDA approval in 1967 for its drug Depo-Provera as an injectable contraceptive, it was denied approval because of the agency's concern over a lack of sufficient evidence demonstrating the drug's safety, particularly in regard to breast and cervical cancer. Upjohn appealed but the denial was reconfirmed in 1983. It was not until 1992 that Depo-Provera was approved in injectable form

by the FDA and by that time ninety other countries had approved it. An implantable contraceptive, Norplant, was approved in 1990, long after other countries had done so.

Condoms had no government control until 1938 when it was found that 75 percent of the condoms then on the market had small pinholes caused either by existence of dust particles in the liquid latex or because they were improperly vulcanized.

The FDA became more active with the passage of the Medical Device Amendment Act of 1976, extending the power of the FDA into setting standards (and thereby control) of many birth control items. The precipitating incident for this was the Dalkon shield tragedy. This marked the full-scale entry of the U.S. government into the contraceptive field because before this act there had been a lack of standards not only for various forms of contraceptives but for many new medical technologies entering the market in ever increasing numbers. The law stipulated among other things that manufacturers of all medical devices on the market before 1976 had to provide the FDA with data on safety and efficacy as well as proof that the device had been marketed in the United States before that year.

Most makers of contraceptives complied, but not all. Lamberts Ltd., the British manufacturer of the cervical cap (there were no U.S. manufacturers), failed to provide the requested data for reasons that are unclear, although probably it was the cost involved in collecting such data. The FDA had no alternative but to place the cap on its Class III list of devices—those that represent a significant risk to the user—and order the seizure of all cap shipments entering the country except for those used at centers engaged in FDA-approved research on contraceptives. Eventually the supporters of the cap, both consumers and physicians, gathered the necessary data, coordinating the research project through the centers comparing the use of the cap and the diaphragms. The project demonstrated that both devices gave equivalent contraceptive protection, and on May 23, 1988, the FDA announced its approval of the Prentif cavity-rim cervical cap for general use.

Earlier, in 1984, the FDA had approved the Copper T IUD after extensive testing, but even with the testing, G. D. Searle had withdrawn the IUD from the market for a time, fearful of legal suits. Injectable contraceptives were approved in 1992.

Because the FDA is a governmental body with many potential bosses, it is not entirely free of governmental interference, and it has not had a good history of approving abortifacients. In recent years, however, it has been more public about abortion and occasionally even acted decisively. In 1999, the FDA approved the use of larger doses of birth control pills as an abortifacient and in 2000, the agency approved Mifepristone (RU-486), although the second Bush administration may attempt to overturn that approval.

See also Emergency Contraceptives; Intrauterine Devices (IUDs); RU-486

References

Butts, H. E. "Legal Requirements for Condoms under the Federal Food, Drug, and Domestic Act." In *The Condom: Increasing Utilization in the United States,* edited by M. H. Redford, G. W. Duncan, and D. J. Prager. San Francisco: San Francisco Press, 1974.

Klitsch, Michael. "FDA Approval Ends Cervical Cap's Marathon." *Family Planning Perspectives* 20 (May/June 1988): 137–138.

Foote, Edward Bliss (1829–1906)

Edward Bliss Foote was the most important American writer on contraception in the last part of the nineteenth century. Born in a village near Cleveland in 1829, he became in succession a printer's apprentice, a compositor, and, while in his twenties, associate editor of the Brooklyn Morning Journal. He then went on to study medicine, graduating from the Pennsylvania Medical University in 1860 and setting up practice in Saratoga Springs, New York. He later moved to New York City. Like many others in the effort to disseminate information about family planning, Foote, in his adult years, had become an advocate of free thought.

Even before he received his medical degree, in 1858 he had written Medical Common Sense, in which he raised the topic of the "best ways to control reproduction." However, he had refused to discuss such methods in a public manner, informing his "married readers" that they could write to him enclosing one dollar, information about their temperaments, and their signatures, and he would send the information. Apparently emboldened by the response, Foote in his 1864 expanded and revised edition added more than one hundred pages devoted primarily to reproductive control and sexual physiology. He gave somewhat lengthy descriptions of four contraceptives that he claimed he had invented: (1) a "membranous envelope," a type of condom made from fish bladders; (2) the "apex envelope," a rubber glans penis cap; (3) a "womb veil," a rubber diaphragm; and (4) an electromagnetic preventive machine that Foote claimed prevented conception by altering the partner's electrical conditions during intercourse. The

American physician and journalist Edward Bliss Foote was a freethinker and advocate of family planning through his newspaper articles. (Archive Photos)

first three would have been effective but the last serves to emphasize just how much medical quackery was part of the practice of many American nineteenth-century physicians. The trouble with the first three, however, was the cost. Condoms were sold for three to five dollars a dozen, the womb veil cost six dollars. The penis caps were somewhat less expensive but the electromagnetic machine cost fifteen dollars. In various reprintings of his book Foote made slight modifications and in the early 1870s mentioned the rubber condom, one of the earliest such mentions.

With the passage of the Comstock laws in the United States in 1873, Foote ceased to print his *Medical Common Sense* but instead incorporated much of it, minus the actual contraceptive advice, in a longer medical advice book, Plain Home Talk. This was frequently revised and issued under a variety of titles but none of them included specific advise on contraception. Instead he told interested married people that they could obtain an important pamphlet on the subject for ten cents either in person at his office or through the mail. The pamphlet was a small, letter-sized one, originally entitled *Confidential Pamphlet for the Married* and later entitled *Words in Pearl*, because it was set in pearl type. It included much of the advice given in his earlier work (and some of the last printings of it mentioned the rubber condom). He was arrested in 1874 for selling such pamphlets and was convicted of distributing obscenity and fined $5,000.

Foote continued to publish somewhat more discrete works on reproductive control and other literature on health reform and forethought, and Janet Farrell Brodie called him the "most successful self-publisher" of the movement for reproductive control in the United States during the last part of the nineteenth century. Recognizing the importance of reaching women with his products, Foote emphasized in his publications both the ease with which women customers could obtain his products and the secrecy with which they could use them. He opened a "Sanitary Bureau," which became a distributing point for his products and publications, including many "not to be found in every respectable drug-store." His wife, Dr. Mary Bond Foote, was also a lecturer and crusader for birth control and women's rights. One of his sons, Edward Bond Foote, continued on in his father's footsteps and wrote his own booklet of contraceptive advice, *The Radical Remedy in Social Science; or, Borning Better Babies through Regulating Reproduction by Controlling Conception*. Another son, Hubert, managed his father's Sanitary Bureau for many years.

Foote was an ardent feminist, and his writings on birth control and sex emphasized women's rights. He believed that every woman had a right to decide just when and how often she would receive the germ of a new offspring. Foote occupied a unique position in the medical history of contraception in that he started as an irregular medical practitioner who won the respect of the established profession. Generally, however, regular physicians did little to advance the birth control cause either by advancing contraceptive technology or educating their female patients about the sexual and reproductive system. Although undoubtedly many physicians gave contraceptive advice or even performed abortions for selected clients, most of them publicly attacked birth control. In a sense they were the devoted guardians of sexuality and morality, but also self-appointed arbiters of situations in which exceptions might need to be made.

See also Comstock, Anthony, and Comstockery; Condoms

References
Brodie, Janet Farrell. *Contraception and Abortion in Nineteenth Century America*. Ithaca, NY: Cornell University Press, 1994.
Bullough, Vern L. "A Brief Note on Rubber Technology: The Diaphragm and the Condom." *Technology and Culture* 22 (January 1981): 104–111.

France and Birth Control

The first country to use birth control as a means of family planning was eighteenth-century France. By the 1830s the country's birthrate had

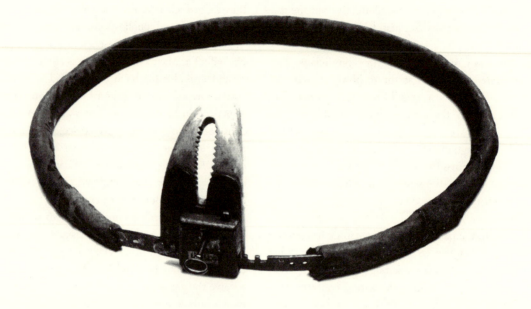

This seventeenth-century chastity belt from France would have deterred any man from attempting sexual intercourse with a young lady. (Bettmann/Corbis)

dropped below thirty per thousand, and most demographers today attribute the decrease to the French use of birth control methods. One of the first to speak out was the Marquis de Condorcet (1743–1794), who argued that it was not enough simply to give existence to future generations but also they must be given happiness, and it was foolish to encumber the world with useless and wretched human beings.

In many parts of France there seemed to be a kind of mind set against large families. This attitude appears in literature, particularly in that of some of the women writers. Some of the reasons appear to be economic: too many children meant that the family resources would have to be divided and minimized. At the same time there was a greater focus on children as individuals, and too large a family seemed to work against this emphasis on the child as an independent person instead of just a member of a unit. Sex for pleasure, instead of just for reproduction, was also being emphasized in the literature

of love. At any rate it became both fashionable and popular not to have very large families.

By far the most common method of birth control was coitus interruptus and detailed descriptions of the practice appear as early as the writings of Pierre de Bourdelles Brantôme (c. 1540–1614). Brantôme reported that the use of such practices allowed both partners to enjoy sex, although both had to be on the look out for the potential "tidal wave." We know that condoms, sponges, and astringents were also used. The sponges were to be soaked in brandy or wine before insertion. Mutual masturbation or interfemoral (nonpenetrative) intercourse was not uncommon.

The French decline in population has become an object lesson for advocates of birth control because it emphasizes that the attitudes of those involved, that is, a determination to have a small family, is an essential part of any effective birth control movement. It is not enough to offer contraceptive information, but rather the important thing is to convince people to want to limit their families.

One reason that many of the efforts of the last part of the twentieth century have concentrated on intrauterine devices, inserts, implants, and sterilization, methods that offer longer periods of infertility without the need of anyone to do anything, is that there are so many accidents through totally voluntary means, perhaps because the commitment of both partners is not as great as it should be.

See also Coitus Interruptus (Withdrawal); Masturbation

References

Fryer, Peter. *The Birth Controllers*. London: Secker and Warburg, 1965.

van de Walle, Etienne. *The Female Population of France in the Nineteenth Century: A Reconstruction of Eighty-Two Departments*. Princeton, NJ: Princeton University Press, 1974.

Freethinkers, Radicals, and Socialists

The earliest advocates of birth control in the United States were for the most part not mainstream medical men but secular reformers of various sorts: utopians, sex radicals, freethinkers, socialists, and others. Some of them used the "science" of the day to argue their case; others did so simply on the basis of women's rights. Many of those who would later be labeled as eugenicists believed that acquired characteristics were inheritable and this was interpreted to mean that a wanted child would be a better child than an unwanted one. Inevitably the goal of many of the advocates was to make motherhood better and more desirable. This goal, however, did not necessarily require the use of birth control devices and there were serious debates about this in the U.S. setting.

The contribution of some of these radicals was summarized by Ben Reitman in a poem he wrote to Norman Himes, who published the first general history of contraception:

My Dear Himes
You made me weep.

Because your article
On the history
Of Birth Control
was inaccurate
Superficial
"Highschoolish"
And you gave no evidence
Of attempting
To learn the facts.
You delved into history,
But failed to get data from living.
Moses Harmon
Was the true father of American Birth Control
His grand Children are living
And have lots of splendid material . . .
You "muffed" all the fine material
In the early Socialist, Anarchist & I.W.W. literature.
The tremendous amount of free Love literature
Passed you by.
There are several hundred pamphlets
On B. C. that you evidently know nothing about.
The technique of B. C. propaganda
In America is a Mystery to you . . .
I mean your prejudice against the
RADICALS
Is so great that you not give them credit.
Emma Goldman
More than any one person in America
Popularized B. C.
She was Margaret Sanger's Inspiration
No that ain't the word.
Margaret imitated her and denied her.
Emma was the first person in America
To lecture on Birth Control
in one hundred Cities . . .
The physicians, Social Scientists, Clergy & etc.
Became interested in B. C.
Only after the Radicals had "broken" the ground.
And gone to jail.
The inclosed pamphlet
Was distributed by the millions.
Free
In hundreds of Cities in America
It went through many editions

Was copied and recopied . . .
The decline in the Birth Rate
Was influenced by this pamphlet.
More than any other one piece of literature
Including Margaret's "Family Limitation" . . .
B. L. R. [Benjamin L. Reitman]
Was arrested
For distributing this pamphlet
In New York City (60 days)
Rochester, NY (freed)
Cleveland, Ohio (six months)
He was picked up by the police in many
cities
But was let go
Big Bill Shatoff
Who was an I. W. W. Organizer
Translated that pamphlet
Into Jewish and most all
Of the Radical Jews had copies
In the early days of the Communists' activity
In Russia this pamphlet
Had a tremendous circulation in Russia . . .
Get this into your Head
This all done as part of the radical
propaganda
Anti War
Anti Marriage
Anti Children by Accident. . . .
I see no hope for your Medical Scientific
group to make any real
Contributions to history or . . . (Quoted by
Gordon, 1990, pp. 217–218).

Probably the pamphlet Reitman referred to
was a four-page one, *Why and How the Poor Should*
Not Have Many Children. It is believed to have
been written by Emma Goldman or Reitman
himself, although it has also been ascribed to
William J. Robinson. It described condoms,
instructing the user to check them for leaks by
blowing them up with air, and it recommended
rubber cervical caps and diaphragms (also called
pessaries or womb veils), all of which could be
purchased in drugstores, although the pamphlet
encouraged seeing a physician before using the
cap and diaphragms to ensure a reliable fit. It
also suggested three homemade contraceptives:
suppositories, douches, and a cotton ball dipped
in borated Vaseline.

Reitman himself was for a time Emma Goldman's comrade and lover. He was a physician
and strong advocate of birth control and other
radical causes. Though Reitman and Goldman
gave specific information in defiance of the
law, Goldman had neither the personality nor
the organizational skills to develop a mass movement in the United States. That task fell to
Margaret Sanger, who, though she started as a
socialist and leftist, ultimately chose to act
independently of any left-orientated groups,
and though originally a freethinker, she also
distanced herself from the freethinkers as
well.

References

Gordon, Linda. *Woman's Body, Woman's Right: Birth Control in America*. New York: Penguin, 1990, pp. 217–218.
(The original poem is in the Himes manuscripts in the Countway Library, Harvard University Medical School, and dated February 13, 1937.)

G

Gamble, Clarence James (1894–1966)

James Reed, in his history of contraception in the United States, regarded Clarence James Gamble, along with Margaret Sanger and Robert Latou Dickinson, as the three major forces in the birth control movement in the first half of the twentieth century. Sanger, he believed, gave expression to a feminist impulse, the desire to give women control over their bodies. Dickinson, on the other hand, believed that the main threat to a stable family life sprang from poor sexual adjustment and he championed birth control as a means of strengthening the family. Gamble was concerned that the poor had more children than those higher up in the social scale and feared that this differential fertility between classes would lead to a welfare state or worse. Gamble devoted much of his energy and money to a search for contraceptives that did not require a physician's expertise for prescribing or fitting. The three often worked together. Their coalition was, in a sense, a fragile one because their own motives and causes had to be submerged in a pragmatic attempt to advance their own goals.

A physician, a millionaire (his family was the Gamble part of the Procter and Gamble Corporation), a dedicated Christian, Gamble started out as a medical researcher. His focus changed in 1929 when he became involved in the establishment of a birth control clinic in Philadelphia. His friends, Stuart and Emily Mudd, had opened the clinic as part of a program of the Committee for Maternal Health Betterment, which they had organized. They assigned Gamble the task of determining which of the contraceptive jellies would be most effective.

In 1929, Gamble also established a contraceptive clinic in Cincinnati, after which he began devoting himself full-time to birth control activities. After the success of the clinic in Cincinnati, Gamble went on to found one in Columbus and elsewhere. Initially he provided all the funds but gradually ceased this practice, insisting that the clinics do their own fund raising, which most did successfully. He supported Elsie Wulkop, a friend, as well as others as sort of missionaries for the establishment of birth control clinics. Even though Gamble was a physician, he opposed the medical monopoly on contraception and in 1934 persuaded the Committee for Maternal Health Betterment to do research directed toward finding better, cheaper, and more widely available contraceptives. He became chair of an American Medical Association (AMA) committee on contraceptives, which began publishing articles on condoms, jellies, and intrauterine devices (IUDs). He was a leader in having the AMA in 1943 define standards for contraceptives.

Gamble, even though a multimillionaire, lacked the resources of a Ford or Rockefeller Foundation. He wanted to initiate a variety of projects but also worried that some might defer to him only because of his money. His one inflexible requirement as a donor was that he be allowed to participate actively in the planning and execution of the projects he sponsored. He preferred a low public profile, but his desire to be part of the action brought him into conflict with those who wanted to mainstream the birth control movement. He often bombarded organizational officials with proposals that they ignored and he found himself in a struggle with the American Birth Control League over what they thought was his unwanted and mischievous actions and he was eventually forced out of the organization. He had similar struggles with the Population Council, the Clinical Research Bureau, and the Committee for Maternal Health Betterment. He often played the rival organizations against each other. When he could not get support for projects, he often went off by himself. For example, Gamble was instrumental in pushing for the IUD over the opposition of most of the professionals in the field. He also played an important role in expanding the testing of the oral contraceptive in Puerto Rico in the 1950s.

Increasingly pushed aside by many of the growing groups of professionals in the field, and as other groups and organizations took over tasks that he had originally started and funded, Gamble in 1957 established his own family foundation, the Pathfinder Fund, to carry out his work. It has since become one of the more important organizations in the field and its expertise has often been used by the U.S. Agency for International Development.

See also Dickinson, Robert Latou; Sanger, Margaret Louise (Higgins)

References

Reed, James. *From Private Vice to Public Virtue: The Birth Control Movement and American Society since 1830.* New York: Basic Books, 1978. (Reed's papers are in the Countway Library in Boston.)

German Medical Contributors

Generally in the nineteenth century, physicians from Europe and the United States as a group steered clear of discussing birth control and abortion. Individual physicians in England and the United States, mostly associated with free thought, utopian, or socialist groups, did write and give advice on the topics but the only organized mainstream physician group that dealt

with those topics in any detail in the nineteenth century was in the German-speaking countries.

Modern medicine might be said to have begun with the discovery of bacteria by Louis Pasteur (1822–1895) and Robert Koch (1843–1910). It was Koch who had the most significant influence on medicine, and his postulates for identifying bacteria causing diseases served as the basis of the medical revolution: (1) the organism should be found in each case of the diseases; (2) it should not be found in other diseases; (3) it should be isolated; (4) it should be cultured; (5) it should, when inoculated, produce the same disease; and (6) it should be recovered from the inoculated animal. Within a few decades causative agents were discovered at a rapid rate. Koch himself discovered the bacillus associated with tuberculosis and cholera. Not so surprisingly, many of the diseases associated with sex were also found to have a bacterial source. Albert Neisser in 1879 discovered the diplococcus of gonorrhea; Augusto Ducrey and Paul Unnas in 1889 found the bacillus causing soft chancre; and in 1905 Fritz Shaudinn and Eric Hofman found the *Spirochaeta Treponema pallidum,* the cause of syphilis; and with these discoveries, August von Wasserman, Neisser, and Carl Bruck were able, through a blood test, to document the existence of a syphilis spirochete.

Not all of the discoveries were made by German-speaking peoples but it was German-speaking physicians who expanded mainstream medicine into dealing with problems of sexuality. Probably the most influential figure in this endeavor was Richard von Krafft-Ebing (1840–1902), whose *Psychopathia Sexualis* opened up the study of variant sexual behavior. But it was not only variant sexual behavior that became an object of study but heterosexual activities and the problems of reproduction. Generally, as has been indicated elsewhere in this book, women played a secondary role in medical thinking. Most of the care of women and their problems often fell into the hands of midwives or other female caretakers, with male experts being summoned when more drastic interventions were needed, as in the case of breech or other difficult births. The development of surgical forceps by the Chamberlen family in England in the seventeenth century, a device that they kept secret for a long period, also enabled physicians to intervene much more effectively on difficult births. Some physicians began to specialize in gynecology and obstetrics, and their entry in full force was a result of two nineteenth-century developments, mainly the perfection of surgical anesthesia, and the new emphasis, following the germ theory, on aseptic techniques in child delivery.

Nineteenth-century German medical experts in women's medicine had been particularly concerned with questions of deformities of the reproductive organs in women and how to cope with this problem, which had a direct bearing on the question of contraception because it led to the question of what to do for women whose lives might be put in danger by pregnancy. One of the earliest of the modern German physicians to discuss the subject in some detail was Friedrich Adolph Wilde in 1838. Wilde believed that some form of birth control might be a medical necessity in such cases. After investigating the various methods used by women to avoid pregnancy, he believed that only four had any real potential: condoms, coitus interruptus (withdrawal), the sponge, and the cervical cap. The difficulty with the first three is that they were so often unreliable: condoms continually broke or tore, the timing of withdrawal was not an easy thing and this made it undependable, and the sponge was often misplaced. Wilde, therefore, advocated the use of a rubber cervical cap specially designed to cover the cervix and to be worn between menstrual periods. The cap for each woman was to be individually made, based on a wax impression taken of the os. The impression was then used as a model to make a rubber pessary. Whether Wilde invented the cervical pessary or adopted it from others is unclear but his is the first clear mention of it. As a last resort,

his final solution for those unable to achieve success with the other methods of contraception was the use of sterilization through the removal of the uterus.

New breakthroughs in rubber technology long after the death of Wilde opened up other possibilities. A method for making liquid latex was developed in 1853 that quickly supplanted the unvulcanized rubber that had been used for various inserts and devices earlier. The most influential writer on the subject was the German Dr. Wilhelm P. J. Mensinga of Flensburgh, and later a professor of anatomy at Breslau University. He sometimes used the pseudonym of C. or K. Hasse. Mensinga in his 1882 study used a latex cover for the top of the vagina. The cover was held in place above the pubic bone by a flat spring, similar to that used in the traditional wind-up spring alarm clocks. It was the Mensinga diaphragm that was later used by his student Dr. Aleta Jacobs, who had opened a contraceptive clinic in the Netherlands in 1881 in connection with her medical practice. The diaphragm was popularized in the United States by Margaret Sanger.

Other German physicians experimented with what came to be called intrauterine devices (IUDs), the development of which was based on the pessaries originally used to deal with prolapsed uterus and other uterine difficulties. Particularly noteworthy was Ernest Graefenberg (1881–1957), a German gynecologist who developed a ring of silkworm gut and silver wire, which might be called the forerunner of most modern IUDs. The difficulty with the early IUDs, as with any entry into the uterus, was the problem of infection. Few physicians prescribed such devices because most feared they would cause pelvic infection, and before the development of antibiotics such infections were not infrequently fatal.

Many of the later German physicians such as Graefenberg and Hans Lehfeld fled to the United States because of the Nazis, and they helped push American physicians into the area of contraceptive medicine. Both Graefenberg and

Lehfeld were significant advocates of the cervical cap. The rise of the Nazis in Germany undercut the German lead both in sexual medicine and in development of contraceptives, because many of the contraceptive pioneers were Jewish and because the Nazis promoted devotion to "kinder, kuchen, kirke" (children, kitchen, church) for non-Jewish women.

See also Cervical Cap; Coitus Interruptus (Withdrawal); Condom; Sponges, Tampons, and Vaginal Inserts

References

Bullough, Vern L. "A Brief Note on Rubber Technology and Contraception: The Diaphragm and the Condom." *Technology and Culture* 22 (January 1981): 104–111.

———. *Science in the Bedroom: A History of Sex Research.* New York: Basic Books, 1994.

Graefenberg, Ernst. "The Intrauterine Silver Ring." In *Report of the International Medical Group for the Investigation of Contraception,* 3rd issue, edited by C. P. Blacker. London: n.p., 1930.

Himes, Norman E. *Medical History of Birth Control.* New York: Schocken Books, 1970.

Mensinga, Wilhelm P. J. *Über facultative Stirilität,* 2 vols. Neuweid and Leipzig: Heuser, 1882.

———. *Das Pessarum Occlusivum und dessen Application.* Neuweid and Leipzig, Heuser, 1882. (This text is a supplement to the above referenced work. There were many reprintings and editions.)

Wilde, Friedrich Adolph. *Das weibliche Gebär-unvermögen.* Berlin: In der Nicolaischen Buchhandlung, 1838.

Goldman, Emma (1869–1940)

Emma Goldman was the pioneer woman advocate of birth control in the United States. Known as "Red Emma," she was an anarchist, rebel, lecturer, publicist, agitator for free speech, and feminist, as well as an advocate of birth control. She greatly influenced Margaret Sanger, who in her later life tried to ignore this, downplaying Goldman's role in her life, perhaps in part because Goldman was one of the most notorious women in America in the early part of the twentieth century and did not fit in with Sanger's concept of how the birth control movement should develop. Goldman was jailed in 1893 for nine months on charges of inciting a riot after she told a New York City crowd of unemployed workers to steal bread if they had no money to buy it.

It was while she was in jail that Goldman trained as a nurse, and after being discharged from prison she went to Vienna, where she picked up a certificate as a nurse and midwife. Returning to New York, she began delivering babies and became increasingly convinced of the importance of contraception. She founded *Mother Earth,* an anarchist feminist journal in 1906, and in it she emphasized the importance of women's sexuality and women's right to sexual pleasure. The first issue of Margaret Sanger's monthly, the *Woman Rebel,* in 1914, included an extract from Emma Goldman's essay, "Marriage and Love," urging the right of women not to have children if they did not want to, because they were not machines.

Goldman herself, who had often given lectures on birth control in 1915, began to include specific instructions on the use of contraceptives, including distributing her pamphlet, "Why

Emma Goldman, anarchist feminist activist, was one of the earliest American advocates of birth control, but was later looked down upon by the birth control "establishment" as too radical. (Library of Congress)

and How the Poor Should Not Have Many Children." She was first arrested in Portland, Oregon, for doing so, but a circuit judge set aside her conviction. She was later arrested in New York City for a similar speech and distribution of her pamphlet, and despite her impassioned courtroom speech in her defense, she was convicted and fined one hundred dollars or fifteen days in jail. She chose the jail term.

Birth control, however, was just one of her many causes. In 1917 she was arrested for opposing military conscription and sentenced to prison for two years. When she completed the sentence, she was stripped of her citizenship and she; her lover, Alexander Berkman; and 147 other "subversives" were deported to the new Soviet Union. Goldman quickly became disillusioned with the Soviet state and after a two-year residence there fled to England, where she continued her activities on behalf of women, contraception, and social causes.

In 1923 she published *My Disillusionment in Russia,* a libertarian critique of the communist regime, and in 1931 she completed, with the help of Berkman, her two-volume autobiography, *Living My Life.* She was allowed a brief visit to the United States in the 1930s, after which she returned to England. She died in Canada, where she had been working on behalf of the Spanish anarchists then fighting Spain's dictator, Francisco Franco.

See also Sanger, Margaret Louise (Higgins)

References

Drinnon, Richard. *Rebel in Paradise: A Biography of Emma Goldman.* Chicago: University of Chicago Press, 1961.

Goldman, Emma. *Marriage and Love.* New York: Mother Earth, 1911. (This was a pamphlet first printed in *Mother Earth* and then separately published.)

———. *Living My Life.* New York: Alfred A. Knopf, 1931.

H

Herbal Contraceptives and Abortifacients

A variety of herbs were believed by peoples in the ancient past to have value either as contraceptives or abortifacients. Some herbs were more effective than others, although effectiveness might well have depended on the dosages. Many of the herbs continued to be used in medieval and modern times and, although they were not always mentioned in the medical literature, there are hints of their usage elsewhere. This implies that in many ways herbs were known to women and midwives and their uses were often not publicized. This also meant that information about them could be lost—at least temporarily, because it was not usually committed to writing—and periodically rediscovered. Many of the herbs have been tested in the twentieth century and found to be effective, although some might be toxic if taken in very large amounts. John Riddle has explored them in some detail and much of the information in this entry is based on his research.

One ancient contraceptive might have been so effective that it became extinct. This is believed to have happened to silphium (a species of giant fennel, *Ferula*), which was widely used as an oral contraceptive in the Greek world and in the ancient Near East. Overharvesting caused its price to rise and by the first century of the modern era it was described as worth more than its weight in silver. Part of the difficulty was that it grew only in a thirty-mile band along the dry mountainside facing the Mediterranean sea and attempts to expand its rate of cultivation failed.

By late antiquity it had become extinct. Although it is impossible to measure its effectiveness today, silphium had a widespread reputation as both a contraceptive and an abortifacient. The standard prescription was for a woman to drink the juice from a small amount of silphium, about the size of a chickpea, with water once a month. It was also used as a menstrual regulator, a euphemism in many an ancient herbal book for abortifacient. Other forms of *Ferula* that are not extinct were also used and have been tested in modern laboratories, but they were not as prized by ancient peoples. One such form is astafeda (*Ferula assafoetida*), which was a common substitute for silphium in the ancient world. Its root sap is what gives the modern Worcestershire sauce its distinctive aroma. Crude alcohol extracts of astafeda and a related plant, *Ferula orientalis,* have been found to inhibit plantation of fertilized ova in rats, and these plants among other varieties seem to have been effective means of birth control in humans.

Sometimes, herbs widely used in some periods are not used in others, perhaps indicative of the nature of oral transmission. The seeds of the pomegranate, for example, were widely used to prevent conception in the ancient world and they are still used in India, East Africa, and the Pacific. Modern animal studies have demonstrated that the seeds do have contraceptive value. Female rats fed pomegranate seed and paired with male rats not fed it had a 72 percent reduction in fertility. Guinea pigs subject to the same diet had a 100 percent reduction. But if it was so effective, why was it not used in medieval or modern Europe or the United States? Perhaps simply because it was not grown in the more temperate climates and there was no widespread trade in it because its use was not known in Europe and the United States.

Listed alphabetically are a number of other herbs:

Aloe (*Aloe vera*) has both contraceptive and abortive effects, and although not so much used in ancient times, it was in later times. In an alcohol extract it apparently prevents implantation of the fertilized egg into the uterus, although its effectiveness depends in part on the dosage.

Artemisia is a plant that grows in widely different parts of the world. In the classical world it was regarded as the plant of Artemis, the goddess of the forest, hills, childbirth, and fertility. Artemisia is also an effective antifertility agent. In a 1979 test on rats, 10 mg of scoparone, a derivative of *Artemisia scoparia,* were fed to rats on days one through seven after coitus; the result was a 100 percent termination of pregnancy.

Asarum (*Asarum europaeum*) is closely related to birthwort and has similar medicinal qualities. The North American counterpart (*Asarum canadense*) appears in folk medicine as a contraceptive made from boiling its roots. It is mentioned in Greek writings and medieval writings as well, and is regarded as a way of inducing menstruation.

Birthwort (*Aristolochia*), a plant used in ancient Egypt to ease a difficult childbirth, also has contraceptive and abortive action. Aristolochia acid, derived from the plant, has been found to be 100 percent effective in blocking pregnancy in mice after a single oral dose on the sixth or seventh day after coitus, with few side effects. Stronger doses interrupted midterm pregnancies. Birthwort was also used to expel dead fetuses.

Celery (Apiceae family) was used as an oral contraceptive in ancient Egypt, and celery seed is found in many traditional medical systems in medieval Europe, India, and Africa. Celery seed apparently is not an effective contraceptive unless taken in very high doses.

Chaste tree (*Vitex agnus-castus*) was said by the Greeks to prevent an erection, suppress sexual desire, and serve as an abortifacient. Some Greek athletic trainers required their men to sleep on a botanical bed of chaste tree twigs supposedly to prevent an erection. Seeds of the chaste tree can cause an abortion if taken early in the pregnancy but are less effective later.

Dittany (*Dictamnus albus*), a herb of the mint family, was believed by the Greeks and Romans to induce menstruation and to expel a dead (or live?) fetus. It has both contraceptive and abortive effects. About 3 g of dittany seeds was given to terminate a pregnancy in the third month, less in earlier months.

Ferns are often mentioned as contraceptives and abortifacients in the pharmacological literature of the ancient world, although which ones are difficult to determine. The fern that Linnaeus called *Capillus veneris,* the hair of love, has been found to be an active inhibitor of egg implantation when taken after coitus. Ferns were also used in ancient China as a contraceptive and abortifacient, as they were in Hungary, New Guinea, and in medieval Europe.

Juniper (*Juniperus communis* or *Juniperus sabina*) appears frequently in ancient and medieval sources as both a contraceptive and an abortifacient. It was rubbed on the penis before insertion, inserted into the woman's vagina, or taken orally. It may also have some toxic side effects, but it remains one of the best documented of herbal remedies for unwanted pregnancies. The cypress (*Cyperus incompleteus*) is closely related to juniper and was regarded as a menstrual regulator as well as an abortifacient. The cypress has estrogenic qualities and was not only used in classical and medieval Europe but in Peru and Paraguay.

Mint (*Mentha*) has a number of varieties with antifertility qualities. Pennyroyal (discussed below), sage, marjoram, thyme, rosemary, and hyssop inhibit gonadotrophic or prolactin secretion and were used as early abortifacients or contraceptives. Usually they were boiled down with other spices such as juniper or cypress chips, mixed with a sweet wine, and drunk.

Myrrh (*Commiphora*) was recognized as an antifertility drug in the ancient world as well as an abortifacient. As of this writing, it still has to be tested in animals.

Pennyroyal (*Mentha pulegium*), a member of the mint family, when taken as a tea acted as an abortifacient. A number of modern animal and human studies have found that pennyroyal contains pulegone, which terminates pregnancies when taken in controlled amounts. This is because if it is taken in too large amount it is toxic to the liver. Because many of the ancient prescriptions are not very precise, pennyroyal might occasionally not only have aborted an unwanted fetus but also killed the mother. There must have been a lot of traditional information about the correct amount.

Queen Anne's lace (*Daucus carota*), sometimes called wild carrot, has a wide geographic range. The seeds, harvested in the fall, are a strong contraceptive if taken orally immediately after coitus. Extract of its seeds have been tested on rats, mice, guinea pigs, and rabbits. The action is such that the implantation process is disrupted and a fertilized ovum either will not be implanted or, if it has been implanted for only a short period, will be released.

Rue (*Ruta graveolens*) is another plant with a wide range. It has a very unpleasant odor and a disagreeable taste but it can cause an abortion. Extract of rue administered to female rats reduced the number of pregnancies from 20 to 75 percent depending on the potency of the extract administered. The active ingredient is chalepensin, toxic in high doses. Other members of the rue and related families, including *Murraya paniculata var. M. sapientum,* are equally if not more effective.

Squirting cucumber (*Ecballium elaterium*) was recommended in a Hippocratic treatise on women's problem as an effective abortifacient. Knowledge of it, however, was not carried over into medieval Europe, perhaps because it is not native to western Europe. Modern tests indicate that extracts of the plant prevent ovulation.

Willow (*Salicaceae* family) bark and leaves, often mixed with honey to lessen the bitterness, were taken in various kinds of concoctions to prevent pregnancy or cause an abortion The tree contains a substance (trihydroxyestrin) that is similar to a female hormone that interferes with ovulation and implantation. Willows belong to the same family as the poplar (*Populus alba*) and some older sources mention it as having contraceptive qualities also.

References
Bhargava, S. K. "Antiandrogenic Effects of a Flavonoid-rich Fraction of *Vitex negundo* Seeds: A Histological and Biochemical Study in Dogs." *Journal of Ethnopharmacology* 27 (1989): 327–339.

————. "Antifertility Agents from Plants." *Filoterapia* 59 (1988): 163–177.

————. "Estrogenic and Pregnancy Interceptory Effects of the Flavonoids of *Vitex negundo* Seeds in Mice." *Plantes medicinales et physiotherapie* 18 (1984): 74–79.

Chandhoke, N. "Scoparone: Effect of Reproductive Processes in Rats." *Indian Journal of Experimental Biology* 17 (1979): 740–742.

Dean, P. D. G., D. Exley, and T. W. Goodwin. "Steroid Oestrogens in Plants: Re-estimation of Oestrone in Pomegranate Seeds." *Phytochemistry* 10 (1971): 2215–2216.

Duke, J. *Handbook of Medicinal Herbs.* Boca Raton, FL: n.p., 1985.

Farnsworth, N. R., A. S. Bingel, G. A. Cordell, F. A. Crane, and H. S. Fong. "Potential Value of Plants as Sources of New Antifertility Agents." *Journal of Pharmaceutical Sciences* 64 (1975): 535–598 (pt. 1), 717–754 (pt. 2).

Gordon, W. P., A. C. Huitric, C. L. Seth, R. H. McClanahan, and S. D. Nelson. "The Metabolism of the Abortifacient Terpene, (R)-(+)-Pulegone, to a Proximate Toxin, Menthofuran." *Drug Metabolism and Disposition* 15 (1987): 589–594.

Guerra, M. O., and A. T. L. Andrade. "Contraceptive Effects of Native Plants in Rats." *Contraception* 2 (1974): 191–199.

Heftmann, E., S.-T. Ko, and R. D. Bennett. "Identification of Estrone in Pomegranate Seeds." *Phytochemistry* 5 (1966): 1137–1139.

Jöchle, Wolfgang. "Menses-inducing Drugs: Their Role in Antique, Medieval, and Renaissance Gynecology and Birth Control." *Contraception* 10 (1974): 425–439.

Khamboj, V. P., and B. N. Dhawan. "Research on Plants for Fertility Regulations in India." *Journal of Ethnopharmacology* 6 (1982): 191–226.

Kon, Y. C., C. P. Lau, K. H. Wat, K. H. Ng, P. P. H. But, K. F. Cheng, and P. G. Waterman. "Antifertility Principle of *Ruta graveolens*." *Planta Medica* 55 (1989): 176–178.

Murthy, R. S. R., D. K. Basu, and V. V. S. Murti. "Antiimplantation Activity of Isoadiantone." *Indian Drugs* 21 (1984): 4, 141–144.

Homosexuality, as this painting of Zeus abducting Ganymede depicts, was common in ancient Greece and served as a form of population control. (The Art Archive/Archaeological Museum Spina Ferrara/Dagli Orti, ca. 470 BC)

Prakash, A. O. "Potentialities of Indigenous Plants for Antifertility Activity." *International Journal of Crude Drug Research* 24 (1986): 19–24.

Riddle, J. M. *Eve's Herbs: A History of Contraception and Abortion in the West.* Cambridge, MA: Harvard University Press, 1997.

Riddle, John M., and J. W. Estes. "Oral Contraceptives in Ancient and Medieval Times." *American Scientist* 80 (1992): 226–233.

Saha, J. C., E. C. Savini, and S. Kasinathan. "Ecobolic Properties of Indian Medicinal Plants." *Indian Journal of Medical Research* 49 (1961): 136–150.

Sharma, M. M., G. Lal, and D. Jacob. "Estrogenic and Pregnancy Interceptory Effects of Carrot *Daucus carota* Seeds." *Indian Journal of Experimental Biology* 14 (1976): 506–508.

———. "Antifertility Screening of Plants. Part I: Effect of Ten Indigenous Plants on Early Pregnancy in Albino Rats." *International Journal of Crude Drug Research* 21 (1983): 183–187.

Thomassen, D., J. T. Slattery, and S. D. Nelson. "Menthofuran-dependent and Independent Aspects of Pulegone Hepatotoxicity: Roles of Glutathione." *Journal of Pharmacology and Experimental Therapy* 253 (1990): 2, 567–572.

Woo, W. S. "Antifertility Principle of *Dictamnus albus* Root Bark." *Planta Medica* 53 (1987): 399–401.

Homosexuality as Birth Control

Because sexual intercourse between members of the same sex cannot result in pregnancy, the toleration or encouragement of homosexuality and lesbianism can be regarded as a means of population control, if not birth control. Almost all humans have a bisexual potential, and how this is allowed to be expressed would, at least theoretically, have an effect on the number of children conceived. Thorkil Vanggaard, utilizing mostly unexplored Scandinavian material, hypothesized that all Indo-Europeans practiced at least initiatory pederasty until their dispersal among the various regions of Europe and Asia. Jan Bremer claimed that all European people, not just Indo-Europeans, engaged in same-sex practices and he traced the initiatory pederasty present in some Melanesian societies to ancient practices and customs. Bernard Sargent found the practice widespread among the Hellenes (Greeks), the Taifales of the Arabian peninsula, the Macedonians, the Albanians, more vaguely the Celts, as well as among many non Indo-European peoples.

The Greeks of the fifth century, who institutionalized pederasty, traced the origin of their custom to the ancient Minoans. Aristotle argued that the people on Crete institutionalized pederasty to cut down on the population explosion. This concept has been adopted by William Percy, who maintains that the system was deliberately instituted as a method of population control. A young man in his twenties took over the education and guidance of a young teenager of his own class and background, regarding himself as the boy's lover, and this relationship lasted until the age of thirty, when the older partner by law was required to marry. The younger man in return took another teenager into his care and guided him until he himself reached thirty. In some places such guardianship emphasized the development of the warrior individual but in Athens it became the vehicle of cultural transmission. It became an intense type of male bonding. It also acted as an effective population control because, as indicated elsewhere, the frequency of sexual intercourse is an important factor in pregnancy.

There were of course other alternatives to boys as loving companions, and the ancient world had a large variety of prostitutes, both female and male, to satisfy the man if he no longer sought sexual companionship with his wife and mother of his children.

See also Pregnancy Potential

References
Aristotle. *Politics* 1272A, edited and translated by Jonathan Barnes, 2 vols. Princeton, NJ: Princeton University Press, 1984. (In this particular translation the reference to homosexuality is somewhat more ambiguous than in some others.)
Bremmer, Jan. "An Enigmatic Indo-European Rite: Paederasty." *Arethusa* 13 (1980): 279–298.
Percy, W. A., III. *Pederasty and Pedagogy in Ancient Greece.* Urbana: University of Illinois Press, 1996.
Sulleres, Robert. *The Ecology of the Ancient Greek World.* Ithaca: Cornell University Press, 1991.
Vanggaard, Thorkil. *Phallós: A Symbol and Its History in the Male World.* New York: Cape, 1973.

Hormones and Their Delivery for Contraceptive Purposes

The first effective delivery system for hormonal contraceptives was the pill, but since then many other means have been used in the United States, from injections to inserts to IUDs to vaginal rings. Currently, other methods are also being explored or used in other countries.

Among the hormonal delivery systems used outside the United States is the Mirena levonorgestrel intrauterine device. This method is called an intrauterine system (IUS) by its manufacturers because it has a hormone reservoir that delivers a daily 20 mcg dose of progestin. It is currently in use by nearly one and a half million women in Europe, Asia, and Latin America. It is the single most effective method now available in the world, followed closely by the Copper T 380-A IUD. Among other things the Mirena IUS dramatically decreases menstrual blood loss, is beneficial in the management of fibroids (leiomyomata), the primary cause of hysterectomies in the United States, and may be used by women on estrogen replacement therapy as the form of progestin they need. It is also useful in the treatment of dysfunctional uterine bleeding. In the United States, Berlex Laboratories of Wayne, New Jersey, is leading the fight for Food and Drug Administration (FDA) approval.

Johnson and Johnson has also developed an intrauterine system in the form of a contraceptive patch. The Evra patch contains the same ingredients as birth control pills and is expected to work just as well. It delivers its hormones through the skin for the duration of a year. Cygnus, Inc., a Redwood City, California, company that specializes in developing drugs delivered through the skin, is also developing a similar product. Interested readers can best keep up with these developments in contraception in the newsletter *Contraceptive Technology Update.*

Reference

www.ahcpub.com/online.html

I

Implants

Implants, like the oral contraceptives, are based upon the administration of hormones and grew out of the same research. Research on an implantable contraceptive began in 1966, although it was not until 1974 that clinical trials were undertaken on a variety of progestins. The trials led to the decision to use levonorgestrel as the form of progestin for the new implants. The most widely known of the early implantables was Norplant, which, after undergoing a series of trials, was recognized as acceptable by Finland. Gradually other nations followed and in 1990 the U.S. Food and Drug Administration approved its use. Norplant is distributed by Wyeth-Ayerst Laboratories.

Under the Norplant system, six flexible capsules (originally they were hard), each about the size of a paper match, are placed just under the skin of a woman's upper arm. Each capsule contains 36 mg of levonorgestrel in crystalline form, and each capsule releases approximately 85 micrograms (mcg) per day, decreasing to 50 mcg per day by nine months, 35 mcg per day at eighteen months, and then 30 mcg per day for the third, fourth, and fifth years. The capsules are timed to release the contents over a five-year period, and for the first year only one woman in every five thousand becomes pregnant. The possibility of pregnancy increases as the Norplant insert ages, but it is still very low. There is a higher failure rate for heavier women (more than 154 pounds) than for those less heavy, but the failure rate has decreased with the use of soft capsules, now the norm.

The best time to insert the implant is when a woman is menstruating but certainly not later than five to seven days after the menses have begun. This ensures that the woman is not pregnant. The skin is infiltrated with a local anesthetic (usually lidocaine) where the implantation is to take place and then a small incision about an inch long is made and the capsules are implanted in an operation that lasts about ten minutes. The incision is covered with a dressing for three to five days. Insertion is not particularly painful for most women. For some, the implants may be visible. Removal of the implants is more difficult than insertion; the same procedure is used but it takes a little longer to locate and extract the implants. If there is not too much swelling or trauma, new capsules can be inserted to replace the old ones.

Implants eliminate the inconvenience of taking pills, positioning intrauterine devices, or inserting spermicides. They are also less expensive than oral contraceptives are and release hormones at a regular, even interval. Because they contain no estrogen, implants do not have any cardiovascular side effects. Infertility is reversed by removing the implants. All study patients ovulated within seven weeks after the implants were removed. Also, the implants can be used by women who breast-feed. Norplant II, an improved version, uses two rods instead of six.

Other inserts have since entered the market. Carpronor, developed by the Research Triangle Institute in North Carolina, also uses levonorgestrel. Carpronor is inserted under the skin of the arm or the hip and is effective for

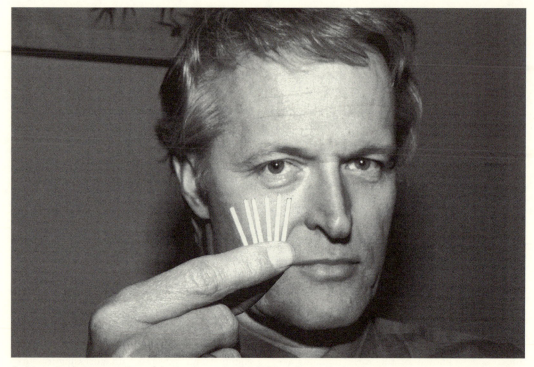

Dr. Wayne Bardin, vice president of the Population Council, holds implants, which when injected into a woman's arm release levonorgestrel, prohibiting conception for a period of up to five years. (Pat Benic / Corbis)

eighteen to twenty-four months. The Population Council developed a progestin and cholesterol pellet of 10 percent cholesterol and 90 percent norethindrone. The pellet is about the same size as a grain of rice and is biodegradable within twelve to eighteen months.

References

Hatcher, Robert L., et al. *Contraceptive Technology.* New York: Irvington Press. (Ongoing editions are published in even-numbered years.)

India and Birth Control

Hinduism, the dominant religion of India, distinguishes between two forms of sexuality. The first is sex for pleasure and procreation; the second is sex in its mystical and magical aspect. In the latter case, power is achieved by control over sexual activity. The first category forms the subject of much of Indian writing on sex, and sexual love is treated as one of the purposes of life and its enjoyment is extolled in numberless passages in Indian literature. Sex in its magical or mystical aspect is also prominent and, as in ancient China, there is great concern that the loss of semen might cause a man to lose his vital energy and sustain a spiritual loss. Two methods are employed to obviate these hazards. One is the ascetic method of absolute continence, and continence is one of the major virtues of the Hindu ethical code. The other method is the technique of nonspilling of the seed and involves the learned technique of coitus reservatus. In modern India, however, it is the concept of sex for pleasure that seems to dominate and the burgeoning population of India is fast heading toward the billion mark.

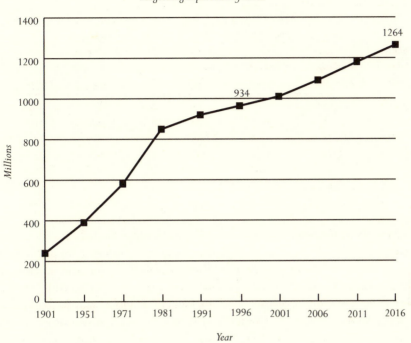

Figure I.1 Population Growth in India

Rapid population growth took place between 1951 and 1981 and was somewhat slower between 1981 and 1991. The rate of population growth has been 2.12 percent per annum and is estimated to grow not less than 1.5 percent per annum during the next twenty years because of the high rate of growth of the already large population base. The Indian population is a young population, with 36.3 percent under fourteen years old and another 10.8 percent between fifteen and nineteen years of age.

Population growth in India cannot be seen in a single and simple perspective because of the nonhomogeneous cultures present in the country. India consists not only of a huge population and a vast geographical area but also has nine major religions, sixteen major languages with four hundred dialects, and more than three hundred castes distributed over twenty-six states, each trying to preserve its separate identity.

As a result of this diversity, states such as Bihar and Uttar Pradesh demonstrate a high total fertility rate and low Human Development Index, whereas states such as Kerala and Tamil Nadu have a low total fertility rate with a high Human Development Index. This aggregate socioeconomic indicator tracks progress in longevity, education, and income as measured against life expectancy at birth, adult literacy, mean years of schooling, and income. The diversity of effects of these factors in India is obvious from Tables I.1 and I.2.

In the context of the heterogeneous character of the Indian population, the sociocultural aspects of life play an important role in population control. According to most anthropologists, culture encompasses learned behavior, beliefs, attitudes, values, and ideas that are characteristic of a particular society or a population. A case study of Kerala and Tamil Nadu on one hand and

Table I.1: Comparison by State of Population Indicators

State	Population in Thousands (1996)	Average Growth Rate in Percentages (1990–1996)	Median Average Age of Marriage 25–49 Female Age Group	High Order Births 4+% Age	Total Fertility Rate	Contraceptive Acceptance % 1991–1993 Spacing	Stopping	Couple Protection Rate
India	934,218	1.98	16.1	23.4	3.5	5.5	30.9	43.9
Bihar	93,005	1.48	14.7	33.7	4.6	2.9	18.6	24.7
U.P.	156,692	2.38	15.1	34.7	5.2	5.4	13.1	33.7
Kerala	39,065	1.24	19.8	6.6	1.7	6.1	48.3	55.4
Tamil Nadu	59,052	1.50	18.1	9.2	2.7	5.7	39.5	57.3

Source: Compiled by author from multiple sources.

Bihar and Uttar Pradesh on the other can elucidate this concept further.

Kerala, the best, and Tamil Nadu, the next best states on the Human Development Index, are both southern Indian states that have had historically very little Muslim influence. Kerala also never came under the influence of Brahmanic culture, in which women were denied education and most of the individual human rights. In Kerala, a predominantly matriarchal state ruled by progressive Indian rajas who always promoted education, a woman played an important role in social life. Today Kerala has the most educated population, with 98.6 percent enrollment in primary schools and 86 percent female literacy. Tamil Nadu, though next best, is not very close to Kerala in overall human development, that is, providing food, clothing, shelter, education, medical aid, and employment to every person. There was no Muslim influence in Tamil Nadu, which came in contact with the West in the nineteenth century. Fast spread of education thereafter helped to liberate Tamil Nadu from the suffocating Brahmanic culture.

Bihar and Uttar Pradesh on the other hand happened to be the hotbeds of Brahmanic counterrevolution, which threw Buddhism out. Bihar, the birthplace of Mahaveer and Gautam Buddha—both rebels against the Brahmanic culture—and the seat of the University of Nalanda (where scholars came to study from all over the East), fell under Muslim domination in the thirteenth cen-

tury, as did Uttar Pradesh. Traditional social life was smothered. Women were pushed behind the purdah and their development stopped completely. These two states continued to remain in the backwaters of India despite the fact that a number of India's national leaders hailed from these two states. Most of the population in Bihar and Uttar Pradesh remained in the clutches of landlords, both Hindu and Muslim. The result has been rampant child marriages, illiteracy, lack of economic development, and discontinuation of traditional beliefs and living styles.

Median average age of marriage in the age group of 25 to 49 years in Kerala is 19.8 and in Tamil Nadu it is 18.1, whereas in Bihar it is 14.1 and in Uttar Pradesh it is 15.1. In Bihar and Uttar Pradesh the total fertility rates are 4.6 and 5.2 per woman, respectively, which are higher than the Indian average of 3.5. Similarly, the high order birthrate (those with four or more children) is 33.7 and 34.7 in Uttar Pradesh and Bihar, respectively, as compared with 6.6 and 9.2 in Kerala and Tamil Nadu, respectively. Contraceptive acceptance in these northern states is also low. Even if we combine spacing methods and sterilization as methods of birth control, in Bihar the rate of women using birth control is 21.5 percent and in Uttar Pradesh it is 18.5 percent, with overall couple protection rates, respectively, of 24.7 and 33.7 percent. The two southern states have a contraceptive acceptance, respectively, of 54.4 and 45.2 percent, with a couple protection rate of

Table I.2: Comparison by State of Development Indicators

State	No. of Women per 1,000 Men	Life Expectancy at Birth 1989–1993 M	F	Adult Literacy 1981–1991 M	F	Maternal Mortality per 100,000 Births 1995	Crude Birth Rate 1992	IMR 1996 M	F	U5 MR M	F	Gender Related Health Index	Reproductive Health Index
India	927	59.0	59.7	62.4	33.9	453	29.1	78	78	119	132	49.82	42.21
Bihar	911	59.7	59.2	55.3	18.2	470	31.7	69	72	117	140	43.51	30.48
U. P.	879	56.5	55.1	53.6	20.6	624	36.0	91	102	145	180	33.39	22.80
Kerala	1,036	68.8	74.7	91.7	86.0	87	17.8	18	13	30	25	88.12	84.61
Tamil Nadu	974	61.4	63.4	65.0	35.8	376	21.8	58	56	79	84	1.21	63.60

Source: Compiled by author from multiple sources.

55.4 and 57.3, respectively. The female literacy rate in Bihar is 18.3 percent and in Uttar Pradesh it is 20.6 percent, and though life expectancy at birth for women has increased, the life of women has not changed—particularly in the rural areas. The political will to change the situation is generally nonexistent all over India and particularly so in Bihar and Uttar Pradesh. In these two states the percentage of people below the poverty level, 54.96 in Bihar and 40.85 in Uttar Pradesh, is also higher than that of the Indian average. All these figures clearly indicate that the general development of the population and particularly the education of women, the crucial factor in contraceptive acceptance, is particularly absent in these two states.

Even when one considers the falling death rate in India, it must be remembered that the death rate did not decrease because of betterment of life per se, but rather it resulted from the cumulative impact of modern drugs, effective epidemic control, and various vaccinations. The Human Development Index continued to remain low, emphasizing a lack of desire to improve the standard of living, a desire that is a key to motivation for reducing the birthrate through contraception strategies. Fault lies in restriction of literacy to only a very few upper class and caste people and a lack of serious efforts to dispel the deep-rooted fatalistic outlook held by the majority of the people who have been deprived of so much for so long. Unfortunately, even by the end of the twentieth century,

this vicious circle of ignorance, poverty, fatalistic attitude, and population growth has not been attacked, and the political leaders have not yet faced the fact that the problem of population growth in India cannot be discussed and managed in isolation but has to be a part of the human development program.

The techniques of contraception are not new to modern India. As early as 1921, Professor R. D. Karve, assisted by his wife Malati, started a Family Planning Clinic in Mumbai (Bombay) and helped many middle-class couples to learn the use of the diaphragm and condom. Karve also emphasized the importance of education in establishing better contraceptive practices, but his movement was primarily restricted to the educated middle class.

In the early 1950s, Pandit Jawaharlal Nehru, India's first prime minister, stated that the population problem was not just one problem but 400 million, at that time the population of India. He emphasized that population issues were part of the overall problem of development—providing food, clothing, shelter, education, medical aid, and employment for everyone. No Indian government has ever quite managed to tie all these elements together. When Nehru's government in 1952 officially adopted the Population Control Program and put it under the Ministry of Health, it was independent of development, that is, government efforts toward population control were separate from government efforts toward other areas of human development. The then-minister

A billboard advertises the family planning program in New Delhi, India. (Courtesy of Planned Parenthood)

of health promoted the rhythm method for preventing pregnancy. This was doomed to fail in an illiterate population that had no scientific knowledge of the menstrual cycle and so had no way to comprehend the concept of a "safe period."

Nongovernmental organizations (NGOs) became active in India. The first countrywide family planning NGO was started in 1952 by Dhanavanthi Rama Rau, who established the Family Planning Association of India, which popularized the use of the diaphragm and condom. These efforts were essentially clinic-based and included little patient education.

Successive governmental programs hardly made any headway in solving the population problem until 1965 when the intrauterine device was accepted officially as a contraceptive and the pill got recognition in 1966. Hospital-based training programs were undertaken to educate the medical profession and family planning officials. Cash incentives were offered to promoters, motivators, and acceptors. Oral contraceptives could be obtained from government hospitals or bought (at a high cost) on the open market. Female sterilization remained mainly a postpartum operation and the husband's written consent (which rarely was granted) was made mandatory.

In 1972, the Medical Termination of Pregnancy Act was passed, legalizing abortions for various reasons, of which "contraceptive failure" happened to be one. It was a virtual and blanket permission for abortion on demand. During 1975 and 1976, the family planning program received its severest setback. The government vigorously promoted (read "forced") vasectomy, giving cash incentives to promoters, clients, and medical personnel involved. Mass sterilization camps for both men and women were organized. Vasectomy centers were set up even on suburban and local railway platforms. The effort was soon perceived by much of the population to be a massive program of coercion and/or corruption, particularly in terms of the bonuses given to promoters and medical personnel. The negative impact of this period brought about the fall of the ruling government.

Since then, no political party has dared to actively propagate any intensive action regarding family planning. In fact, "family planning" was renamed "family welfare" and later became a part of the Maternal and Child Health Program. These programs then became part of the Child Survival and Safe Motherhood Program and later the Reproductive and Child Health Program. The association of family planning combined with development, proclaimed at least as an ideal by Nehru, disappeared, even though at the Bucharest World Congress on Population in 1974 the Indian delegation promoted as its slogan: "Development is the best contraceptive." The concept of family planning as an integral part of development efforts has remained neglected even today.

An overview of the governmental Population Control Program in the last three decades summarizes the attempts to spread some form of population control, though not always successfully.

1) Uniform and centrally planned program for the entire country is executed through the central government.

2) Existing state government infrastructure is used in varied sociocultural grass-roots environments.

3) Information about various methods of contraception is delivered through a health delivery network of 20,719 primary health centers and more than one million subcenters in rural India (1992).

4) Contraception information and methods are delivered by primary health care workers of different categories such as auxiliary nurse midwives, village health guides, community health volunteers, multipurpose workers, and traditional birth attendants. The terminology of these categories of workers varies at different places due to lack of coordination.

5) In urban areas these services are provided through a network of government or municipal (city) hospitals and clinics and also the urban welfare centers specially established for this purpose. Private-sector hospitals, clinics, and dispensaries also provide family welfare services.

6) Until as late as 1998, health practitioners at all levels were given targets for the number of intrauterine device placements and sterilization operations they were to perform.

7) Cash incentives are being given to clients and motivators.

8) Laparoscopic female sterilization has been promoted so much that vasectomy has stopped receiving any serious attention.

9) Media publicity is restricted only to slogans and so-called benefits of family planning. There are hardly any explanatory demonstrations of use of contraceptive devices, probably because of the (imaginary) belief of promoting permissive sexual behavior. No relevant educational programs such as sex education, marriage counseling, and contraceptive promotion are undertaken by the concerned agencies.

10) Cash incentives are given to couples getting sterilized after having one or two daughters.

11) Condoms are publicized more as an AIDS preventive measure than as a contraceptive.

It is possible that each one of the above actions could be counterproductive, or at least ineffectual, from the point of view of population control strategy.

Surveys of socioeconomic characteristics continue to demonstrate that the percentage of unmet needs for family planning remains especially high for the following segments of the population: rural men and women, illiterate women, illiterate husbands, Muslim women, tribal women, and women not yet exposed to media messages on family planning.

The unmet need for child spacing, however, varies according to age, number of living chil-

Indian women wait their turn at a birth control clinic. (Hulton Getty Collection/Archive Photos, ca. 1965)

Table I.3: Education of Husband and Wife and Average Number of Conceptions

Education	Number of Men	Percentage	Number of Conceptions	Number of Living Children
Nil	278	29.4	3.122	2.399
Primary	467	49.4	3.077	2.441
Secondary	154	16.2	1.9991	1.370
Higher	26	2.7	1.981	1.700
	Number of Women			
Nil	616	65.0	3.105	2.072
Primary	271	28.7	2.631	2.092
Secondary	44	4.6	2.009	1.705
Higher	11	1.1	1.454	1.173

Table I.4: Total Fertility Rate by Population Group

Annual Income in Rupees	TFR	Adult Literacy Group	TFR	Village Development Group	TFR
Up to 20,000	4.9	None Literate	5.3	Low	5.3
20,000–40,000	3.8	Female Literate	2.9	Medium	4.2
40,000–62,000	3.5	Male Literate	5.0	High	3.4
62,000–86,000 +	3.2	Both Literate	3.3	All India	4.3

Source: Shariff 1999. Reprinted with permission.

dren, number of living sons, and to some lesser extent by child loss. Dr. Radhadevi et al. found that among currently married women with unmet needs for family planning only 26 percent intend to use contraceptives for spacing. Of the 74 percent who did not intend to do so, 62 percent give as their reason that they want more children. This emphasizes that simply revamping the family planning services would not make much difference to contraceptive acceptance unless there are effective educational programs demonstrating the importance of child spacing.

In 1969 to gauge community perception about family planning, Streehitkarini conducted a family and fertility survey of nine hundred families in the slums of central Bombay. The survey demonstrated that women's education was the key factor in population control. The level of the woman's education influenced the number of conceptions as well as the child survival, both essential for reducing the need for more chil-

dren. Other studies have continued to emphasize the importance of female education, as Abusaleh Shariff reports in Tables I.3 and I.4.

It has been the experience of birth control workers worldwide that no educated woman would deprive her children of education. Education leads to self-confidence and enhances decisionmaking power, and this in turn leads to social change. Jawaharlal Nehru was correct many years ago when he emphasized the need to address development and population problems together. Social change in India is needed urgently. For more than two centuries Western experts have known that women play a crucial role in social change as well as in population growth. It is difficult not to connect greater literacy with rising hope and expectations. This transition has yet to happen in Indian society.

Other countries have faced the problem of controlling population growth more effectively than India has. For example, the experience in

A customer walks out of a birth control store in Calcutta, India (Archive Photos)

both Indonesia and Iran shows that family planning programs have to be an integral part of the national strategy for development. In the Indonesian program at least six ministries are involved. Ministers of health, religious affairs, information and broadcasting, education, industry, and the home ministry all work together. At no time were any incentive payments made to induce participation in the family planning effort. The only promise was that of a "small, prosperous and happy family" to those who become regular program participants.

In Iran total acceptance of all methods of contraceptives was only 37.0 percent in 1976 but by 1997 it had risen to 72.9 percent. The birthrate per 1,000 population was 43.4 in 1986, and in less than a decade it declined to 24.3, reaching 20 by the time it was presented to the Conference on Population and Family Planning at Tehran. Female literacy and other factors played a role in this success. In 1976 only 36 percent of the females above the age of six were literate but by 1996 this increased to 74 percent. For rural women it was 62 percent in 2000. More Iranian women are working or intending to work once they finish school, which also influences people's attitude toward family size. Perhaps the most important contribution toward the family planning program success has been the interest, support, and guidance of the religious leaders. Their backing developed within a context of the religious flexibility regarding social issues. There is little doubt about the effectiveness of the positive *fatwa* (direction given by Islamic leaders), originally issued by Ayatollah Khomeini in 1980, regarding the use of contraceptives.

These two examples from so-called underdeveloped countries should stimulate the Indian government to apply itself seriously to women's education and human development rather than merely to propagation of family planning services. NGOs should play a more meaningful role, not only in demanding more equitable laws but also in finding more innovative ways to bring about changes in education and health care systems. A few NGOs are working at this but, com-

pared with the size of the country and the population, they seem to be getting lost in the sea of ignorance and poverty. The innovations and experiments carried out by some of these NGOs are publicly applauded but never replicated or put into practice on a large scale, which could be done only by the governmental agencies. The fault lies with the bureaucratic and mechanical approach in training grass-roots personnel.

Dr. Ashish Bose, a demographer, has described India's family planning program as having three major gaps: communication, credibility, and creativity. The communication gap exists because the thinkers, intellectuals, sociologists, and workers have no direct communication with the illiterate masses. They instead depend upon the politicians to communicate the right message. The politicians, because of their vested interests, never talk adequately about the family planning program lest their outspokenness affect their vote banks.

The credibility gap exists because the belief in family planning programs in India is at a nadir because neither the politicians, bureaucrats, nor even the people who are likely to derive the benefit are taking responsibility for population control. The focus is misdirected when it is only toward the so-called Minimum Needs Program while development is ignored. Even the Minimum Needs Program remains mostly on paper.

The last gap that Bose describes is "the creativity gap," by which he means that we have failed to generate new ideas, look for innovation, and tackle bold initiatives, even at the cost of failure. The safe policy that is being pursued has taken its toll and made the Indian masses continue to live in misery and inhuman conditions.

In an interview in the *Times of India—Mumbai* on World Population Day, Indian scientist Dr. Vasant Gowarikar, former director of Vikram Sarabhai Space Centre and a member of the Central Population Committee of India, said

> The crucial breakthrough in India's population growth pattern occurred between 1981–91 when the birth rate declined faster than the death rate.

We are currently witnessing the first stage of transition, which will lead to a stabilized population growth by early next century. . . . When I claim that India has turned the corner it is a claim about choice [I mean] . . . people are increasingly choosing to have fewer children.

Gowarikar does not deny the valuable role played by literacy in checking the population growth but yet asserts the overriding role played by people's wisdom. He further says, "If we are given only two things to choose I would go on war-footing to make India fully literate and [give it an] energy surplus within three years." These two goals would help people without hurting any interest groups and ideology.

People's development is the crucial factor in population control. As the pioneer in contraceptive service, Dr. R. D. Karve, cited earlier, said more than fifty years ago, "No one will practice birth control to meet the danger of growth in population. People will practice it for their individual good." India needs, as Nehru said, to improve the quality of life of the individual. Providing education and making quality contraceptive services available to every person is a start. Crucial in this is upgrading the role and status of women. In the Streehitkarini survey in 1988, 98 percent of the women surveyed wanted to educate their daughters so that they would not have to face the same drudgery that they themselves had to. To be free to develop, a woman needs education, contraceptives, and an income of her own. This would start the much-needed social change that would help India to overcome the population crisis.

Acknowledgments

For assistance with this entry, I would like to acknowledge the contributions of Dr. Ramesh Potdar; Ms. Sanjeevani, Ms. Rajashree, Shri. Praveen; Dr. Sumati Kulkarni; Dr. Jeeban Mukhopdhyay, editor, Statistical Outline of India 1998–1999, Tata Services Ltd.; and Smt. Rupa Rege, Nitsure, ICICI.

Dr. Indumati Parikh

See also Condom; Diaphragm; Oral Contraceptives

References
Aghajnin, Akbar, and Amir Merhyar. "Activity in Islamic Republic of Iran." *Family Planning Perspective* 25(2) (June 1993): 102.
Bose, Ashish. "India's Quest for Population Stabilization: Progress, Pitfalls, and Policy Options." *Demography India* 18 (1989): 261–273.
Ember, Carol R., and Melvin Ember. *The India Report—Anthropology.* New Delhi: Prentice Hall, 1990.
Forward Looking Strategies for the Advancement of Women to 2000. New Delhi: Centre for Women's Development Studies, 1986.
Parikh, Idumati. *An Experiment in Community Involvement in Family Planning in Metropolitan Slums.* New Delhi: Center for the Study of Social Change, 1978.
Radha, D., S. R. Rastogi, and Robert D. Rethorford. "Unmet Need for Family Planning in Uttar Pradesh." *National Family Health Survey Subject Report No. 1.* Honolulu, HI: India East-West Center in Program on Population, 1978, p. 24.
Rohde, Jon, Meera Chatterjee, and David Morley. *Reaching Health for All.* New Delhi: Oxford University Press, 1998, pp. 482–488.
Shariff, Abusaleh. *A Profile of Indian States in 1990.* New Delhi: Oxford University Press, 1999.
Toward Population and Development Goals—UNFPA—United Nations System in India. New Delhi: Oxford University Press, 1997.

Infant Mortality

In the past, high infant mortality rates compensated somewhat for high birthrates. Although infant mortality figures of the past are notoriously difficult to determine accurately, our best estimates are that somewhere between 25 and 40 percent of the infants born before the nineteenth century did not live beyond their first birthday. In medieval Europe it is estimated that only about half of the population reached the age of twenty.

Adding to the statistics was infanticide. Although infant mortality certainly cuts down population growth, it is not a form of birth control. Still, considerable evidence shows that the high mortality rate of newborns and infants in many societies is not entirely a result of natural causes but has resulted from actions that would either consciously or unconsciously have led to a high death rate. This is not technically infanticide even though various practices subtly and some not so subtly are likely to lead to death. A good example of this is the practice of wet nursing as it existed in the eighteenth and nineteenth centuries in Paris and elsewhere. Infants who were in the well-to-do families and who survived the first three or four weeks (during which the mortality rate is the highest) were removed from the mother and sent to the country to be fed by other women who usually kept them for a year or so. Because wet nurses by definition usually had infants of their own to feed, and the parents of the boarded infant did not live nearby, the care varied tremendously and the mortality rate was very high, much higher than it would have been had the mother fed her own infant. One study estimated that of those infants sent out to wet nurses, some 25 percent died by the end of the year. This would put the infant mortality rate of French infants (including those who died before being boarded out) at the high end of infant mortality, that is, over 40 percent.

Other practices that put the baby at risk, such as sleeping in the same bed as the infant and accidentally rolling over on the baby, also were not infrequent.

See also Infanticide

References

McKeown, Thomas. *The Modern Rise of Population.* New York: Academic Press, 1976.

Sussman, G. D. "Parisian Infants and Norman Wet Nurses in the Early Nineteenth Century: A Statistical Study." *Journal of Interdisciplinary History* 7 (Spring 1977): 537–553.

————. "The Wet-nursing Business in Nineteenth Century France." *French Historical Studies* 9 (1975): 304–328.

Infanticide

Probably the traditional solution to threats of overpopulation or to unwanted children was infanticide, literally the killing of newborn babies. The anthropologist Ralph Linton wrote in a personal letter to Norman Himes that it was possible to argue that infanticide more effectively met the need of some groups than the practice of contraception, which at heart is practiced by an individual. Contraception results in an uncontrolled, hit-or-miss limitation of population. Infanticide not only made limitation to food supply certain, but also was a conscious way of exercising control of the sex ratio—important where there was a division of labor on sex lines. Linton held that infanticide in the past contributed to group survival in a certain state of cultural evolution.

Certainly infanticide was widely practiced and justified in a variety of ways. Linton reported that in Madagascar all children born on certain unlucky days were put to death to prevent them from bringing bad luck to their families. He reported that in at least one tribe all children born on three different days of the week were killed. Note that the infanticide was not necessarily regarded as infanticide but as a necessity for avoiding bad luck.

Many societies practiced infanticide in order to maintain their mobility rather than because of a desire to check population. In nomadic societies the problem of transporting small children is great and could possibly slow down the group to a dangerous extent. Some Australian tribes killed every child born before its elder sibling could walk. Among the Pima of Arizona a child born after the death of its father was killed so that the widowed mother would not be burdened with an extra child when she had to support her family alone.

The ancient Greeks also practiced infanticide, although usually rather than being killed outright the infant was abandoned. If it was found and adopted by someone, it was because the gods had willed that the child not die. The story of Oedipus is a story about just such a case. The practice also continued in Rome; although it was later made illegal in the third century, it was rarely prosecuted. Tacitus, for example, who wrote in the second century of the modern era, found it odd and foolish that the Jews did not practice infanticide. Early German law specified that the mother was entitled to decide whether or not to keep the baby. In the medieval period, infant abandonment, a form of infanticide, was not unusual, and though the Christian church later set up foundling homes to deal with the issue, most of those abandoned probably died even in the foundling homes. The very existence of such institutions, however, probably helped ease the consciences of the women who abandoned them.

Various reasons have been given by informants for justifying the practice. Some commentators on Polynesian culture reported that women had been known to kill their infants in order not to have to suckle them, as they wanted to preserve the beauty of their breasts. Probably most societies used different criteria. Many women exposed their babies to avoid the stigma of having a child out of wedlock, others simply felt overburdened, and for others the child was probably regarded as too sickly to survive. In eighteenth- and nineteenth-century France, infants in certain classes were sent out to wet nurses in the country to live away from their families until they were weaned. The mortality rate was exceedingly high but the family could justify the practice as in the best interest of the infant because conditions in the country were regarded as so much better than those in the city.

Police and others in Western countries regularly find abandoned infants, many of them still alive, although now it seems more an act of desperation than any well thought out process. If it occurs in today's world, when there are so many other alternatives, from active programs of birth control to abortion to adoption, it is perhaps easier to understand how peoples in other societies justified their actions.

See also Infant Mortality

References

Engels, D. "The Problem of Female Infanticide in the Graeco-Roman World." *Classical Philology* 75 (1980): 112–120.

Gordon, Linda. *Woman's Body, Woman's Right: A Social History of Birth Control in America,* 2d ed. New York: Penguin Books, 1990.

Linton, Ralph. "Letter to Norman Himes." In *Medical History of Contraception,* by Norman E. Himes. New York: Schocken Books, 1970, p. 52.

Shaw, Brent D. "The Family in Late Antiquity: The Experience of Augustine." *Past and Present* 115 (1987): 46.

Infibulation

Infibulation, the practice of the fastening of the prepuce or the labia with clasps or stitches to prevent copulation, has been used by some groups to prevent pregnancy. A nineteenth-century German physician and staunch Malthusian urged that boys, from age fourteen onward and until they had enough money to marry and found a family, be required to wear a ring through the prepuce. He advised pulling down the prepuce over the head of the penis and a lead wire perforating the prepuce be twisted, soldered, and stamped with a seal that would be retained so that the ring could be unfastened only when the stamp could be duplicated.

Actually such a method was described centuries earlier by the Roman medical writer Celsus, who reported that the Romans used such a practice. Two threads were drawn through the prepuce and moved backward and forward each day until two openings had been made into which a ring could be inserted.

Much more common in history and today is female infibulation, sometimes called female circumcision, Pharaonic circumcision, or perhaps more accurately female sexual mutilation. It is an ancient blood ritual of obscure origin and was described by western travelers such as Richard Burton in the nineteenth century. Among some peoples, partial or complete clitoridectomy is customary. Other groups additionally excise the inner lips of the vulva. The most drastic procedures are found among the peoples along the horn of Africa in Somalia, northern and central Sudan, southern Egypt, Djibouti, Mali, parts of Kenya, and Ethiopia. Here the clitoris is excised, the labia minora is removed, and the skin of the labia majora, scraped clean of its fleshy layers, is then sewn together over the wound. When the wound has healed, the labia are fused so as to leave only a small opening that is most valued by the cultures if it does not exceed the circumference of a match stick. The result of this procedure, which virtually obliterates the external genitalia and the introitus, is an artificially created chastity belt of thick, fibrous scar tissue.

The age at which a girl is subjected to the procedure varies from early infancy to the birth of her first child, depending on the prevailing custom in the area or tribe. In the last part of the twentieth century, however, the tendency is to perform the surgery at younger ages because a small girl is more easily managed.

When a girl has been infibulated, she must thereafter pass her urine and menstrual blood through the remaining tiny opening until her infibulation is partially torn or cut open when she marries. Giving birth is complicated by the infibulation scar, which in the most drastic cases prevents dilation beyond four of the ten centimeters usually required to pass the fetal head. The infibulation must therefore be cut in an anterior direction, and after birth has taken place it must be resutured. The birth process itself becomes progressively more difficult as scar tissues accumulate to hamper it. In effect the more drastic forms of infibulation are surgically induced means to prevent premarital intercourse, and afterward, to limit the number of pregnancies a woman might have.

Infibulation, in the societies that practice it, has been used as a measure that the woman is decent and respectable. Without being infibulated, a girl cannot marry, and an unmarried woman has virtually no rights in most of the societies where circumcision and infibulation are practiced.

References

Abdalla, R. M. D. *Sisters in Affliction—Circumcision and Infibulation of Women in Africa.* London: Zed Press, 1982.

Burton, Richard. *Love, War, and Fancy: Notes to the Arabian Nights.* London: Kimber, 1954.

Himes, Norman. *Medical History of Contraception.* New York: Schocken Books, 1970.

Lightfoot-Klein, Hanny. *Prisoners of Ritual: An Odyssey into Female Genital Circumcision in Africa.* New York: Haworth Press, 1989.

Injectables

Although injectable contraceptives, based on chemical formulations similar to those of the oral contraceptive, were developed soon after the pill, questions about their safety were raised in the United States while their lack of availability limited their use in most countries where different standards existed. The major exceptions were Indonesia and Thailand and their use gradually spread from these countries. It was not until 1992 that the first injectable was approved by the U.S. Food and Drug Administration (FDA). By 1995 more than a hundred countries had approved some form of injectable contraceptive and the list has continued to grow.

An injectable form of progestin had been developed by the German pharmaceutical firm Schering and appeared on the market in 1957 as Noristerat (the technical name was norethindrone enanthate), even before the oral contraceptive, but the battle for approval in the United States was waged by Upjohn, which had synthesized another form of progestin, medroxyprogesterone acetate (Provera), in the late 1950s and which they used in their injections. Clinical trials began in 1963 on the depot (i.e., injectable form), hence the name Depo-Provera. When Upjohn applied for FDA approval in 1967, however, it was denied. This occurred in spite of the fact that progestin-only contraceptives seemed to be very promising. The grounds for the FDA disapproval were that Upjohn had not presented sufficient evidence demonstrating safety with regard to breast and cervical cancer. Upjohn appealed the denial but it was reconfirmed in 1983 on the grounds that the beagle dogs used by Upjohn to test their injectables developed breast tumors, and endometrial cancers appeared in some of the monkeys used in the trial. The validity of the use of these animals was questioned by many, but it was not until the 1980s that several epidemiological studies could assess the risk of cancer on women using injectables in other parts of the world. The largest of these studies was the World Health Organization Collaborative Study of Neoplasia and Steroid Contraceptives, conducted in ten countries between 1979 and 1988. This study found that there was no overall increased risk of breast cancer, although young women had a statistically significant increase in breast cancer within the first five years. The injection, however, was not believed to have caused the cancer, although it might well have accelerated the growth of existing tumors because older women had no such increase. Another explanation is simply detection bias. Researchers were looking for breast cancer and perhaps found it earlier than they otherwise might have. There was no increased risk of cervical, ovarian, or liver cancer, and, as for endometrial cancer, the progestin injectables had a protective effect. As a result of these and other findings, the FDA in 1992 approved the use of Provera in its injectable form, and other injectables have since followed. Several of the newer ones are combinations of progestin and estrogen, similar to the combinations in oral contraceptives.

The progestin-only injectables include Depo-Provera and Megestron. Both have the same technical name, depot medroxyprogesterone acetate and require injection of 150 mg, but each has a different manufacturer. They are injected at three-month intervals (some countries use a weekly schedule; others, longer ones). They are the two most widely available injectables as of this writing. Noristerat and Doryxus are also progestin injectables but with a different formula, norethindrone enanthate, and require a 200-mg injection every two months, although in some countries injections are given every two months for the first six months and every three months thereafter.

The combination progestin and estrogen injections are usually given every month and are of lower dosages: 55 mg, 80 mg, and 160 mg, depending on the formulation. These combination injectables include Cyclofem and Cyclogeston, first available in Mexico, Peru, Thailand, and Guatemala; Mesigyna, originally registered in Argentina, Brazil, and Mexico; Pelutan, Topasel, Agurin, Horprotal, and Unco-Ciclo, available in many Latin American countries as well as Spain; and Anafertin and Yectames, also originally available in Latin America. The Chinese developed a progestin-estrogen combination that they call Chinese injectable No. 1. It requires two injections of 255 mg in the first month, and then one every month. Not all combination injectables

have been approved in the United States but, because their use is increasing, predictably more will be available. All require injection into muscle tissue without prior massaging.

Injectables are almost completely effective and have reliable reversibility. Once a woman desires to become pregnant, she quits taking the injection, although usually she has to wait several months for the pregnancy to occur, longer than those who go off the pill or have an intrauterine device removed. Side effects seem to be minor in most women, with most of the problems occurring in the first year, after which most women have normal bleeding patterns. Some report weight gain, and a small number report headaches, dizziness, abdominal discomfort, acne, and moodiness, all of which are plausible reactions to hormones.

References

Bullough, Vern L., and Bonnie Bullough. *Contraception: A Guide to Birth Control.* Amherst, NY: Prometheus Books, 1997.

Hatcher, Robert L., et al. *Contraceptive Technology.* New York: Irvington Press. (Ongoing editions are published in even-numbered years.)

"New Era for Injectables." *Population Reports,* ser. K, no. 5 (August 1995), vol. 23, no. 2.

Intercourse, Age, and Pregnancy Potential

Theoretically, when a couple engages in intercourse without using contraceptive methods (and the woman is not already pregnant), there is a 3 percent chance that pregnancy will occur. In simple terms this means that, on the average, pregnancy results once every thirty-three or thirty-four times the couple engages in random or unplanned intercourse.

Though we have little data for the frequency of intercourse for men in the historical past, Alfred Kinsey and his associates gathered some statistics that can serve as a more recent guide. They found that the greatest period of sexual activity in married American males occurs between the ages of sixteen and twenty. These data would be hard to replicate today because a much smaller percentage of males in today's world get married before they are twenty. That the male sex drive is at its height in the sixteen to twenty age group only emphasizes the difficulties of a program that stresses total abstinence as a way of avoiding teenage pregnancy. This age group in the Kinsey study engaged in intercourse more than 3.0 times a week compared with 1.7 times a week for the forty-one to forty-five age group. From this it seems clear that the age of the male partner has some bearing on how many pregnancies a woman will have, because not only is intercourse less frequent with older men but the sperm count also declines as men age. Similarly, the older the woman at marriage, the fewer pregnancies she will have because she is fertile for fewer years.

One form of birth control then is having men and women marry at considerably older ages than those in the Kinsey sample. This is the custom in Ireland and it was also the custom in ancient Greece and elsewhere. The older marriage age, however, assumed that the women, at least, will not engage in sexual intercourse until they are ready to marry. Such assumptions, however, are not usually made about the sexual activity of the man, who is free to visit prostitutes or engage in other forms of casual sex. The delay in marriage works most effectively in countries with strong double standards of sexual conduct or where government or religious control and interference in the private lives of its citizens is the greatest.

See also Age at Pregnancy

References

"Age at Marriage and Fertility." *Population Reports,* ser. M, no. 4 (November 1979), vol. 7, no. 6.

Kinsey, Alfred C., Wardell B. Pomeroy, and Clyde E. Martin. *Sexual Behavior in the Human Male.* Philadelphia: W. B. Saunders, 1948, pp. 336 and 356, tables 81 and 88.

International Meetings and Congresses

From the beginning of the twentieth century, there was an attempt to make the birth control message an international one. The first steps were initiated by the British, who kept the term "Malthusian," after their own Malthusian League, and some six International Neo-Malthusian and Birth Control Conferences were held irregularly between 1900 and 1925. These conferences brought together various individuals involved in issues of birth control and helped focus on some of the problems. For example, at the fifth conference, held in 1922, one of the issues discussed was the need for an accurate understanding of when in the menstrual cycle the woman was likely to be most fertile. The term "Malthusian," however, was repulsive to many. Moreover, eugenicists themselves were not united on the birth control issue since their purpose was to increase the birthrate of the "fit" and decrease that of the "unfit." Many were concerned that "selfish" women of the "fit" category would use birth control to limit their families and the "unfit" would refuse to use it. The sixth and last conference of the group was held in New York City and it was organized by Margaret Sanger, who increasingly was becoming the international emissary of the birth control movement. The New York conference led to the organization of the International Federation of Birth Control Leagues, a somewhat different concept because it emphasized the growing spread of the birth control movement.

Sanger was also the organizer of the first World Population Conference, held in Geneva in 1927. This conference brought together demographers, scientists, sociologists, physicians, and others, and two scientific organizations emerged from it, the International Union for the Scientific Study of Population and the International Medical Group for the Investigation of Contraception.

In effect, the birth control movement had become international. Further international movements and even meetings were handicapped, first by the depressed economic conditions of the 1930s and then by the onset of World War II.

Margaret Sanger organized many international meetings and conferences to promote her cause; here she meets with Mahatmas Gandhi of India. (Library of Congress)

In 1948, Sanger was instrumental in bringing together delegates from twenty-six countries to form the International Committee on Planned Parenthood. Four years later the group changed its name to the International Planned Parenthood Federation and Margaret Sanger was one of the honorary presidents. Other more specialized international groups also formed with special emphasis on fertility, population, sexuality, and other issues that impinged directly on birth control.

See also Eugenics; Malthus, Thomas Robert; Neo-Malthusians; Sanger, Margaret Louise (Higgins); Sterile Period (Rhythm Method)

References

Clarke, Adele E. *Disciplining Reproduction.* Berkeley: University of California Press, 1998.

Fryer, Peter. *The Birth Controllers.* London: Secker and Warburg, 1965.

Ledbetter, Roseanna. *A History of the Malthusian League, 1877–1927.* Columbus: Ohio State University Press, 1976.

Pierpont, Raymond. *Report of the Fifth International Neo-Malthusian and Birth Control Conference.* London: William Heinemann, 1922.

Intrauterine Devices (IUDs)

Intrauterine devices (IUDs) have a long history. Most of the early devices, however, were not technically designed for contraceptive use but rather as pessaries to be placed in the vagina with a stem extending through the cervical opening into the uterus. Although nominally inserted to correct uterine positions (prolapse or other difficulties), they also induced abortions as well as prevented pregnancies. In the United States, where technically contraceptive devices could not be patented, pessaries could, and in the last part of the nineteenth century many pessaries were widely advertised and clearly were used as a means of contraception.

Robert Latou Dickinson promoted IUDs as a contraceptive device in the United States as early as 1916. The devices were widely discussed at the Fifth International Conference on Birth Control in 1922, in part because of the efforts of Ernst Grafenburg, who began experimenting with various types of IUDs in 1909, although he did not begin publishing on the topic until the 1920s and 1930s. Grafenburg developed a ring of gut and silver wire that became popular in Germany in the 1920s. One of the feared problems with such inserts and the one that delayed their widespread use was the problem of infection. It was only after the discovery of antibiotics, from the 1940s onward, that a pelvic infection that might result could be dealt with easily. Earlier such an infection might well have become fatal.

Still, there was experimentation. In 1930, Tenrei Ota of Japan introduced gold and gold-plated silver intrauterine rings, which he claimed were both more effective and less prone to transmit infection than the Grafenburg device. Both inserts were used but after a period of initial enthusiasm both quickly ran into difficulty. The Japanese government for a time even prohibited the use of Ota's device, whereas Grafenburg abandoned his ring because of opposition of European physicians. It, however, continued to be used in Israel.

In the post–World War II era, encouraged by the development of the new antibiotics, more physicians began to experiment with IUDs. The major turning point occurred at an international conference on IUDs held in New York City in 1962 under the auspices of the Population Council. Physicians from the United States, Israel, Germany, and elsewhere reported on their favorable experiences with IUDs. Equally important as the ability to control infection in encouraging the use of IUDs was the development of polyethylene, a biologically inert plastic that could be molded into any desired configuration. It was flexible (thus easily inserted into the uterus) and could spring back after insertion to its predetermined shape.

One of the key figures in the development of a safe, functional IUD and in bringing about an attitude change regarding its use was Jack

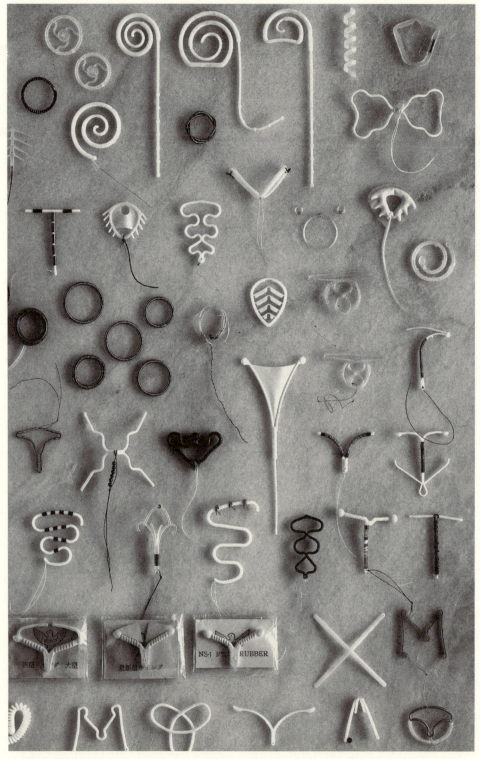

A display of intrauterine devices at the Museum of Contraception in Toronto, Ontario, Canada (Courtesy of Janssen-Ortho, Inc.)

Lippes, a gynecologist from Buffalo, New York. Influenced by the reports of the successful use of IUDs (19,000 using the Ota ring in Japan and 866 using the Grafenberg ring in Israel), Lippes inserted the Grafenberg ring—made from silkworm gut—on twenty of his patients. Lippes soon ran into problems, primarily when trying to remove the device, because it lacked a tail and required him to use an instrument similar to a crochet hook for retrieval. This worried him because in the process it might also scratch the lining of the uterus, increasing the risk of infection. Lippes experimented with the Ota ring as well and to aid in its removal he attached a string that dangled through the cervix. Although this facilitated removal, in about 20 percent of his cases the Ota ring would rotate, winding the string up into the uterine cavity.

As he continued his experiments, Lippes turned to polyethylene that he formed into a double loop with a monofilament thread of the same material hanging from it. Initially this caused some problems because the thread was difficult to see in the vagina, but after dying the thread blue he found he could see it and thus easily remove the IUD. The existence of the blue thread also allowed women to check that the device was still in place. Though there were other competitors such as the Margulies Spiral and the Binberg Bows, the Lippes Loop became the best known and most widely used device in developing countries outside of China. The loops were available in four types from the smallest, A, to the largest, D, and they served as a standard for evaluating other IUDs.

How IUDs Work

Originally, it was difficult to explain why IUDs prevented pregnancy. Animal studies were not as helpful as they could have been because the way IUDs prevented pregnancy varied from species to species. In sheep and chicken, they blocked sperm transport; in the guinea pig, rabbit, cow, and ewe, they interfered with the function of the corpus luteum (the yellow egg sac in the ovary that secretes progesterone). Obviously several things appeared to be happening at the same time. Ultimately research demonstrated that the IUDs had an effect on both ova and sperm in a variety of ways. The IUD stimulates a foreign body inflammatory reaction in the uterus, not unlike the reaction experienced with a splinter in the finger. The concentration of white blood cells, prostaglandins, and enzymes that collect in response to the foreign body then interferes with the transport of sperm through the uterus and fallopian tubes and damages the sperm and ova, thus making fertilization impossible.

Problems

Unfortunately, not all the IUDs marketed in the 1960s and 1970s were tested as thoroughly as the Lippes Loop. As drug companies tried to compete with each other, they often did not test the product themselves. A problem arose over the Dalkon Shield, a poorly designed, relatively untested device that was rushed onto the market by a major pharmaceutical firm, the A. H. Robins Company, to capture a share of the growing IUD market. Robins purchased the right to the Dalkon Shield, developed by Hugh Davis and his business associates in the 1970s. In rushing the Dalkon Shield to the market, Robins relied upon reports by Davis and his colleagues. Apparently most of these were not particularly accurate and were in violation of professional ethics because Davis was doing both the testing and the marketing. Though questions were raised about the Dalkon Shield almost as soon as it appeared on the market—insertion was particularly painful and there was a high rate of infection—complaints were initially ignored by Davis and his associates as well as by Robins. By 1976, seventeen deaths had been linked to its use, but Robins took no action until 1980, when it finally advised physicians to remove the shield from women who were still wearing it. The company's failure to act resulted in a large number of lawsuits, which ultimately led to Robins declaring bankruptcy.

In the aftermath of the Robins failure, other companies marketing IUDs were also sued, and although the lawsuits were not particularly successful, the liability insurance rates had risen so much that all companies in the United States ceased to distribute any IUD device for a time. The devices, however, were available in Canada and most of the rest of the world. A major reason for the difference between the use of IUDs in the United States and the rest of the world is that the United States is practically alone among the countries of the world in relying almost totally on private enterprise for its pharmaceuticals even though much of the research is paid for by the government. Obviously, private pharmaceutical companies want to sell IUDs for a profit. Because only a small percentage of American women used the device—approximately seven percent in 1982–1983—and because IUDs are long lasting, profits from any IUD after the initial adoption were modest. The Lippes IUD, for example, cost only a few pennies to manufacture, and though it required the services of a physician to insert, few drug companies would gain any profit from selling it, and it simply ceased to be distributed in the United States. One good effect of the Dalkon Shield episode, however, was that it led the U.S. government to finally establish standards for IUDs. Because they originally had been regarded as devices rather than drugs, they required no prior approval from the Food and Drug Administration (FDA), but they now do.

A second generation of IUDs—however, now with FDA approval—appeared on the market and the medicated ones promised a somewhat higher return to the drug manufacturers. Some of these released copper, other released steroids into the uterine cavity, having the same effect as the birth control pill. The copper devices had considerable advantages over the Lippes Loop because the copper devices are less likely to be expelled, produce less menstrual blood loss, are better tolerated by women who have not yet delivered babies, are more likely to stay in place after postpartum or postabortion insertion, and are slightly more effective. They originally needed to be replaced more often and cost more, hence allowing for more profit for the maker, but the newer ones such as the Copper T 308 has less than a 2 percent failure rate in the first year of use and is almost 100 percent effective after that for up to ten years. It is one of the most effective contraceptives ever developed. Interestingly it was approved for sale by the FDA in 1984 but it took several years before a company, Gyno Pharma, Inc., was willing to market it in the United States because of the Dalkon Shield incident.

The steroid-releasing IUDs release either progesterone or synthetic hormones called progestins into the uterus. The effective doses of steroids released from IUDs are substantially lower than doses required for oral administration, and the systemic side effects are less frequent. First on the market was Progestasert, which has a reservoir containing 38 mg of progestin, released at a rate that requires its replacement after one year. There is a longer-lasting IUD that releases 20 mg of levonorgestrel per day and has a reservoir holding up to a five-year supply. Others will undoubtedly appear on the market. Interestingly, the Lippes Loop is still widely used in many of the developing countries of the world.

Early studies indicated that an IUD increased the risk of pelvic inflammatory disease (PID), an infection of the upper genital tract that can cause infertility. Later studies indicated that the risk was usually limited to the first four months after IUD insertion and to those women who have been exposed to a sexually transmitted disease. The levonorgestrel IUD seems to be particularly effective against PID. There are contraindications, however. For example, a copper IUD should not be inserted into a woman who has a copper allergy or Wilson's disease (a rare inherited disorder of copper excretion). Women who fall into any of the following risk categories should not use the IUD: those who are pregnant or have had PID, those with a history of ectopic pregnancy, those with gynecological bleeding disorders, women in whom there is a suspected malignancy of the genital tract or a congenital uterus abnormality, or women with fibroids that prevent proper IUD insertion. Insertion of an IUD in the initial stage of a pregnancy will cause the fetus to abort. Women who have passed the menopause should have their IUDs removed because narrowing and shrinking of the uterus may make later removal difficult and increase the chances of infection. The user should also periodically check for the IUD string and return for follow-up care if she cannot locate the string or if she misses a period.

The IUD, in summary, is a particularly good choice for a parous woman (one who has been pregnant and delivered at least once) who does not want to be bothered with taking pills daily. In some women who have never been pregnant, an IUD increases the menstrual flow, causes pain, and irritates the cervix, thus making it a less desirable choice. The absence of the IUD from the U.S. market for several years was a result of panic on the part of the drug companies when the A. H. Robins Company was sued by so many people. The other IUDs were never banned by the FDA and the current devices on the market are safe and effective.

See also Pessary

References

Bullough, Vern L., and Bonnie Bullough. *Contraception: A Guide to Birth Control.* Amherst, NY: Prometheus Books, 1997.

Grafenburg, Ernst. "An Intrauterine Contraceptive Method." In *The Practice of Contraception: An International Symposium and Survey,* edited by Margaret Sanger and Hannah Stone. Proceedings of the Seventh International Birth Control Conference, Zurich, Switzerland, September 1930. Baltimore, MD: Williams and Wilkins, 1931, pp. 33–47.

Himes, Norman E. *Medical History of Contraception.* New York: Schocken Books, 1970.

Lippes, Jack. Interview by author in Buffalo, New York, 1987.

———. "PID and IUD." Unpublished paper presented at the World Congress of Gynecology and Obstetrics, Tokyo, October 1979.

Mintz, Morton. *At Any Cost: Corporate Greed, Women, and the Dalkon Shield.* New York: Pantheon Books, 1985.

Ota, T. "A Study on Birth Control with an Intrauterine Instrument." *Japanese Journal of Obstetrics and Gynecology* 17 (1934): 33–47.

Rybo, Goran, Kerstin Anderson, and Viveca Odlind. "Hormonal Intrauterine Devices." *Annals of Medicine* 25 (1993): 143–147.

Southam, Anna L. "Historical Review of Intra-Uterine Devices." In *Intra-Uterine Contraception,* edited by S. J. Segal, A. L. Southam, and K. D. Shafer. Proceedings of the Second International Conference, International Congress Series No. 86. Amsterdam: Excerpta Medica Foundation, 1965, pp. 3–5.

Tietze, Christopher, and Sarah Lewit eds. *Intra-uterine Contraceptive Devices.* Proceedings of the Conference, International Congress Series No. 54. New York City, April 30–May 1, 1962. Amsterdam: Excerpta Medical International, 1962.

World Health Organization. *Mechanization of Action, Safety, and Efficacy of Intrauterine Devices.* Technical Report Series 753D. Geneva: World Health Organization, 1987.

Islam

Islam could be classed as a sex-positive religion. Though Islam holds many beliefs in common with Judaism and Christianity, and many characters and events portrayed in the Christian and Jewish scriptures appear in the Koran, Islamic laws relating to marriage, divorce, fornication, abortion, contraception, and sexually related matters are different.

Abortion, for example, according to most Islamic theologians is acceptable as long as the fetus is not fully formed, usually determined as taking place 120 days after conception. Various means of birth control are also permitted providing it is acceptable to both parties. In recent times there have been a number of *fatwas* (legal decisions) to this effect issued by the councils of *ulamas* affirming traditional legal opinion on such matters. Ulamas are those recognized as scholars or authorities of Islam, namely, the imams of important mosques, judges, teachers in the religious faculties of university, and in general, the body of learned persons competent to decide upon religious matters, at least in Sunni Islam. In Shi'ite Islam, the ayatollah has more independent authority and can make autonomous judgments and statements that might vary from mainstream Islam or even from another ayatollah.

This tolerance of contraception allowed the Arabic medical writers (not all of whom were Muslims) to include much more discussion of contraception and abortion than existed in the Christian west.

Muhammad ibn Zakariya al-Razi (or Rhazes 860–921) in a section of his *Quintessence of Experience* reflects attitudes of Islamic physicians. He examined several approaches to birth control. One way is to prevent the entrance of the semen into the uterus. Among methods for doing this, he listed coitus interruptus and coitus reservatus. The uterine aperture could also be blocked by suppositories made up of a number of ingredients including ear wax from animals, tamarisk gum, the inner skin of the pomegranate, elephant dung, pitch, colocynth pulp, and ox bile.

According to Rhazes, a second way to prevent conception is to expel the seed. He advises applying to the os of the uterus drugs such as sal ammoniac, sugar candy (lead), potash, bamboo concretions, and other drugs that bring on the menses. He also advises the woman to rise quickly, sneeze, blow her nose several times, and call out in a loud voice. She should jump violently backward seven to nine paces, smell foul odors, or fumigate her vagina.

If this has failed and the semen has become lodged, he advises that the woman insert into her womb a probe and said the root of the mallow is a good source to make one from. One end of the probe should be tied to the thigh so that it may not penetrate too deeply. It is to be left there all night. The woman is advised not to use force, not to hurry, and not to repeat the operation. Other probes include those made of paper smeared with ginger and dried.

Other writers on contraceptives included the Persian Ali ibn Abbas (d. 994), who wrote an encyclopedic treatise of medicine, the *Almaleki,* or "Royal Book," which included a chapter on prevention of conception. Among methods that he advised to prevent conception was for the women to insert rock salt into her vagina or for the man to coat his penis with tar. Women also might use cabbage seeds, juice of rue, and leaves or fruit of the weeping willow. Probably the use of rock salt was effective because it acted as an astringent, although the tar (which the woman could also insert into her vagina) might also be somewhat effective.

Probably the greatest of the Muslim physicians was Ibn Sina (980–1037), known in the west as Avicenna. His *Canon of Medicine* served as the basic medical text in the west until well into the eighteenth century, and his section on contraceptives and abortifacients continued to be read in the nineteenth century. He advised coating the penis with white lead or pitch and putting the pulp of pomegranate mixed with alum into the vagina. Also recommended was a suppository made of willow leaves or, failing that, one made of colocynth pulp, mandrake, iron dross, sulfur scammony, and cabbage seed. Avicenna wrote that inserting pepper after coitus prevented conception. Elephant dung either by itself or as a fumigant was also recommended. According to John Riddle, Avicenna included all the contraceptives and abortifacients known to medicine and found in any of the other ancient and medieval sources.

Numerous other Arabic and Muslim writers wrote on contraceptives and abortifacients, and many of their works entered Europe first in Latin translations by Constantine Africanus (1085). Although Constantine included the sections on abortifacients and contraceptives, some of the copiers of his manuscript left out key chapters. Still, most of the data came into the West although Western medical writers did not always mention such things in their own writings.

Clearly the Islamic world knew about coitus interruptus and coitus reservatus, used a wide variety of suppositories or tampons, believed in a safe period for intercourse when pregnancy was not possible (but are not very clear on when that period was), knew how to do abortions and did them, but also recognized that there were a lot of things beyond their control. As a result they also usually included various magical procedures such as wearing an amulet or writing magical words on a piece of paper. There were also exercises of dubious validity such as jumping backward, sneezing, raising the thigh, or anointing the penis with various salves, oils, and juices. As in the Western world, it was probably the midwives who were most involved with disseminating contraceptive advice. They certainly were much freer to do so, and perhaps more knowledgeable, than their Western counterparts. At least in the Islamic world, knowledge was more readily available.

References

Bouhdiba, Abdelwahab. *Sexuality in Islam.* London: Routledge Kegan Paul, 1985.

Himes, Norman E. *Medical History of Contraception.* New York: Schocken Books, 1970.

Musallam, Basim F. *Sex and Society in Islam: Birth Control before the Nineteenth Century.* Cambridge, UK: Cambridge University Press, 1983.

Riddle, John. *Contraception and Abortion from the Ancient World to the Renaissance.* Cambridge, MA: Harvard University Press, 1992.

J

Jailed

Many birth control activists, particularly in the United States, were jailed for their advocacy of birth control. Linda Gordon estimated that at least twenty besides Margaret Sanger and her immediate group served some time in jail. Carlo Tresci, an Italian-American anarchist, was sentenced to a year and a day for advertising a book on contraceptives written in Italian in his radical labor paper, *Il Mantello.* Intervention by the American Civil Liberties Union got his sentence commuted after he served four months. Emma Goldman was jailed several times for giving out contraceptive information. Jessie Ashley, Ida Raugh Eastman, and Bolton Hall were arrested for distributing birth control pamphlets at mass meetings in Carnegie Hall. The police, however, were selective regarding whom they arrested, and Rose Pastor Stokes, who was involved in the same demonstration but whose husband was a millionaire, was not arrested because the police were fearful that her arrest would bring on a greater amount of unwanted publicity. Carl Rave was jailed in San Mateo for three months for selling Sanger's book, *Family Limitation.* When Agnes Smedley was arrested and sent to jail in 1918, she used the occasion to spread birth control information among the other prisoners. Ben Reitman served sixty days in New York and six months in Cleveland and was arrested in other cities but let go, all for distributing information about contraception.

Arrests took place not only in the twentieth century but in the nineteenth, when Charles Knowlton was arrested and so was Edward Bliss Foote. In England, Annie Besant and Charles Bradlaugh were arrested; others who were threatened with arrest lessened their activity. Generally, however, in the twentieth century it was those most associated with radical political movements who were arrested, including originally Margaret Sanger.

See also Besant, Annie; Bradlaugh, Charles; Foote, Edward Bliss; Goldman, Emma; Knowlton, Charles; Sanger, Margaret Louise (Higgins)

References
Gordon, Linda. *Woman's Body, Woman's Right: A Social History of Birth Control in America.* New York: Penguin Books, 1990.

Judaism and the Jewish Tradition

Coitus interruptus is mentioned in the biblical story of Onan:

> And Er, Judah's first born, was wicked in the
> sight of the Lord;
> and the Lord slew him.
> And Judah, said unto Onan, Go in unto thy
> brother's wife,
> and marry her, and raise up the seed to thy
> brother.
> And Onan knew that the seed should not be his;
> and it came to pass, when he went in unto his
> brother's wife,
> that he spilled it on the ground,
> lest that he should give seed to his brother.
> And the thing which he did displeased the Lord;
> whereupon he slew him also (Genesis
> 38:7–10).

Though this story has often been regarded as a prohibition against masturbation, the act described is coitus interruptus; moreover, the punishment seems to be not so much for spilling the seed as for the refusal to obey the levirate requirement that Onan take his brother's wife as his own. Not all commentators agree with this interpretation. Most importantly, however, the passage emphasizes that the ancient Jews knew about coitus interruptus, and that it was so publicized in the Christian Bible helped disseminate information about it to future generations of both Christians and Jews.

In Judaism, the Talmud (the collection of Jewish law and tradition consisting of the Mishnah and the Gemara) and the Midrash (a commentary on biblical texts) mention such things as abortions and potions for sterility frequently enough that it is evident that both abortion and some form of birth control were used by the ancients. Although Judaism emphasized the duty of propagating and expanding the tribe of believers, it also emphasized the joys and importance of sex and recognized that pregnancy is not always desirable. For the most part, Judaism put the burden of birth control on women, although not entirely.

Coitus interruptus seems to have been permitted at certain times. For example, Rabbi Eliezer, who flourished in the first century of the modern era, said that during the twenty-four months that women are nursing their babies, the man should "thresh inside and winnow outside." This tolerance of coitus interruptus, however, was to be permitted only under specific circumstances, otherwise it was condemned. Interestingly, however, other types of nonprocreative intercourse such as anal or oral, however, are not technically forbidden, although they are labeled unnatural.

Some rabbis suggested the use of a *mokh,* a spongy substance, and absorbent material, something like cotton, by women trying to avoid pregnancy. The Babylonian Talmud listed three categories of women who should use a sponge: a minor (a girl between eleven and twelve), a pregnant woman, and a woman who nurses a child. The minor was to use one because she might become pregnant and die; a pregnant woman, because the fetus might be compromised; and the nursing mother, because pregnancy might kill the child (*Yebamot,* 12b, 100b; *Ketubbot,* 39a; *Nedarim,* 35b; *Niddah,* 45a).

There was also a belief among some of the commentators that the semen once deposited in the vagina could be removed by violent movements, although this would not necessarily be very effective. Abortifacients were also known, as indicated by the story of Judith, the wife of Rabbi Hiyya. Judith came to her husband after a difficult childbirth and asked, "Is a woman commanded to propagate the race?" When he replied in the negative, she drank a potion that was held to make one sterile. When the rabbi learned of her actions, he complained that she had not given him one more birthing (*Yebamoth,* 65b). By implication, knowledge of potions must have been widespread, and some must have been fairly effective.

A kind of folktale in the Midrash tells how at the time of the great flood a man used to marry two women, one to give him children and another for sexual intercourse only. The latter took "the cup of roots," which was believed to cause sterility. Among other things the mixture included alum, an astringent. In general the Talmudic tradition is not against the use of contraceptives and does not forbid birth control, at least as used by a woman. It does require every Jew to have at least two children in fulfillment of the biblical command to propagate the members of the faith, but there are certain conditions when a man may be exempt from this, as when he is engaged in religious work and fears he may be hindered by the responsibilities of a family; or when a man, because of love or other consideration, marries a woman who is incapable of having children; or when a man is married to a woman whose health is such that it is dangerous for her to have children.

Some modern Jewish commentators, such as David Feldman, based on the passages cited above as well as others, have concluded that the Jewish tradition tends to support birth control and abortion, albeit with many qualifications. Many recent commentators agree with him.

See also Coitus Interruptus (Withdrawal)

References
Babylonian Talmud, edited by I. Epstein. London: Soncino Press, 1936 ff.
Feldman, David M. *Marital Relations, Birth Control, and Abortion in Jewish Law.* New York: Schocken Books, 1968.
Gordis, Robert. *Sex and the Family in Jewish Tradition.* New York: Burning Bush Press, 1978.
Himes, Norman E. *A Medical History of Contraception.* New York: Schocken Books, 1970.
Riddle, John M. *Contraception and Abortion in the Ancient World and in the Renaissance.* Cambridge, MA: Harvard University Press, 1992.

K

Kaufman, Alvin Ratz (1885–?)

Alvin Ratz Kaufman was president of the Kaufman Rubber Company in Kitchener, Ontario. Long an advocate of birth control services, Kaufman established the Parents' Information Bureau in 1931 to distribute contraceptive supplies to low-income Canadian families. In 1936, one of Kaufman's home visitors, who distributed such supplies, was charged with unlawfully advertising various methods of contraception. After a highly publicized trial, she was acquitted on the grounds that her action had served the public good. Kaufman was also instrumental in establishing birth control clinics in Toronto and Windsor, but as a result of higher costs and a smaller number of clients that could be reached, these clinics were closed in favor of the home visiting service. The Parents' Information Bureau was still operating in 1966 when Canada's House of Commons' Standing Committee on Health and Welfare held public hearings on birth control. The committee recommended that birth control be removed from the Criminal Code, that the wording of the Food and Drugs Act be amended to include contraceptive devices, and that control over marketing and advertising of contraceptives should be included in the Food and Drugs Act regulations. Such a bill was finally passed in 1969.

Brenda Margaret Appleby

See also Canada and Birth Control

Knowlton, Charles (1800–1850)

Charles Knowlton was the first person in the history of the birth control movement to go to prison for advocating and writing a pamphlet on birth control. It probably was the most influential nineteenth-century tract on the subject. Born in rural Worcester County in Massachusetts to a moderately well-off family, Knowlton attended the local school and was apparently a more or less average student. He began worrying in his teens about his proclivity for what we would now call wet dreams and was convinced that he had a serious illness. In his hypochondria, he consulted numerous physicians, and despite faithfully following their advice, he remained a pale, debilitated, nervous, and gloomy young man. He seemed to get better when he underwent electric shock treatment. He then married the daughter of the person who administered the shocks and made a quick recovery from almost all of his ailments. Inevitably he advised marriage as the remedy for the disorder that had afflicted him.

Knowlton studied medicine with various physicians, but believed he needed a better anatomical knowledge, so he broke into the local graveyard, took out a recently deceased subject, and dissected the corpse after first removing the teeth and any possible identifying marks. Apparently he continued to do illegal dissection because he later spent two months in jail for illegal dissections. His father paid more than $250 in costs to prevent his remaining there any longer. Knowlton went on to attend lectures at the Dartmouth Medical School, from which he received his medical degree in 1824.

Extremely ambitious, Knowlton conceived himself to be a new John Locke, and to demonstrate he wrote and self-published his book, *Ele-*

ments of Modern Materialism. When it did not sell anywhere near the 1,000 copies he had ordered, he had to sell all his household goods to satisfy his creditors. He returned to medicine and opened up a practice in Ashfield, a town of about 1,800 people in Massachusetts. Like many of the other nineteenth-century advocates of birth control, Knowlton was a freethinker who liked to scandalize the local churchgoers by playing his violin on Sunday mornings while they were going to church.

Early in his medical career, Knowlton had come to believe not only that young couples often suffered financial burdens because of too frequent births but that the too frequent births also led to ill health in the mother as well. He began giving out contraceptive advice and also wrote a manuscript that he handed out. He decided to make his advice available to a large public and in 1832 published anonymously in New York a booklet entitled *Fruits of Philosophy, or the Private Companion of Young Married People by a Physician.* No copy of the first edition is believed to have survived but there are extant copies of the second published in 1833. It was probably the most influential tract of its kind, although unfortunately his methods were not equal to his influence. Knowlton relied chiefly on douching, which consisted of syringing the vagina with some liquid soon after the male emission into it, which would not merely dislodge nearly all the semen, as simple water would do, but which would destroy the fecundating property of any portion of semen that remained (Knowlton, 1937, p. 60).

For a douching Knowlton recommend a solution of alum with infusions of almost any astringent herbs such as green pea, raspberry leaves, or white oak or hemlock bark. For some cases he recommended the use of sulfate of zinc in combination with alum salts. Actually alum would have been fairly effective as a spermatocide but the same cannot be said for zinc sulfate. He also recommended the use of salt water, vinegar, and bicarbonate of soda. For even alum to be effective it would have had to be used almost immediately after intercourse and even then it would not be entirely successful.

Knowlton urged his readers to pay careful attention to what he wrote because the subject was of such a great and abiding importance that it deserved study and pondering. He said that some people might believe that the knowledge of the practices he advocated would lead to illicit intercourse, but he replied that if a woman's chastity could be overcome, it could be overcome without the knowledge he wanted to impart. Knowlton said that some had also claimed that such practices were against nature, but he answered that civilized life was one continuous battle against nature, and birth control methods would not change that. Rather conception control would prevent overpopulation; mitigate the evil of prostitution; reduce poverty, ignorance, and crime; help prevent hereditary diseases and preserve and improve the species; reduce the number of artificial abortions and diminish infanticide; and prevent ill health caused to women by excessive childbearing or habitual abortion.

Knowlton had some difficulty in getting his book accepted. He was fined in 1832 at Taunton, Massachusetts, and in 1833 he was jailed at Cambridge for three months for attempting to distribute it. A third attempt to convict him in Greenfield, Massachusetts, led to disagreement between two different juries and the dropping of the case. As in many other cases of attempted censorship, the effect of his trial was to so publicize his work that by 1839 it had sold 10,000 copies. The book continued to be published throughout the nineteenth century, many times by free thought presses, and so popular was it that others used the title and basic content to add their own remedies to the book. The last authorized U.S. edition was published in 1877 but the book continued to be published in England after that. Knowlton himself more or less retired from the fray and in

1844 was elected a Fellow of the Massachusetts Medical Society. He continued to write articles on a variety of medical topics until his death.

References

Fryer, Peter. *The Birth Controllers.* London: Secker and Warburg, 1965.

Himes, Norman Edwin. *Medical History of Contraception.* New York: Schocken Books, 1970.

Knowlton, Charles. *Fruits of Philosophy,* commentary by Norman E. Himes and Robert Latou Dickinson. Reprinted from the 10th edition. Mount Vernon, NY: Peter Pauper Press, 1936.

M

Male Contraceptives

Research and discussion for much of history has concentrated on what the woman can do to avoid getting pregnant. Comparatively little attention has been given to men. Coitus interruptus and coitus reservatus have long been used by men, although the motivating factor was not always to avoid impregnating the female partner. The condom was originally conceived as a prophylactic, a way of avoiding sexually transmitted diseases, but it was also recognized that it had contraceptive value. Still today, the condom is recognized as much as a prophylactic device as a contraceptive one. In recent years, male sterilization has become an acceptable means of birth control, although sterilization surgery is less frequently done on men than on women.

Most of the recent research dealing with contraceptives for men has concentrated on either hormonal suppression of sperm production or chemical interference at the sites of sperm production. The key to hormonal suppression is controlling the luteinizing hormone and the follicle stimulating hormone, which regulate sperm production. One method is to deliver an agonist (an opponent) of the luteinizing releasing hormone, which will suppress sperm production. The problem is that when sperm production is suppressed so is testosterone production, which affects the male libido and potency and sometimes brings about changes in secondary sex characteristics such as breast enlargement. To counter this a synthetic androgen (MENT) was added but such a pill has not yet been approved by the U.S. Food and Drug Administration.

Experiments are also being conducted on an antifertility vaccine that neutralizes hormones required for sperm production or sperm maturation. The vaccine is combined with a MENT implant to provide androgen replacement needed for normal sex drive and behavior.

Androgens (male sex hormones) and two types of female sex hormones, progestins and estrogens, inhibit production of the pituitary hormones in men and thus control sperm production. Most promising are androgens given alone or combined with progestin. Two major problems remain, namely, that complete sperm suppression cannot be achieved in all men and the testosterone compounds tested so far must be given as weekly injections.

Experiments have also been conducted on levonorgestrel/testosterone enanthate and desogestrel/testosterone enanthate. Injections seemingly reduce the sperm count to nothing, but also allow it to return fairly rapidly when the person stops taking the enanthate.

A mechanical intervention being researched in India involves injecting a nontoxic polymer (styrene maleic anhydride) into the vas deferens to block the passage of the sperm. The blockage can later be removed by injection of another substance, dimethyl sulfoxide, which dissolves the first, and thus makes the procedure reversible, much more so than a vasectomy.

Research has also been carried out on plant compounds that interfere with male fertility. The best known of these is gossypol, derived from cottonseed oil and which inhibits an enzyme that has a critical role in the metabolism of sperm and

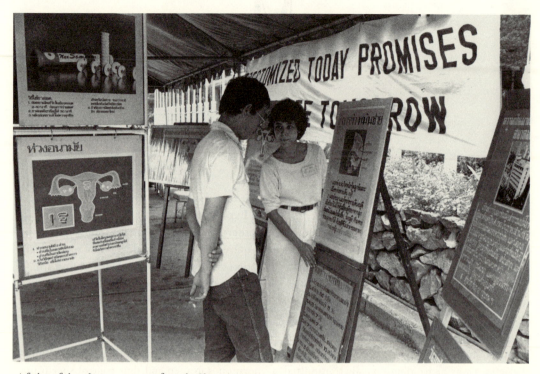

A father of three listens as a nurse from the Planning Association in Bangkok, Thailand, explains the vasectomies it offers for free to celebrate U.S. Independence Day, July 4, 1986. (Reuters / Apichart Weerawong / Archive Photos)

the cells that make sperm. Gossypol first came to attention as a potential antifertility agent as a result of an effort to explain extremely low fertility rates in a particular geographical area of China. Researchers eventually related the comparative sterility of inhabitants to the exclusive use of crude cottonseed oil for cooking. The oil contains the phenol compound gossypol, which is found in the seed, stem, and root of the plant and which inhibits sperm production. Clinical trials began in China in 1972 but two problems emerged in the longer term studies. First, some men developed hypokalemia (low potassium concentration in the blood), a problem that could be remedied by the administration of potassium. Second and more important, sperm production in some men did not resume when they stopped taking gossypol. Since then, the Chinese have taken to experimenting with other plants including *Tripterygium*

wilfordii, a vine native to southern China. Other botanicals are also being tested by other countries, but as of this writing none has entered the market.

See also Coitus Interruptus (Withdrawal); Coitus Reservatus

References
Hatcher, Robert A., et al. *Contraceptive Technology,* latest edition. New York: Irvington publishers, updated biennially.

Male Potential for Impregnating

If a man impregnated a woman every time he had heterosexual intercourse, he theoretically could have thousands of children. In reality this does not happen, although at least one man in history had more than a thousand children. The record holder seems to be the polygamous

Moulay Ismail (1672–1727), the last Sharfan emperor of Morocco. He was reported to have had 525 sons and 342 daughters by 1703, and in 1721 he recorded the birth of his seven hundredth son. Apparently by then he no longer bothered to record the number of his daughters. Because all of his children were considered legitimate, it was easier for him to keep track of them than for those men whose sexual activities had resulted in the casual fathering of children with a variety of female companions (Young, 1994). The western male with the most progeny might well have been Augustus the Strong (1670–1733), king of Poland and elector of Saxony. His nickname "The Strong" came from his ability in the bedchamber and not from his military skills. He was the father of 365 children whom he recognized, only one of whom was legitimate. One of the better known of his illegitimate offspring was Maurice de Saxe who became a marshal of France (Wolf, 1951).

References

Wolf, J. H. *The Emergence of the Great Powers.* New York: Harper, 1951.

Young, Mark C., ed. *Guinness Book of Records, 1995.* New York: Facts on File, 1994.

Malthus, Thomas Robert (1766–1834)

Thomas Robert Malthus (1766–1834), an English economist and demographer, is best known for his theory that population increases faster than the means of subsistence. Born in 1766 to a middle-class family that lived near Dworking, he was largely educated at home. He attended Jesus College and Cambridge University, was made a fellow of his college in 1793, and took holy orders in 1797.

In 1798 he published anonymously his classic, *An Essay on the Principle of Population As It Affects the Future Improvement of Society, with Remarks on the Speculations of Mr. Godwin, M. Condorcet, and Other Writers.* Malthus was an economic pessimist, viewing poverty as the inescapable lot of humans. Within the economic traditions of the time, he was a Liberal defending capitalism and regarding inequality and widespread poverty as inevitable and necessary to the maintenance of a high culture. Opposed to him were the traditional mercantilists, who sought to secure a nation's supremacy over other states by the accumulation of precious metals and by exporting the largest possible quantity of products while importing as little as possible. But within the advocates of capitalism he also had opponents who had a more democratic and somewhat egalitarian version of liberalism; this radical wing was far more optimistic than was Malthus, daring to assert the possibility of the perfection of society.

In the first edition of his work, Malthus rather crudely argued that infinite hopes for social happiness are vain because population will always tend to outrun the growth of production and the increase of population will take place, if unchecked, in a geometrical progression (1, 2, 4, 8, 16), whereas the means of subsistence could increase only arithmetically (1, 2, 3, 4, 5). When population had reached the limit of its expansion, it would be held in check by famine, war, and ill health.

He expanded on his ideas in subsequent editions of his book (there were six) and by his sixth edition, published in 1826, Malthus had added much factual material and illustrations of his thesis, but his logic was often faulty and his handling of actual data was not very sophisticated. For example, his claim that deliberate birth limitation could not work had already been proven false in France, where birthrates had been falling for many decades. His data never had the empirical validity that he claimed but his theories nonetheless had great significance and served as a justification for forcing laborers into jobs at subsistence wages since this was just an inevitable result of natural laws. His influence was most felt in the British Poor Laws of 1834, which abolished "outdoor relief," forcing the poor either to enter workhouses or to take low-paying factory jobs.

It was Malthus, however, who first set Charles Darwin on the path of reasoning that led to his principle of natural selection. Malthus is also one of the founders of demography. His economic ideas were incorporated into the system of David Ricardo and used to justify a theory of wages that made the minimum cost of subsistence of the wage earner a standard of judgment and discouraged charity.

In spite of his views that any intervention into the reproductive life cycle was a vice to be deplored, he was unintentionally one of the founders of the birth control movement. His only solution to the problems he raised was the adoption of moral restraint, that is, abstinence and later marriages. Those who came to believe, as he did, that overpopulation was a major cause of poverty but who wanted to intervene more directly through birth control to limit such growth called themselves Neo-Malthusians and were regarded as being in opposition to the "true" Malthusians.

The early Neo-Malthusian movement was a low-key propaganda effort by men active in other radical causes as well, such as trade unionism and worker education. The Neo-Malthusian movement had great influence in Britain and dominated the British birth control movement until well into the twentieth century. It had somewhat less influence in the United States, however. Many of the Neo-Malthusians also became associated with the eugenics movement.

See also Eugenics; Neo-Malthusians

References

Malthus, Thomas R. *An Essay on the Principle of Population As It Affects the Future Improvements of Society, with Remarks on the Speculations of Mr. Godwin, M. Condorcet, and Other Writers.* London: Johnson, 1986 [1798].

Smith, Kenneth, *The Malthusian Controversy.* London: Routledge and Kegan Paul, 1951.

Masturbation

Masturbation can be defined in various ways, and though it can involve more than one person, it is most simply defined as any action of deliberate self-stimulation that brings about sexual arousal. Such stimulation may or may not be pursued to the point of orgasm, and it may not even have orgasm as its ultimate objective. In the past, etymologists generally held that the word "masturbation" had been formed from a combination of the Latin words *manus,* meaning hand, and *stuprare,* meaning to defile. This seems to impart a negative judgment to the practice, which the Romans would not have done. As a result, many modern etymologists link *manus* with the Latin verb *turbare,* meaning to agitate, disturb, or arouse, a more descriptive term.

What we mean by masturbation today, however, is not necessarily what those who used the term earlier meant. Coitus interruptus has been called masturbation, as has also mutual foreplay in the sex act. In fact, like the term "onanism," it has had many meanings and some in the past have used it to describe all nonprocreative sexual activities.

See also Coitus Interruptus (Withdrawal); Onanism

Maternity Ratio, Total

Statisticians like to talk of a "total maternity ratio," which is defined as the average number of previous live births per women now age forty-five or older, regardless of whether a particular woman has children (not all women can or do have children). This ratio varies with different groups and societies. For the Ashanti of Ghana, the total maternity ratio has been estimated at approximately six; for the Sioux, eight; and for certain groups of Eskimos, less than five. Only a minority of people have ever approached a rate as high as ten. The highest rate recorded in history was 10.7 among the Hutterite in the first half of the twentieth century. The Hutterite are a communal religious group dating from the sixteenth century who settled in South Dakota between 1874 and 1877. They now live in more than a hundred different religious colonies in the Dakotas, Montana, and Washington in the United States and in Alberta, Saskatchewan, and Manitoba in Canada. It should be added that the Hutterite total maternity rate has been declining since 1950.

Note that the total maternity ratio is based upon live births, which means that abortions are excluded, whether they are spontaneous (i.e., miscarriages) or induced, and so are still births.

References

Bullough, Vern L., and Bonnie Bullough. *Contraception: A Guide to Birth Control.* Amherst, NY: Prometheus Books, 1997.

Eaton, J. W., and A. J. Mayer. "The Social Biology of Very High Fertility among the Hutterite: The Demography of a Unique Population." *Human Biology* 25 (1953): 206–264.

McCormick, Katharine Dexter (1875–1967)

Katharine Dexter McCormick campaigned nearly her entire life for a woman's right to self-determination. As a leader in the suffrage movement, as a patron of women's higher education, and as a key supporter of the U.S. birth control movement, McCormick dedicated her efforts and considerable financial resources to helping women gain decision-making power within and outside of the family. Her most significant contribution to women's liberation came late in life when she joined forces with Margaret Sanger to support research that directly resulted in the oral contraceptive pill, the first major breakthrough in contraceptive technology since the advent of vulcanized rubber in the mid-nineteenth century.

Katharine Dexter was born in Dexter, Michigan, where her father, Wirt Dexter, made his fortune as a prominent Chicago corporate attorney. After the deaths of her father in 1889 and brother in 1894, Katharine and her mother, Josephine Moore Dexter, formerly a schoolteacher, moved to Boston, where they had deep family ties. Equipped with a wide-ranging intellect and liberating affluence, Katharine Dexter flourished in elite society but never settled for predictable comforts or traditional expectations. Setting her sights on the impractical (for a woman in 1900) pursuits of science and medicine, she enrolled in the Massachusetts Institute of Technology (MIT) in 1900 after three years of preparatory studies.

One of the first women to receive a science degree from MIT, Dexter graduated with a B.A. in biology in 1904.

That same year she suspended any career pursuits to marry childhood friend Stanley McCormick, comptroller of the International Harvester Corporation and an heir to the family business fortune. Not long after their wedding, Stanley McCormick exhibited signs of severe mental illness; by 1906 he was hospitalized and in 1909 declared incompetent with what was later diagnosed as schizophrenia. This stunning blow for Katharine McCormick, still in her early thirties and faced with an impaired, childless marriage, seemed to act as a catalyst for her activism and philanthropy. She retreated from society life to focus on curing her husband's illness and addressing the inequities that women everywhere shared, regardless of class or circumstance.

In pursuit of a treatment for her husband, McCormick became a prominent and demanding medical philanthropist, supporting the work of several notable psychiatrists and physicians and later pouring money into research in endocrinology—she established the Neuroendocrine Research Foundation at Harvard in 1927—believing that her husband's disease could potentially be cured by hormone treatments. Stanley McCormick never emerged from his illness and lived out his life in a grand Santa Barbara estate and under constant medical care until his death in 1947. Endocrine research failed to help her husband, but McCormick's interest and education in this emerging medical field enabled her to accept the plausibility of a hormonal anovulant pill many years later.

Around the time McCormick had her husband declared incompetent and began a long battle with the McCormick family over control of his fortune, she joined forces with Boston suffragists. In 1909 she spoke at the first outdoor woman suffrage rally in Massachusetts. Early in the next decade she and the suffragist and birth control pioneer Mary Ware Dennett organized suffrage rallies and lobbying campaigns through-

Katharine Dexter McCormick, a suffragist and birth control advocate, joined forces with Margaret Sanger late in her life to spur research that led to the oral contraceptive pill for women. (Courtesy of the Sophia Smith Collection, Smith College)

out the Boston area. Later in the decade McCormick became vice president and treasurer of the National American Woman Suffrage Association, working closely with Carrie Chapman Catt with whom she cofounded the League of Women Voters in 1920.

McCormick's association with Mary Ware Dennett, who began organizing for legalized birth control in 1915, and other feminists who were active beyond the suffrage battle exposed her to the early trials of the birth control movement. Her marital predicament may have also convinced her of the necessity for safe and reliable contraception; she expressed a strong belief in thwarting congenital disease. McCormick first met Margaret Sanger in 1917 and served

that year on the Committee of 100, a group of prominent women organized to publicly promote legalized birth control and support Sanger after her arrest in 1916 for opening the first birth control clinic in the United States. Though it is unclear when her financial support of birth control began, McCormick served on the National Council of the American Birth Control League, founded by Sanger in 1921, which included many large donors to the league. She helped Sanger in less conventional ways as well: acting as an illegal courier in the 1920s, McCormick smuggled diaphragms from Europe to Sanger's Clinical Research Bureau in New York; and in 1927 she let Sanger use her family's Geneva Chateau as a meeting place for delegates to the World Population Conference.

McCormick continued to lend moderate financial support in the interwar years to Sanger's clinic in New York, but her drawn-out, contentious battle with her in-laws over control of Stanley McCormick's fortunes restricted her philanthropy. In 1950, after the settlement of her husband's estate, McCormick, with an infusion of new wealth, contacted Sanger about prospects for contraceptive research. Sanger had long sought a more effective and less intrusive contraceptive and sponsored, since the 1930s, hormonal research aimed at finding and developing a method of inhibiting ovulation—an idea that even in 1950 was dismissed by many experts. McCormick, however, continued to believe in the medical potential of hormones. After he rejected several proposals for McCormick's money, she and Sanger converged on the biologist Gregory Pincus, codirector of the Worcester Foundation for Experimental Biology (WFEB) and an expert on hormonal aspects of mammalian reproduction.

Since 1948 the Planned Parenthood Federation of America (PPFA) had given small grants to Pincus to study progesterone as an ovulation suppressant. Sanger met him in 1951 and came away impressed with his confidence and his success in the laboratory. She wrote enthusiastically to McCormick, knowing that no other individual or organization possessed the proper combination of compassion, scientific knowledge, and financial resources to take on the considerable risk of funding a pharmaceutical contraceptive. Meanwhile McCormick had recently renewed ties to Hudson Hoagland, Pincus's partner at the WFEB and whom she had consulted years earlier in seeking a hormonal treatment for her husband. In 1953 McCormick, Sanger, and Pincus met for the first time at the WFEB in Worcester, Massachusetts.

Pincus was also engaged in research on synthetic steroids for G. D. Searle, but the pharmaceutical company failed to encourage his research on the hormonal manipulation of the female reproductive cycle, seeing little promise of a marketable drug. Likewise, PPFA failed to exhibit much enthusiasm for Pincus's early findings on progesterone. McCormick, however, was impressed with Pincus's resolve and trusted the WFEB to bring together the right combination of scientists for such a momentous project. She gave Pincus and Hoagland ample social justification for their mission, educating them on the urgent need for a simple and effective contraceptive.

McCormick provided the WFEB with an initial sum of $20,000 and then an annual contribution of $150,000 or more a year until her death in 1967 (additionally, in her will she left five million dollars to PPFA and another one million dollars to the WFEB). She gave a total of at least two million dollars, both through PPFA and later directly to the WFEB, in support of research and testing that led to the synthetic amalgam of progesterone and estrogen marketed by Searle as Enovid in 1960 and immediately heralded as "the pill." Searle had changed its position as the research progressed. Apart from the money, McCormick kept the project focused through her close contact with the WFEB and her skill at managing personality conflicts and excitable egos.

Katharine McCormick died in 1967 and, like Margaret Sanger, who died a year before her, lived just long enough to see the pill succeed as a popular alternative to barrier methods of birth control and give women greater sexual autonomy than at any other time in history.

Peter Engelman

See also Pincus, Gregory Goodwin; Sanger, Margaret Louise (Higgins)

References

Most biographical details about McCormick emanate from "A Tribute to Katharine Dexter McCormick" (comments delivered at MIT, Cambridge, Massachusetts, March 1, 1968—copy available in the MIT Historical Collections). Most of McCormick's correspondence with Sanger, spanning approximately thirty years, is located in the Sophia Smith Collection, Smith College, and published in Esther Katz et al., eds. *The Margaret Sanger Papers Microfilm Edition: Smith College Collection Series.* Bethesda, MD: University Publications of America, 1995.

McLaughlin, Loretta. *The Pill, John Rock, and the Church: The Biography of a Revolution.* Boston: Little, Brown, 1982.

Reed, James. *From Private Vice to Public Virtue: The Birth Control Movement and American Society since 1830.* Princeton, NJ: Princeton University Press, 1978.

Reynolds, Moira Davison. *Women Advocates of Reproductive Rights: Eleven Who Led the Struggle in the United States and Great Britain.* Jefferson, NC: McFarland, 1994.

Medieval Europe

Though one often thinks of the Christian Church when one thinks of medieval Europe, the Christianization of Europe in terms of changing traditional ways of thinking was a slow process. Christianity in the Roman Empire had been primarily an urban religion, centered in the cities, and medieval Europe in its beginning was far more rural as the great cities of the Roman Empire went into decline. Although the kings and rulers of the Germanic kingdoms eventually accepted and pushed Christianity, the rural areas were slow to change and adjust. The very word pagan, which is commonly used to describe non-Christians, is derived from the term meaning rural dweller.

Although Christianity might well have provided the Romans and Germans with common religion, its moral influence on the family was initially very limited. Neither the Greeks nor the Romans, nor the Germanic and Celtic peoples, as far as we can tell, had regarded contraception or abortion as immoral. Christianity, both in its theology and its laws, attempted to modify this nonrestrictive role but it was not particularly effective in this for much of the Middle Ages. Nor was it more effective in enforcing other aspects of the Christian moral code. Charlemagne, for example, had a number of concubines, and many of the Germans practiced polygamy. It was not that the church officials did not try. Christian authorities regularly denounced polygamy, concubinage, and incest, gradually attempting to advance a theory of monogamous and indissoluble marriages. Jack Goody has argued, in fact, that the church officials recognized that the key to undermining paganism was to take control over marriage.

Though the marriage age was apparently fairly early among the German migrants into western Europe, the age gradually rose over the course of the Middle Ages, and the system that emerged was marked by both the late age of marriage of the bride and the small gap of a few years between her age and that of the groom. It is clear, however, that even by the end of the medieval period many males never married and neither did numerous females. Unmarried women sought refuge in religious foundations and convents or lay sisterhoods, although this was not true everywhere in Europe. In England, for example, convents were closed to peasant girls. What eventually emerged in western Europe was what can be called a bilineal family structure, consisting of a strong-bonded pair, weak kin, and an exogamous marriage pattern in which a woman moved into the family of her husband.

These changes did not happen overnight but were part of a gradual process and probably for a time two different models of marriage existed, what George Duby has called the profane and the religious. In the profane the idea was to protect the patrimony and ensure the continuation of the family, whereas in the religious there was an increasing attempt to view marriage as a weapon against lust and to make it a sacrament.

Still, there was an inherent bawdiness in the medieval period that was difficult to repress. Rapid procreation took place once a woman was married or regarded as the right age for having children, and this was especially true among the elite. Up to a quarter of first births took place before nine months of marriage. The public applauded vigorous marital sexuality. Obscenities were shouted at the marriage ceremony and the relatives took the wedding couple to their marriage bed and stayed to view the stained sheets the next day. Thus though premarital sex was common, rates of illegitimate births were low.

Medical sources regarded sex as natural and important, and there were a variety of methods and potions to encourage pregnancy, excite passion, facilitate pregnancy, prevent miscarriage, and so forth. Impotence was a grounds for annulment of a marriage. The church encouraged births, and at the same time greatly feared female sexuality. Female masturbation was regarded as a more serious sin than was male masturbation. Marriage in a sense was designed to protect men from female domination, and the doctrine of the immaculate conception of Mary highlighted the gulf that separated real, sexually dangerous women and the female paragon.

Yet, for all of this, birthrates throughout the Middle Ages were not high, although there are exceptions; for example, Blanche of Castile married Louis VIII of France when she was twelve and had her first child at nineteen and twelve more before she was forty. Note, however, the delay between marriage and consummation. Eleanor of Aquitaine had been divorced by the king of France, in part because she regarded him as more a "monk" than king, and in part because, although she gave birth to two daughters, she had not given him a son. After the annulment of her marriage on the grounds of consanguinity, she married Henry II of England, some eleven years her junior, and gave birth to three more daughters and five sons. So many children, however, caused disputes over inheritance, and few future queens followed her example. In fact, once a powerful family had a male heir, there seems to have been a deliberate attempt to avoid having other legitimate ones. The husband, if interested in sex, turned to concubines. The wife contented herself with other pursuits. It is argued that the emergence in the eleventh century of the principle of primogeniture, that is, the replacing of partible inheritance, eased pressures against having larger families because the family estates would be held together, no matter the size of the family.

Reproductive years for most women was limited, particularly as marriage age was raised. The average length of a marriage has been estimated to have been only between fifteen and seventeen years, after which one of the partners had probably died. Family size was not large because high infant mortality depleted the number of surviving children. Across Europe it is estimated that only half of the population reached age twenty. Most of the women stopped having children in their thirties after brief periods of high fecundity earlier. One possible explanation for this is the anemic condition most medieval women found themselves in after a series of pregnancies and as a result of the lack of much protein in their diet.

Other limitations probably came about from deliberate attempts at birth control. Some suggestion of this comes from the courtly love stories of the mid-twelfth century in which no births are reported as due to seductions. This might be a fictional device rather than reality but there are hints that some of this is based on reality. Chaucer says as much in "The Nun's Priest's Tale" when he reported that the couples bedded "moore for delit than world to multiplye."

Women were regarded, especially by the clergy, as the ones who attempted to control procreation. Saint Bernardino wrote:

And I say this to the women who are the cause that the children that they have conceived are destroyed; worse, who also are among those who arrange that they cannot conceive, and if they have conceived, they destroy them in the body. You (to whom this touches, I speak) are more evil than murderers . . . [These women are] like the Sodomite, are the cause for the shrinking of the world; between you and him there is no difference (Quoted from Herlihy and Klapische-Zuber, p. 251).

Abortion, however, was defined somewhat differently in the medieval period than it later came to be, in part because of the question about when the fetus became human, and was not simply an animal. Medieval theologians taught that the fetus was transformed from a vegetative state to a human being when the soul entered the fetus to make a human body. Albertus Magnus in the twelfth century and Saint Thomas Aquinas and others in the thirteenth century argued that the soul was created by God, not by humans, and its entrance into the human embryo was the key development, which coincided with quickening. Were the embryo to perish before the soul entered the body, there would be no soul to have perished because a soul cannot exist without a body. Otherwise, the soul would be denied the opportunity of resurrection because it would never have had a body from which to resurrect. When this happened is not clear but in many of the penitentials there was a distinction between a woman taking some kind of "maleficium," a word associated with black magic, forty days after she was pregnant compared with her taking one earlier. It was the difference between a large and a small sin. Aquinas accepted Aristotle's idea that in procreation "the active power of generation belonged to the male, and the passive to the female," but rejected the Aristotelian view that women were misbegotten men. However, Aquinas and other scholastics were often puzzled by God's motives in creating women. The answer seems to be that they were created for the purpose of procreation. Thus Aquinas and other scholastics condemned contraception, whether through coitus interruptus (defined as a "sin against nature") or through herbs and drugs.

The references to contraceptives in medieval writings are both direct and indirect, such as references to menstrual regulators. Many herbs are mentioned. Saint Hildegard of Bingen (1098–1117) mentions "haselwurtz," or *Asarum europaeum*, and that she used a German term rather than a Latin one was interpreted by the historian John Riddle to mean that she had not learned about this from books but from women in her circle. Other herbs mentioned include tansy (a well-known abortifacient in modern medicine), which was not known to the classical writers. Also mentioned by medieval writers are artemisia, juniper, and others that are mentioned by the classical writers. Interestingly, menstrual regulators are also mentioned by Albertus Magnus, who in his theological works opposed contraception and abortion but in his works on natural philosophy gave practical advice on what drugs to use for these purposes.

Contraceptive advice became more sophisticated after the translation of the Arabic writers such as Avicenna, who had compiled information from many classical writers and added his own as well. Avicenna also recommended barrier contraceptives or suppositories of cedar oil, pomegranate, alum, willow, pepper, and cabbage. He argued that he was including these methods, which included therapeutic abortion, in order to overcome women's fears of pregnancy. Most of his Latin translators and commentators passed on the information in their medical treatises.

There were no medieval secular laws that made abortion criminal, although one law promulgated by Edward I (1271–1307) of England held that anyone who assisted with an abortion for a woman whose pregnancy was "formed and animated" was guilty of a homicide, but the actual meaning of the law is unclear. The pregnant woman involved, however, was not held liable. Physicians obviously did intervene occasionally because William of Saliceto (d. c. 1280) advised that the physician, despite the general provisions about abortion, had to take into account the needs of the patient. When conceiving presented a dangerous risk to the woman because of her health, debilities, or extremity of youth, William held that she should be given information about contraception and abortion.

As the church became more powerful as an institution through the development of canon law and an effective bureaucracy, it gave increasing attention to marital contraception. Its use was even grounds enough to nullify a marriage. Although the ecclesiastical writers never specified what the means of contraception were, James Brundage is of the opinion that coitus interruptus was "presumably the most effective technique available in the period," at least it was the one that involved both partners in the relationship. What women did by themselves was harder for the clerics to determine and to rail against specifically.

The church, however, increasingly condemned coitus interruptus, and that might be because coitus interruptus was being more widely used than before. Moreover, in spite of the high death toll of the plague, those women who survived certainly were able to have more protein and iron in their diet than before, perhaps emphasizing the need for more effective family planning to keep family size down. John T. Noonan argued that the church, which had always opposed sensuality, was reinvigorated by a rebirth of Augustinianism and by the threat of the dangers of heresy, namely, Catharism, which opposed procreation altogether. This led the church, in a sense, to defend procreation but not sensuality and to follow Augustine in emphasizing and defending childbearing as the only justification of marriage.

It was not only medieval Roman Catholicism that was hostile to contraception, but so was the Eastern Orthodox Church centered in Byzantium. As did western Christianity, the Eastern Orthodox Church maintained that sexual activity within marriage was to be restricted to certain times and positions and never to involve hindrances to procreation, although, as in the Roman Catholic Church, there were gradations of sinfulness. Some of the Slavic churches, particularly those of Russia, had an extremely negative opinion of all sexual relations. Many didactic tracts cast all sexual relations as unnatural and desire as coming from the devil. An unconsummated marriage was regarded as the best, and one of the motifs common in Russian saints' lives is of a saint being conceived of a pious and abstinent mother and born of a miracle rather than normal marital intercourse. Children were viewed as the result of God's will rather than of intercourse. Menstruating women could not enter church or take communion.

Medieval women as well as medical and theological writers knew about contraceptives and abortifacients and there are indications that they were certainly used, but most of what we know comes from indirect evidence rather than actual descriptions of their use.

See also Anemia, Diet, and Pregnancy; Canon Law and Contraception; Herbal Contraceptives and Abortifacients; Islam; Quickening

References

Aquinas, Thomas. *Summa Theologiea,* translated by English Dominicans. New York: Benziger Brothers, 1947, Ia. 118, art. 1–2.

Biller, R. P. A. "Birth Control in the West in the Thirteenth and Early Fourteenth Centuries." *Past and Present* 4 (1982): 22–25.

Chaucer, Geoffrey. "The Nun's Priest's Tale," line 3345.

Duby, George. *The Knight, the Lady, and the Priest: The Making of Modern Marriage in Medieval France,* translated by Barbara Bray. New York: Pantheon, 1983.

Gold, Penny S. *The Lady and the Virgin: Image, Attitude and Experiences in Twelfth Century France.* Chicago: University of Chicago Press, 1985.

Goody, Jack. *The Development of Family and Marriage in Europe.* Cambridge, England: Cambridge University Press, 1983.

Helihy, David, and Christiane Klapische-Zuber. *Tuscans and Their Families: A Study of Florentine Catasto of 1427.* New Haven, CT: Yale University Press, 1985.

Huby, Pamela M. "Soul, Life, Sense, Intellect: Some Thirteenth Century Problems." In *Human Embryo: Aristotle and the Arabic and European Traditions.* Exeter, UK: Exeter University Press, 1990.

Lemay, Helen Rodnite. "Human Sexuality in Twelfth to Fifteenth Century Scientific Writings." In *Sexual Practices and the Medieval Church,* edited by Vern L. Bullough and James Brundage. Buffalo: Prometheus Books, 1982.

McLaren, Angus. *A History of Contraception.* Oxford, England: Basil Blackwell, 1990.

Noonan, John T. *Contraception: A History of Its Treatment by the Catholic Theologians and Canonists.* Cambridge, MA: Harvard University Press, 1966.

Riddle, John M. *Contraception and Abortion from the Ancient World to the Renaissance.* Cambridge, MA: Harvard University Press, 1992.

———. "Contraception and Early Abortion in the Middle Ages." In *Handbook of Medieval Sexuality,* edited by Vern L. Bullough and James Brundage. New York: Garland, 1996.

Russel, Josiah Cox. *The Control of Late Ancient and Medieval Populations.* Philadelphia: American Philosophical Society, 1985.

Mineral Contraceptives and Abortifacients

Various herbal contraceptives and abortifacients have been used throughout history; some minerals were also used. Alum, or aluminum and potassium sulfate, a colorless, crystalline substance with stringent and styptic property, is often mentioned as a vaginal suppository. Used internally it acts as an emetic and an astringent. The most widely mentioned mineral, however, is copper.

Two works in the Hippocratic corpus, *Diseases of Women* and *On the Nature of Women,* mention drinking *misy,* a copper compound, probably copper sulfate. The use of a copper compound, however, is not mentioned again in any of the medical writings until the sixth century of the modern era, when Aetius of Amida mentions it. So far, little experimentation has taken place on ingested copper, although copper intrauterine devices today are part of the armory of contraceptives. Trace elements of copper in the uterus are harmful to sperm and seriously handicap conception. Modern experiments found that copper wires inserted in utero corroded 6 mg a month (0.2 daily) for up to eighty months and thereafter 0.014 daily. Experiments with rabbits indicate that copper did not necessarily prevent fertilization, although there was spermicidal action, but rather copper salts inhibited the lysis (dissolving) of the semen coagulum. Action apparently took place in the endometrium, where implantation occurs, because the tissue there absorbed copper ions.

It has been hypothesized that copper metal inhibits enzyme activity at very low concentration, possibly through prostaglandin synthesis. Copper increases prostaglandin production and prostaglandins increase inflammation of the endometrium, discouraging the fertilized egg from attaching. Others have argued that copper sulfate is absorbed in the human fibroblast, which inhibits growth of proteins necessary for early cellular growth.

Still another metal mentioned in ancient recipes is white lead, or lead acetate. This is probably a distillation of lead, a sweet white basic salt that is astringent, relieves pain, and dissipates easily. It was used as a vaginal suppository and was believed to be an antifertility agent.

See also Classical Medical and Scientific Writers on Birth Control; Herbal Contraceptives and Abortifacients

References

Hippocrates. "Diseases of Women," 1.176; "On the Nature of Women," 98. In *Oeuvres completes d'Hippocrate*, edited by Emile Littr, 10 vols. Paris: Bailliere, 1839–1861.

Oster, G., and M. P. Salgo. "The Copper Intrauterine Device and Its Mode of Action." *New England Journal of Medicine* 293 (1975): 432–438.

Riddle, John. *Contraception and Abortion from the Ancient World to the Renaissance.* Cambridge, MA: Harvard University Press, 1992.

Zhu, Shou-Min. "The Copper Intrauterine Device: Copper Corrosion in Uterus and the Effect of the Copper Ion on Some Enzyme Activities." In *Recent Advances in Fertility Regulation,* edited by Chang Chai Fen, David Griffin, and Aubrey Wollman. Geneva: Atar, 1981, pp. 248–264.

Modernity and Falling Birthrates

The "demographic transition" central to thinking on population is the belief that in premodern societies an equilibrium existed between high fertility and high mortality. As societies modernized, improved sanitation and nutrition brought the death rate down, thereby disrupting the equilibrium and causing the population to grow. Finally, in fully modern societies, the birthrate will gradually decline until it is once more in equilibrium with the death rate.

A number of discrepancies exist between this model and reality. First, controlled birthrates—and not simply uncontrolled death rates—curbed population growth long before the demographic transition. This was notably the case in western Europe, where late marriage and prolonged breast-feeding and other developments greatly restrained fertility from at least the fourteenth century on. Such practices, however, stemmed not from a desire to keep fertility and mortality in balance but, as Seccombe argues, rather from the limited resources for family formation. Children had to wait for their parents to retire before they could take over the farm, marry, and have children of their own. Understandably, the age of marriage fell whenever plague or conquest freed up land for settlement.

Second, Europe's demographic transition of the eighteenth and nineteenth centuries brought not only lower death rates but also higher birthrates. This was particularly true in England, where rising fertility contributed over twice as much to population growth as falling mortality. Fertility also rose in the Netherlands, largely because couples were marrying younger. In both countries, then, larger families were a deliberate choice and not a result of overestimating how many children would survive to adulthood. Admittedly, growth elsewhere in Europe, notably France, was due almost entirely to falling death rates. It would be hard, however, to attribute lower French fertility to an earlier entry into modernity. France trailed England and the Netherlands on such yardsticks of modernization as expansion of the market economy, improvements in sanitation and nutrition, and migration to the cities. France was more modern only in a political and ideological sense.

Third, the twentieth century decline in birthrates throughout the Western world has shown no signs of bottoming out. After the World War II baby boom, fertility began to decrease around 1964, and by 1975 most of Europe and North America had fallen below the replacement threshold of 2.1 children per woman. Far from leveling off, the trend has continued. In the last decade of the twentieth century,

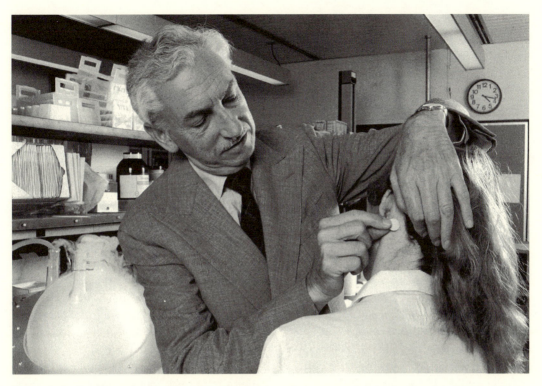

New methods of birth control, especially ones that last several months or years, are causing birth rates to fall in industrialized countries. Here, Dr. Alejandro Zaffaroni attaches a contraceptive patch, which contains the same ingredients as the birth control pills developed by Johnson & Johnson. (Roger Ressmena / Corbis)

fertility had dropped to 1.2 children per woman in Italy, Spain, the Czech Republic, and Latvia. It had fallen below 1.0 in the eastern parts of Germany, Spain's Basque country, and twenty-four of Italy's ninety-five provinces. There is no reason to believe the decline has stopped and it will certainly not bottom out at 2.1.

Yet the demographic transition model is correct on one point: clearly, a premodern regime of high fertility has given way to a postmodern one of low fertility. What is less clear is the relationship between the decline in fertility and the preceding decline in mortality. It looks increasingly fortuitous and may simply reflect some kind of common cause, that is, the same modern culture that has cut death rates through better sanitation and medical care has also caused a shift in priorities away from procreation.

An alternative model attributes the decline in fertility to the emergence of a less coercive social environment. Women face less pressure from their husbands, relatives, and society to bear children. Improved educational and career opportunities have given them a broader range of life choices. Finally, easier access to contraception and abortion prevents unwanted pregnancies. Support for this model comes from the Muslim world, where surveys show that women bear more children than they actually want. On the other hand, birthrates rose in Sweden when that country expanded its system of daycare facilities while still maintaining easy access to family planning services and a strong commitment to gender equality at home and at work. This seems to indicate the existence of an unrealized fertility potential in Western countries.

The demographic transition is therefore not simply the end of a regime where more children are born than desired but also the beginning of one where fewer are born than desired.

Quebec makes an interesting case study because the birthrate plummeted from 3.67 children per woman in 1962 to 1.82 in 1972. It entered a second decline in the early 1980s, falling from 1.75 in 1979 to 1.40 in 1986. In the late 1980s, it rose modestly in response to increases in the family allowance, notably for the third child. This gain, however, had all but disappeared by the late 1990s.

Gauthier and Bujold link the decline of birthrates in the 1960s to the end of coercive factors in Quebec that made people have more children than they would if the choice had been entirely their own. Legalization of contraception and sterilization, combined with the introduction of free medical care, made it easier to postpone or terminate childbearing. The cultural environment also became markedly less natalist and profamily, notably with the waning influence of the Roman Catholic Church. In the diocese of Montreal, church attendance fell from 61 percent in 1961 to 30 percent in 1971. The weakening of religious constraints on life goals, together with the prosperity of the 1960s, facilitated a wider range of aspirations, most of which were unrelated to family formation. Finally, this freer and more open environment allowed people to construct new forms of solidarity and sociability. The family unit, which was transgenerational in nature, now had to compete with social settings constructed around the workplace or the school and encompassing people of roughly the same age with similar interests. People no longer had to choose social relationships that necessarily involved long-term reciprocal obligations of dependency and responsibility.

Gauthier and Bujold, however, paint a strikingly different picture for the fertility decline of the early 1980s. Birth control did not become more accessible or reliable. The proportion of women in college and in the labor force did not increase. Cultural values did not change as they had in the 1960s. The two authors, however, did find one major "marker" from this time period: youth unemployment and impoverishment of young families. With the onset of the 1982 recession, high unemployment hit young adults much harder than it did older age groups. The jobs of young adults were also lower paying and less secure (part-time work, short-term contracts, freelancing, etc.). The effects of the recession were particularly hard on young families, among whom the poverty rate rose from 23.1 percent in 1981 to 31.5 percent in 1982.

It may seem obvious that young adults, like all new entrants to the labor force, will bear the brunt of any economic recession. Yet this has been true only in recent times. In 1931, at the height of the Great Depression, the burden of unemployment was spread more or less equally among all age groups (Table M.1).

The end of the 1982 recession did not mark a return to normal. Young adults remained overwhelmingly concentrated in service sector jobs that paid lower wages and provided less secure working conditions. When another downturn came in 1989, their earnings fell much more than those of older cohorts and, as with the 1982 recession, the ensuing years have only partially reversed the widening of the income gap. Everything being taken into account, average incomes since the 1970s have steadily risen for those forty-five to fifty-four years old and fallen for those twenty to twenty-four years old. Households of those in the twenty to twenty-four year age group earned 20 percent less in 1994 than they did in 1975. This phenomenon has been noted in other Western countries.

The weaker economic position of young adults can be ascribed to the spread since the 1940s of a number of labor practices. Foremost among these are seniority clauses in union contracts, notably LIFO (last in, first out) and LOFI (last out, first in). Another one is attrition, that is, a firm that is wishing to downsize will protect its existing employees by freezing all outside hiring and filling vacancies, as they come up, from a list of laid off personnel. The costs of downsizing are thereby externalized onto new entrants to the labor force. The results may be seen in the Quebec civil service; in 1999, less than 1.4 percent of its regular employees are under thirty years old, compared with 21.4 percent of all Quebec workers.

The 1989 recession saw the advent of another age-sensitive labor practice: two-tiered wage agreements. Under this kind of arrangement, employers and unions agree to maintain existing wage rates for anyone hired before a certain date while paying substantially less to anyone hired afterward. Although two-thirds of these agreements disappeared with the end of the recession, they are now once again on the rise, more than doubling in number from 1991 to 1997.

These new labor practices have helped convert the union movement into a vehicle for the aspirations of older workers. To some degree, the process feeds upon itself: because fewer young adults hold unionized jobs, they are less likely to influence decision making in the unions. Less than 15 percent of the membership of Quebec's largest trade union is under thirty years of age. Older workers thus have the power to shift the costs of economic insecurity onto younger entrants to the labor force. Although a dichotomy between "insiders" and "outsiders" is not new to Quebec, the lines of inclusion and exclusion were traditionally drawn in terms of ethnicity, religion, and lineage. People saw their interests as lying in entities that were necessarily transgenerational in nature and that continually recycled resources from older to younger members. The rise of modernity has emancipated older adults from this system, thus allowing them to use their greater share of decision-making power for their own benefit. This situation does not seem to be isolated to Quebec.

In premodern societies, people sought to optimize not so much their own well-being as that of their present or prospective family. In general, resources tended to be transferred from older, more productive members to

Table M.1: Unemployment Rates in Quebec, 1931 and 1982, by Age Group

Age Group	1931	1982
20–24	17.1	20.6
25–34	16.6	13.4
35–44	15.3	10.2
45–54	17.1	8.7
55–64	20.0	9.0

Sources: Census of Canada, 1931, vol. 6, "Unemployment" Table 6, p.8; Labour Force Annual Averages 1982, Table 2, p. 23, Statistics Canada.

younger or still unborn ones. Because decision making was disproportionately vested in older family members, decisions on resource allocation tended to be suboptimal for the person making them. When faced with several alternatives that seemed equally beneficial, people would opt for the one that maximizes benefits for present and future children. For example, personal gain alone did not seem to motivate the Irish emigrants of the late nineteenth century:

> . . . it is not surprising that nine times as many people opted for emigration as remained permanently celibate in Ireland. Economic motives alone provide an insufficient explanation for the exodus. The Irish immigrants generally achieved enough economic success to marry and have families, but they generally filled menial, low-status jobs with long working hours and often faced a diminished life expectancy. The standard of living on the home farm did not necessarily compare unfavorably with the standard of living achieved in the destination countries. We propose that the chief difference was that emigration offered greater marital and reproductive prospects. (Strassmann and Clarke, p. 48)

The family has since declined as a factor in personal decisionmaking. It is perhaps no coincidence that this decline parallels the expansion of the market economy and, accordingly, the increase in freedom to leave economic relationships that no longer serve one's interest. This "market discipline" has the merit of terminating unproductive or inefficient relationships. Unfortunately, it also works against nonmarket entities, such as the family, that necessarily redistribute resources from more productive to less productive members.

In sum, it can be argued that the ultimate cause of the decline in birthrates has been the withering away of both coercive and noncoercive social supports for fertility. Traditional societies invest massively in family formation and reproduction, often to the detriment of adults. From the mid-nineteenth century on, these supports began to dissolve with the shift from a "vertical" lineage-based model of society to a "horizontal" age-class model. Today, resources are being redistributed in the opposite direction, away from young-age classes and toward older workers and retirees.

Peter Frost

References

Bachand, R., and M. Boutet. *Relever les défis de l'emploi. Rapport du Chantier.* Quebec City: Bureau du Sommet du Québec et de la Jeunesse, 1999.

Chesnais, J.-C. "Fertility, Family, and Social Policy in Contemporary Western Europe." *Population and Development Review* 22 (1996): 729–739.

Conseil permanent de la jeunesse. *Interdire les clauses "orphelins": Une question d'équité intergénérationnelle.* Brief presented to the Commission de l'économie et du travail, 1998.

Duval, L. *Aspects économiques de la vie des jeunes familles biparentales.* Sainte-Foy, Quebec: INRS-Culture et société, 1997.

Gauthier, M., and J. Bujold. *Les antécédents et les conséquents de la baisse de la fécondité au Québec, 1960–1970.* Quebec City: Institut québécois de recherche sur la culture, 1993.

Gauthier, M., and L. Mercier. *La pauvreté chez les jeunes.* Quebec City: Institut québécois de recherche sur la culture, 1994.

Golini, A. "How Low Can Fertility Be? An Empirical Exploration." *Population and Development Review* 24 (1998): 59–73.

Seccombe, W. *A Millennium of Family Change.* London: Verso, 1992.

Strassmann, B. I., and A. L. Clarke. "Ecological Constraints on Marriage in Rural Ireland." *Evolution and Human Behavior* 19 (1998): 33–55.

Trudel, C. À. "75 ans, la CSN doit penser aux jeunes." *Le Devoir* A3, May 21, 1996.

Mothers' Clinic and Its Successors

On March 17, 1921, Marie Stopes (1880–1958) founded the Mothers' Clinic in London, with the aims of providing poor women with the latest contraceptive methods and demonstrating its effect on their health and marital relations. As such, Stopes's clinic was a practical application of *Married Love,* her 1918 best-selling sex manual. Stopes's clinic was decidedly nonmedical in its orientation. The atmosphere in the clinic was friendly and sympathetic, with staff chosen for their ability to make the patients feel at home. The clinic itself resembled a parlor more than a medical facility, with photographs of Stopes's family and the children of patients adorning the walls.

Stopes and her husband Humphrey Roe funded the clinic personally and created the Society for Constructive Birth Control and Racial Progress to maintain it. They hired midwives and nurses as the staff. These women talked to patients about their marriages and families and then examined and fitted them with cervical caps designed to Stopes's criteria. Patients were seen by a consulting doctor only when there was some medical condition that required additional expertise. Though few women came initially, by 1924 Stopes's *First Five Thousand* (1925) testified to the clinic's success. Stopes publicized the work of the clinic aggressively and saw it as a model for what she hoped would be a chain of publicly funded birth control clinics.

Other birth control clinics were founded in the years directly after the Mothers' Clinic was founded, but not by the government. Birth control leagues began opening rival clinics, and their staffs were often critical of Stopes's work. These physicians and birth control reformers organized their work in a more medical way, insisting that all patients must be seen by a doctor. Many also claimed that Stopes's cervical cap was not as effective a method of contraception as the more widely used "Dutch cap," or diaphragm. Lay and medical rivals attacked Stopes's methods of computing success rates as unscientific and self-serving. Stopes defended her work as pure science and continued her practices unabated.

In 1927 she created the nation's first mobile contraceptive clinic, called the Caravan Clinic, which traveled to rural northern England to aid women who could not easily reach London. A year later, the clinic was burned by Elizabeth Ellis, a Catholic opponent of Stopes's work, but the resultant publicity enabled Stopes to gain a donation to open two clinics to replace it.

Stopes published the next clinic report, *Ten Thousand Cases,* in 1930. In the following decade, she expanded the clinical work by opening branches in Aberdeen (1934), Belfast (1936), Cardiff (1937), Leeds (1934), and Swansea (1943). Clinics in South Africa, Australia, and New Zealand also became affiliated with the Mothers' Clinic. Despite this rapid growth, the Mothers' Clinics were outpaced by the clinics of the National Birth Control Association, and by the mid- to late 1930s Stopes was no longer a leader of the national movement. Doctor-controlled contraceptive clinics became the norm in the United Kingdom.

During World War II, shortages of staff and rubber hampered all birth control clinics, forcing most to suspend their work. Stopes's Mothers' Clinic pressed on; despite taking bomb damage twice during the 1940 blitz, it remained open. When Stopes died in 1958, she left the Mothers' Clinic to the Eugenics Society, which ran it from 1960 to 1976. In these years contraceptive clinics underwent rapid change and, functioning through the Marie Stopes Memorial Clinic, the Eugenics Society began offering services to unmarried and young patients, as well as providing vasectomies and abortions. The Eugenics Society gave up the clinic in 1976, when the government finally took over the responsibility for contraception as part of the National Health Service. The clinic was taken over by Marie Stopes International, which continues to provide private family planning services and fosters reproductive rights around the world.

Marie Stopes's papers, including the clinic records, are located at the British Museum and the Wellcome Institute for the History of Medicine. Several biographies have been published, none of which cover the clinic in any great depth. Stopes's own published reports, *The First Five Thousand* and *Ten Thousand Cases,* provide the best descriptions of the clinic and its work.

Cathy Moran Hajo

See also Cervical Cap; Diaphragm; Stopes, Marie Charlotte Carmichael

References

Peel, Robert A., ed. *Marie Stopes, Eugenics, and the English Birth Control Movement.* London: The Galton Institute, 1997.

Rose, June. *Marie Stopes and the Sexual Revolution.* New York: Faber and Faber, 1992.

N

National Birth Control League

The National Birth Control League (NBCL) was a short-lived organization founded by Mary Ware Dennett, Clara Gruening Stillman, and Jessie Ashley. Though she never held the post of president, Dennett was the driving force behind the league, defining its tactics and legislative focus. The NBCL was formed in New York City in March 1915. At its founding, birth control was considered immoral by many, and individuals who associated with it took risks with their reputations. With the NBCL, Dennett tried to carve out a respectable forum for men and women to support contraceptive reform. Her organization focused on legislative lobbying for the removal of the term "prevention of conception" from the obscenity act.

The NBCL staked out its territory in October 1915, when it refused to aid Margaret Sanger's defense on obscenity charges related to the publication of the *Woman Rebel*. The NBCL held itself as a law-abiding organization and would not support Sanger's direct-action challenges to the Comstock Act. Though its members later asked Sanger to join the NBCL, the rift had already been formed and she refused. Drawing from free speech advocates, suffrage supporters, and society women, the NBCL rejected all associations with sex reform. Instead it framed its discussion of the topic in terms of the right to free speech.

Despite its claims of being a national organization, the NBCL actually operated in a very small geographic area, centered around New York City. Although Dennett drafted legislative amendments to correct both the federal and New York State censorship codes, the NBCL's only practical campaign centered on Albany. In 1917 the NBCL circularized New York State legislators, held meetings around the state, and unsuccessfully attempted to introduce a bill to amend Section 1142 of the State Penal Code. The NBCL concluded that much more educational work was needed among legislators before another bill would be successful.

After Margaret Sanger's return to the United States in October 1915, the NBCL had to vie with her and her often adversarial campaign for birth control. With superior flair for publicity, Sanger's efforts were more widely known. She opposed the NBCL's efforts in Albany in 1917 and succeeded in having a bill introduced that exempted physicians from existing obscenity laws. Though the bill never made it through committee, it offered an alternative that many found more palatable than the "clean repeal" that Dennett and the NBCL sought.

In 1918, Dennett took on full-time work as the paid executive secretary of the NBCL. The league, never financially sound, had a difficult time raising sufficient funds, despite numerous appeals to members. By 1919 Dennett had determined that the focus should be on federal legislation and wanted to embark on a Washington-based campaign. Instead the board voted to cut back the work of the league, eliminating Dennett's full-time position in favor of a voluntary one. Dennett resigned in March 1919, founding the Voluntary Parenthood League shortly afterward to take up the federal work.

The NBCL did not survive the loss of its most active member and leader and closed shortly afterward.

Mary Ware Dennett's papers, *Papers of Mary Ware Dennett and the Voluntary Parenthood League,* including a small amount of NBCL material, are at the Schlesinger Library, Harvard University, and available on microfilm: *Sexuality, Sex Education, and Reproductive Rights* (Bethesda, MD: University Publications of America, 1994).

Kathy Moran Hajo

See also Dennett, Mary Coffin Ware; Sanger, Margaret Louise (Higgins)

References

Chen, Constance. *"The Sex Side of Life": Mary Ware Dennett's Pioneering Battle for Birth Control and Sex Education.* New York: The New Press, 1996.

Gordon, Linda. *Woman's Body, Woman's Right: A Social History of Birth Control in America.* New York: Penguin Books, 1976.

Native Americans of California

Birth control and abortion practices differed among various groups of Native Americans. The most diverse of the Native American groups were those in California, who spoke at least one hundred different mutually unintelligible languages and who were organized into five hundred or so different groups. Generalities can be made among the groups because they had much in common, yet generalities do not necessarily apply to any particular group because there was variance among cultures.

Because indigenous peoples in the United States did not leave a written record, information about them comes from either the reports of others or remembered traditions kept alive over the centuries. Because the quality of Native American existence began to deteriorate almost immediately after colonization, all reports of Native American prehistory reflect this impact. Anthropologists did not begin to work among them until 1871. Further complicating the issue is that American and European understanding of Native Americans has been a fairy-tale view of them as living in a wild and beneficent world in which they had only to take what they needed. A deeper look at Native American life reveals that, although Native Americans had a rich environment, they controlled and managed their resources very carefully. They had an intimate and extensive knowledge of plants, animals, weather, astronomical phenomena, and medicine. With such a considered lifestyle, it is no wonder that they were also sensitive to the management of human birth, which affected the balance of life directly. B. W. Aginsky, for example, reported that the Pomo people had developed and imposed birth control methods to keep their population within the limits of the food supply of the valley. This same effort was more or less normative among all tribes. Among the various means used to control population were sexual restrictions, coitus interruptus, infanticide, abortion, and various recipes for menstrual regulation or birth control as well as songs and rituals.

Elimination of unwanted young is known to have occurred among the Yurok, Pomo, Wappo, Wintun, Yana, Sinkyone, Kato, Klamath, Hupa, and Yuma. Undoubtedly it was a general procedure among all California tribes and tribes elsewhere, although its frequency varied. Thus it was often normative practice to kill one of a pair of twins, and deformed infants were similarly disposed of. Generally, abortion was used to prevent the arrival of illegitimate and unwanted children.

Malcolm Margolin wrote that "sexual restrictions were so pervasive throughout California, that they certainly helped reduce the uglier agents of population control that have plagued other cultures: disease, famine and warfare."

Probably the most widely used method of birth control was abstinence, which was built into the societal fabric through a long list of forbidden times and occasions to have sexual intercourse. Among the northern tribes, men and women had separate dwellings three quarters of the year, and abstinence during that time was the inevitable outcome of these household arrangements. Cohabitation was confined largely to the

Native American wise women like this Athapaskan Hupa female shaman often held the collective medical wisdom of their tribe regarding birth control practices. (Edward Curtis/Library of Congress, 1923)

late summer and fall, when the family camped out together. This meant that most children were born in the spring. This was also a time when food was more plentiful.

Abstinence was often regarded as a necessary part of the healing process, and much of the treatment for illness involved setting standards for abstinence. Abstinence was also required when special tasks were to be performed or special jobs undertaken. For a man to go near a pregnant or menstruating woman, or in fact a woman of sexually ripe age at such a time, would not only invalidate the candidate's power, but make him ill. It might also cause the death of an unborn child and bring illness and death to infants and children. These then were powerful taboos, requiring not only abstinence but complete avoidance. Preparation for deer hunting, for example, required a period of fasting and sexual continence. Sex was taboo when eating bear meat. After a couple had a child, the husband was not to touch his wife until the child could stand alone on its feet, otherwise the couple would have no more children. Mourners were not to have sex. Abstention was called for while a woman was menstruating and there were taboos against intercourse for mothers who were nursing.

Among many Native American tribes there were men, in the past called "berdaches" by European reporters and investigators, who lived as women, performed the role of women, and had intercourse with men. These men-women were regarded as having special powers in some societies, and their existence as "wives" to other men of society certainly allowed them to be also classed as a factor in limiting population growth.

The Native Americans had a enormous pharmacopeia of plants, many of which were associated with short-term sterility or menstrual regulation. Included in the list were drinks made from the roots of *Lithospermum rudedrale,* a low-growing shrub, and which apparently results in short-term sterility. Most of the contraceptive drugs taken, however, have not been tested in modern animal studies, but that the Native Americans believed

that the drugs acted to prevent pregnancy emphasizes the Native Americans' wish to limit their population. Supernatural and magical means including songs, prayers, and ritual actions were used to prevent pregnancy and to enhance the effectiveness of other methods.

Abortion was practiced among unmarried women who were pregnant. Various means of abortion have been described, ranging from putting hot stones on the abdomen of a woman, to lifting heavy weights, to jumping off high places, to hitting the stomach. Some tied tight belts around their waist. Abortion inducers were also used that were made from various ingredients including horehound (*Marrubium vulgare*), silk tassel bush (*Garrya elliptica*), and mistletoe (*Phoradendron flavescents va. Villosum*). Many tribes tolerated abortion because they believed the child did not get its spirit until after birth. In fact, often special preparations had to be taken during the first ten days of life to make sure the vulnerable spirit of the newborn was firmly lodged in the infant's body and it could become human. Neglecting such procedures was at least mentally infanticide. Infanticide was not uncommon but was not as morally acceptable as abortion. A common way of performing infanticide reported by informants was for a woman to simply sit on the unwanted child. Strangulation was not uncommon.

There is some debate as to whether the infanticide and abortions reported by European observers were at the same level among the Native Americans before the Europeans appeared. It has been speculated that reports of widespread abortion and infanticide might well have been a response to the degradation the Native Americans suffered at the hands of the Europeans. This is the argument of Sherburne Cook, who believed that abortion and infanticide were clear-cut responses to unfavorable environmental circumstances. They were acts on the part of an individual performed under definite and usually extreme provocation as part of the Native American resistance to the European invasion and dominance. The missionaries, who controlled the

Native Americans in California, for example, wanted an increase in population to gain both more workers and more converts. Abortion or infanticide provided escape for the child and resistance to a system that was eager to increase the population. Women who had a miscarriage or failed to conceive, in fact, were regularly punished by the priests. They were flogged; had their heads shaved; and were forced to dress in sack cloth, cover themselves with ashes, and carry a doll or wooden image of a child painted red if abortion were suspect. On Sundays the accused woman stood before the mission church and received the taunts and jeers of churchgoers even though she might well have become pregnant through rape by nontribal members.

One Catholic priest quoted by Kennedy wrote in 1801:

> Knowing full well the inhuman crimes these Native American women so often commit . . . how they commit abortions and are guilty of suffocating their infants, we employ for their correction all care and vigilance, all the expedients, and all the diligence that a matter of such importance demands.

Sarah Hopkins, who lived among the Paiutes in the mid-nineteenth century, wrote:

> My people have been so unhappy for a long time they wish now to *disincrease* instead of multiply. The mothers are afraid to have more children, for fear they shall have daughters, who are not safe even in their mother's presence.

Such statements are not unusual and force a different view of abortion and infanticide, namely, as a means of protest, perhaps the only means that many women could take, to the conditions under which they were forced to live. When a fetus was aborted or an infant died, the same forms of mourning were expressed as in response to any other death.

Lois Robin

References

Aginsky, Bernard W. "Population Control in the Shanel Tribe." *American Sociological Review* 4 (1939): 2:209–216.

Aginsky, Bernard W., and Ethel G. Aginsky. *Deep Valley.* New York: Stein and Day, 1967.

Bean, Lowell, ed. *California Indian Shamanism.* Menlo Park, CA: Ballena Press, 1992.

Bean, Lowell, and Dorothea Theodoratus. "Western Pomo and Northeastern Pomo." In *Handbook of American Indians,* vol. 8, edited by Robert Heizer. Washington, DC: Smithsonian Institution, 1978, pp. 289–305.

Buckley, Thomas. "Yurok Doctors and the Concept of Shamanism." In *California Indian Shamanism, edited by Lowell Bean.* Menlo Park, CA: Ballena Press, 1992.

Cook, Sherburne F. *The Conflict between the California Indian and White Civilization.* Berkeley: University of California Press, 1976.

Elsasser, Albert. "Mattole, Nongatl, Sinkyone, Lassik, and Wailaki." In *Handbook of American Indians,* vol. 8, edited by Robert Heizer. Washington, DC: Smithsonian Institution, 1978, pp. 190–230.

Goodrich, Jennie, Claudia Lawson, and Vana Parrish Lawson. *Kashaya Pomo Plants.* Berkeley, CA: Heyday Books, 1980.

Gutierrez, Ramon A., and Richard J. Orsi, eds. *Contested Eden: California before the Gold Rush.* Berkeley: University of California Press, 1998.

Heizer, Robert, ed. *Handbook of North American Indians,* 8 vols. Washington, DC: Smithsonian Institution, 1978.

Heizer, Robert F., and Albert B. Elsasser. *The Natural World of the California Indians.* Berkeley: University of California Press, 1980.

Hopkins, Sarah Winnemucca. *Life among the Paiutes, Their Wrong and Claims.* Bishop, CA: Chalfant Press, 1969.

Kelly, Isabel. "Coast Miwok." In *Handbook of North American Indians,* vol. 8, edited by Robert Heizer. Washington, DC: Smithsonian Institution, 1978, pp. 414–425.

LaPena, Frank. "Wintu." In *Handbook of North American Indians,* vol. 8, edited by Robert Heizer. Washington, DC: Smithsonian Institution, 1978, pp. 324–348.

Margolin, Malcolm. *The Ohlone Way.* Berkeley, CA: Heyday Books, 1978.

Ohlone elder, taped conversation at Watsonville, CA, February 2000.

Pilling, Arnold R. "The Yurok." In *Handbook of North American Indians,* vol. 8, edited by Robert Heizer. Washington, DC: Smithsonian Institution, 1978, pp. 127–154.

Robin, Lois. Personal communication with Bernice Torres, Carmel and Carmel Valley, CA, 1993.

Sarris, Greg. *Keeping Slug Woman Alive.* Berkeley: University of California Press, 1993.

Smith, Charles R. "Tubatulabal." In *Handbook of North American Indians,* vol. 8, edited by Robert Heizer. Washington, DC: Smithsonian Institution, 1978, pp. 437–440.

Thompson, Lucy. *Che-na-wh weitch-ah-wen: To the American Indian, Reminiscences of a Yurok Woman.* Berkeley, CA: Heyday Books, 1991.

Walker, Philip L., and Travis Hudson. *Chumash Healing.* Banning, CA: Malki Museum Press, 1993.

Wallace, William J. "Hupa, Chilula, and Wkilkut." In *Handbook of American Indians,* vol. 8, edited by Robert Heizer. Washington, DC: Smithsonian Institution, 1978, pp. 173–179.

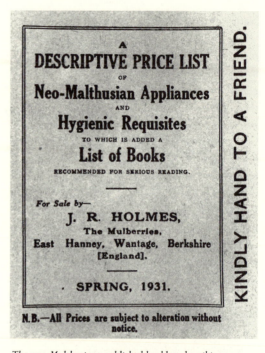

The neo-Malthusians published booklets describing contraceptive techniques, as the cover of this 1931 booklet demonstrates. (Courtesy of the Sophia Smith Collection, Smith College)

Neo-Malthusians

In simple terms, Neo-Malthusians are Malthusians who believed that population could be controlled and that control could provide a key to the creation of a more perfect society. They were strong advocates of some forms of birth control, but they also generally were anticlerical, antimystic, and freethinkers. They strongly believed that developments in science and technology would make the world a better place to live and human nature could at least be manipulated by human effort. They provided the dominant intellectual justification for contraception in the British Isles and ultimately were more influential there than in the United States.

Part of the reason is that the United Sates, at least at the beginning of the nineteenth century, was far behind the British Isles in industrialization and was more optimistic in the long run. The birth control movement in the United States initially was also strongly influenced by utopian socialists, and it was transmitted to future generations through radicals and reformers including feminists. Neo-Malthusians were also influenced by perfectionism.

Nineteenth Century Fertility Trends in England and the United States

Fertility rates that had remained fairly stable through the sixteenth to the end of the eighteenth centuries in Europe and in what was to become the United States began to drop in the nineteenth century. Although the drop in family size could be partly explained by lengthy periods of continence and extended periods of breast-feeding, that women stopped giving birth at much earlier ages than in the past indicates that some sort of family planning was involved. The fertility rate in the United States, for example, dropped 50 percent between 1800 and 1900. The decline in the fertility rate was first noticeable in France at the end of the eighteenth century, and it was slower to appear in the rest of Europe, but it gradually did so.

Some have explained this through what is called an adjustment theory, that is, the number of births per family went down because of changes in living conditions. One such change is hypothesized to be a decline in the rate of infant mortality. Even if this was a factor, it does not explain why the decline in the French birthrate began in the eighteenth century and why even in industrializing countries, such as England and

Belgium, marital fertility fell before infant mortality figures declined.

On the other hand are those who are called the innovations theorists. They have been more interested in what men and women thought than in census tables indicating what they did. An individual who believed in the possibility of controlling nature would, it has been argued, be more likely to limit family size than the one who felt powerless and alienated. As evidence for this, the innovations theorists point out that those most likely to be the first users of birth control would be the self-confident, future-oriented individuals in society. According to this theory, the impetus would come from the enlightened upper classes, and then a generation or so later they would be followed by other groups as middle-class mores were diffused.

Unfortunately, there are holes in the theory when the actual historical data are examined. In France, for example, limitation of family size took place among the peasant classes in the eighteenth century. Such a decline in birthrate has been attributed to the peasant's desire to avoid dividing land among heirs. A similar decline in birthrate among the bourgeoisie has been explained as an effort to maintain a more comfortable lifestyle. Other explanations have been offered for other countries and subgroups, but that it happened might indicate what J. A. Banks and others have called a cultural innovation. Those who first restricted births did not do so to escape poverty, but to protect new-found prosperity, in effect carrying out a revolution of rising expectations. The result was a kind of trickle-down theory in which the lead of the upper classes would be followed by the lower classes as they too began to anticipate that a change for the better might be in store for them. Also important was the growing urbanization, which meant greater mobility and also greater secularization. Traditional family ties were weakened and the influence of the traditional village attitudes diminished. Inevitably urban family size declined before rural but it is also true that the economic value of children as workers declined and they increasingly had less value in the urban setting than they did in a rural one, where the family farm could not function without the whole family being involved in production.

As McLaren has pointed out, even though such suppositions are true and all classes and ethnic groups ultimately saw the wisdom of adopting the small family model, they might well have had different reasons. Women and men view fertility controls differently, so does the church, the medical profession, and even the state. Did people in the past want the large number of births that occurred? There was, as the various entries in this encyclopedia indicate, always among women some interest in various means of preventing pregnancy or achieving an abortion. Although the methods used were not necessarily effective, some were far more effective than others. Many, if not most, women who wanted to avoid pregnancy tried some of the contraceptive formulas and then, if they did not work, and if the fall back on abortion did not work either, they accepted the inevitable. Infanticide and abandonment would be a final out.

At the end of the eighteenth century, while individuals such as the Marquis de Condorcet (1743–1794) wrote of the need to constrain population, the person who made population control seem to be a critical necessity was Thomas Malthus. The pessimistic Malthus emphasized that poverty could not be eliminated by charitable acts or individuals, but was a problem caused by the poor and which they would have to address themselves. He saw only misery for them unless they could keep their family size down by abstinence. The nineteenth-century British reformers who took up the cause of improving the lot of the poor, and who accepted Malthus's ideas about the problems of population growth, wanted to intervene more positively and turned to advocating various methods of family planning. Even before Malthus had written, Jeremy Bentham (1748–1832) had declared that population could be controlled by using such devices as a sponge, and it was the Bentham example that the reformers followed.

Certainly the reformers were motivated to try to alleviate the growing misery and hunger, which Malthus and predicted would occur, and the answer to them was also to educate the poor, who might previously not have known about birth control. These reformers are known collectively as the Neo-Malthusians because, although they accepted Malthus's predictions, they did not accept his solution. Francis Place began the movement by distributing handbills in 1823 describing the use of the sponge; and in at least one version of his handbill, coitus interruptus. After this initial effort, Place turned to other things but his efforts were continued by his disciples, most notably Richard Carlile. In 1826 in the first book published in England on birth control, *Every Woman's Book: or, What Is Love,* Carlile described the use of the sponge, partial withdrawal by the male, coitus interfemora (between the thighs), and the use of the condom (baudruche, or glove).

The Neo-Malthusian movement in the United States was not far behind. It was initiated by Robert Dale Owen and Charles Knowlton, each of whom had been influenced by Place and Carlile. Owen believed that Carlile was wrong in advocating partial withdrawal (he was) and instead advocated complete withdrawal, or coitus interruptus. He had little use for Carlile's other contraceptive advice as well because Owen believed that the sponge was not particularly effective and that it was disagreeable, whereas the condom was inconvenient.

Knowlton's discussion is far more comprehensive, and Norman Himes called it the most important account on the topic since Soranos wrote in the classical period. This is somewhat of an exaggeration because Knowlton primarily espoused douching. He is, however, important historically for the difficulties he had in disseminating his information, including some time in jail; his role in popularizing the cause; and for his book, which was widely known at the time of his death.

Probably the most influential of the early books was that by George Drysdale, whose initial book on sex education, *The Elements of Social Science,* was published anonymously in 1854. He devoted five and a half pages to ways of preventing conception, recommending the use of a sponge and then after intercourse a clear water douche. He disapproved of coitus interruptus because it might lead to mental and physical illness, and he believed that the condom was unaesthetic, dulled enjoyment, and might even produce impotence. He also considered the so-called safe period and believed that, although it was not infallible, it might reduce the likelihood of pregnancy.

All the early public advocates of contraceptives were political radicals and mostly freethinkers. They believed they not only had a mission to serve the poor but also to challenge the moral and religious hypocrisy of the time. This made them suspect to most of the political establishment. George Drysdale, for example, worked closely with Charles Bradlaugh, an outspoken advocate of freethinking. In his newspaper, the *National Reformer,* which was founded in 1860, Bradlaugh attacked British social, religious, and sexual prejudices, declaring himself a republican, an atheist, and a Malthusian. Drysdale contributed regularly to the newspaper, and his message about birth control as well as the book by Charles Knowlton on the subject were regularly printed in England.

In 1876, Henry Cook a Bristol bookseller, was sentenced to two years at hard labor for publishing an edition of Knowlton's book, and the prosecution claimed that the book was adorned with "obscene" illustrations, probably illustrations of the male and female genitals. Knowlton's book had been published in London without interference for some forty-three years by a number of booksellers, including Charles Watts (1836–1901), a free-thought publisher. After the successful Bristol prosecution, Watts, to avoid jail himself, pleaded guilty to publishing an obscene book and was given a suspended sentence and cost provided he did not do so again.

As indicated elsewhere, this led to the Brad-laugh-Besant trial, which among other things gave widespread publicity to the birth control movement. Annie Besant, unimpressed by the advice in the Knowlton book, wrote *The Law of Population,* the first book by a woman on the subject. Her advice was judicious and accurate. She said the safe period was uncertain, coitus interruptus was all right but she was not enthusiastic about it, douching with a solution of sulfate of zinc or of alum might work but it was up to the individual's preference, the condom was acceptable as a guard against disease and might also be used as a contraceptive, but the sponge was the most desirable.

In the aftermath of the trial, the Malthusian League, which had been formed by Drysdale in the 1860s, was reinvigorated and reorganized and George Drysdale's brother, Charles R. Drysdale, became its president. He was succeeded as president by Dr. Alice Vickery, his wife, emphasizing again the entrance of women into the movement. The league continued to publish the *Malthusian* until 1921, when it changed its name to the *New Generation.* It changed it back to the *Malthusian* in 1949 and ceased publication in 1952. In spite of the attention given to it by historians, the membership of the Malthusian League was never very large, usually less than one hundred active members, although the circulation of the journal was larger. Most of the league's arguments were concentrated on economic and social arguments for family limitation. It did not publish a leaflet giving practical details of contraceptive techniques until 1913.

In the United States, the birth control movement ran into difficulty with the passage of the Comstock Act, which had devastating effects, and people such as Edward Bliss Foote, whose books and pamphlets on the subject of birth control were widely read, had to turn to other methods than books and pamphlets to reach an audience. It was not until the second decade of the twentieth century that the birth control movement could form anew.

See also Besant, Annie; Bradlaugh, Charles; Bradlaugh-Besant Trial; Carlile, Richard; Coitus Interruptus (Withdrawal); Comstock, Anthony, and Comstockery; Condom; Drysdale, George; Foote, Edward Bliss; France and Birth Control; Knowlton, Charles; Malthus, Thomas Robert; Modernity and Falling Birthrates; Owen, Robert Dale; Sponges, Tampons, and Vaginal Inserts; Sterile Period (Rhythm Method)

References
Banks, Joseph A. *Prosperity and Parenthood: A Study of Family Planning among the Victorian Middle Classes.* London: Routledge and Kegan Paul, 1954.
Carlile, Richard. *Every Woman's Book; or, What Is Love.* London: R. Carlile, 1826. (This is called the fourth edition but no earlier one has survived.)
Cole, A. J., and S. C. Watkins, eds. *The Decline of Fertility in Europe.* Princeton, NJ: Princeton University Press, 1986.
Condorcet, A. N. de. *Esquisse d'un tableau historique de progres d l'esprit humain,* edited by O. H. Prior. Paris: J. Vrin, 1933.
Drysdale, George. *Physical, Sexual, and Natural Religion, by a Student of Medicine.* London: Edward Truelove, 1854. (The later editions, usually also published by Truelove, were entitled *The Elements of Social Science.*)
Himes, Norman. *Medical History of Contraception.* New York: Schocken Books, 1970.
McLaren, Angus. *A History of Contraception.* Oxford, England: Blackwell, 1990.
Owen, Robert Dale. *Moral Physiology; or a Brief and Plain Treatise on the Population Problem,* 4th ed. New York: Wright and Owen, 1831.
Sennet, R. *Families against the City: Middle Class Homes of Industrial Chicago, 1872–1890.* Cambridge, MA: Harvard University Press, 1970.

Noyes, John Humphrey (1811–1886)

John Humphrey Noyes popularized coitus reservatus in the United States. Noyes had begun his personal sexual experiment after his wife had survived four stillbirths. In his efforts to avoid both unwanted children and the physical burdens women endured during repeated pregnancies, he sought nonintrusive methods of birth control. He said he wanted to avoid "propagative" sex and replace it with "amative" sex. In his scheme of controlled ejaculation, also called by other names such as male continence, Karezza, and the magnetation method, the couple engaged in normal intercourse but the man deliberately avoided ejaculation by stopping his

John Humphrey Noyes, a social reformer who established the Oneida community in New York in 1848, popularized the "withdrawal method" in late-nineteenth-century America. (Archive Photos)

thrusting before climax. Detumescence then is allowed to take place in the vagina, after which the activity can be resumed. The process can be repeated until the couple wants to terminate it. The method required great self control on the part of the man, and some training (often helped by putting the finger against the vas deferens to prevent ejaculation) was essential.

Noyes was an adherent of a belief of Protestantism called "perfectionism." The perfectionists did not regard humans as naturally depraved as did the Calvinists, but rather held that human perfection could best be realized when people entered into communal life in which all private property was abolished. Noyes did not believe that all men were equal in every respect but that "every man, woman and child should be surrounded by circumstances favoring the best

development of heart, mind, and body." He gathered together a group of like-minded individuals in Putney, Vermont, and in 1843 the groups under his leadership established a commune. In some ways his community was similar to that of the Shakers but Noyes feared that celibacy would bring stagnation and eventual death to the community. The physical passions, in his mind, must be channeled to serve the community. Thus Noyes encouraged sexual union between the sexes but attempted to keep as much physical passions from the relationship as possible. Noyes supervised the pairing of couples and expelled from the community those who ignored his advice. It was to avoid the problem of unintentional pregnancy and to control passion that he developed his concept of male continence and spread it among his followers. He taught that each member of the community was married to all others of the opposite sex and coitus reservatus was the key to harmonious relationships.

In 1847, when he returned from a convention of perfectionists, he found his neighbors in Putney in an uproar over the reports of sexual improprieties taking place in the community. He was accused of committing adultery, arrested, and allowed out on bail. Once out of jail, he jumped bail and ended up in Oneida, New York, where in 1848 he founded the Oneida Community, which flourished in the last part of the nineteenth century. The community began to disintegrate after his death but elements of it survived until well into the twentieth century. The company he founded as a community company was secularized in 1935 and renamed Oneida, Ltd., and continued to produce silver plate products as well as stainless steel tableware, china, and industrial items.

The description of Noyes's method of intercourse was first put into writing in 1866 when persistent inquiries about the method led Noyes to publish a leaflet outlining it. In 1872 a much longer tract appeared. Noyes did not originate the concept of coitus reservatus, as some have claimed, because it was known and practiced by the ancient Chinese as well as other peoples long before. Noyes did, however, popularize it among Americans, as well as others. In his writings he rejected condoms, sponges, and lotions as unnatural, unhealthy, and indecent, as well as destructive of love. Obviously there were times when members of the Oneida Community did not practice coitus reservatus and there were probably failures even when they did, but the community welcomed wanted children. Noyes himself had believed that propagation was a decision that had to be mutually arrived at but sexual intercourse need not necessarily lead to pregnancy.

See also Coitus Reservatus

References

Klaw, Spencer. *Without Sin: The Life and Death of the Oneida Community.* New York: Penguin Books, 1993.

Muncy, Raymond Lee. *Sex and Marriage in Utopian Communities.* Bloomington: Indiana University Press, 1973.

Noyes, John Humphrey. *Male Continence.* Oneida, NY: Office of the Oneida Circular, 1872.

———. *Male Continence: or Self Control in Sexual Intercourse. A Letter of Inquiry Answered.* Oneida, NY: Oneida Circular, 1872.

O

Onanism

Onanism is based on the biblical account of
Onan, the son of Judah and the brother of Er,
Judah's first born son. The Lord had killed Er
because of his wickedness, and according to the
levirate law, because Er's wife was childless,
Onan was supposed to get her with child.
Rather than do so, he spilled his seed on the
ground and because of this the Lord slew him
also (Genesis 38:8–10).

How commonly the practice of coitus interruptus was employed in the past is debatable,
but under the term "onanism," it was condemned in the medieval penitentials and other
writings, it appears in the Venetian police
records in the fifteenth century, and was condemned by both Protestant and Catholic writers. Such condemnations did not prevent its
practice but probably taught many people about
it. This is evident in an early anonymous eighteenth-century tract entitled *Onania,* which
went through at least eighteen editions. To condemn the practice required some explanation of
what was involved and there are horrific
accounts of the fate of those who engaged in it,
some of them married couples who did so to
prevent further pregnancies. Included in some
editions, however, was a defense of onanism by
an individual who practiced it:

> My conscience seems to clear me of ONAN's
> Crime, for what he did was out of spite and ill-
> will, and contrary to an express Command of
> raising up Seed to his Brother, in Contradiction to
> the Method of Our Redemption: Whereas mine is

pure necessity in respect both of Body and
Soul . . . (*Onania,* 1726, p. 103).

Angus McLaren called this the first public
defense made of coitus interruptus. Certainly
the practice was widely used in the eighteenth
century.

Onanism, however, soon came to mean more
than coitus interruptus. Rather it became a
ubiquitous term applied to all nonprocreative
intercourse. This was particularly the case in
many of the medical theories of the eighteenth
century, which often classed what had been
regarded as sinful as a medical pathology and
subject to medical treatment and investigation.
The justification for such classifications was the
assumption of the theorists that good health was
the result of a kind of equilibrium and this condition of homeostasis could be upset by activities
that caused a drain on the body. Although theorists disagreed in their assumptions about how
the body worked, they all emphasized the need
to keep it in balance; output was supposed to
match intake. Sexual activity of any type was
thought to challenge the body's equilibrium, as
did any abnormal bodily loss such as diarrhea or
vomiting. Intercourse was essential to continue
the species, but it was the nonprocreative sexual
activities that were dangerous to one's health.
Two factors contributed to such a phenomenon.
One is the observable phenomenon that orgasm
in the man results not only in the ejaculation of
semen but also in a brief feeling of lassitude. This
led many, if not most, physicians to believe that
the rash expenditure of semen could result in

growing feebleness and even insanity. They did not say much about women in this respect but assumed they too faced dangers. Adding to this assumption was a second observation, namely, that many sexually promiscuous individuals seemed to have serious disabilities as they aged. Although we know today that much of what was attributed to sexual activity itself was the result of third-stage syphilis, which can result in insanity, paralysis, heart problems, skin lesions, as well as other symptoms, all of this was attributed to an overactive sex life.

Particularly influential in focusing medical attention on onanism was the Lausanne, Switzerland, physician S. A. D. Tissot (1728–1797), who concluded that all sexual activity was potentially dangerous because it caused blood to rush to the head. Such a rush of blood, he believed, starved the nerves, making them more susceptible to damage, thereby increasing the likelihood of insanity or various other physical disabilities. Although he recognized the necessity of procreation for the survival of humans, Tissot believed that nonprocreative sex of every kind must be controlled. His influence on the medical profession was profound, and during the last part of the eighteenth century until well into the twentieth century the dangers of onanism, that is, masturbation, coitus interruptus, coitus reservatus, and all nonprocreative sex (including the use of contraceptives and even same-sex relationships), were classed as pathological by large segments of the medical community.

Increasingly in the nineteenth century, the term "onanism" was replaced in the United States by the term "masturbation," but included under masturbation were a host of sexual activities because it was believed that masturbation itself was an initiating factor in homosexuality and other "pathological" sex acts. Thus coitus interruptus, coitus in os (oral sex), coitus interfemora, pederasty, bestiality, mutual stimulation in foreplay, and self-stimulation were all lumped together under masturbation. Some even designated the use of contraceptives as a form of masturbation.

See also Coitus Interruptus (Withdrawal)

References

Bullough, Vern L., and Bonnie Bullough. *Sexual Attitudes: Myths and Realities.* Buffalo: Prometheus Books, 1995.

McLaren, Angus. *A History of Contraception.* Oxford, England: Blackwell, 1990.

Onania: or the Heinous Sin of Self-Pollution and All Its Frightful Consequences in Both Sexes, 11th ed. London: Thomas Crouch, 1726. (Pagination differs from edition to edition, and in this one, the page is 103. There is a modern reprinting of the eighth edition (1723) of this in *Marriage, Sex, and the Family in England, 1660–1800,* edited by Randolph Trumbach, New York: Garland, 1985.)

Tissot, S. A. D. *Onanism: A Treatise Upon the Disorders Produced by Masturbation,* translated by A. Hume. London: J. Pridden, 1776. (The original was in Latin but it was quickly translated into most of the secular languages of Europe and went through many printings and editions. This particular edition was reprinted by Garland in a series, *Marriage, Sex, and the Family in England,* edited by Randolph Trumbach, New York: Garland, 1985.)

Opponents of Birth Control and Abortion in the Nineteenth Century

In both England and the United States there were opponents to the dissemination of information about birth control. In England, many of the opponents of the initial efforts of Francis Place and Richard Carlile to disseminate such information came from editors of working-class newspapers, although many of them also supported the concept. Many of the most vocal opponents were physicians. A Dr. Ewing Whittle in 1868 urged physicians to "proclaim loudly that medicine is not the science of the day that points out the way to infidelity and vice; and that, as a profession, we abhor the unnatural projects which have been proposed" (Quoted by Fryer, p. 127).

Medical men believed they were the guardians of public health and, by implication, public morals. *Lancet,* a major medical journal of the time, said that women who contemplated the use of various means of contraception had a mind similar to that of a prostitute. As late as 1904, the president of the British Gynecological Society was convinced that chronic disease and other dangers could be produced by the use of birth control and held that those using such methods and devices were engaged in onanistic practices that were every bit as dangerous as masturbation itself. Various medical journals periodically continued to condemn contraception as a sin against physiology, and some medical groups tried to prevent advertisements and sales of contraceptives. Nowhere, however, was the medical opposition to both birth control and abortion as vehement as it was in the United States.

During the last part of the nineteenth century, there was a strong movement led by the college-educated, or "regular," physicians to make abortion illegal. Before that time it had been treated according to the common-law tradition in which abortions before quickening were not punishable, and those procured later, might, if the woman died, be high misdemeanors but not felonies. The effect of the medical campaign was to drive abortion underground. Because this movement coincided with the enactment of the Comstock Act, which made dissemination of contraceptive information through the mails a felony, "regular" physicians joined in this campaign as well. Many states legislated not only against abortion but in terms of contraception they often went further than the federal law.

Deeply involved in the campaign were medical professionals. They were the most visible single group seeking to tighten the laws against abortion and incidentally contraception. The campaign was as much a campaign to raise the status of the "regular" physicians by establishing minimal licensing requirements for medical practitioners as it was a campaign against abortion and birth control. The "regular" physicians implied that it was only the uneducated midwives and the various sectarians and irregulars who administered abortions or campaigned for contraception. The answer to the problem was to severely curtail the practices of hordes of people who claimed medical expertise. This had been a problem since the 1830s, when the existing licensing laws for physicians had been successfully attacked by a variety of medical practitioners, many with little or no training or schooling, many of them belonging to various sects such as naturopaths, and all of whom in the minds of the "regular" physicians were undermining the medical profession. In order to persuade hesitant state legislators to reinstate licensing laws, the college-educated physicians needed to persuade the public of their expertise and their "moral" integrity. The dangers posed by abortion and, after the passage of the Comstock laws, the use of birth control, were the means by which they did so.

The leader, if there was one, in the medical campaign was Horatio Robinson Storrer, a Massachusetts physician who equated the use of contraceptives with abortion. The only solution for those who wanted to space children was abstinence or the utilization of the safe period. Coitus interruptus, he said, could make men impotent, whereas other methods used by women threatened the health of the woman and potentially might make her sterile. In a sense the antiabortion and anticontraceptive movement was also an antiwomen movement, particularly against the strong-minded married women of the new middle class who were regarded as shirking their natural roles as wives and mothers. A large number of physicians called upon their "scientific" background to argue that women were specially designed by their nature to be childbearers and mothers and anything else was a perversion of their role.

Many religious groups were opposed to contraception as well, but the most vehement and well-organized opposition came from the Catholic Archbishop of New York City.

See also American Medical Association; Carlile, Richard; Catholic Church (American) and Birth Control; Comstock, Anthony, and Comstockery; Masturbation; Onanism; Quickening

References

Brodie, Janet Farrell. *Contraception and Abortion in Nineteenth Century America.* Ithaca, NY: Cornell University Press, 1994.

Fryer, Peter. *The Birth Controllers.* New York: Secker and Warburg, 1965.

Gordon, Linda. *Woman's Body, Woman's Right: A Social History of Birth Control in America.* New York: Grossman, 1976.

Mohr, James C. *Abortion in America: The Origins and Evolution of National Policy, 1800–1900.* New York: Oxford University Press, 1978.

Reed, James. *From Private Vice to Public Virtue: The Birth Control Movement and American Society since 1830.* New York: Basic Books, 1978.

Smith-Rosenberg, Carroll. "The Abortion Movement and the AMA." In *Disorderly Conduct: Visions of Gender in the United States.* New York: Alfred A. Knopf, 1985.

Oral Contraceptives

Oral contraceptives are derived from synthetic hormones that prevent pregnancy. They were first approved by the U.S. Food and Drug Administration (FDA) in 1960. Although the FDA approval was not then necessary for contraceptive devices, it was for pharmaceuticals, and so the pill, in effect, was the first contraceptive approved by the U.S. government. This marked a breakthrough in what had previously been governmental inaction in the field of contraception.

The development of the pill was dependent upon discovery and isolation of hormones. This research was an international effort involving Americans such as Edgar Allen and Edward A. Doisy, Germans such as Adolf Butenandt, British such as Guy F. Marrian, as well as investigators from the Netherlands and other countries. These researchers isolated various hormones beginning with estrone and estriol, which turned out to be excreted metabolites of estradiol, the active hormone produced in the ovaries. These discoveries were followed by the isolation of progesterone and of testosterone.

The isolation of the hormones led to the understanding of how the female menstrual cycle worked and it was this that laid the groundwork for the pill. The earliest application of some of the hormonal research was an effort to control menstrual pain. After the hormone progesterone had been isolated, it was found as early as 1936 that daily injections of it prevented the estrus cycle (when the female is in heat) in rats. Further research with humans demonstrated that a combination of both estrogen and progesterone was more effective in preventing ovulation and dysmenorrhea (painful menstruation) than either hormone alone.

Early hormones had been laboriously extracted from animal urine and this was not only expensive (progesterone was selling at eight dollars a gram in 1943) and time-consuming but both the progesterone and estrogen derived from animals tended to be destroyed by enzymes in the human body. A cheaper source of estrogen was found by Russell Marker in the yam plant in Mexico, and some of the other hormones became less expensive after another breakthrough occurred when Carl Djerassi in 1952 developed an orally active analogue of progesterone. It was this that formed the basis for the oral contraceptive.

Even though research scientists had the basic tools for developing an oral contraceptive, most were reluctant to do so because of the controversial nature of such a development. Gregory Pincus, however, had become somewhat immune to criticism after he had suffered more or less scientific ostracism in 1934 when he announced that he had achieved in vitro fertilization of rabbit eggs inside a test tube. He was denied tenure at Harvard and in the popular literature became symbolic of the mad scientist playing with nature, though he managed to continue his research with private financial support. In 1944, Pincus set up the Worcester Foundation for Experimental Biology to conduct research about hormones and by this time had managed to overcome his early notoriety and gain worldwide recognition for his research. Among other things he was editor of the annual *Progress in Hormone Research.*

Pincus was convinced that there was a possibility of an oral contraceptive, and he and Margaret Sanger met together at the New York apartment of Abraham Stone (the husband of the late Hannah Stone), who was then medical director and vice president of the Planned Parenthood Federation. Not present at the meeting but influential was Katharine Dexter McCormick, who had earlier supported work by Pincus and who very much believed in the

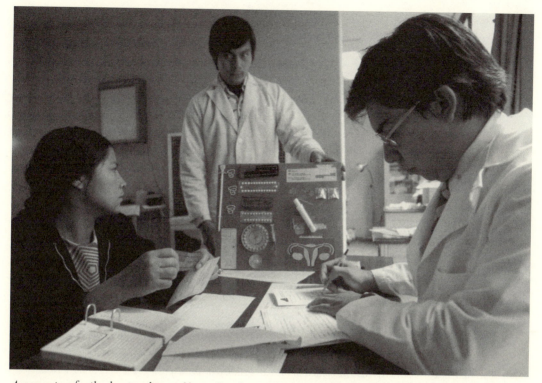

A woman in a family planning clinic in Mexico City chooses birth control pills from among the variety of birth control options shown her. (Tom Nebbia/Corbis)

possibility of an oral contraceptive. The result of the meeting was a decision to proceed, with McCormick later promising the Worcester foundation $20,000 a year, soon increased to $125,000 and then to $180,00 a year for the rest of her life. McCormick also left the foundation one million dollars in her will.

Pincus, assisted by his long-time associate Min Chueh Chang and working with the obstetrician John Rock, set out to test various compounds as potential oral contraceptives, mostly those submitted by Searle Pharmaceuticals, with whom Pincus had been working.

Rock had been included in the team because a physician was needed to test out contraceptive regimens for women. Rock tested Pincus's progesterone regimens on fifty infertile but regularly ovulating women to determine if the dosages would repress ovulation or perhaps even cause the women to become pregnant. One of the batches of 19-norprogestin turned out to be contaminated by a tiny amount of estrogen, but when this defect was remedied the researchers found there was a higher incidence of breakthrough bleeding toward the end of the ovulation-inhibiting cycle of medication. The result was a decision to combine progestin and estrogen in the daily dosages. They used Enovid (norethynodrel) for the progestin component and 1.5 percent mestranol for the estrogenic component. Rock had also found that his patients, once they had quit taking the pill, resumed their normal patterns of ovulation.

The next step was to do a mass study, and Pincus selected Puerto Rico, in part because Dr. Edris Rice-Wray, medical director of Puerto Rico's Family Planning Association, was willing to undertake the exacting and demanding task of

"The pill" revolutionized women's reproductive options in the late 1960s, contributing to a second wave of the women's movement that engendered many social reforms. (Hulton Getty Collection/Archive Photos)

supervising the series of prolonged experiments. The study began in April 1956 in a suburb of San Juan, and by January 1957, when the preliminary trial records were reviewed, 221 women of proven fertility had taken Enovid as directed for periods varying from one to nine months, and not a single one had become pregnant.

Although the women were warned that they might experience nausea, vomiting, dizziness, abdominal pain, diarrhea, or other side effects, they volunteered in good numbers; however, not all the women proved able to endure the side effects, which varied from individual to individual. Some twenty-five women had quit taking the pill either because they were frightened by the side effects or because their priest or personal physician advised them against it. Others appeared to have been confused about what they

were supposed to do. One woman took the tablets only when her husband was not traveling. Another, who became pregnant, complained that the pills had not worked at all even though she had made her husband take them every day.

After the preliminary reports indicated success, Rice-Wray opened up her enrollments and the project was extended elsewhere in Puerto Rico under the gynecologist Adeline Pendleton Satterthwaite. Later another clinic involved in the study was opened in Haiti. Trials also spread to the United States and in 1960 the FDA allowed Enovid to be marketed.

Oral contraceptives work by interfering with the hormonal system, thus controlling ovulation and related reproductive functions. The normal menstrual cycle is regulated by an area in the brain called the hypothalamus, which works through the pituitary to regulate ovarian function. The pituitary gland secretes two hormones: the follicle-stimulating hormone, which signals the follicle in the ovary to develop, and the luteinizing hormone, which signals the follicle to release the egg (ovum). These two hormones travel through the bloodstream to reach the ovary.

In response to the follicle-stimulating hormone an ovarian follicle (or egg sac) develops in the ovary. This follicle releases the hormone estrogen while the egg is ripening. During the first few days of the menstrual cycle the rate of release is slow, but as the follicle develops, the supply of the estrogen level rises precipitously. When the estrogen secretions reach a certain level, the hypothalamus sends a message to the pituitary gland, which in turns secretes luteinizing hormone, thereby triggering ovulation. After ovulation, the follicle that held the egg is renamed the corpus luteum (literally, yellow body). It produces both progesterone and estrogen. The progesterone stimulates the lining of the uterus (the endometrium) to expand, which allows the fertilized egg to be attached to it. If no fertilization takes place, both the estrogen and progesterone diminish and this build-up of the uterine lining is shed during menstruation.

Oral contraceptives, as synthetic hormones, replace and suppress the hormones that the body would have produced. Because oral contraceptives are administered in a constant dosage or in some other pattern differing from the normal cycle described, a false signal is transmitted to the hypothalamus, with the result that the signal triggering the ovulation process is not delivered. In addition, the hormones in the oral contraceptives alter the tubal transport system, change the cervical mucus, and modify the endometrium so that fertilization is not possible.

Over the years the amount of estrogen and progesterone contained in the pills have been lowered as lesser doses were found to be effective; combinations vary by manufacturers. Only two estrogenic compounds are used, ethinyl estradiol and mestranol. Ethinyl estradiol is pharmacologically active, whereas mestranol must be converted into ethinyl estradiol by the liver before it becomes pharmacologically active.

As of this writing, there are basically three types of oral contraceptives: combination pills, which include both estrogen and progestin; triphasic pills, which include these same elements but in differing amounts during the cycle; and "mini-pills," which are low-dose progestin (without estrogen). The combination pills are the most popular and probably the most reliable. Current dosages usually include 1 mg or less of progestin and 35 to 50 mg of estrogen.

When the combined estrogen-progestin pills are used perfectly, that is, taken the same time every day, and when other instructions relating to their side effects such as diarrhea or vomiting are followed, their level of effectiveness reaches 100 percent (about one pregnancy per thousand women). The progestin-only pills are associated with a slightly higher pregnancy rate but one that is still less than 1 percent. The pill is not for everyone. Women with a history of stroke, coronary artery disease, embolisms, diabetes, thrombophlebitis, or other blood vessel problems should not take oral contraceptives, nor should women who smoke heavily. It is known that pills make one less likely to have uterine or ovarian cancer and slightly more likely to have cervical cancer and perhaps breast cancer, particularly if a woman begins taking the pill when she is young.

For those who miss a day, it is possible to use the pills as a morning-after contraceptive. The first dose must be swallowed no later than seventy-two hours after unprotected sex, and the second dose must be taken twelve hours after the first. The number of tablets taken, usually either two or four, depends on the brand.

See also McCormick, Katharine Dexter; Sanger, Margaret Louise (Higgins); Stone, Hannah

References
Bullough, Vern L. *Science in the Bedroom: A History of Sex Research*. New York: Basic Books, 1994.

Bullough, Vern L., and Bonnie Bullough. *Contraception.* Amherst, NY: Prometheus Books, 1997.

Hatcher, Robert A., et al. *Contraceptive Technology.* New York: Irvington Publishers. (Regularly updated editions are issued biennially in even-numbered years.)

Pincus, Gregory. *The Control of Fertility.* New York: Academic Press, 1965.

Pincus, Gregory, et al. "Fertility Control with Oral Medication." In *Benchmark Papers in Human Physiology: Contraception,* edited by L. L. Langley. Stroudsburg, PA: Dowden, Hutchinson, Ross, 1973, pp. 413–426.

Robert Dale Owen, a U.S. House Representative who was scurrilously attacked for spreading information about birth control, decided to do just that. (Archive Photos)

Owen, Robert Dale (1801–1877)

Robert Dale Owen was one of the pioneer advocates of birth control in the United Sates. He was the son of a well-known social reformer, the industrialist Robert Owen, who is best known for his association with the progressive textile mill at New Lanark in Scotland and the utopian colony that he founded in New Harmony, Indiana. The younger Owen was important in his own right. He settled in the United States, served as a congressman, and while in Congress, drafted the bill founding the Smithsonian Institution. In Indiana, he was instrumental in securing a married woman's property law, a common free school system, and more freedom in divorce laws.

Owen had read and owned a copy of Richard Carlile's *Every Woman's Book* and in 1827 had loaned it to a friend, who urged him to publish it. Owen refused but the friend issued a prospectus about the book (intent to publish), printed on Owen's own press. Owen objected and made a public statement about why he was not publishing it. In it he said he was not a physiologist and could not decide the merits of the book, his printers were young boys and should not come in contact with such information, and the public prejudices against such a book would be so strong that they would probably destroy its usefulness. He agreed that the book was bold and plain and calculated to benefit humanity, but feared that in the United States it might be circulated secretly and fall into the hands of the wrong people.

Owen's statement did not end the matter. Two years later, one of his political enemies pub-

lished a pamphlet in New York City reprinting Owen's statement in full but then went on to accuse him of approving of an obscene work that could destroy conjugal happiness and encourage promiscuous intercourse. Later, the New York Typographical Society rejected a gift Owen had sent them of an illustrated sample of a new typography that he had received from England. Even though the illustrations included the Lord's Prayer and other religious material and there was nothing about birth control in it, his opponents used the opportunity to read aloud from Carlile's *Every Woman's Book,* charging Owen with being a "moral incendiary" who was engaged in an effort "to degrade, nullify and destroy" the "holy conjugal relation" and from whom even seemingly innocent gifts should be suspect.

Owen, under attack for something he had not done, decided that he might as well do what he was under attack for doing. First he published three articles in his newspaper, *The Free Inquirer,* summarizing the economic and sociological case for birth control, and this was followed in 1831 by a seventy-two-page booklet, *Moral Physiology; or a Brief and Plain Treatise on the Population Question*. Most of the booklet is devoted to the social and health arguments for family limitation, but in the first three U.S. editions, all published in 1831, Owens discussed three methods of birth control. The first, coitus interruptus, he defined as total withdrawal, and he then went on to argue that most men have enough control over their passions to practice it. He included some case studies—what Peter Fryer called the first birth control case studies to ever be published—demonstrating the good effects of such a method. He next turned to the vaginal sponge but reported he knew of three men who had their partners try it but without success. Lastly he discussed the use of a condom. He claimed that its efficacy is certain but that it is nonetheless disagreeable to use because of cleanliness issues. He also added that because a condom could be used only once, and cost a dollar, it would be unaffordable by most men. In the fourth edition of his book (second edition in England), Owen relegated both the sponge and condom to a footnote, and in still later editions neither are mentioned at all. Some 75,000 copies of the book had been sold in American and English editions by his death.

Owen's great importance was in breaking the barrier of silence in the United States about birth control and in influencing others to write on the topic.

See also Carlile, Richard

References

Fryer, Peter. *The Birth Controllers*. London: Secker and Warburg, 1965.

Hime, Norman E. *Medical History of Contraception*. New York: Schocken Books, 1970.

Owen, Robert D. *Moral Physiology: or, A Brief and Plain Treatise on the Population Question*. New York: Wright and Owen, 1831. (This text was still being printed in the 1880s.)

P

Pessary

Technically a pessary is an instrument placed in the vagina to support the uterus or rectum. They were used to support a prolapsed (fallen) uterus or to alleviate symptoms of abnormal retroversion (a backward displacement of the uterus), anteversion (anterior displacement of the uterus), anteflexion (bending forward of the neck of the uterus), or related problems. Because a tipped uterus does not ordinarily cause problems, the variety of devices designed in the nineteenth century to deal with such conditions might seem puzzling to today's readers. If, however, many of them are seen as devices that also have contraceptive implications, then they become much easier to understand. For example, those designed to correct a displacement included a splint to press the uterus forward or backward, which could have served the same function as an intrauterine device. Rings designed to cover the entrance to the uterus, many of which had domes fitted over them, acted in the same way as a modern diaphragm or cervical cap. Other pessaries were developed to provide a roof to the vagina to hold a prolapsed uterus in place, and this also could act in the same way as a diaphragm. In retrospect, in fact, it seems that many of the so-called female complaints of the past, which led physicians and surgeons to prescribe such devices, were efforts to find some socially acceptable way of avoiding pregnancy. Historians can easily trace the developments of such pessaries in the United States because they could be patented and advertised, whereas devices claiming to have contraceptive value were not protected and were in fact regarded as obscene until well into the twentieth century.

The term "pessary" also was applied to a medicated vaginal suppository that could also be regarded as a contraceptive. The U.S. Patent Office, for example, issued patents for a number of pessaries in the last few decades of the nineteenth century, but nowhere are they ever described as useful for birth control. Both the diaphragm and the cervical cap were originally marketed as pessaries.

One of the first pessaries to be designed for contraceptive purposes was a cervical rubber cap specially molded to fit each individual patient. This was described by a German, Friedrich Adolph Wilde (1838), in his book on obstetrics. He argued that an attempt to prevent a pregnancy was medically necessary in certain cases, such as in the case in which a woman whose pelvis was such that she could not deliver a baby naturally and would be exposed to the dangers of a cesarean section, the success of which was not very high in the nineteenth century. Wilde contended that the methods known to him such as withdrawal, the condom, and the sponge were not reliable, and continence was not practical. For such women he developed a specially molded cervical cap made of resin or rubber—what now would be called unvulcanized rubber. The diaphragm developed much later because it depended on the vulcanization of rubber.

The use of pessaries as a contraceptive seemed obvious and as early as 1846 a John B.

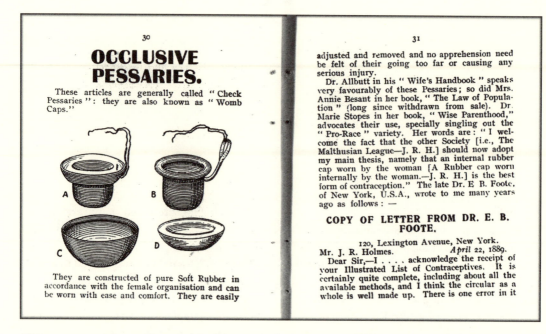

These pessaries, or early cervical caps and diaphragms, were illustrated in A Descriptive Price List of Neo-Malthusian Appliances and Hygienic Requisites *in 1931. (Courtesy of the Sophia Smith Collection, Smith College)*

Beers of Rochester, New York, requested a patent on a "wife's protector," the design of which was clearly intended to prevent conception. His device was a hoop, 1.5 inches in diameter, covered with "oil-silk or some other membranous substance" attached to a thin 8-inch-long metal handle, either to help insert or withdraw the device. Caution was needed in disseminating information about such devices and in 1847 Dr. Walter Scott Tarbox was tried in Boston for transgressing the obscenity act by printing and circulating a pamphlet for "Dr. Cameron's Patent Family Regulator or Wife's Protector." Though he was convicted, the decision was later overturned on a technicality. In 1864, Edward Bliss Foote advertised his "Womb Veil," made of rubber, which was to be placed in the vagina before copulation and which spread a thin film of rubber before the cervix to prevent "the seminal aura from entering." Some of the pessaries were designed for long-time wear, although it is not evident if there was a clear contraceptive intent. In the twentieth century

the Mensinga diaphragm became the pessary of choice in the United States.

Those pessaries with a clearer contraceptive intent went by a variety of names, such as "check pessary," "womb guard," "mechanical shield for ladies," and "closed-ring pessaries," names designed to pass the censorship of the Comstock Act. William Rothacker, a Cincinnati physician, in 1883 described the "pessaire preventif" as only one model of a large variety of appliances whose function was to cover the mouth of the womb and prevent the passage of spermatozoa into the uterine cavity.

See also Cervical Cap; Comstock, Anthony, and Comstockery; Diaphragm; Foote, Edward Bliss

References

Brodie, Janet Farrell. *Contraception and Abortion in Nineteenth Century America.* Ithaca, NY: Cornell University Press, 1994.

Bullough, Vern L. "A Brief Note on Rubber Technology: The Diaphragm and the Condom." *Technology and Culture* 22 (January 1981): 104–111.

Foote, Edward Bliss. *Medical Common Sense.* New York: Self-published, 1864.

Wilde, Friedrich Adolph. *Das weibliche Gebr-unvermgen. Eine medicinisch-juridische Abhandlung zum Gebrauch für practische Geburtshelfer, Aerzte und Juristen*. Berlin: Nicholai'schen Buchhandlung, 1838, p. 317.

Physiology of Reproduction

The question of how pregnancy occurs is one that was unanswerable for much of human history. It was obvious that it had some connection with sexual intercourse. The mating of animals when the female is in estrus would have made this clear, but not all acts of intercourse in humans led to pregnancy, and so it was reasonable to conclude that other forces were involved as well. Some investigators, such as Sir Henry Maine (1822–1888), held that prehistoric man believed he played no part in conception but that instead, through some magical means, ancestral spirits in the form of living germs found their way into the maternal body. Maine classified the stages of human cultural development into ascending stages from anarchy, to matriarchy, to patriarchy, claiming that patriarchy, which he regarded as the highest stage, began when males discovered they were the key factor in the whole pregnancy process and were the initiating factor for the miracle of birth. Such a supposition is highly unlikely, but in history it is not always what really happened that matters but what some influential people say happened, and Maine's thesis could neither be proven nor disproved even though few would now accept it.

From strictly observational criteria, not only the reproductive habits of animals, but simply that semen is visible and the ovum is not, it is easy to understand why throughout recorded history the man assumed that he was primarily responsible for procreation. This does not mean the woman was entirely excluded from the male perception of who was responsible for procreation. Excluding her would have been a difficult thing to do in terms of the biology of reproduction, but she was often conceptualized as only carrying and nourishing the seed planted by the man.

Plato had argued that pregnancy was almost a necessity for women, otherwise they might become hysterical. He wrote that the uterus was "an indwelling creature desirous of child-bearing. [When] it remains barren too long after puberty, it is distressed and sorely disturbed, and straying about in the body and cutting off the passages of the breath, it impedes respiration and brings the sufferer into extreme anguish and provokes all manners of diseases besides."

Aristotle gave women a slightly more important role than some of his predecessors in that he believed the fetus was formed from the union of sperm and menstrual blood. Still, he held it was the man who furnished the active principle, whereas the woman supplied the passive element.

The writer of the Hippocratic work on generation, who wrote about the same time as Aristotle, held that the woman had a seed also (two-seed theory) and equated it with vaginal secretions. This view was more or less accepted by Galen, the second-century medical writer, who held that both male and female seeds had coagulative power and receptive capacity for coagulation but that one was stronger in the male and the other in the female. This was modified somewhat by the Arabic medical writer Avicenna, a commentator on Aristotle, in the early part of the eleventh century, who said the male agent was equivalent to the clotting agent of milk and the female "sperm" was the coagulum. Just as the starting point of the clotting was in the rennet, so the starting point of the clot that was to become a human was in the man. Avicenna's interpretation of Aristotle was adopted with modifications in the thirteenth century by Saint Albertus Magnus, who held that female semen was only that in an equivocal sense and that the male contributed the essential material for generation. Saint Thomas Aquinas, his pupil, agreed, stating that the female generative power was imperfect as compared with the male generative power.

Better understanding of the process depended on more effective knowledge of the human body. In this, the anatomical work of Andreas Vesalius in the sixteenth century proved important, as did the more specialized studies on female anatomy by Gabriele Falloppio, his younger contemporary. Falloppio described the clitoris as well as the tubes that bear his name. Falloppio was also important in the understanding of male anatomy because he described the arteria profunda of the penis, which helps explain why it becomes erect. Anatomical studies also demonstrated that there was no foundation for the traditional belief in the wandering womb, which had been advanced by Plato. Nevertheless the folk myth persisted even as the sixteenth century anatomists challenged it.

The first major challenge to the dominance of the male in reproduction came from William Harvey, the seventeenth-century physician, best known for his demonstration of the circulation of the blood. Harvey also did major research on animal reproduction, primarily on chick embryos and those of deer. He believed the egg was all important and, although he could not see the egg in the deer, he hypothesized that one must exist. He formulated his dictum that "an egg is the common primordium of all animals." This was later summed up by the Swedish biologist Carl Linnaeus as *Vivum omne ex ovo,* or all life comes from the egg.

The growing number of the ovists ran into an obstacle with the studies of Anton van Leeuwenhoek (1632–1723), who used the newly developed microscope to observe all kinds of new creatures. Johan Ham brought him a vial of semen that he had taken from a sick man and in which he had observed numberless little creatures in it. Leeuwenhoek confirmed their existence and then tested semen from other sources and found that the "spermatozoa" existed in such great quantity and were so small that there were literally thousands, probably millions, in a space the size of a grain of sand. Leeuwenhoek described them as having round bodies with tails five or six times the size of their body and making swimming movements like that of an eel. He found that the sperm died within twenty-four hours if kept in cold temperature but survived several days if kept in warm conditions.

The debate between the ovists and the spermaticists continued throughout the eighteenth and much of the nineteenth centuries. Although biologists could disagree on interpretation of the data, they were also influenced by their own world views. Many could not accept that the existence of so many sperm implied that God was playing Russian roulette, taking a chance on what happened, and that this argued against an individual soul. If embryos developed mechanically, God, it was implied, had no part. Still, as research continued, the existence of sperm was confirmed in most animal species, the mammalian egg was finally discovered in 1827, and in 1875 Oscar Hertwig observed the sperm entering the egg of the sea urchin. The Mediterranean sea urchin provided an almost unique opportunity for such observation because the eggs are transparent, occur in large numbers, and develop rapidly. Under such conditions it was fairly easy for Hertwig to observe the coming together of two nuclei in the egg, leading him to surmise he had observed fertilization. Not until a year later did Herman Fol actually observe the spermatozoa penetrate an egg.

To understand further the process of fertilization in humans, it was essential to know more about female physiology, particularly the place the menstrual cycle played in it. By 1920, after several false starts and assumptions, a theory of menstruation was beginning to develop. The essentials were that menstruation occurred because the lining of the uterus, after being prepared for implantation of the ovum, would degenerate if fertilization of the egg did not occur. This theory required that ovulation and the corpus luteum formation precede the premenstrual change. The whole process was found to be triggered by what eventually came to be called hormones. The female hormone estrone was isolated in 1929 and was being produced commercially within a short time. Estriol was isolated in 1930. But the two forms of estrogen were not the only female hormones and by 1934 progesterone had also been isolated. Such discoveries, through the work of numerous investigators, led to a greater understanding of the physiology of reproduction and its hormonal regulation.

By the 1930s researchers divided the menstrual cycle into four or five phases. The five-phase description was generally adopted because it tended to be more descriptive of what women experience, namely, (1) the follicular phase, (2) ovulation, (3) the luteal phase, (4) the premenstrual phase (not included in the four-phase cycle), and (5) either menstruation or pregnancy. During the follicular phase, which lasts from six to fourteen days, several follicles (from which the phase gets its name) begin to ripen and mature within an ovary. This process is mediated by a hypothalamus decapeptide that was originally called gonadotropin-releasing hormone but is now usually called luteinizing hormone-releasing hormone (LH-RH) or luteinizing hormone-releasing factor (LH-RF). The release of LH-RH is in response to low levels of estrogen in the bloodstream. LH-RH in turn stimulates the pituitary to secrete follicle-stimulating hormone (FSH) and LH. FSH stimulates the follicle to produce and secrete estrogen into the bloodstream (the follicular phase). As the level of estrogen in the bloodstream rises, it signals the pituitary to stop releasing FSH. This then leads to the second stage, ovulation, which involves the rupture of a mature follicle from the ovary. When the egg is released from the follicle, it begins its journey through the fallopian tube, at the end of which the egg reaches the uterus, where it may or may not be fertilized by a sperm. Some women are able to feel the rupturing of the egg (*mittelschmerz*), but most do not. The result is the third phase, the luteal phase, because the empty follicle, now referred to as the corpus luteum (yellow body), secretes progesterone. Progesterone leads to an increase in the growth of the endometrium (uterine lin-

ing) in preparation for the egg in case it is fertilized (premenstrual phase). After four to six days, the corpus luteum begins to disintegrate, leading to a decrease in the levels of both progesterone and estrogen, and finally, if fertilization has not taken place, to menstruation, the disintegration and discharge of the uterine lining. As the estrogen level drops, the cycle starts over again. If, however, pregnancy takes place, the placenta begins to produce human chorionic gonadotropin (hCG) at rapidly increasing levels for the first six weeks; hCG delays the onset of menstruation and replaces LH. The placenta also produces estrogen and seems to be the chief source of estrogen during pregnancy. Progesterone is also present in the placenta. The ability to detect hCG was the explanation for the success of the first pregnancy tests.

The whole cycle is marked by variations in body basal temperature, with the temperature rising slightly during the later part of the menstrual cycle. This rise begins one to two days after ovulation in response to rising levels of progesterone, and it is on this fluctuation in body temperature that some women chart their fertility cycle. Other changes take place in the cervical mucosa, which has also been used to plot safe periods for sexual intercourse. By the 1950s, after thousands of years of speculation, the physiology of reproduction was finally understood.

See also Sterile Period (Rhythm Method)

References

Aristotle. *Generation of Animals*, translated by A. L. Peck. London: Heinemann, Loeb Classical Library, 1953, 729A, 25–34.

Avicenna. *Canon of Medicine*, translated by O. Cameron Gruner. London: Luzak and Company, 1930, I, 196, p. 23.

Bullough, Vern L. *Science in the Bedroom: A History of Sex Research*. New York: Basic Books. 1994.

———. *Sexual Variance in Society and History*. Chicago: University of Chicago Press, 1976.

Hippocrates. *On Intercourse and Pregnancy*, translated by T. U. H. Ellinger. New York: Henry Schuman, 1952, pp. 21 ff.

Maine, Henry. *Ancient Law*. London: Murray, 1861.

Plato. *Timaeus*, translated by R. G. Bury. London: Heinemann, Loeb Classical Library, 1961, 91C.

Pincus, Gregory Goodwin (1903–1967)

Gregory Goodwin Pincus is the inventor of the birth control pill. Pincus, a pioneer in hormone research, was more or less ostracized by many of his contemporaries. This is because as an untenured professor at Harvard, Pincus received national publicity in 1934 when he announced that he achieved in vitro (inside a test tube) fertilization of rabbit eggs. Unfortunately, in the aftermath the *New York Times* portrayed him as a sinister character bent on hatching humans in bottles, similar to the character of Professor Bokanovsky, created by Aldous Huxley in the novel *Brave New World* (1932), which was then being widely read. A popular magazine article on Pincus concluded that he was threatening the American male.

Shortly after this Pincus was denied tenure at Harvard and was unable to get another academic position. He eventually ended up at Clark University, although not with an academic appointment. In 1944, he had reestablished himself enough to set up the Worcester Foundation for Experimental Biology to conduct research into steroids. Eventually G. D. Searle Pharmaceutical Company supported his research. Pincus also began on his own to test the contraceptive value of steroids and had decided that the most promising of these hormones was progesterone, which caused the lining of the uterus to thicken. His work came to the attention of Katharine Dexter McCormick and Margaret Sanger and with funding from them he pushed on to develop the oral contraceptive.

See also McCormick, Katharine Dexter; Oral Contraceptives; Sanger, Margaret Louise (Higgins)

References
Bullough, Vern L. *Science in the Bedroom: A History of Sex Research.* New York: Basic Books, 1994.
Reed, James. *From Private Vice to Public Virtue: The Birth Control Movement and American Society since 1830.* New York: Basic Books, 1978.

Place, Francis (1771–1854)

Francis Place, an English reformer, was the first person to attempt to reach large numbers of people with a message about birth control. To do so he developed what might be called a social theory of contraception. Place, who had learned to read and write, was apprenticed as a tailor at age thirteen. He became a journeyman at age seventeen and was successful enough at nineteen to marry Elizabeth Chadd. The couple had fifteen children, ten of whom survived infancy. Place became radicalized during a strike of the journeyman tailors and became one of the leaders, an activity that got him blacklisted when the unsuccessful strike ended. The couple pawned everything that could be pawned and borrowed from landlords and others in order to survive. Place was almost ready to find a new means of supporting himself when finally one of his old employers contracted him to do some tailoring. Place and his wife worked long days to pay off their debts and recover their pawned possessions.

Although he was unemployed, Place had engaged in some serious reading, borrowing books by Adam Smith, John Locke, and David Hume, learning algebra and geometry, and studying history. He continued his organizing activities in spite of the difficulties that had beset him and became secretary of the Breeches Makers' Benefits Society. When the workers finally achieved their long-sought raise, Place was out of a job because the organization was dissolved. Interestingly he was opposed to labor unions (not benefit societies) because he believed that unionism turned one class against another; and he wanted to suppress class consciousness. Continuing his political activities, however, he went on to establish a successful tailoring establishment that paid him well.

He worked on a number of causes before becoming assistant and adviser to a member of Parliament, a position he used to get major reform legislation enacted. Much of his action was done anonymously. He wrote his *Illustrations and Proofs of the Principles of Population* in 1822 and, although he believed in Malthus's predictions about population, Place urged contraceptive measures as a substitute for Malthus's ideas of "moral restraint."

Francis Place, neo-Malthusian author of Illustrations and Proofs of the Principles of Population, *advocated birth control as a means toward better quality of life for families. (Archive Photos)*

Place wrote several handbills on the subject of contraception: "To the Married of Both Sexes," "To the Married of Both Sexes in Genteel Life," and "To the Married of Both Sexes of the Working People," all three of which survive in printed form, plus a fourth, "To the Mature Reader of Both Sexes," that exists in draft. In each of them he advised his readers to use a soft sponge tied by a bobbin or penny ribbon that was to be inserted into the vagina just before sexual intercourse and withdrawn afterward. The sponge was to be washed before it was used again. In one handbill he recommended coitus interruptus but apparently came to rely entirely on the sponge in later editions. He distributed the pamphlets widely and had others assist in the pro-

ject. Interestingly Place was not prosecuted for the distribution of the pamphlets even though at least one person complained to the attorney general about a bundle of handbills she had received. The movement that Place began came to be called the Neo-Malthusian movement because, although most of its advocates accepted most aspects of the Malthusian thesis, they believed in contraception. Theologically most of the Neo-Malthusians disagreed with Malthus because his doctrines tended to be anticlerical, antimysticism, and even to some extent anti-Christian.

When Place went on to other endeavors, some of his disciples took up his work, among them Richard Carlile, Richard Hassell, and William Campion.

Place's personal life did not end happily. His wife died of cancer in 1827, and Place in 1830 married again, this time not so happily and the two separated after twelve years and many quarrels. In 1844, Place suffered a stroke, after which he complained about his inability to think clearly. He died in the early hours of January 1, 1854, but his life passed unrecognized at the time and it was only later that he was given credit for his work in contraception. His papers are in the British National Library.

See also Carlile, Richard

References

Fryer, Peter. *The Birth Controllers.* London: Secker and Warburg, 1965.

Himes, Norman E. *A Medical History of Contraception.* New York: Schocken Books, 1970.

Place, Francis. *Illustrations and Proofs of the Principle of Population . . ..* Reprinted and edited by Norman E. Himes with comments. London: Allen and Unwin, 1930.

Plastic Wrap

Because in today's world it is general knowledge that erecting a barrier at the mouth of the cervix, thereby closing its entrance to sperm, is a form of contraception, various devices other than the standard barriers of condom, diaphragm, and cap have been tried, often by teenagers. One frequently reported by birth control clinics is plastic wrap. It is not effective because it does not stay in place and does not fit tightly enough to prevent the entrance of sperm.

Polygamy

Polygamy is derived from the Greek word *gamia,* the act of marrying, and so literally means many acts of marriage, either for a man or woman. To distinguish these, the more technical terms polygyny, many wives, and polyandry, many husbands, are also used, although polygamy is still the most widely used term even though multiple wives are far more common than multiple husbands. In fact, polygyny might be said to have been the normative form of marriage at one time or another for many people in more than three-fourths of the world's traditional cultures. Polygyny also was a major form of birth control because one man with many wives would reduce the pregnancy potential of his wives, and more importantly it would mean that many men did not have a wife or regular female companion, only an occasional prostitute.

In many Asian countries in the past, plurality of legal wives was customary, although not all could afford it. In China, however, tradition was to allow only one wife, although the number of concubines depended upon a man's ability to afford them, a practice that lasted until the twentieth century, as the 1931 Pearl Buck novel, *The Good Earth,* so effectively illustrated. According to Islamic law, polygyny is acceptable but a man is allowed to have no more than four wives at one time, although divorce is easy and the number of concubines is not restricted. Several of the modern Islamic nations have prohibited plural marriages but many have not. Hinduism traditionally allowed men to have as many wives as they pleased and many high-caste people had hundreds. Polygyny was and still is the rule in many of the African tribes and in the past was common

in Australia and in Polynesia. In ancient civilizations polygyny was acceptable and was, for example, a common practice among the ancient Hebrews. Men who could afford them kept numerous wives and concubines simultaneously, and monogamy was common because of poverty, not principle. Josephus (d. 96 M.E.), the ancient Jewish historian, in discussing the tangled marital affairs of King Herod (37–4 B.C.E.) and his nine wives, observed that "It is an ancestral custom of ours to have several wives at one time"(Josephus, 17.9–25, 29–33). In ancient Hebrew society, and in many others, there was the levirate tradition, a requirement that a man marry his brother's widow and to make certain she had children to support her in her old age.

The major exception to widespread polygynous marriage in the ancient world was among the Greeks. Greek marriage was monogamous, and in fact monogamy was believed by the Greeks to be a distinguishing feature of their culture in contrast to "barbarian" ones. Hermione in Euripides's *Andromache,* emphasizes this difference in her speech, stating that in Greece, as compared with the rest of Asia, there is not one man teaming up with two wives, rather "clean-living husbands love and honor one, gluing affectionate eyes only on her." The Romans similarly were monogamous, although marriage in both Greek and Roman civilizations could easily be dissolved by divorce.

Germanic law codes treated marriage as a union created by cohabitation rather than by formal act. Marriage was a social fact, not a legal status, and polygyny was a common feature, although most men probably contented themselves with a single wife because they could not afford to do otherwise. Polygyny continued to be a fact of Germanic society for several centuries after most of its population was converted to Christianity.

Early Christianity followed the Greek and Roman monogamous ideals. So hostile were many of the early Christians to sexual intercourse, that even monogamy was regarded as only second best to total abstinence and a non-

A single family from the fundamentalist Mormon community of Short Creek, Arizona, where state police arrested all the men on charges of polygamy in 1953. The Church of Jesus Christ of the Latter Day Saints (Mormon Church) has excommunicated all known polygamists. (Hulton Getty Collection / Archive Photos)

marital life. In this emphasis on abstinence and celibacy, Christianity was not alone because when it appeared upon the religious scene there was a new emphasis on sexual abstinence among Stoics, Neo-Platonists, Gnostics, and others, all of whom identified sexual self-denial as evidence of spiritual strength and venerated virgins as sources and symbols of power. The difficulty Christians had in insisting on at most one wife came from their acceptance of the Hebrew scriptures because the stories of polygynous prophets and patriarchs were incorporated into the Christian Bible. Generally, the justification for these early practices by the Christian Fathers of the Church was that there had been a need during the early period of human existence to fulfill the command to increase and multiply, something they believed was no longer necessary. Thus, although the orthodox Fathers of the Church in the second and third centuries tended to accept marriage as an option, the ideal life was one of celibacy, and even married Christians were urged to restrict the role of sex in their life. The ultimate authority for the western church was Saint Augustine (d. 430), who held that the ideal for Christians should be lifelong abstinence. Marriage was an acceptable alternative only for those unable or unwilling to live the celibate life. Sex in marriage, however, was to be restricted to attempts to procreate, and any interference with this aim was sinful. Augustine also stipulated that sexual intercourse should be conducted with the woman on the bottom and the man on top and only in the proper orifice (vagina) and with the proper instrument (penis). Any other position or orifice or instrument was condemned.

Polygamy was not to be tolerated; neither for that matter was divorce. There was even considerable debate about remarriage after the death of a spouse. Although many early church writers wanted to prohibit it, regarding it as bigamous, in general the church came to recognize subsequent marriages of widows and widowers as valid and lawful, even if, because of subsequent deaths, other remarriages resulted.

Saint Thomas Aquinas (1225–1274), the authoritative theological writer of the modern Catholic Church, maintained that polygyny was contrary to natural law. He did, however, concede that in the past the practice had been allowed among the biblical patriarchs. Interestingly, one of his reasons for condemning it was that it tended to create family stress and complicated marital relationships. As secular law developed in the later Middle Ages, it reflected traditional Christian doctrines on polygamy, writing into secular law what had been the concepts expressed in canon law. In general this has continued to be true of western-oriented nations and religions although the illegality of the practice has not eliminated polygamy and occasional religious groups have insisted on its validity, mainly because of the biblical precedents. In the sixteenth century some of the Protestant writers such as Bernardino Ochino (1487–1564) conditionally defended the plurality of wives. Even Martin Luther was willing to tolerate polygyny as a lesser of two evils. Philip, the Landgrave of Hesse, a major supporter of Martin Luther, had an invalid wife with whom he apparently was unable to have sex. With his wife's consent, he sought to marry a second time, rather than commit adultery, and both Martin Luther and Philip Melancthon approved, although not as doctors of theology but as personal friends. When Philip's bigamy became widely known, Luther expressed sorrow that it could not have been kept secret and advised Philip to remain calm because the controversy would subside or perhaps one of his wives would die.

Perhaps the most notorious of modern examples of polygamy within the Christian tradition has been that of the Church of Jesus Christ of Latter Day Saints, commonly known as the Mormon Church. So hostile to the practice were many of the people in communities around Nauvhoo, Illinois, then headquarters of the Church, that it became a major factor in the assassination of the prophet Joseph Smith, founder of Mormonism. After his murder, most of his followers left the United States for the Spanish territories in the West, although before they reached the territories they had been annexed to the United States. As news of their continued polygamous practices circulated and hostility grew, the United States sent an army of occupation to deal with such "horrendous" practices, and the struggle continued. Federal authorities ultimately forced the Mormons to sacrifice their religious principles as a necessary condition of Utah's statehood and the courts upheld the constitutionality of Utah's outlawing of polygamy.

Polyandry, the linking of a woman to two or more men in a marriage contract, was never as common at polygyny. Interestingly, all the societies that have allowed such practices have also allowed polygyny as well as monogamous relationships. Probably the most common form of polyandry is what has been termed fraternal polyandry. This involves the simultaneous marriage of a family's brothers to one wife, as found described in the Indian epic *Mahabharata*. In special circumstances the husband in the marriage takes a second wife himself, with sisters commonly preferred as cowives (sororal polygyny). Husbands and wives form a single household in the husband's village.

Polyandrous practices seem to be disappearing more rapidly than polygynous ones, in part because they have been more identified with rural areas. A good example is the case of the Nayars in Kerala (India), where until well into the twentieth century Nayar households were formed around siblings rather than around married couples. Children were raised by their mothers and maternal uncles, and ancestry was traced through women. A woman maintained concurrent sexual relationships with several men, one of whom would claim paternity when she became pregnant. A man, similarly, would have several wives at a time.

In many communities the continuing polyandrous relationships might better be described as secondary marriage. In northern Nigeria and in the northern Cameroon, women in some communities were (and still are) encouraged to contract subsequent marriages while maintaining their first. Women, however, reside with only one husband at a time, whereas the men marry additional wives, all of whom reside with them. The marriage careers of men and women are different and there is a complex relationships of in-laws.

Despite that polygamy is technically illegal in the United States, it continues to flourish and has seemingly grown in recent yeas. Although many polygamist groups are associated with the Mormons, much to the embarrassment of the current generation of authorities of the Church of Jesus Christ of Latter Day Saints, the law seems unable to deal with polygamy effectively. One reason for this is that many of those in polygamous relationships are not legally married to more than one wife and so are not technically in a bigamous or polygamous relationship. Instead they have emphasized that the additional women living with them are spiritual wives, and although they have been united with them in the eyes of God, they did not bother to get a marriage license. Government attempts to arrest polygamous husbands have usually been thwarted by the refusal of wives to testify against them and the willingness of whole families of the incarcerated polygamist to go on welfare, straining state resources.

In American society, where divorce is widespread, serial marriages common, and extramarital activity not unusual, government officials are increasingly reluctant to intervene in what essentially is a private relationship. Problems arise, however, especially with marriage of underage girls. Currently the strongest weapon that law enforcement officials have to use against some of the polygamists is that they have taken teenagers as spiritual wives and had intercourse with them. Because the girls were under the age of consent, which in most states is now eighteen, their male consorts are in effect guilty of statutory rape. Increasingly, some of the wives who come from polygamous communities or families and who believed they were forced by relatives or community pressure to enter into a polygynous union have been willing to testify against their unwelcome spouses and to effect an escape from their communities. Other than the statutory rape potential, however, it is difficult to secure convictions. Although many polygamists live in small rural communities and are open about their relationships, many others prefer anonymity and take great care to establish separate households in cities such as Los Angeles for each of their polygamous wives and visit them on a regular circuit. Others simply live together as an extended family. Many, if not most, of those engaged in polygamous liaisons today in the United States probably have no religious motives at all. It is the isolated rural polygamous communities that receive the most publicity and where community pressure often forces some into polygamous relationships who do not want them.

Why have polygamy? Some have suggested that men have a greater disposition for variety in sexual partners than do women. There is little empirical support for such a belief but if it is true it still does not explain polygamy because there are many other options open to men interested in a variety of sexual partners than taking another wife. One of the major arguments against such a belief is that, if polygamy was a solution to "male sexual drives," why did so comparatively few people in history become polygamists, namely, the well-to-do? It has also been suggested that polygyny evolved in response to lengthy postpartum sex taboos because polygyny would allow the husband outlets during the forbidden period. There are, however, other alternatives such as having a lover or a prostitute or simply bar hopping, rather than seeking an additional wife, and it is not clear that an additional wife would provide more sexual access. This is because women who live in close proximity to each other tend to have synchronized menstrual periods, and this means that, if the husband attempts to treat his wives equally, more than one of his wives is likely to becoming pregnant at the same time.

The existence of a low sex ratio, that is, a scarcity of men in relation to women, has also been advanced as a possible explanation for polygyny. Certainly polygyny maximizes the opportunities for women to marry in a society where adult males are in short supply, and this might justify polygamy in certain situations, but such shortages are not usually long lasting. Socrates, in monogamous Athens, allegedly took a second wife, technically a concubine, in order to contribute to taking care of the large number of widows resulting from the wars during his lifetime. Moreover, in most societies where polygamy has been practiced it has been restricted to the rich and powerful, and the result has been to deprive many men of the opportunity to marry. In Utah, where American polygamous practices received the most attention, there were many more men than there were women. There was, however, probably an excess of Mormon women over Mormon men because so many of the men in the territory were miners, ranch workers, and workers on the railroad and were not members of the Mormon Church. To further complicate the issue, however, polygyny in the Mormon Church in the nineteenth century was highly restricted, limited to those whom the Church authorized to join in polygamous unions. The overwhelming majority of the nineteenth-century Mormon families were monogamous ones.

In some societies, a polygamous family is a sign of status. Wives of the many biblical patriarchs represented alliances with other families or countries. It is also perhaps the ultimate sign of male machismo to be surrounded by women ready to comply with any wish, although this is obviously fantasy. In fact, it would be simpler to have concubines or lovers; they could more easily be discarded than another wife. Still, in many societies multiple wives had economic value. Where women's economic contribution is essential to the welfare of the family, as in gathering and agricultural economics, polygamy is a source of workers. Was this the justification for polygamy? Probably not, because polygyny has also been found in hunting and fishing economies, where potential female contribution is low. In the later case it has been suggested that multiple wives were valued for the number of sons that would result and contribute to the family income. But again, is polygyny the best solution to this? It might well be that some individuals enjoy and want the feeling and freedom of belonging to a large family unit. In an unpublished interview, conducted by this writer, of a polygamous family in the 1960s, most of the wives worked outside of the home (one was a lawyer), and a lesser number stayed home taking care of the children and household tasks. They all lived together in a compound, and the husband was kept busy managing his properties and keeping his wives happy. One of the wives reported that polygamy gave her a feeling of independence, and at the same time the tremendous support from the other wives allowed her to escape the more demanding tasks of motherhood and concentrate on her career. This might be described as seeing polygamy naively because, in the past, few women in polygynous relationships had much of a choice in the matter. Polyandry seems to have worked best in situations where men have difficulty in supporting a family. That polyandry is so much scarcer than polygyny seems to emphasize the greater control men have had over women in the past (and in large parts of the world still do) in both monogamous and polygamous arrangements.

Rarely mentioned in the discussion of polygamy is that it is a form of birth control. It tends to cut down the number of children each woman has, simply because of the inability of one man to realize the fertile potential of so many wives. This is true even though the record for the number of children is held by the polygamous Moulay Ismail. His harem, however, included thousands of women, many of whom failed to have any children at all. Even if he faithfully took a different sexual partner each day or sometimes two, the total pregnancy rate of the total number of women was low probably because he had sex with each only once or at most twice a year. Even men with smaller harems would have a lower pregnancy rate than if they only had one wife. Polygamous families might have large numbers of

children, but each woman had many fewer pregnancies than she might have had in a monogamous relationship. The removal of the polygamous wives from the list of eligible female partners also made for a shortage of potential wives for other men, thereby cutting down their probability of fathering children.

See also Augustine, Saint; Christian Hostility to Birth Control; Male Potential for Impregnating

References

Arrington, Leonard J., and Davis Bitton. *The Mormon Experience.* New York: Alfred A. Knopf, 1979.

Beal, C., and M. C. Goldstein. "Tibetan Fraternal Polyandry: A Test of Sociobiological Theory." *American Anthropologist* 83 (1981): 5–12.

Boserup, E. *Women's Role in Economic Development.* London: Allen and Unwin, 1970.

Brundage, James. *Law, Sex, and Christian Society in Medieval Europe.* Chicago: University of Chicago Press, 1987.

Buck, Pearl. *The Good Earth.* New York: John Day, 1931.

Bullough, Vern L. *Sexual Variance in Society and History.* Chicago: University of Chicago Press, 1976.

Crook, J. H., and S. J. Crook. "Tibetan Polyandry: Problems of Adaptation and Fitness." In *Human Reproductive Behavior: A Darwinian Perspective,* edited by L. Betzig, M. Borgerhoff Mulder, and P. Turke. Cambridge, UK: Cambridge University Press, 1988.

Ember, M. "Warfare, Sex Ratio, and Polygyny." *Ethnology* 13 (1974): 197–206.

Epstein, Louis M. *Marriage Laws in the Bible and the Talmud.* Cambridge, MA: Harvard University Press, 1942.

Euripides. *Andromache,* edited and translated by J. Frederick Nims. In *The Complete Greek Tragedies,* vol. 4, edited by David Grene and Richmond Lattimore. Chicago: University of Chicago Press, 1956.

Fuller, C. J. *The Nayars Today.* Cambridge, UK: Cambridge University Press, 1976.

Goody, Jack. "Polygyny, Economy, and the Role of Women." In *The Character of Kinship,* edited by Jack Goody. London: Cambridge University Press, 1973.

Heath, D. "Sexual Division of Labor and Cross Cultural Research." *Social Forces* 37 (1958): 77–79.

Hiatt, L. R. "Polyandry in Sri Lanka: A Test Case for Parental Investment Theory." *Man* 15 (1980): 573–602.

Josephus. *Jewish Antiquities,* edited and translated by H. St. J. Thackeray. London: Heinemann, Loeb Classical Library, 1930.

Levine, Nancy E. *The Dynamics of Polyandry: Kinship, Domesticity, and Population on the Tibetan Border.* Chicago: University of Chicago Press, 1988.

Levine, N. E., and W. H. Sangfree. "Women with Many Husbands: Polyandrous Alliances and Marital Flexibility in Africa and Asia." *Journal of Comparative Family Studies* (Special Issue, 11, 1980).

Mahabharata, translated by M. N. Dutt. London: n.p., 1929.

Muhsam, H. F. "Fertility of Polygamous Marriages." *Population Studies* 10 (1956–1957): 3–16.

Murdock, G. "World Ethnographic Sample." *American Anthropologist* 50 (1957): 664–687.

Westermarck, E. *A Short History of Marriage.* London: Macmillan, 1926.

Whiting, J. "Effects of Climate on Certain Cultural Practices." In *Explorations in Cultural Anthropology,* edited by Ward Goodenough. New York: McGraw-Hill, 1964.

Polygyny and Sex Ratios

Sex ratio is the ratio of males to females in a particular population at a particular time or for a particular cohort. The normative ratio is roughly about 106 males to 100 females, although at conception the sex ratio appears to be three males to two females. Various social factors affect sex ratios. A high sex ratio implies a male surplus, whereas a low one implies a female surplus. In sub-Saharan Africa sex ratios seem to be low, and this has implications for population growth. Interestingly the sex ratios are also low in African diaspora populations (e.g., African Americans) not only in the United States, but in the West Indies, Britain, and Latin America. Sex ratios are significantly lower in black Americans than in white Americans even when birth order, socioeconomic status, paternal age, and paternal education are controlled.

The question is how this can be explained, and one reason might be the widespread existence of polygyny (many wives) among native Africans south of the Sahara. A study of seven different Kenyan ethnic groups has found that polygynous relationships produce proportionately more daughters than do monogamous ones. It is suggested that women bear more daughters when they experience less frequent sexual intercourse (maternal effect), as appears to be the case in polygynous relationships. Low sex ratios may thus reflect the "generalized" polygyny (20 percent of all sexual unions) that prevails in 85 percent of sub-Saharan African societies.

Why are low sex ratios associated with polygyny? Perhaps they offset the wife shortage that results when some men have more than one wife. No such compensatory effect, however, has been found in nonhuman polygynous species. Although the subordinate females in such species usually bear more daughters, the dominant females bear more sons, so the overall sex ratio remains more or less equal. Apparently, the wasted reproductive potential of unmated males goes underutilized because it is confined mainly to subordinate individuals with limited reproductive value. The benefit of bearing a daughter does not outweigh that of bearing a son—who may become a dominant male with better reproductive success.

In sub-Saharan Africa, however, polygyny is primarily determined not by reproductive quality but by age:

> Inequality between old and young men was general in African lineage systems. Although a young man might often work harder than his father or other elders, access to wives was determined not by current earnings but by access to prestige goods. The young man knew, however, that some day he would inherit his father's wealth, take more wives, and assume authority over his sons in turn. (Curtin et al., 1978, pp. 160–161)

Traditionally, young men had to delay marriage until they could save up enough bride-wealth. Young warriors were often completely barred from marriage. This age rule may have arisen to contain the disruptive social effects of male-male competition for mates. In a sense, the competition was externalized because young celibate warriors had opportunities to capture women.

It was thus age, and not lifetime reproductive value, that distinguished single men from their married counterparts. Because single men were younger and could expect to live longer, they may actually have been worth more to a prospective mate. As a result, natural selection would tend to have compensated by lowering the sex ratio, the actual mechanism apparently being a maternal effect mediated by the frequency of sexual relations experienced by the mother.

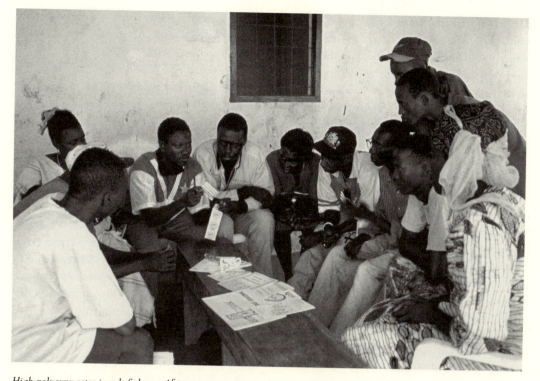

High polygyny rates in sub-Saharan Africa over generations mean more daughters are born than sons. Here, health workers give contraception information to young men in Gambia. (Lisa Taylor/Corbis, 1996)

How do we account, then, for low sex ratios in the African diaspora, notably in the United States? Young African American men are not barred from sexual relations, at least not like their counterparts in traditional African societies. Nor, for that matter, is there evidence for a maternal effect. Children with white mothers and black fathers have the same sex ratio at birth as children with two black parents This would seem to indicate a paternal effect, possibly mediated by the proportion of Y-bearing sperm in the father's semen.

To be sure, the same selection pressures that produced one mechanism could conceivably have produced another. The wife shortage resulting from polygyny might initially have favored a lowering of the sex ratio via a flexible mechanism, that is, a maternal effect mediated by coital frequency. If the situation persisted long enough, natural selection would eventually have favored means to keep the sex ratio permanently low, via heritable traits.

Although it is notoriously difficult to raise or lower the sex ratio by selective breeding, small but significant heritable differences have been achieved in bulls, pigs, and albino rats. Sustained selection, in the order of twenty-five generations, appears to be required.

Has generalized polygyny existed long enough among sub-Saharan Africans for such selection to operate? Several lines of evidence indicate that the practice has existed for a long time. Genetically, sub-Saharan Africans display much lower Y chromosome/X chromosome variability than do other populations, apparently because proportionately fewer men have contributed to the gene pool.

Linguistically, reconstruction of proto-Bantu, spoken approximately 3,000 years ago, has uncovered a specific term for "taking a second wife." Physically, over time, too many men competing for too few women should favor the evolution of physical robustness. Such male-male competition might be reflected in the increased sexual dimorphism of African Americans for weight, chest size, arm girth, and leg girth. In contrast, a small, graceful, and almost childlike body characterizes Khoisans and Pygmies, the only sub-Saharan populations with a low incidence of polygyny.

According to mitochondrial DNA and Y-chromosome dendrograms, Khoisans are the oldest living population in sub-Saharan Africa, followed by Pygmies. Among these hunter-gatherers of Namibia and Botswana, only 6 percent of the men practice polygyny. The sex ratio at birth, 105 males to 100 females, is comparable to that of non-African populations. Thus, Africa's high polygyny rates and low sex ratios are probably a derived condition and not an ancestral one.

Modern black Africans seem to be a recent adaptive radiation from an ancestral Pygmy population. This radiation probably occurred somewhere in West Africa, given the absence of black Africans from the continent's central, eastern, and southern regions before the Bantu expansion of the last 3,000 years. Black Africans were also absent from the middle Nile until about 4,000 years ago, when they first appear in paintings from Pharaonic Egypt and in skeletal remains from Nubia. Murdock attributes this expansion out of West Africa to the development of the Sudanic food complex some 6,000–7,000 years ago near the Niger's headwaters, where a wide range of cultivated plants (sorghum, pearl millet, cow pea, etc.) were developed independently of the Southwest Asian food complex. Other authors, such as Shaw, postulate a larger area of origin in West Africa. The Sudanic complex seems to be the culmination of a long period of proto-agriculture, during which hunter-gatherers protected fields of wild grains and made clearings for wild yams and oil palms. Tending of wild edible species is suggested by unusually abundant *Canarium* (pili nut) leaf impressions from a southern Ghanaian site dated to 8000–9000 B.C.E.

Some form of agriculture is also apparent in reconstructed words of proto-Niger-Congo, probably spoken c. 10,000 B.C.E.

At first glance, a West African origin for this agriculture-driven expansion seems inconsistent with genetic evidence for the common ancestry of black Africans and Pygmies. The latter now live only in central Africa. They seem, however, to have once inhabited the entire rain forest zone, including the Guinea coast of West Africa, as indicated by finds of Sangoan artifacts—widely linked to Pygmy hunter-gatherers.

From the outset, these Guinea coast hunter-gatherers may have displayed some reproductive isolation, and hence genetic differentiation, because of the Dahomey Gap—a mosaic of savanna and woodland separating the rain forest on the Guinea coast from that of central Africa. The thinning of the rain forest during the last ice age may have increased their isolation and, more importantly, made it easier for them to manage food production from wild yams and oil palms. Indicative of a shift in subsistence is the appearance of hoe-like implements at Guinea coast sites as early as 12,000 B.C.E. The end of the ice age and the return of less open forest by 9000 B.C.E. may have compelled these protoagriculturalists to move out into mosaic environments to the north and east. Such a migration may correspond to the breakup of proto-Niger-Congo, estimated at 10,000 B.C.E. The first language group to branch off was proto-Mande; its descendent languages occupy an area centered on the Niger's headwaters—the same area that Murdock sees as the cradle of the Sudanic food complex.

Sudanic agriculture developed primarily out of female gathering and only secondarily out of male hunting. It thus greatly enhanced women's contribution to food provisioning, the corollary being a reduction in the costs of polygyny to men. As polygyny became more frequent, male-male competition would have grown keener for the shrinking pool of potential mates, the result being an intensification of sexual selection for larger, stronger, and more muscular males, as in nonhuman polygynous species.

Such a scenario leaves surprisingly little time for the morphogenesis of true black Africans. The beginnings of protoagriculture cannot be pushed back much further than 12,000 B.C.E. A tall, clearly Negroid skeleton (Asselar Man) has been dated to 6500 B.C.E. This leaves a window of not much more than six thousand years for the changes that differentiate Pygmies from black Africans, that is, a shift from a gracile, almost childlike body to a much more robust one, with attendant increases in stature, weight, and muscle mass.

As development of the Sudanic complex allowed these agriculturalists to expand out of mosaic environments and into the savanna, the ratio of female to male participation in food provisioning should have declined. The savanna is more demanding on women's time, particularly for obtaining water and firewood, so successful penetration of this environment would have required greater male involvement in agriculture. In the savanna regions of Ghana, Goody states that "women planted grain and helped with the harvest, but they were not concerned with yam cultivation, and did not carry out the many hoeing activities that were connected with cereal agriculture." Yet, surprisingly, polygyny was as common as in the mosaic environments and rain forests further south, a fact leading him to conclude: "Although hoe agriculture, female farming and polygyny are clearly associated in a general way, there seems little evidence directly to connect variations in rates of polygyny with differences in the role of women in farming or in trade."

High polygyny rates in Africa may thus reflect not so much existing conditions as preexisting ones whose adaptations have been maintained through cultural lag, notably by keeping a large sex difference in the age of first marriage. In addition, natural selection may have favored an increased predisposition to polygyny that persists even when the adaptive landscape has changed.

It is likely, then, that generalized polygyny in sub-Saharan Africa goes back some 12,000 years, that is, to the beginnings of protoagriculture in West Africa. If selective breeding in non-human species is any indication, this would be enough time for selection of heritable differences in the sex ratio at birth. Some questions still remain. If agriculture led to generalized polygyny in West Africa, why did it not elsewhere? Part of the answer is that animal husbandry, which developed out of male hunting, played a greater role elsewhere in agricultural development, thus lowering women's contribution to food provisioning and raising the costs of polygyny. As well, in other world regions, agriculture set off a process of social differentiation and state formation: (1) it created a food surplus that could be stored for future consumption; (2) more powerful individuals appropriated the surplus and used it to become even more powerful (by using food as payment to servants, officials, and soldiers); and (3) eventually, both power and polygyny became largely confined to a small ruling class (Testart 1982). In sub-Saharan Africa, this process took much longer or remained incomplete.

Some qualifications must be made:

1. In some African populations, this maternal effect may be confounded by a paternal effect, that is, men who are inclined toward polygyny will father more daughters even before they take a second wife. An attempt was made to control this factor by studying mothers who had lived with the same man before and after he had taken a second wife. In five of the ethnic groups, the sex ratio at birth was lower for children born during the polygynous phase of the marriage; in two ethnic groups, it was actually higher. Unfortunately, the author does not state the statistical significance of these differences, nor the ethnic groups involved. Domestication of food sources primarily involved plants and not animals. The guinea fowl is the only domestic animal that clearly originated in sub-Saharan Africa. Domestic cattle were introduced at a late date, probably after 6000 B.C.E.

2. Polygyny has been found to correlate with male stature in human populations. It does not, however, seem to correlate with an increase in male stature over female stature, perhaps

because insufficient time has elapsed for enough sex-linked alleles to be produced through mutation and retained through selection.

Peter Frost

References

Blench, R. "Recent Developments in African Language Classification and Their Implications for Prehistory." In *The Archaeology of Africa,* edited by T. Shaw, P. Sinclair, B. Andah, and A. Okpoko. London: Routledge, 1995, pp. 126–138.

Camps, G. *Les civilisations préhistoriques de l'Afrique du Nord et du Sahara.* Paris: Doin, 1974.

Cavalli-Sforza, L. L. "African Pygmies: An Evaluation of the State of Research." In *African Pygmies,* edited by L. L. Cavalli-Sforza. Orlando: Academic Press, 1986, pp. 361–426.

Ciocco, A. "Variation in the Sex Ratio Birth in the U.S." *Human Biology* 10 (1938): 36–64.

Clutton-Brock, J. "The Spread of Domestic Animals in Africa." In *The Archaeology of Africa,* edited by T. Shaw, P. Sinclair, B. Andah, and A. Okpoko. London: Routledge, 1995, pp. 61–70.

Clutton-Brock, T. H., and G. R. Iason. "Sex Ratio Variation in Mammals." *Quarterly Review of Biology* 61 (1986): 339–374.

Coon, Carleton Stevens. *The Origin of Races.* New York: Alfred A. Knopf, 1962.

Curtin, Philip, S. Feierman, L. Thompson, and J. Vansina. *African History.* Boston: Little, Brown, 1978.

Davies, O. "The Origins of Agriculture in West Africa." *Current Anthropology* 9 (1968): 479–487.

Ehret, C. "Historical/Linguistic Evidence for Early African Food Production." In *From Hunters to Farmers: The Causes and Consequences of Food Production in Africa,* edited by J. Desmond Clark and Steven A. Brandt. Berkeley: University of California Press, 1984, pp. 26–35.

Erickson, D. "The Secondary Sex Ratio in the United States, 1969–71: Association with Race, Parental Ages, Birth Order, Paternal Education, and Legitimacy." *Annals of Human Genetics* 40 (1976): 205–212.

Excoffier, L., E. S. Poloni, S. Santachiara-Benerecetti, O. Semino, and A. Langaney. "The Molecular Diversity of the Niokholo Mandenkalu from Eastern Senegal: An Insight into West Africa Genetic History." In *Molecular Biology and Human Diversity,* edited by A. J. Boyce and C. G. N. Mascie-Taylor. Cambridge, UK: Cambridge University Press, 1996, pp. 141–155.

Feitosa, M. F., and H. Krieger "Some Factors Affecting the Secondary Sex Ratio in a Latin American Sample." *Human Biology* 65 (1993): 273–278.

Gaulin, S., and J. Boster. "Cross-cultural Differences in Sexual Dimorphism: Is There Any Variance To Be Explained?" *Ethology and Sociobiology* 6 (1984): 219–225.

Gluckman, M. "The Kingdom of the Zulu of South Africa." In *African Political Systems,* edited by M. Fortes and E. E. Evans-Pritchard. London: Oxford University Press, 1940, pp. 25–55.

Goody, Jack. *The Character of Kinship.* Cambridge, UK: Cambridge University Press, 1973.

Gray, J. P., and L. D. Wolfe. "Height and Sexual Dimorphism of Stature among Human Societies." *American Journal of Physical Anthropology* 53 (1980): 441–445.

Holden, C. "Southern African 'Eve'." *Science* 286 (1999): 229.

Howell, Nancy. *Demography of the Dobe !Kung.* New York: Academic Press, 1979.

James, W. H. "The Sex Ratio of Black Births." *Annals of Human Biology* 11 (1984): 39–44.

Junker, H. "The First Appearance of the Negroes in History." *Journal of Egyptian Archaeology* 7 (1921): 121–132.

Khoury, M. J., J. D. Erickson, and L. M. James. "Paternal Effects on the Human Sex Ratio at Birth: Evidence from Interracial Crosses." *Annals of Human Genetics* 36 (1984): 1103–1111.

Maley, J. "The Climatic and Vegetational History of the Equatorial Regions of Africa during the Upper Quaternary." In *The Archaeology of Africa,* edited by T. Shaw, P. Sinclair, B. Andah, and A. Okpoko. London: Routledge, 1995, pp. 43–52.

Martin, J. F. "Changing Sex Ratios. The History of Havasupai Fertility and Its Implications for Human Sex Ratio Variation." *Current Anthropology* 35 (1994): 255–280.

Meikle, D. B., B. L. Tilford, and S. H. Vessey. "Dominance Rank, Secondary Sex Ratio, and Reproduction of Offspring in Polygynous Primates." *The American Naturalist* 124 (1984): 173–188.

Murdock, G. P. *Africa: Its Peoples and Their Cultural History.* New York: McGraw-Hill, 1959.

Oliver, R. "The Problem of the Bantu Expansion." *Journal of African History* 7 (1966): 361–376.

Penny, D., M. Steel, P. J. Waddell, and M. D. Hendy. "Improved Analyses of Human mtDNA Sequences Support a Recent African Origin for Homo Sapiens." *Molecular Biology and Evolution* 12 (1995): 863–882.

Polome, E. C. "The Reconstruction of Proto-Bantu Culture from the Lexicon." In *L'Expansion bantoue 2,* edited by L. Bouquiaux. Paris: Centre national de la recherche scientifique, 1977, pp. 779–791.

Posnansky, M. " Early Agricultural Societies in Ghana." In *From Hunters to Farmers: The Causes and Consequences of Food Production in Africa,* edited by J. Desmond Clark and Steven A. Brandt. Berkeley: University of California Press, 1984, pp. 147–151.

Romaniuk, A. "The Demography of the Democratic Republic of the Congo." In *The Demography of Tropical Africa,* edited by William Brass, A. J. Coale, P. Demeny, D. F. Heisel, F. Lorimer, A. Romaniuk, and E. van de Walle. Princeton, NJ: Princeton University Press, 1968, pp. 241–341.

Scozzari, R., F. Cruciani, P. Malaspina, P. Santolamazza, B. M. Ciminelli, A. Torroni, D. Modiano, D. C. Wallace, K. K. Kidd, et al. "Differential Structuring of Human Populations for Homologous X and Y

Microsatellite Loci." *American Journal of Human Genetics* 61 (1997): 719–733.

Shaw, T. "Hunters, Gatherers and First Farmers in West Africa." In *Hunters, Gatherers, and First Farmers beyond Europe,* edited by J. V. S. Megaw. Leicester, England: Leicester University Press, 1980, pp. 69–125.

Spurdle, A. B., M. F. Hammer, and T. Jenkins. "The Y Alu Polymorphism in Southern African Populations and Its Relationship to Other Y-specific Polymorphisms." *American Journal of Human Genetics* 54 (1994): 319–330.

Stahl, A. B. "Intensification in the West African Late Stone Age: A View from Central Ghana." In *The Archaeology of Africa,* edited by T. Shaw, P. Sinclair, B. Andah, and A. Okpoko. London: Routledge, 1995, pp. 261–273.

Strandskov, H. H. "Birth Sex Ratios in the Total, the 'White' and the 'Coloured' U.S. Populations." *American Journal of Physical Anthropology* 3 (1945): 165–175.

Teitelbaum, M. S. "Factors Affecting the Sex Ratio in Large Populations." *Journal of Biosocial Science* 2 (1970): 61–71.

———. "Factors Associated with the Sex Ratio in Human Populations." In *The Structure of Human Populations,* edited by G. A. Harrison and A. J. Boyce. Oxford, UK: Clarendon Press, 1972, pp. 190–199.

Testart, A. "The Significance of Food Storage among Hunter-Gatherers: Residence Patterns, Population Densities, and Social Inequalities" *Current Anthropology* 23 (1982): 523–537.

Todd, T. W., and A. Lindala. "Dimensions of the Body: Whites and American Negroes of Both Sexes." *American Journal of Physical Anthropology* 12 (1928): 35–101.

Torroni, A., O. Semino, R. Scozzari, G. Sirugo, G. Spedini, N. Abbas, M. Fellous, et al. "Y-Chromosome DNA Polymorphisms in Human Populations: Differences between Caucasoids and Africans Detected by 49a and 49f Probes." *Annals of Human Genetics* 54 (1990): 287–296.

van de Walle, E. "Characteristics of African Demographic Data." In *The Demography of Tropical Africa,* edited by William Brass, A. J. Coale, P. Demeny, D. F. Heisel, F. Lorimer, A. Romaniuk, and E. van de Walle. Princeton, NJ: Princeton University Press, 1968, pp. 12–87.

van den Berghe, P. *Human Family Systems.* New York: Elsevier, 1979.

Visaria, P. M. "Sex Ratio at Birth in Territories with a Relatively Complete Registration." *Eugenics Quarterly* 14 (1967): 132–142.

Watson, E., K. Bauer, R. Aman, G. Weiss, A. von Haeseler, and S. Pääbo. "mtDNA Sequence Diversity in Africa." *American Journal of Human Genetics* 59 (1996): 437–444.

Watson, J. S. "On Artificially Selecting for the Sex Ratio." *Ethology and Sociobiology* 13 (1992): 1–2.

Whiting, J. W. M. "The Effect of Polygyny on Sex Ratio at Birth." *American Anthropologist* 95 (1993): 435–442.

Wolff, G., and M. Steggerda. "Female-male Index of Body Build in Negroes and Whites: An Interpretation of Anatomical Sex Differences." *Human Biology* 15 (1943): 127–152.

Population Control and Organization

Population control has had at least two different meanings. Generically, it has been the attempt in modern history to lower birthrates on national or regional scales, for the purpose of improving the standards of living of large groups. Specifically, it is the programs and policies advanced primarily by the United States, sometimes through international organizations such as the United Nations, and later nationally by other nations such as China and India.

A number of American foundations in the twentieth century became interested in the issue, many of them originally backers of eugenic research, who reoriented their thinking to support research about overpopulation. The pioneer group was not American-inspired but British-inspired, the International Neo-Malthusian and Birth Control Conferences, six of which were held between 1900 and 1925, the last one in New York City. In retrospect, some of the American efforts seem to have been openly racist such as the Kellogg-sponsored Race Betterment Foundation established in 1913 and which held several Race Betterment Conferences. Some had more neutral titles such as the Scripps Foundation for Research in Population Problems (founded in 1922). Margaret Sanger herself was the force behind the First World Population Conference in Geneva in 1927, although she was forced by the male physicians who dominated to take a back seat at the actual conference, which brought together American eugenicists with European Neo-Malthusians.

Gradually the eugenics establishment merged into the population control movement, and American foundations became a dominant force. It is one of the great contradictions of American philanthropy that even though research into contraception and population control was still stigmatized, so much so that many American scientists refused to do such research, so much of the research and development money was given by American foundations. The Milbank Memorial Fund, founded in 1928, and one of the main backers of eugenic research, began to support research about overpopulation in underdeveloped countries. The Rockefeller Foundation joined the Milbank Foundation in 1936 in setting up an office of Population Research at Princeton University. In 1952 John D. Rockefeller III founded the Population Council. He had been frustrated in his efforts to lead the larger Rockefeller Foundation into more extensive, programmatic, and applied efforts in reproduction, population, and contraception, and so set up his own foundation. The Population Council focused on contraceptives requiring medical rather than user initiative such as the intrauterine device and long-acting hormonal implants such as Norplant. The Population Council was for many years the dominant force in bringing international attention to the issues of reproduction and population. It was later joined by the Ford Foundation, which also became extremely influential in international reproduction and population issues. A growing number of foundations such as Mellon, DuPont, Sloan, and others also entered the field.

In 1948 Margaret Sanger, with the help of the Brush Foundation and others, founded the International Planned Parenthood Federation. International organizations such as the World Health Organization also moved into the field, in part supported by American foundations. So did the U.S. government after 1960, encouraged by the private foundations, and federal appropriations skyrocketed from a total of $19 million in the period 1961–1965 to more than $183 million in the period 1970–1974. The U.S. government has continued to be a major factor on the international scene. Within the National Institutes of Health, funding was initially provided through the National Institute of Child Health and Human Development. In 1968 the National Institutes of Health founded the Center for Population Research to focus research. Money was also channeled through the Office of Population of the U.S. Agency for International Development.

During the presidency of Ronald Reagan, funding for international efforts by the U.S. government was severely curtailed, as was money for local family planning agencies. Most of the cuts were later restored, particularly under President William Clinton. The United Nations itself established the United Nations Family Planning Agency, and many nongovernmental organizations (NGOs) participate in its activities.

References

Cleland, John, and John Hobcraft. *Reproductive Change in Developing Countries.* New York: Oxford University Press, 1985.

Potts, Malcolm, and Pouru Bhiwandilwa, eds. *Birth Control: An International Assessment.* Lancaster, UK: MTP, 1979.

Pregnancy Potential

Pregnancy is a natural biological process for most women, and normally a woman who engages in sexual activity with any regularity could spend most of the years of her life between the ages of fifteen and forty-five either pregnant or nursing a newborn infant. It is estimated that under favorable circumstances the average woman could become pregnant every other year during her reproductive life. This would mean that the average woman, provided she did not give birth to twins or have other forms of multiple births, could give birth to fifteen children during her lifetime. Obviously some women would become pregnant more often than others, with a theoretical maximum of about twenty pregnancies for one woman. But what is theoretical is not always actual. The largest number of live births recorded for any one woman is sixty-nine by the first wife of Feodor Vassilyev (her first name does not appear in the records), a peasant from the village of Shula, 150 miles east of Moscow. She had twenty-seven pregnancies. Included among her children were sixteen pairs of twins, seven sets of triplets, and four sets of quadruplets, all born between 1725 and 1765. Almost all the offspring survived beyond the first year.

The most prolific mother of the twentieth century was Leontina Espinosa Albina (b. 1925) of San Antonio, Chile. In 1981 she gave birth to her fifty-fifth and last child, although earlier reports had her giving birth to fifty-nine. Forty of the children, twenty-four boys and sixteen girls, were still alive in 1995.

References

Young, M. C., ed. *Guinness Book of Records 1995.* New York: Facts on File, 1994.

Protestantism in the Sixteenth and Seventeenth Centuries

The Protestant movement, which began in the sixteenth century, was not simply a theological movement, but rather one deeply associated with the political, economic, and social issues of the time. Many of the leaders who accepted Lutheran or Calvinist teachings did so in part out of desires to end the economic and political power of the papacy in their territories, or, in Germany, to oppose the power of the Holy Roman Emperor. Nobles in France saw it as a way to combat the power of the monarchy as well as the papacy, and in England Henry VIII clearly recognized that a confiscation of church property would swell the royal treasury.

Martin Luther (1481–1546) was the spark that began of the revolt against Catholicism but he was not alone; a host of others included Ulrich Zwingli (1484–1531) in Zurich and John Calvin (1509–1564) in Geneva. As communities and political jurisdictions broke with Rome, the churches they established came to be called Protestant after a 1529 document issued by princes who followed Luther and who protested a papal order that they abandon their religious innovations. Attempting to preserve Catholicism was the Holy Roman Emperor, and the issue of which countries and areas would be Catholic and which Protestant was eventually decided by the wars of religion that dominated the last part of the sixteenth and first part of the seventeenth centuries.

Sex was an integral part of the Protestant movement because all segments of the reformers abandoned the idea of clerical celibacy. Luther himself conspicuously demonstrated his opposition to celibacy in 1525 by marrying Katherine von Bora, who had fled her convent. The Protestants, however, were no less interested in regulating sexuality than the Catholics had been, and both Calvin and Zwingli established courts to handle marriage and morals cases. Though the Protestants rejected traditional canon law, Luther even burning a canon law book, they still followed most of its traditions regarding sex and marriage. The Protestants were also strong Augustinians, and Luther, as the Catholic theologians before him, linked original sin and sexual desires. He differed, as did most Protestants, however, in emphasizing that marriage was the ideal state for almost everyone.

Calvin went further than Luther by taking some of the initial steps in empowering women. Calvin taught that the primary purpose of marriage was social rather than generative. Woman had not been created simply to be man's helper in procreation, nor was she just a necessary remedy for his sexual needs caused by the corruption of human nature by the Fall. Rather, woman had been created as man's inseparable associate in life as well as in the bed chamber. Although Calvin agreed that the scriptures emphasized men instead of women, he questioned whether it should be concluded that "women are nothing." Instead he held that women were included under the generic term "men," although he believed that women clearly should be subordinate to men. He did not deal with contraception in any detail but he stated that coitus interruptus was monstrous.

Luther, Zwingli, Calvin, John Knox (1513–1572), and many other reformers were known as "magisterials" because they believed that the church should work with the state and its officials, and in many matters this meant that civil law took over many of the issues previously held to be matters of canon law. Both Luther and Calvin, for example, rejected the concept of marriage as a sacrament. They, however, did not believe in the separation of church and state, and still assumed that laws and church teachings would be the same.

Though procreation was held by almost all Protestant groups not to be the only reason for marital sex, some modicum of control over sexual passion was to be exercised. In England, Puritan leaders such as Robert Cleaver in the seventeenth century held that when men and women raging with "boiling lust" meet together as "brute beasts" it would be a just judgment of God to send them either monsters or fools as offspring.

But Protestant groups were not united and there were many radical groups, many of them linked together by the term "Anabaptist" because they refused to allow their children to be baptized and instead held that baptism was something reserved for those old enough to truly believe. The Anabaptists were vigorously denounced by Luther, Zwingli, and Calvin and severely persecuted by both Roman Catholics and Protestants. Some of the more radical Anabaptist groups were so concerned with the biblical injunction to be fruitful and multiply that they accepted polygamy as a necessity. Other groups such as one known as the "Dreamers" emphasized the goodness of all aspects of sex and sexuality. The eighteenth century Moravians sang hymns to Jesus's penis as well as to Mary's breasts and uterus. Count Nikolaus Zinzendorf (1700–1760) defended such hymns by asserting that shame about the sex organs was a denial of the full humanity of Christ. Some of the more radical groups saw the Christian message as giving them an inner light, freeing them from existing religious and secular laws and reverting to an early Christian heresy known as antinomianism. The early antinomian groups of believers had taught that Christians are by grace set free from the need of observing any moral law. The seventeenth century Ranters in England, for example, proclaimed that

> What act soever is done by thee in light and love, is light and lovely, though it be that act called adultery . . . No matter what Scripture, saints, or churches say, if that within thee do not condemn thee, thou shalt not be condemned. (Quoted by Weisner-Hanks, p. 67)

Eventually the very diversity of Protestantism made divergent views of sex more possible, and the increasing emphasis put on women as partners, particularly by the American Puritans, made limitation of family size a conjoint effort and created an attitude more receptive to some means of birth control.

In the United States, many of the early settlements were by religious groups attempting to establish disciplined moral and sexual utopias where God's law, as they interpreted it, would be the basis of all social and legal institutions in ways that were impossible in the more decadent Europe. This was true of the Puritans in Massachusetts, the Amish in Pennsylvania, the Shakers in northeastern parts of the United States, and later the Hutterites in the Dakotas and upper midwest, the Mormons in Utah, and even the groups of the more secular utopias such as New Harmony in Indiana and the Perfectionists in Oneida, New York. Catholicism also had its "utopian" groups, especially among the Jesuit mission settlements in Canada and Latin America. For brief periods such communities may have been the most sexually disciplined communities in the Christian world, but their isolation was difficult to maintain for long, and those who objected to such discipline went elsewhere, again creating a more receptive audience for effective family planning. It was perhaps no accident that the secular movement for birth control originated mainly in Protestant-dominated areas, which were somewhat less hostile to the concept. It is important to emphasize, however, that the birth control movement spread also to Catholic areas and to other parts of the world, and France, for example, was a pioneer in practicing such methods although not in public discussion of them.

References

Bullough, Vern L. *Sexual Variance in Society and Culture.* Chicago: University of Chicago Press, 1976.

Bullough, Vern L., and Bonnie Bullough. *The Subordinate Sex.* Urbana: University of Illinois Press, 1973.

Wiesner-Hanks, Merry E. *Christianity and Sexuality in the Early Modern World.* New York: Routledge, 2000.

Q

Quickening

Quickening was believed to be the time the soul entered the body—the time when human life began. But when did this occur? One of the issues in any discussion of abortion or child-bearing is that of when life begins. Neither ancient nor medieval people believed that the soul originated with conception. A male conceptus was not an ensouled being according to Hippocrates until after thirty days; Aristotle held that it was forty days. The Greeks believed that the conceptus of the female was thinner than that of the male, took longer to coagulate and was not ensouled until after eighty or ninety days. The male fetus began to move at three months; the female, at four. Thus, though the fetus could be viewed as being alive earlier, it was alive in the same sense that a vegetable was. Jewish tradition followed this same reasoning and thus, although Exodus 21:22–23 provides for fines for damage to the fetus, this only happens if the fetus is determined to be alive, that is, after movement.

Even then, the fetus was never more than potentially human and was regarded as part of the mother until its birth. This interpretation meant that abortion, at least in the early phases of pregnancy, was not the moral problem for the ancient peoples within the Greek tradition that it became for twenty-first century Americans. This classical view continued in the medieval world, and one of the major writers, Albertus Magnus, believed, as did Aristotle, that the embryo or fetus developed like other animals until a time when it came to be con-

nected with the Divine Intellect, or God. It was at this time that the soul entered the body. This separate existence was necessary because, according to Saint Thomas Aquinas, the soul was created by God and was not created by the act of conceptus, but entered only at a later date. Thus, though the Christian church condemned abortion, there was always a question of whether all abortion was condemned or that which took place only after the soul had entered the body. Roman law, as preserved in the Justinian code in the sixth century of the modern era and compiled long after Christianity had become the legal religion of the Empire, did not regard abortion before forty days as a crime.

Popularly the entrance of the soul was believed to be marked by quickening. A fetus that was spontaneously or otherwise aborted before the soul entered the body would have no soul, and no soul could have perished because a soul cannot exist without a body. Technically then, early abortion in the medieval period was tolerated but not sanctioned. This ambivalence continued to exist among Catholic Christians, with one interruption, until the nineteenth century. The interruption occurred in 1588 when Pope Sextus V by a bull, *Effraenatum,* declared all abortions murder regardless of when they took place and required excommunication for those involved. Less than three years later, however, his successor, Pope Gregory XIV revoked the penalties on the grounds that the edict had not had the hoped-for effect, and the old system was reestablished. The major change came under

Pope Pius IX, who in 1869 declared that ensoulment began at conception. In a sense the pope was trying to establish consistency because in 1865 he had proclaimed the dogma of the Immaculate Conception of Mary, who he decreed had been free from all stain of original sin "from the first moment of conception."

It is also possible that the pope was reacting against the growing use of contraceptives, particularly in France, and to new developments in biology. Gradually secular laws in England and in the United States also began to change.

See also Canon Law and Abortion

References
Huby, Pamela M. "Soul, Life, Sense, Intellect: Some Thirteenth-Century Problems." In *The Human Embryo: Aristotle and the Arabic and European Traditions,* edited by G. R. Dunstan. Exeter, UK: University of Exeter Press, 1990, pp. 132–133.
Noonan, John T., Jr. *Contraception.* Cambridge, MA: Harvard University Press, 1965.

R

Robinson, William Josephus (1867–1936)

William Josephus Robinson, M.D., was the first American physician to demand that contraceptive knowledge be taught to medical students and was a strong fighter against moral reformer Anthony Comstock. Robinson was probably the most influential and popular of the American physicians writing on birth control in the first three decades of the twentieth century, carrying on the work begun by Edward Bliss Foote and others. Robinson was, however, much more a part of the medical establishment. Until 1912 the American Medical Association for the most part supported the Comstock law, which, among other things, suppressed the distribution of contraceptive information, and part of Robinson's mission was to educate his medical colleagues.

Robinson made a strong case against legal interference with the physician-client relationship and believed that the physician had a right to prescribe contraception to a patient desiring it and that such an action was medically and socially desirable. In the journals that he edited, the *American Journal of Urology* and the *Medico-Pharmaceutical Critic and Guide* (1898–1915), afterward the *Medical Critic and Guide,* he constantly editorialized on the importance of contraception. He baited Comstock and the censors in his popular manual published in 1904 entitled *Fewer and Better Babies; or, The Limitation of Offspring.* Deliberately left blank were five pages in two chapters entitled "The Best, Safest, and Most Harmless Means for the Prevention of Conception" and "Means for the Prevention of Conception Which are Disagreeable, Uncertain, or Injurious," but that included a statement that he would include such information as soon as the "brutal" Comstock laws were removed from the statute books. Robinson wrote that the kind of censorship preventing him from giving his readers such information was as "real and as terrifying as any that ever existed in darkest Russia." He believed that it hung like a Damocles sword over the head of every honest radical writer, and even worse than not being permitted to mention the safe and harmless means of contraception was that a physician could not even discuss the unsafe and injurious means that so many women had attempted to use.

Robinson also wrote a leaflet in 1904 aimed at physicians and describing contraceptive techniques. He later wrote a popular book entitled *Practical Prevenception.* He is said to have induced Dr. Abraham Jacobi, the founder of pediatrics in the United States, to include a discussion of contraception in his 1912 Presidential Address to the American Medical Association, the first time that organization broached the subject. In addition to his work on contraception, Robinson also wrote widely on sexological subjects and spoke out strongly against the nineteenth century emphasis on continence. He held that the sexual instinct was natural and important and he proved to be a significant force in eliminating the limitations put on the topic of sexuality by prudish ignorance. His son, Victor Robinson, also a physician, was also active in the campaign for contraception, although not as much as his father had been.

See also Comstock, Anthony, and Comstockery

References

Fryer, Peter. *The Birth Controllers*. London: Secker and Warburg, 1965.

Robinson, W. J. *Fewer and Better Babies; or, The Limitation of Offspring*. New York: Critic and Guide, 1924.

————. *Practical Prevenception*. Hoboken, NJ: American Biological Society, 1929.

————. *What Doctors Have Learned about Birth Control*. Girard, KS: Haldeman-Julius, 1931.

RU 486 (Mifepristone)

Abortion became an increasingly divisive struggle in the United States at the end of the twentieth century. A symbol of this struggle was the battle over RU 486 (mifepristone), which had less to do with the pill itself than the politics of abortion. The compound was isolated by a team led by Etienne-Emile Baulieu at the French pharmaceutical company Roussell Uclaf in 1980. RU 486 (the test number given by the drug company) blocked the female hormone progesterone, making it impossible for the body to sustain a pregnancy. RU 486 was tested and tried in France beginning in 1982 and by 1988 the French government approved the use of mifepristone when combined with a drug designed to induce uterine contractions to bring about an expulsion of the sloughed uterine substance. As controversy mounted over the use of RU 486 as an abortion pill, Roussell Uclaf attempted to rid itself of the controversy by trying to abandon the drug but was forbidden to do so by the French government.

As knowledge about the drug spread, some 700,000 Americans signed a petition, which was carried to France by Eleanor Smeal and Peg Yorkin, the founders of the Feminist Majority, urging the company to market the drug in the United States. The U.S. Food and Drug Administration (FDA), under prompting from President George Bush, almost immediately placed the drug on an import alert list. Roussell Uclaf was reluctant to get involved in any controversy in the United States and still remained a reluctant manufacturer in France. In spite of this the drug was approved for use in Great Britain in 1991, and other European states followed.

One of the first acts of President William Clinton in 1993 was to instruct the Department of Health and Human Services to promote "the testing, licensing, and manufacture in the U.S." of mifepristone. Roussell Uclaf, however, still refused to enter the U.S. market and instead donated its U.S. rights to the drug to the Population Council, a New York nonprofit group. Roussell Uclaf also gave up its patent rights in France and the rest of Europe to avoid a threatened boycott of its products. When no major U.S. pharmaceutical firm appeared willing to undertake the manufacture of the product, the Population Council encouraged Joseph Pike, an investor and lawyer, to put together a group to manufacture, test, and market the pill. Pike, however, was later forced out by the Population Council, and ultimately the newly founded Danco Laboratories in New York City began to arrange for the manufacture, distribution, and testing of the pill. Most of the names of those involved in manufacturing and testing the drug, however, were kept secret because of the fear of personal attacks on the employees and on agencies and companies involved. By the end of 1996, a total of 2,121 American women had participated in the experiment at seventeen sites around the country. Though the FDA ruled that the drug was safe and effective, it asked for more information about manufacturing and labeling. Such information was submitted but it took until October 2000 to approve the pill and allow it to enter the market. By that time the pill had been in use by over half a million women in some thirteen countries. RU 486 had been approved by the American Medical Association, American Medical Women's Association, American College of Obstetrics and Gynecologists, and many other groups.

The U.S. procedure for administration of the pill followed the French example, which involves swallowing three pills in the presence of a physician or qualified medical personnel in a clinic or hospital. Two days later the woman

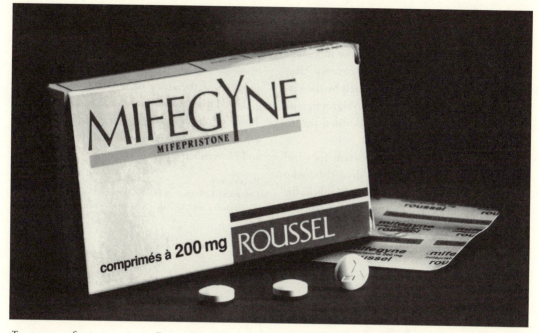

Twenty years after its invention in Europe, RU 486 was finally approved by the U.S. Food and Drug Administration in the year 2000. (Corbis)

returns to receives a dose of another drug, prostaglandin, which causes the uterus to contract. In the majority of cases, the sloughed off material is expelled within a few hours and the woman remains in the clinic for two or three hours. She is then given another prostaglandin pill and held for another hour. She returns to the hospital five or six days later for a physical checkup to be certain the expulsion of the material is complete. Etienne-Emile Baulieu, the inventor of the pill, believes the pill does not resolve the ethical issues surrounding abortion, but rather makes the process less invasive for the pregnant woman.

Obviously the pill is not for everyone. In France it is the personal preference of 20 percent of women who have abortions, whereas in Britain only 6 percent opt for it. Its advocates assume that many physicians who otherwise have been reluctant to be involved in abortion issues will be more likely to turn to this method

because it simply involves prescribing a pill and not engaging in any invasive procedures. This might especially be true in areas where there are few abortion clinics or few physicians willing to be publicly associated with abortion. The use of RU 486 is very much a private affair, and 97 percent of those women who have used it reported they would recommend it to a friend. The FDA approved it for use during the first forty-nine days after a woman's last menstrual period, when the embryo's size varies from that of a pencil point to that of a grain of rice.

It should be added that RU 486 is not the only pill that can be used to induce an abortion, and as indicated in the entry on oral contraceptives, many of these can also serve as a morning-after pill. They, however, operate on a different principle. The so-called morning-after pills, Preven and Plan B, essentially high-dose birth control pills, were approved by the FDA in 1998, and as of this writing there is serious consideration of making them available without a prescription. In fact, the American Medical Association has urged that this be done. Although the morning-after pill has aroused less controversy than mifepristone, it has been condemned by the Vatican, and as of this writing Walgreen, the nation's largest drug chain, has decided not to offer it at its pharmacies.

Although some of the antiabortion foes had indicated they would punish druggists who accept prescriptions for mifepristone, this in the long run would be counterproductive because the drug is also likely to become a major tool in the treatment of progesterone-encouraged cancers in the brain and other parts of the body because of its ability to inhibit progesterone.

Much of the story of mifepristone has been gathered from newspapers such as the *Los Angeles Times* and the *New York Times* and from news magazines such as *Newsweek* and *Time* from October and November 2000.

Reference

Lader and Laurence. *A Private Matter: RU-486 and the Abortion Crisis.* Buffalo, NY: Prometheus Books, 1995.

S

Sanger, Margaret Louise (Higgins) (1879–1966)

Margaret Sanger was born in Corning, New York, to Irish-born Michael Higgins, a free-thinker and stonemason, and his Irish-American wife, Anne Purcell Higgins, a devout Roman Catholic. Margaret Louise, the sixth of the eleven Higgins children, sought a way out of the working-class fate of her parents, and with the support of her two older sisters, attended Claverack College and Hudson River Institute. She was forced to leave school before graduating in order to attend to her mother, who was suffering from tuberculosis. Her mother died shortly after, at the age of fifty, a premature death that young Margaret attributed to her mother's frequent pregnancies. In 1900, Margaret showed an interest in medicine and enrolled in White Plains Hospital to train as a nurse, but left before completing her third and final year in order to marry aspiring architect and artist, William Sanger. The two settled down in Hastings, New York, where Margaret Sanger led a quiet domestic life. Though suffering from a recurring tubercular condition, probably contracted from her mother, she became the mother of three children (Stuart, b. 1903; Grant, b. 1908; and Peggy, b. 1910).

By 1910, the couple, each interested in socialist politics, decided to move to New York City, the center of a pre–World War I community of radical activists. The couple quickly became active in the New York branch of the Socialist Party, with Margaret Sanger being hired as a paid organizer for the Women's Committee. She soon became mired in the bureaucracy of party politics and turned to the Industrial Workers of the World (IWW). The IWW's commitment to radical change and working-class empowerment through militant action appealed to her. She participated in several IWW labor actions, notably the 1912 strike at Lawrence, Massachusetts, and the 1913 strike at Paterson, New Jersey.

Margaret Sanger also threw herself into the bohemian world of Greenwich Village with its artists, writers, journalists, and feminists, many of whom sought to free themselves from Victorian repression by espousing social and sexual liberation, as well as economic revolution. When her husband began pursuing a growing interest in painting, Margaret Sanger helped support her family by resuming her nursing, taking cases for the Visiting Nurse Association among the immigrants of New York's Lower East Side. She also began writing articles for the socialist daily, the *New York Call,* particularly on issues relating to the health and hygiene of the working-class women and children she was treating. Among these articles was a 1912–1913 series on sex education, "What Every Girl Should Know," that drew the attention of the U.S. Post Office, which in 1913 suppressed her article on venereal disease on the grounds of obscenity.

Sanger was shocked by this action. Through her nursing work and her association with the children of women on strike, Sanger also became upset at the toll taken by frequent childbirth, miscarriage, and self-induced abortion. Increasingly, Sanger's primary interest turned to

Margaret Louise Sanger, who worked as a nurse among poor immigrants in New York City, saw the need for women to limit their family size and founded the modern birth control movement. (Library of Congress)

helping those working women who lived hard lives and died early, as her own mother had. She found that most of these women had few contraceptive options. Withdrawal and condoms were the most widely used methods, methods that required the cooperation of their sexual partners. Awakened by her anarchist colleagues such as Emma Goldman to the connection between limiting family size and working-class empowerment, Sanger began to focus her efforts on providing these women with a wider range of woman-controlled contraceptive options. However, contraception was defined as obscene and was legally prohibited by the 1873 federal Comstock Act and a host of state laws. Sanger knew that middle- and upper-class women could circumvent these legal prohibitions and was convinced that only by liberating *all* women from the risk of unwanted pregnancy could fundamental change be effected.

Sanger decided to address the plight of working women in March 1914 by launching the *Woman Rebel,* a radical monthly that advocated militant political action and female empowerment. Among the issues she espoused was the right of every woman to be "absolute mistress of her own body." Only birth control, a term first used in the *Woman Rebel,* would free women from the tyranny of uncontrolled childbirth. Although she did nothing more in the *Woman Rebel* than advocate birth control, postal authorities suppressed five of its seven issues. Sanger, who had begun to view birth control as part of a larger free-speech issue, defied authorities by continuing publication of the monthly. She also began preparing her assault on the Comstock Act by writing *Family Limitation,* a sixteen-page pamphlet that provided birth control information in the form of detailed evaluations and graphic descriptions of various contraceptive methods. The pamphlet listed syringes filled with foam acid powders; vinegar-soaked sponges to absorb sperm; spermicidal douches made of such easily purchased ingredients as vinegar, copper, nitrate of silver, Lysol, and boric, citric, and tartaric acids; recipes for vaginal suppositories made of cocoa butter or quinine (later manufactured and labeled as Quinseptikons); and Mizpah cervical caps. In August 1914, Sanger was indicted for publishing obscene material in the *Woman Rebel.* Unwilling to risk a potentially long prison term, she jumped bail in October and, using an alias, set sail for England. En route, she ordered the release of her *Family Limitation* pamphlets in the United States.

Sanger spent much of her 1914–1915 exile in England, where contact with the British Malthusian League, which sought to control population growth by promoting contraception, helped her to formulate more sophisticated socioeconomic justifications for birth control. She also came under the tutelage of noted British sexual theorist, Havelock Ellis, who became her friend, lover, and most influential mentor. Under his influence, Sanger found intellectual justification for rationalizing birth control as a tool for free-

Margaret Sanger was arrested and tried for opening the first birth control clinic in America in 1916; here several mothers brought their families to the courtroom to support Sanger's cause. (Library of Congress)

ing women from Victorian sexual repression and linking the inequality of sexual experience with all other gender inequities. Birth control, she now argued, would liberate women not just by making sexual intercourse safe, but also pleasurable. During these eleven months abroad she also published three additional methods pamphlets that summarized birth control practice in England, the Netherlands, and France (*English Methods of Birth Control; Dutch Methods of Birth Control;* and *Magnetation Methods of Birth Control,* respectively).

Upon her return to the United States in October 1915, Sanger found that birth control had made headlines. Her husband, William Sanger, whose January 1915 arrest, and subse-

quent conviction and thirty-day jail sentence for inadvertently giving a copy of *Family Limitation* to a Comstock agent, had escalated interest in birth control as a civil liberties issues. As she launched a campaign to refocus attention on her own case, Sanger received an unexpected blow when her five-year-old daughter, Peggy, died suddenly on November 6. In the wake of the sympathetic publicity and positive press coverage Sanger received, the government decided not to prosecute her. Denied the platform of a public trial, Sanger embarked on a cross-country tour in 1916 to promote her cause, a trip marked by volatile confrontations with local authorities, several arrests, and national publicity for Sanger and her cause.

Sanger returned to New York in the summer of 1916 once again ready to challenge the laws prohibiting the distribution of birth control information and services. On October 16, 1916 she opened the nation's first birth control clinic in Brownsville, Brooklyn. Some four hundred women received instruction in sexual hygiene and various contraceptive methods from suppositories and douches to pessaries. Nine days later police closed the clinic and arrested Sanger and her two coworkers. She was tried and convicted in February 1917 for violating the New York State Comstock Law's ban on the dispensation of birth control information and services and spent thirty days in the Queens County Penitentiary. On appeal, Sanger's conviction was upheld but in its 1918 decision the New York State Appellate Court exempted physicians from the prohibition on distributing birth control to women when medically indicated. This landmark ruling provided Sanger with the legal loophole through which she could open a network of doctor-staffed clinics, similar to the contraceptive delivery system she had seen in Holland during her 1915 exile.

With the collapse of the radical left after World War I, Sanger, who had grown increasingly disillusioned by the disinterest she found among socialist and feminists, began to shift away from the radical/socialist stance and broaden the movement's base of support. She turned to an expanding circle of wealthy women who, mobilized by her arrest and trial, began volunteering their time and money in support of birth control. With their support, she began promoting the social and economic benefits of birth control in a new monthly journal, the *Birth Control Review,* which she launched in 1917. In 1921 she founded the American Birth Control League, which undertook an educational and public relations campaign to cultivate mainstream respectability. Sanger also tried to enlist the support of the liberal wing of the eugenics movement, championing birth control for those with genetically transmitted mental or physical defects, and even supporting forced sterilization for the mentally incompetent and those with hereditary physical defects or transmissible congenital diseases. Like most liberal eugenicists, she did not advocate the elevation of any one racial group over others nor any other race- or class-based efforts to limit population growth. She also consistently refused to encourage population growth among white, native-born middle and upper classes. Her belief in eugenics, including sterilization policies, stemmed from her conviction that a stronger, healthier population would both alleviate human suffering and reduce the financial burden on the state. Nevertheless, Sanger's reputation would be permanently tainted by her association with the racist eugenics of the 1920s and 1930s.

Critical to Sanger's efforts to gain respectability for birth control was her securing support from the medical and scientific community. In Holland she had been introduced to the Mensinga diaphragm, or "Dutch cap," an occlusive diaphragm that needed to be fitted and required medically skilled and individualized instruction. Previously an exponent of contraceptive self-help, Sanger now became convinced that the proper use of these devices needed professional supervision and monitoring. In 1923, she opened the Birth Control Clinical Research Bureau (later renamed the Margaret Sanger Research Bureau), staffed by a licensed female physician, who provided an array of gynecological and contraceptive services, though the clinic relied heavily on the use of the Mensinga diaphragm in conjunction with a spermicidal jelly.

In 1926, Sanger published *Happiness in Marriage,* a marriage manual that argued for contraception as the best means to reduce abortion, promoted doctor-controlled contraceptive services, and continued to endorse the diaphragm and contraceptive jelly method as the most effective for the majority of women. In an effort to persuade physicians, as well as lawmakers and social workers, of the impact and safety of contraceptives, the bureau kept extensive patient records, compiled statistics tracking the effectiveness of contraceptives on women's health, and sought to become the model for a nationwide system of doctor-staffed clinics. Ten thousand patients were studied, providing the first clinical trial of birth control methods. Of the patients monitored over an extended period of time, the safety and effectiveness of the diaphragm was clearly demonstrated. These studies, coupled with the educational programs she established, enabled Sanger to convince many physicians that diaphragms were both practical and safe. However, on April 15, 1929, at the urging of the city's Catholic leaders, the clinic was raided by police, who arrested the staff and seized its confidential medical records. This blatant violation of patient confidentiality raised the ire of the medical community, who came to Sanger's defense, and the city finally dropped its charges.

In 1929 Sanger formed the National Committee on Federal Legislation for Birth Control to lobby for a federal "doctors-only" bill, legislation granting doctors exclusive right to disseminate contraceptives. Yet even those physicians who supported birth control continued to distrust Sanger, a lay person with a history of militant action, while most remained hostile to birth control as illegal, immoral, and unnecessary. It was not until 1937 that the American Medical Association responded to Sanger's intense lobbying by formally endorsing birth control. Sanger, for her part, courted the support of doctors, but resisted the efforts of the medical community to take control of her clinic and her movement.

In these years, Sanger reorganized her personal life in accordance with her belief in sexual freedom and equality for women. Having separated from William Sanger in 1913, she embarked on a series of intimate liaisons with several men, including Havelock Ellis and H. G. Wells. In 1922 she married wealthy oil producer, James Noah H. Slee, but only after he agreed to accept her demand for personal autonomy and promised to provide support for the birth control movement. The marriage thrust the

working-class woman from Corning into a world of money and privilege. Sanger suddenly had lavish homes, the means to put her two sons through private preparatory schools and Ivy League universities, and a new source of money to pursue her cause. Though Sanger continued to pursue a remarkably autonomous personal life, the marriage was in its own way successful and lasted until Slee's death in 1943.

From the start Sanger sought to cultivate global support, and her frustration with the resistance of physicians to her efforts to promote birth control led her to begin focusing more intently on international work and the hope of discovering new contraceptives abroad. She organized several international birth control conferences, including the ground-breaking World Population Conference in Geneva in 1927 and the Seventh International Birth Control Conference in Zurich in 1930, during which more than a hundred scientists, physicians, and clinicians were brought together by Sanger to discuss not the moral, ethical, and political aspects of birth control, but to focus on technical appraisals of contraceptive techniques and devices, and a review of birth control work in each nation. Sanger lectured on birth control throughout Europe and Asia. Her 1922 trip to China and Japan helped nascent birth control efforts in those countries. A 1927 trip to Germany, during which she combined lectures with demonstrations on fitting diaphragms, helped to spur the formation of the German Committee for Birth Control. Similarly, her 1936 tour of India, which included a widely reported debate with Mahatma Gandhi, helped to launch the Indian birth control movement. Sanger also cultivated an extensive worldwide network through the London-based Birth Control International Information Centre, which she cofounded in 1929 with British activist Edith How-Martyn. However, the pronatalist policies of the rising fascist regimes in Europe and Japan impeded their work and by 1937 the centre was closed.

With her expanding global interests, growing involvement in the Birth Control Clinical Research Bureau, and the money and power her new marriage gave her, Sanger's interest in the administrative aspects of the movement began to wane, leading to rising tensions between Sanger and other members of the American Birth Control League. In 1928 she resigned from the league amid a great deal of anger and animosity over her leadership approach, and she resigned as editor of the *Birth Control Review* the following year. Sanger now focused much of her energies not only on the clinic, but on her legislative efforts. But despite her intense lobbying and her success in cultivating public support, continued public resistance and powerful opposition from the Catholic Church led to the failure of her legislative work in the United States. She also was unable to secure government funding for birth control as a public health measure. But she did succeed in overturning a key element of the Comstock Act's ban on birth control. Having been forced to smuggle birth control devices and materials into the United States for testing and for use at her clinic, until she could sponsor a company to manufacture them in the United States, Sanger decided in 1932 to challenge the prohibition on the importation of contraceptives by having a case of diaphragms shipped to her clinic from Japan. The package was seized by U.S. Customs as a violation of the 1930 Tariff Act (an outgrowth of the 1873 Comstock Act), which prohibited all persons from importing into the United States from any foreign country "any article whatsoever for the prevention of conception." Sanger and her attorney, Morris Ernst, contested the seizure, and the case, officially known as *United States v. One Package Containing 120, more or less, Rubber Pessaries to Prevent Conception,* began a long journey through the courts that ended in 1936 when the U.S. Court of Appeals ruled that physicians were exempt from the ban on the importation of birth control materials. This decision effectively legalized the distribution of birth control for medical use, though the prohibition on importing contraceptive devices for personal use was not lifted until 1971.

In courting an alliance with establishment forces, Sanger provided the birth control movement with the financial support and social rationale needed to battle significant opposition. Yet her pragmatic approach also led to a subtle but steady change in the direction of the movement. As the number and influence of conservative supporters increased, Sanger's initial focus on women's personal autonomy and empowerment was subordinated. The new leaders of the American Birth Control League began to emphasize selective population control, introducing programs aimed at child-spacing, problems of infertility, and the maintenance of traditional, middle-class values. The movement's new leaders, a growing number of them men, viewed Sanger's radical history, militant tactics, and persistently feminist focus as a liability in their efforts to win mainstream acceptance. Sanger's legislative failures further compromised her leadership of the movement. In 1939, tired and discouraged, Sanger agreed to merge her clinic with the American Birth Control League to form the Birth Control Federation of America, but her position in the new organization was largely honorific. She was even more dismayed when the new leadership decided that even the term "birth control" was too radical and in 1942 the Birth Control Federation of America was renamed the Planned Parenthood Federation of America. Sanger went into semiretirement at her home in Tucson, Arizona.

Sanger was propelled back into the movement when she recognized that the post–World War II alarm over population growth and its relationship to economic development and social stability, particularly in the Third World, would help launch a revival and expansion of an international birth control movement. Among her first goals was the resuscitation of the Japanese birth control movement, which she had helped mobilize during her 1922 visit. Although barred from entering occupied Japan in 1950, a steep hike in the Japanese birthrate and an alarming number of abortions in Japan created a new consensus on birth control, and in 1954 Sanger was invited to address the Japanese Diet. She was the first American woman to be so honored.

But Sanger's primary goal after 1946 was to establish an international organization to foster family planning on a global scale. In 1948 she helped form the International Committee on Planned Parenthood (ICPP), which sought to revive the family planning movement after the devastation of the war. In 1952, Sanger contacted Indian birth control leader, Lady Rama Rau, and suggested that she host an international conference in Bombay. This effort eventually led to the establishment of the International Planned Parenthood Federation (IPPF). Sanger played a critical role in this effort, cajoling an impressive array of world figures such as Albert Einstein to lend their names to the effort, then she raised money to bring delegates to India and procured the public and organizational support required to mount the event. Although her IPPF colleagues were often annoyed by her sometimes imperious behavior and proclivity for unilateral action, they acknowledged her significant contributions and worldwide reputation by electing her as their first president. Sanger, though in her seventies and increasingly frail, nevertheless tried to direct the growth of the infant organization to reflect her unwavering conviction that, by reducing the number of unwanted children, birth control would facilitate more efficient allocation of economic and social resources. As IPPF president, she opposed all efforts to broaden its mission beyond the dissemination of birth control. At the same time she also resisted efforts to impose mandatory, government-controlled measures that ignored the needs and requirements of women. When Sanger relinquished the presidency in 1959, the IPPF, with twenty-six member nations, was the largest private international organization devoted to promoting family planning.

Throughout these years, Sanger also persisted in her pursuit of a simpler, less costly, more reliable female contraceptive. Although Sanger initially was among the most active proponents of "doctorless" birth control promoting inexpensive methods such as douches and suppositories, her support of doctor-controlled delivery of contraceptives led her to focus more attention on promoting the use of the spring-form diaphragm. But although the diaphragm was very effective when properly fitted and used, many women found it unpleasant. Poorer women found it burdensome because it required a doctor's visit for proper measuring, fitting, and follow-up; some degree of privacy to insert and clean; and hygienic conditions to properly maintain. Sanger continued to search for cheaper more accessible methods, and as early as 1920 visited war-torn Germany to investigate reports of the development of a new chemical contraceptive. By the mid-1930s, she was allocating increased time and resources to research and testing of new contraceptives, primarily in two forms: spermotoxins (substances that would immunize women against sperm) and hormonal compounds aimed at inhibiting ovulation. She also investigated promising anecdotal evidence on several other contraceptive home remedies, including a variety of herbal mixtures that reportedly caused sterility in both men and women.

Sanger held out hopes for a pill or injection that would preclude barrier methods and spermicidal solutions, but in the interim pursued and promoted alternate versions of barrier methods that would eliminate both the need for physicians and the discomfort associated with the diaphragm. She financed a number of efforts aimed at creating and testing spermicidal jellies, foam powders, sponges, and finally hormonal contraceptives. Vindication for her persistence came in the 1950s when she played a critical role in promoting research on an oral contraceptive for women. Starting in the early 1950s, Sanger orchestrated the various links and working associations necessary to carry out research on the contraceptive use of steroids and secured from Katherine McCormick substantial monetary support, which enabled Gregory Pincus to develop the first effective anovulant contraceptive—the birth control pill.

Margaret Sanger died in Tucson in 1966, six years after the U.S. Food and Drug Administration formally approved Enovid, the first birth control pill, and only one year after the U.S.

Supreme Court affirmed the right of married couples to use birth control, a right extended to unmarried couples in 1972 in *Einsenstadt v. Baird,* a case originally brought by William R. Baird against the state of Massachusetts.

Sanger's papers are available on microfilm in *The Margaret Sanger Papers: Smith College Collections Series* (83 reels) and *Collected Documents Series* (18 reels), edited by Esther Katz, Peter Engelman, and Cathy Moran Hajo. Bethesda, MD: University Publications of America, 1995, 1996. An additional 145 reels are available at the Library of Congress.

Esther Katz

See also American Birth Control League; Brownsville Birth Control Clinic; Clinical Research Bureau; Comstock, Anthony, and Comstockery; Eugenics; Goldman, Emma; Malthus, Thomas Robert; McCormick, Katharine Dexter; Pincus, Gregory Goodwin; *United States v. One Package*

References

Chesler, Ellen. *Woman of Valor: Margaret Sanger and the Birth Control Movement in America.* New York: Simon & Schuster, 1992.

Gordon, Linda. *Woman's Body, Woman's Right: A Social History of Birth Control in America.* New York: Grossman, 1976.

McCann, Carole R. *Birth Control Politics in the United States, 1916–1945.* Ithaca, NY: Cornell University Press, 1994.

Reed, James. *From Private Vice to Public Virtue: The Birth Control Movement and American Society since 1830.* Princeton, NJ: Princeton University Press, 1978.

Sanger, Margaret. *Margaret Sanger: An Autobiography.* New York: W. W. Norton, 1938.

———. *Motherhood in Bondage.* New York: Brentano, 1928.

———. *My Fight for Birth Control.* New York: Farrar & Rinehart, 1931.

———. *The Pivot of Civilization.* Washington, DC: Scott-Townsend, 1922.

———. *What Every Girl Should Know.* New York: Madx N. Maisel, 1920.

———. *What Every Mother Should Know.* New York: Truth Publishing, 1921.

———. *Woman and the New Race.* New York: Blue Ribbon Books, 1920.

Self-help Literature in the Nineteenth Century

The United States saw a wide dissemination of popular literature dealing with various medical problems including marriage and family ones in the nineteenth century. Much of it was written by unorthodox medical practitioners who appeared in great numbers. The more traditionally trained physicians founded the American Medical Association in 1846 to assert professional standards for medicine, but it was not until the twentieth century that they gained the control over medicine that they long sought. Until they did, all kinds of medical practitioners appeared. Many Americans in much of the nineteenth century resented officially trained physicians, believing them to be an elite group monopolizing knowledge that would best be widely diffused.

Among the largest of the medical sects that flourished in the nineteenth century were the Thomsonians, a system patented by Samuel Thomson in 1813. Thomson was opposed to the "heroic" blood letting and other interventionist practices of orthodox medicine and urged instead natural botanical remedies taken according to a strict regimen. He also advocated regular douching and his agents sold douching syringes and spermicides among other things. There were also strong advocates of hydrotherapy. They encouraged Americans to drink more water, to use a variety of sitz baths, and to wrap themselves daily in wet sheets for an hour or so. Other popular healers emphasized colonic enemas. Still others, such as John Harvey Kellogg, developed special diets (e.g., corn flakes) at their sanitaria. There were homeopaths, naturopaths, chiropractors, and many others. Many of the newly emerging American religious groups were also concerned with health. Mary Baker Eddy and the Christian Science church with its own practitioners, the Seventh Day Adventists with their dietary restrictions, and the Mormons with their Word of Wisdom, which discouraged the use of alcoholic beverages all helped popularize the new campaign for health. The result was a plethora of popular health manuals, many of which by the 1850s included references to contraception, menstrual regulation, and even abortion. Titles such as *A Confidential Letter to the*

Married; The Wife's Secret of Power; Science of Repro-duction and Reproductive Control; The Marriage Guide; How Not To and Why; and *Conception: The Pro-cess, Method of Prevention without Any Expense or Any Hindrance to Perfect Intercourse* were widely avail-able. Much of the newly available literature was pamphlet sized and focused specifically on con-traception and abortion, although the lines were increasingly blurred between sober advice tracts and lengthy advertising booklets for birth con-trol products or services. Interestingly many of the pamphlets are no longer available and their existence is known only by their titles in card catalogues or by references to them in court records.

As reproductive control became commercial-ized after 1850, and as some women became increasingly able to assert a degree of indepen-dence over their fertility, a reaction set in, play-ing upon the ambivalence that many felt about any kind of control of reproduction. The social purity movement became a crusade that result-ed in state laws altering two hundred years of American custom and public policy toward abortion and toward contraception, with the result that both went underground.

See also Comstock, Anthony, and Comstockery

References

Brodie, Janet Farrell. *Contraception and Abortion in Nineteenth Century America.* Ithaca, NY: Cornell University Press, 1994.

Serena

Serena, or Service de regulation des naissances, an organization in French-speaking Canada, grew out of a movement begun in 1955 by Gilles and Rita Breault of Lachine, Quebec. Aid-ed by a grant from their provincial government, teams of lay Catholics were trained to teach the techniques for using the "sterile" period to pre-vent conception. It was an early grass-roots movement in Quebec that taught couples how to take daily body temperature and the other techniques that became available to determine the timing of ovulation in women and when not to engage in intercourse. In 1962, this move-ment became known as Serena. The organization in 1966 gave testimony in favor of decriminaliz-ing Canadian birth control services.

Brenda Appleby

Social Purity Movement

The underlying philosophy behind most of the opposition to both contraception and abortion was that promulgated by the social purity movement. The deep ambivalence that Ameri-cans felt toward the growing industrialization, the vast increase in emigrants, the rapid growth of cities, the commercialization of contracep-tion, the increase in prostitution, and a number of similar issues led to what historians have called the social purity crusade in the last part of the nineteenth century. The crusade, as Janet Farrell Brodie has emphasized, was led by "energetic, driven men" backed by the profes-sional organizations of white, middle-class, native-born men and women who assumed the role of custodians of the public good. They had the backing of most state and federal officehold-ers and the result was an enactment of federal and state legislation that among other things criminalized contraception and abortion, both of which had long been legal.

Underlying these growing restrictions was the belief that it was necessary to restrict sexuality itself. Many reformers believed that the growing commerce in cheap sexually oriented literature was inciting unhealthy passion in the young, leading them ultimately to corruption and depravity. This goal fitted the growing feminist movement, which espoused a need to curb male sexuality and give women greater sexual "self ownership." Many feminists were ambivalent about contraceptives because they failed to restrict male sexuality, whereas others simply believed that women should have a higher moral standard, which would include greater absten-tion from sex. Among the leaders of the social purity movement's campaign against abortion and contraception were physicians.

See also American Medical Association

References

Boyer, Paul. *Purity in Print.* New York: Scribner, 1968.

Brodie, Janet Farrell. *Contraception and Abortion in Nineteenth Century America.* Ithaca, NY: Cornell University Press, 1994.

Pivar, David J. *Purity Crusade, Sexual Morality, and Social Control, 1868–1900.* Westport, CN: Greenwood Press, 1973.

Spermicides

Spermicides, as indicated by the various historical entries in this encyclopedia, are among the oldest and simplest of all techniques used to prevent conception. From ancient times to the present, various substances, usually highly acidic ones with pasty or sticky bases, have been employed. The sticky base plus an acid remain important elements in current spermicides. The historical efforts are particularly interesting because they started long before sperm were seen with the microscope and before the reproductive process was fully understood. Spermicides developed through a trial-and-error basis, and that ancient spermicides exist attests to long-standing needs and desires for some kind of fertility control.

Among the first, if not the first, of the commercial spermicide products were the quinine pessaries developed by the English pharmacist Charles Rendell in 1885. These suppositories consisted of soluble cocoa butter plus quinine sulfate. Cocoa butter—a yellowish, hard, brittle, vegetable fat obtained from the seeds of the *Theobroma* plant—contains about 30 percent oleic acid and 40 percent stearic acid, as well as other fatty acids. Cocoa butter was a good vehicle for a spermicide suppository because of its low melting point, and the cocoa butter itself probably served to block the cervix with an oily film. The quinine sulfate, however, was not a particularly potent spermicide and in some individuals it might have resulted in a toxic reaction.

Other chemical combinations used as the active ingredient including chinosol, lactic acid, and boric acid.

It was not until the 1920s that research into spermicides began seriously, and although the Rockefeller Foundation was one of the main supporters of such research it had to go to England and Europe to find researchers willing to conduct tests because the stigma attached to scientists in America who engaged in contraceptive research was so great. European pharmaceutical firms also did research on their own.

Several refinements made spermicides somewhat more effective. The first was the development by a German pharmaceutical firm of a spermicide in combination with an effervescent tablet that foamed when it came in contact with moisture. The foam allowed widespread dispersal of the spermicide in the vagina. In 1937, phenylmercuric acetate, a far more effective spermicide than quinine sulfate, was first used in the production of Volpar. Although this compound has since been banned from the U.S. market because of concerns about the safety of mercury, it proved very effective.

A major breakthrough came with the introduction of surfactants, surface-active agents, in the 1950s. These agents act primarily by disrupting the integrity of the sperm membrane. Because surfactants are not strongly acidic, they are rarely irritating to the vagina or penis and they have become the principal active ingredient in spermicidal products. They can also be combined with different bases to make a wide variety of spermicides including jellies, suppositories, foaming tablets, and foam in pressurized containers.

Different types of spermicides vary in their ability to provide rapid and expansive coverage. Foams and jellies are dispersed best. Suppositories need body heat to melt. Foaming tablets need moisture to produce the foam, and distribution in the vagina may depend in part on coital movements. Thus solid preparations may require as long as fifteen minutes between insertion and coitus to ensure melting or foaming action. Dispersal, however, is also dependent on the amounts of vaginal fluids, and this varies from woman to woman.

Spermicides can be purchased in the pharmacy (as can condoms) without a prescription. Although prices vary, they are relatively inexpensive, costing approximately fifty cents to a dollar per use. They are not difficult to use and are completely safe. These qualities are particularly important to first-time users. When combined with other easily available contraceptives, such as condoms, they are even more effective than when used alone. Many jellies, in fact, are designed to be used with barrier contraceptives. Currently on the market are foams, suppositories or tablets, creams or gels, and a film. The latter is a paper-thin sheet of film that should be inserted near the cervix (or inside the diaphragm) at least five minutes before intercourse in order to allow time for it to melt.

Laboratory tests show that most spermicides do immobilize sperm but clinical studies and use surveys yield failure rates from as low as 3 percent to more than 50 percent. This means that spermicides used alone, as of this writing, do not meet the standards for study design and analysis and make comparison with other means of contraceptives difficult and not meaningful. They are valuable as an emergency contraceptive but most effective when used with barrier contraceptives such as a condom or diaphragm. Even with their failure rate, spermicides are more effective than coitus interruptus, fertility awareness techniques (i.e., rhythm method), douches, or simple chance. Some spermicides also offer some protection against sexually transmitted diseases such as gonorrhea, syphilis, chlamydia, herpes, hepatitis B, and even to some extent human immunodeficiency virus (HIV).

See also Douching; Sterile Period (Rhythm Method)

References

Bullough, Vern L. *Science in the Bedroom.* New York: Basic Books, 1994.

Bullough, Vern L., and Bonnie Bullough. *Contraception: A Guide to Birth Control.* Amherst, NY: Prometheus Books, 1997.

Hatcher, Robert A., et al. *Contraceptive Technology.* New York: Irvington Publishers (Updated every other even-numbered year).

Voge, Cecil I. B. *The Chemistry and Physics of Contraception.* London: Jonathan Cape, 1933.

Sponges, Tampons, and Vaginal Inserts

One of the early references to the insertion of a spongy substance into the vagina is in the Babylonian Talmud, an encyclopedia of Jewish tradition supplementing the Scriptures and written over a period of several centuries, being finally completed in the fifth century of the modern era. Some of the writers mention a *mokh,* a spongy substance made of absorbent material, something like wads of cotton that women could insert in their vagina to avoid pregnancy (Yebamot 12b, 100b; Kettubot 39a; Nedarim 35b, and Niddah, 45a, in the Talmud, 1935–1952). It does not seem likely that the use of such inserts was restricted to Jews and it probably reflects practices in existence at least in the eastern parts of the Roman Empire if not throughout it at the beginning of the common era. Norman Himes speculated that the use of *mokh* might be similar to the use of lint mentioned in Egyptian sources and, if so, it indicates an old tradition even though mention of it has not been found in other surviving sources.

Aristotle mentioned that women anointed their vaginas with oil of cedar or with ointments of lead or frankincense mixed with olive oil when they wanted to avoid pregnancy. Tradition has it that they also used a sponge soaked in citrus juice but the practice is known as having been traditional only in Constantinople at a later date. Chaucer mentions vaginal inserts in his *Parson's Tale* (lines 575–576). Sponges are specifically mentioned in a number of sixteenth-, seventeenth-, and eighteenth-century English and French sources including a recommendation for the sponge by Jeremy Bentham in his "Situation and Relief of the Poor" in 1797 to keep down the birthrates of the poor. Francis Place, the founder of the English birth control movement, in his handbills in the 1820s recommended the use of the sponge, implying that the sponge was in wide use among some people. He wrote:

> What is done by other people is this. A piece of soft sponge is tied by a bobbin or penny ribbon, and inserted just before intercourse is to take place, and is drawn as soon as it has taken place. Many tie a piece of sponge to each end of the ribbon and they take care not to use the same sponge until it has been washed.
>
> If the sponge be large enough, that is: as large as a walnut or a small apple, it will prevent conception, and thus, without diminishing the pleasures of married life, or doing the least injury to the health of the most delicate women, both the woman and her husband will be saved from all the miseries which too many children produces (Quoted by Himes, 1970, pp. 216–217).

The sponge became one of the first methods, if not the first, to be popularized by the emerging birth control movement, and if individuals had not known about it before, information about it quickly spread, even though it was not as effective as Place had promised.

Tampons are mentioned in Sanskrit sources, although the tampon was supposed to be inserted after intercourse rather than before to prevent pregnancy, and this would not be particularly effective. The *azego,* mentioned in Japanese sources, is a tampon made of soft paper and rolled into a ball. Rhazes (d. c. 923–924) mentions a number of possible ingredients for such tampons or suppositories including elephant dung, tamarisk gum, pitch, ox gall, pomegranate skin, and ear wax of animals. Beeswax tampons or suppositories have been noted in Germany, Hungary, and elsewhere, and the sponge was also used in much of Europe.

Other items were also used. Giovanni Giacomo Casanova, for example, in 1760 reported that he bought some gold balls that he said he used for several years. He advised placing a ball, after soaking it in an alkaline solution, at the os of the cervix, to which it will then adhere, although one has to be careful that it is not displaced. Apparently the weight of the ball would hold it in place and block the cervix, and although Casanova attested to its efficacy, there is no real evidence it would be very effective.

See also Place, Francis

References

Aristotle. *History of Animals,* Bk. VII (3:20–27; 531A). In *The Complete Works of Aristotle,* edited by Jonathan Barnes, 2 vols. Princeton, NJ: Princeton University Press, 1984.

Chaucer, Geoffrey. "Parson's Tale." In *The Poetical Works of Chaucer,* edited by F. N. Robinson. Boston: Houghton-Mifflin, 1933.

Epstein, Isidore, ed. and trans. *Talmud, The Babylonian.* London: Soncino Press, 1935–1952.

Himes, Norman E. *A Medical History of Contraception.* New York: Schocken Books, 1970.

Sterile Period (Rhythm Method)

That intercourse during some phases of the female menstrual cycle was more likely to lead to pregnancy than during other times has long been recognized, although for much of history there was not much agreement on when these periods of sterility occurred. Neither the understanding of how reproduction occurred nor the physiology involved was advanced enough to give definitive answers. Existence of such periods are mentioned in the Hippocratic corpus, but probably the best summary of information on the subject is in the work of Soranus, the Roman physician who wrote in the second century of the modern era. He held that the uterus shortly before menstruation and during menstruation was unsuitable for conception because it was already receiving material, making it difficult to also receive the seed. He believed that the best time for conception was at the end of menses, and this meant that those interested in preventing conception should not have intercourse at that time. This mistaken fixing of the moment of high conception was a problem that plagued any effective use of what some have called natural contraception until the twentieth century.

We know that members of the Manichaean faith, a rival of Christianity, believed in a sterile period, although it apparently did not always work for them. Still, Saint Augustine, a former Manichaean himself, condemned the use of any such method. This makes for an interesting contradiction in western Christian history because, in spite of the Augustinian condemnation, it is the one method of avoiding pregnancy officially accepted by the Catholic Church today. Mostly discussion about the sterile period remained theoretical until the nineteenth century, when Karl Ernst von Baer published his discovery of the human ovum, which revolutionized the understanding of human reproduction. Catholic theologians applied themselves to this new discovery, particularly Auguste Joseph Lecomte (1824–1881), a faculty member at Louvain University in Belgium. He espoused that married couples with sufficient reason to avoid conception might use the sterile period, which he believed was much better than withdrawal, or what he called onanism. Debate and discussion on the issue continued within the Catholic Church until Pope Pius XII, in a speech to an Italian association of midwives on October 29, 1951, referred to the method as acceptable if there were serious reasons to avoid conception.

Technically, it was not until the third decade of the twentieth century that Kyusaku Ogino in Japan and Herman Knaus in Austria independently identified the time of ovulation in relation to the menstrual cycle that any kind of periodic abstinence was more effective in controlling births than pure chance. Because the period of fertility coincides in general with ovulation, it should be simple to plot the cycle on a calendar and have intercourse only during the nonfertile phases to avoid pregnancy. Unfortunately, this timing is based upon estimating when ovulation will occur or has occurred, and this date can be definitely known only after the next menstrual period begins, which is some fourteen days after ovulation. Some women have regular periods at intervals of twenty-eight or twenty-nine days, whereas others experience much more variation.

Because this is the case, there are long periods in the cycle in which abstinence is required if pregnancy is to be avoided. To cut down on abstinence, much effort has been expended in trying to calculate more accurately when ovulation will or has occurred. Interestingly, the very methods developed to help predict ovulation for purposes of contraception, in fact, are very helpful to those people who are trying to get pregnant because this is when they should concentrate their sexual activity.

The original method by both Ogino and Knaus was based upon a calendar rhythm method. Most used was the calendar calculation of Ogino rather than that of Knaus, even though Ogino stipulated additional days of abstinence to allow for a longer possible fertile period resulting from variation in the time of ovulation. According to the Ogino formula, a woman estimates the beginning of her fertile period by subtracting eighteen days from the shortest previous six to twelve menstrual cycles, and she estimates the end of the fertile period by subtracting eleven days from the longest cycle. This does not mean that she is actually fertile all of those days but that the fertile period will fall into that time span.

As an illustration, the average length of the menstrual cycle for a woman whom we will call Mary has ranged from twenty-three to thirty-one days over the past twelve months. Her calculations would be: $31 - 11 = 20$ and $23 - 18 = 5$.

This means that Mary's fertile period could take place any time from five days after the beginning of her menses until twenty days after. The couple, in order to prevent conception, should not engage in intercourse from the fifth day after the beginning of the menses (calculations are always from the beginning of the menses) until the twenty-first day after, requiring an abstinent period of sixteen days.

A second subject, whom we will call Juanita, has a more regular menstrual cycle with a range between twenty-seven and twenty-nine days over the past twelve months. Her calculations would be: $29 - 11 = 18$ and $37 - 28 = 9$.

The couple would abstain beginning nine days after the onset of the menses and could begin intercourse again on the nineteenth day, and thus need only have a ten-day period of abstinence. This is the minimum amount of abstinence possible under the calendar system.

The problem with the straight calendar method is that, even for those who practice it devotedly, success is not guaranteed, simply because even women who are usually very regular can have their cycles go askew because of tension, illness, anxiety, stress, and other factors. It also requires the dedicated cooperation of both the individuals involved. For those using the straight calendar method, the failure rate has been estimated at about 18.87 percent, that is, nearly one in five women become pregnant within the first year of using the calendar method. This, however, is a lower rate than would have occurred without using the method because it estimated that anywhere from 50 to 85 percent of sexually active women who have intercourse regularly would become pregnant within a year if no method at all were used.

Recognizing the failure rate led others to develop new methods of determining the sterile period. It had been observed as early as 1868 that a woman's basal body temperature (BBT), that is, the temperature of the body at rest, rises slightly during the later part of the menstrual cycle. In the 1930s this rise was linked to ovulation, whereupon daily recording of temperatures was suggested to users of the calendar rhythm method as an additional way of identifying the fertile period. The woman using the BBT method charts her temperature regularly at the same time each day and abstains from intercourse between the first day of menstruation and the third consecutive day of elevated temperature. The three-day wait after the temperature rise is intended to ensure that the ovum is no longer fertilizable. Used by itself the method allows for about ten safe days of intercourse every cycle before the menses begins again. When combined with the calendar method, it has the advantage of allowing an earlier resump-

tion of sexual activity and would also permit intercourse during and immediately after the menses, allowing for fewer days of abstinence. To assist clients, special thermometers with expanded scales that allow slight change to be more easily detected have been developed because the temperature rise is slight from two-tenth to four-tenths of a degree Centigrade or four-tenths to eight-tenths of a degree Fahrenheit. Temperature taken rectally is the most accurate but it must be taken at roughly the same time every morning after at least three to five hours of uninterrupted sleep. Any deviation from the routine or from a regular pattern of behavior can alter the BBT, as can a mild illness or extreme changes in environmental temperature. Although some rely entirely on the BBT method, most users prefer to combine it with the calendar method, which allows for more safe days.

Just as there are changes in BBT, changes also take place in the cervical mucus in response to the changing hormonal levels. Two Australian physicians, John and Evelyn Billing, developed a method of periodic abstinence based solely on the cervical mucus changes. In a typical menstrual cycle, the secretory cells in the cervix produce two kinds of mucus at two different phases, and each type has its own cellular and chemical components as well as physical structure. During most of the cycle the mucus is designed to act as a barrier to the entrance of sperm, but after ovulation, the purpose is to encourage entrance of the sperm. Once menstrual bleeding has stopped, there is little or no mucus for a few days. Then a white or cloudy and tacky mucus is discharged; the amount increases over the next few days. The mucus then becomes thinner and clearer and it increases in amount. There are one or two days when the mucus is thin, like raw egg white, slippery and elastic. Because of its stretchability it has been termed *spinnbarkheit* mucus. It most resembles the fluid produced during sexual arousal. Ovulation occurs at the end of this clear mucus period. After ovulation the mucus thickens, becoming cloudy and white. It also loses its elasticity.

Changes in the mucus are a result of changing hormone levels. During the preovulatory and ovulatory phases, the mucus is type E, or estrogenic. It is responding to ovarian secretions of estrogen. After ovulation, when progesterone is produced, the mucus is known as type B, or gestagenic, and this marks the beginning of the safe period. A woman using this method has to learn to distinguish between two types of mucus, both by feeling inside her vagina as well as by visual inspection. To confirm her feeling sensations, she should remove the excretions from her vagina with a tissue or her finger in order to check the appearance and stretchiness. Learning to recognize mucus patterns takes some time (often even months of instruction and practice) and abstinence is recommended during the entire first month of instruction. To be effective, abstinence should begin on the first day after menses that mucus is observed (wet mucus, type E, appears first) and continue three days after the *spinnbarkheit* type of mucus disappears.

The method is difficult to learn and many women feel uncomfortable with it. Because sperm may survive in the reproductive tract up to three days (and perhaps longer), the advent of the *spinnbarkheit* may come too late to warn the couple who attempted coitus during the first part of the cycle. Mucus also can be affected by a variety of physiological and psychological problems.

For those determined to use the sterile period, a combination of the methods, known as the STM, or sympto-thermal method, probably is the most effective. It uses the calendar calculation and supplements this by using the thermal (temperature) and mucus changes. To do so requires active record keeping, set times to do the required procedures, and continued dedication.

As more is known about the fertility period, improvements are continually being made to determine it. As of this writing, there are diagnostic kits on the market developed for determining ovulation. Enzyme immunoassays for measuring urinary estrogen and pregnanediol glucuronide have appeared on the market that can easily be used at home at minimal cost and require minimal time to perform. Such tests have to be performed by the woman about twelve days each month, but they should reduce the number of days of abstinence required. Most of the current kits on the market detect a hormonal change that occurs a day or two before ovulation, the interval when intercourse is most likely to result in pregnancy. The test detects the spike in the level of the luteinizing hormone (LH) that occurs in the middle of a woman's menstrual cycle. The LH surge, which can last for just hours or for as long as two days, triggers the ovary to release the mature egg for its journey into the fallopian tube, where fertilization takes place. Identifying the start of the surge requires testing urine samples for several days in mid-cycle. The devices differ but all indicate the presence of LH with a colored line, dot, or test area, the intensity of which has to be compared against a reference. Because women vary widely in how much LH they produce at the time of the surge, it is important to pick a product that is as sensitive as possible. *Consumer Reports* in the past has tested such kits and some detect much better than others.

New techniques are still being developed. One technique being studied is the testing of glucuronide levels in urine, a rise in which would indicate that the woman should not have intercourse. Other researchers are attempting to measure the water content in cervical mucus, the existence of preovulatory estrogen, or changes in electrical resistance of body fluids. The difficulty with research in the field is that the pharmaceutical companies have so far not found much profit in natural planning methods. If they do, many other methods will probably be developed in the future. In fact, the driving factor behind current research is not determining sterility but fertility because the same tests can be used to get pregnant as to avoid pregnancy. Even the best tests requires great dedication to use successfully.

See also Augustine, Saint

References

Billings, Evelyn, and Ann Westmore. *The Billings Method: Controlling Fertility without Drugs or Devices.* New York: Random House, 1980.

Billings, John. *Natural Family Planning: The Ovulation Method.* Collegeville, MN: Liturgical Press, 1973. (This is a thirty-eight-page pamphlet based on an earlier Australian one.)

Brown, J. B., et al. "Natural Family Planning." *American Journal of Obstetrics and Gynecology* 157 (1987): 1082–1089.

Ferin, J. "Determination de la periode sterile premensturelle par la courbe thermique." *Bruxelles medica* 27 (1947): 86–93.

Hatcher, Robert A., et al. *Contraceptive Technology.* New York: Irvington Publishers. (This is an ongoing series published biennially in even-number years and is the best source for keeping up to date on developments.)

Knaus, Herman. *Periodic Fertility and Sterility in Woman,* translated by Kathleen Kitchen. Hobart, IN: Concip Company, 1934. (Knaus's original work appeared in 1931. Apparently it was only after he published that he realized the existence of Ogino's work, which was then published in German.)

Noonan, John T. *Contraception: A History of Its Treatment by the Catholic Theologians and Canonists.* Cambridge, MA: Harvard University Press, 1966.

Ogino, Kyusaku. *Conception Period of Women,* translated by Yonez Miyagawa. Harrisburg, PA: Medical Arts Publishing, 1934. (The original work appeared in Japanese in 1924 and Ogino received an award from the Japanese Obstetrical Society for his work, which came to be known in Europe only after the publication of Knaus's work in 1931.)

"Ovulation Tests." *Consumer Reports* 61 (October 10, 1996): 49–50.

"Periodic Abstinence." *Population Reports,* ser. I, no. 3 (September 1981), vol. 9, no. 4.

Squire, W. "Puerperal Temperatures." *Transactions of the (London) Obstetrical Society* 9 (1868): 129.

Trussell, J., and L. Gummer-Strawn. "Contraceptive Failure of the Ovulation Method of Periodic Abstinence." *Family Planning Perspectives* 22(2) (1990): 67–75.

Sterilization

The simplest form of male sterilization, castration, is an old practice and probably began with animals. Because most domestic animals tend to flock together and produce roughly the same number of male and female offspring, and one male was all that was actually needed to service dozens of females, castration to early herders served to be the ideal solution to the fighting and competition that resulted from male animals seeking to mate with as many females as possible. Some individuals even became specialists at castrating, and in the early Vedic record of India, the term *vadhyrsava* (literally "he who castrated horses") appears.

There are many methods for castrating animals but it is safest to do so shortly after the testicles descend in the newborn male. The mortality rate is not particularly high if castration is carried out on the young. It is higher when adult animals are castrated. If a string or horse hair is tied tightly around the scrotum, the testicles turn black and drop off in about three weeks. Among the many other methods is biting of the testicles with one's teeth (as was often done with lambs by sheepherders). Some species of animals were castrated so frequently that they developed special names such as gelding or ox.

In humans, the castration process originally was probably quite brutal with a slash of a sword cutting off the penis and testicles. Because this is such a vascular area, the mortality was extremely high and such drastic methods were also regarded as painful and symbolic ways of killing an enemy. When males were first castrated for religious purposes or to become the neutered servants or bureaucrats of the powerful has been lost to history but it was done in many ancient civilizations. Many of the imperial servants in China were castrated, having not only their testicles removed but their penis as well. One of the religious groups that emphasized male castration was the hijras of India. Renunciation of sex desires was held by the believers in the cult to emphasize their commitment to the gods. The emasculation operation itself is called *nirvan,* a term for the state of mind in which the individual is liberated from the finite human consciousness and approaches the dawn of a higher consciousness. Many of the slaves in ancient Rome were castrated, and the practice continued in the Byzantine and Islamic empires. In the Byzantine Empire many of the key court officials, even generals, were castrated, because only a man with testicles could be installed as ruler. In the Islamic harems, the servants in the harems were eunuchs, and some units of the military were comprised of eunuchs. Few of those in the Byzantine or Islamic world underwent total castration but simply had their testicles removed or crushed. Some forms of castration were more painful than others. A tortuous form of castration involving splitting the penis is discussed in the Hindu *Arthavaveda*.

As far as females are concerned, female sterilization is mentioned as occurring among the ancient Lydians but what this implied is unclear. Although there was early recognition of the female "testicles" (ovaries), there is little record of them being removed. Female circumcision, however, which involves in its more drastic form not only the removal of the clitoris but of the labia minora and majora and the sewing up of the vaginal entrance to allow only the expelling of urine and menses, was and is common in parts of Africa and the Middle East. The earliest mention of a human ovariectomy dates only from the end of the seventeenth century, when a Dutch sow gelder reportedly had successfully effected the removal of both ovaries from his own daughter to prevent her from "gadding" about at night. Whether this is medical folklore or reality is unclear, but it is evidence that female ovariectomies were being done on animals. It is not clear when such procedures began. It was not until the end of the eighteenth century that the first successful ovariectomy is recorded by a surgeon who did so to remove a tumor.

Even in the Western world, however, castration and genital mutilation took place at the end of the nineteenth century in countries such as the United States in order in extreme cases to "avoid the dangers of masturbation." It was also widely used in the twentieth century as a punishment for sex crimes and under much of the eugenic legislation for sterilizing both the mentally retarded and handicapped. It was not, however, until the end of the nineteenth century, with the recognition of the importance of asep-

sis and the use of anesthesia that surgeons were at all willing or able to deal with any invasion of the body cavities with any chance of success, that the incidence of female sterilization increased.

It was only in the twentieth century that the voluntary sterilization movement developed, and at the present time it is the most effective method of birth control known. It is also the most widely used method of contraception not only in the United States but in the world and it has become the method of choice for couples who decide that they have completed their family and do not want any more children. The major problem with sterilization is that it is difficult although not impossible to reverse, something those contemplating the surgery should keep in mind.

The standard method for sterilizing males is the vasectomy. It is one of the safest, simplest, and most effective methods of contraception. Interestingly, many of the techniques associated with it in the early twentieth century were perfected by Eugen Steinach (1861–1944), who originally advocated it as a method of sexual rejuvenation. He believed, like the ancient Chinese, that the secretions associated with ejaculation would flow back into the body if he cut and ligated (tied) the vas deferens. Though his idea was discredited when it was pointed out that the secretion simply flowed back into the urine, his method was adopted as a way of sterilizing males. Vasectomy is widely used in China and elsewhere. It is sponsored by Planned Parenthood, and in the United States it is endorsed and encouraged by the Association for Voluntary Sterilization.

Vasectomy is a simple, minor surgical procedure, usually performed under local anesthesia, that takes from ten to fifteen minutes to perform. The surgeon makes a small opening in the scrotum and severs the vas deferens either by tying it, blocking it, or cutting out a small piece. He or she then repeats the operation on the other side because there are two vas deferens, one for each testicle. Some surgeons prefer to make only one incision. Some seal the ends of the vas by ligation (tying it); others, by coagulating it with electricity; and still other, by using clips.

Regardless of the method, the incision is then closed, usually with an absorbable suture such as catgut, although some surgeons make such small incisions that no suturing is required. Postoperative care is relatively simple and involves the patient resting for one or two hours in the clinic and then at home for several more hours. The man should avoid hard work or strenuous exercise for two or three days after surgery and wear a scrotal support for seven or eight days. Sometimes there is mild discomfort, which can be relieved by taking aspirin or other mild painkillers. Usually the incision heals in about a week. Sexual intercourse can be resumed at any time during or after the healing process but contraceptives should continue to be used because infertility is not immediate. In fact, it may take ten weeks or more before the male is infertile. This is because sperm have been stored in the reproductive tract on the urethral side of the obstruction and these must be expelled before it is safe to have intercourse without using some other method of contraception. Part of the usual procedure is to have the semen checked for sperm six to eight weeks after the vasectomy; if they are still present another check is called for within a few weeks, and if they are still present, another surgical procedure might be necessary.

The major obstacle in male sterilization seems to be psychological, which is why careful and accurate counseling is essential before the surgery is performed. Some men, however, should not have a vasectomy or should have it delayed for physical reasons, for instance, if there are local skin infections, a varicocele (enlarged veins in the spermatic cord), a large hydrocele (accumulated fluids in the testes), inguinal hernia (protrusion of the hernial sac containing the intestine through the inguinal opening of the scrotum), filariasis (a chronic disease caused by the existence of thread worms), or the presence of scar tissue from previous surgery. Some systemic disorders such as diabetes also suggest caution, as does a recent heart attack. The failure rate is low, about .15 per 100 person years for those who have an active sex life. This means that there are 15 pregnancies every year for every 10,000 operations. Usually these were a result of surgical errors.

The number of requests for reversals is low, probably not more than two in every 1,000 cases; still this adds up to a significant number. Success with the reversal depends on both the condition of the tissue and the skill of the surgeon, with success being determined by the patient's ability to impregnate his partner. Even though the vas can be restored, pregnancy is often not guaranteed because a vasectomy leads to decreased sperm count. The longer the vas has been ligated, the less the chance of success.

Other methods of occluding the vas that make the procedure more reversible are being experimented with. The Chinese, for example, inject into the vas a liquid polyurethane or silicone, which provides a solid plug to block the passage when the injected substance hardens. In the United States the silicone plug is being used because the polyurethane apparently releases a chemical that causes cancer in rats. Contraceptive plugs can also be surgically inserted in the vas. Something called the Vassoclude uses one or two medical clips in each vas. As experiments continue, new methods will appear and the would-be candidate should investigate the method best suited for him.

One of the standard methods of female sterilization in the middle of the twentieth century was a hysterectomy, the removal of the uterus and ovaries. The nominal reason for this was a prolapsed uterus or some other kind of uterine difficulty, but in retrospect it seems that many were done as a means of preventing pregnancy. Although hysterectomies are still performed, usually now for reasons other than sterilization, almost all methods of voluntary female sterilization in some way or another block the fallopian tubes, which transmit the ova from the ovaries into the uterus.

Tying the tubes (tubal ligation) is one of the oldest forms of tubal occlusion. Traditionally, it was performed by making a 3- to 4-inch (10-cm) incision (a laparotomy) in the abdomen and tying, dividing, resecting (removing), or crushing the tubes or burying the stumps in the muscular wall of the uterus. Simple ligation (tying off), which dates from 1880, is seldom performed today because of the high failure rate (up to 20 percent). The most widely used procedures are those involving removal of a segment of the tube and ligation of the end. A number of variations to this method are of interest to the specialist, but the most widely used technique is one developed by Ralph Pomeroy, who used it early in the twentieth century, although no description of it was published until after his death. It is the technique recommended by the International Planned Parenthood Federation Panel of Experts. The procedure involves picking up the tube near the midportion to form a loop, tying (ligating) the base of the loop with an absorbable suture, and cutting off (resecting) the top of the loop. As the suture material is absorbed, the ends of the tube pull apart. The failure rate is low (0–0.4 percent), although the rate is higher if the procedure is performed at the same time as a cesarean section because the tissues are traumatized.

Since 1960, the procedure has been simplified with the development of the minilaparotomy and laparoscopy. The minilaparotomy, sometimes called the "minilap," can be performed under local anesthesia. A small insertion of about 2 cm (approximately l inch) is made. Each fallopian tube is then pulled up into the incision in order to be cut and tied, blocked with rings or clips, and allowed to slip back into place. Laparoscopy involves inserting a laparoscope into the abdomen. The laparoscope is a long tube, somewhat like a telescope, through which the surgeon locates the tubes, severs them, and closes the end by cautery, clips, or rings. The incision is smaller than for a minilaparotomy and can be made close to the umbilicus (navel), normally leaving no scar visible. It is easier, however, to make the incision at a spot somewhat lower in the abdomen because this brings the scope closer to the target organs.

It is also possible for the surgeon to enter the abdomen through the vagina (a colpotomy), with or without the scope, to carry out the procedure. This approach has been used extensively in India but is less popular in the Untied States. All of the procedures can be carried out on an outpatient basis under local anesthetic and can be completed in about ten to twenty minutes. If a general anesthetic is used, hospitalization is required and the risk of such surgery is increased substantially because of the inherent risk of anesthesia.

The Chinese developed a method of sterilization in the 1960s through chemical occlusion, that is, obstructing the tubes by chemical burning. This method can be done without surgery and without anesthetic. It involves the insertion of a cannula (a tube) through the cervix and uterus up into the fallopian tubes where phenol (carbolic acid) solution is injected. This results in a scarring of the tubes, which ultimately closes the opening. One of the side effects is mild to moderate pain. The phenol preparation can also cause minor fever, dizziness, nausea, pelvic inflammation, and vaginal discharge. An occasional perforation of the uterus or peritonitis (an infection of the serous membrane that lines the abdominal wall) can occur as well. Chemical occlusion is a very low cost method of sterilization but it is not reversible.

Experiments have been conducted on other chemical compounds: quinacrine, a hardening and thickening agent that damages the tissues of the tubal lining, and methyl cyanoacrylate, a tissue adhesive that turns from a liquid to a solid when it comes in contact with fluid in the tubes, and thus blocks them. New kinds of clips are also being developed that can be inserted either through a minilaparotomy or through various vaginal approaches. The tubal ring can also be installed in the same way. Once the ring is installed, it expands, blocking the tubal opening. Restoring fertility has a higher probability when rings have been used. Like the vasectomy in men, the method of female sterilization is a subject that the woman should discuss with her physician before deciding on the method.

One of the dangers of any kind of tubal sterilization is ectopic pregnancy, that is, the implantation of fertilized ovum outside the uterine cavity. Though the statistical incidence of this is very low, a substantial percentage of those pregnancies that do occur in sterilized women are ectopic ones, and they require surgical removal.

Women with a vaginal or pelvic infection should not undergo sterilization but can proceed when the infection has cleared up. Some kinds of procedures also cannot be used where there are adhesions or scars from previous surgery or infections. Few women in today's world should undergo any major surgery such as hysterectomy or bilateral oophorectomy (removal of the ovaries) to become sterile, although there might be other reasons, such as cancer, which would justify such drastic surgery.

Some forms of tubal ligation are more reversible than others, and this is something the individual needs to take into consideration if sterilization seems to be the most desirable means of birth control. Sterilization is increasingly the method of choice for those persons who have decided that they have completed their families and, as indicated, is the most widely used family planning method in the world. Female sterilizations, however, far outnumber male sterilizations, even though males can be more easily sterilized than females can. As with so many other forms of contraception, the answer as to why such differences exist lies more in the sphere of human psychology than in techniques or in knowledge.

This article deals with voluntary sterilization. Unfortunately, for a good part of the twentieth century, there was also involuntary sterilization of both sexes. This was part of the eugenic movement discussed elsewhere in this encyclopedia. In most of the fifty American states, and in many European countries, individuals who were diagnosed as mentally deficient or socially maladjusted were sterilized. Involuntary sterilization was conceived as a therapeutic method of improving the quality of the "race" and the health of the individual. Involuntary sterilization was first legalized in Indiana in 1907 and by the 1930s, some 27 states had such laws on their books. The Supreme Court affirmed the constitutionality of Virginia's law on the subject in 1927 in *Buck v. Bell*.

Decisions about who was to be sterilized varied by jurisdiction and mostly affected disenfranchised people in the United States. Under such programs, a disproportionate number of African Americans, Native Americans, welfare mothers, prison inmates being discharged, people with mental illnesses or physical handicaps, and others who did not conform to middle-class values and standards were sterilized. While there was some opposition to such practices, the real opposition to them was set off by the excesses of Nazi Germany in World War II. The practice then began to decline, although in California the practice was not officially ended until the 1960s.

It should be emphasized that voluntary sterilization means the individual has chosen to terminate his or her reproductive capacity; it is not to be confused with sterilization imposed on others by government or administrative edict.

See also China

References

Bullough, Vern L. "Eunuchs in History and Society." In *Eunuchs,* edited by Shawn Tougher, in press.

Bullough, Vern L., and Bonnie Bullough. *Contraception: A Guide to Birth Control Methods.* Amherst, NY: Prometheus Books, 1997.

Hatcher, Robert A., et al. *Contraceptive Technology.* New York: Irvington Press. (Regular biennial updates are published in even-number years.)

Lull, C. B. "The Pomeroy Method of Sterilization." *American Journal of Obstetrics and Gynecology* 59 (1950): 1118–1123.

Reilly, Philip R. *The Surgical Solution: A History of Involuntary Sterilization in the United States.* Baltimore: Johns Hopkins University Press, 1991.

"Vasectomy." *Population Reports,* ser. D., no. 5 (March 1992), vol. 20.

"Voluntary Female Sterilization." *Population Reports,* ser. C, no. 10 (November 1990).

Stone, Hannah (1893–1941)

Hannah Stone, a physician, became medical director of the Birth Control Clinical Research Bureau in 1925. Stone, who had a staff affiliation with

Physician Hannah Stone was forced to resign her position at a New York hospital when she became the director of the Birth Control Clinical Research Bureau in 1925. (Library of Congress)

records were recovered. Stone was also involved in the *United States v. One Package* decision, in which a ruling by the U.S. Court of Appeals for the Second Circuit allowed the importation of contraceptives by physicians. Stone was the physician to whom the package had been addressed. Emily H. Mudd, who used the services of the clinic, in the 1930s called her the "Madonna" of the clinic.

Stone viewed the birth control clinic as part of a broad program to improve the quality of life. She believed that the clinic should serve as a source of information and advice concerning many problems of parenthood ranging from fertility to sterility, and even marital relations. She wrote not only on contraception, but with her husband Abraham she also authored *A Marriage Manual,* in the form of a conversation between a physician and patient. She edited with Margaret Sanger the proceedings of the Seventh International Birth Control Conference held in Zurich, Switzerland, in 1930. When Hannah Stone died in 1941, her husband, Abraham Stone, succeeded her as medical director.

See also Clinical Research Bureau; *United States v. One Package*

References

Reed, James. *From Private Virtue to Public Vice.* New York: Basic Books, 1978.

Sanger, Margaret, and Hannah Stone, eds. *The Practice of Contraception: An International Symposium and Survey.* Baltimore: Williams & Wilkins, 1931.

Stone, Hannah. "Therapeutic Contraception." *Medical Journal and Record* CXXVII (March 21, 1928): 7–17. (Robert L. Dickinson provided the introduction.)

Stone, Hannah, and Abraham Stone. *A Marriage Manual: A Practical Guide Book to Sex and Marriage.* New York: Simon & Schuster, 1935.

Stone, Hannah, and Abraham Stone. "Maternal Health and Contraception: A Study of 2,000 Patients from the Maternal Health Center, Newark, NJ," in two parts. *Medical Journal and Record* CXXXVII. (April 19, 1933): 7–15 and (May 3, 1934): 7–13.

Lying-in Hospital, was forced by that institution to resign her affiliation as a result of her appointment and she was also denied membership in the New York County Medical Society for many years. One of her early accomplishments was to publish the first systematic follow-up of the effectiveness of clinical dissemination of contraceptives.

In April 1929, Stone and another physician were arrested at the Clinical Research Bureau for violating Section 1142 of the criminal code, namely, disseminating contraceptive information. The police were particularly obnoxious, dumping files, seizing others, barging into examination rooms, and confiscating patient case histories. In the aftermath it was found that the raid had been instigated by the precinct magistrate on the urging of Catholic social workers and religious officials. Ultimately the chief of police apologized for the raid, but not all the

Stopes, Marie Charlotte Carmichael (1880–1958)

Marie Charlotte Carmichael Stopes differs from most of the other advocates of birth control in

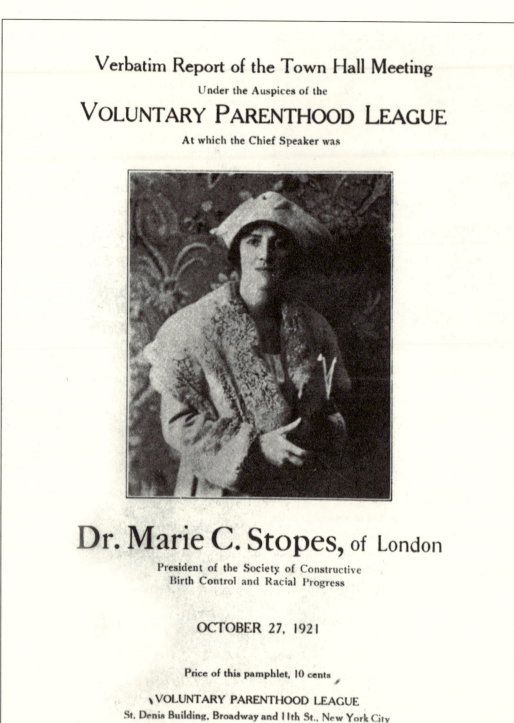

Verbatim Report of the Town Hall Meeting

Under the Auspices of the

VOLUNTARY PARENTHOOD LEAGUE

At which the Chief Speaker was

Dr. Marie C. Stopes, of London

President of the Society of Constructive
Birth Control and Racial Progress

OCTOBER 27, 1921

Price of this pamphlet, 10 cents

VOLUNTARY PARENTHOOD LEAGUE
St. Denis Building, Broadway and 11th St., New York City

Marie Stopes, an enthusiastic advocate of women's right to enjoy their sexuality, opened the first birth control clinic in the United Kingdom in 1921. Here she lectured at the Voluntary Parenthood League the same year. (Courtesy of the Sophia Smith Collection, Smith College)

that she made sexuality very much part of her mission. Her 1918 publication, *Married Love,* became a manifesto for woman's rights to sexual enjoyment and sold more than a million copies. After this was published, she moved into the birth control movement.

A graduate of the University College, London, she earned a Ph.D. in paleobotany from the University of Munich and on her return to England she was one of the first women to hold a faculty position in science. She married in 1911 and soon discovered that her husband was impotent. Scientist that she was, Stopes began researching the problem and in the process solidified her own ideas about a woman's right to sexual enjoyment. It was not until after the marriage was annulled in 1916 that she published *Married Love,* the book that made her famous.

She wrote:

> Where the acts of coitus are rightly performed, the pair can disagree, can hold opposite views about every conceivable subject under the sun without any ruffling or disturbance of the temper, without any angry scenes or desire to separate. They will but enjoy each other's differences. Contrariwise, I am sure that they can have ninety-nine per cent of all their qualities and attributes in perfect harmony, and if the sex act is not properly performed; if they fail to adjust themselves to each other; if they are ignorant of the basic laws of union in marriage, all that harmony and suitability in other things will be of no avail and they will rasp each other apart in sentiment, until they but endure each other for some extraneous motive, or they desire to part (Stopes, 1931, p. 21).

She remained a virgin, however, until her marriage to Humphrey Verdon Roe in 1918, which included a contract that allowed her to keep her maiden name. Roe was an enthusiastic advocate of birth control, something that Stopes had not paid much attention to in her book. Her interest was also aroused because, as a result of her books, she had received a number of letters from women readers asking for information about methods of birth control. The response was a short book, *Wise Parenthood,* in which she recommended the use of the cervical cap, preferably combined with a soluble quinine pessary or a small wet sponge with its pores filled with powdered soap or alternatively a pad of cotton wool smeared with Vaseline. She did not favor the use of the condom, coitus interruptus, douches, or the safe period, the latter because the only time available for intercourse was, in her mind, when a woman had less physiological benefit from the sex act.

A woman with almost a missionary zeal, Stopes once wrote that she did her birth control work because "I feel that the responsibility for the unborn whom I had not helped would be unbearable if I were not to carry it on" (Maude, 1924, pp. 192–193). She with her husband opened the first birth control clinic in the British Empire, in Islington, London, in 1921. The clinic had a fourfold purpose: to help the poor gain information, to test the belief that the working class was hostile to birth control, to obtain information about contraceptive practices, and to collect data on the sex lives of women. Though the clinic was criticized by the medical profession because, among other things, there was no gynecologist present, Stopes ignored the criticism. Instead she relied upon nurses, who usually made a vaginal examination, fitted the client with a pessary, and showed her how to use it. If the nurse believed there was something unusual or abnormal about the case, she referred the patient to a woman physician affiliated with the clinic as a consultant. Referrals occurred in about two percent of the cases. Such a practice would not have been allowed in the United States.

Influenced by the Neo-Malthusian doctrines, Stopes was somewhat contradictory in pushing birth control for the laboring class while urging more children for the upper classes, but she regarded her mission as educating the ordinary woman who had to be taught birth control in order to fulfill her duties as a citizen. Stopes emphasized the family as important and was strongly opposed to abortion.

Stopes was a ruthless antagonist. When a physician denounced her and in the process publicly quoted another physician, Dr. Anne Louise McIlroy, as saying that the cap was the most harmful method of birth control that she had experienced, Stopes sued for libel. The legal battle lasted more than two years and cost her opponents more than ten thousand pounds in legal fees (Stopes as the victim relied upon the crown attorneys). McIlroy, the expert witness for the defense, declared that rubber check pessaries could cause occlusion of the womb, although she admitted that she had never had a case of a woman who had worn the cap. The jury gave an ambiguous verdict, that the words were defamatory but true in substance and fact, although they were not a fair comment. The judge awarded Stopes one hundred pounds. The confusing decision led to an appeal by her opponents, and on eventual appeal to the House of Lords, Stopes lost. Incensed by this, Stopes began investigating and found that McIlroy herself was fitting caps on her patients at the Royal Free Hospital, something Stopes demonstrated by presenting herself in disguise to McIlroy and getting fitted with a cap. In her clinic, and to those she advised, Stopes insisted on using the rubber cervical cap and was opposed to the use of the diaphragm. She took it upon herself to draw up the specifications for the cap and made certain that the manufacturers followed her instructions. In her later years, Stopes became extremely autocratic, alienating most of the other workers for birth control in the United Kingdom. She, however, could be winning and supportive when it suited her needs. It was this combination of characteristics that made her so successful and that helped change world opinion regarding birth control. Stopes was extremely multitalented, and under her own name and other various pseudonyms (Erica Fay, Harry Buffkins, Marie Carmichael) wrote plays, poetry, and novels; compiled a collection of fairy stories; and early in her career published a textbook on ancient plants, as well as prepared a catalog of Cretaceous flora for the British Museum.

Probably, as one of her biographers wrote, if Stopes had been less individualist, less tenacious in her views, less outspoken, less touchy, less impatient with those who did not share her vision, her achievements would have been commensurately less. Stopes, more than anyone else in Britain, broke the "barrier of convention and theological prejudice" about birth control.

See also Cervical Cap

References

Briant, Keith. *Marie Stopes: A Biography.* London: Hogarth Press 1962.

Fryer, Peter. *The Birth Controllers.* London: Secker and Warburg, 1965.

Hall, Ruth. *Passionate Crusader: The Life of Marie Stopes.* New York: Harcourt Brace Jovanovich, 1977.

Stopes, Marie. *Married Love.* London: Fifield, 1920.

———. *Radiant Motherhood.* London: Putnam's, 1920.

———. *Wise Parenthood.* London: Fifield, 1918.

Stopes, Marie Carmichael. *Enduring Passion,* 4th ed. New York: Putnam's, 1931.

U

United States v. One Package

Even after the death of Anthony Comstock and the growing acceptance of birth control, the Comstock legislation, prohibiting importation of contraceptive devices or the sending of them through the mails, remained on the books. Margaret Sanger had been impressed by a new pessary designed by a Japanese physician whom she had met at a conference on contraceptive technique that she had organized in Zurich in 1930. This was part of her regular activity because over the years she had collected various devices and hoped to carry out experiments on them. Morris Ernst (1888–1976), then general counsel for the American Civil Liberties Union as well as for the American Birth Control League, and an attorney in private practice as well, saw the new pessaries as an opportunity to challenge the old Comstock prohibitions. In fact Sanger had set up a National Committee on Federal Legislation for Birth Control to encourage such cases, and at the time a number of court cases were in the works.

Margaret Sanger set up the National Committee on Federal Legislation for Birth Control to try cases that would lift the Comstock Law against distributing birth control devices through the U.S. mail. (Library of Congress)

It was arranged for Hannah Stone, a physician, to have 120 Japanese pessaries sent to her for her private practice in 1932. To make certain that the customs officials knew what was happening, officials were informed of the action, and they confiscated the materials in what can only be called a carefully scripted court case. On December 7, 1936, the U.S. Court of Appeals for the Second Circuit ruled on the issue in *United States v. One Package* in a decision by Judge Augustus Hand. Hand ruled that the Comstock statute could not be applied in ways that obstructed public health, which in essence meant that such devices could be imported at least by physicians for use in cases where a physician believed that avoidance of pregnancy would be beneficial to a woman's health.

In short, the decision opened the mails to contraceptive materials mailed to physicians. The right of individual citizens to bring such devices into the country for personal use, however, was not established until 1971.

See also Sanger, Margaret; Stone, Hannah

Reference
Garrow, David J. *Liberty and Sexuality.* New York: Macmillan, 1994.

V

Vaginal Rings

The vaginal ring relies upon the sustained release of hormones, either progestin alone or in combination with estrogen, and they act on the reproductive system in the same ways as the oral contraceptives do. The only advantage they have over the pill, injections, or intrauterine devices (IUDs) is the ease with which the patient can place the ring and remove it. The disadvantage is that the efficacy rate is lower than that of the injectables, implants, or medicated IUDs, and many women find vaginal rings uncomfortable. They can also be expelled during urination or defecation, particularly by women in the Third World countries who are accustomed to squatting while defecating. Many users also report that rings interfere with coitus.

The levonorgestrel ring was developed by the World Health Organization and World Health Council and began undergoing tests in 1972. Worn around the cervix, the ring releases levonorgestrel, a synthetic hormone of the progestin family, which makes the cervical mucus virtually impregnable to the sperm. The ring is designed to stay in place for three weeks, whereupon the woman removes it for a week during menses and then reinserts it. The same ring can be used for three months. A progesterone ring was also developed by the Population Council for use by breast-feeding mothers so that they would not be exposed to synthetic hormones that might affect the composition or quantity of their breast milk. Several other combinations are being tested.

See also Sponges, Tampons, and Vaginal Inserts

References

Hatcher, Robert A., et al. *Contraceptive Technology.* New York: Irvington Publishers. (Biennially updated in even numbered years.)

Violence against Abortion Providers

Barnett Slepian, M.D., Buffalo, New York, obstetrician, gynecologist, and abortion provider, was assassinated in his Amherst, New York, home on October 23, 1998. Slepian, fifty-two, had returned from a synagogue service honoring his late father, and was relaxing in his kitchen with his wife and four sons, when a sniper's round smashed through a kitchen window and struck him in the back. The bullet pierced his heart, killing him in minutes. An outspoken pro-choice activist and frequent target of antiabortion protesters, Slepian was the second U.S. abortion physician killed by a sniper, the first being David Gunn in Pensacola, Florida, in 1993. The killing heightened awareness of antiabortion terrorism and was widely condemned. But not everyone was critical; Reverend Donald Spitz, founder of Pro-Life Virginia, celebrated the assassination and praised the killer for ending Slepian's "bloodthirsty practice."

Slepian was born in Cambridge, Massachusetts, and grew up in Rochester, New York. He attended medical school at the Autonomous University of Guadalajara, Mexico, graduating in 1978. During his Buffalo residency he met and married nurse Lynne Breitbart. They had four sons. Slepian established a

James Charles Kopp was on the U.S. Federal Bureau of Investigation's top-ten wanted criminal list for allegedly shooting Barnett Slepian to death in his New York home. Kopp was arrested in France on March 29, 2001. (AFP/Corbis)

successful obstetrical/gynecological practice in Buffalo and was widely recognized for providing skilled, compassionate obstetrical care. He also performed abortions at two Buffalo clinics, which made him a target of vociferous protests. He was often harassed in public and reportedly received two hundred death threats. In one 1988 incident, Slepian lashed out at protesters picketing his home during Hanukkah, damaging a protester's van with a baseball bat. In 1994 he wrote an eerily prescient letter to the editor of the local newspaper predicting that escalating antiabortion rhetoric in the area might lead to the shooting of an abortion provider. After Slepian's death, the family established a memorial fund to support training of medical stu-

dents in abortion techniques and reproductive health care.

The assailant eventually charged in the murder was James Charles Kopp of St. Albans, Vermont, born in 1954. A devout Roman Catholic, Kopp was a longtime antiabortion activist associated with the most radical and violent wing of the pro-life movement. Canadian authorities also charged Kopp in the nonfatal shootings of three abortion doctors in that country; like the Slepian murder, these attacks occurred in the fall, close to the Canadian veterans' holiday Remembrance Day, which has been adopted as a focus of antiabortion activism. He was one of the U.S. Federal Bureau of Investigation's Ten Most Wanted Fugitives and was also sought by the Royal Canadian Mounted Police until his arrest in France in 2001. Rewards offered for his arrest and conviction total more than one million dollars.

Slepian is the latest in a line of abortion doctors and others targeted by antiabortion radicals. As the antiabortion movement has failed to eliminate abortion through legal or political means, its radical wing has opted increasingly for the use of force. Abortion physicians who were killed and wounded before Slepian's murder include Jack Fainman (Winnipeg, Manitoba, November 1997), shot and wounded at home, allegedly by James Kopp; an unnamed doctor (Perinton, New York, October 1997), shot and wounded at home by an unknown assailant; Calvin Jackson (New Orleans, December 1996), stabbed outside his clinic by a pro-life activist; Hugh Short (Ancaster, Ontario, November 1995), shot and wounded at home, allegedly by James Kopp; George Klopfer (Indiana, 1995), shot by an unknown assailant while driving his car; and Garson Romalis (Vancouver, British Columbia, November 1994), severely wounded at home, allegedly by James Kopp. In July 1994, pro-life activist Paul Hill shot and killed John Bayard Britton outside a Pensacola, Florida, clinic, also killing volunteer escort James Barrett and wounding Barrett's wife. Hill gave himself up on the scene and was convicted of murder. Also in 1994, Paul Hackmeyer was shot in the chest in an ambush outside his home; he survived the attack. In August 1993, George Patterson, who had performed abortions at the Florida clinic where Dr. Britton died, was found shot to death in Mobile, Alabama; it is unclear whether this attack was a robbery or was related to Patterson's abortion practice. In August 1993, George Tiller, a Wichita, Kansas, provider known for providing therapeutic third-trimester abortions, was shot in both arms outside his clinic by Rachelle ("Shelley") Shannon, a member of the antiabortion extremist group Army of God. Tiller returned to work next day; Shannon was jailed. In March 1993, David Gunn was shot in the back and killed outside the same Pensacola, Florida, clinic where Dr. Britton and his escort would die sixteen months later. The assailant, pro-life activist Michael Griffin, surrendered on site and was convicted of murder. In late 1992, Douglas Karpen was nonfatally shot by an unknown assailant in a parking garage near his clinic, an attack that was not recognized as abortion-related until several years later. The first incident of violence against an abortion doctor may be the 1982 abduction of an Illinois physician and his wife by Don Benny Anderson, alleged founder of the Army of God. Anderson held his captives at gunpoint in a bunker for eight days before releasing them unharmed. Anderson remains jailed.

Violence against abortion doctors is part of a larger pattern: since 1977, U.S. abortion clinics have been the targets of 154 arsons, 39 bombings, and 99 acid attacks. Since 1991, there have been fifteen attempted murders of abortion clinic personnel, from doctors to support staff. At least seven clinic personnel died between 1993 and 1998. Though roundly condemned by most in the pro-life movement, the campaign of violence is succeeding in doing what pickets and clinic blockades could not: reducing American women's access to abortion services. As a result in part to rising fears of violence, the number of abortion doctors has plunged about 15 percent since 1980—in rural areas, 55 percent. In 84 percent of the nation's counties there are no abortion doctors. Pro-choice activists and medical educators have begun modifying medical school curricula, establishing scholarship funds, and forming activist organizations such as Medical Students for Choice to help ensure that tomorrow's doctors will acquire the knowledge and the determination to keep safe, legal abortion available for women who choose it.

Tom Flynn

Voluntary Parenthood League

The Voluntary Parenthood League (VPL) was founded in 1919 by Mary Ware Dennett after her resignation from the National Birth Control League. In many ways the VPL served as the organizational base for Dennett's ideas on birth control, despite that others often held more prestigious titles. With the VPL, the focus on removing birth control from obscenity statutes was at the federal level.

The VPL based its legislative program on the right to free speech. They argued that the men and women of the United States were being denied access to vital information by Section 211 of the U.S. Criminal Code (known as the Comstock Act). This law lumped contraception with abortion and obscene writings and devices, forbidding their distribution through the mails. The VPL argued that the ban limited the availability and quality of information and that the ban was outdated. Their proposed amendment was simple—the removal of the words "prevention of conception" from the list of obscene materials.

Finding a sponsor for their bill proved to be difficult. From 1919 to 1921 Dennett met with legislators in Washington, finding them "coarse, ignorant and impatient." Many feared any issue that bore the taint of immorality or controversy, and others feared opposition from Catholic constituencies. Dennett's tactics did not endear her to the medical profession. She decried attempts to exempt physicians from the obscenity ban because the result would be a creation of a medical monopoly on contraceptive information. In 1920, the New York Academy of Medicine refused her support, in part because the VPL's bill would intrude on what they felt was their professional territory.

After 1921, the VPL faced a rival birth control organization, the American Birth Control League, organized by Margaret Sanger. Though Sanger promised to leave the field of federal legislation to the VPL, her group supported "doctors only" legislation, and by 1925 began their own federal lobbying campaign. This competition split the already weak support for birth control on Capitol Hill.

In 1922 Dennett tried a different tactic and sought the aid of the liberal postmaster, William Hays, who was considering a major overhaul of postal codes. After months of lobbying, Dennett's plans were dashed when Hays resigned his post. The new postmaster, Dr. Hubert Work, opposed any loosening of the laws on birth control.

Forced back to Congress to seek a sponsor for the VPL's "open" bill, Dennett secured Senator Albert Cummins of Iowa and Representative John Kissel of New York. On January 10, 1923 they introduced the Cummins-Kissel Bill, but it was never debated because of an overcrowded calendar. Before the next session of Congress was convened, Kissel had been defeated for reelection and Dennett was forced to search for another sponsor. She found Representative William Vaile of Colorado and on April 8, 1924 the Cummins-Vaile Bill was introduced to Congress. It was the first birth control bill to reach debate. In the Judiciary Subcommittee hearings held on the bill, Reverend John Ryan of the National Catholic Welfare Council and other opponents attacked the bill vigorously, and when the bill was finally reported out of the committee in January 1925, the committee had declined to recommend it to the full Congress. Despite intense pressure put on congressmen by

Dennett to vote on the bill, Congress failed to vote before the end of the legislative session in March 1925. The Cummins-Vaile bill was dead.

Dennett's failure cost the VPL dearly. Both congressmen and some VPL officers disagreed with Dennett's aggressive tactics and her insistence that the bill was not about birth control per se, but free speech. Worn out by the work, Dennett resigned from her position as executive director. Her salary was in arrears and there was every indication that Sanger's better-funded American Birth Control League was about to enter the legislative fray. Dennett's position was not replaced and the VPL never mounted another lobbying campaign. Instead they focused on promoting Dennett's *Birth Control Laws* (1926), which outlined their views on the legal status of birth control and attacked not only the position of birth control opponents, but also the supporters of the "doctors only" legislation.

By 1927, the VPL was essentially moribund, but its officers were unwilling to disband it and leave the federal field to Margaret Sanger. They maintained a correspondence address and a voluntary staff that responded to inquires on birth control. As time went by, they grew less and less active. When queried, as late as 1940, officers claimed that the VPL had shifted its focus and now worked to educate influential leaders in the hopes of changing attitudes about birth control. The archives of the Voluntary Parenthood League form part of Mary Ware Dennett's papers, held at the Schlesinger Library, Harvard University, and available on microfilm.

Cathy Moran Hajo

See also American Birth Control League; Dennett, Mary Ware; National Birth Control League

References

Chen, Constance. *The Sex Side of Life: Mary Ware Dennett's Pioneering Battle for Birth Control and Sex Education.* New York: The New Press, 1996.

Sexuality, Sex Education, and Reproductive Rights: Papers of Mary Ware Dennett and the Voluntary Parenthood League. Bethesda, MD: University Publications of America, 1994.

W

Witchcraft, Contraception, and Abortion

Fear of witches and witchcraft reached epidemic proportions at the beginning of the early modern period in Europe. Though the fear of witches had existed in the later Middle Ages, the greater fear in medieval times had been of heresy. Although heresy remained a major problem for the Catholic Church, it was the fifteenth century rise of neo-Platonism with its acceptance of a magical world view that encouraged a belief in magic and evil powers. Undoubtedly, a major contributing factor was the disastrous effects of the Black Death that had swept Europe in the fourteenth century and continued to devastate Europe for several centuries. Inevitably the Inquisition, which originally had been established to deal with heresy, became active against magicians and diviners and against those associated with certain sexual activities.

Pope Innocent VIII (1484–1495) in his bull issued December 5, 1494, stated that it had been called to his attention that members of both sexes were using incantations, charms, and conjurations that allowed them "to suffocate, extinguish and cause to perish the births of women" and that "men beget not, nor women conceive" and they "impede the conjugal action of men and women" (Bullough, pp. 420–421). The persons most responsible for the papal proclamation were Heinrich Institor (Kramer) and Jakob Sprenger, who were running into opposition for their witch-hunting activities. Using the bull as a justification, the two wrote a handbook for all witch-hunters, the *Malleus Malleficarum,* or "Hammer of the Witches," published in 1486.

Though neither contraceptive practices nor abortion were specifically mentioned by Kramer and Sprenger, the papal bull clearly raised the question of abortion. Witchcraft soon came to be associated with impotence, infertility, abortion, and various means of preventing pregnancy. Women, in fact, were the primary objects of witchcraft persecutions because they were believed to be more susceptible to demonic possession than men.

Interestingly, George Hummel in his investigation of witchcraft held that one of the cures frequently offered to women who were believed to be possessed was emmenagogic medicines, medicines that not only encouraged the onset of menstruation but also brought about abortions. In fact, one measure of the success of the treatment was if a woman's uterus dropped and her menses began. Whether those giving the exorcism treatment realized that they might be aborting a woman is highly debatable, but that is what might well have happened.

In the sixteenth and seventeenth centuries the whole process of pregnancy was often caught up with witchcraft. Though Margaret Murray, an early investigator of witchcraft, concluded that the better the midwife the better the witch, this is somewhat of an exaggeration but with a strong kernel of truth. Among the women accused of witchcraft in the Salem witch trials in New England were two midwives, Anne Hutchison and Jane Hawkins.

Women and girls who knew how to control their reproductive lives were often accused of witchcraft. Here, the slave woman Tituba taught a few "magic tricks" to several young girls in her care. (North Wind Picture Archives)

It seems contradictory that the witch-hunters were using abortifacients to remove the evil spirit, and yet midwives were accused of being witches for bringing about menstrual regulations. Certainly midwives were widely believed to know how to cause an abortion and which herbs might prevent conception. In those areas of Europe where midwives were licensed, midwives were often required to take an oath that they would not use any witchcraft or charms in their practices nor, in some cases, administer any drugs or potions that had not been prescribed by a Latin-reading surgeon or physician. The requirement of the surgeon or physician in this case, however, might indicate the results of a turf war because by the end of

the seventeenth century male medical professionals were increasingly moving into the obstetrical business, particularly among the rich and powerful.

This struggle continued in the United States until well into the twentieth century and one of the charges that the medical profession used against midwives was that they were the abortionists in society, and the campaign to replace them was also a campaign against abortion.

References

Bullough, Vern L. *Sexual Variance in Society and History.* Chicago: University of Chicago Press, 1976.

Hummel, George. *Medicinal Exorcisms: The "Ritual Virtues" of the Remedia Efficacissims, and the Work of Giralom Menghi.* Unpublished Ph.D. Dissertation, University of Connecticut, 1999.

Kramer, H., and J. Sprenger. *Malleus Malleficarum,* translated by Montagu Summers. New York: Dover, 1971.

Murray, M. A. *The Witch Cult in Western Europe.* Oxford: Clarendon Press, 1921.

Riddle, John M. *Eve's Herbs: A History of Contraception and Abortion in the West.* Cambridge, MA: Harvard University Press, 1997.

Women and the Control of Reproduction

Birth control has been part of the folklore and folk culture of nearly all societies. It has primarily been a woman's issue, and not one with which men were often much concerned. Since much of the knowledge of women never reached the printed page, it was passed on through the generations by what might be called an underground of midwives, wise women, and healers. Most of the herbal remedies mentioned in this encyclopedia were found by women and the authors of the medical tracts in which they have been recorded often received their knowledge from midwives and other women. Clearly some contraceptive remedies were more effective than others, and none of them were as effective as modern methods. Still the historical remedies are important because they document the efforts of women to have some control over their own bodies; even a method that has only a small percentage of effectiveness can have a great impact on the birth rate.

In many preliterate societies, and even in many literate ones, magic played a role in reproduction and women made sacrifices to the gods, recited incantations, took potions and philters, performed dances and pantomimes to get pregnant, to avoid pregnancy, and to abort. Probably many of these rituals had little practical effect but some did, and certainly there are psychogenic factors involved in pregnancy even today. There were both passive methods such as prayer and more active ones that might involve magic but that emphasized the importance of intervention.

Most cultures and periods have regarded women as having a sexuality, but it was not to be expressed as openly as that of men. In the Christian tradition in the West, a woman's "place" was to become a wife and thereby bear children and satisfy her husband's sexual desire. Not all theologians agreed entirely and even the most misogynistic had to agree that women were God's children. Protestants in the sixteenth century followed traditional Catholic views on this although John Calvin and the Calvinists placed less emphasis on the childbearing duty of women than did Martin Luther. Protestants in general had a far more favorable view of sex than did Catholics who found chastity ideal.

Traditional family units were considerably weakened by changes in work patterns brought about by industrialization beginning in the eighteenth century. Industrial production and commercial change increasingly took men out of their homes to workplaces, and husbands and wives often spent the greater part of their days separated from one another. Moreover, as industry began to produce outside the home what women had previously made by hand, the work at home came increasingly to emphasize cleaning, repairing, consuming, and child rearing. As men and women increasingly led separate lives, both sex and marriage was redefined to these changing needs. The double standard of sexuality, which probably had always existed, was more effectively institutionalized, and Victorian moralists even argued that sex should be indulged in only for purposes of procreation. In response, men of all classes often patronized brothels rather than seeking sex with their wives, and "proper" women were taught to regard sex as dirty, immoral, and undignified. Associated with this new emphasis on prudery was a cult of motherhood, a romanticization of women as mothers. While pregnancy has always been regarded as a more or less natural event in women's lives, in nineteenth and twentieth century America, it was often called "confinement" and pregnant women were not supposed to be seen in public.

Margaret Sanger's work directly benefited thousands of women, like these with her at a Tucson, Arizona clinic in 1936. (Courtesy of Sophia Smith Collection, Smith College)

But motherhood itself was extended beyond the child raising functions to embrace maternal virtues in the family setting: soothing, comforting, and succoring their husbands and the men in their lives. Women, though perceived as inferior to men in most ways, were accepted as morally superior. People during the Victorian era believed that this greater holiness came from women's innate capacity to nurture. Female chastity was accepted as a woman's destiny as a "naturally" asexual being; men were merely asked to moderate the extremes of their powerful sexual urge. It was against this restrictive moral environment that the birth control campaigners of the nineteenth century had to struggle. Most of these early reformers were men since increasingly the "public" sphere belonged to men and the "private" sphere was the province of women.

Victorianism was a philosophy not only defined by the clergy and political philosophers of the day but also by the medical professionals, who not only embraced the idea of women's special biological status (often described as "the weaker sex"), but used it to condemn midwifery and other women's healing arts, which they associated with abortion. The doctors thereby justified excluding women from college and higher education because of their need for protection and "purity." Women bought into the idea, in part because they had no real economic alternatives, but their status as "women on pedestals" became, ironically, a basis of their own growing power in this two-tiered world of males and females. They could campaign against alcohol, slavery, and child labor because they needed to "raise" the level of male morality to that of their own.

One of the reasons women persuaded the male-dominated society to give them the vote was a belief that it would raise the level of society. It was on the issues of abolition of slavery and woman suffrage that women in America first spoke out at the Seneca Falls Convention in 1849 and similar meetings (even though in some states it was illegal for women to speak in public), but then their concerns were extended to child labor, to education, and a whole host of other issues. The more radical women, many of them socialists and freethinkers, also began to make a full scale assault on the male-dominated institutions, even though they did not always receive support from their male colleagues.

Increasingly in the twentieth century, the ability to control the spacing of children and even the number of children became a feminist agenda, and whereas males had been the first strong advocates and speakers on the issue, once women gained their own voice, they became the leaders in social change. In the process birth control and family planning went public, and ultimately even open discussion of abortion became possible.

References

Bullough, Vern, and Bonnie Bullough. *The Subordinate Sex.* Urbana: University of Illinois Press, 1974.

Gordon, Linda. *Woman's Body, Woman's Right: Birth Control in America.* 2d. ed. New York: Penguin Books, 1990.

Y

Yarros, Rachelle Slobodinsky (1869–1964)

Rachel Slobodinsky was the first woman admitted to the College of Physicians and Surgeons in Boston in 1890 but she finished her education at Woman's Medical College of Pennsylvania, receiving the M.D. degree in 1893. She married Victor S. Yarros, like her a Russian immigrant, and the couple moved to Chicago, where Rachelle Yarros began an obstetrical and gynecological practice. She became an unsalaried instructor at the medical school of the University of Illinois at Chicago and continued her relationship with the college until 1928, reaching the rank of associate professor. She was, among other things, an associate director of the Chicago Lying-in Hospital at the University of Chicago. From 1907 to 1927 Yarros and her husband lived at Hull House and she became very much identified with the reform movements emanating from Jane Addams and others. Yarros was active in the social hygiene movement in its efforts to eradicate prostitution and eliminate venereal disease through education and legislation, but most importantly she was the Chicago leader in the birth control movement. Shortly after the beginning of World War I in Europe, Yarros persuaded the Chicago Women's Club, to which she belonged, to establish a birth control committee. This committee evolved into the Illinois Birth Control League, which Yarros directed for many years. In 1923, at the urging of Margaret Sanger, Yarros opened the nation's second birth control clinic close to Hull House on Chicago's west side. She also campaigned for greater access to sex information for women and to this end she wrote *Modern Woman and Sex* (1933), which was reissued in 1938 as *Sex Problems in Modern Marriage*. Yarros also published a number of articles on birth control. Like many others in the birth control movement, she was both a socialist and an agnostic. The Yarroses had no children born to them but adopted a daughter, Elise Donaldson.

APPENDIX 1
World Survey of
Birth Control Practices

Most of the information for this survey is compiled from the web site of the International Planned Parenthood Federation (IPPF) at <http://www.ippf.org/regions/countryprofiles>. Some of the information is also dependent on data from the United Nations Population Information Network. Data are believed to be accurate to 1998 except where noted. The World Factbook 1997–1998 filled in information for countries with a population over one million that have no IPPF affiliate. The references to crude birth rate are births per 1,000 population in a given year; the total fertility rate as used here is the average number of live births for women between ages fifteen and forty-nine. For example, at current rates in the United States, the total fertility rate is 2. Since the replacement rate for a population is 2.1, if this rate holds, there will be an eventual leveling off of the population in the United States and an ultimate decline, unless of course, the rate of immigration overcomes the low fertility rate. Most countries have a higher total fertility rate than the United States, but the ideal for a leveling and ultimate decline in population growth is 2.1 or less. The other data are self-explanatory, except complete information is not always available. The major nongovernmental organization (NGO) involved in family planning, usually an affiliate of the IPPF, is listed for each country for which such information is available.

Major countries with populations of more than 10 million are listed first in alphabetical order, then countries with populations of less than 10 million by their geographical areas.

Countries over 10 Million Population

Afghanistan

North of Pakistan in southwestern Asia, Afghanistan, after about twenty years of war, has a Muslim government that strictly enforces shariah (Islamic law). It is a very poor, landlocked country that is dependent on subsistence farming and raising livestock. It has a family planning group—the Afghan Family Planning Association. Address: PO Box 545, Kabul, Afghanistan; telephone: 93 22659; cable: FAMILYGUIDE KABUL.

Population (millions, 1996 est.)	22.7
Birth rate (1996 est.)	43
Total fertility rate (1996 est.)	6.14

Algeria

The government of Algeria, a country in northwestern Africa, has attempted since 1983 to bring about a reduction in population growth by, among other things, increasing contraceptive use. The Association Algérienne pour la Planification Familiale (AFPA) was formed in 1987 to disseminate information, carry out public education, and work with government and religious groups to encourage contraception. Address: 49 rue des Jardins Hydra, Alger, Algeria; telephone: 213 (2) 603 168; fax: 213 (2) 604 975; telex: (0408) 55257 AAPFDZ.

Population (millions)	30.2
Crude birth rate	31
Total fertility rate	4.4

Women 15–49 using any
 method of contraception   47 percent
Women 15–49 using modern
 methods of contraception   43 percent

Angola

Angola is a country in equatorial Africa bordering the Atlantic Ocean. Since its independence from Portugal in 1975, Angola has been in a state of continual civil war. Despite rich natural resources, including oil, gold, rich soil, diamonds, fisheries, and forests, the economy is in disarray and the people are poor. The important organization concerned with contraception is Associação Angolana para o Bem Estar da Familia. Address: Rua C-6 No. 36, Rangel, Luanda, Angola; telephone: 244 (2) 33 94 21 or 33 85 67; fax: c/o Paulo Pombolo, IEC Director: 244 (2) 32 11 05; telex: 3226 MINSA, AN/4186Mirexan/3202.

Population (millions)	12
Crude birth rate	51
Total fertility rate	7.2

Argentina

Argentina, a large country in southern South America, enacted a law in 1986 making the states responsible for providing family planning services. However, lack of human and material resources and the controversy surrounding the law have acted to prevent the execution of the law. Attempting to fill this gap and also lobbying to get the state more active is the Asociación Argentina de Protección Familiar (AAPF). It maintains a pilot medical center in Buenos Aires and offers its services through nearly 200 medical offices associated with public hospitals and health centers. Among adolescents under age twenty, contraceptive use varies between 30 and 50 percent and is related to level of education and availability. Telephone of the AAPF: 54 (1) 826 1216; fax: 54 (1) 824 8416; e-mail: aapf@ciudad.com.ar.

Population (millions)	36.1
Crude birth rate	19
Total fertility rate	2.5
Women 15–49 using any method of contraception	74 percent

Australia

The government of Australia, a continent between the Pacific and Indian Oceans, provides funding for family planning, usually through Family Planning Australia, a representative national body for the independent state organizations that run Family Planning Programs throughout Australia. The organization provides community education, dispenses contraceptive information, and also deals with sexually transmitted diseases. It also manages a number of regional training programs in the South Pacific and Southeast Asia. Address: 9/114 Maitland St., Hackett ACT 2602, Australia; telephone: 61 (2) 6230 5255; fax: 61 (2) 6230 5344; e-mail: fpa@actonline.com.au; web: <http://www.actonline.com.au/fpa>.

Population (millions)	18.7
Crude birth rate	14
Total fertility rate	1.8
Women 15–49 using any method of contraception	76 percent
Women 15–49 using modern methods of contraception	72 percent

Bangladesh

A very poor country in Southeast Asia, Bangladesh has a government strongly committed to family planning. It has prioritized a National Population Program to reduce fertility to the replacement rate by 2005. Services are provided by the government through a network of Union Health and Family Welfare Centers, satellite clinics, and field workers as well as by the complementary work of nongovernmental organizations. Contraceptive supplies, however, are erratic, and the government is attempting to foster contraceptive manufacturing in the private sector. The high level of public awareness of family planning is not matched by contraceptive use, since there is a social preference for early marriage, large families, and male offspring.

The Family Planning Association of Bangladesh (FPAB), the oldest and largest nongovernmental organization in family planning in Bangladesh, contributes around 7 percent of the national family planning success. It emphasizes female empowerment as part of family planning but at the same time tries to increase male involvement. Address: PO Box 3714, 1000 Dhaka, Bangladesh; telephone: 880 (2) 416

1346, 880 (2) 417 5523; fax: 880 (2) 83 3008; telex: 632379 IFICB, BJ/642940 ADAB BJ; cable: BAFAM-PLANSDHAKA; e-mail: fpab1@citechco.net.

Population (millions)	123.4
Crude birth rate	25.6
Total fertility rate	3.3
Women 15–49 using any method of contraception	49 percent
Women 15–49 using modern methods of contraception	42 percent

Belgium

The government of the western European country of Belgium has never developed an explicit family planning policy. Such services are provided by different organizations that are funded by regional government, and the cost of certain contraceptives (oral contraceptives and sterilization) is refunded by the federal health insurance system. First-trimester abortion on the request of the woman is legal. There are two federations of family planning groups, one for each language group. Federatie Centra voor Geboortenregeling en Seksuele Opvoeding (CGSO Trefpunt) originally was a federation of fourteen family planning centers in the Flemish-speaking part of Belgium. There is still cooperation between it and the now thirty centers providing such service, although generally it acts as a center of expertise providing services for professionals and information to the general public as well as developing sex education materials and lobbying the government of Flanders. Telephone for CGSO Trefpunt: 32 (9) 221 0722; fax: 32 (9) 220 8406; e-mail: cgso@xs4all.be; web: <http://www.cgso.be>.

The French-speaking portion of Belgium works through the Fédération Francophone Belge pour le Planning Familial et l'Education Sexuelle (FFBPFES). It runs some thirty-seven family centers and lobbies the Wallonian government, the major source of its funding, for women's reproductive health rights, conducts training for health personnel, and conducts educational campaigns. Telephone for FFBPFES: 32 (2) 502 8203 or 32 (2) 502 6800; fax: 32 (2) 502 2613.

Population (millions)	10.2
Crude birth rate	12
Total fertility rate	1.6

Brazil

Brazil, the largest country in South America, is on the Atlantic Ocean. Although more than half of all sexually active women use modern contraceptives, there are significant differences between those who live in urban and rural areas, those with different educational levels, and those who live in different regions of the country. Abortion is allowed only in case of rape or to save the life of the mother, but there is a high rate of illegal abortion, which is responsible for 12 percent of all maternal deaths. Female sterilization (40 percent) and oral contraceptives (21 percent) are the most commonly used contraceptives.

The Sociedad Civil Bem-Estar Familiar no Brasil (BEMFAM) is the largest nonprofit organization providing reproductive health services in the country. With twelve clinics and twenty government programs, it provided 3,098,897 consultations in 1994. Services include gynecological consultation, contraceptive counseling, Pap smears, prenatal care, and education about sexually transmitted diseases. Address: CEP 20031-170, RJ, Centro Rio de Janeiro, Brazil; telephone: 55 (21) 210 2448 or 55 (21) 262 3933; fax: 55 (21) 220 4057; telex: 3912130634 BEMFAM; e-mail: info@bemfam.org.br.

Population (millions)	162.1
Crude birth rate	22
Total fertility rate	2.5
Women 15–49 using any method of contraception	77 percent
Women 15–49 using modern methods of contraception	70 percent

Burkina Faso

One of the world's least developed countries, landlocked Burkina Faso is located north of Ghana in West-Central Africa. Contraceptive use is low, although the government is favorable to family planning as part of primary health care and social wellbeing. It was not until 1986 that the country replaced the French colonial law outlawing contraception, and in 1991 a population policy was finally adopted that was designed to increase contraceptive prevalence by 60 percent by the year 2005. The country has 2 national hospitals, 10 regional ones, 72 medical centers, 628 health and social centers, 132 dispensaries, and 16 maternity hospitals. There is, however, still little information about contraceptives available.

Abortion is very limited, and backstreet abortions are common. It was only in 1997 that the government banned female genital mutilation. One of the groups attempting to carry out educational programs is the Association Burkinabé pour le Bien-Etre Familial. Address: BP 535, Ouagadougou, Burkina Faso; telephone: 226 310598; 226 317510; telex: 1111; e-mail: ABBEF@fasonet.bf.

Population (millions)	11.3
Crude birth rate	47
Total fertility rate	6.9
Women 15–49 using any method of contraception	15 percent
Women 15–49 using modern methods of contraception	8 percent

Cambodia

Cambodia, a country in Southeast Asia, adopted a pronatalist policy in 1979 to overcome the heavy loss of population in the wars of the 1970s. By early 1990, however, the government began a birth spacing policy that established the right of every individual to family planning information and services. Family planning services are offered in most public-sector hospitals throughout the country, and many private physicians offer intrauterine device insertion services. In 1997, the National Assembly adopted an abortion law allowing abortions if women request such services.

Implementation of family planning in rural areas, however, is difficult because of the underdeveloped transport and communication infrastructure and because women have a low level of literacy. Following the work of a USAID-funded Family Health and Spacing Project that began in 1994, the Reproductive Health Association of Cambodia (RHAC) was established as an independent indigenous nongovernmental organization. It receives support from the government, members of the European community, and various international family planning groups. It has four clinics, a network of approximately 400 Health Development Team agents, and nearly 100 staff members. The clinics offer family planning services as well as treatment of sexually transmitted diseases and prenatal care. RHAC introduced Norplant in Cambodia in 1996 and in 1997 established a comprehensive reproductive health program for youth. The postal address for the group is House #6, Road 150, Sanguat Veal Vong, Khan 7 Makara, Phnom Penh,

Cambodia; telephone: 855 (23) 36 62 95; fax: 855 (23) 36 61 94; e-mail: rhac@bigpond.org.kh.

Population (millions)	10.8
Crude birth rate	38
Total fertility rate	17

Cameroon

A West-Central African country bordering Nigeria, Cameroon has a large population with no access to public health services and a high level of illiteracy. In 1992 the government adopted a population policy calling for responsible parenthood in fertility decisions and for education programs, but implementation is difficult because of traditional pronatalist attitudes and the lack of effective infrastructure. Abortion is allowed only in case of risk to a woman's life, of fetal defects, or of rape or incest.

The Cameroon National Association for Family Welfare is a nongovernmental organization organized to support government efforts not only in dissemination of contraceptive information but also in nutrition, parasite control, general welfare issues, and sexually transmitted diseases. It distributes condoms and other nonprescriptive contraceptives. In 1999, however, only 16 percent of the women between ages fifteen and forty-nine were using any method of contraception, and only 4 percent were using modern methods.

Address: CAMNAFAW, BP 11994, Yaound, Cameroon; telephone: 237 23 7984; fax: 237 23 7984; telex: 8512 or 1140; e-mail: camnafaw@icc-net.cm.

Population (millions)	14.3
Crude birth rate	41
Total fertility rate	5.9
Women 15–49 using any method of contraception	16 percent
Women 15–49 using modern methods of contraception	4 percent

Canada

The fertility rate of Canada in North America is at an alltime low, and, if present trends continue, annual deaths could equal or surpass births by 2020. Provincial governments are responsible for providing family planning in each province, and some, such as Ontario, have excellent programs whereas others, such as Prince

Edward Island, have no family planning clinics at all. Abortion is available. The federal government has eliminated the family planning division of the Health and Welfare Department, although it gives minimal support to the Planned Parenthood Federation of Canada (PPFC). The Canadian International Development Agency provides support to family planning in the developing world. Telephone of PPFC: 1 (613) 241 4474; fax: 1 (613) 241 7550; e-mail: admin@ppfc.ca; web: <http://www.ppfc.ca>.

Population (millions)	30.6
Crude birth rate	12
Total fertility rate	1.6
Women 15–49 using all methods of contraception	73 percent

Chile

Chile is a long strip of land along the Pacific Ocean in South America. It has one of the lowest fertility rates and one of the fastest-falling birth rates in Latin America. There is, however, a high rate of teenage pregnancy. Abortion is illegal, but it remains a leading cause of maternal mortality. Almost all births take place in institutions with professionals in attendance. The government supports a policy of family planning and recognizes it as a human right.

The Asociación Chilena de Protección de la Familia, founded in 1962, was the first family planning organization in Chile to focus on small programs in underserved and impoverished areas. It is not supported by the state and is chronically underfunded. Address: Cassila 16504, Correo 9, Santiago, Chile; telephone: 56 (2) 334 8246, 56 (2) 334 8227, or 56 (2) 234 3931; fax: 56 (2) 334 8235; e-mail: aprofa@interacess.ci.

Population (millions)	14.8
Crude birth rate	19
Total fertility rate	2.4
Women 15–49 using any method of contraception	43 percent

China

A large country with a huge population, China lies between Korea and Vietnam in eastern Asia. The target of the Chinese government between 1991 and 2000 has been to keep the annual rate of natural population below 1.5 percent in the decade and to stop

the population growth at 1.3 billion. This they did by promoting family planning, late marriages, and fewer but healthier births with the ideal of one child per couple. Abortion is legal, and prostaglandins, especially mifepristone, are widely available.

The success of the family program has been handicapped by the traditional preference for sons and large families and by the spread of the population to remote, mountainous, and poverty-stricken areas where family planning and services are not made easily available. The nongovernmental organization that plays a significant role in China's family planning program is the China Family Planning Association. Its target audience is women of reproductive age in economically less-developed areas. Telephone for the China Family Planning Association: 86 (10) 6441 7612; fax: 86 (10) 6442 7612; telex: 211231 CFPA CN; e-mail: cfpa@public.fhnet.cn.net.

Population (millions)	1,242.5
Crude birth rate	17
Total fertility rate	1.8
Women 15–49 using any kind of contraception	83 percent
Women 15–49 using modern methods of contraception	81 percent

Colombia

In Colombia, which lies in northern South America, the birth rate dropped by half in the last twenty-five years of the twentieth century. Contraceptive use has gone from being almost nonexistent to 72 percent in 1999. The 1991 national constitution included an article about the right to family planning, although family planning services provided by the central government are still marginal.

The Asociación Pro-Bienestar de la Familia Colombiana (Profamilia), founded in 1965, has thirty-five centers in thirty-one cities and a national marketing program with thousands of retailers. It provided directly and indirectly most of the family planning in Colombia, although in 1999 the percentage fell somewhat due to the 1993 health law, Law 100, which forced all private and public health institutions in the country to supply family planning services. Also, international support for Colombian efforts, much of it channeled through Profamilia, declined since its success meant that it was no longer seen as a priority country. Profamilia relied heavily on intrauterine device insertion, Norplant, and voluntary female and male sterilizations. Profamilia telephone: 571-338-31-60; fax: 571-338-31-59; e-mail: DireccionEjectiv@profamilia.or.co or Relaciones-Publicas @profamilia.org.co; web: <http://www.profamilia.org.co>.

Population (millions)	40
Crude birth rate	26
Total fertility rate	2.7
Women 15–49 using any method of contraception	82 percent
Women 15–49 using modern methods of contraception	59 percent

Congo, Democratic Republic of

The Democratic Republic of Congo (formerly Zaire), in central Africa northeast of Angola, is one of the largest and most populous countries on the African continent. Its years of economic crisis, poor infrastructure, and political instability have had a negative impact on family health. Like many other countries where French influence was strong, it had a colonial law banning contraception. In 1972, however, the government encouraged a policy of birth spacing (called desirable births) and in 1982 launched an official project toward this end. Although other policies have been drafted, most have never been formally adopted, and much of the effort has fallen on volunteer organizations supported by religious groups or foreign governments, including a USAID project.

The Association pour le Bien-etre Familial has attempted to extend information on reproductive health and family planning to semiurban and rural communities. One of its emphases is training nongovernmental organization representatives not only in sexual and reproductive health and social rights of women, but encouraging such groups to engage in income-generating activities to help support themselves. Address: BP 15313, Kinshasa, Dem. Rep. of Congo; telephone: 243 (12) 44598; fax: 243 (88) 70703; telex: 21537 LASCO ZR, attn: AZBEF.

Population (millions)	49
Crude birth rate	48
Total fertility rate	0.6
Women 15–49 using any method of contraception	8 percent

Women 15–49 using modern methods of contraception	3 percent

Côte d'Ivoire

Côte d'Ivoire borders Mali, Burkina Faso, Ghana, and Liberian West Africa. Its government favors family planning and works in collaboration with the Association Ivoirienne pour le Bien-Etre Familial (AIBEF) to increase the use of contraceptives. Information and education about population matters are provided by the Ministry of Public Health and Social Affairs as well as the Ministry of Women's Affairs. Maternal and child health along with family planning services are provided through thirty-five health centers across the country. Contraceptives are also distributed by more than thirty private clinics and by most pharmacies and drug stores. The population's attitude, however, remains pronatalist, and lack of family planning facilities and a shortage of equipment and of trained staff have impeded progress. The address of the AIBEF is 01 BP 5315, Abidjan, Côte d'Ivoire; telephone: 225 25 1811 or 225 25 1812; fax: 225 25 1868; telex: 23930/23927 CABIN CI.

Population (millions)	15.6
Crude birth rate	39
Total fertility rate	5.7
Women 15–49 using any method of contraception	11 percent
Women 15–49 using modern methods of contraception	4 percent

Cuba

A Caribbean archipelago south of Florida, Cuba is said to be in its "final phase" of a demographic transition, although it is still categorized as a developing country. The fertility rate is below the replacement rate. The government has made health care for women and children a main priority in its public health policy. Handicapping the population policy, however, has been an insufficient supply of some contraceptive methods and a lack of choice of methods. Abortion is legal and institutionalized within the country, but the rate of abortion has been falling over the years. The Sociedad Cientifica Cubana para el Desarrollo de la Familia (SOCUDEF) operates 114 community-based family planning delivery units in government-owned clinics. This accounts for 45 percent of the contraceptive service delivery as well as the services for infertility. SOCUDEF has more than 500 volunteers and more than 1,700 community activists, the majority of whom are women. It provides information, guidance, education, and services, and also maintains a youth training center in Cienfuegos province aimed at adolescents; similar projects, although not on the same scale, exist in other provinces. Telephone: 53 (7) 24 2436 or 53 (7) 24 2119; fax: 53 (7) 24 2545; e-mail: socudef@cenial.inf.cu.

Population (millions)	11.1
Crude birth rate	14
Total fertility rate	1.4
Women 15 49 using any method of contraception	70 percent
Women 15 49 using modern methods of contraception	68 percent

Czech Republic

The Czech Republic is located in central Europe southeast of Germany. Family planning services are provided in hospitals as well as in nongovernmental clinics. The traditional model of family formation and reproductive behavior has been replaced by a pattern of later marriage and delayed childbearing. Modern contraceptives are available, and first-trimester abortion on request is legal. The incidence of abortion has been declining. The Czech Society for Family Planning and Sex Education (SPRSV) runs clinics offering a range of contraceptive and counseling services. It also offers lectures on sex education and reproductive health. SPRSV telephone: 420 (2) 2423 2552; fax: 420 (2) 2423 2553; e-mail: planrod@login.cz.

Population (millions)	10.3
Crude birth rate	9
Total fertility rate	1.2
Women 15 49 using any method of contraception	69 percent
Women 15 49 using modern methods of contraception	45 percent

Ecuador

Ecuador lies in northwestern South America between Colombia and Peru. The constitution guarantees family planning as well as the right of parents to have the number of children they can support and educate. Family planning is provided through government maternal and child health programs. Abortion is ille-

gal. The Asociación-Pro Bienestar de la Familia Ecuatoriana (APROFE), founded in 1965, works closely with the government, sponsoring workshops and lectures around the country. The APROFE has clinics in most of the major cities, providing a variety of contraceptives as well as sterilization and family planning. The APROFE sells contraceptives at subsidized prices from a variety of shops and offices in the country. It pays special attention to young men and women. Address: PO Box 09-01-5954, Guayaquil, Ecuador; telephone: 593 (4) 419 666 or 593 (4) 400 888; fax: 593 (4) 419 667; cable: APROFE; e-mail: aprofe@aprofe.org.ec.

Population (millions)	12.2
Crude birth rate	28
Total fertility rate	3.6
Women 15 49 using any method of contraception	57 percent
Women 15 49 using modern methods of contraception	46 percent

Egypt

Egypt, an ancient country on the Mediterranean Sea between Libya and the Gaza Strip, took some tentative steps toward population planning in the 1950s, but an explicit policy did not emerge until 1985 with the establishment of the National Population Council. Out of this arose the Egyptian Family Planning Association, which from 1995 began establishing a number of family planning clinics. Strong government support has made it the major family planning organization working in collaboration with the government. One of its priority targets is rural areas, where the prevalence of contraceptive practices is the lowest. Telephone: 20 (2) 270-6374 or 20 (2) 270-7250; fax: 20 (2) 270-6372; telex: 091 22950EFPA UN; cable: GEEPLAN CAIRO; e-mail: efpa@idsc.gov.eg.

Population (millions)	65.5
Crude birth rate	28
Total fertility rate	3.6
Women 15–49 using any method of contraception	48 percent
Women 15–49 using modern methods of contraception	46 percent

Ethiopia

Ethiopia lies in eastern Africa, west of Somalia. The government officially adopted family planning as a health-promoting measure for mothers and children in 1980 and integrated family planning services with maternal and child health in 1,628 health institutions run by the Ministry of Health. The transitional government in 1993 continued the policy. The program, however, has been handicapped by political instability.

The Family Guidance Association of Ethiopia has focused its efforts on educational campaigns. It also operates a Saturday youth clinic in Addis Ababa to reach adolescents with its message. Address: PO Box 5716, Addis Ababa, Ethiopia; telephone: 251 (1) 51 89 09 or 251 (1) 51 41 11; fax: 251 (1) 51 21 92; telex: 21473 FGAE; cable: BETESEB; e-mail: fgae@telecom.net.et.

Population (millions)	58.4
Crude birth rate	46
Total fertility rate	7
Women 15–49 using any method of contraception	4 percent
Women 15–49 using modern methods of contraception	3 percent

France

France lies in western Europe between Belgium and Spain. It has no explicitly formulated policy on family planning, but such services are available in government-regulated centers. Such centers are, however, sparse in rural areas. Prescriptive contraceptives are available from licensed pharmacies, and condoms are available from a wide variety of outlets. First-trimester abortion on request is legal. The law does not recognize sexuality in a minor, since contraception is available freely and anonymously without any condition as to age. A girl can go through pregnancy and give birth without parental consent, but an unmarried minor needs parental consent or a judge's approval to obtain a legal abortion.

The Mouvement Français pour le Planning Familial is a feminist movement that cites its activities in the wider context of combating social inequalities and sexual oppression. It is a leading member of the High Council for Information on Sex, a national umbrella organization for nongovernmental organizations working in the broad field of sexual and reproductive rights. It is affiliated with the International Planned Parenthood Federation. Telephone: 33 (1) 48 07 29 10; fax: 33 (1) 47 00 79 77; e-mail: MFPFConf@aol.com or MFPDoc@aol.com.

Population (millions)	58.8
Crude birth rate	12
Total fertility rate	1.7
Women 15–49 using any method of contraception	75 percent
Women 15–49 using modern methods of contraception	68 percent

Germany

Germany lies in central Europe between the Netherlands and Poland. It has a temperate climate and many natural resources. It ranks third in the powerful economies of the world. The International Planned Parenthood country file on family planning is currently being updated.

Population (millions, 1996)	83.5
Birth rate (1996)	9.66
Total fertility rate (1996)	9.3

Ghana

Ghana lies in western Africa between Côte d'Ivoire and Togo. It developed a population policy in 1969 designed to lower the high fertility level through voluntary use of modern contraceptive methods and also to reduce the high infant and maternal mortality rates and ensure a more balanced spatial development in all regions of the country. In 1994, the National Population Council was set up to apply a revised policy that included coordinating, monitoring, and evaluating all the population programs in the country and integrating a comprehensive program into the overall national development plan. It also aimed to eliminate female genital mutilation, Konte (whereby a girl-child is forced into marriage and released when pregnant), early pregnancy, and unhealthy or dangerous child delivery practices.

The nongovernmental organization working most closely with the government is the Planned Parenthood Association of Ghana. It concentrates on reaching marginalized groups and encouraging male participation in the family planning programs.

Population (millions, 1996)	17.7
Crude birth rate	35
Total fertility rate	4.59

Greece

Greece is located in southern Europe between Albania and Turkey. The government has no declared policy on family planning and provides no dedicated services. Contraceptives, however, are widely available, often without prescriptions, but the use of modern methods remains low. Abortion is legal on request in the first trimester and is widely practiced.

The Family Planning Association of Greece focuses on information and education, particularly aimed at young people. It collaborates with the government to create a network of research, studies, projects, and specific programs. It also has a youth group. Telephone: 30 (1) 38 37 592; fax: 30 (1) 38 06 390; e-mail: eop-fpag@ath.forthnet.gr.

Population (millions)	10.5
Crude birth rate	10
Total fertility rate	1.1

Guatemala

Guatemala is in Central America between Honduras and Belize. Guatemala's 1986 constitution recognized the right of a couple to freely decide the number and spacing of their children. The Ministry of Health offers family planning services through government clinics, although there are periodic attacks by religious and anti-family planning groups. The Asociación Pro-Bienestar de la Familia de Guatemala offers family planning services in twenty-eight clinics throughout the country and works with 106 private physicians. It concentrates much of its effort in rural areas, running information and educational campaigns and family life education programs. Address: Apartado Postal 1004, Guatemala, 01001, Guatemala; telephone: 502 230 5488 or 502 251 3096; fax: 502 251 4017; e-mail: aprofam@guate.net.

Population (millions)	11.1
Crude birth rate	39
Total fertility rate	5.1
Women 15–49 using any method of contraception	31 percent
Women 15–49 using modern methods of contraception	27 percent

Hungary

Hungary is a landlocked country of central Europe east of Austria and west of Romania. The government supports family planning services through the national health service. However, there is inadequate nationwide sex education and inadequate services for young adults. Thus, women are still relying on abortion as a method of birth control. The Pro Familia Hungarian Scientific Society (HSS) focuses primarily on education and advocacy and running training courses on contraceptive methods and sexually transmitted diseases. Telephone: 36 (1) 316 55 17; fax: 36 (1) 316 55 17; telex: 224308 STATI H.

Population (millions)	10.1
Crude birth rate	10
Total fertility rate	1.3
Women 15–49 using any method of contraception	73 percent
Women 15–49 using modern contraception	68 percent

India

India is the largest country in South Asia, stretching from the Himalayas to the Indian Ocean. It is one of the most heavily populated countries in the world. The government supports a national family planning program including maternal and child health, family welfare, and nutrition. Sexually transmitted diseases are widespread. The average age for women to marry is twenty, and female infanticide is still extant.

The Family Planning Association of India (FPAI) has programs all over India, providing reproductive health services, a contraceptive retail sales program, and education on family planning and prevention of sexually transmitted diseases. It even has women's empowerment groups and income generation programs. Telephone: 91 (22) 202 9080 or 91 (22) 202 5174; fax: 91 (22) 202 9038/204 8513; cable: FAMPLAN BOMBAY; e-mail: fpai@glas-bm01.vsni.net.in; web: <http://www.fpaindia.com>.

Population (millions)	988.7
Crude birth rate	26
Total fertility rate	3.5
Women 15–49 using any method of contraception	41 percent
Women 15–49 using modern methods of contraception	36 percent

Indonesia

Indonesia is an archipelago in Southeastern Asia between the Indian Ocean and the Pacific Ocean. Indonesia has the fourth highest population in the world and is the world's largest archipelago. Of its 17,000 islands, 6,000 are populated, and the population is becoming increasingly urban. The government has a policy of improving the quality of life of the people, including decreasing mortality, improving the health of mothers and children, and decreasing the birth rate. Abortion, illegal but often performed, accounts for a large number of maternal deaths. Illiteracy, poverty, and differences in language, culture, and religion makes an effective family planning program difficult. The Indonesian Planned Parenthood Association (IPPA) since 1957 has started several projects targeting young couples, sex workers, health of mothers and children, and dispensing contraceptive information. Address: PO Box 6017, 12120, Jakarta Selatan, Indonesia; telephone: 62 (21) 720 7372 or 62 (21) 739 4123; fax: 62 (21) 739 4088; cable: IPPA JACARTA; e-mail: pkbinet@idola.net.id.

Population (millions)	207.4
Crude birth rate	24
Total fertility rate	2.7
Women 15–49 using any method of contraception	55 percent
Women 15–49 using modern methods of contraception	52 percent

Iran

A Muslim country of Southwest Asia, Iran is between Iraq and Pakistan in the Middle East. After the revolution of 1979, Iran had government policies that improved primary health care but encouraged a rapidly growing population. Recognition of the problems connected with such an increase in population led to a change in government policy and consequently a dramatic drop in population growth. Abortion is illegal unless the mother's life is in danger. Although sexual health issues for young people are not covered adequately, the Iranian government has set up a network of primary care facilities that provides free family planning. The government encourages a maximum of three children per family, three years between children, and pregnancy between ages eighteen and thirty-five. Families receive no additional health benefits for a fourth child, and men are

encouraged to be sterilized. The Family Planning Association of the Islamic Republic of Iran (FPAIRI) complements the network of health care facilities by providing education, training, and research. Address of FPAIRI: PO Box 19395-3518, Tehran, 19119, Iran; telephone: 98 (21) 222 3944 or 98 (21) 222 1479; fax: 98 (21) 225 7746; e-mail: FPAIRI@neda.net.

Population (millions)	64.1
Crude birth rate	19
Total fertility rate	2.5
Women 15–49 using any method of contraception	71 percent
Women 15–49 using modern methods of contraception	56 percent

Iraq

An ancient country in southwestern Asia, Iraq has no official population policy, but it does have a pronatalist stance. Contraceptives, however, are freely given, and the government supports the Safe Motherhood Initiative. Since the Gulf War and the subsequent embargo, contraceptives and medical supplies have been inadequate, although the United Nations has given special permission to import some to the Iraq Family Planning Association (IFPA). This popular organization does its best to cope with the great shortage of funds and supplies, but mortality rates for infants and mothers has increased. The IFPA provides information and services through clinics of the Ministry of Health. Address: PO Box 6028, Al-Mansour, Baghdad 12605, Iraq; telephone: 9964 (1) 422 9202; fax: 9964 (1) 477 4970; cable: ALMANSOUR BAGHDAD.

Population (millions)	21.8
Crude birth rate	38
Total fertility rate	5.7
Women 15–49 using any method of contraception	18 percent
Women 15–49 using modern methods of contraception	10 percent

Italy

Italy, which includes the islands of Sardinia and Sicily, is a southern European country that juts south into the Mediterranean Sea. The government supports family planning, and contraceptives and first-trimester abortions are readily available. Many citizens in this Roman Catholic country, however, use only natural family planning, and there is some illegal abortion. The Unione Italiana Centri Educazione Matrimoniale e Prematrimoniale (UICEMP) provides information and training for health and social workers who staff the state family planning clinics and for other workers servicing young people. Address of UICEMP: Via Eugenio Chiesa I, Milan 20122; telephone: 0039/02/5456687; fax: 1139/02/5456687; e-mail: uicemp@tin.it.

Population (millions)	57.7
Crude birth rate	9
Total fertility rate	1.2

Japan

An archipelago off the east coast of Asia, Japan is very much a first-world country. Pronatalist, it has no policy concerning population or family planning. Sex education and family planning have low priority in the Ministry of Health and Welfare. Most modern contraceptives have not been approved for use, although oral contraceptives are prescribed for some 200,000 women for "therapeutic" reasons. Abortion is legal and much used. Use of the condom is common. The Family Planning Federation of Japan is thus very important in educating family planning workers, in espousing reproductive health as human rights, in disseminating information about birth control and sexual health, and in lobbying officials.

Population (millions)	126.4
Crude birth rate	10
Total fertility rate	1.4
Women 15–49 using any method of contraception	64 percent
Women 15–49 using modern methods of contraception	57 percent

Kazakhstan

Formerly a part of the Soviet Union, the Republic of Kazakhstan is in central Asia northwest of China. Its deserts, plains, and mountains are polluted with radioactivity and chemicals, but it has large untapped supplies of petroleum and minerals, and it has agricultural potential. It has no affiliation with International Planned Parenthood.

Population (millions, 1996 est.)	16.9
Birth rate (1996 est.)	19.02
Total fertility rate (1996 est.)	2.36

Kenya

Kenya lies between Somalia and Tanzania in eastern Africa, bordering the Indian Ocean. It has multiple large problems: deforestation, desert encroachment, unsafe water, soil exhaustion. For humans, life expectancy is under age fifty, infant and maternal mortality rates are high, female genital mutilation is practiced among many of the thirty ethnic groups, and HIV/AIDS is prevalent. On the positive side, three-quarters of people over fifteen are literate, and the government, through the Ministry of Health, is cooperating with various nongovernmental organizations in the area that are trying to alleviate these problems.

The Family Planning Association of Kenya (FPAK) supplements the work of the Ministry of Health and other nongovernmental organizations by providing affordable, accessible family planning and reproductive health information. It has many special programs for youth and for men. Address of FPAK: PO Box 30581, Nairobi, Kenya; telephone: 25 (2) 215 676; fax: 254 (2) 213 757; cable: FAMPLAN; e-mail: fpak@ken.healthnet.org.

Population (millions)	28.3
Crude birth rate	33
Total fertility rate	4.5
Women 15–49 using any method of contraception	33 percent
Women 15–49 using modern methods of contraception	27 percent

Korea, North (Democratic People's Republic of Korea)

Lying in the northern part of the Korean peninsula in east Asia, North Korea was hit by a series of natural disasters in the 1990s that seriously affected the food supply, and consequently famine relief has impeded the plans and good intentions of the national health care system. Abortion is legal, and hospitals and clinics all over the country give free family planning advice, but lack of effective transportation and communication affects accessibility. A further problem is a lack of trained personnel. The Family Planning and Maternal and Child Health Association (KFP and MCHA) is active. It tries to reach people in the large mountainous mining areas. Address of KFP and MCHA: Puksong-2-Dong, Pyonchon District, Pyongyang City, Democratic People's Republic of Korea; telephone: 850 (2) 422 3450; fax: 850 (2) 381 4660; telex: 37001 Bogen KP; cable: POP CENTRE, PYONGYANG.

Population (millions)	22.2
Crude birth rate	18
Total fertility rate	1.9

Korea, South
(Republic of Korea)

Lying on the south end of the Korean peninsula in east Asia, South Korea is a densely populated, largely urban country. It has achieved its demographic growth target of 1 percent and is now looking at the issues arising from urbanization and from an aging population. Continuing problems are the preference for male children that results in abortions of female fetuses and reaching the people who live in relatively inaccessible remote islands. The Planned Parenthood Federation of Korea (PPFK) is one of three active groups that provide good family planning information and services. Address of PPFK: Youngdeungpo PO Box 330, Seoul, 150–650, Republic of Korea; telephone: 82 (2) 634 8211; fax: 82 (2) 671 8212; e-mail: ppfk@unitel.co.kr.

Population (millions)	46.1
Crude birth rate	15.1
Total fertility rate	1.6
Women 15–49 using any method of contraception	80.5 percent
Women 15–49 using modern methods of contraception	70.0 percent

Madagascar

An island country of southern Africa, east of Mozambique, Madagascar is one of the poorest nations of the world. Most of the agrarian populace has no access to potable water. Their love of children and their belief that infertility is a curse contribute to the 3 percent growth rate. The Ministry of Health is integrating family planning into its many nationwide health centers, which also provide basic education about hydration, vaccination, and nutrition. The National Population Policy seems to be getting the better of the 1920 anticontraception law of this pronatalist county.

The Fianakaviana Sambatra (FISA) promulgates family planning as a human right. It has targeted underserved groups and tried through education to promote community involvement. It is also creating an effective management information system. FISA address: BP 703, 101, Antananarivo, Madagascar; telephone: 261 (20) 224 0347 or 224 1812; fax: 261 (20) 224 1813; telex: 22445 FPAFS MG; e-mail: fisa@simicro.mg.

Population (millions)	14
Crude birth rate	44
Total fertility rate	6
Women 15–49 using any method of contraception	19 percent
Women 15–49 using modern methods of contraception	10 percent

Malaysia

Malaysia consists of the north third of the island of Borneo and the north part of the peninsula it shares with Indonesia in Southeast Asia. Malays, Chinese, and Indians have lived together for centuries in this wet, tropical land. The government has forged detailed family planning policies that are supposed to slowly lower the fertility rate. The Ministry of Health and the National Population and Family Development Board (NPFDB) operate clinics for women and children and offer gynecological services in the main centers of the country. Services are limited in the remote, mountainous areas of the country. The Federation of Family Planning Associations of Malaysia (FFPAM) is one of the effective agencies in providing family planning services to Malaysians. It has targeted specific groups, such as youth in particular areas and the Malaysian aborigine village of Kampung Tisong. Address of FFPAM: 81-Bjalan 55 15/5A, Subang Jaya, 47500 Petaling Jaya, Selangor, Malaysia; telephone: 60 (3) 733 7516, 733 7528, or 733 7514; fax: 60 (3) 734 6638; e-mail: ffpam@po.jaring.my; web: <http://www.ffpam.org.my>.

Population (millions)	22.2
Crude birth rate	26
Total fertility rate	3.2
Women 15–49 using any kind of contraception	48 percent
Women 15–49 using modern methods of contraception	31 percent

Mali

A poor, landlocked country in the middle of central Africa, Mali is desert in the north, grasslands in the center, and humid agricultural land in the south. More than half the people are under twenty, and about 10 percent are nomads. Women, who have low status in this pronatalist country, marry early and have many children. The government has set national health policies regarding women, education, and the environment. The Association Malienne pour la Promotion et la Protection de la Famille (AMPPF) supports the government in family planning issues, providing education and clinical service in local communities. It has ambitious plans for distributing contraceptives and recruiting workers. Address of AMPPF: BP 105, Bamako, Mali; telephone: 223 22 4494; fax: 223 23 7755/22 2618; telex: 1201 (attn: AMPPF); e-mail: amppf@mal.healthnet.org.

Population (millions)	10.1
Crude birth rate	51
Total fertility rate	6.7
Women 15–49 using any method of contraception	7 percent
Women 15–49 using modern methods of contraception	5 percent

Mexico

South of the United States on the North American continent, Mexico has a population that increases by 2.3 million people a year despite the fact that the country is gradually lowering its birth rate because of its national family planning program. The government works with various private organizations to provide the best services in Latin America, but only 30 percent of women in urban slums and rural areas use contraceptives, and young adolescents add 500,000 babies a year to the population. The economy cannot support such a large and growing population. Many people live at or below the poverty level. A functional, effective organization is Fundación Mexicana para la Planeación Familiar (MEX-FAM), which provides education and medical services in most of the thirty-two Mexican states. It focuses especially on providing services in rural areas and urban slums. One of its special programs is with male factory workers. Telephone of MEX-FAM: 52 (5) 573 7100, 573 7348, or 573 7070; fax: 52 (5) 573 2318 or 655 1265; e-mail: mexinfo@ mexfam.org.mx; web: <http://www.mexfam.org. mx>.

Population (millions)	97.5
Crude birth rate	27
Total fertility rate	3.1
Women 15–49 using any method of contraception	65 percent
Women 15–49 using modern methods of contraception	56 percent

Morocco

A country on the Mediterranean Sea next to Algeria in northern Africa, Morocco is an Arab country with a minority nomadic Berber population in the eastern mountains. Current population policies set up in 1966 support family planning and aim at reducing the birth rate. The Association Marocaine de Planification Familiale (AMPF) works with political and religious leaders to implement family planning policies. It provides services and education, often targeting rural areas. Improvement of the status of women is one of its goals. Address of AMPF: PO Box 1217, Rabat RP, Morocco; telephone: 212 (7) 20 362 or 21 224; fax: 212 (7) 20 362; cable: FAMPLAN RABAT.

Population (millions)	27.7
Crude birth rate	24
Total fertility rate	3.3
Women 15–49 using any method of contraception	50 percent
Women 25–49 using modern methods of contraception	42 percent

Mozambique

Mozambique lies on the Indian Ocean between Tanzania and South Africa. Its social and fiscal structure have been ruined by drought and a lengthy civil war, so the people lack safe water, access to health care, and education. The average life expectancy of these Bantu people is forty-four years. Traditional patterns of living trap women into multiple pregnancies. The Associação Moçambicana para Desenvolvimento da Família (AMODEFA) is a nongovernmental organization that cooperates with government and other nongovernmental organizations to increase the knowledge and availability of family planning. It has trained staff and volunteers who have fielded many special projects, such as home health care of people with HIV/AIDS and setting up a women's education center. Address of AMODEFA: CP 1535, Maputo, Mozambique; telephone: 258 (1) 493 864; fax: 258 (1) 491 236; telex: 6239 MO; e-mail: amodefa@zebra.uem.mz.

Population (millions)	18.6
Crude birth rate	41
Total fertility rate	5.6
Women 15–49 using any method of contraception	6 percent
Women 15–49 using modern methods of contraception	5 percent

Myanmar

Myanmar (formerly Burma) lies between the Tibetan plateau and the Malay peninsula, bordering India, China, and Thailand. The largely Buddhist population is literate, and 60 percent have access to health care. There are problems with pollution and with clean water. Myanmar Maternal and Child Welfare Association is one group that offers services to the public. It has special education programs for women and has set up day care centers. It has also trained a large group of volunteers. Health and Welfare Services gives care to pregnant women, encourages breast feeding, and educates people concerning sexually transmitted diseases. Address of MMWCA: Corner of Than thu mar Road and Parami Road, South Okkalapa Township, Yangon, Myanmar; Telephone: 951 571123 or 571758; fax: 951 572104.

Population (millions)	47.1
Crude birth rate	30
Total fertility rate	3.5
Women 15–49 using any method of contraception	17 percent
Women 15–49 using modern methods of contraception	14 percent

Nepal

A landlocked country of South Asia between China and India, Nepal is one of the ten poorest countries on earth. The three topographical areas of mountains, hills, and plains contain many remote areas that are hard to service. The government wants to reduce the population growth rate, but individual families want male children and put young brides under consider-able pressure to produce them. Consequently, not many families use the contraceptives that are freely available. Abortions are illegal except to save the life of the mother. Female literacy is low. The largest nongovernmental organization and the only provider of full family planning services is the Family Planning Association of Nepal (FPAN). With eight hundred staff members and nine thousand volunteers, it provides services through both urban and rural clinics. Address of FPAN: PO Box 486, Kathmandu, Nepal; telephone: 977 (1) 524 648, 524 440, or 524 670; fax: 977 (1) 524 211; telex: 2307 FPAN NP /2270 NATRAJ NP; e-mail: fpandg@mos.com.np.

Population (millions)	21.8
Crude birth rate	34.54
Total fertility rate	4.43
Women 15–49 using any method of contraception	28.5 percent
Women 15–49 using modern methods of contraception	28.8 percent

Netherlands

A western European country on the North Sea, the Netherlands has a highly literate population with a high standard of living and a long life expectancy. Agricultural products, including flowers, cheese, and milk, are its major products. The government is committed and the people observe the international conventions of basic freedoms and human rights, so all family planning services are available and the teenage pregnancy rate is low. Abortion is available. Thus the Rutgers Foundation (Rutgers Stichting, or RS), the family planning organization, gives services to groups that are often neglected—migrants, raped women, sex offenders, people with psychosexual problems, and the mentally handicapped. It also offers training to family planning providers from eastern Europe, Asia, and Latin America. Address of RS: Oudenoord 176–178, PO Box 9663, Utrecht, 3506 GR, Netherlands; telephone: 31 (30) 231 3431; fax: 31 (30) 231 9387 (local) or 31 (30) 236 4665 (intl. div.) e-mail: Intdiv@Rutgers.nl; web: <http://www.rutgers.nl/internationaal.html>.

Population (millions)	15.7
Crude birth rate	12
Total fertility rate	1.5
Women 15–49 using any method of contraception	74 percent

Women 15–49 using modern
   methods of contraception   71 percent

Niger

More than half of Niger, a landlocked country in the middle of Africa, is Sahara Desert, so most of the polygamous Muslim population live in the savannas of the south. Drought, overuse of the land, and decline of the exchange rate have created acute economic problems. The average life span is only forty-seven years. The government has increasingly supported family planning since 1985. Niger now has a population policy by which nurses dispense various kinds of contraceptives in selected areas, and strategies for birth spacing are gradually being disseminated. Severe problems exist because of male attitudes, high female illiteracy, inadequate clinics, and inadequate supply of contraceptives. There is an active nongovernmental organization, Association Nigérienne pour le Bien-Etre Familial (ANBEF), which is educating target influential groups. They have also focused on informing youth about sexually transmitted diseases and on training volunteers.

Population (millions)	10.1
Crude birth rate	53
Total fertility rate	7.4
Women 15–49 using any method of contraception	4 percent
Women 15–49 using modern methods of contraception	2 percent

Nigeria

The Federal Republic of Nigeria has a larger population than any other country of Africa, and it includes 250 different ethnic groups. About half are Christian and half Muslim, with shariah (Islamic law) observed in parts of the north. Also some traditional beliefs remain, as evidenced by Sadaka marriages in some communities, in which older men marry very young girls. The country has good agricultural land and very large supplies of oil and natural gas. The newly elected democratic government faces very large problems. From 1983 to 2000, Nigeria was ruled by a series of unpopular military rulers who were not good economic or environmental managers. For many years there has been an awareness that the high population growth rate was not good for the country, and the governments have tried to introduce voluntary fertility regulation. The Ministry of Health, with nongovernmental organizations, has tried to distribute contraceptives. Unstable governments, lack of transportation, deficient health care systems, the cost of services, and traditional pronatal beliefs in rural areas hamper successful family planning. The Planned Parenthood Federation of Nigeria (PPFN), the largest nongovernmental organization dealing with family planning and reproductive health in Nigeria, provides about 10 percent of family planning services in the country. They have had a strong program that trains traditional healers in nonprescriptive contraceptives, basic hygiene, human anatomy, and prevention of sexually transmitted diseases. Address of PPFN: PMB 12657, Lagos, Nigeria; telephone: (234.1) 497.5254; fax: (234.1) 820.526; telex: 27604 NG; cable: PLANFED LAGOS; e-mail: ppfn@rcl.nig.com.

Population (millions)	121.8
Crude birth rate	45
Total fertility rate	6.5
Women 15–49 using any method of contraception	15 percent
Women 15–49 using modern methods of contraception	7 percent

Pakistan

Pakistan, which lies between India and Iran in South Asia, has the seventh largest population in the world. The great number of people erodes any effective economic policy and creates a growing number of very poor people. It has a family planning program, but it is ineffective because the Islamic religious party opposes family planning, female trained medical personnel are inadequate, and medical services are not available throughout the country. The low status of women and the practice of purdah (seclusion) means that most women cannot travel away from home. Only 24 percent of women are literate, gynecological knowledge is minimal, and female health workers must be accompanied by men. The major actor in family planning in Pakistan is the Family Planning Association of Pakistan (FPAP). It focuses on reproductive health, on women's status, and on educating youth, providing services all over the country. They also train paramedics and traditional practitioners. Telephone of FPAP: 92 (42) 631 4621 or 631 4625;

fax: 91 (42) 636 8692; telex: 44877 PEARL,
PK/44167 PEARL PK; e-mail: fpapak@brain.
net.pk.

Population (millions)	130.6
Crude birth rate	39
Total fertility rate	5.4
Women 15–49 using any method of contraception	23.9 percent
Women 15–49 using modern methods of contraception	16.9 percent

Peru

Peru, which lies in South America on the Pacific
Ocean between Ecuador and Chile, has major industries of agriculture, fishing, and mining, but most of
the people make their living in the service area.
Healthy economic growth has taken place, but job
creation is not keeping up with the birth rate and
health and nutrition levels are inadequate. Seventy
percent of urban women use modern contraceptives,
compared with only thirty-eight percent of rural
women. Eleven percent of pregnancies are among
teenagers. The concerned government has assigned
the implementation of the right to responsible parenthood to a special Council on Population. The nongovernmental organization Instituto Peruano de
Paternidad Responsable (INPPARES) has an elabo-
rate family planning program that extends to all parts
of the country. It works with the Ministry of Health
and with local doctors, health personnel, and community groups. It educates the public concerning
contraception, family health, and sexually transmitted diseases. An effective educational environment
has been health fairs held in the open air, with music,
food, and family planning booths. Address of
INPPARES: Casilla Postal 2191, 11, Lima, Peru; telephone: 51 (1) 261 5310, 261 5533, or 261 5522; fax:
51 (1) 261 7885; e-mail: postmast@inppar.org.pe;
web: <http://www.inppares.org.pe>.

Population (millions)	26.1
Crude birth rate	28
Total fertility rate	3.5
Women 15–49 using any method of contraception	64 percent
Women 15–49 using modern methods of contraception	45 percent

Philippines

Of the thousands of tropical rain-forested islands that
make up the Philippines, 880 are inhabited. With one
of the highest population growth rates in Southeast
Asia (2.3 percent), a concerned government has set
up a strong family program that includes family planning; reproductive health of men, women, and adolescents; prevention and treatment of infections and
diseases of the reproductive tract; education on sexuality; prevention of violence against women; and
treatment of infertility. Difficulties in effecting this
ambitious program come from the inaccessibility of
remote areas and from the strong opposition of the
Roman Catholic Church to family planning programs. The strongest nongovernmental organization
is the Family Planning Organization of the Philippines (FPOP). It has modeled some experimental
programs in specific areas that have been adopted by
the government. Its goals are to provide family planning services, to increase adolescent and male knowledge and responsibility concerning sexuality, and to
defend the individual right to family planning.
Address of FPOP: PO Box 1279, Manila Central Post
Office, Manila 1052, Philippines; telephone: 63 (2)
721 7302, 721 7101, or 722 6466; fax: 63 (2) 721
4067; telex: 63320 ETPPMO PN c/o Eastern Tele;
cable: FPOPHIL MANILA; e-mail: dpop@wpi.
webguest.com.

Population (millions)	75.3
Crude birth rate	30
Total fertility rate	3.7
Women 15–49 using any method of contraception	48 percent
Women 15–49 using modern methods of contraception	30 percent

Poland

In Central Europe, east of Germany, Poland has good
farmland in the plains and central highlands before
reaching the Carpathian Mountains in the south. It has
many mineral resources, and its chemical and ship-
building industries produce jobs but also very polluted
air. A fundamentalist Catholic climate is not conducive
to family planning, so the availability of sex education
is erratic. Contraceptives are available in pharmacies,
but not many people use them. Sixty percent of the
public approve of abortion for social reasons, but
strong Catholic pressure removed that option. The

nongovernmental organization Towarzystwo Rozwoju Rodziny (TRR) in its ten branches and eight counseling centers educates teachers, parents, and youth about sexual health and human reproduction. It espouses reproductive health and sexual rights. It publishes a journal and educational pamphlets, and it provides psychological, legal, and family counseling. Address of TRR: ul. Sewerynow 4, 00-331 Warszawa, Poland; telephone: 4822 828 6191; fax: 4822 828 6192; e-mail: zgtrrw@free.ngo.pl; web: <http://www.waw.pdi.net/~polfedwo>.

Population (millions)	38.7
Crude birth rate	11
Total fertility rate	1.6

Portugal

The Portuguese Republic, which includes the islands of Madeira and the Azores, lies on the Atlantic coast of southwestern Europe. The democratic revolution of 1974 enabled Portugal to change from one of the poorest countries of Europe to a respected member of the European Union. Its economy is based on agriculture, services, and industry. With the revolution came family planning as a human right. Family planning information and sex education are available to all. Contraceptives and abortions are accessible. The Associação para o Planeamento da Família (APF), established in 1967, trains health professionals and youth workers and publishes materials on sexual health. It has a research center and conducts research on adolescent sexual behavior. It also has projects on sexual abuse, prostitutes, and people with disabilities. Telephone of APF: 351 (1) 385 3993; fax: 351 (1) 388 7379; e-mail: apfportugal@mail.telepac.pt; web: <http://www.apf.pt>.

Population (millions)	10
Crude birth rate	11
Total fertility rate	1.4

Romania

A country bordering the Black Sea in southeastern Europe, between Ukraine and Bulgaria, Romania has since 1990 been struggling to recover from the previous communist dictatorship. It has serious political, economic, and social problems, among them the violent treatment of the Romanian gypsies. The government now provides free education and free health care, and, instead of the former criminalization of contraception and abortion, a family planning service is under development. Government services are uneven, but the Societatea de Educatie Contraceptiva si Sexuala (SECS) has created model clinics, trained health personnel, fostered awareness of women's reproductive rights, and produced materials for youth. Telephone of SECS: 40 (1) 411 6661 or 410 1108; fax: 40 (1) 410 1097; e-mail: secs@ starnets.ro.

Population (millions)	22.5
Crude birth rate	10
Total fertility rate	1.3
Women 15–49 using any method of contraception	57 percent
Women 15–49 using modern methods of contraception	14 percent

Russia

An enormous country extending from eastern Europe through the Urals and Far East into Siberia, Russia stretches through eleven time zones that contain mountains, forests, plains, and tundra. It has an educated populace, but since the 1991 collapse of the Soviet Union and the subsequent struggle toward a stable democratic government and a market economy, Russia has had economic and social instability. Since 1955, abortion has been the most common form of birth control. The government supports family planning, and gradually services are becoming available in selective areas. The quality and supply of contraceptives is uneven. The Russian Family Planning Association (RFPA) trains personnel to work with the public, produces informational materials, and educates youth. Telephone of RFPA: 7 (95) 973 1559; fax: 7 (95) 973 1917; e-mail: rfpa@dol.ru.

Population (millions)	146.9
Crude birth rate	8.6
Total fertility rate	1.23
Women 15–49 using any method of contraception	67 percent
Women 15–49 using modern methods of contraception	24.6 percent

Saudi Arabia

A wealthy Middle Eastern country bordering the Red Sea and the Persian Gulf, Saudi Arabia is a dry desert kingdom with more oil reserves than any other country. It is a firmly Muslim country with strong ties to the United States.

Population (millions, 1996 est.)	19.4
Birth rate (1996 est.)	38.32
Total fertility rate (1996 est.)	6.45

Serbia and Montenegro

Serbia and Montenegro in southeast Europe formed a shaky joint state after the breakup of Yugoslavia. There is no affiliation with International Planned Parenthood.

Population (millions, 1996 est.)	10.6
Montenegro	.64
Serbia	10
Birth rate (1996 est.)	
Montenegro	11.86
Serbia	13.98
Total fertility rate (1996 est.)	
Montenegro	1.53
Serbia	2

Somalia

A humid desert country on the Indian Ocean east of Ethiopia, Somalia is a very poor, undeveloped country with few resources. The largely nomadic and seminomadic population raises livestock. Because of ongoing civil war in this country where clans and warlords held power in the past, there is now no government. There is a Somali Family Health Care Association (SFHCA). Address: PO Box 3783, Mogadishu, Somalia; telephone: 252 (1) 22 438; telex: 9099 3785 INTERACT SM; cable: SFHCA, BOX 3430, Mogadishu.

Population (millions)	10.7
Crude birth rate	50
Total fertility rate	7
Women 15–49 giving live birth each year	21 percent

South Africa

On the southern tip of Africa between the Indian and Atlantic Oceans, South Africa is a multiracial country rich in natural resources (gold, coal, diamonds, uranium). Mining, agriculture, and manufacturing are vigorous industries, but the legacy of apartheid leaves unemployment among the 75 percent black majority as a huge problem. Since the dismantling of apartheid, the National Department of Health has tried to give education and services to the whole family. The philosophy is that information and services and privacy are due to all. Safe abortions are available and contraceptive use is the highest in sub-Saharan Africa. The country is wrestling with the rapid spread of HIV/AIDS. Planned Parenthood Association of South Africa (PPASA) has been active since the 1930s, but the new black government is suspicious of nongovernmental organizations. The PPASA is now working to complement government services through training health workers and studying reproductive needs. Its numerous projects include Men as Partners, the New Crossroads Youth Center, and training Lifeskills teachers. Address of PPASA: PO Box 1008, Melville, 2109, South Africa; telephone: 27 (11) 482 4601 or 482 4661; fax: 27 (11) 482 4602 or 331 3412; e-mail: PPASA@WN.APC.ORG; web: <http://www.ppasa.org.za>.

Population (millions)	38.9
Crude birth rate	27
Total fertility rate	3.3
Women 15–49 using any method of contraception	53 percent
Women 15–49 using modern methods of contraception	52 percent

Spain

South of France and between the Atlantic Ocean and the Mediterranean Sea, Spain is a highly urbanized country with a mixed capitalist economy and a 22 percent unemployment rate. There is no stated family planning policy in this strongly Roman Catholic country, and family planning services are not part of the health system. The government has initiated legal means of dealing with wife abusers. Contraceptives are legally available, but abortions are available only under special circumstances. The information and service facilities offered by the Federación de Planificación Familiar de España (FPFE) include advocating reproductive rights for women; setting up youth centers in Barcelona, Madrid, and Santiago; and counseling on abortion and AIDS.

Telephone of FPFE: 34 (1) 319 92 76 or 308 22 86; fax: 34 (1) 308 15 89; e-mail: fpf@adv.es.

Population (millions)	39.4
Crude birth rate	9.0
Total fertility rate	1.2
Women 15–49 using any method of contraception	49 percent
Women 15–49 using modern methods of contraception	69 percent

Sri Lanka

A large island south of India, Sri Lanka is a densely populated agricultural country with citizens from many ethnic and religious backgrounds. An ongoing civil war makes parts of the north and east inaccessible. The government has worked diligently to improve the health and welfare of the citizens, making primary health care available to all and encouraging fewer children per family. It wants to reduce the birth rate even more to decrease poverty and increase the well-being of the people. The average age at marriage is twenty-five, and women, as well as men, can own property, although the society is traditionally male dominated. Infant, child, and maternal mortality are much lower than they were a few decades ago. Abortion is illegal, despite the fact that women in general use only traditional methods of contraception. Except in the north and east of the country, oral contraceptives and condoms are available from community health personnel. The citizenry is served by the network of public health nurses and midwives. The Family Planning Association of Sri Lanka (FPASL) supplements and works with the government health system. The clinic in Colombo offers a wide range of reproductive services, including subfertility counseling, alternative methods of birth control, and retail sales of contraceptives. It has many special projects, especially for youth, and it lobbies political and religious leaders for liberalization of abortion laws. Telephone of FPASL: 94 (1) 58 4153, 58 4157, or 59 4203; fax: 94 (1) 58 0915; cable: FAMPLAN COLOMBO; e-mail: dayafpas@sltt.lk.

Population (millions)	18.9
Crude birth rate	18
Total fertility rate	2.2
Women 15–49 using any method of contraception	66 percent
Women 15–49 using modern methods of contraception	44 percent

Sudan

Sudan is south of Egypt in Northern Africa, bordering the Red Sea. It exists with civil war, unstable government, high inflation, and unfavorable weather. In part because it produces food for a cash crop, it does not have enough food for its population, which is growing because of refugees as well as a high birth rate. Nutritional diseases and epidemics are common.

In family planning matters, the country has only the Sudan Family Planning Association (SFPA), which tries to make the people aware of the social and economic benefits of family planning. It has ninety-three clinics and many community distribution centers. It trains volunteers in order to increase service in remote areas, and it encourages the education and vocational training of women. It resists the female genital mutilation that is common in rural areas. Address of SFPA: PO Box 170, Khartoum, Sudan; telephone: 249 (11) 471095; fax: 249 (11) 471095; telex: (0984) 22069 SHECO SD/2228AMGP; cable: FAMPLAN KHARTOUM SOUTH.

Population (millions)	28.5
Crude birth rate	35
Total fertility rate	5
Women 15–49 using any method of contraception	10 percent
Women 15–49 using modern methods of contraception	7 percent

Syria

On the Mediterranean Sea between Lebanon and Turkey, Syria is a Muslim country deeply involved in the complex politics of the Middle East. The high birth rate and Palestinian refugees increase economic problems. It is an industrialized country with oil, but also with significant soil erosion, water pollution, desertification, and deforestation. The government has no official population policy, but it supports the nongovernmental organizations engaged in family planning activities. The Syrian Family Planning Association (SFPA) has eighteen clinics and forty-seven other outlets for providing education and services. It works with the Women's Union, and it uses mass communication to get its message to the people. Address of SFPA: PO Box 2282, Damascus, Halbouny, Syria; telephone: 963 (11) 223 0871; fax: 963 (11) 222 5676; telex: 0492 412823 SFPASY SY; cable: FAMPLAN DAMASCUS (SYRIA).

Population (millions)	15.6
Crude birth rate	33
Total fertility rate	4.6
Women 15–49 using any method of contraception	40 percent
Women 15–49 using modern methods of contraception	28 percent

Taiwan

Islands of eastern Asia off the southeastern coast of China, Taiwan has an energetic capitalist economy based on industry and foreign trade. There is no recorded affiliation with International Planned Parenthood.

Population (millions, 1996 est.)	21.47
Birth rate (1996 est.)	15.01
Total fertility rate (1996 est.)	1.76

Tanzania

An east African country on the Indian Ocean bordering Mozambique and Kenya, Tanzania has a coastal plain, a central plateau, and inland mountains. Marginal agricultural land, inadequate potable water, deforestation, and desertification make it one of the poorest countries of the world.

AIDS and thousands of Rwandan refugees make much worse its already unfortunate situation. The government has tried to set up a National Family Planning Program, but the numbers of illegal abortions, teenage pregnancies, HIV/AIDS cases, and incidences of domestic violence have increased. The Uzazi na Malezi Bora Tanzania (UMATI) supports the government family planning program, giving counseling and services in various communities, including the refugee community. Address of UMATI: PO Box 1372, Dar-es-Salaam, Tanzania; telephone: 255 (51) 111 638, 111 639, or 125 491; fax: 255 (51) 807 297; telex: 41780 UMATI; cable: UMATI; e-mail: Umati@wilken.dsm.com.

Population (millions)	30.6
Crude birth rate	42
Total fertility rate	5.7
Women 15–49 using any method of contraception	20 percent
Women 15–49 using modern methods of contraception	13 percent

Thailand

Situated in Southeast Asia on the Indo-Chinese peninsula, tropical Thailand is a forward-looking developing country with good natural resources and a strong manufacturing sector. Its vehicles and manufacturing cause air pollution, and its infrastructure is sluggish. A large shift in social patterns, caused in part by government policy, has resulted in lowering the population growth rate to 1.2 percent. There has, of course, also been an increase in unsafe abortions, in unwanted pregnancies, and in sexually transmitted diseases, including HIV/AIDS. The Ministry of Health provides family planning services throughout the country, and the Planned Parenthood Association of Thailand (PPAT) supports them by providing special activities directed to target groups, such as the hill tribes, college students, or slum communities. It also reaches people through its many media programs. Address of PPAT: 8 Soi Vibhavadi-Rangsit 4 Super Highway Ladyao, Chatuchak, Bangkok 10900; telephone: 66 (2) 597 1665; fax: 66 (2) 597 9559; e-mail: ppat@samart.co.th.

Population (millions)	61.1
Crude birth rate	17
Total fertility rate	2
Women 15–49 using any method of contraception	72 percent
Women 15–49 using modern methods of contraception	70 percent

Turkey

A large, ancient country bridging Europe and Asia, the Republic of Turkey borders the Black, the Aegean, and the Mediterranean Seas as well as several European and Asian countries.

Its economy is based on a mixture of modern industry and commerce in the cities and traditional agriculture and crafts in the villages. It is increasingly tied to the economy of Europe. It is almost 100 percent Sunni Muslim. There is no affiliation with International Planned Parenthood.

Population (millions, 1996 est.)	62.48
Birth rate (1996 est.)	22.26
Total fertility rate (1996 est.)	2.58

Uganda

A tropical plateau inside a rim of mountains, Uganda is a landlocked country of eastern Africa, west of

Kenya. Although it has problems with poaching, deforestation, and overgrazing, it has good climate and soil for agriculture, and it has significant deposits of copper, cobalt, limestone, and salt. A very poor country, Uganda subsists through export of coffee and cotton. With a low literacy rate and a high fertility rate, HIV/AIDS is widespread and polygamy and female genital mutilation are common. Ugandans have strong pronatalist attitudes, and they are suspicious of modern contraception. The government, with the help of various nongovernmental organizations, is trying to create a comprehensive family planning program. The Family Planning Association of Uganda (FPAU) works with the government and other nongovernmental organizations to provide quality sexual and reproductive health services. Opposing traditional cultural and political barriers, FPAU promotes the rights of individuals, especially women, to make their own choices concerning reproductive and sexual issues. It has many special programs, including one addressing female genital mutilation and several addressing youth. FPAU runs seventeen permanent clinics and forty-seven outreach clinics. Address of FPAU: PO Box 10746, Kampala, Uganda; telephone: 256 (41) 54 0658 or 54 0665; fax: 256 (41) 54 0657; telex: 61301 SAMPAN/ 61168 FOODBEV; e-mail: Fpau@swiftuganda.com.

Population (millions)	21
Crude birth rate	48
Total fertility rate	6.9
Women 15–49 using any method of contraception	15 percent
Women 15–49 using modern methods of contraception	8 percent

Ukraine

On the Black Sea between Russia and Poland, the Republic of Ukraine is mostly fertile plains and plateaus with some mountains. Meat, milk, grain, and vegetables come from its farms, and it can supply equipment and raw materials to industry. Since the breakup of the Soviet Union, the government has tried to institute reform, but bureaucrats and citizens have resisted. Inflation has been a severe problem. Ukraine has no affiliation with International Planned Parenthood.

Population (millions, 1996 est.)	50.86

Birth rate (1996 est.)	11.17
Total fertility rate (1996 est.)	1.6

United Kingdom

Islands west of France between the North Sea and the North Atlantic Ocean, the United Kingdom (UK) consists of England, Scotland, Wales, Northern Ireland, and some small islands. The UK is highly industrialized, and almost 30 percent of the land is good farmland. A Eurostat study indicates that the UK has more single, poor, less educated mothers than most of the European Union, probably because of immigration from former colonies. Contraceptives are easily available in the UK, and abortion is available up to 24 weeks. The United Kingdom Family Planning Association (UKFPA) does research, as well as the usual information, education, and training. Various publications target special topics, such as sexually transmitted diseases, kinds of contraception, and legal issues. Telephone of UKFPA: 44 (171) 837 5432; fax: 44 (171) 837 3042; e-mail: 1006353. 125@compuserve.com.

Population (millions)	59.1
Crude birth rate	13
Total fertility rate	1.7
Women 15–49 using any method of contraception	72 percent
Women 15–49 using modern methods of contraception	68 percent

United States of America

A large country in North America, the United States stretches east and west from the Atlantic Ocean to the Pacific Ocean, and north and south from Canada to Mexico, and separately it has tropical Hawaii in the Pacific and arctic Alaska west of Canada. It has the most powerful, diverse, advanced economy in the world with the largest per capita income. It is the world leader in technology. However, there is an increasing gap between the rich and the poor; there is growing poverty among many groups, especially unskilled workers; and homelessness and drug abuse are real problems. Despite advanced knowledge of treatment and prevention, the United States has the highest rate of sexually transmitted diseases in the industrialized world. Abortion is legal, but its status is being continually challenged. Forty-four percent of unintended pregnancies end with abortion.

Contraceptives and family planning information are readily available through pharmacies, private doctors, or clinics. The Planned Parenthood Federation of America (PPFA) is pushing for an increase in contraceptive use to alleviate the tension between the proabortion and antiabortion groups. PPFA provides reproductive health care services all over the country in its clinics. A range of services targets the varied communities of the United States. Telephone of PPFA: 1 (212) 541 7800; fax: 1 (212) 245 1845; cable: PARENTHOOD; e-mail: communication@ppfa.org; web: <http://www.plannedparenthood.org>.

Population (millions)	270.2
Crude birth rate	15
Total fertility rate	2
Women 15–49 using any kind of contraception	71 percent
Women 15–49 using modern methods of contraception	68 percent

Uzbekistan
The Republic of Uzbekistan is in central Asia, north of Pakistan. It is mostly sandy desert with dunes and some irrigated river valleys. The Aral Sea is drying up because of chemical pollution and natural salts. Uzbekistan is an important cotton exporter and a significant producer of machinery, chemicals, gold, and natural gas. After the Soviet breakup, Uzbekistan tried to retain tight control of production and prices, but high inflation is forcing the government to introduce some reform. The country has no affiliation with International Planned Parenthood.

Population (millions, 1996 est.)	23.42
Birth rate (1996 est.)	29.86
Total fertility rate (1996 est.)	3.69

Venezuela
A South American country bordering the Caribbean Sea, Venezuela is a land of mountains, plains, highlands, and lowlands. Only 3 percent of the land is arable, but it has considerable resources (petroleum, iron ore, gold, bauxite, diamonds, and hydropower). Venezuela is a developing country that struggles to control inflation and retain the value of its currency. Oil supports the economy. The gap between rich and poor is growing, with 36.3 percent of the people living in extreme poverty. Government family planning programs reach only 14 percent of women of childbearing age, although since the 1970s women have reduced the average number of children from six to three. The government has passed laws to protect women against violence, and, with the United Nations, is educating the public about HIV/AIDS. The Asociacion Civil de Planificacion Familiar (PLAFAM) has three clinics that have clinical, surgical, and educational programs. The educational programs target poverty areas. Address of PLAFAM: Ajparetado 69592, Las Mercedes 1063-A, Caracas, Venezuela; telephone: (582) 693-9358 or 693-5262; fax: (582) 693-9757; e-mail: plafam@etheron.net.

Population (millions)	23.3
Crude birth rate	26
Total fertility rate	3.1
Women 15–19 giving live birth each year	8 percent

Vietnam
The Socialist Republic of Vietnam is a long, narrow country in Southeast Asia between China and Cambodia. Since the Vietnam War, it has attracted foreign capital. Its economy is based in part on exporting crude oil and manufactured goods, but most of the people work in agriculture. Urban expansion and population pressure, however, are reducing the agricultural output. The government encourages women to have only one or two children and aims for a growth rate of 1.7 percent. Abortion is common and sexually transmitted diseases, including HIV/AIDS, are increasing, as is domestic violence. Problems are the traditional preference for male children, the lack of male concern for family planning, and transportation and communication problems in mountainous and rural areas. The Vietnam Family Planning Association (VINAFPA) supports the government by supplying reproductive information and services. Its 914 community distributors reach 311 communities. Address of VINAFPA: 138A Giang vo Street, Hanoi, Vietnam; telephone: 84 (4) 846 1142 or 846 1143; fax: 84 (4) 844 7232; cable: VINAGOFPA; e-mail: vinafpa@netnam.org.vn.

Population (millions)	78.5
Crude birth rate	19
Total fertility rate	2.3

Women 15–49 using any method of contraception	75 percent
Women 15–49 using modern methods of contraception	56 percent

Yemen

A Middle East country on the Arabian Sea between Oman and Saudi Arabia, the Republic of Yemen has moderate oil reserves, fish, rock salt, marble, and some deposits of other minerals. It has high inflation, however, and political subdivisions that hinder positive economic growth. Its large public debt and high population growth block progress. Thirty-six percent unemployment, the illiteracy of three-quarters of the women, and the maternal mortality rate of 1.4 deaths per 1,000 live births demonstrate the need for education and family planning. The government adopted a population policy in 1991. It includes increasing the use of contraceptives and setting up effective family planning and health care. The Yemen Family Care Association (YFCA) has been important in implementing these goals. Since it is the main distributor of services, in both urban and rural areas, it receives support from the government. It supplies contraceptives to forty-five clinics throughout the country, and it lobbies religious and political leaders. In 1997 it started a mobile clinic with a physician, a midwife, and a social worker. Address of YFCA: PO Box 795k Sana'a, Yemen; telephone: 967 (1) 28 81 45 of 27 09 48; fax: 967 (1) 27 09 48; telex: 0895 2965 YFCA YE; cable: FAMPLAN SANA'A.

Population (millions)	15.8
Crude birth rate	44
Total fertility rate	7.3
Women 15–49 using any method of contraception	7 percent
Women 15–49 using modern methods of contraception	6 percent

Zaire

The Republic of Zaire is primarily a tropical low-lying plateau, 3 percent arable, 4 percent meadows and pastures, and 78 percent forest and woodland. Its inhabitants belong to more than 200 ethnic groups, mostly Bantu. It is one of the poorest countries in the world although it has large mineral and agricultural potential. Families survive through subsistence farm-

ing and small trade. Zaire has no affiliation with International Planned Parenthood.

Population (millions, 1996 est.)	46.5
Birth rate (1996 est.)	28.1
Total fertility rate (1996 est.)	6.64

Zimbabwe

Zimbabwe, a landlocked republic north of Botswana and South Africa, is a country of high plateaus and some mountains. With 7 percent arable land and 13 percent meadows and pastures, most of the people work in agriculture, although mining is significant. AIDS, other sexually transmitted diseases, hepatitis, and malaria have caused the life expectancy to drop precipitously. The government established the Zimbabwe National Family Planning Council (ZNFPC) to space children, help with welfare, and limit family size. Supported by International Planned Parenthood, it has thirty-four clinics and a community-based distribution system. Address of ZNFPC: PO Box 220, Harare, Zimbabwe; telephone: 263 (4) 620 281 or 620 285; fax: 263 (4) 620 280; telex: 16521 ZW7.

Population (millions)	11
Crude birth rate	35
Total fertility rate	4.4
Women 15–49 using any method of contraception	48 percent
Women 15–49 using modern methods of contraception	42 percent

Countries under 10 Million Population, by Geographical Area

Africa

Benin

The Republic of Benin in west-central Africa extends north from the Gulf of Guinea and borders Nigeria on the east. It is one of the poorest countries in the world, and less than a fifth of the population has access to health services. Although the government issued a population policy declaration in 1996 ensuring availability of education for everyone and aimed at substantially increasing the life expectancy, dissemination of information about contraceptives is primarily through private clinics (although the University Clinic of Gynecology and Obstetrics offers family planning). To receive family planning, however, women have to be authorized to request it by their husbands, and this, combined with strong religious opposition to such practices, makes it difficult. The major volunteer group is the Association Béninoise pour la Promotion de la Famille (ABPF), which has mounted an educational and information campaign about family planning. Address of ABPF: BP 1486, Cotonou, Benin; telephone: 229 320 049; fax: 229 323 234; telex: 5030 Cotonou (Rp du BENIN).

Population (millions)	6
Crude birth rate	45
Total fertility rate	6.3
Women 15–49 using any method of contraception	16 percent
Women 15–49 using modern methods of contraception	3 percent

Botswana

Botswana adjoins the republic of South Africa on the south and Zimbabwe on the west. There is no official population policy as yet, although the government has committed itself to the provision of voluntary planning services and services have been organized under the Ministry of Health. Since there is a shortage of trained health personnel, nongovernmental organizations assist in providing educational and counseling services. The Botswana Family Welfare Association (BOFWA) distributes nonprescriptive contraceptives and carries out an educational campaign. Telephone for BOFWA: 267 300489; fax: 267 301222; e-mail: bofwa@info.bw.

Population (millions)	1.4
Crude birth rate	33
Total fertility rate	4.3
Women 15–49 using any method of contraception	33 percent
Women 15–49 using modern methods of contraception	32 percent

Burundi

A landlocked central African country bordered by Zaire, Tanzania, and Rwanda, Burundi had to suspend the implementation of its drafted population policy (1993) due to the sociopolitical crisis in the government. In theory, however, family planning services are offered through government health centers and private clinics. All government health centers offer family planning methods. Abortion is illegal except for medical reasons, but many clandestine ones take place. A major group in attempting to provide reproductive health information and services is the Association Burundaise pour le Bien-Etre Familial. Address: BP 5232, Bujumbura, Burundi; telephone: 257 2 25047; fax: 257 2 27617; telex: 5131 MINISANBDI.

Population (millions)	5.5
Crude birth rate	43
Total fertility rate	6.6
Women 15–49 using any method of contraception	9 percent
Women 15–49 using modern methods of contraception	1 percent

Cape Verde

A group of islands off Mauritania in northwestern Africa, Cape Verde has a population growing at the rate of 2.9 percent a year. Associação Caboverdiana para a Protecção da Familia (VerdeFam) is a nongovernmental association concerned with, among other things, family planning. Address: CP 503, Praia, Cape Verde; telephone: 238 61 20 63; fax: 238 61 20 42; e-mail: verdefam@mall.cytelecom.cv.

Population (millions)	0.4
Crude birth rate	36
Total fertility rate	5.3

Central African Republic

Another of the least developed countries in the world, the Central African Republic is in east-central Africa. There is no official government policy on population, and family planning activities are integrated into the Maternal and Child Health Services in health centers located throughout the country. Contraceptive services are supposed to be provided through five regional hospitals, fourteen provincial hospitals, and sixty-five health centers, but few of the rural centers offer family planning services. Women's access to contraceptive service is subject to their husbands' authorization. Large families are still often associated with prestige. The Association Centrafricaine pour le Bien-Etre Familial attempts to assist the government in reducing infant and maternal mortality rates and in providing family planning services in semiurban and rural areas. Address: BP 1366, Bangui, Central African Republic; telephone: 236 61 54 35; fax: 236 61 67 00; telex: 5217 RC.

Population (millions)	3.4
Crude birth rate	38
Total fertility rate	5.1
Women 15–49 using any method of contraception	16 percent
Women 15–49 using modern methods of contraception	4 percent

Chad

A country in east-central Africa, Chad borders Libya on the north and Sudan on the east. An anticontraception law enacted by the French in 1920 was finally rescinded in 1993. The country adopted and promulgated a National Population Policy in July 1994, but the large size of the country, the poor communication infrastructure, and the difficulty of attending health facilities are major impediments to family planning. Complicating the issue is the requirement that the presence of the husband is required to get contraceptive services. Adolescents require authorization from parents or guardians. The Association Tchadienne pour le Bien-Etre Familial is a nongovernmental organization attempting to influence the government policies on sexually transmitted diseases and on contraception. Address: BP 4064, N'Djaména, Chad; telephone: 235 51 43 37 or 235 51 45 48; fax: 235 51 41 83; telex: 1116 KD/5228.

Population (millions)	7.4
Crude birth rate	50
Total fertility rate	6.6
Women 15–49 using any method of contraception	4 percent
Women 15–49 using modern methods of contraception	1 percent

Comoros

Comoros comprises a group of volcanic islands in the North Mozambique Channel between Mozambique and Madagascar that were under French control from 1843 until they became independent. Association Comorienne pour le Bien-Etre de la Famille is a non-

governmental organization concerned with family issues. Address: B 524, Moroni, Comoros; telephone: 269 (73) 5301; fax: 269 (73) 5301.

Population (millions)	0.5
Crude birth rate	37
Total fertility rate	5.1
Women 15–49 using any method of contraception	21 percent
Women 15–49 using modern methods of contraception	11 percent

Congo

Congo is located between Angola and Gabon in western Africa. Family planning is recognized by the Congolese government as one of the eight components of primary health care and is regarded as a fundamental right for every Congolese citizen. Still, pronatalist attitudes are very strong, and poor communication infrastructures, strong male resistance, inadequate understanding of the family planning messages, and the opposition of the Catholic Church are major obstacles to effective family planning. The 1920 French anticontraception law is still on the books (although it is not enforced), and there is a shortage of trained personnel, contraceptives, health facilities, and financial resources.

The nongovernmental organization is the Association Congolaise pour le Bien-Etre Familial, which supports the government's family planning efforts and attempts to provide accurate family planning information to male members of the security forces and to train staff and volunteers in resource mobilization and in program management. Address: BP 945, Brazzaville, Congo; telephone: (242) 815806/ 412523; fax: (242) 815891/815806/ 810330.

Population (millions)	2.7
Crude birth rate	39
Total fertility rate	5.1

Djibouti

Djibouti is surrounded by Somalia, Eritrea, and Ethiopia. Reproductive health was not considered a national priority until well into the 1990s. The first indication of any change was 1991, when the minister of health in a speech stressed the importance of a balanced family, although there were no specific provisions or programmatic policy developed at that time.

In 1999, the government took the first steps to establish programs for maternal and child health, including birth spacing. The Association Djiboutienne pour l'Equilibre et la Promotion de la Famille was founded in 1994 and has since attempted to carry out educational programs on reproductive health and to facilitate access to reproductive and sexual health services. It maintains a close relationship with the Ministry of Public Health and Social Affairs, and in 1997 they joined together to open the first reproductive health clinic. Its postal address is BP 4440, Djibouti, Djibouti; telephone: 253 354 667; fax: 253 353 991; e-mail: adepf@bow.intnet.dj.

Population (millions)	0.7
Crude birth rate	39
Total fertility rate	6.08

Equatorial Guinea

Located in west-central Africa between Cameroon and Gabon, Equatorial Guinea does have a family planning association. Address: Apartado 984, Malabo, Equatorial Guinea; telephone: (240) 94.824; fax: (240) 93.313.

Population (millions)	0.43
Crude birth rate	44
Total fertility rate	5.9

Eritrea

Eritrea is on the Red Sea, east of Sudan and north of Ethiopia. The government is strongly in favor of family planning, but it has been handicapped by war, first fighting to establish its independence from Ethiopia and later by competing factions within the country. It is one of the world's poorest countries. The Planned Parenthood Association of Eritrea, formed in 1992, is practically the only organization providing concerted family planning services. The Ministry of Health is collaborating with UNICEF in a safe motherhood program, and the Ministry of Labor and Human Welfare works closely with the Planned Parenthood Association. It has concentrated much of its resources on training health workers, on sexual and reproductive health needs, and on educational projects. Address of Planned Parenthood Association: PO Box 226, Asmara, Eritrea; telephone: 291 (1) 127 333; fax: 291 (1) 120 194.

Population (millions)	3.4
Crude birth rate	38
Total fertility rate	6.1
Women 15–49 using any method of contraception	8 percent
Women 15–49 using modern methods of contraception	4 percent

Gabon

A small coastal country of western Africa lying on the Equator, Gabon is a former French colony that became an independent republic in 1960. Although the country has serious economic problems, it is better off than most of sub-Saharan Africa because of oil, timber, and manganese. The people are largely Christian (55–75 percent) and animistic. Gabon has problems with deforestation and poaching, but it has a manageable birthrate. It has no organized affiliation with International Planned Parenthood.

Population (millions, 1966 est.)	1.7
Birth rate (1996 est.)	28.2
Total fertility rate (1996 est.)	3.89

Gambia

Gambia, a small tropical country bordering the North Atlantic Ocean, is surrounded by Senegal. The economy in this land of wooded savanna and rainforests depends on peanuts, livestock, and tourism. Gambia's traditional culture values women through their production of babies, especially male babies. Health services are available, but potable water is limited. Government policy is to better the status of women through laws concerning discrimination, minimum age for marriage, inheritance, and records of marriage and divorce. The low literacy rate and difficult terrain make application of these goals challenging. The government increasingly calls on the Gambia Family Planning Association (GFPA) to teach the populace the benefits of family planning. For example, the GFPA connects health with income by teaching members of the family, especially women, skills like sewing and knitting. Another project is getting citizens involved in the social marketing of contraceptives. Address of GFPA: PO Box 325, Kanifing, Banjul, Gambia; telephone: 220 39 1473 or 39 1945; fax: 220 92463; telex: 2290 BOOTH; cable: FAMPLANASS; E-MAIL: gfpa@ggfpp.gm.

Population (millions)	1.2
Crude birth rate	43
Total fertility rate	5.9
Women 15–49 using any method of contraception	12 percent
Women 15–49 using modern methods of contraception	7 percent

Guinea

Guinea borders the Atlantic Ocean in west-central Africa. Contraceptive use is low, although the government has a favorable attitude toward it and works closely with the nongovernmental organization in the field. Abortion is illegal except for therapeutic reasons. Although the government promulgated a National Population Police in 1992, the guidelines for integration of family planning in maternal and child health activities have not yet been issued. The key nongovernmental organization is the Association Guinéenne pour le Bien-Etre Familial. It conducts education campaigns, organizes workshops, maintains family planning service in four health centers, runs a model clinic designed to serve as an educational institution for midwives and others, and also disseminates information. It is attempting to expand its contraceptive services to other clinics. Address: BP 1471, Conakry, Guinea; telephone: (224) 442.363/462.365; fax: (224) 414.321; telex: 23229 AGBEF GE.

Population (millions)	7.5
Crude birth rate	43
Total fertility rate	5.7
Women 15–49 using any method of contraception	2 percent
Women 15–49 using modern methods of contraception	1 percent

Guinea-Bissau

Guinea-Bissau is on the west coast of Africa between Senegal and Guinea. Its population has little knowledge of modern contraception, although traditional methods are widely used. There is little reliable demographic and fertility data. The Associação Guineense para o Bem-Estar Familiar aims to intensify family planning through education and sensitization projects. It also works to persuade the government to initiate family planning programs. It has trained field workers in family planning and is work-ing to provide family planning services to fifty villages throughout the country. Address: Apartado 2, Bissau Codex, 1041, Guinea-Bissau; telephone: 245 22 24 94; fax: 245 22 24 94.

Population (millions)	1.1
Crude birth rate	42
Total fertility rate	5.8

Lesotho

Lesotho is a small, mountainous, agrarian enclave in South Africa. Problems are erosion, unsafe water, and inaccessible services due to mountainous terrain. Male preference, pronatal traditions, and poverty make family planning difficult. The government does, however, support and provide family planning services. Clinics of the Roman Catholic Church provide natural family planning, but the Lesotho Planned Parenthood Association (LPPA) is the country's leader in family planning services. It provides integrated services for women, men, and youth, works to establish gender-sensitive policies in this country that has considered women to be minors, and collaborates with the government and other groups to provide services and education. Address of LPPA: PO Box 340, Masru, 100, Lesotho; telephone: 266 313 645; fax: 266 310 328; telex: 4570 LO.

Population (millions)	2.1
Crude birth rate	33
Total fertility rate	4.3
Women 15–49 using any methods of contraception	23 percent
Women 15–49 using modern methods of contraception	19 percent

Liberia

A western African country on the Atlantic Ocean between Côte d'Ivoire and Sierra Leone, Liberia since 1990 has seemed to be in a perpetual state of civil war, so the largely agricultural economy and government and nongovernment services to inhabitants have been largely nonfunctional and many inhabitants have fled the country. Only about one-third of the populace have access to health care and less than half can get clean water. Before the civil strife, the government, working with the Family Planning Association of Liberia (FPAL), had a national system that provided basic health services with emphasis on maternal and child health. Now, there is low contraceptive use, many illicit abortions with their attendant problems, and rampant HIV/AIDS. The FPAL is trying to set up clinics and services in small communities, to distribute condoms, to publicize gender issues, and to raise money to support these much-needed activities. Address of FPAL: PO Box 938, Monrovia, Liberia; telephone: (231) 227.117; fax: (231) 226.591.

Population (millions)	2.8
Crude birth rate	43
Total fertility rate	6.2
Women 15–49 using any method of contraception	6 percent
Women 15–49 using modern methods of contraception	5 percent

Libya

Libya is a Muslim country on the Mediterranean Sea between Egypt and Tunisia. Its economy is primarily dependent on its oil revenues.

Population (millions, 1996 est.)	5.4
Birth rate (1996 est.)	44.4
Total fertility rate (1996 est)	6.3

Malawi

Located in southern Africa between Zambia and Mozambique, the Republic of Malawi is a landlocked, relatively undeveloped, largely agricultural country that depends on outside assistance to survive. Deforestation and erosion are problems. They do have a National Family Welfare Council. Address: Private Bag 308, Capital City, Lilongwe 3, Malawi; telephone: 265 780 826; fax: 265 744 187; telex: 44361 COMSER MI.

Population (millions)	9.8
Crude birth rate	42
Total fertility rate	5.9
Women 15–49 using any method of contraception	22 percent
Women 15–49 using modern methods of contraception	14 percent

Mauritania

A country on the North Atlantic Ocean bordering Mali and Senegal, Mauritania hosts the Sahara Desert on two-thirds of its land and has dry grasslands in the south. Most people live in the southwest by a tributary of the Senegal River. The government has established a Center for Demography and Social Studies to plan and execute a population program, and other agencies have organized seminars on family planning to push for changes in attitudes. The Association Mauritanienne pour la Promotion de la Famille (AMPF), which opened its first clinic in 1990, takes an active role in educating the public about the advantages of birth spacing and improving the status of women. Address of AMPF: BP 3127, Nouskchott, Mauritania; telephone: 222 (2) 56 078.

Population (millions)	2.5
Crude birth rate	40
Total fertility rate	5.4
Women 15–49 using any kind of contraception	3 percent
Women 15–49 using modern methods of contraception	1 percent

Mauritius

Mauritius is one major and a number of smaller islands of southern Africa in the Indian Ocean east of Madagascar. It has a relatively high standard of living due to the export of labor-intensive manufactured textiles and to tourism. Government policy is to reduce fertility by encouraging use of contraceptives, although abortion is banned. Government and private agencies promote family planning and run clinics. Cultural and religious traditions, however, disapprove of any discussion of sexuality in homes, schools, or media. The Mauritius Family Planning Association (MFPA) promotes the right of each individual to make his or her own choices regarding reproduction and has programs to educate people of all ages. Their programs include education about sexually transmitted diseases and AIDS. Telephone of MFPA: 230 211 4101/4105; fax: 230 208 2397; telex: 4364 MFPA IW 4361; cable: MFPA; e-mail: mfpa@intnet.mu.

Population (millions)	1.2
Crude birth rate	17
Total fertility rate	2
Women 15–49 using any method of contraception	75 percent

Women 15–49 using modern
   methods of contraception   60 percent

Namibia

On the Atlantic Ocean between Angola and South Africa, Namibia was occupied by the apartheid South African regime until 1990, so the new government faced great problems in education and health of the indigenous population. The Ministry of Health and Social Services has been providing some family planning services to the public, but much more is needed, especially because HIV/AIDS is rampant. The Namibia Planned Parenthood Association (NAPPA), established in 1996, has been targeting areas and issues to promote reproductive health. They have raised money and reached out to donor agencies. Address of NAPPA: PO Box 41, Windhoek, Namibia; telephone: 264 (61) 21 7621; fax: 264 (61) 26 2786/21 5590; telex: 724 WK.

Population (millions)	1.6
Crude birth rate	36
Total fertility rate	5.1
Women 15–49 using any method of contraception	29 percent
Women 15–49 using modern methods of contraception	26 percent

Réunion

Réunion is a 2,500-square-kilometer island in southern Africa, east of Madagascar. It is a tropical, mountainous island with some arable land, sugar cane being the most important crop. Being an overseas department of France was an advantage until 1993 when France became part of the European Common Market. There is considerable unrest in Réunion due to high unemployment and the social tensions arising from the large economic gap between the well-to-do white and Indian people and the poor indigenous people. Address of Association Orientation Familiale du Département de la Réunion (AROF): BP 93, St. Denis, 97400, France.

Population (millions)	0.7
Birth rate	24
Total fertility rate	2.72

Rwanda

A landlocked country in central equatorial Africa, Rwanda has the physical conditions for successful agriculture—climate, rainfall, and soil—but the large population has led to deforestation and erosion. Worse, ethnic hostility among the native Hutu, Tutsi, and Twa has led to the death or refugee status of millions of people. The government, with the help of various nongovernmental organizations (the United Nations Children's Fund, the United Nations Population Fund, and the World Health Organization) is trying to resuscitate the health structure by setting up family planning services and educational programs about AIDS prevention. The Association Rwandaise pour le Bien-Etre Familial (ARBEF) promulgates positive information about family planning, helps to facilitate delivery of services, and fosters responsible sexual attitudes among youth. Address of ARBEF: BP 1580, Kigali, Rwanda; telephone: 250 76 127; fax: 250 72 828; telex: 22504.

Population (millions)	8
Crude birth rate	39
Total fertility rate	6
Women 15–49 using any method of contraception	21 percent
Women 15–49 using modern methods of contraception	13 percent

São Tomé and Príncipe

The west African island of São Tomé sits on the Equator. It is a poor country that exists largely on subsistence agriculture. It grows cocoa and coffee for export but has to import food for daily living.

Population (millions)	0.14
Birth rate	34.39
Total fertility rate	4.33

Senegal

On the western coast of Africa, Senegal is a country of rolling hills and tropical climate with five months of rain and seven months of dry weather. Early marriage and polygamy are common in this 92 percent Muslim country. One of the poorest countries in the world, unemployment is about 43 percent, more than half the population are under twenty, and half the women have a child by twenty. The government, which has a population policy and a family planning policy, and various nongovernmental organizations, are trying to implement family well-being and women's development, including banning female genital mutilation. Problems include pronatalist attitudes, polygamist jealousies, a preference for male children, and inadequate distribution and quality of services. The Association Sénégalaise pour le Bien-Etre Familial (ASBEF) is helping the country recognize that family planning can improve the well-being of the populace. Its many endeavors include getting men involved in family planning projects, educating people about HIV/AIDS, and using media for education. Address of ASBEF: BP 6084, Dakar, Senegal; telephone: 221 (8) 245 261 or 245 262; fax: 221 (8) 245 272; telex: 51470 ASBEF SG; e-mail: asbef@telecomplus.sn.

Population (millions)	9.0
Crude birth rate	43
Total fertility rate	5.7
Women 15–49 using any method of contraception	13 percent
Women 15–49 using modern methods of contraception	8 percent

Seychelles

The tropical Seychelles islands of East Africa northeast of Madagascar consist mostly of rocky hills or elevated coral reefs. The economy depends on tourism, farming, fishing, and small-scale manufacturing.

Population (millions)	0.1
Crude birth rate	21
Total fertility rate	2.1
Women 15–49 giving live birth each year	4 percent

Sierra Leone

Sierra Leone, a small country on the western coast of Africa has a tropical savanna climate and about twenty ethnic groups that make their living largely by subsistence farming. Deforestation is a problem, but an even bigger one is the social disorder and displacement caused by the shifting war zones. The government has a population policy focusing on family planning and improving maternal and child health. Large displaced portions of the population living in camps, early sexual activity and marriage, a growing number of HIV/AIDS cases, and Muslim negative views toward family planning are all major problems in Sierra Leone. The Planned Parenthood Association of Sierra Leone (PPASL) supports government efforts in pro-

viding education and services on family planning and reproductive health. It has held workshops and created media presentations of women's issues, childcare, AIDS, family planning, and condoms. Address of PPASL: PO Box 1094, Freetown, Sierra Leone; telephone: 232 (22) 22 27 74; fax: 232 (22) 22 44 39; telex: 3210 (Attn: PPASL).

Population (millions)	4.6
Crude birth rate	49
Total fertility rate	6.5
Women 25–29 giving live birth each year	21 percent

Swaziland

A small monarchy in southeastern Africa almost completely surrounded by South Africa, Swaziland is a mountainous country with considerable natural resources. Most of the Swazi people make their living through subsistence agriculture or livestock, which has resulted in soil depletion and overgrazing. Women must get husbands' approval before using contraceptives, and the culture has a negative attitude toward family planning. Women, always subject to male family members, are pressured to produce male children. The Family Life Association of Swaziland (FLAS) has initiated a high-quality reproductive program especially designed for this culture. It has a skilled staff and dedicated volunteers who encourage the belief in the free choice of individuals in sexual matters. It has a help line, many kinds of education projects, and counseling. One project of FLAS was to distribute information on family planning and AIDS to male industrial workers. Address of FLAS: PO Box 1051; Manzini, Swaziland; telephone: 268 53 586, 53 082, or 53 088; fax: 268 53 191; e-mail: flas@iafrica.sz.

Population (millions)	1
Crude birth rate	43
Total fertility rate	5.6
Women 15–49 using any method of contraception	21 percent
Women 15–49 using modern methods of contraception	19 percent

Togo

Situated on the Gulf of Guinea between Benin and Ghana, Togo is a country with large social, economic, and tribal groups. Its forty ethnic groups live largely through subsistence farming. Two-thirds of the women are illiterate. Only a quarter of the country's many health centers offer any family planning service, but several other organizations give such services. The Association Togolaise pour le Bien-Etre Familial (ATBEF), one such organization, tries to convince leaders, parents, and teachers of the importance of family planning, and it trains volunteers. Address of ATBEF: BP 4056, Lomé, Togo; telephone: 228 21 41 93 or 228 22 06 95; fax: 228 22 02 66; telex: 5046 (Attn. ATBEF); e-mail: atbef@cafe.tg.

Population (millions)	4.9
Crude birth rate	46
Total fertility rate	6.8
Women 15–49 using any method of contraception	12 percent
Women 15–49 using modern methods of contraception	3 percent

Tunisia

On the Mediterranean Sea between Algeria and Libya, Tunisia has a diverse economy based on agriculture, tourism, manufacturing, and mining. The World Bank in 1996 declared Tunisia to be its "best student in the region," and in 1986 it was declared a model for family planning programs and for training personnel from other Arab countries. A balance between economic growth and population growth was achieved by Tunisia. The Association Tunisienne du Planning Familial (ATFP) complements the government program, providing family planning services in rural areas and providing information about sexually transmitted diseases, including AIDS. Telephone of ATPF: 216 (1) 23 2419; fax: 216 (1) 767 263; cable: FAMPLAN TUNIS.

Population (millions)	9.5
Crude birth rate	26
Total fertility rate	3.2
Women 15–49 using any method of contraception	60 percent
Women 15–49 using modern methods of contraception	49 percent

Zambia

Zambia is a landlocked country in southern Africa, east of Angola. An ancient but very poor country, it has more than seventy Bantu-speaking ethnic groups. Copper mining and subsistence agriculture barely sustain them. The government tries to control the high rate of population growth by promulgating family planning methods, but not many women use them, probably because of the low status of women, the wide demand for spousal consent, difficulty of transportation, and the rural belief in large families. More homeless orphans live in Zambia than any other place in the world—90,000 on the streets of Lusaka. The Planned Parenthood Association of Zambia (PPAZ) tries to influence national policies. Its aim is quality reproductive health care for everyone. It puts out information through the media, distributes contraceptives, and trains health workers. Address of PPAZ: PO Box 32221, Lusaka, Zambia; telephone: 260 (1) 228 178 or 220 198; fax: 260 (1) 228 165; telex: 45070, NCRZAM/40293, PLAPAZ ZA; cable: PLAPAZA LUSAKA; e-mail: ppaz@zamnet.zm.

Population (millions)	9.5
Crude birth rate	42
Total fertility rate	6.1
Women 15–49 using any method of contraception	26 percent
Women 15–49 using modern methods of contraception	14 percent

Asia

Armenia

Armenia, a country in southeastern Asia east of Turkey, has a high plateau with mountains and a fertile river valley: about 17 percent is arable and 20 percent is good for meadows and pastures. There are problems with chemical pollution of the soil, with deforestation, and with river pollution. Since the breakdown of the Soviet system, there have been blockade and other difficulties with neighbors, in part because of Armenian nationalism. International Planned Parenthood does not have an affiliate in Armenia.

Population (millions, 1996 est.)	3.46
Birth rate (1996 est.)	16.27
Total fertility rate (1996 est.)	2.06

Azerbaijan

Azerbaijan is a dry steppe country on the Caspian Sea in southwestern Asia. Its considerable petroleum resources, now being developed by Western companies, will aid its transition to a market economy. Azerbaijan is very unsettled because Armenians in the Nagorno-Karabakh section are separatists. There is no International Planned Parenthood affiliation.

Population (millions, 1996 est.)	7.68
Birth rate (1996 est.)	22.28
Total fertility rate (1996 est.)	2.64

Bhutan

Bhutan, a mountainous country with some fertile valleys, lies between China and India in southern Asia. The small, undeveloped economy is based on subsistence agriculture, herding, forestry, and some tourism. The government is concerned with the environment, with cultural traditions, and with social welfare. There is no International Planned Parenthood affiliation.

Population (millions, 1966 est.)	1.82
Birth rate (1966 est.)	38.48
Total fertility rate (1966 est.)	5.33

Georgia

The Republic of Georgia is a mountainous country on the Black Sea between Russia and Turkey. Traditionally, the country's economy has been based on Black Sea tourism, agriculture (citrus fruits, tea, grapes), mining (manganese and copper), and industry (wine, chemicals, machinery, textiles). Civil strife, however, has seriously interfered with the economy. International Planned Parenthood does not have an affiliate there.

Population (millions, 1996 est.)	5.21
Birth rate (1996 est.)	12.81
Total fertility rate (1996 est.)	1.69

Kyrgyzstan

The Republic of Kyrgyzstan in central Asia west of China is situated in the mountains of Tien Shan and its associated valleys. The economy of this poor country depends on cotton, wool, and meat, though it also has some gold, mercury, uranium, and hydropower exports. It has carried out difficult market reforms in its adjustment to the breakup of the Soviet Union. Citizens have had a difficult time. Foreign aid has

helped considerably. Kyrgyzstan is not affiliated with International Planned Parenthood.

Population (millions, 1996 est.)	4.53
Birth rate (1996 est.)	26.02
Total fertility rate (1996 est.)	3.22

Laos

Laos, a country in southeastern Asia, northeast of Thailand, is composed mostly of jagged mountains with some plains and plateaus. Deforestation, soil erosion, and inadequate infrastructure hamper the communist government's attempts to make the country self-sufficient. Private enterprise, encouraged since 1986, has helped the economy. The people live by subsistence agriculture (vegetables, coffee, sugar cane, cotton, animals, opium, marijuana) with some foreign aid. Laos is not affiliated with International Planned Parenthood.

Population (millions, 1996 est.)	5.0
Birth rate (1996 est.)	41.94
Total fertility rate (1996 est.)	5.87

Maldives

Over a thousand islands in twenty-six atolls, the Republic of Maldives lies in the Indian Ocean southwest of India. All the inhabitants live on about two hundred islands, although most live in the capital of Male, and about half the population are under age fifteen. This Muslim country forbids abortion except for medical emergency, and use of any kind of contraception, including condoms, requires a prescription. A fatal blood disease, thalassemia, affects about 20 percent of the population. There are some health workers (at a ratio of about 14,000:1), and the introduction of HIV / AIDS education has made discussion of sexual issues more acceptable. The Society for Health Education (SHE), begun by four women in 1988, is the only nongovernmental organization involved in family planning, and it has a good relationship with the government. SHE is trying to increase services, to educate the populace, and to train more health workers. Telephone of SHE: 960 32 71 17 or 960 31 50 42; fax: 960 32 22 21; e-mail: she8804@dhivehinet.net.mv.

Population (millions)	0.26
Crude birth rate	32

Total fertility rate   6.4
Women 15–49 using any method
   of contraception   15 percent

Mongolia

A landlocked country between China and Russia, Mongolia is a country of extreme climate—hot in summer and cold in winter. Half the population is urban, but most of the rest is seminomadic. Both the market system and the health system are having some difficulties creating a new structure after sixty-five years of dominance by the Soviet Union. During that time abortion and contraception were illegal and women were rewarded for having many children because of the sparse population of the country. Beginning in 1989, contraception and abortion became available, and the large-family policy has been modified by encouragement to space children. Inadequate information and counseling on contraception have led to many cheap, illegal abortions and consequent maternal deaths and chronic health problems. The incidence of sexually transmitted diseases is increasing.

There is an active nongovernmental organization— the Mongolian Family Welfare Association (MFWA). It cooperates with the government to provide family planning services and information in selected areas throughout the country. It has trained thousands of volunteers. Address of MFWA: Chingeltei Duureg, 6-r Khooroolol, 5-r Khoroo, Build 7, Room 41, Ulaanbaatar, Mongolia; telephone: 9761 313514; fax: 9761 369244; e-mail: monpf@old.magicnet.mn.

Population (millions)   2.4
Crude birth rate   24
Total fertility rate   3.1
Women 15–49 using any method
   of contraception   57 percent
Women 15–49 used modern
   methods of contraception   41 percent

Singapore

Singapore's geographical location between Malaysia and Indonesia on main trade routes helps these islands thrive commercially, and consequently the main island is very densely populated. The government's family planning program, adopted when its two-child norm failed to reduce the population, is selectively "three or more if you can afford it." The Ministry of Health pro-

vides services for the whole population, and abortion is accessible. The Singapore Planned Parenthood Association (SPPA), the only nongovernmental organization engaged in family planning, focuses on educating the public about reproductive health issues. A special project has been the reproductive health of handicapped persons. Address of SPPA: Block 3A, Holland Close, #01-55, Singapore 272 003; telephone: 65 775 8981; fax: 65 776 8296; e-mail: sppassn@singnet.com.sg.

Population (millions)   3.9
Crude birth rate   15
Total fertility rate   1.7
Women 15–49 using any method
   of birth control   65 percent

Tajikistan

A country in central Asia, next to China, the Republic of Tajikistan is a land of mountains and valleys. It is also a land of civil conflict, caused by deep regional, religious, and clan-based differences. It has inadequate potable water and inadequate sanitation facilities. Most of the people farm, but the standard of living is low, and the birth rate is high. The country is dependent on foreign aid. It is not affiliated with International Planned Parenthood.

Population (millions, 1996 est.)   5.92
Birth rate (1996 est.)   33.78
Total fertility rate (1996 est.)   4.38

Turkmenistan

Turkmenistan borders the Caspian Sea, lying between Kazakstan and Iran. Flat to rolling sand in the north rising to mountains in the south means it has meadows and pastures but little arable land, and the land is polluted with chemicals. It is an important world producer of cotton. The promise of its immense petroleum reserves has not been fulfilled because of a tribal social structure, an authoritarian regime, and the inability of its formerly Soviet customers to pay for oil. Turkmenistan has no affiliation with International Planned Parenthood.

Population (millions, 1996 est.)   4.15
Birth rate (1996 est.)   29.12
Total fertility rate (1996 est.)   3.62

Caribbean Islands

Anguilla

Anguilla is a small island of the lesser Antilles. It has a low population growth rate and a low infant mortality rate but a high adolescent pregnancy rate. The government has a national family planning program that provides family planning in conjunction with maternal and child health care in all government clinics. Abortion is illegal unless there is a risk to the life or the physical or mental health of the mother. There is also the Anguilla Family Planning Association (AFPA) staffed by volunteers, which assists the government by providing contraceptives and clinical supplies. Address of AFPA: PO Box 168, The Valley, Anguilla; telephone: 1 (264) 497 2702; fax: 1 (264) 497 2050; telex: 3179329 IDMITCH LA; e-mail: mitchellm @anguillanet.com.

Population (millions, in 1966)	10.4
Birthrate (1996)	17.8

Antigua and Barbuda

Antigua and its dependency Barbuda are islands in the Lesser Antilles. In 1984, the government began providing family planning services free of charge in all its maternal and child health clinics, although adolescents cannot receive family planning services without parental consent. In addition, the Antigua Planned Parenthood Association maintains a clinic at its headquarters. Voluntary sterilization is performed by private clinics or in government hospitals but not by the association. It has concentrated much of its attention in recent years on meeting the needs of adolescents. Address: PO Box 419, St. John's, Antigua and Barbuda; telephone: 1 (268) 462 0947; fax: l c/o C&W (268) 462 1187; cable: FAMPLAN.

Population (millions)	0.1
Crude birth rate	17
Total fertility rate	1.7
Women 15–49 using contraceptives of any kind	53 percent
Women 15–49 using modern methods of contraception	51 percent

Aruba

Aruba is next to the Antilles in the eastern Caribbean. The government does not have an explicit population policy, but it supports family planning and provides the Foundation for the Promotion of Responsible Parenthood (FPRP) with the majority of its total budget. Contraceptive prescriptions or devices are not included in the free services given by the government, and FPRP attempts to meet this need through cooperating physicians and clinics. The most widely used methods of contraception are oral contraceptives and condoms. Also used are injectables and intrauterine devices; 5.7 percent of couples have chosen sterilization. Address of FDRP: PO Box 2256, San Nicolaas, Aruba; telephone: 297 (8) 48 833 ext. 219, 220, 225; fax: 297 (8) 41 107; e-mail: arfamplan@setarnet.aw.

Population (millions)	0.08
Crude birth rate	17
Total fertility rate	6.8

Bahamas

The Bahamas are Caribbean islands just southeast of Florida. In 1995 the government announced that it intended to implement a national family planning program, and as a result such services are provided at the public hospital, at seven government satellite clinics, and through private clinics. Abortion is illegal except when there is a risk of life and health of the mother or fetus, or in the case of rape. Helping to extend services is the Bahamas Family Planning Association, which offers counseling, Pap smears, contraceptives, HIV/AIDS counseling, medical services, and Norplant insertions and removals. It works with the government to provide family planning in clinics of fifteen of the islands in the Bahamas archipelago. Address: PO Box N-9071, Nassau, Bahamas; telephone: 1 (242) 325 1663 or 1 (242) 323 6338; fax: 1 (242) 325 4886; e-mail: bahfpa@bateinet.bs.

Population (millions)	0.3
Crude birth rate	23
Total fertility rate	2
Women 15–49 using contraception (all methods)	65 percent
Women 15–49 using modern methods of contraception	63 percent

Barbados

The government of Barbados in the eastern Caribbean fully supports family planning and assists the Barbados Family Planning Association (BFPA) by providing approximately 60 percent of its budget, as well as by tax concessions, rent-free premises, and free access to all government institutions. Family planning services were established in all public clinics between 1993 and 1995. In an effort to reduce teenage pregnancy and child abuse, the government provides clinic-based family life education and school outreach programs. Abortion is available under certain medical regulations included within the Medical Termination of Pregnancy Act. The Barbados Family Planning Association was founded in 1954 and, in addition to working with government clinics, it has eighty-one community delivery centers around the country to increase access to family planning. Currently 55 percent of women of childbearing age use some form of contraceptive. Telephone: 1 (246) 426 0271 or 1 (246) 426 2027; fax: 1 (246) 427 6611; telex: FAMPLAN.

Population (millions)	0.3
Crude birth rate	14
Total fertility rate	1.7
Women 15–49 using contraception (all methods)	55 percent
Women 15–49 using modern methods of contraception	53 percent

Bermuda

Bermuda is a group of islands in the Atlantic east of North Carolina. The government began providing family planning services in 1937 and continues to maintain most of the clinical family planning services. Some services are offered by physicians and pharmacies. Abortion is illegal except on therapeutic grounds. Closely linked to the department of health is the Teen Services, which is also affiliated with the Caribbean Family Planning Association. Address: PO Box HM 1324, HM FX Hamilton, Bermuda; telephone: 1 (441) 292 4598; fax: 1 (441) 295 7164.

Population 1998 (millions)	0.06
Crude birth rate	14.92
Total fertility rate	1.79

Dominica

Dominica, an independent republic within the British commonwealth, lies halfway between Puerto Rico and Trinidad in the Caribbean Sea. The government,

since 1984, has provided contraceptive service through approximately fifty health centers across the country. Aiding and cooperating with the government program is the Dominica Planned Parenthood Association (DPPA), founded in 1976. For many years the DPPA provided mainly information and education to support the government's clinical services, but it also operates a clinic in Roseau, the capital. The most popular contraceptive methods are pills (58 percent) and injectables (34 percent). Teenage pregnancy has been declining from a high of 20 percent of all births in 1992, but it still remains high and the DPPA has adopted this area as one of its priorities. Address of DPPA: PO Box 247, Roseau, Dominica; telephone: 1 (767) 448 4043; fax: 1 (767) 448 0991; e-mail: dppa@cwdom.dm.

Population (millions)	0.1
Crude birth rate	19
Total fertility rate	2
Women 15–49 using any method of contraception	50 percent
Women 15–49 using modern methods of contraception	48 percent

Dominican Republic

The Dominican Republic shares the Caribbean island of Hispaniola with Haiti. Infant mortality is high, and in 1999, 41 percent of the children hospitalized had malnutrition. There is a high rate of teenage pregnancy. The government supports family planning and has established a number of policies and programs to lower the fertility level, but it has lacked the funds to carry out many of them. This has left the Asociación Dominicana Pro-Bienestar de la Familia to take greater responsibility for family planning. PROFAMILIA, as it is called, runs three urban clinics that provide prenatal and infant care, laboratory tests, contraceptives, voluntary sterilization, and infertility counseling and provides technical assistance and contraceptives to one hundred private clinics. Contraceptives are available at subsidized prices in pharmacies and other stores, and as the price of the contraceptives have dropped, their use has increased. Address of PROFAMILIA: Apartado 1053, Santo Domingo, Dominican Republic; telephone: 1 (809) 689 0141 or 1 (809) 689 4209; fax: 1 (809) 686 8276; telex: (326) 4112 SDGTXDR; cable: DOMBIEFA; e-mail: profamilia@codetel.net.do.

Population (millions)	8.3
Crude birth rate	27
Total fertility rate	3.2
Women 15–49 using any method of contraception	64 percent
Women 15–59 using modern methods of contraception	59 percent

Grenada

In Grenada, the most southerly Windward Island in the Lesser Antilles, 90 percent of the citizens have a knowledge of contraceptives. The government supports family planning as an essential component of maternal and child health care. A population council has been established to implement this policy, and family planning services are provided at no cost to the client at government health science stations. The Grenada Planned Parenthood Association, founded in 1964, works in close association with the government. It operates three clinics that also offer comprehensive reproductive health services and counseling. However, it charges a small fee for its services and supplies. It also operates thirteen contraceptive retail sales outlets and carries out public information and educational campaigns. Abortion is illegal unless the life of the mother is at risk. Postal address: PO Box 127, St. George's, Grenada; telephone: 1 (473) 440 3441 or 1 (473) 440 2636; fax: 1 (473) 440 8071; cable: GPPA.

Population (millions)	0.1
Crude birth rate	20
Total fertility rate	3.8
Women 15–49 using any method of contraception	54 percent
Women 15–49 using modern methods of contraception	49 percent

Guadeloupe

Guadeloupe is a chain of seven small islands southeast of Puerto Rico in the eastern Caribbean Sea. The government supports family planning, sex education, and women's development. Access to family planning, including minors, is guaranteed by law. The most popular contraceptive method is the pill. Abortion upon request is given on social, economic, therapeutic, and medical grounds. The Association Guadeloupéenne pour le Planning Familial (AGPF) was the sole provider of family planning for a decade

until the government became involved in 1975. The AGPF continues to provide family planning services in its clinics, and it conducts information and education activities in family planning and cooperates fully with the government. Address of AGPF: BP 134, Cédex, Pointe-à-Pitre, Guadeloupe; telephone: 590 82 2978; 590 82 1712; fax: 590 91 5988.

Population (millions)	0.4
Crude birth rate	18
Total fertility rate	2
Women 15–49 using any method of contraception (estimated)	50–55 percent

Haiti

Haiti, which shares the Caribbean island of Hispaniola with the Dominican Republic, has the highest maternal mortality rate in the Western Hemisphere. Eighty percent of the population lives below absolute poverty standards. The Association pour la Promotion de la Famille Haïtienne (PROFAMIL) and other nongovernmental organizations have made inroads in educating women about modern contraceptives, but the growth rates of sexually transmitted diseases, tuberculosis, malaria, and AIDS are high. PROFAMIL gives training, awareness workshops, and talks to community leaders and runs a daily clinic for men in Port-au-Prince. Address of PROFAMIL: Delmas 31, Rue Edmond La Forest #8, Boîte Postale 1493, Port-au-Prince, Haiti; telephone: 509 (2) 490 149; fax: 509 (2) 490 149.

Population (millions)	7.5
Crude birth rate	34
Total fertility rate	4.8
Women 15–49 using any kind of contraception	18 percent
Women 15–49 using modern methods of contraception	14 percent

Jamaica

A Caribbean country in the Greater Antilles, Jamaica has a high unemployment rate and a population with almost half the households headed by single women. The National Family Planning Board strongly supports family planning, providing clinical services and education. The pill is the most common contraceptive, and female sterilization is common. Abortion is available, but unsanitary conditions often result in complications. The Jamaica Family Planning Association (JFPA), founded in 1957, led the way in family planning services, helping to set up the government program and providing services to outlying communities. Since cultural norms accept male promiscuity, JFPA has focused on teaching safe sex to women and has worked for male involvement by educating its drivers and by setting up condom distribution points in rural areas. Address of JFPA: PO Box 92, St. Ann's Bay, Jamaica; telephone: 1 (876) 972 2515 or 1 (876) 972 0260; fax: 1 (876) 972 2224; cable: JFPA; e-mail: FAMPLAN@cwjamaica.com.

Population (millions)	2.6
Crude birth rate	23
Total fertility rate	3
Women 15–49 using any kind of contraception	66 percent
Women 15–49 using modern methods of contraception	60 percent

Martinique

A French colony for almost three hundred years, Martinique was an overseas department of France from 1945 to 1993, when the European Common Market dulled the advantages of being a department. The government has five clinics that provide plentiful maternal and child care. Women can get legal abortions up to eight weeks. With the support of the government, family planning is provided by the Association Martiniquaise pour l'Information et l'Orientation Familiales (AMIOF). It gives sex education in the schools, distributes family planning information through radio and television, and runs contraception clinics. Telephone of AMIOF: 596 714 601; fax: 596 715 682.

Population (millions)	0.4
Crude birth rate	15
Total fertility rate	1.7

Netherlands Antilles

The Netherlands Antilles, composed of two island groups, is an autonomous part of the Kingdom of the Netherlands. Curaçao, the administrative center, and Bonaire are north of Venezuela, and Dutch St. Maarten, St. Eustatius, and Saba are east of the Virgin Islands. The Foundation for the Promotion of Responsible Parenthood (FRPR) (in Dutch, Stichting

tot Bevordering van Verantwoord Ouderschap) provides information and services about family planning through its clinics and in cooperation with the government in other clinics. Abortion is legal. There is a problem with teenage pregnancy that accounts for a disproportionate number of abortions. Address: PO Box 308, Curaçao, Netherlands Antilles; Telephone: 599 (9) 461 1323 or 599 (9) 461 1487; fax: 599 (9) 461 1024.

Population (millions)	0.2
Crude birth rate	19
Total fertility rate	2.2

Puerto Rico

A Caribbean Island east of the Dominican Republic, Puerto Rico is a commonwealth of the United States, which means that Washington controls finance, defense, currency, and foreign relations. The economy depends on tourism, agriculture, and the manufacture of pharmaceuticals and alcoholic beverages. Puerto Ricans are U.S. citizens, so many emigrate to the mainland because of the poverty and high unemployment rate. AIDS is a serious problem because of multiple sex partners by both men and women, because most people do not use safe sex, because of multiple use of drug needles, and because of perinatal transmission. The Ministry of Education teaches physiology, but does not teach anything about attitudes toward sex and gender. The large number of people living at the poverty level have no public access to family planning services. PROFAMILIA (Asociación Puertorriqueña Pro-Bienestar de la Familia) was the first family planning organization in the Western Hemisphere. It provides education and services to low-income people, a telephone hotline for adolescents, and training programs for professionals. Address of PROFAMILIA: Apartado Postal 192221, 000919-2221, San Juan, Puerto Rico; telephone: 1 (787) 767 960 or 765 7373; fax: 1 (787) 766 6920; e-mail: profampr@mailhost.tid.net.

Population (millions)	3.9
Crude birth rate	18
Total fertility rate	2.1

St. Kitts and Nevis

St. Kitts and Nevis, two wet, tropical, hilly islands in the Windward Islands of the Lesser Antilles, have a growing tourist industry and, for the Caribbean, a low unemployment rate. The government is encouraging people to grow more agricultural products than sugar cane so that the need for imports will be reduced. Because of male emigration, almost half the households with children under fifteen are headed by women. Multiple sexual relationships seems to be a cultural pattern, so siblings in the same household likely have different fathers. Teen pregnancy is a major problem. The government has tried to alleviate some of the health and social problems through offering family planning services. A nongovernmental family planning association, St. Kitts Family Life Services Association (SKFLSA), is active on each island. Address: PO Box 358, Basseterre, St. Kitts and Nevis; telephone: 1 (869) 465 2918; fax: 1 (869) 465 7657.

Population (millions)	0.04
Crude birth rate	19
Total fertility rate	2.6

St. Lucia

The east Caribbean island of St. Lucia, independent from Great Britain since 1979, has an economy dependent on agriculture (especially bananas), tourism, and foreign aid. Of the total population, 25 percent live in poverty. The cultural attitude toward marriage is significant: Single mothers head 40 percent of households, and 83 percent of babies are born to unmarried mothers. The infant mortality rate and the fertility rate have been dropping, but the fertility rate among teenagers is still above 80 per 1,000 population. Community health nurses are the primary provider of reproductive health services. In a 1991 study, the National Population Council indicated that the country needs to provide more jobs and education for teenagers. The dominant Roman Catholic Church strongly discourages modern methods of family planning. Clinical and nonclinical information and services are available to all through the Santa Lucia Planned Parenthood Association (SLPPA). It provides services in shops and factories and also disseminates information through various media. They even have trained facilitators who conduct group dialogues about reproductive and sexual concerns. Telephone of SLPPA: 1 (758) 453 7284 or 452 4335; fax: 1 (758) 453 7284; cable: PARENTHOOD.

Population (millions)	0.1

Crude birth rate	25
Total fertility rate	2.7
Women 15–49 using any method of contraception	47 percent
Women 15–49 using modern methods of contraception	46 percent

St. Vincent and the Grenadines

Income for St. Vincent and the Grenadines, Caribbean islands north of Trinidad, comes from agriculture and tourism. The poverty level of 41.9 percent is largely due to underemployment. Twenty-two percent of births occur to teenagers. The government has established a population policy and a family life education program, but the family planning activities are inadequate. Cooperating with the government, the St. Vincent Planned Parenthood Association (SVPPA) provides education for the public and also operates a family planning clinic. The education program includes classes in public schools, media presentations, postpartum talks with new mothers, and staff members' conversations with people at factories, clubs, and churches. Address of SVPPA: PO Box 90, Kingstown, St. Vincent and the Grenadines; telephone: 1 (809) 456 1793; fax: 1 (809) 457 2738; cable: VINPLAN.

Population (millions)	0.1
Crude birth rate	22
Total fertility rate	2.4
Women 15–49 using any method of contraception	58 percent
Women 15–49 using modern methods of contraception	55 percent

Trinidad and Tobago

Trinidad and Tobago, Caribbean islands northeast of Venezuela, have a relatively advanced economy based on crude and refined oil, but they also have income from manufacturing, from agriculture, and from tourism. They have problems with water, air, and oil pollution. The people, who are primarily of African or East Indian descent, accept family planning and are familiar with contraceptives. The Family Planning Association of Trinidad and Tobago (FPATT) provides full reproductive health services in three clinics, including Pap smears, breast and pelvic examinations, contraceptives, voluntary sterilization, and prostate examinations. It uses media to try to get its contraceptive message to youth. Telephone of FPATT: 1 (868) 625 6533, 623 4764, or 627 6732; fax: 1 (868) 625 2256; cable: PLANFAM; e-mail: fpattrep@wow.net.

Population (millions)	1.3
Crude birth rate	14
Total fertility rate	1.9
Women 15–49 using any method of contraception	53 percent
Women 15–49 using modern methods of contraception	44 percent

Europe

Albania

Albania is on the Adriatic Sea in southeastern Europe. The Family Planning Association of Albania was founded in 1992 to combat what had been a strong pronatalist policy, one result of which was that Albania had the highest infant and maternal mortality rates in the world. Following the foundation of the Family Planning Association of Albania, the Ministry of Health began to integrate family planning services in the 165 women's and maternity centers. The State Secretariat for Women and Youth also came out in support of family planning. Nonprescriptive contraceptives are available in pharmacies at regulated prices. First-trimester abortion on request is legal. There remains considerable opposition to family planning, but nonetheless there have been significant reductions in maternal and infant mortality as well as increased contraceptive use. Address of the Family Planning Association of Albania: Rr. "Marsel Kashen," pallatet e Lanes, Pall. 1, Shk 1 Ap. 1, Tirana, Albania; telephone: +355 42 26256; fax: +355 42 24269; e-mail: postmaster@fpa.tirana.al.

Population (millions)	3.3
Crude birth rate	17
Total fertility rate	2

Austria

In Austria, a country in central Europe, family planning services are funded by the Ministry of Family Affairs, and contraceptives are widely available from general practitioners. About three hundred family and partner counseling centers are run by different groups, ranging from conservative to feminist, and some offer contraceptive services. First-trimester abortion on request is legal. Not all areas of the country provide equal access to services, since there is strong opposition in some.

Österreichische Gesellschaft für Familienplanung runs six clinics in Vienna and one in Lower Austria specializing in fertility regulation services, mainly for young people, migrants, and people with disabilities. It also lobbies for more effective planning services and counseling. Address: Postfach 125, Vienna, 1183, Austria; telephone: 43 (1) 478 5242; fax: 43 (1) 478 5242 22; e-mail: e.pracht@oegf.at.

Population (millions)	8.1
Crude birth rate	11
Total fertility rate	1.4
Women 15–49 using contraception (all methods)	71 percent

Bosnia and Herzegovina

Bosnia and Herzegovina, two parts of the former Yugoslavia, formed the Croat Federation of Bosnia and Herzegovina in 1994. It has considerable natural resources, but many problems: the warring factions created many casualties and displacement of people and destroyed much infrastructure; in addition, this area has much air pollution and is subject to earthquakes. International Planned Parenthood has no organized subsidiary there.

Population (millions, 1996)	2.7
Population growth rate (1966 est.)	2.84
Birth rate	6.34
Total fertility rate	1.0

Bulgaria

Bulgaria, located in southeastern Europe on the Balkan peninsula, provides family planning services in health centers and hospitals as well as in nongovernmental clinics. Contraceptives are available, but in irregular supply. First-trimester abortion on request is legal, provided it takes place in a state medical institution. The advocacy, information, and education body in Bulgaria is the Bulgarian Family Planning and Sexual Health Association (BFPA). It runs comprehensive sexual and reproductive health care clinics in Sofia and has eight branches. Telephone: 359 (2) 943 3052; fax: 359 (2) 943 3710; e-mail: bfpa@online.bg.

Population (millions)	8.3
Crude birth rate	9
Total fertility rate	1.2
Women 15–49 using any method	
of contraception	76 percent

Croatia

A prosperous and industrialized part of the former Yugoslavia, Croatia now has many problems resulting from the war and the previous communist inefficiency: large numbers of refugees, a severely damaged infrastructure, a large foreign debt, and upheaval of the old trade patterns. International Planned Parenthood has no organized subsidiary there.

Population (millions, 1996 est.)	5.0
Population growth rate (1996 est.)	0.58
Birth rate (1996 est.)	9.83
Total fertility rate (1996 est.)	1.4

Denmark

Denmark lies in northern Europe north of Germany. Couples there increasingly take the option of living together rather than marrying. Still, marriage between people of the same sex has been authorized by law since 1989. Divorce also is increasingly common. Family planning services are integrated in the national health service, with responsibility for service delivery assigned to county clinics and local general practitioners. Information on contraception is distributed by the Ministry of Health through the family planning association (Foreningen Sex og Samfund) and the Health Information Committee. School sex education has been obligatory since 1970 and was integrated into health education in 1991. First-trimester abortion on request is legal.

The Foreningen Sex og Samfund is the leading association in Denmark in the field of sex and reproductive health. It has been a longstanding advocate of quality sex education for all the population. It is recognized by the government as a partner in issues related to sexual and reproductive rights. The Ministry of Health funds family planning information on contraception, and its clinics are supported by local governments. The association runs a counseling helpline, Sexlinien, for young people. Telephone: 45 (33) 93 10 10; fax: 45 (33) 93 10 09; e-mail: danish-fpa@sexogsamfund.dk; web: <http://www.sexlinien.dk> and <http://www.sexogsamfund.dk>.

Population (millions)	5.3
Crude birth rate	13
Total fertility rate	1.8
Women 15–49 using any	
contraceptive	78 percent
Women 15–49 using modern	
methods of contraception	71 percent

Estonia

In eastern Europe bordering the Baltic Sea, Estonia has had successful economic growth after bottoming out in 1993. The International Planned Parenthood country file is currently being updated.

Population (millions, 1966 est.)	1.5
Population growth rate (1966 est.)	1.1
Birth rate (1966 est.)	10.7
Total fertility rate (1966 est.)	1.55

Finland

Finland lies in northern Europe between Sweden and Russia. The government supports family planning. Service is an integral part of the primary health care system, which involves general practitioners, nurses, and the schools. Contraceptives are widely available and used. Oral contraceptives and intrauterine devices are the most popular methods. First-trimester abortion on request is legal. The abortion rate per 1,000 live births in 1999 was 172. The abortion rate per 1,000 women under age twenty is 9.6. The government, through the Department of International Development Cooperation, supports family planning and reproductive health programs internationally. Sex education is provided in the schools.

The Family Federation of Finland (Väestöliitto), founded in 1941, is a central organization of twenty-six organizations in the fields of health, social affairs, and research. It offers counseling, does research on a range of population and family issues, and serves as an advocacy group. Address: PO Box 849, Helsinki 00101, Finland; telephone: 358 (9) 228 050; fax: 358 (9) 612 1211; e-mail: jouko.hulkko@vaestoliitto.fi; web: <http://www.vaestoliitto.fi>.

Population (millions)	5.2
Crude birth rate	12
Total fertility rate	1.7

Iceland

Lying just south of the Arctic Circle, the island nation of Iceland is the westernmost state of Europe. Family planning services and contraceptives are available, and sex education is provided from primary school age. The age of sexual consent is 14, and the average age of first sexual intercourse is 15.4. The Icelandic Association for Sexual and Reproductive Health (IcASRH) focuses on young people, providing lectures and hosting discussion groups. Address: PO Box 7226, Reykjavik, 127, Iceland; telephone: 354 (5) 69 4980; fax: 354 (5) 69 4963.

Population (millions)	0.3
Crude birth rate	15
Total fertility rate	2

Ireland

A Roman Catholic country in the British Isles, Ireland has some family planning services available, although it has no official policy. Pharmacies carry contraceptives, and women can legally travel to the United Kingdom for abortions. Active "pro-life" groups oppose family planning. The pro-choice Irish Family Planning Association (IFPA) provides contraceptives and some counseling, and it also trains nurses to counsel women about making their own choices about sexual and reproductive health. In addition, it has a telephone hotline for young people. Telephone: 353 (1) 878 0366 or 353 (1) 872 5394; fax: 353 (1) 878 0375; e-mail: ifpa@iol.ie; web: <http://www.ifpa.ie>.

Population (millions)	3.7
Crude birth rate	14
Total fertility rate	1.9

Latvia

A small European country on the Baltic Sea between Estonia and Lithuania, Latvia has four distinct ethnic regions, strong folk traditions, and a negative birth rate. Health education is taught in about a third of the schools. There is a national reproductive health program, and the quality of contraceptives and health care is improving. The Latvian Association for Family Planning and Sexual Health (LAFPSH) has active education and training programs that focus especially on advising and training young people. Telephone of LAFPSH: 371 724 2700 fax: 371 782 0605; e-mail:

ifpa@mailbox.riga.lv;   web: <http://www.papardeszieds.lv>.

Population (millions)	2.4
Crude birth rate	8
Total fertility rate	1.2

Lithuania

The Baltic state of Lithuania, lying between Latvia and Russia, has thousands of lakes and streams but an increasing amount of pollution. The strong Roman Catholic religion, the high abortion rate, and the negative population growth have made the country resistant to family planning and sex education. The Family Planning and Sexual Health Association of Lithuania (FPSHA) has given classes for health personnel and published newsletters and pamphlets on contraception and reproductive rights. Telephone of FPSHA: 370 (2) 79 03 19 or 73 16 30; fax: 370 (2) 79 03 19; e-mail: lithfpa@puni.osf.lt.

Population (millions)	3.7
Crude birth rate	11.
Total fertility rate	1.4
Women 15–49 using any method of contraception	20 percent

Luxembourg

Located in western Europe between France and Germany, the Grand Duchy of Luxembourg has a female Minister of Family Welfare who is actively promoting the equality of women and the protection of women from violence. The independent Mouvement Luxembourgeois pour le Planning Familial et l'Education Sexuelle (MLPFES) has concentrated on individual counseling and on working with other organizations. Telephone of MLPFES: 352 48 59 76; fax: 352 40 02 14.

Population (millions)	0.4
Crude birth rate	14
Total fertility rate	1.8

Macedonia

Landlocked and mountainous, Macedonia was the poorest republic of the former Yugoslavia, and it is still relatively undeveloped. It does produce enough food and coal to fill its own needs. International

Planned Parenthood has no organized subsidiary there.

Population (millions, 1996 est.)	2.1
Population growth rate (1996 est.)	0.46
Birth rate (1996 est.)	13.3
Total fertility rate (1996 est.)	1.8

Moldova

A landlocked east European country northeast of Romania, Moldova has an economy based largely on agriculture and livestock. The rich soil is countered by the bacterial or chemical pollution of the water. The country is poor, and though health services for women and contraception are legal, most people cannot afford them and not much is even available; consequently, sexually transmitted diseases and first-trimester abortions are common. A national family planning program is being developed, and the Family Planning Association of Moldova (FPAM) is trying to educate the public, especially teachers, parents, and psychologists. Telephone of FPAM: 373 (2) 54 12 07; fax: 373 (2) 54 12 08; telex: 373 2 233 425; cable: D.Pitzini UNDP; e-mail: fpam@cri.md.

Population (millions)	4.2
Crude birth rate	12
Total fertility rate	1.8
Women 15–49 using any method of contraception	22 percent

Norway

Most of the population of mountainous Norway, which includes the largest glacial field in Europe, live in the south around Oslo. One-third of the country's revenue comes from North Sea oil. Family planning, in which fathers participate as much as mothers, is an integral part of life in Norway. Paid maternity/paternity leave is routine, and free family health care, including contraceptives and abortions, is available. Given the extensive family care by the government and other nongovernmental organizations, the Norwegian Association for Sexuality and Reproductive Health (NSSR) acts as a linking, training, and administrative organization, and it is involved with foreign aid, especially in Africa, the Baltic states, and Russia. Telephone of NSSR: 47 63 84 02 76; fax: 47 22 24 95 91; e-mail: kristina.totlandsdal@ helsetilsynet.dep. telemax.no.

Population (millions)	4.5
Crude birth rate	14
Total fertility rate	1.8
Women 15–49 using any method of contraception	76 percent
Women 15–49 using modern methods of contraception	65 percent

Slovakia

Located in central Europe south of Poland, Slovakia became a republic separate from the Czech part of Czechoslovakia. The most obvious topographical feature is the Carpathian Mountains with its forests, making forestry the main industry. It also has oil, natural gas, zinc, and industries, which have made industrial pollution a problem. The people are mostly Slovaks, but there are also many Gypsies, Hungarians, and other minorities. In 1998 the unemployed were 14 percent of the population. Although there is no explicit family planning policy, services and contraceptives are available, and first-trimester abortion is legal. Strong pronatal opposition exists in the Roman Catholic Church and the Christian Democratic Party. The Slovak Association for Family Planning and Parenthood Education (SSPRVR), backing reproductive and sexual rights, centers its efforts on education and training and runs four clinics giving specific services. It publishes a quarterly bulletin and runs advice columns in magazines. There is a decrease in abortion and an increase of contraceptive use in Slovakia. Address of SSPRVR: PO Box 206, Bratislava, 814 99, Slovakia; telephone: 421 (7) 43423880; fax: 421 (7) 43423880; e-mail: ssppr@netlab.sk.

Population (millions)	5.4
Crude birth rate	11
Total fertility rate	1.5
Women 15–49 using any method of contraception	74 percent
Women 15–49 using modern methods of contraception	42 percent

Slovenia

A part of the former Yugoslavia, Slovenia lies in southeastern Europe south of Austria. Compared to other central and east European countries, it is doing well economically. International Planned Parenthood has no organized subsidiary there.

Population (millions, 1996 est.)	2.0
Population growth rate (1996 est.)	0.27
Birth rate (1996 est.)	8.27
Total fertility rate (1996 est.)	1.13

Sweden

Situated on the east side of the Scandinavian peninsula in Europe, Sweden ranks very high (ninth) in the Human Development Index. The high living standard of its people comes from forests, iron mines, and paper mills in the north and from wheat, sugar beets, and livestock in the south. Sweden is highly industrialized. Supported by the strong belief in human rights, Sweden has a full range of family planning, contraceptive, abortion (up to eighteen weeks), and maternity services, all subsidized or free of charge. The Swedish help with family planning in many countries. The Riksförbundet för sexuell upplysning (RFSU) promotes sexual and reproductive health rights and enjoyment of sexuality. For example, it has produced a film, Sexuality across Cultural Borders, and a video on masturbation techniques. It conducts seminars on gender roles and language characteristics of the genders. Address of RFSU: PO Box 12128, Stockholm, 102 24, Sweden; telephone: 46 (8) 692 0700; fax: 46 (8) 653 0823; telex: 14359 RFSUS; e-mail: kerstin.strid@rfsu.se; web: <http://www.rfsu.se>.

Population (millions)	8.9
Crude birth rate	10
Total fertility rate	1.6
Women 15–49 giving live birth each year	1 percent

Switzerland

A landlocked mountainous country between France, Italy, and Germany, Switzerland has a high standard of living, a high education level, and low infant and maternal mortality rates. The varied economy includes precision instruments, chemicals, textiles, foodstuffs, and tourism. The government has no official policy about family planning, and services vary among the four language regions. The Association Suisse de Planning Familial et d'Education Sexuelle (ASPFES) directs its efforts toward education and promotion of sexual rights and health care.

A survey funded by the Federal Health Department underscored the variation in service and training standards and the need for more consumer information. It has published booklets on reproductive health for migrant women, on organizations and services for health professionals, and on sexual and reproductive health rights for youth. Telephone of ASPFES: 41 (21) 661 22 33; fax: 41 (21) 661 22 34; e-mail: aspfes@bluewin.ch.

Population (millions)	7.1
Crude birth rate	12
Total fertility rate	1.5
Women 15–49 giving live birth each year	0.5 percent

Latin America

Belize

Belize, which borders Mexico and Guatemala in Central America, has a government that supports family planning by other agencies but does not do much on its own. It does provide some family life education in the primary schools. Abortion is illegal unless the pregnancy constitutes a risk to the life or to the physical and mental health of the woman or her existing children. There is active opposition to family planning programs from the Catholic Church.

The Belize Family Life Association (BFLA), the only organization in the country dedicated primarily to family planning, was founded in 1985. It maintains four centers dedicated primarily to family planning as well as an outreach program using mobile clinics that travel across the country. It also conducts family life education in primary and secondary schools and organized youth awareness workshops for teenagers. Address for the BFLA: PO Box 529, Belize City, Belize; telephone: 501 (2) 44 399 or 501 (2) 31 018; fax: 501 (2) 32 667; e-mail: bfla@bti.net.

Population (millions)	0.2
Crude birth rate	33
Total fertility rate	4.1
Women 15–49 using contraception (all methods)	47 percent
Women 15–49 using modern methods of contraception	42 percent

Bolivia

Bolivia, a country in northern South America, has one of the highest maternal mortality rates in the world, and, although it is estimated that 89 percent of women of childbearing age have said they have heard of either traditional or modern contraceptive methods, only a minority have had access to them. Of those 16.5 percent of the women who do use modern contraceptives, the most common method is the intrauterine device, with about 42 percent using it. A smaller number have had tubal ligations, taken the pill, relied on condoms for their partners, or had injections. The second largest number of those using some form of contraceptive (22 percent) relied on the rhythm method, abstinence, or early withdrawal. CIES—Salud Sexual y Reproductiva—was created in 1988 as a not-for-profit organization to improve the health conditions of Bolivians of all ages and to provide education in sexual and reproductive health. In 1999 it had nine health clinics that provided integrated sexual and reproductive health care services in eight capital cities as well as one smaller one. It also has a pilot mobile health care project for rural areas to provide services and information about health and contraception. A number of private physicians also provide sexual and reproductive services. Address of CIES: Casilla 9935, La Paz, Bolivia; telephone: 591 (2) 36 1609, 591 (2) 36 1604, or 591 (2) 36 1668; fax: 591 (2) 36 1614; e-mail: ciesofce@caoba.enteinet.bo.

Population (millions)	8.1
Crude birth rate	32
Total fertility rate	4.2
Women 15–49 using contraceptives all methods	48.3 percent
Women 15–49 using contraceptives modern methods	25.2 percent

Costa Rica

Costa Rica lies in Central America between Nicaragua and Panama. There has been a sustained drop in the fertility rate since 1985, although rates are lower in urban areas than in rural ones. Contraceptives almost free of charge can be obtained from the government, including the social security system and the Ministry of Health, and from company physicians. The dominant nongovernmental organization is the Asociación Demográfica Costarricense, which conducts public information campaigns, conducts training programs, and works with public and private institutions interested in public policies. Address:

Apartado Postal 10203-1000, San Jose, Costa Rica; telephone: 506 231 4425 or 506 231 4211; fax: 506 231 4430; telex: 303 2604 ASDECO; cable: ASDECO; e-mail: demograf@sol.racsa.co.cr; web: <http://www.adc.or.cr>.

Population (millions)	3.5
Crude birth rate	23
Total fertility rate	2.8
Women 15–49 using all methods of contraception	75 percent
Women 15–49 using modern methods of contraception	65 percent

El Salvador

El Salvador is in Central America between Guatemala and Honduras. Even though the government proposed a comprehensive population policy in 1974, the official starting of such a policy dates from the constitution of 1983, which established demographic policies designed to ensure the maximum welfare of the population. The twelve-year civil war, which ended in 1992, made any implementation of policy difficult. The Ministry of Health and Social Assistance's Reproductive Health Division includes a family planning program that provides almost half of the contraceptives used. Working independently of the government so far has been the Asociación Demográfica Salvadoreña, which operates a clinic with professional counselors and trains volunteers. It also operates reproductive health units in private companies. It runs a national media communication and information education program aimed at the population under twenty-five. This seems to be particularly important, because in the past women in relationships have started using contraception only when they are about twenty-three years old and already have had an average of two living children, more in the rural areas. The association also has about 1,500 rural promoters who distribute contraceptives, and a number of physicians serve as backup to this program. Address: Apartado Postal 1338, San Salvador, El Salvador; telephone: 503 225 0588 or 503 225 0435; fax: 503 225 0879; cable: DEMOSAL; e-mail: ads_mis@sal.gbm.net.

Population (millions)	5.8
Crude birth rate	29
Total fertility rate	3.9

Women 15–49 using any method of contraception	53 percent
Women 15–49 using modern methods of contraception	48 percent

Guatemala

Guatemala lies in Central America just south of Mexico. Guatemala's 1986 constitution recognized the right of a couple to freely decide the number and spacing of their children. The Ministry of Health offers family planning services through government clinics, although there are periodic attacks by religious and antifamily planning groups. The Asociación Pro-Bienestar de la Familia de Guatemala offers family planning services in twenty-eight clinics throughout the country and works with 106 private physicians. It concentrates much of its effort in rural areas and runs information and educational campaigns and family life education programs. Address: Apartado Postal 1004, Guatemala, 01001 Guatemala; telephone: 502 230 5488; 502 251 3096; fax: 502 251 4017; e-mail: aprofam@guate.net.

Population (millions)	11
Crude birth rate	39
Total fertility rate	5.1
Women 15–49 using any method of contraception	31 percent
Women 15–49 using modern methods of contraception	27 percent

Guyana

Guyana lies in northern South America between Venezuela, Brazil, and Suriname. The government has no formal population policy but it does support family planning. Abortions are allowed. The government works with the Guyana Responsible Parenthood Association, founded in 1974. It is the leading agency in the country providing family planning service. It offers services in all ten of the administrative regions of Guyana, provides a full range of contraceptives, and has a program offering voluntary sterilization for men and women. It also offers low-cost contraceptives through several private clinics and pharmacies, and works with other family planning groups to educate teenagers. Telephone: 592 (2) 532 86 or 592 (2) 57 583; fax: 592 (2) 521 44; cable: GUYRESPAR; e-mail: grpafpa@sdnp.org.gy.

Population (millions)	0.7
Crude birth rate	24
Total fertility rate	2.7

Honduras

Honduras, located in Central America between Nicaragua and El Salvador, has 75 percent of the households living at or below poverty level. Many, especially the indigenous people, have no access to health care. The government has no population policy, but the national health program includes family planning, and women can get free oral contraceptives. Abortion is illegal except when a woman's health is involved. The Associación Hondureña de Planificacion de la Familia (ASHONPLAFA) has six regional clinics and twenty community clinics, including some separate clinics for women and men. Address: Apartado Postal 625, Tegucigalpa, Honduras; telephone: 504 232 3225, 504 232 3959, or 504 232 6449; fax: 504 232 5140; cable: ASHONPLAFA; e-mail: central@ashonplafa.com; web: <http://www.ashonplafa.com>.

Population (millions)	5.9
Crude birth rate	33
Total fertility rate	4.4
Women 15–49 using any method of contraception	50 percent
Women 15–49 using modern methods of contraception	41 percent

Nicaragua

A small country in Central America, Nicaragua is struggling toward economic and political stability after a prolonged civil war. Poverty and unemployment are problems, especially in rural areas. Sixty-three percent of married women report using contraceptives, but pregnancy among teenagers is high. Officials are becoming aware of the relationship of population and economic development. Still, governmental support of family planning services is not consistent. The Ministry of Health does have nine hundred places that distribute contraceptives. Nicaragua has several active nongovernmental organizations, among them the Asociación Pro Bienestar de la Familia Nicaragüense (Profamilia), which has one thousand centers where women can get contraceptives. Voluntary sterilization is the most requested, followed by injectable and oral contraceptives.

Profamilia trains teachers and parents and tries especially to educate adolescents. Address: Apartado Postal No. 4220, Managua, Nicaragua; telephone: 505 (2) 78 0841, 505 (2) 67 0263, or 505 (2) 78 5629; fax: 505 (2) 77 0802; e-mail: profamil@tmx.com.ni.

Population (millions)	4.8
Crude birth rate	38
Total fertility rate	4.6
Women 15–49 using any method of contraception	49 percent
Women 15–49 using modern methods of contraception	30 percent

Panama

In Central America between the North Pacific Ocean and the Caribbean Sea, Panama generates most of its income from shipping in the Panama Canal. Almost half the population live in poverty, and 42 percent are under age nineteen. The teenage pregnancy rate is high, and abortion is illegal. The government does provide maternal and child services, but the quality and availability are uneven.

There are nongovernmental organizations, including the Associación Panameña para el Planeamiento de la Familia (APLAFA). It focuses on education on family planning and human sexuality for the young and subsidizes contraceptive services. It has also offered vocational training for women. Address of APLAFA: Apartado Postal 46375, Panamá City, Panama; telephone: 507 236 4428, 260 7005, or 260 3139; fax: 507 236 2979; cable: APLAFA: e-mail: aplafa@orbi.net.

Population (millions)	2.8
Crude birth rate	22
Total fertility rate	2.7
Women 15–49 using any method of contraception	49 percent

Paraguay

A small, landlocked country in South America, Paraguay has a 9.4 percent unemployment rate but a large number of inhabitants living in rural poverty. The number of children per woman aligns with the level of education: women with two or fewer years of education average 6.9 children, and those with twelve or more years average 2.4 children. The most common

contraceptive is an herbal tea drunk daily. The government has a small family planning program, and knowledge of contraceptives is gradually growing among the populace. The Centro Paraguayo de Estudios de Población (CEPEP) is the only nongovernmental organization providing subsidized family planning services. Its clinics provide common gynecological services, train volunteers, and educate the public. Telephone of CEPEP: 595 (21) 491 627, 490 162, or 497 503; fax: 595 (21) 444 503; e-mail: cepep@pla.net.py.

Population (millions)	5.1
Crude birth rate	32
Total fertility rate	4.4
Women 15–49 using any method of contraception	51 percent
Women 15–49 using modern methods of contraception	41 percent

Suriname

On the northeast coast of South America, Suriname is a country of mostly rolling hills and a swampy coastal plain. Ethnically diverse (East Indian, Javanese, European, African, Amerindians) and officially Dutch speaking, the Surinamers have lived through years of political and economic instability. The government and Stichting Lobi, the Planned Parenthood affiliate, collaborate to encourage family planning. Lobi runs two clinics and also works through forty-nine government clinics, giving basic services such as Pap smears, sexually transmitted disease and fertility tests, and contraceptives. Lobi teaches sex education in many schools, trains volunteers, and does fund raising. It has created a computerized system of cost analysis to run its business affairs efficiently. Abortion is illegal in Suriname. Address of Stichting Lobi: Postbox 9267, Paramaribo Suriname; telephone: 597 400 444 or 401 215; fax: 597 400 960; cable: LOBI; e-mail: lobi@sr.net.

Population (millions)	0.4
Crude birth rate	24
Total fertility rate	2.6
Women 15–49 giving live birth each year	5 percent

Uruguay

Located on the Atlantic Ocean in South America between Argentina and Brazil, Uruguay is a country of rolling plains, a fertile coast, and a good climate. High inflation and abrupt changes in economic conditions have impeded progress. Uruguay has a high abortion rate, a high rate of contraceptive use, and, among the very poor, a high fertility rate. Family planning is not part of the curriculum of universities, nor is it part of the health services of the government or insurance companies. Thus, it is up to the Asociación Uruguaya de Planificación Familiar (AUPF) to provide information and services on family planning. It gives family planning services in its own clinics to armed service groups, to workers' groups, and even in the women's jail. It distributes contraceptives to private physicians and publicizes women's issues in the media. It trains teachers and parents. In a model clinic it has an operating room for performing contraceptive surgical procedures. One of its clinics is in Santa Rita, the lowest-income area in Montevideo. Address of AUPF: Casilla de Correos, 10.634, Sucursal 60, Montevideo, Uruguay; telephone: 598 (2) 707 7479, 707 7481, or 707 7480; fax: 598 (2) 707 7482; cable: AUPFIRH; e-mail: aupfiec@netgate.comintur.com.uy.

Population (millions)	3.2
Crude birth rate	18
Total fertility rate	2.4
Women 15–19 giving live birth each year	5 percent

Middle East

Bahrain

Bahrain is an archipelago east of Saudi Arabia in the Arab Gulf. Although there is no national population policy or family planning program, there are no restrictions on the supply and use of contraceptives, and abortion is allowed for health reasons. Family planning services are integrated into primary health care. In 1995, some 54 percent of the women of reproductive age were using some method of family planning but only 26 percent of them were using modern contraceptives. The Bahrain Family Planning Association (BFPA) was created in 1975 and since then has been campaigning to increase family planning. The government through the Ministries of Health, Social Affairs, and Labor supports the undertaking of the BFPA in its educational campaign. Address of the BFPA: PO Box 20326, Manama, Bahrain; telephone: 973 232 233 or 973 256 622; fax: 973 276 408/244 671; telex: 0490 8200 BAFPA.

Population (millions)	0.6
Crude birth rate	23
Total fertility rate	3.2
Women 15–49 using any method of contraception	62 percent
Women 15–49 using modern methods of contraception	31 percent

Cyprus

Cyprus is an island in the eastern Mediterranean. Since the 1974 Turkish invasion, the people of Cyprus have maintained two separate communities, one Greek, the other Turkish. The Turkish portion is part of Turkey, and information for it is not reported here. The Greek-speaking government of the republic is basically pronatalist and does not operate family planning services in state hospitals. It does, however, subsidize family planning practices offered by the Family Planning Association of Cyprus, which runs a family planning clinic in Nicosia. The association advocates relaxation of the abortion laws, runs workshops on sex education and sexuality awareness for young people, and provides prenatal classes at maternity wards. Telephone for the FPAC: 357 (2) 751093; fax: 357 (2) 757495; e-mail: famplan@spidernet.com.cy.

Population (millions)	0.7
Crude birth rate	15
Total fertility rate	2.1

Israel

Between Egypt and Lebanon on the Mediterranean Sea, Israel is a country of disparate peoples—about 82 percent Hebrew-speaking Jews, including migrants from various parts of the world, and 14 percent Arabic-speaking Muslims. The fertility rate of 2.9 is lower among peoples of European and American descent. Although Israel is pronatalist, abortion and modern contraceptives are readily available. The Israel Family Planning Association (IFPA) runs counseling centers and family planning clinics, including some for new immigrants from Ethiopia and Russia, training programs for counselors, and HIV/AIDS projects. Telephone for IFPA: 972 (3) 510 1511 or 972 (3) 510 1512; fax: 972 (3) 510 2589; e-mail: ziegler@tx.technion.ac.il.

Population (millions)	6
Crude birth rate	21
Total fertility rate	2.9

Jordan

Situated between Israel and Saudi Arabia, Jordan is a Muslim country with many seminomadic citizens and a relatively high literacy rate. Traditional religious opposition to birth control gives this desert nation a growth rate of 4.4 percent a year, the highest in the Arab world. The government has no general population policy, but since 1975 there has been a National Population Commission, which complements the work of the Jordan Association for Family Planning and Protection (JAFPP). The association runs fifteen clinics where people can go for advice and contraceptives. Address for JAFPP: PO Box 212302 or 8066, Amman, Jordan; telephone: 962 (6) 5160999 or 962 (6) 5161032; fax: 962 (6) 5161020; telex: (0493) 23046 JO; cable: FAMPLAN AMMAN-JOR; e-mail: JAFPP@nol.com.jo.

Population (millions)	4.6
Crude birth rate	30
Total fertility rate	4.4
Women 15–49 using any method of contraception	53 percent
Women 15–49 using modern methods of contraception	38 percent

Kuwait

A small desert country strategically situated on the Persian Gulf between Saudi Arabia and Iraq, Kuwait has 10 percent of the world reserves of petroleum. Kuwait has no arable land, it has both air and water pollution, and it depends on desalinization for usable water. It has generous health and education programs for its citizens. It has no affiliation with International Planned Parenthood.

Population (millions, 1996 est.)	1.95
Birth rate (1996 est.)	20.28
Total fertility rate (1996 est.)	2.82

Lebanon

The small Mediterranean country of Lebanon, lying next to Syria and Israel, is recovering from a crushing sixteen-year civil war (1975–90). In 1983, the government tried to integrate family planning into primary health care services, but under the circumstances, long-term family planning had little success. The Lebanon Family Planning Association (LFPA) has played a pioneering small-scale role in educating communities. It is giving training to both governmental and nongovernmental personnel. Changes can be expected as the country becomes independent and stabilized. Address of LFPA: PO Box 118240. Beirut, Lebanon; telephone: 961 (1) 311 978; fax: 961 (1) 318 575; telex: 20426 LEFPA: e-mail: ifpa@cyberia.net.lb.

Population (millions)	4.1
Crude birth rate	23
Total fertility rate	2.3

Oman

Strategically located between Saudi Arabia and the Arabian Sea, Oman has four billion barrels of oil reserves. The economy is almost entirely dependent on oil, although the government is encouraging private investment. There is no International Planned Parenthood affiliate there.

Population (millions, 1996 est.)	2.19
Birth rate (1996 est.)	37.86
Total fertility rate (1996 est.)	6.09

Palestine

The Occupied Territories' status as a war area for so long means that war-related medicine, not family planning, has received government attention. Thus, nongovernmental organizations are the providers of family health care and planning. The Palestinian Family Planning and Protection Association (PFPPA) focuses on the poor, training workers and providing family planning information. Through such things as films on hygiene, nutrition, and family planning, attitudes toward women and family planning are slowly changing. Address of PFPPA: PO Box 19999, Jerusalem; telephone: 972 2 234 8732 or 972 2 234 2728; fax: 972 2 234 2729; telex: 25656 FPPJSM IL/25379 LORNCIL; cable: FPA address; e-mail: pfppa@painet.com.

Population (millions)	2.9
Crude birth rate	45
Total fertility rate	6.3
Women 15–49 using any method of contraception	45 percent
Women 15–49 using modern methods of contraception	31 percent

United Arab Emirates

A small desert country on the Persian Gulf next to Saudi Arabia and Oman, United Arab Emirates is strategically placed near the Strait of Hormuz. It depends on desalinization plants for water. Its oil and natural gas make it a wealthy country, and its citizens have a high standard of living. It has no affiliation with International Planned Parenthood.

Population (millions, 1996 est.)	3.06
Birth rate (1996 est.)	26.43
Total fertility rate (1996 est.)	4.46

Oceania

American Samoa

Tiny islands in the Pacific halfway between Hawaii and New Zealand, American Samoa has one of the best deepwater harbors on the South Pacific. The American Samoa Planned Parenthood Association is active there. Address: PO Box 1043, Pago Pago, American Samoa.

Population (millions)	0.06
Crude birth rate	34.7
Total fertility rate	4.3

Cook Islands

The fifteen tropical and subtropical Cook Islands in Polynesia have a "free association" with New Zealand. Family planning is not part of any specific government policy, but contraceptive and related health services have been available since 1984 as part of the government's family health program. Family planning, however, remains controversial, in part because of religious beliefs, and implementation is difficult because of the geographical barriers. The Cook Islands Family Welfare Association complements government efforts in family planning, concentrating on distributing contraceptives and performing public education. Address: PO Box 109, Rarotonga, Cook Islands; telephone: 683 23 420; fax: 682 23 421; e-mail: cifwa@oyster.net.ck.

Population (millions)	0.02
Crude birth rate	24.3
Total fertility rate	3.3
Women 15–49 using any method of contraception	50 percent

Fiji

Fiji consists of several large islands as well as three hundred volcanic and coral islets and atolls, of which only one hundred are inhabited. It is one of the wealthier island nations. The government does not have an explicit population policy, and child services in the national health infrastructure are available free. There is, however, a lack of trained personnel, and communication is difficult because of the geographic spread of the population. The nongovernmental organization in Fiji is the Reproductive and Family Health Association of Fiji, which was established in 1996. It concentrates on nationwide information and education for all aspects of reproductive health. Address: 12 Pier Street, 2nd Floor, Rooms 3–5, GB Hari Building, Suva, Fiji; telephone: 679 30 61 75; fax: 679 30 61 78.

Population (millions)	0.8
Crude birth rate	24
Total fertility rate	2.8

French Polynesia

Papeete on the island of Tahiti is the capital of the group of islands, atolls, and islets making up French Polynesia in the Western Pacific Ocean about halfway between South America and Australia. There is a nongovernmental organization, Comité pour le Planning Familial de la Polynésie.

Population (millions)	0.2
Crude birth rate	23.

Kiribati

Kiribati consists of one island and thirty-two atolls lying along the Equator in the Pacific Ocean. It has high rates of population growth, of serious eye problems caused by deficiency of Vitamin A, of sexually transmitted diseases (including HIV/AIDS), and of infant mortality. Although there is no official government policy, the Kiribati Family Health Association (KFHA) is active and family planning is generally accepted. Difficulties have arisen because of the distance of outlying atolls and because of the opposition of church groups to reproductive education. Address of KFHA: PO Box 345, Tarawa, Kiribati; telephone: 686 28 749; fax: 686 28 728.

Population (millions)	0.082

Crude birth rate	31
Total fertility rate	3.2

New Zealand

New Zealand consists of two large islands in the South Pacific southeast of Australia. Most of the largely urban, European population live on the coastal plains that surround the central mountains. About 15 percent of the population are indigenous Maori and about 6 percent are other Polynesian people. Unemployment rates—about 6 percent for the country—are high among these native peoples. New Zealand people are knowledgeable about family planning, and services are available from private and public organizations and practitioners. The government has established free sexual health clinics and some free contraceptive services. The New Zealand Family Planning Association (NZFPA) has thirty-two clinics across the country, and they work closely with Te Puawai Tapu, an organization that educates young Maoris. Address of NZFPA: PO Box 11-515, Wellington, New Zealand; telephone: 64 (4) 384 4349; fax: 64 (4) 382 8356; cable: FAMPLAN.

Population (millions)	3.8
Crude birth rate	15
Total fertility rate	2

Papua New Guinea

Made up of the eastern half of the island of New Guinea and many smaller islands, Papua New Guinea is the largest country in the South Pacific. Its nineteen provinces and Capital District contain great linguistic, cultural, and geographical diversity. Most of the people are dependent for a livelihood on subsistence agriculture and on the cash crops of cocoa, coffee, and palm oil. The rich timber, fish, and mineral resources do not benefit the general population. Women are undervalued and educated even less than men. The government is not now meeting the health, education, and economic needs of its people, yet the population is growing at a rate of 2.4 percent. The Papua New Guinea Family Health Association (PNGFHA), started in 1996, has implemented several projects: a condom mail order service; dissemination of educational pamphlets, radio programs, posters, etc.; training programs for volunteer leaders from remote areas; family planning clinics in Lae and Rabaul; and lobbying of influential leaders in government. Address of

PNGFHA: PO Box 839, Lae 411, Morabe Province, Papua New Guinea; telephone: 675 472 6827; fax: 675 472 6296; e-mail: pngfha@datec.com.pg.

Population (millions)	4.3
Crude birth rate	34
Total fertility rate	4.8
Women 15–49 using any method of contraception	26 percent
Women 15–49 using modern methods of contraception	20 percent

Samoa

The tropical islands of Samoa, lying about one-third of the way between Hawaii and New Zealand, have narrow plains on the coast and rugged volcanic mountains inland. Agriculture (copra and coconut) and tourism are the main sources of income, but the greater amount of imports means the country needs foreign aid and money sent from emigrants. Though not living in extreme poverty, the people are poor, and there is high youth unemployment. The primary social unit is the extended family (aiga) headed by a chief (matai), which stresses group rather than individual achievement. The government's Family Welfare Center offers general health services, including family planning, at three hospitals, and it sends district nurses to make monthly visits to women's committees. The Samoa Family Health Association (SFHA), working closely with the Family Welfare Center, provides specific contraceptive services, including running a mobile unit to outlying islands. Address of SFHA: PO Box 3029, Apia, Samoa; telephone: 0685 26929; fax: 685 24560; telex: 219 GOLDSTAR SX; e-mail: sfha@lesamoa.net.

Population (millions)	0.2
Crude birth rate	29
Total fertility rate	4.2
Women 15–19 giving live birth each year	2 percent

Solomon Islands

The Solomon Islands, a Melanesian archipelago consisting of mountainous islands and dying coral atolls, lie two thousand kilometers northeast of Australia. Major economic activities are subsistence farming and fishing, although the islands have considerable natural resources—lead, zinc, nickel, and gold. They import most manufactured and petroleum products, and the government is barely financially solvent. The very high population growth rate of 3.2 percent (1998) has led to high unemployment and inadequate health care. Attempting to reduce this growth rate, the government promotes family planning. Problems are many: low status of women, difficult terrain, shortage of contraceptives and of trained personnel, and opposition of religious groups. The Solomon Islands Planned Parenthood Association (SIPPA), working with the Ministry of Health, is embarked on a five-year Population Education and Youth Family Life Campaign. SIPPA provides education and services through radio programs, through teacher training, and through distribution of contraceptives. Address of SIPPA: PO Box 554, Laambi Cress, Honiara, Solomon Islands; telephone: 677 22991 or 677 23727; fax: 677 23653.

Population (millions)	0.4
Crude birth rate	37
Total fertility rate	5.4
Women 15–49 giving live birth each year	9 percent

Tonga

An archipelago about two-thirds of the way from Hawaii to New Zealand, Tonga is a Polynesian kingdom with an economic base in subsistence agriculture (bananas, copra, coconut), tourism, and money sent from abroad by emigrants. Tonga has a relatively high birth rate, but so many people emigrate because of high inflation and unemployment that the population is decreasing. The government encourages family planning and gives contraceptives free of charge in its hospitals and clinics. Divorce and the incidence of sexually transmitted diseases are rising. The Tonga Family Planning Association (TFPA), operating discretely within cultural norms, has a network of clinics through which it provides family planning services and information. Address of TFPA: PO Box 1142, Nuku'Alofa, Tonga; telephone: 676 22 770; fax: 676 23 766; e-mail: fpatonga@ kalianet.to.

Population (millions)	0.1
Crude birth rate	26
Total fertility rate	4.2
Women 15–49 using any method of contraception	39 percent

Tuvalu

A group of nine coral atolls about halfway between Hawaii and Australia, Tuvalu has poor soil and no natural resources. The people survive through subsistence farming and fishing. The country has a good health system, which runs a family planning clinic. The Tuvalu Family Health Association (TUFHA) works with the government clinic and provides information services. Address of TUFHA: c/o Medical Division, PO Box 92, Funafuti, Tuvalu; Telephone: 688 20411; fax: 688 20410; telex: GOVT TV 4803.

Population (millions)	0.01
Crude birth rate	28
Total fertility rate	3.3

Vanuatu

A group of islands three-quarters of the distance from Hawaii to Australia, Vanuatu (formerly New Hebrides) is a wet, tropical Melanesian republic. It has active volcanoes and many earthquakes. Its people are strongly traditional, with chiefs and church leaders playing important roles. Women lack education and political and economic power, and men have negative attitudes toward contraception. The Vanuatu Family Health Association (VFHA), endorsed by the government, provides family planning services such as vasectomies, and it trains student nurses. It has tutored a network of counselors to serve outlying communities. Address of VFHA: Private Mail Bag 0065, Port Vila, Vanuatu; telephone: 678 22 140; fax: 678 24 627.

Population (millions)	0.2
Crude birth rate	35
Total fertility rate	4.7

APPENDIX 2
Print and Nonprint Resources

In addition to the various references listed at the end of most of the entries in this encyclopedia, information can be found elsewhere. This appendix is designed as a guide to such material. Researchers looking for information about birth control have an advantage in that a limited number of English words and phrases typically are used to describe key areas. In searching for information, consider—depending on what you are looking for—the following key words, any or all of which may be used in indexes, catalogs, and search engines: abortion; birth control; contraception; contraceptives (condoms, intrauterine contraceptives or intrauterine devices or IUDs, oral contraceptives, etc.); family planning; natural family planning; pro-choice or pro-choice movement; pro-life or pro-life movement; sterilization (sometimes this term will yield materials on laboratory sterilization techniques, not reproductive sterilization); tubal ligation; and vasectomy.

In general searches, be sure to try birth control, contraception, and family planning, since some sources may concentrate entries under one of these terms, while others may use all three, with little overlap between entries. If a specific term like condom yields no entries, try a more general term like birth control or contraception. For some types of questions concerning demography, the terms population and fertility may be useful.

Note that considerable information is available on natural family planning—not always recognized at a time in history when the pill and the condom get the most media attention. Note also that most forms of noncoital sex or "outercourse" prevent pregnancy, but the techniques are not always mentioned in information materials about birth control. For a discussion of noncoital sex, see Marty Klein and Rikki Robbins, *Let Me Count the Ways: Discovering Great Sex without Intercourse* (New York: Tarcher/Putnam, 1998); or Cathy Winks and Anne Semans, *The New Good Vibrations Guide to Sex* (San Francisco: Cleis, 1997).

Books and Library Resources

Many of the sources of information described in this appendix may be accessed via the Internet or by simply buying books or using the telephone. Others are available only through libraries: public libraries, university libraries, medical libraries, or law libraries. Anyone can use reference materials in public libraries—a library card is needed only to check out books. University, medical, and law libraries have varying policies concerning the public. Some have open access at certain times, requiring only that the visitor show an ID to use materials on site free of charge. Others charge user fees. Usually public library staff can help you find out what other kinds of libraries are nearby and what their access policies are.

Always feel free to ask library staff for help—in person or over the telephone. Not all librarians are unfailingly courteous and helpful, but most try to be. Librarians can usually find ways of getting information that might not occur to you. Do be aware, however, that some types of library services—such as interlibrary loan—take time. You may be able to find the information you need as quick as a mouse click—or you may not.

A great deal of reference material about birth control can be found on the Internet, and such information is listed throughout this appendix. For searching in print, do not neglect the *Encyclopedia Americana* and *Encyclopedia Britannica* as a first stop. In encyclopedias, there are comprehensive overviews, such as that under "Birth Control" in Britannica's *Macropedia;* also be sure to look up narrower topics such as "Margaret Sanger." Beyond the general encyclopedias, several useful handbooks and overviews have been published in this area.

Audiovisuals

Another option is to purchase a tape. Some organizations have their conferences taped and then sell the tapes of the individual sessions. Call the organization and ask. The best source for identifying videos about birth control is *Bowker's Complete Video Directory* (R. R. Bowker), available in libraries.

Books in Print

The reference *Books in Print* may be found in virtually all libraries and has a Subject Guide section in multiple volumes. Use the key words listed above to search the subject guide. Information is available on titles, publishers, and price—but if a book looks interesting, the actual book should be consulted, or more details obtained from the Internet.

If a specific book is needed and a nearby library does not have it, it can be made available through interlibrary loan (ILL). Some books about birth control might take a historical approach to the subject. Others may be primarily area studies or consumers' guides to methods, or may discuss empowerment and advocacy from a particular viewpoint such as pro-life, or may describe medical and clinical aspects for health professionals. To identify titles appropriate to your search, it is necessary to use several approaches.

The references listed below are primarily for professionals, but are useful for the public:

Abortion: A Reference Handbook, 2nd ed. Edited by Marie Costas. Santa Barbara, Calif.: ABC-CLIO, 1996.

All about Birth Control: A Personal Guide. John Knowles and Marcia Ringel of the Planned Parenthood Federation of America. New York: Three Rivers Press/Crown Publishers, 1998. Clear and detailed discussion of methods, including abstinence and outercourse, plus background on human reproductive anatomy/physiology and on Planned Parenthood.

An Atlas of Contraception. Pramilla Senanayaka and Malcolm Pots. New York: Parthenon Publishing Group, 1995. A volume in the *Encyclopedia of Visual Medicine Series.* Brief medical discussion of contraceptive techniques and human sexuality, with historical background. Many color illustrations, graphs, tables, and charts.

Contraception: A Guide to Birth Control Methods, 2nd. ed. Vern L. Bullough and Bonnie Bullough, Amherst, New York: Prometheus Books, 1997. Description of methods, including abstinence and outercourse, plus sections on the history of contraception and on human reproductive anatomy/physiology.

Contraceptive Technology. Edited by Robert A. Hatcher and others. New York: Irving Press. Updated regularly in even-numbered years. An extensive guide to methods, including abstinence and natural methods (but very little outercourse), how they work, advantages/disadvantages, supporting data and references, plus additional information about reproductive anatomy/physiology, sexually transmitted diseases, fertility, and adolescent reproductive behavior. Designed for physicians and those who run clinics. There is also a monthly newsletter for health professionals, *Contraceptive Technology Update,* available online at <http://www.ahcpub.com/online.html>.

Catalogs

The catalog of a local public, university, or medical library usually gives only titles and bibliographic information, but the "expanded" or "full" record format in online catalogs gives further clues about the content of the subject. The catalogs of many libraries are searchable on the Internet. Call the library and ask for the uniform resource locator (URL) of the home page.

The Internet

Several Web sites are especially useful. To identify books by subject, author, or title, regardless of whether or not the book is in print, use the Library of Congress catalog, <http://www.loc.gov/catalog>. For in-print titles primarily, try the large Internet bookstores such as Amazon, <http://www.amazon.com>, and Barnes & Noble, <http://www.bn.com>. To buy out-of-print books, try Alibris, <http://www.alibris.com>, Powells, http://www.powells.com, and Half.com <http://www.half.com>.

The "Full Record" listing of records in the Library of Congress catalog gives the subject terms assigned to use as clues to content. The Internet bookstore records often have tables of contents, reviews, or readers' comments, and it is not necessary to buy books to access this information. In addition, many of the Web sites of organizations listed below have bibliographies and may even sell books over the Internet.

Reference Books on Product Information

Most contraceptive products are made and sold by the pharmaceutical industry. For detailed information about contraceptive products themselves, there are useful sources that all medical libraries, as well as many public and academic libraries, have. See also *Contraceptive Technology Update* in this appendix.

Health Devices Sourcebook (ECRI): Lists only devices rather than drugs or substances and provides information about the manufacturer. The index heading contraceptive devices includes fallopian tube clips (used in surgical sterilization), condoms (male and female type), implants, intrauterine devices, diaphragms, and sponges.

Physicians' Desk Reference ("PDR," Medical Economics Company): Lists pharmaceutical products currently available; ingredients, usage, effectiveness, side effects, warnings, and much other information as supplied by the manufacturer, plus information about manufacturers. The index heading contraceptives includes "devices" (diaphragms and intrauterine devices), implants, injectable contraceptives, and oral contraceptives. No coverage of over-the-counter creams, jellies, etc.

Physicians' Desk Reference for Nonprescription Drugs and Dietary Supplements (Medical Economics Company): Similar information to PDR; includes over-the-counter contraceptives, jellies, and suppositories.

Special Libraries

The major reference for special-topic library collections is the *Directory of Special Libraries and Information Centers* (Gale Group), available in most libraries. The index to the 24th edition, 1999, for example, listed forty-five libraries under birth control and thirty-one under abortion. Ten of these appear under both headings, but the actual overlap is much larger. Many of the collections listed under birth control are within headquarters and affiliates of the International Planned Parenthood Federation and Planned Parenthood Federation of America, which also collect materials on abortion. Many of the entries under *abortion* are those for in-house libraries of local pro-life organizations, which often have holdings on natural family planning. Special libraries and collections have different procedures about services and public access. Before visiting a library, check the directory for applicable procedures and then call ahead to verify. Some will provide services by telephone, mail, or web site.

Journals, Magazines, and Newspapers

Periodicals include newspapers, magazines, and scholarly/technical journals, and usually can provide more up-to-date information than books. Periodical articles can be found by scanning issues of key periodicals or by using indexes and databases.

To retrieve an article from a periodical that is not in a nearby library, try interlibrary loan. If it is still not available, there are a number of document delivery services that can send you a copy for a fee, such as Information on Demand (McLean, Va.). Some libraries have directories of fee-based information services, and some libraries have their own fee-based document delivery.

Conferences and Proceedings

Scholars and other professionals working in the birth control and related fields have many conferences to exchange information about trends and work in progress. Such information, which is presented orally (sometimes with typescript versions) constitutes the conference paper or "proceedings." Conference papers can be tedious rehashes of received wisdom or can announce fascinating breakthroughs.

To find out about work presented at a conference, it is generally necessary to identify conferences of key organizations and attend the conference. There are, however, less expensive and less time-consuming options. One is to request the preliminary conference program from the sponsoring organization and select presentations of interest, then write or call the presenters after the meeting and request a print version. Not all presenters prepare print versions, but many will send out the text of their slides or a bibliography. Contact presenters through the sponsoring organization or track down the telephone number for their affiliation if it is listed in the conference program.

Current Awareness Services

Some periodical-type publications list titles and sometimes abstracts for articles in specific areas. One relevant to birth control is: *Studies in Family Planning*, published quarterly by The Population Council, One Dag Hammerskjold Plaza, New York, NY 10017, website <http://www.popcouncil.org/sfp>.

Databases

Some databases do not contain titles or texts of articles or books but statistics and data:

CDC's Reproductive Health Information Source (Centers for Disease Control and Prevention): <http://www.cdc.gov/nccdphp/drh/surveil.htm>—Access to information and statistics on birth control, pregnancy, and other aspects of reproductive health.

Data Archive on Adolescent Pregnancy and Pregnancy Prevention (Sociometrics): <http://www.socio.com/data.htm>—Original data and text from over 130 research studies. Sociometrics has other data sets on family topics.

National Center for Health Statistics (Centers for Disease Control and Prevention): <http://www.cdc.gov/nchs>—Access to vital statistics of many types, including birth and pregnancy rates.

Directories

To identify key periodicals, check the large directories in the public and academic libraries. For *Ulrich's International Periodicals* directory (R. R. Bowker), use "Birth Control" as your major search term. Abortion titles (pro-choice and pro-life) are also included here. Many medical titles, however, are listed under "Medical Sciences—Obstetrics and Gynecology." The heading "Population Studies" may also have titles of interest. *Ulrich's* includes short descriptions for most entries, as well as how to subscribe and which document delivery service provides copies of articles. If you want to find out which libraries carry a periodical, ask a librarian to search the Online Computer Library Center (OCLC) database.

Educator's Update

Published six times a year by the Education Department of the Planned Parenthood Federation of America (New York). Lists and annotates recent books, articles (in journals not entirely devoted to birth control topics), videos, upcoming conferences, and web sites.

Indexes

To identify specific periodical articles, consult abstracting and indexing ("A&I") services: databases, print, and/or CDs. Some of the major scholarly A&I services include:

BIOETHICSLINE (National Reference Center for Bioethics Literature, Kennedy Institute of Ethics, Georgetown University): <http://www.georgetown.edu/research/nrcbl>—Searchable for free via Grateful Med (below).

Contemporary Women's Issues <http://www.cwidb.com>—International; abstracts and some full texts.

ERIC (Educational Resources Information Center): <http://www.ericsp.org>—Education-related topics, searchable for free on the Internet.

Family Studies Database (formerly Inventory of Marriage and Family Literature until 1974).

LEXIS <http://www.lexis-nexis.com>—Law, full texts, available in law libraries and most university libraries.

MEDLINE (National Library of Medicine): Grateful Med <http://igm.nlm.nih.gov> and Pub Med <http://http://www.ncbi.nlm.nih.gov/PubMed>—Searchable for free on the Internet.

New York Times Index—Newspaper abstracts.

PAIS International **<http://www.pais.org>—Public affairs, contemporary business, and social issues.**

Periodical Abstracts—Includes popular, academic, and business journals plus newspapers, some full text.

POPLINE (Johns Hopkins University)—Family planning and populations studies, available free through Grateful Med.

Population Index (Office of Population Research, Princeton University): <http://popindex.princeton.edu>—Available free on the Internet.

PsycINFO (American Psychological Association): <http://www.apa.org/psycinfo>—Psychology and life sciences.

Readers Guide to Periodical Literature—These can usually be accessed via both university and public libraries—ask the librarian which are available and how to use them. Some have both scholarly and popular materials.

Sage Family Studies Abstracts <http://www.sagepub.com>.

Westlaw <http://www.westlaw.com>—Law, full text, available in law libraries.

Women's Resources International—Citation only.

Organizations

The United States has thousands of organizations concerned with every conceivable issue, including birth control. In addition, many international groups have birth control as a major focus. Many of these organizations provide pamphlets, bibliographies, library services, referrals, educational courses, conferences, speakers bureaus, lobbying and advocacy, statistics, periodicals, books, or other publications. Some services are free, by mail or telephone or on the Internet, or at minimal charge. Organizations are also sources of expert information.

The guidebook for up-to-date access to most of these organizations is the *Encyclopedia of Associations* (Gale Research), found in all libraries. A separate two-volume set covers international organizations. Some useful keywords in the index of these volumes include abortion (933 entries), demography (26 entries), family planning (200 entries), fertility (11 entries), natural family planning (910 entries), population (115 entries), reproductive freedom (1 entry), reproductive health (8 entries), reproductive medicine (29 entries), reproductive rights (23 entries), and right to life (81 entries). Many affiliates of Planned Parenthood and other family planning organizations outside the United States are listed in the international volume. Some of the larger key organizations include:

Advocates for Youth <http://www.advocatesforyouth.org>—To reduce teen pregnancy and sexually transmitted diseases: advocacy, resource guides, conferences, curricula, issues and policy analysis, library, periodicals, reports, research, speakers' bureau, statistics/data.

Alan Guttmacher Institute <http://www.agi-usa.org>)—To promote voluntary fertility control: issues and policy analysis, periodicals, publications, research, statistics.

American Life League <http://www.all.org>—To provide pro-life information and education: library, meetings and courses, periodicals, publications, speakers' bureau.

Association of Reproductive Health Professionals <http://www.arhp.org>—Membership organization for physicians and health professionals: advocacy, conferences and courses, library, periodicals, publications and audiovisuals, speakers' bureau.

AVSC International <http://www.avsc.org>—To ensure access to voluntary contraception, especially sterilizations: conferences, periodicals, publications.

Catholics for a Free Choice <http://www.cath4choice.org>)—To support and advance pro-choice Roman Catholic perspectives worldwide, acting as a focal point, voice, and advocate: advocacy, issues, policy analysis, education, publications, research.

Center for Reproductive Law and Policy <http://www.crlp.org>—To secure reproductive freedom for women in the United States and worldwide: advocacy, issues and policy analysis, library, litigation, periodicals, publications.

Common Ground Network for Life and Choice <http://www.sfcg.org>—To bring pro-life and pro-choice supporters together in dialogue for creative problem-solving and joint action: position papers, action projects, conferences, audiovisuals.

Couple to Couple League <http://www.ccli.org>—To promote marital chastity through natural family planning: bibliography/catalog, conferences and courses, periodicals.

Focus on the Family <http://www.family.org>—To promote traditional Judeo-Christian values and strong family ties; offers three free pro-life resource lists: Pro-Life Materials, Materials for Right to Life Organizations, and Material for Crisis Pregnancy Centers.

Human Life International <http://www.hli.org>—To provide research and information for the pro-life movement: conferences, library, periodicals, publications, research, speakers' bureau, statistics/data.

Johns Hopkins University Communication Programs <http://www.jhuccp.org>)—To promote public awareness of family planning, AIDS prevention, and maternal and child health primarily in developing countries: workshops, sponsorships, POPLINE bibliographic database, publications.

Kaiser Family Foundation <http://www.kff.org>—To serve as an independent voice and source of facts and analysis on health care issues, including reproductive and sexual health: education, issues and policy analysis, publications, research.

National Abortion and Reproductive Action League <http://www.naral.org>—To maintain a pro-choice political constituency: advocacy, issues and policy analysis, periodicals, speakers' bureau, statistics.

National Abortion Federation <http://www.prochoice.org>—Forum for abortion service providers: conferences and courses, curricula, hotline, issues and policy analysis, library, referrals, publications, statistics/data.

National Right to Life Committee <http://www.nrlc.org>—To educate and advocate for pro-life: advocacy, conferences, library, periodicals, publications, research, speakers' bureau.

Pathfinder International <http://www.pathfind. org>. Dedicated to expanding availability and quality of reproductive health services.

Planned Parenthood <http://www.plannedparenthood.org> (United States); <http://www.ippf.org> (international)—National and international federation of local and national organizations providing access to contraception, abortion, sterilization, and infertility services: clinical services plus advocacy, conferences and courses, libraries, speakers' bureaus, periodicals, publications; links to other organizational web sites at <http://www.plannedparenthood.org/library/EXTERNALLINKS/contraception.html>.

Population Council <http://www. popcouncil.org>—To improve reproductive health and achieve balance between people and resources: advocacy, conferences and courses, issues and policy analysis, library, periodicals, publications, research.

Zero Population Growth <http://www.zpg.org>—To educate and mobilize support to stop population growth; advocacy, conferences and courses, issues and policy analysis, library, periodicals, publications, research, speaker's bureau, statistics/data.

People

"People sources" come in one or a combination of three types: subjects for interview and questionnaire studies, colleagues, and experts. Locating subjects for scholarly studies is beyond the scope of this appendix. Colleagues and experts may be found by joining appropriate organizations listed above and making contact with others doing interesting work. Attending conferences is one way to meet such people. Another is to track down someone's affiliation, contact the organization for the e-mail and/or address of the person, and then write to them. "Cold" telephone calls can sometimes lead to friendly conversations, but the better known the person, the less likely he or she will be willing to respond spontaneously to a stranger unless referred by a mutual acquaintance.

There are several shortcuts to tracking down addresses. You can write to any recently published author in care of the publisher—if the publisher's address is not in the book, it can be obtained through the "Publishers" section of *Books in Print*. Anyone who teaches at a U.S. college or university can usually be found in the National Faculty Directory (Gale Research), available at libraries.

Martha Cornog

Special thanks is due to Susanne Pichler, librarian for the Katharine Dexter McCormick Library at Planned Parenthood Federation of America, New York City.

INDEX

ABOUT THE EDITORS
AND CONTRIBUTORS

Brenda Appleby, Ph.D., is a bioethicist who teaches in the departments of medicine and religious studies at Queen's University in Kingston, Ontario, Canada.

Gwen Brewer, Ph.D., is professor emeritus of English at California State University–Northridge in Northridge, California.

James Brundage, Ph.D., is Ahmanson-Murphy Distinguished Professor of History Emeritus at the University of Kansas in Lawrence, Kansas.

Vern Bullough, R.N., Ph.D., is clinical professor of nursing at the University of Southern California, distinguished professor of history and sociology at the State University of New York, and professor emeritus of California State University–Northridge.

Martha Cornog, M.A., M.S., is manager of membership services for the American College of Physicians in Philadelphia, Pennsylvania.

Stacy Elliott, M.D., is a sexual medicine consultant at Vancouver Hospital and clinical associate professor of medicine at the University of British Columbia in Vancouver, British Columbia, Canada.

Peter Engelman, Ph.D., is assistant editor of the Margaret Sanger Papers Project at New York University.

Fan Fu Ruan, M.D., is a teacher and administrator at the Academy of Chinese Culture and Health Sciences in Oakland, California, and professor at the Institute for the Advanced Study of Human Sexuality in San Francisco, California

Tom Flynn is editor of *Free Inquiry* magazine and lives in Buffalo, New York.

Peter Frost, Ph.D., is a researcher at Groupe d'Etudes Inuit et Circumpolaires (GETIC) at Université Laval in Sainte-Foy, Quebec, Canada.

Cathy Moran Hajo is a Ph.D. candidate and assistant editor and assistant director of the Margaret Sanger Papers Project at New York University.

Esther Katz, Ph.D., is editor and director of the Margaret Sanger Papers Project and adjunct professor of history at New York University.

Idumati Parikh, Ph.D., is president of the Government Colony, Bandra East, at the Centre for the Study of Social Change in Mumbai, India..

Lois Robin is an independent scholar specializing in the culture of Native Americans. She lives in Santa Cruz, California.